1983

EXTINCT AND VANISHING MAMMALS OF THE WESTERN HEMISPHERE

WITH THE MARINE SPECIES OF ALL THE OCEANS

John Charles Phillips

EXTINCT AND VANISHING MAMMALS

of the

WESTERN HEMISPHERE

with the

MARINE SPECIES OF ALL THE OCEANS

by

GLOVER M. ALLEN

Special Publication No. 11

COOPER SQUARE PUBLISHERS, INC.
NEW YORK
1972

Originally Published, 1942
Reprinted 1972 by Cooper Square Publishers, Inc.
59 Fourth Avenue, New York, N. Y. 10003
International Standard Book Number 0-8154-0433-6
Library of Congress Card Catalog Number 72-85661

Printed in the United States of America

IN MEMORY OF

John C. Phillips

(1876–1938)

NATURALIST, CONSERVATIONIST
AND SPORTSMAN IN THE
HIGHEST SENSE

FOREWORD

MAY 1, 1942, is likely to be a significant date in the history of conservation, for on that day the "Convention on Nature Protection and Wildlife Preservation in the American Republics" came into effect for the seven American countries, including the United States, that had deposited ratifications with the Pan American Union. Twelve other Republics have now signed the Treaty, and it is hoped that their ratifications are soon to follow.

Publication of the present volume, devoted to the extinct and vanishing mammals of the New World, including certain marine mammals of all the oceans, is therefore particularly timely. Its author, Dr. Glover M. Allen, of the Museum of Comparative Zoology at Harvard University, who died on February 14, 1942, was one of the great naturalists of his day. His profound knowledge of mammals and birds was the result not only of a life-time study in museums but also of intimate observation of animals in their native habitats—in Africa, Australia, the Caribbean, and South America, as well as in many parts of his own country. The final preparation of this report was one of the last projects that Dr. Allen completed before his untimely death. We know that he thought of it as one might think of the clearing of a new trail into a virgin forest. It will, indeed, be the opening of the way to a wider understanding of the genuine need for international cooperation, if the vanishing wildlife of the Americas is to be preserved for the benefit of future generations.

This volume is dedicated to Dr. Allen's friend Dr. John C. Phillips, founder and first chairman of the American Committee for International Wildlife Protection. It was largely due to Dr. Phillips's vision that in May 1936 a project for a comprehensive study of the recently extinct and vanishing mammals of the world was undertaken under the auspices of the American Committee. Information on this subject had never been assembled, and it was felt that such a report, if carefully prepared, would be invaluable to the work of the Committee in helping to determine those species of mammals most urgently in need of protection and, at the same time, to estimate factors that might have caused the extinction of species. Basic information was needed to substantiate proposals for the protection of vanishing species in their native habitat through the establishment of adequate national parks and reserves. The material for the preparation of such a report was widely scattered, and assembling and evaluating it involved a great deal of correspondence with zoologists, game wardens, nature protection societies, and governments in many parts of the world, as well as a survey of widely scattered articles in popular magazines, books on sport and travel, and scientific literature.

Dr. Francis Harper, of Philadelphia, under arrangements made by Dr. Phillips, undertook this work and devoted many months of careful research to the preparation of material on the Old World mammals, treating in his report (as yet unpublished) about 400 forms. Dr. Allen made use of a special bibliography of references to literature collected by Dr. Harper, and with this as a basis prepared the present work on the New World and marine mammals, assembling much additional material to complete it.

The Harper-Allen study could never have been brought to its present state of completion had it not been for the most generous financial assistance received in the form of gifts from many individuals over a period of seven years, a special grant from the Penrose Fund of the American Philosophical Society (1937, No. 195), and a publication grant from the Boone and Crockett Club and the Conservation Committee of the New York Zoological Society. The American Committee takes this opportunity to express its gratitude to Dr. Allen and to Dr. Harper for their months of work in the preparation of material for reports on recently extinct and vanishing mammals of the world. We wish also to thank the forty financial contributors of information from many parts of the world. We are indebted further to the Academy of Natural Sciences of Philadelphia, whose famous library proved of inestimable assistance, and to the Museum of Comparative Zoology, at Cambridge, for the use of its library and other facilities. Thanks are due also to Dr. John Eric Hill, of the American Museum of Natural History, for his contributions to Dr. Allen's volume, and to Mr. Paul H. Oehser, editor of the United States National Museum, for the editorial supervision of this volume through the press and for the preparation of the index. The drawings for the illustrations were made especially for this work by Mr. Earl L. Poole, of the Reading Public Museum and Art Gallery.

In these dark days, when even man is fighting to save himself from extinction, let us hope that this book, inspired by a great sportsman and conservationist and written by a great naturalist "whose gentleness and purity of spirit were beyond all praise," will in some measure be helpful in promoting a wider understanding of the need for preserving the wildlife heritage of the American republics for the enjoyment and wise use of generations to come. "Natural beauty," in the words of Trevelyan, "is the highest common denominator in the spiritual life of today." And what a great destiny lies ahead for the peoples of the Americas if, in winning their struggle for world freedom, they keep faith with their birthright of natural beauty, as well as with the wild creatures over which they have dominion and with the earth that sustains them!

HAROLD J. COOLIDGE, Jr.
(for the Committee)
Washington, D. C.
June 12, 1942

Publication Committee:
CHARLES M. B. CADWALADER
HAROLD J. COOLIDGE, Jr.
ALEXANDER WETMORE

CONTENTS

ILLUSTRATIONS

INTRODUCTION

THE accounts that follow are intended to cover, first, those species of New World mammals that have been exterminated or seriously depleted by human agency during the past four and a half centuries; and second, the oceanic species of world-wide distribution, mainly cetaceans, seals, and sea-lions, that within the historic period have suffered similar reduction, some of them over a longer term. The method followed is to give the common name, the current Latin name, reference to original description with type locality, the important synonyms, and references to figures of the exterior or the skull, or both. Following a brief description there are given the geographic range past and present and a short description of each species from the viewpoint mainly of its economic or commercial use, present status, protective measures, and other facts pertinent to a better understanding of its control or encouragement or other special needs. The introductory paragraphs to each of the major groups were prepared by Dr. J. Eric Hill, of the American Museum of Natural History, and are signed with his initials.

Full acknowledgment is due Dr. Francis Harper for the large share of the bibliographic work for the present volume that he had already accomplished in connection with his work on the Old World species preliminary to the preparation of the final accounts, and which he has handed on to me. In laying out the work Dr. Harper selected for inclusion those mammals that have been wholly or in part extirpated or have been greatly restricted in range or numbers by clearing and settlement or by intensive hunting for food, fur, or other economic and commercial purposes. In a search through literature and by extensive correspondence Dr. Harper had already accumulated a considerable mass of information concerning the past and present status of many of these species, and of this I have made

1

full use. To the list of species he selected I have added a few
others that, as the work progressed, seemed to require treatment. Possibly others should have been included, such as the
three-banded armadillo, which though still found in parts of
Brazil, seems now to have an interrupted range and may have
been locally exterminated for food. ˙ ˈPossibly, too, various
species of mammals have been in part exterminated by pre-
historic peoples, if the evidence now accumulating is to be
trusted that primitive weapons found in association with
skeletons of extinct species of bison and mammoth in parts of
our West are proof of the killing of some of the survivors of
these species by human contemporaries.˙ There is some evidence, though of a rather uncertain nature, that in southern
South America prehistoric man was contemporary with species
of ungulates, now extinct, the remains of which date from the
Pampean time of late Pleistocene. Such animals have been
omitted, however, since the present inquiry does not extend so
far back into the past.

Although few modern species of New World or marine
mammals have been directly exterminated by man, it is nevertheless true that almost any of those having a considerable
value for food, fur, oil, or other products, as well as those
having a less tangible interest as game animals for trophies,
are likely to be endangered increasingly with the more intensive
methods of modern times and with the growth of populations
and consequent reduction of areas available for their support.
With the settlement of this hemisphere by Europeans, the
control measures they imposed on the native mammals were
naturally directed first against the larger predators—wolves,
pumas, bears—that menaced their meager flocks or even at
times endangered their own lives. Clearing of forests for
agricultural purposes had an immediate effect in reducing the
available food and shelter for sylvan species and thus indirectly
in driving out or eliminating some of these. Probably this
factor has been a potent one in the extinction of various fruit-
eating bats of the West Indian islands. The growing demands
of the fur trade, with its increasing inroads on the fur bearers,
have resulted in great reduction of native stocks in many regions, even those remote from civilization where professional
trappers have for long periods pursued the more valuable
species unremittingly. The large game animals, which fur-

nished dependable supplies of meat and hides, were drawn heavily upon during pioneer stages and later were intensively pursued, in part for sport and in part for incidental food purposes. • Finally the oceanic species, particularly the larger cetaceans and seals, have been hunted with increasing vigor and improved devices the world over, until at the present day many of the regions formerly productive now no longer repay the effort or expense of pursuit.

Protective legislation in aid of certain species of commercial or economic importance, began early, as in colonial New England, but in most cases did not come till much later, sometimes too late to be of much avail. On the other hand, there have been some mammals that have proved more adaptive or have responded more quickly to a release of the pressure put upon them, and with proper management may prove a dependable asset for a long time to come. Any facts that will serve to bring out the needs of those species worth conservational treatment should be of value as a guide to future management of these natural resources. The last decade has seen much progress in these matters and a wider awareness that the time has come when immediate steps are necessary to preserve such assets before their depletion has gone too far.

A long step forward in the preservation and protection of American wildlife was made when, on October 12, 1940, through the agency of the Pan American Union, representatives of the nations of the Western Hemisphere affixed their signatures to the Convention on Nature Protection and Wildlife Preservation in the American Republics, thus pledging their countries "to adopt measures for the protection of useful, harmless and ornamental species of plant and animal life. They have thus given formal recognition to the fact that many such species know no national boundaries, and that true conservation of the gifts of Nature should begin before these resources have been dissipated by thoughtless or selfish destruction" (from the statement of Dr. Héctor David Castro, Minister of El Salvador). The Senate of the United States ratified this convention on April 7, 1941. In the "Annex" to the Convention, three mammals are included the protection of which is declared to be of special urgency and importance in the United States and is to be as nearly complete as possible, namely, the woodland caribou, the sea otter, and the manatee (see Congressional Record—Senate, for April 7, 1941). Similar lists are to be submitted by the other countries.[1]

GLOVER M. ALLEN

February, 1942.

[1] For a full account of this and other related matters see HAYDEN, SHERMAN STRONG, The International Protection of Wild Life, an examination of treaties and other agreements for the preservation of birds and mammals, 246 pp. Columbia University Press, 1942.

NORTH AMERICA AND THE
WEST INDIES

Order INSECTIVORA: Moles, Shrews, and Their Relatives

INSECTIVORES are primitive mammals of moderate or small size, with long pointed muzzles and sharp-cusped chewing teeth. They feed chiefly on insects and other invertebrates, but some prey on small mammals or fish. The New World insectivores belong to the suborder Lipotyphla and include two groups differing in important dental characters.

The archaic insectivores, with V-shaped molar teeth, are represented in the West Indies by two families; all are either extinct or threatened with extinction:

(1) Nesophontidae, five primitive species from the islands of Puerto Rico, Haiti, and Cuba. These are extinct, so far as known.

(2) Solenodontidae, two species of long-snouted heavy-bodied insectivores, found in the islands of Haiti and Cuba.

The more modern insectivores, with W-shaped molar teeth, are represented by two families, both of which are widely distributed in the Old World and North America, but only one extends into Central or South America:

(3) Talpidae, moles. None of these are discussed here.

(4) Soricidae, shrews. A single species is considered to be in danger of extinction because of rarity.—J. E. H.

Family NESOPHONTIDAE: Extinct Antillean Insectivores

NESOPHONTES EDITHAE Anthony

Nesophontes edithae Anthony, Bull. Amer. Mus. Nat. Hist., vol. 35, p. 725, 1916 ("Cueva Catedral, near Morovis, Porto Rico").

FIGS.: Anthony, H. E., 1916, pl. 23 (cranium); 1918, pp. 366–375, figs. 17–23 (skull and larger bones).

Our first knowledge of this remarkable genus and species is due to Dr. H. E. Anthony, who, during his investigation of cave deposits in Puerto Rico, brought to light abundant remains of the species that he named *Nesophontes edithae*, including many nearly complete skulls and other parts of the skeleton from caves at Morovis and Utuado. It apparently lived on the island until comparatively late, perhaps post-Columbian, times.

This is the largest of the species at present known from the Greater Antilles, but since no living examples have been found, only the skeletal characters have been described. It was probably about the size of a chipmunk. In life, the snout was probably elongate and flexible, the head long and slender, the eye small, the limbs only moderately long and probably with five clawed toes on each; the thorax seems to have been narrow instead of widened as in *Solenodon*, and the tail was probably about as long as the body. The tubular skull lacked the jugal bone. The anterior pair of incisors is not greatly enlarged as it is in that genus; the canine is double-rooted and retains its primitive large size, while the upper molar teeth have high cusps, forming a V-shaped pattern. Only one of the original four premolars is missing so that the tooth formula is: $i\frac{3}{3}$, $c\frac{1}{1}$, $pm\frac{3}{3}$, $m\frac{3}{3} = 40$. The humerus shows the entepicondylar foramen, the pubic bones are not united below, and the tibia and fibula are nearly separated, becoming slightly united distally in adults. "No living insectivore has such an assemblage of generalized characters," a fact that makes the group of unusual interest. It was made by Anthony the type of a separate family, Nesophontidae, and is regarded by Winge as somewhat ancestral to the moles. The skull length is about 40–44 mm. The abundant remains found by Anthony represent a larger and a smaller size, the former of which are taken to be of males, the latter of females, an unusual difference among the insectivores.

Among the rugged and tree-covered hills of Puerto Rico, this mammal must once have been a common species and doubtless was preyed upon by owls, through the agency of which its remains were probably brought into the limestone caves where they have been found. Why this large species should be found on this island alone, while on Cuba and Hispaniola only small forms occur, or how it originally reached these islands at all, are questions still unsolved. Nor is it clear that the introduction of rats from Europe, or the burning of forests with intensive cultivation, is alone responsible for its disappearance. Presumably it lived up till the earlier post-Columbian times. Hitherto no representative of the genus is known from Jamaica or other West Indian Islands except Cuba and Hispaniola. That so primitive and interesting a type should have wholly died out within Recent times is to be regretted.

NESOPHONTES MICRUS G. M. Allen

? *Nesophontes micrus* G. M. Allen, Bull. Mus. Comp. Zool., vol. 61, p. 5, pl., fig. 14, Jan. 1917 ("Cavern in the Sierra of Hato-Nuevo, Province of Matanzas, Cuba").
FIGS.: Allen, G. M., 1917, pl., fig. 14 (jaw); 1918, pl., figs. 7–10; Anthony, H. E., 1919, pl. 37, figs. 8, 9, 11, 12 (crania).

NESOPHONTES LONGIROSTRIS Anthony

Nesophontes longirostris Anthony, Bull. Amer. Mus. Nat. Hist., vol. 41, p. 633, 1919 ("Cave near the beach at Daiquiri, Cuba").
FIGS.: Anthony, 1919, pl. 37, figs. 10, 13 (cranium).

These two Cuban *Nesophontes* are at first glance very similar, though *N. longirostris* has a slightly longer rostrum, and the upper premolars are spaced instead of being in contact. They are both known from skeletal remains only, the former from both western and eastern Cuba, the latter from the type locality in the eastern part of the island.

These closely similar species differ remarkably from *N. edithae* of Puerto Rico in their very much smaller size. Otherwise they are much alike, although a number of minor characters separating them have been pointed out by Anthony (*op. cit.*, p. 633), such as the greater size of the first as compared with the second upper premolar, whereas in *N. edithae* these are equal; again, in the lower jaw, the second premolar is only about half as large as the two others instead of equaling them. Length of palate from postpalatal notch to alveolus of first incisor, about 14.1–15.3 mm. in *N. micrus;* 14.7 in *N. longirostris*, contrasted with 20.5 in *N. edithae*. Cranial length of *N. micrus*, 28 mm.

Nothing is known of *N. longirostris* except that it occurred in eastern Cuba up to relatively recent times. Since this end of the island still harbors various species that are absent from the western end, it is likely that this was a local species, differing only slightly from *N. micrus*, the remains of which are now known from recent cave deposits on the Isle of Pines as well as from both eastern and western Cuba itself. No doubt, as

Dr. Anthony has suggested, the remains of these insectivores in the cavern deposits are due to the agency of owls, such as the Cuban barn owl, which even at the present time is building up in some of these caves deposits of bones of introduced rats as well as of bats. These bones, especially skulls, are more or less broken so that complete crania are rare among the deposits. Anthony adduces some evidence that the *Nesophontes* were abundantly represented in the deposits prior to the deposition of rat bones, so that the introduction of the rats may have been the decisive factor in extermination of the insectivores. Thus the latter may have been extinct only since white occupation.

NESOPHONTES PARAMICRUS Miller

Nesophontes paramicrus Miller, Smithsonian Misc. Coll., vol. 81, no. 9, p. 3, 1929 ("Large cave near St. Michel, Haiti").

FIGS.: Miller, 1929a, pl. 1, fig. 1 (skeletal remains); 1930, pl. 2, figs. 2, 3 (rostrum).

NESOPHONTES HYPOMICRUS Miller

Nesophontes hypomicrus Miller, Smithsonian Misc. Coll., vol. 81, no. 9, p. 4, 1929 ("Deep cave near the Atalaye plantation [near St. Michel], Haiti").

FIGS.: Miller, 1929a, pl. 1, fig. 2 (skeletal remains); 1930, pl. 2, fig. 1 (rostrum).

NESOPHONTES ZAMICRUS Miller

Nesophontes zamicrus Miller, Smithsonian Misc. Coll., vol. 81, no. 9, p. 7, 1929 ("Large cave near St. Michel, Haiti").

FIG.: Miller, 1929a, pl. 1, fig. 3 (skeletal remains).

These three insectivores, apparently extinct and known only from skeletal remains found in Hispaniolan caves, may be discussed together. They have no common names.

They are differentiated from one another largely on size characters. In body dimensions they approximated mice or small rats.

"Insectivores of the genus *Nesophontes* are abundantly represented in the Haitian caves. They have not previously been recorded from the island of Hispaniola. In the superficial layer of the cave floors the bones of these animals occur in undisturbed material along with remains of *Epimys rattus* [roof rat] and *Mus musculus* [house mouse]. This association is so intimate that there appears to be no reason to doubt the simultaneous occurrence of the insectivores and the introduced rodents. Some of the jaws of *Nesophontes* are more fresh in appearance than some of the jaws of *Epimys* near which they were found. Whether or not *Nesophontes* now exists alive is a question which for the present cannot be answered. No bones of insectivores have been found in any of the numerous fresh owl pellets which I have examined. It seems not improbable, however, that if any part of the island remains uninvaded by the roof rat, the native animal might now be found to exist there" (Miller, 1929a, p. 3).

Wetmore and Swales write (1931, p. 238): "It seems probable that the deposits [made by the extinct owl in the Haitian Caves] were accumulated over a long period of years extending perhaps from four hundred to two thousand or more years ago." They record the finding of skulls of *Nesophontes* in a supposed nesting site of this owl in a sink-hole on La Selle, Haiti.

Miller also records (1929c, p. 4) remains of *N. paramicrus* and *N. hypomicrus* from a deposit made by the extinct owl, *Tyto ostologa*, in a cave on the islet San Gabriel in the Samaná Bay region of the Dominican Republic.

The occurrence of remains of these insectivores with those of the introduced roof rat and house mouse indicates their survival to post-Columbian times, while their usual absence from fresh owl pellets suggests their extinction.

In the following year, Miller (1930) found bones of both these species in material collected earlier in 1930 about 10 kilometers southwest of Constanza, Dominican Republic. This consisted of a mass of owl pellets, apparently those of the small living barn owl, found "in a shelter under an overhanging ledge about 100 feet up the northern flank of Monte Culo de Maco" in the rain-forest region where disintegration may take place much sooner than in the drier parts of the island. Some of the bones were so fresh as to retain bits of dried tissue while the brain case of one of the skulls was found to be "packed full of hair by the action of the owl's stomach." From this evidence Miller concludes that these insectivores as well as two associated genera of rodents may still exist in that region. It is hoped that future exploration may confirm this suggestion.

Family SOLENODONTIDAE: Solenodons

HISPANIOLAN SOLENODON

SOLENODON PARADOXUS Brandt

Solenodon paradoxus Brandt, Mem. Acad. Imp. Sci. St. Pétersbourg, ser. 6, vol. 2, p. 459, 1833 (Haiti).

FIGS.: Brandt, 1833, pls. 1, 2; Allen, G. M., 1910, pls. 1–3 (colored), 4–9 (anatomy).

First made known by the Russian zoologist Brandt, a little over a century ago, this large insectivore was supposed to be nearly or quite extinct in its island habitat until 1907, when A. Hyatt Verrill found that it was still living in the interior of northeastern Hispaniola.

It is a stoutly built animal, with a total length of about 22 inches, of which the strong tapering tail constitutes about 10 inches. Males and females are alike in size and in color, which varies from a mixed blackish and buff dorsally, with clearer yellowish sides, to a deep ferruginous tint, darkest and clearest on the lower throat. Characteristic is a small squarish spot of white in the middle of the nape. The tail is nearly naked and dusky in color except at the base, which is flesh-color. The feet and distal part of the limbs are nearly hairless and pale-tinted. The muzzle is provided with a long cartilaginous snout, supported at its base by a small round bone (the os proboscidis). The feet are armed with strong, slightly curved claws for digging, five on each foot. In its long tubular skull it somewhat resembles *Nesophontes* and the Madagascar tenrec, but the teeth show wide divergence from the former, in that the anterior upper pair of incisors and the second lower incisors are remarkably enlarged, the latter deeply grooved on the inner side. This enlargement is suggested by the generic name ("sword tooth"). The upper and lower canines are somewhat reduced, the former about equaling the second incisor. Except for the loss of one premolar, the full placental tooth formula is present: $i\frac{3}{3}$, $c\frac{1}{1}$, $pm\frac{3}{3}$, $m\frac{3}{3} = 40$.

Although this solenodon is said by Verrill to go under various names in Hispaniola, as *orso, hormigero, juron*, these are merely Spanish equivalents for "bear," "anteater," and "ferret." Hearne (1835, p. 105), however, in presenting a specimen to the Zoological Society of London in 1835, declared that in Haiti it was known to the people as *agouta*. Verrill writes that in the Dominican Republic it is called *milqui*.

Following its rediscovery by Verrill in 1907, five living animals were sent to the zoological gardens at Washington and New York from the Dominican Republic, and others including four living adults were received by the Museum of Comparative Zoology at Cambridge. The last came from a locality in the interior of the northeastern part of Hispaniola known as La Vega. Since that time a German collector, Paul Thumb, by the aid of a well-trained dog, succeeded in 1935 and 1936 in securing a number, about 20 in all, which he shipped alive to the zoological garden at Hamburg, Germany. Of these, several survived the voyage and formed the subject of three short papers by Dr. Erna Mohr (1936–37) concerning their ways in captivity, with a number of photographic illustrations. Herr Thumb secured his solenodons mainly in rocky and wooded country in the vicinity of San José de las Matas. In life the solenodon is a rather slow-moving creature, constantly on the move with a shuffling gait, sniffing everywhere with its long nose, and scraping and scratching here and there with its long claws, exploring for food. It is capable of delivering a sharp bite if too much disturbed, however.

According to Dr. Mohr (1937a), Herr Thumb found solenodons in dens among broken rock for the most part, or occasionally in hollow logs. In the former case the depth varied according to conditions of the rocks. The holes he dug out in 1935 were packed with the empty shells of a snail, but this was not the case with those examined in the next year; while at the

Hispaniolan solenodon (*Solenodon paradoxus*)

Hamburg gardens, Dr. Mohr found the solenodons quite
indifferent to live snails presented to them. Thumb found as
many as eight solenodons in a single burrow. In captivity it
was ascertained that the female may have one to three, usually
two, young at a birth and may bring forth twice in a single
year, though showing no particular breeding season. The
group of eight in a den may thus be accounted for as the two
parents with their young of two successive litters. Three of
the families dug out by Thumb consisted of the adult pair and
their single young. A family secured for the Museum of Comparative Zoology in 1937 by W. J. Clench was of similar constitution. These were from southwest of Sabana, Dominican
Republic.

At the present time it appears that this solenodon is in no
immediate danger of extinction, but is still present in areas of
stony forest in northeastern Dominican Republic. If, however,
such areas are extensively encroached upon through clearing
and cultivation, it will no doubt be reduced in numbers.

CUBAN SOLENODON; "AYRE"; "ALMIQUI"

SOLENODON CUBANUS Peters

Solenodon cubanus Peters, Monatsb. Königl. Preuss. Akad. Wiss. Berlin, 1861, p. 169,
    1862 (mountains near Trinidad and Bayamó, Cuba).
FIGS.: Peters, 1863, pls. 1–3 (exterior and anatomy); Mohr, 1937a, figs. on pp. 7, 8.

The Cuban solenodon was probably the animal first made
known by Oviedo as the *ayre* in his famous "Historia General y
Natural de las Indias," 1535, but it remained for the Cuban
naturalist Felipe Poey to bring it to the notice of modern
scientists, in a newspaper report in *El Plantel* in 1838, a
century ago. It was not till nearly 25 years later, however,
that Peters was able to compare a specimen with the Hispaniolan species and point out its distinctive characters.

In size this is slightly smaller than the species *S. paradoxus*,
about 20 inches long, tail about 7 inches, and is quite different
in color. In place of the blackish and buffy to ferruginous back,
the Cuban solenodon is blackish brown in color, with a varying
amount of white, or buffy, which may include only the base of
the muzzle, the cheeks, and a mark on each shoulder, as in a
specimen in the Museum of Comparative Zoology, or may be

more extensive, to include the entire head and lower surfaces, and extend back along the side of the neck to the shoulder, whence it continues in scattered long white hairs to the haunches. There is no distinct white mark on the nape.

The first definite knowledge of this species is due to Poey, who obtained specimens in the mountains east of Bayamó, where it was said to be well known, and he published an account of it with a colored plate in his "Memorias sobre la Historia Natural de Cuba" in 1851. He, however, supposed it to be the same as the species of Hispaniola, and after search in the earlier accounts of Cuban animals, failed to identify it with any known to the early historians of the country. For this reason, he proposed that it be called the *almiqui*, a name derived from that of one of the mountains near where his specimens were taken, in the region east of Bayamó. Gundlach subsequently obtained it near Trinidad, about halfway of the length of the island of Cuba, to the westward. In 1886, he sent three to the United States National Museum that he secured from the high mountains about 30 miles from Bayamó. One of these was exhibited alive at a meeting of the Biological Society of Washington (Proc. Biol. Soc. Washington, vol. 4, p. x, 1886). It was the surviving adult male of a family of three, of which the adult female and her young one succumbed during the journey from Cuba, and was said by Dr. F. W. True (1886) to be destined for the zoological garden at Philadelphia. Even at that time the animal seems to have become rare, for Gundlach wrote that it had been secured only after "the promise of many years" by the same person who had supplied specimens previously to himself and Poey. No more are known to have been captured until 1909, when two Swedish engineers secured a live one in the mountains of eastern Cuba. This animal died soon after, and its remains were sent to the Riksmuseum at Stockholm. Two photographs taken before its death are reproduced by Dr. Erna Mohr (1937a) and are apparently the only ones that show the living animal. At about the same time a second specimen (or possibly the same one) was in captivity in the possession of M. Bofell, director of the Municipal Museum of Santiago. According to Paul Serre (1910) it had been captured by laborers near Baracoa, in extreme eastern Cuba, in the course of road construction. Its owner is said to have refused various offers to buy it, but its subsequent fate

is unknown.   In the 30 years that have since elapsed I have
no knowledge of the capture of any others.   Efforts of various
naturalists to discover it in eastern Cuba have been unavailing,
and even Herr Thumb, who was so successful in finding *S.
paradoxus* in the Dominican Republic with the aid of his dog,
failed to find it when in 1937 he hunted for it in that region.

Very little is known of its habits.   It was believed to have
lived in caves, but, curiously, the researches of Dr. H. E.
Anthony and others in cave excavations have revealed very
little even in the way of recent remains, although bones of the
much smaller *Nesophontes* are common.   The Museum of
Comparative Zoology, however, has a lower jaw from a cave
at San Lucas, near Maisi, eastern Cuba.   This paucity of cave
fragments may indicate that the animal was little preyed upon
by owls, perhaps on account of its size and strength, but was
rather secure in holes among rocks such as the Hispaniolan
species makes use of.   Captive animals are said to have eaten
the meat of chickens, either raw or cooked, while the one
captured by the Swedish engineers ate freely of raw beef given
in small pieces.   With the introduction and spread of the Burmese mongoose in Cuba, it is very possible that this voracious
carnivore may already have exterminated the last of the
solenodons.   The loss of either of the two species is greatly to
be deplored, since they are in the New World the last living
representatives of the group of insectivores with triangular
instead of squarish molars, the Zalambdodonta, found elsewhere at the present time only in Africa (the potamogale) and
on the island of Madagascar (the Madagascar hedgehog and
its relatives).

Family SORICIDAE: Shrews

WHITE MOUNTAINS DWARF SHREW

SOREX MYOPS Merriam

Sorex tenellus myops Merriam, Proc. Biol. Soc. Washington, vol. 15, p. 76, Mar. 22,
   1902 (Pipers Creek [Cottonwood Creek], near main peak of White Mountains,
   altitude 9,500 feet, Mono County, California).
FIGS.: Jackson, H. H. T., 1928, pl. 3, fig. B'; pl. 6, fig. R (skull).

Few specimens of this tiny shrew are known.   In color the
back is drab, the lower parts pale smoke gray tinged with pale

olive-buff (Jackson); tail buffy brown to tawny olive above, below nearly "tilleul buff, darkening toward tip." It is said to be thus paler than its near relatives of the *ornatus* group, and its skull is smaller than in any except *Sorex tenellus* and *S. nanus* of Owens Valley, California, and Colorado, respectively. Total length, 98 mm., tail, 41; hind foot, 12; length of skull, 15.2.

This small shrew is regarded by Dr. H. H. T. Jackson (1928) as a distinct species, though its relationship to *S. tenellus* is doubtless close. For many years it was represented only by the two specimens in the collection of the U. S. Biological Survey. Dr. Jackson believed it was probably confined to the White Mountains of California, "where it is seemingly rare and may even be exterminated by the destruction of its habitat through sheep grazing." More recently, however, Dr. William H. Burt (1934) has discovered it in the Charleston Mountains of southern Nevada, where he considers it common "along the small streams at altitudes of 8,000 feet or above" up to 10,000 feet, not far from water. The possibility that grazing has already much restricted its habitat in the White Mountains makes its inclusion here excusable.

Order CHIROPTERA: Bats

The bats form a large complex order; they are the only mammals that truly fly. There are two suborders:

Megachiroptera, fruit bats or flying-foxes. There is a single family, found in southern Asia, Africa, Australia, and many of the oceanic islands. They are characterized by blunt cheek teeth and a second claw in the expanded wing-hand.

Microchiroptera, insectivorous bats (several are secondarily fruit-eating or carnivorous and one family is specialized for a diet of blood). Sixteen families are usually recognized, of which six are restricted to the New World and two are common to both hemispheres. The New World families follow:

(1) Noctilionidae, primitive bats, found in tropical America. They are related to the Old World Rhinopomidae and Emballonuridae. Two genera are recognized; neither is here considered endangered.

(2) Phyllostomidae, New World leaf-nosed bats. These do not appear to be closely related to any Old World group, but

probably developed in South America. Most of the species of this large family have lancetlike nose-leaves; those that do not show this character have cutaneous growths on the lower jaw. Fifty-two genera are recognized, of which seven (including 13 species) are discussed in this volume, as either extinct or extremely rare.

(3) Desmodontidae, vampire bats. The blood-drinking bats are restricted to the American tropics. They are related to the preceding family and have a rudimentary nose-leaf. None is discussed in this work.

(4) Natalidae, long-legged bats. These small, delicately built bats are found in the American tropics, north to the Bahama Islands and central Mexico. One species is believed to have become extinct in historical times.

(5) Furipteridae. Two genera, closely related to the long-legged bats, are found in tropical South America. Neither genus is discussed here.

(6) Thyropteridae. A single genus, with large suction disk on the thumb, is restricted to tropical America. This bat is not considered endangered.

(7) Vespertilionidae, common bats. They are found in both hemispheres to the limit of tree growth and on the oceanic islands to Samoa and Hawaii. Three species are here considered in danger of extinction.

(8) Molossidae, free-tailed bats. Found in the warmer parts of both hemispheres. None of these bats is thought to be a vanishing form.—J. E. H.

Family PHYLLOSTOMIDAE: Leaf-nosed Bats

Puerto Rican Long-nosed Bat

Monophyllus frater Anthony

Monophyllus frater Anthony, Bull. Amer. Mus. Nat. Hist., vol. 37, p. 565, 1917 (cave near Morovis, Puerto Rico).

Figs.: Anthony, H. E., 1917c, pl. 56, figs. 5, 6; 1918, p. 349, fig. 8 (skull).

Of the various genera of bats confined to the West Indies and unknown from the neighboring mainland, the long-tongued members of *Monophyllus* are remarkable, for they are found in almost all the islands of the entire Antillean chain. Because those on the several islands can usually be distinguished from their neighbors by minute characters, they have been given distinctive names. Thus we have as the oldest named form, *M. redmani* of Jamaica; others are *M. cubanus* of Cuba, *M. cubanus ferreus* of Haiti, *M. portoricensis* of Puerto Rico, an allied form on Antigua, *M. luciae* on Santa Lucia, *M. plethodon* on Barbados, and *M. clinedaphus* from an unknown locality. All are living, and no doubt vary in abundance on the several islands. On Puerto Rico, however, in recent years, Dr. H. E. Anthony has discovered a second and larger species, which he has distinguished as *M. frater;* on each of the other islands only one form is known to occur.

Members of this genus of the subfamily Glossophaginae are likely to be confused with *Glossophaga* of the mainland (and some of the Antillean islands). They are small species with long snouts surmounted by a small lancet-shaped nose-leaf and are provided with a long extensible tongue for feeding on fruit juices and perhaps in part upon nectar or pollen of flowers. The teeth are peculiar in that the lower incisors are minute and the cheek teeth are slightly elongate and spaced. The cusps of the latter are low and the outer ones are placed close to the edge of the crown so that the usual W-shaped pattern of the cusps is obscured. The dentition includes, on each side, two incisors above and below, a canine, two upper and three lower premolars, and three molars above and below. Externally it is easily distinguished from *Glossophaga* by the longer tail, which is about half as long as the femur and projects beyond the edge of the narrow interfemoral membrane, whereas in the latter genus the tail extends barely to the middle of the wide interfemoral membrane.

The species *M. frater* is known only from five fragmentary skulls excavated in the large Cathedral Cave near Morovis, Puerto Rico, by Dr. H. E. Anthony some years ago. With these was associated a skull of the living species still found in Puerto Rico, *M. portoricensis*, showing that the two were contemporaries and represented distinct species. *M. frater* is considerably larger than the latter, with a narrow elongate rostrum. This larger size is obvious from the comparative measurements: Length of the upper cheek teeth (alveoli), 6.8–7.1 mm. as against 5.3; in the smaller species, length of palate 12.4–12.7 mm. as against 9.3. In spite of much collecting done in Puerto Rico, no living examples of this larger species have yet come to light. While it is quite possible that it may eventually be found, it seems more likely that it is now extinct, perhaps as a result in part of extensive clearing and agriculture. As Anthony points out, the interesting thing about this species is that it affords another instance of two closely related species from the same region, differing most obviously in little but size. A similar case is afforded by the bats of the genus *Chilonycteris*, of which three species occur in Cuba.

JAMAICA LONG-TONGUED BAT

REITHRONYCTERIS APHYLLA Miller

Reithronycteris aphylla Miller, Proc. Acad. Nat. Sci. Philadelphia, 1898, p. 334 ("Jamaica").

FIGS.: Miller, 1898, figs. 2b (head), 3 (skull), 4 (section of palate), 5a (tongue).

The present species seems most closely related to *Phyllonycteris*, which it may represent in Jamaica. Externally and in its dentition it resembles *Phyllonycteris poeyi* but is at once distinguished by the vestigial nose-leaf, which instead of forming an erect lancet is reduced to almost nothing and appears as a short piglike snout, set off by an encircling groove. The ears, too, are shorter, and the tragus shows four notches on its outer margin; the hind foot is large, three-fourths as long as the tibia, and with strong claws; calcar absent, as in *Phyllonycteris;* and tail shorter than tibia. Color light yellowish brown (in alcohol). The genus differs remarkably from *Phyllonycteris*, however, in that the floor of the brain case is elevated out of its usual position in such a way that the roof of the posterior nares is formed "by two longitudinal folds given off probably by the pterygoids and nearly meeting in the median line." The skull has the rostral portion relatively broader, and there is less contrast in both diameter and height of the upper incisors. Total length, 88 mm.; tail, 12; tibia, 17; forearm, 48; skull length, 26.

The only known specimen of this genus and species is the type, a male preserved in the Museum of the Institute of Jamaica. Its further history is not recorded, but it was taken in that island some time prior to 1898; no fragments were found by Dr. H. E. Anthony in the course of his explorations for cave fossils in Jamaica, so that nothing is known of its haunts, habits, or present status. Very likely, however, it is on the way to extinction if it has not already gone.

Dominican Hairy Bat

Ardops nichollsi (Thomas)

Stenoderma nichollsi Thomas, Ann. Mag. Nat. Hist., ser. 6, vol. 7, p. 529, 1891 (Island
of Dominica, Lesser Antilles).

Montserrat Hairy Bat

Ardops montserratensis (Thomas)

Stenoderma montserratensis Thomas, Proc. Zool. Soc. London, 1894, p. 133 (Island of
Montserrat, Lesser Antilles).

St. Lucia Hairy Bat

Ardops luciae (Miller)

Stenoderma luciae Miller, Proc. Acad. Nat. Sci. Philadelphia, 1902, p. 407 (Island of
St. Lucia, Lesser Antilles).

Guadeloupe Hairy Bat

Ardops annectens Miller

Ardops annectens Miller, Proc. Biol. Soc. Washington, vol. 26, p. 33, Feb. 8, 1913
("Island of Guadeloupe, Lesser Antilles").

So far as known, the bats of this genus are confined to the
islands of the Lesser Antilles, where they appear to be rare, for
few specimens seem to be preserved in collections. They are at
present known to inhabit St. Lucia, Dominica, Guadeloupe,
and Montserrat only, and on each seem to be represented by a
slightly differing race. In time, with clearing of wooded areas,
their habitat is likely to be more and more restricted, with the
possibility of their final extermination; hence they may be
considered here collectively.

All the four known "species" are of similar appearance and
of medium size, about 3 inches long from nose to tip of tail,
with rather long loose pelage of a light-brown color. The fur
of the body extends thickly over the hind limbs to the ankles
and out along the border of the lateral membrane for a short
distance; on the arms the hair extends thickly out to the wrist.
The interfemoral membrane is very narrow, and there is a
short calcaneum. The head is short and blunt; the ears are
not much longer than the distance from their base to the end
of the nose. The genus is closely related to *Phyllops* and
Ariteus, of Cuba and Jamaica, respectively. It is smaller than

the species of *Artibeus* found in the same islands and differs conspicuously in the skull by having the palate deeply emarginate posteriorly and in the great development of the postglenoid process. In each jaw are two incisors, a canine, two premolars, and three molars. The crown of the inner upper incisor is short and thick, scarcely or not higher than long. Additional details of the teeth are given fully by Miller (1907, p. 151).

The first-described species, *A. nichollsi*, of Dominica, is small, with a forearm of about 46 mm.; *A. montserratensis*, of Montserrat, is slightly larger, with a forearm of 51.5 mm.; the Guadeloupe form, *A. annectens*, is of intermediate size, with a forearm of 48 mm.; while the most southerly one, *A. luciae*, of St. Lucia, is very little larger than *A. nichollsi*, forearm 47 mm., and has a small white spot on the shoulder and distinctly bifid inner upper incisors. If, as seems likely, the genus once occurred on Martinique, it has probably now been extirpated with clearing and volcanic destruction.

These bats are evidently tree-living, rather than cave-haunting, which implies not only that they are somewhat solitary and so easily escape observation, but also are more difficult to find on account of living among the leaves by day. Of the Montserrat species, Thomas records that it is said to hang by day underneath branches of trees, and to do much damage to the cocoa plantations. It seems likely, however, that it can hardly be common enough to be very destructive, and that the larger *Artibeus* is the real culprit. Of the Guadeloupe form, Miller mentions five specimens, implying a small group captured. Dr. G. K. Noble, who secured an adult female and well-grown young in Guadeloupe in 1914, writes me that he found these hanging together directly over the path he was following through the woods near Sainte Rose. Later his guide caught another one, so that they must occur in some numbers still. *Ardops* is a member of the fruit-eating group of leaf-nosed bats; hence it must depend for a living upon the soft fruits of various forest trees, and these in turn must occur in sufficient variety to provide a continuous supply throughout the year. It is evident, therefore, that any important change in the forest cover, whereby such trees are destroyed or replaced by other kinds that do not produce the desired fruit, must inevitably affect these local species. One may surmise that as already indicated, such changes have taken place on Martinique and possibly too on St. Vincent, where otherwise one might expect the genus to occur. Of its status on the other Lesser Antillean islands practically nothing is known.

FALCATE-WINGED BAT

PHYLLOPS FALCATUS (Gray)

Arctibeus falcatus Gray, Ann. Nat. Hist., vol. 4, p. 1, 1839 ("Cuba").
SYNONYM: *Stenoderma albomaculatum* Gundlach, Monatsber. Königl. Preuss. Akad. Wiss. Berlin, 1861, p. 155.
FIGS.: Dobson, 1878, pl. 28, figs. 3, 3a (dentition); Anthony, H. E., 1917b, pl. 34, fig. 3 (skull).

LESSER FALCATE-WINGED BAT

PHYLLOPS VETUS Anthony

Phyllops vetus Anthony, Bull. Amer. Mus. Nat. Hist., vol. 37, p. 337, 1917 ("Cave at Daiquiri, Province of Oriente, Cuba").
FIGS.: Anthony, 1917b, pl. 34, figs. 4–6 (skull).

HISPANIOLAN FALCATE-WINGED BAT

PHYLLOPS HAITIENSIS (J. A. Allen)

Ardops haitiensis J. A. Allen, Bull. Amer. Mus. Nat. Hist., vol. 24, p. 581, Sept. 11, 1908 (Caña Honda, Dominican Republic).
FIGS.: Anthony, H. E., 1917b, pl. 34, fig. 2 (skull).

The small fruit-eating bats of this genus much resemble those of the genus *Ardops* of the Lesser Antilles, but so far as known they are confined to Cuba and Hispaniola. Their superficial resemblance to the larger *Artibeus*, common in the same islands, may at times have caused them to be overlooked, yet from the paucity of known specimens they are probably actually fewer in numbers, or even, in the case of *P. vetus*, are already extinct.

Similar in size to the members of the genus *Ardops*, and like them with a short blunt rostrum, hairy limbs and wing-border, they may be at once distinguished by the fact that the deep emargination at the posterior part of the palate is continued forward in a converging V-shaped outline, which extends about to the level of the middle of the second molar, whereas in *Ardops* this indentation is a narrow, parallel-sided arch. In *Phyllops*, also, the crown of the inner upper incisor is slender, noticeably higher than long, whereas in *Ardops* and in *Ariteus* the crown of this tooth is short and thick, scarcely or not higher than long (Miller, 1907). In contrast to the related genus *Stenoderma*, the rostrum of the skull rises above the level of the low supraorbital ridges and the nasal opening extends much less than halfway back to the point of union of these ridges. In addition, the third upper molar is still more minute, and the second upper molar is scarcely three-fourths the size of the first instead of nearly equaling it in crown area. In *P. falcatus* the head and body measure about 1.9 inches; the tail is absent; forearm, 1.65 inches; tibia, 0.6 inch; hind foot, 0.4 inch. The fur is described as gray-brown, with dark tips; the lower side is slightly paler.

The species described from Cuba as *P. vetus* is smaller than *P. falcatus* in its skull, the palatal emargination is narrower, and the small third upper molar is nearly circular instead of oval. The Hispaniolan species, *P. haitiensis*, is of about the same size as *P. vetus* but differs in the sudden contraction of the V-shaped palatal emargination near its tip and in the apparent lack of the shallow pits in the basioccipital.

Very little is known of the habits or status of these three bats. Both *P. falcatus* and *P. vetus* are Cuban, while *P. haitiensis* is at present known from Hispaniola only. The first was sent by MacLeay to the British Museum, in 1838 or 1839, with the note, "Killed in my bedroom." Gundlach mentions specimens from Matanzas and Cárdenas, and in 1914 I examined two skulls taken from owl pellets in eastern Cuba by Dr. Charles T. Ramsden. In 1917, Dr. H. E. Anthony, in the course of excavations in a cave at Daiquiri, eastern Cuba, secured seven fragmentary skulls and four mandibles. Although he did not find the species alive, he mentions "an almost perfect skull taken from an owl pellet collected by Mr. Barnum Brown . . . at the 'Cueva de los Machos' near Cienfuegos." "The material," he writes (1919), "is, for the most part, fresh in appearance and not deeply discolored, some of it very recent in fact." In addition, there is a specimen in alcohol in the U. S. National Museum from Santiago, Cuba. Of *P. vetus*, discovered by Dr. Anthony in the cave deposits at Daiquiri, eastern Cuba, about 40 skulls were obtained. He states that it was "found as a fossil and judging from the condition of the specimens evidently has not been frequenting this region since the more recent animal remains, bats of the present day, were deposited. Therefore, while it is quite possible that this bat may be discovered living on some part of the island I am led to believe that it is truly extinct, a fossil of an earlier period than the very recent." Since, like its living relative, this was in all probability a tree-dwelling and fruit-eating species, it may have had a rather precarious foothold in this drier eastern part of Cuba. In a note in his paper of 1919, Anthony adds that a further comparison of the specimens of the two species, *P. falcatus* and *P. vetus*, confirms his belief that the latter was an older inhabitant of the region for the bones "are all more ancient in appearance, more deeply stained and discolored"; while the fact that the owls that prey upon these bats have not brought them in to add to the more recent deposits is indicative of the same thing.

Of the Hispaniolan species still less is known, for beyond the original specimen from Caña Honda, Haiti, it has elsewhere been recorded only from owl deposits. These are: near Constanza, in the mountainous interior of the Dominican Republic, where "in a shelter under an overhanging ledge about 100 feet up the northern flank of Monte Culo de Maco," Herbert W. Krieger secured a broken skull and a mandible (Miller, 1930, p. 6); in a large cave near St. Michel, ten skulls and several mandibles; one skull from the deep cave and a mandible from the crooked cave near the same place; and a skull from owl pellets in the cave at Diquini, Haiti. These were found at all levels from the surface to a depth of two feet (Miller, 1929a).

These small, heavy-bodied, fruit-eating bats may have been easily taken by their enemy the barn owl. Probably the species still persists in wooded regions of this island.

"DUSKY NASEBERRY BAT"

ARITEUS ACHRADOPHILUS (Gosse)

Artibeus achradophilus P. H. Gosse, Naturalist's Sojourn in Jamaica, p. 271, footnote 1851 (Content, Jamaica).

SYNONYMS: *Artibeus sulphureus* P. H. Gosse, *op. cit.*, p. 271, footnote, 1851; *Ariteus flavescens* Gray, Proc. Zool. Soc. London, 1866, p. 117.

FIGS.: Gosse and Hill, 1851, pl. 6, fig. 4 (nose leaf); Peters, 1867, pp. 433–434, pl. 2.

For practically all we know of this bat, we are indebted to P. H. Gosse who first described it in his "Naturalist's Sojourn in Jamaica," the island to which it is confined.

The species is one of the group of West Indian fruit-eating bats, of which the genera *Ardops*, *Phyllops*, and *Stenoderma* are related members. Of about the same size and appearance as these, it may at once be distinguished by the possession of only two instead of three upper molars (the minute third molar of the other genera having been lost in *Ariteus*) and by the presence of a "minute though evident metaconid" in the first lower molar. As in the related genera, the nose-leaf is lanceolate with a distinct midrib; the short interfemoral membrane is concave behind and like the legs is covered with rather long hair, forming a fringe along the posterior margin. It is said to be light reddish brown in color, paler beneath, and with a small white patch on each shoulder. There are no facial stripes, and the tail is lacking. Length of head and body, 2.2 inches; forearm, 1.6 inches; tibia, 0.6 inch; hind foot, 0.4 inch.

This genus may be regarded as the representative in Jamaica of the genus *Phyllops*, from which the above characters distinguish it. Gosse (Gosse and Hill, 1851) writes that the first specimen he secured came in at the open window of a house at the Vineyard, near Black River, where he was staying. He supposed that, like other bats that flew in and out, it was in search of insects attracted by the lights. Three others he succeeded in shooting in the early evening at Content, and these are presumably the specimens listed by Dobson as in the collection of the British Museum. Here a large and fruitful naseberry tree (the *níspero* of the Spanish colonists)—*Achras sapota*—attracted many bats by its large fruits, resembling "a very rough russet apple, firm and fleshy, of a rich sugary sweetness." At about a quarter of an hour after sunset the bats began to visit the tree. "First one comes, takes a rapid flight around the tree, darts once or twice through the dense foliage, and winging away is lost in the light of the sky. Another and another comes immediately, and performs the same evolutions . . . By carefully following the flight of an individual with the eye, we perceive that now and then he alights for a moment on some object at the extremity of a bunch of leaves; but no sooner has the eye rested on the spot than the sooty wings are again spread, and he is pursuing his giddy course with his fellows. The object of his visit is a ripe naseberry, nestled in the midst of that rosette of leaves. Occasionally the weight of the suspended Bat dislodges the ripe fruit, and it falls to the ground, splitting with the shock. On picking it up we see that it has been just bitten, not gnawed as by the rodent incisors of a mouse, but nibbled in a ragged manner." No doubt several species of fruit-eating bats visit these trees for the feast.

What may be the present status of this bat does not seem to be known. However, it is evidently rare in collections, whether from actual scarcity or through failure of visitors to capture it. On account of its island habitat and the intensive agriculture carried on in Jamaica, it is likely to become reduced in numbers as time goes on.

STENODERMA RUFUM Geoffroy

Stenoderma rufum E. Geoffroy, Description de l'Égypte, vol. 2, p. 114, 1818 (locality unknown).

SYNONYM: *Artibaeus undatus* Gervais, in Expéd. Amér. du Sud de Castelnau, Zool., Mamm., p. 35, pl. 9, fig. 3 (teeth), 1855.

FIGS.: Peters, 1876, pl. 1, figs. 1–3; Anthony, H. E., 1918, fig. 10 (skull and teeth).

This small fruit-eating bat was described 125 years ago from a specimen in the Paris Museum, but unfortunately there was no record of its place of origin. Since that time no other living specimen has been taken, and its habitat has remained unknown. In 1918, however, Dr. H. E. Anthony recorded the discovery of over two dozen "good-sized fragments of skulls, some nearly complete," during his excavations in the Cathedral Cave near Morovis, Puerto Rico. The presumption is thus strengthened that the real home of the species was the Greater Antilles, perhaps Puerto Rico.

In life this bat doubtless resembled somewhat the larger *Artibeus*, found in the same region, but the skull differs markedly in its short, broad rostrum, which, with its parallel and short tooth rows, is nearly square as seen from below. The median notch of the palate extends far forward to the level of the middle of the first molar. The incisors and upper canines form together a nearly transverse row, while the last molar, both above and below, is very small. The first two upper molars are broad for crushing and show little trace of the four primitive cusps. Total length of skull, exclusive of incisors, 23.1 mm.; zygomatic width, 15.7.

Since no other living examples of this small fruit bat have been found since it was first made known by Geoffroy, it is believed now to have become extinct during the last century. Anthony's interesting discovery of its remains in the Cathedral Cave in Puerto Rico indicates not only that this island may have been its home but also that it was fairly common there. The curious shape of the rostrum, so short and square, with heavy anterior molars, may indicate that it was adapted for feeding on some special kind of fruit, the abundance of which has been seriously affected through the clearing and burning of the original forest cover with cultivation on the island. Coincident with such restriction of food, the bat may have been much reduced in numbers until its final extinction. Anthony mentions the possibility that it may still be found on other islands but has been overlooked on account of a certain resemblance to the common *Artibeus*.

PUERTO RICAN LONG-TONGUED BAT

PHYLLONYCTERIS MAJOR Anthony

Phyllonycteris major Anthony, Bull. Amer. Mus. Nat. Hist., vol. 37, p. 567, Sept. 7, 1917 (cave near Morovis, Puerto Rico).
FIGS.: Anthony, 1917c, pl. 56, figs. 1, 2; 1918, p. 356, figs. 12, a-d (skull).

HAITIAN LONG-TONGUED BAT

PHYLLONYCTERIS OBTUSA Miller

Phyllonycteris obtusa Miller, Smithsonian Misc. Coll., vol. 81, no. 9, p. 10, Mar. 30, 1929 ("Cave near the Atalaye plantation, about 4 miles east of St. Michel, Haiti").

The bats of this genus are known only from Cuba, Puerto Rico, and Hispaniola of the Greater Antilles, where slightly differing local forms have developed on each island. On Cuba the living species, *P. poeyi*, though apparently not very common, nevertheless occurs in numbers in suitable caves, as at Guanajay, where Palmer secured a large series in 1900 (Miller, 1904), Baracoa, or in the Sierra de Hato Nuevo, where in 1917 Dr. Thomas Barbour found a large colony. On the other hand, in Puerto Rico it is unknown in the living state, though found in the superficial cave deposits, and the same is true of the Hispaniolan form; both are therefore included here among species nearly or quite gone.

These are small bats with long narrow skulls and long protrusible tongues, which are useful in licking up fruit pulp and juices on which they largely feed. Probably pollen and flower nectar are also eaten. A small hastate nose-leaf is present at the tip of the snout, and the interfemoral membrane is narrow, extending only to the middle of the tibia. The calcar is absent altogether. In each jaw, both upper and lower, there are two incisors, a canine, two premolars, and three molars. The last are rather weak and rounded, the second and third lower molars without cusps, a character contrasting with the condition in the related genus *Erophylla*, occurring in the same regions. The Puerto Rican *Phyllonycteris major* is decribed as closely related to the Cuban *P. poeyi*, but "noticeably larger, with wider brain case and heavier dentition"; greatest length of skull, 27–28 mm.; breadth of brain case, 11.4 mm. The form from Haiti, *P. obtusa*, is described as very similar to the Cuban species "but incisive foramina smaller and anterior border of premaxillaries as viewed in palatine aspect less narrowly curved." Greatest length of skull, 22.2 mm.; breadth of brain case, 10.2 mm.

During the course of his investigations in Puerto Rico caves, Dr. H. E. Anthony found no evidence that *P. major* is still living in that island. In only one cave, that near Morovis, did he find its remains, including about 60 skulls and many jaws. This may indicate not only that it was a cave-dweller, like its Cuban relative, but also that its choice of caves and perhaps even its numbers were limited. "It was contemporaneous with *Nesophontes* as well as with *Stenoderma rufum* and other bats to be found living today." Concerning the Hispaniolan *P. obtusa*, Miller (1929a) writes that remains were found in three distinct places: "The crooked cave near the Atalaye plantation, St. Michel, Haiti," a skull and mandible; a skull from a cave near Port-de-Paix; and a skull from owl pellets found in a cave at Diquini. The last implies that the skulls were fairly recent, and very likely the species may still be found there living, although none of the various collections of bats made in Hispaniola has hitherto yielded specimens. It is, as in other cases, difficult to assign an exact reason for the decline of such a species. Nevertheless, since it depends on a constant supply the year around of various fruits and berries in their season, it is obvious that any material changes in the forest or shrub covering, if this eliminated or reduced any one species of fruit even for a short critical season, might have a disastrous effect.

Concerning the Cuban species, *P. poeyi*, Palmer (*in* Miller, 1904) found it "very abundant in a wet, ill-ventilated cavern on Guanajay Mountain. On entering this cave, the vertical opening of which, about 12 feet across, was concealed by bushes, we descended about 25 feet, and were then standing some 20 feet above the lowest level. The slight noise which we made disturbed the bats in the inner chambers, and we could distinctly hear the rumbling made by their wings. As we proceeded this sound increased, until, when we reached the inner and thickly populated chambers, it became a grand, rushing roar of thousands on thousands of wildly flying animals. To reach the inner chamber it was necessary for us to descend from the first landing to the real floor of the cavern, and there light our candles, for not a ray of light and very little fresh air penetrated so far. From the floor we worked our way over many guano-covered, damp bowlders and through arches and narrow passages up to a sloping shelf, where, owing to the low roof, a man could not stand upright. By this time the bad air and excessive warmth was [were] telling on us, and we were in a most profuse perspiration. The bats were now thoroughly aroused, and the noise of their wings was astounding. Many were darting out through the passage by which we had entered . . . We began swinging a dip net in every direction, trusting to chance to secure specimens. About fifteen minutes of such work usually resulted in the capture of 20 to 30 bats, nearly all of this species . . . Before June 7, all the females were big with a single young, but after this date we found the pink, almost hairless little ones of different sizes hanging to the roof and scattered over much of its surface. On our last visit, late in June, the cave was so hot as to be unbearable . . . Among the specimens captured at the mouth of the damp cave near Baracoa . . . were many of this species . . . On one side of the vertical opening of this cave grew a large tree whose roots descended like a stream into the cavity. The people of the neighborhood assured me that the majás (the Cuban boa, *Epicrates angulifer*) coil themselves among these roots and grab at the bats as they fly out. I was told that a snake frequently secures a bat in this manner."

Family NATALIDAE: Long-legged Bats

CUBAN YELLOW BAT

NATALUS PRIMUS Anthony

Natalus primus Anthony, Bull. Amer. Mus. Nat. Hist., vol. 41, p. 642, Dec. 30, 1919 ("Daiquiri, Cuba," in the Cueva de los Indios).

The bats of the family Natalidae are small and delicately formed and have noticeably long and slender legs and distinctly funnel-shaped ears. The ample interfemoral membrane is supported in part by the tail, which extends to its border. In distribution the members of this family are confined to tropical America and occur on some of the West Indies, to which three of the genera are confined: *Chilonatalus* (on the Bahamas, Greater Antilles, and Old Providence Island), *Nyctiellus* (the Bahamas and Cuba), and *Phodotes* (island of Curaçao). The genus *Natalus* is the only one occurring on the mainland from tropical South America north to central Mexico, as well as in both the Greater and the Lesser Antilles. In the latter it is known living from the island of Dominica (*N. dominicensis* Shamel) and Antigua; in the former, from the Dominican Republic (*Natalus major* Miller). It is thus especially interesting that in the course of his cave investigations in eastern Cuba, Dr. H. E. Anthony should have found the present species represented by mandibles associated with *Nesophontes* and *Boromys* in the Cueva de los Indios at Daiquiri, "buried but a short distance under the surface. The bone is stained a very dark brown and probably represents an extinct form." From *N. major*, of the Dominican Republic, hitherto the largest known member of the genus, "it may be known by its even greater length of mandible and noticeably heavier teeth. The first lower molar is especially 'plump' in contour and the tooth extends externally considerably beyond the alveolar border." The mandible on which the description is based measured 14.4 mm. in greatest length or about a millimeter more than in the large form of the Dominican Republic, of which it may be regarded as the Cuban representative. The color in life was perhaps yellowish, as in some of its near relatives.

Nothing further is known of the species, but since it has not been found living by any of the various collectors who have searched for bats in Cuba, it is probably, as Anthony says, extinct.

In this connection it may be surmised that the present sporadic distribution of this genus in the West Indies, with one living form on Dominica, one in Hispaniola, and a third probably recently extinct in Cuba, implies that it may once have been more widespread over this area—and has already died out on other islands. Of this, however, there is at present no evidence. The other related genera, too, may be thought of as in a restricted situation. The little *Nyctiellus*, one of the smallest of bats, and formerly believed to be confined to Cuba and the Isle of Pines, has in late years been found in numbers in some of the Bahamas (G. M. Allen and Sanborn, 1937) and is probably in no present danger. The somewhat larger *Chilonatalus* is found, in several closely allied races, on Cuba, Jamaica, the Bahamas, and on Old Providence Island, dwelling in caves. Wherever its small colonies exist it does not seem especially difficult to find and may be fairly safe for the present, since it is insectivorous like the others of the family, and there would seem to be no lack of sustenance for it. Of the genus *Phodotes*, a close relative of *Natalus*, practically nothing is known beyond Miller's original description based on a specimen from the island of Curaçao, off the coast of Venezuela. If, as supposed, it is peculiar to that island, its future status may well be somewhat precarious on account of changes taking place with intensive cultivation.

Family VESPERTILIONIDAE: Simple-nosed Bats
SPOTTED BAT; "DEATH'S-HEAD BAT"
EUDERMA MACULATUM (J. A. Allen)

Histiotus maculatus J. A. Allen, Bull. Amer. Mus. Nat. Hist., vol. 3, p. 195, 1891 (near Piru, Ventura County, California, probably at mouth of Castac Creek).
FIGS.: Miller, 1897a, pl. 1, fig. 11 (ear); pl. 3, fig. 3 (wing); 1907, p. 226, fig. 37 (skull); Bailey, V., 1931, pl. 21, B; Grinnell, H. W., 1918, pl. 16, fig. 9 (photograph).

For 12 years after its first discovery in Ventura County, Calif., this bat remained unique; then a second one was found in the biological laboratory of the College of Agriculture and Mechanic Arts at Mesilla Park, N. Mex. Since that time only six additional specimens have been discovered, all in the Southwestern United States. This apparent rarity has led to the belief that the species is actually a waning one, and for this reason it is here included.

This is a fairly large bat with a total length of about 110 mm.; tail, 50; forearm, 50. In color the fur is deep black, with three large white spots: one at each shoulder and one on the lower part of the back, giving a striking contrast. The lower side is washed with white. The very long ears measured 34 mm. in one specimen. The two upper and two lower premolars, the nostrils simple instead of opening upward or in connection with nasal swellings, and the distinctive color and long ears will serve to identify it easily.

An account of the skeleton with figures of the important bones has been given by E. R. Hall (1934), who in a later note (1939) adds an eighth to the list of known individuals taken. The localities are: Piru, Ventura County, Calif.; Mesilla Park, N. Mex.; Yuma, Ariz.; Mecca, Kern County, and Yosemite Valley, Calif.; Reno, Nev.; and Salt Lake City, Utah (see Durrant, 1935, p. 226). In every instance only a solitary individual has appeared, and in such unexpected places as clinging to a fence rail, or the under side of a rock, under the eaves of a schoolhouse, in a biological laboratory (!), or on the side of a building. One was found dead in the overflow of a railway water tank. From these few instances it has not been possible to deduce what is the natural resting place of the species by day. Possibly the one found clinging to the lower side of a rock indicates more nearly the sort of place they normally seek for shelter. The area outlined by these eight known instances takes in roughly the arid region of the Great Basin of the Southwestern United States, to which probably the species is confined. Other than the scanty information supplied by the eight specimens hitherto discovered, nothing whatever is known of its habits. It is, however, not at all impossible that it may somewhere be found in greater numbers. Its evidently solitary disposition and its liking for outside resting places make it seem unlikely that it is a colonial and cave-dwelling bat.

Whether this is a species in danger of eventual extermination can not now be told with certainty, nor does it appear that anything can at present be done to foster it.

GALÁPAGOS ISLANDS RED BAT

LASIURUS BRACHYOTIS (J. A. Allen)

Atalapha brachyotis J. A. Allen, Bull. Amer. Mus. Nat. Hist., vol. 4, p. 47, Mar. 25, 1892 ("Chatham Island," Galápagos Islands).

This, the only bat at present known from the Galápagos Islands, is one of the red-bat group, found on the American continents from north-temperate to south-temperate latitudes. It is a smaller relative of the hoary bats of the American continents and Hawaii and like them has a hairy tail-membrane, short rounded ears, and only a single upper incisor.

The Galápagos bat is said to resemble closely its mainland representative in its rusty-red coloring and minutely frosted tipping to the hairs, but the ears are smaller and the wings slenderer, the dentition lighter, with shorter canines. Forearm length, 39 mm.

Of this bat almost nothing is known. Dr. George Baur, who collected the type specimen about 50 years ago, wrote at the time of its capture (Allen, 1892): "On Chatham Island, at an elevation of about 1700 feet, where the hacienda is placed, we observed bats nearly every evening." The specimen was the only one he succeeded in capturing, and it is at present in the Museum of Comparative Zoology (its skull, however, unfortunately lost). Dr. Baur adds: "Bats have been observed on Indefatigable Island by Dr. Habel, and I observed one on South Albemarle." It is, of course, uncertain whether all these represented the same species of bat. Red bats are known to reach Bermuda in their migrations in eastern North America, so that it is not surprising that this strong-flying species should have reached the Galápagos at some distant period. Whether it will continue to survive the arid conditions and restriction of forest growth on the islands can not at present be told.

HAWAIIAN HOARY BAT; "OLEPE"

LASIURUS SEMOTUS (H. Allen)

Atalapha semota H. Allen, Proc. U. S. Nat. Mus., vol. 13, p. 173, Sept. 9, 1890 (Kauai, Hawaiian Islands).

SYNONYM: *Lasiurus grayii* in part, J. E. Gray, Proc. Zool. Soc. London, 1862, p. 143.

This is the Hawaiian representative of the continental hoary bat, which as a species ranges from north-temperate and sub-boreal latitudes to south-temperate climates, thus covering a wide latitudinal extent. It is migratory in northern United States and southern Canada; hence perhaps one may assume that the ancestor of the Hawaiian form reached that group of islands by flight over sea at some time in the distant past, coming from the American continent. Although at one time believed to be the same as the continental *L. grayii* of Chile, the Hawaiian form is darker, and in the red phase lacks to a large extent the hoary tips to the hairs of the upper surface found in that race and in the North American *L. cinereus*.

In the Hawaiian hoary bat the color of the fur above may be either gray as in *L. cinereus* or dark red, almost blackish brown, with the middle portions of the hairs dull whitish, showing through if the fur is disturbed. On the lower flanks, legs, and interfemoral membrane above, the color of the back in the red phase passes gradually into a bright chestnut or mahogany red, with practically no white tipping to the hairs. Below, the color is paler, with chin and upper throat buffy white, and an indistinct half-collar of darker, set off by white tips to the hairs, from the dull-brown belly. Fur along the under side of forearm and at base of fingers clear buffy. A minute tuft of short white hairs at base of thumb and of digit 5, and a third white tuft on the inner side of the forearm just beyond the elbow. Forearm measures about 50 mm. (in the original description it is given as 40, but G. S. Miller, Jr. (1939) shows that this is a misprint for 50 as shown by an examination of the lectotype in the U. S. National Museum).

This bat was first reported from the Hawaiian Islands by J. E. Gray in 1862, who, however, believed it identical with the Chilean race, which Tomes had earlier named *Lasiurus grayii*. Harrison Allen in naming it as a distinct form, had eight specimens from the "Sandwich Islands," only two of which had the more precise locality of Kauai. Perkins (1903, p. 465) writes that it chiefly frequents the mountains where, presumably, more forested areas remain. He adds that it is locally common in the uplands of Hawaii, and he has seen it, though rarely, on the islands of Kauai and Oahu. Bryan, writing in 1915, says: "They have always been rare, but are apparently still to be seen in the uplands of Hawaii." There are four specimens in the museum at Tring, England, from Hawaii taken in 1891, and the Museum of Comparative Zoology has a specimen taken in 1937 at Waimea, island of

Hawaii, by Miss Barbara Lawrence, who says that the boys sometimes find them hanging among the fronds of tree ferns in the lowland valleys.

While at present the species may be in no particular danger, it is likely that any considerable changes, such as reduction in the amount of sheltering tree growth, will affect the species adversely. As the only bat at present known to inhabit this group of islands, this species is of particular interest, and its obvious derivation from the American Continent makes it further noteworthy from the distributional viewpoint.

Order EDENTATA: Edentates

The New World edentates belong to the suborder Xenarthra. Two groups are recognized:

(1) Cingulata, the armadillos and their relatives. A race of the widely distributed nine-banded armadillo is restricted in its range to a small West Indian island and may be easily exterminated.

(2) Pilosa, sloths, ground sloths, and American anteaters. Of these the ground sloths have become entirely extinct; five species are thought to have persisted into historic times in Puerto Rico, Haiti, and Cuba.—J. E. H.

Family DASYPODIDAE: Armadillos

GRENADA ARMADILLO

DASYPUS NOVEMCINCTUS HOPLITES G. M. Allen

Dasypus novemcinctus hoplites G. M. Allen, Bull. Mus. Comp. Zool., vol. 54, p. 195, July, 1911 ("Hills back of Gouyave, island of Grenada," West Indies).

This is a small race of the continental nine-banded armadillo, but it may be included in this account since any island race represented by a relatively small population is liable to further reduction if in the course of years the conditions change greatly through fire, settlement, or other causes that may further restrict the available habitat.

Externally this is a somewhat smaller replica of the ordinary nine-banded armadillo, with the usual external bony cuirass consisting of a shoulder shield, a rump shield, and nine intermediate half-rings on the body. The tail is covered with a series of 12 complete bony rings, and the color in life is light flesh-color. From the posterior free edges of the transverse body-rings project three or four short bristles from each scale and similar but smaller bristles are present at the posterior margins of the scales on the shields of body and tail. On the under side of the body there are transverse rows of small round scutes, each in the center of a cluster of yellowish bristles. The skull in addition to being smaller than that of the mainland representative has one or two less teeth in each series, usually six or seven instead of eight. Total length, up to 678 mm.; tail, 82; hind foot, 37; greatest length of skull, 85.5.

At the present day this armadillo is confined to the rough country covered with rain forest on the hills in the central part of the island of Grenada. Probably, too, the armadillo found on the island of Tobago is very similar if not identical. It is more or less hunted by the local Negroes who esteem its flesh. They not only hunt the armadillos with dogs but catch them in deadfalls set in the runways. Whether the armadillo naturally occurred in these islands or whether it was introduced there long ago is uncertain, but in either case it has been native for a long enough time to allow its development into a distinct dwarf race. De Rochefort, writing in 1658, mentions the "Tatou" as a native of Tobago, especially calling attention to the small size. Soon after, Du Tertre in the 1667 edition of his work on the history of the French Islands, was the first to record it from Grenada, where he says it was then common. It was unknown on any of the other French islands, and apparently all attempts to introduce it in Martinique from Grenada had ended in failure. Labat in 1742, however, mentions having eaten the flesh of armadillos that had been brought to Martinique from Grenada, and in 1700 had several times eaten it on the latter island.

At the present time I know of no reason to suppose that this armadillo is in any danger of extinction. When I visited the island in 1910, I found it well known to the people and a Mr. John Branch assured me that often the Negroes might capture several in a single night, hunting with dogs, in the forest back of Victoria. The animal is fairly prolific and should survive without difficulty if conditions remain substantially unchanged.

Family MEGALOCHNIDAE: Ground Sloths

SMALLER PUERTO RICAN GROUND SLOTH

ACRATOCNUS ODONTRIGONUS Anthony

Acratocnus odontrigonus Anthony, Ann. New York Acad. Sci., vol. 27, p. 195, Aug. 9, 1916 ("Cueva de la Ceiba, near Utuado, Porto Rico").

FIGS.: Anthony, H. E., 1916, pls. 7–10, pl. 11, fig. 1; 1918, figs. 43–48, 50–54 (except those of *A. major*); pl. 69, figs. 1a–c; pl. 70, figs. 2–6; pl. 71, figs. 1, 3–6; pl. 72, figs. 1, 3, 4; pl. 73, figs. 1–3, 5, 7; pl. 74, figs. 1–4 (skeletal parts).

LARGER PUERTO RICAN GROUND SLOTH

ACRATOCNUS MAJOR Anthony

Acratocnus major Anthony, Mem. Amer. Mus. Nat. Hist., ser. 2, vol. 2, p. 412, 1918 ("Cave . . . near Utuado, Porto Rico").

FIGS.: Anthony, H. E., 1918, figs. 42, 43, 48, 49, 51, 53 (parts pertaining to No. 17169); pl. 69, figs. 2a–c; pl. 70, figs. 1, 7, 8; pl. 71, fig. 2; pl. 72, figs. 2a–b, 5; pl. 73, figs. 4, 6.

HISPANIOLAN GROUND SLOTH

ACRATOCNUS (?) COMES Miller

Acratocnus (?) *comes* Miller, Smithsonian Misc. Coll., vol. 81, no. 9, p. 26, Mar. 30, 1929 ("Large cave near St. Michel, Haiti").

FIGS.: Miller, 1929a, pl. 5, fig. 2; pl. 6, fig. 2; pl. 8, fig. 1; pl. 10, fig. 1 (limb bones and atlas).

Among the most interesting finds of recent years is the discovery of bones in the caves of Puerto Rico and Haiti representing a small ground sloth, which was evidently contemporary with aboriginal culture. It was approximately the size of a two-toed sloth but represented the ground-living group, known from the mainland of North America by the gigantic mylodons of the Pleistocene era. The nearest relatives seem to be the small ground sloths of the genus *Hapalops* from Miocene formations of Patagonia, although there are various differences. Their presence on both Puerto Rico and Hispaniola is additional evidence of the faunal affinities of these two islands, and since the three forms hitherto described seem closely allied, they may be considered under a single head.

The smaller ground sloth of Puerto Rico was the first described and is the best known, from abundant skeletal remains found in the cave earth during excavations originally undertaken in the course of archeological research. As in the living tree sloths, the premaxillae were toothless, and the incisors and canines of the lower series are also lacking. The skull is relatively long and narrow instead of globular as it is in the tree-living types, the rostrum is short and broad, and there is a well-developed median crest extending forward from the wide occipital ridge to the frontal region, where a lower branch goes to each of the short postorbital projections. The large tusklike upper canines are strongly triangular in section, followed by a diastema of nearly the same length as the diameter of the tooth or somewhat longer, then four cheek teeth in two parallel rows, each tooth approximately oval in section, with the broader end on the lingual side. In the lower jaw, there is a large tusklike first premolar corresponding to the upper canine, then a space, followed by three cheek teeth much like those of the upper series. The humerus has a slender shaft, a wide distal expansion, and a large entepicondylar foramen. The femur is wide in front view, but not thick, and shows a low third or outer trochanteric ridge. The tibia is short and stout and the fibula is free. The calcaneum or heel bone is broadly hatchet-shaped, and the terminal phalanges were evidently provided with stout claws. The tail is believed to have been short but rather stout. Dr. Anthony gives the following dimensions of the major skeletal elements: Skull length, tip of rostrum to occipital condyles, 136.2 mm.; breadth of brain casé, 28.5; greatest breadth across postorbital processes, 47.5; alveolar length of upper molar series, 35.5; longest humerus, 145; ulna, 160; radius, 128.8; longest femur, 163.3; longest tibia, 128.

Among the remains of this species recovered in caves in Puerto Rico were a few indicating a similar sloth of slightly larger size, which Dr. Anthony in a later communication decided must represent a second and larger species of the same genus. This he named *Acratocnus major*, and defined it as being very similar to *A. odontrigonus* but "larger and heavier and with different skull characters"; it has "proportionally a much broader muzzle and an elevated basioccipital region," and a larger upper canine. No complete measurements of the skull are available, but the breadth across postorbital processes is 66 mm.; length of ulna, 171; length of tibia, 133. By comparison with the corresponding measurements given above for the smaller species, the obvious size difference may be appreciated.

The Haitian species, *A. (?) comes,* was based on a femur from a large cave and represents an animal much like *A. odontrigonus,* weighing perhaps 50 pounds. The bone differs from the corresponding one of the latter in having the neck of the articular condyle shorter and less bent outward and forward so that it diverges less noticeably from the general contour of the shaft. In describing the species, Miller refers to it a few other fragments, including several caniniform teeth from Gonave Island, off the coast of Port-au-Prince, Haiti, but the complete skull is as yet unknown.

In Puerto Rico, remains of this type of ground sloth occur in dry caves in the limestone of the mountainous parts of the island. "Caves up on the sides of small hills yielded the most bones and the size of the cave was immaterial. The cave that contained the greatest amount of Ground Sloth material was a small one with the entrance on a rather steep hillside and opening out on a sheer front of limestone. Inside, the cave did not open out very wide but had a deep fissure at the left toward which the floor sloped abruptly. This fissure was richly packed with bones of the sloth and the large rodent [*Elasmodontomys*], the bones beginning at near the surface and continuing down some nine feet when excavations had to be given up because of the impossibility of reaching any deeper. This cave had the appearance of a trap for any animal that wandered into it and certainly would have proved so for any old or sick animal that had strength enough to crawl up through the cave entrance."

Concerning the remains of this genus and a larger sloth found in Hispaniola by Miller, the latter states (1929a): "That one or both of these sloths continued to exist on the island until after the advent of man I have no doubt. The facts that have led me to this conclusion are as follows: (a) In the two caves near St. Michel most of the sloth remains were found within two feet of the surface; and human bones and pottery occurred to the same depth without any indication that they had been dug in. (b) Near the entrance to the smaller of the two main caves bones of ground sloths (certainly two and perhaps more individuals) were inextricably mixed with bones of man (adult and infant) and domestic pig. The remains were scattered among the small fragments of limestone which made up the greater part of the floor material, and I was unable to determine any definite level-relationship among them. (c) Near the entrance to the large cave I unearthed with a trowel, in fine, soft, undisturbed material at the bottom of a trench two feet deep, the femur of a ground sloth, and, about 18 inches from it, a fragment of coarse dark pottery . . the bone and pottery had every appearance of having been deposited on the former surface of the cave floor and subsequently covered by the gradual accumulation of detritus . . In general the ground sloth bones were associated with the human remains in exactly the same manner as the bones of *Isolobodon* and *Plagiodontia*, rodents which are positively known to have been contemporary with man." The external appearance of these animals may only be conjectured, for no fragments of hide or hair are known to be preserved.

Larger Hispaniolan Ground Sloth

Parocnus serus Miller

Parocnus serus Miller, Smithsonian Misc. Coll., vol. 81, no. 9, p. 29, Mar. 30, 1929 ("In a large cave near St. Michel, Haiti").
Figs.: Miller, 1929a, pl. 7; pl. 8, fig. 2; pl. 9; pl. 10, figs. 2, 3.

Large Cuban Ground Sloth

Megalocnus rodens Leidy

Megalocnus rodens Leidy, Proc. Acad. Nat. Sci. Philadelphia, 1868, p. 180 (Cuba).

Miller, in describing the larger ground sloth from Haiti, believed there was good evidence that it lived to be the contemporary of man, since its remains were found in close association with pottery and in layers of cave earth at no great depth. Judging from the size of the few bones found, he surmised it to have been an animal weighing upward of 150 pounds and more heavily built that *Acratocnus*. The femur, on which the description mainly rests, is at once distinguishable by the absence of the lesser trochanter, "as well as by its greater size and the much more noticeable antero-posterior flattening of the upper portion of the shaft." No skulls have yet been found sufficiently well preserved to give much idea of the cranial characters. An important feature of the humerus seems to be the lack of an entepicondylar foramen, of which no trace is visible in the figure published by Miller. The humerus measures 200 mm.

in greatest length. Three calcanea are essentially similar to the calcaneum of *Mylodon*.

While *Acratocnus* and *Parocnus* did not perhaps become extinct till fairly recent times, possibly not until after the discovery of the West Indies by Europeans, the Cuban ground sloths may have died out at an earlier time. Their remains are known in some abundance in deposits around a warm spring at Ciego Montero, associated with bones of a crocodile and a giant tortoise. Another important locality is the Casimba in the Sierra de Jatibonico, in central Cuba, a fissure spring at the bottom of a ravine, where many bones have been found. Although a full account of these remains was in preparation by the late Dr. W. D. Matthew and Prof. Carlos de la Torre, this seems to have been indefinitely postponed through the death of the former. Nevertheless, in preliminary papers (Torre and Matthew, 1915; Matthew, 1918, 1931) they distinguish no less that four genera, to which names are given. Matthew (1918, p. 660) restricts *Megalocnus* to the largest of these, "about the size of a black bear"; the smallest is *Microcnus*, "about the size of a cat, and there are two of intermediate size, *Mesocnus*, with a rather long, narrow muzzle, and *Miocnus*, with a broad, square muzzle." To this last genus *Acratocnus* of Puerto Rico and Hispaniola is said to be related. Possibly, too, *Parocnus* may be found to be closely related to one of the two intermediate genera or even identical with it, when better material is assembled and restudied. The three other genera, *Megalocnus*, *Microcnus*, and *Mesocnus*, have large tusks of a "peculiar dished shape, with a tendency to approach toward each other like the incisors of rodents." Matthew regards the Cuban ground sloths and the Puerto Rican *Acratocnus odontrigonus* as descendants of a common ancestral type of Upper Miocene or Lower Pliocene age, related to that of *Megalonyx*. Matthew adds that "there is so much individual and age variation in ground sloths that it is difficult to say how many species of these genera are present. *Megalocnus* occurs abundantly both at Ciego Montero and the Casimba, but apparently only one species at Ciego Montero, while at the Casimba there may be two or three. The species found at the eastern end of the island agree better with the Casimba forms than with the Ciego Montero species. Of the smaller forms there are clearly two species of *Mesocnus*, but I see no proof of more than one of *Miocnus* or *Microcnus*." So far nothing seems to have been discovered that would indicate that ground sloths in Cuba were contemporaneous with early man.

Order RODENTIA: Gnawing Mammals

The rodents, here considered to include the rabbits and pikas, are the largest order of mammals, both in number of species and of individuals. They are characterized by chisel-like incisor teeth, usually a single pair above and below, but with a second pair of upper incisors in the rabbits. They are mostly small mammals, with large populations and rapid rates of reproduction. There are four suborders:

(1) Lagomorpha (Duplicidentata): The rabbits and hares, found in all zoogeographical regions, except the Australian, and pikas of Asia and western North America. Rabbits have been introduced into Australia and elsewhere.

(2) Sciuromorpha: This includes the squirrel family, which is world wide, except for the oceanic islands and the Australian Region; the scaly-tailed African "flying squirrels," the African springhaas; the beaver, found in Europe, northern Asia, and North America; and the sewellel of the Pacific coast of North America.

(3) Myomorpha: The rats, mice, jerboas, and their relatives; representatives of this group occur in all regions, although human agency is doubtless responsible for their presence on some oceanic islands.

(4) Hystricomorpha: The porcupines, cavies, chinchillas, and their relatives; representatives of this group are found in all regions, except the Australian and the oceanic islands.

The vanishing or extinct North American rodents are the following:

(1) Sciuridae, squirrels, four forms of a single genus.

(2) Castoridae, beavers, eighteen races of the single American species.

(3) Cricetidae, native rats and mice, eight species of three genera.

(4) Echimyidae, hystricoid spiny rats, twenty species and subspecies of nine genera.

(5) Heptaxodontidae, the unique species, thought to have become extinct about the time of Columbus.

(6) Dinomyidae, giant hystricoid rats, two species of two genera.

(7) Dasyproctidae, agoutis, three insular species of the typical genus.

The last four families belong to the New World Hystricomorpha and have their relatives in South America, where they probably originated.—J. E. H.

Family SCIURIDAE: Squirrels

KAIBAB, OR WHITE-TAILED, SQUIRREL

SCIURUS KAIBABENSIS Merriam

Sciurus kaibabensis Merriam, Proc. Biol. Soc. Washington, vol. 17, p. 129, 1904 ("Head of Bright Angel Creek, top of Kaibab Plateau, north side of Grand Canyon of Colorado, Arizona").

FIGS.: Nelson, 1918, p. 448, lower fig. (col.); Goldman, 1928, p. 127, pl. 16 (photograph).

This is perhaps the handsomest of the North American squirrels, a close relative of Abert's squirrel, with long-tufted ears, which ranges from Colorado into Mexico. The white-tailed squirrel has become isolated on the north side of the Grand Canyon in the high Kaibab Plateau and has developed striking color characters, such especially as its large white tail. Because of its restricted habitat and conspicuousness it may be included here.

In its general appearance it resembles Abert's squirrel, but the under parts are mainly black instead of white, and the tail is practically all white instead of on the under side only. The back is dark grizzled gray, with a wash of ferruginous from shoulders to rump. The ears are blackish in summer but rimmed anteriorly with gray in winter; the ear tufts are black, the face, fore feet, and toes mixed gray and black; hind feet in summer mainly gray but in winter mainly black. The tail is ample and bushy, white, with an indistinct buffy-gray stripe down the middle of the upper side. Size about that of a gray squirrel.

The Kaibab squirrel is found in a restricted area about 40 miles in length and 20 miles in greatest width, at the broadest (southern) part of the Kaibab Plateau. Isolated here from its nearest allies of the south side of the Grand Canyon, it is confined to the portions of the plateau where the yellow pine

(*Pinus ponderosa*) is found. It is largely dependent on this tree for food and shelter as are its relatives of the Abert's squirrel type, which, wherever they occur, "are rarely or never seen beyond the local range of this tree. On the Kaibab Plateau the altitudinal range is mainly from 7,000 to 8,500 feet" (Goldman, 1928). Major Goldman (1928) writes: "Yellow pines are rarely hollow and I have never seen one of these squirrels enter a hole. Dome-shaped nests, about 2 feet in diameter, made of cut pine branches, are usually well concealed among crowded limbs in the upper part of a tree. Like most squirrels, the white-tail is most active during the early morning and late afternoon, but may be found abroad at any time of day. Practically nothing seems to be known of its breeding habits." Although it depends partly for food upon the seeds of the yellow pine, which it extracts by gnawing away the scales, this supply is more or less precarious in years when the crop is poor. Its main reliance is therefore the cambium beneath the bark of the newer twigs of the yellow pine, which provides an unfailing food supply. "In feeding, the leaf-bearing branch tip is commonly severed and allowed to drop to the ground. A subterminal section of tender stem 2 to 4 inches in length is cut off, scaled, and when the cambium sought as food has been neatly removed, the peeled wood remaining is also dropped . . . In summer, however, they evidently indulge in a more varied diet. Much time is spent in foraging upon the ground and I have at various times observed them feeding upon mushrooms and other funguses, and they doubtless eat many other things."

Although it is known that these squirrels are occasionally taken by hawks, Major Goldman believes that their numbers are no more seriously affected by these enemies than are those of other forms of Abert's squirrel. "The destruction of much ground cover through overbrowsing by deer may, however, expose the squirrels to some additional danger from hawks. Squirrels everywhere vary in numbers from year to year owing to causes imperfectly understood, but at present there seems to be no great danger of the extinction of the white-tail. These beautiful squirrels are objects of great interest to tourists along the Grand Canyon highway that bisects the Kaibab plateau, and efforts should be made to establish them in other yellow pine forested areas." He adds the caution that care should be taken in such an enterprise, not to introduce them into other areas already occupied by races of Abert's squirrel, since hybridization would inevitably tend to the loss of the distinctive and conspicuous characters of this particular form. At the present time the Kaibab squirrel is completely protected by law and should be fairly well safeguarded, but any influences that might tend to impair the growths of yellow pine to which it is restricted would react unfavorably on its welfare in the limited area in which it is found.

BLACK MANGROVE SQUIRREL

SCIURUS NIGER AVICENNIA A. H. Howell

Sciurus niger avicennia A. H. Howell, Journ. Mammalogy, vol. 1, p. 37, Nov. 1919 ("Everglade, Lee County, Florida").

There are few less-inviting places for mammals than a mangrove swamp. The clean trunks and branches offer little in the way of food or shelter; the soft ooze from which the trees grow is daily washed by the tides and thus is unsuitable for groundlivers; while the suckerlike stems and rooting tips form a tangle almost impossible for the larger species to penetrate. It is therefore the more remarkable that a depauperate form of the southern fox squirrel has made the mangrove belt of the southwest coast of Florida its home and become adapted to a life in this apparently unfavorable environment.

The mangrove squirrel is described as smaller and darker (more tawny) both above and below than the typical race, with the feet clearer white and less tinged with buff. The type is in the so-called buff phase or at least is not of the entirely black sort, with white face and ears. The head and back are black sprinkled with cinnamon but more abundantly on lower back; sides shading to orange-cinnamon; nose, lips, front of face, and ears white; fore legs blackish washed with orange-cinnamon, the feet and toes white; hind legs with more orange-cinnamon than black, the feet edged with white. Tail orange-cinnamon above, mixed with black, and shading on the sides to hazel; under side rich tawny, with a submarginal band of black. Under parts dull orange-cinnamon washed on throat and breast with black and white. A black phase also occurs, in which the nose, ears, paws and sometimes the end of the tail are white, while elsewhere the pelage is deep shining black, with a few pale hairs on the under side. Total length of an adult male (the type), 535 mm. (21.25 inches); tail vertebrae, 260 (10.25 inches); hind foot, 75 (about 3 inches); skull, occipitonasal length, 65.5.

This squirrel is confined to "the damp, dark forests of black and red mangrove which extend practically without a break from Marco Pass to Cape Sable and around the southern end of the peninsula" of Florida, "to the shores of Biscayne Bay on the east coast." Here it is apparently not common, for Howell writes that "several days spent in hunting through these mosquito-infested forests resulted" in only a brief glimpse of one, while the type specimen he secured through an Indian boy who knew where its home tree was located. A small series of specimens, however, was secured by W. S. Brooks in the spring of 1920, for the Museum of Comparative Zoology, mostly in the black phase. I am indebted to Dr. Thomas Barbour for a few notes on this squirrel. He tells me that it is well known to the residents of the region, though not regarded as common, and that it may be found on even some of the isolated keys grown up to mangroves. Its feeding habits are remarkable for, instead of depending on nuts and other seeds, it lives on the buds and bark of the mangroves, gnawing the latter from twigs which it cuts. Dr. Barbour reports that after the hurricane that passed over this region a few years ago its numbers seem to have been lessened. Evidently it is very difficult to secure satisfactory estimates of the size and extent of this squirrel population, since the swamps can hardly be penetrated except by canoes along small waterways. While this race of fox squirrel may be in no very immediate danger at the present time, it might easily be affected by any large-scale attempts to alter the local ecologic conditions.

BRYANT'S FOX SQUIRREL; PENINSULA FOX SQUIRREL

SCIURUS NIGER BRYANTI H. H. Bailey

Sciurus niger bryanti H. H. Bailey, Bull. Bailey Mus. and Library of Nat. Hist., no. 1, p. 1, Aug. 1, 1920 ("Cambridge, Dorchester County, Maryland").

Dorchester County, Md., lies on the southwestern side of the large peninsula, nearly cut off from the mainland on the east by Delaware Bay and Delaware River and on the west by the long estuary formed by Chesapeake Bay. Isolated in the

area near the tip of this peninsula is a small population of fox
squirrels, which differ from the eastern fox squirrels in coloration by lacking the buff and russet tints. They form a local
race, named by H. H. Bailey in honor of the ornithologist
Walter E. Bryant.

In a small series of specimens of this squirrel the coloration is
remarkably uniform. The entire dorsal surface of the body is a
hoary gray, the result of abundant white-tipped hairs mixed
with black hairs. On the forehead the black hairs slightly predominate. The under surfaces from chin to root of tail are
white. Feet and ears dull white, sometimes with a faint tinge
of buffy. Tail mixed black and white both above and below,
the black forming a narrow and continuous submarginal
border on the under side.

Although, according to Bailey, the local gunners secure a
few each season in Dorchester County, this race is so localized,
with little or no likelihood of its increasing its range, that it
must be thought of as like an island form threatened with
gradual encroachment on its available habitat. For this reason
it is likely in time to become more and more restricted, with
little possibility of long survival unless given special protection.

Concerning the present status of this squirrel, I am indebted
for a few details to David V. Black, manager of the Blackwater
National Wildlife Refuge, Cambridge, Md., who in response to
inquiries writes, under date of March 21, 1941: "I have talked
with several persons in Dorchester County about the fox
squirrels found here, and they all seem to be of the opinion
that they are fairly abundant and are found in all parts of the
county. There is no particular protection given to Bryant's
fox squirrel. It is hunted indiscriminately with other squirrels
during the open seasons in the State. I do not think that it is
threatened with extermination as yet. Most of the timber
has been cut out in the county, and what little remains seems
to be in the process of cutting with small portable sawmills, so
that the natural habitat for squirrels and other woods dwellers
is continually diminishing. The squirrels do occur on the
refuge, where, of course, no hunting is allowed."

EASTERN FOX SQUIRREL; NORTHERN FOX SQUIRREL

SCIURUS NIGER NEGLECTUS (Gray)

Macroxus neglectus Gray, Ann. Mag. Nat. Hist., ser. 3, vol. 20, p. 425, 1867 (Wilmington, Delaware).

SYNONYMS: *Sciurus vulpinus* Schreber, Säugthiere, vol. 4, p. 772, 1792 (preoccupied by *Sciurus vulpinus* Gmelin) (Baltimore, Maryland); *Sciurus ludovicianus vicinus* Bangs, Proc. Biol. Soc. Washington, vol. 10, p. 150, 1896 (White Sulphur Springs, West Virginia).

FIGS.: Audubon and Bachman, 1849, Quadrupeds of North America, vol. 1, pl. 17 (col.) (as *Sciurus cinereus*); Bangs, 1896, pl. 8, fig. 3 (skull).

The fox squirrels are typical of open heavy forests in the eastern half of the United States and extend in various sub-species from New England west to the plains region in South Dakota, and south to southern Florida, and to Texas and northeastern Mexico. In the more thickly settled areas of the East their numbers have been greatly reduced locally, and especially in the Northeast they have reached nearly the point of complete extirpation. The typical form, *Sciurus niger niger*, is still fairly common in the southeastern States, from southern South Carolina to Florida, frequenting chiefly the open "piney woods." The northeastern race, *S. niger neglectus*, however, is gone from its more northern outposts and is in danger of complete wiping out east of the Alleghenies.

The eastern fox squirrel is slightly larger than that of the Southeast and somewhat resembles a large gray squirrel. The upper parts of the head and body are a grizzled buffy and black, slightly darker on the forehead; cheeks, ears, forearms and feet, the lower hind legs and hind feet pale rufous; under side of body white; tail about as long as body, mixed black and buffy above, rufous below and on the sides. Total length, about 2 feet; tail, 11 inches; hind foot, 2.75 inches (73 mm.). Distinguished from the more western race, *rufiventer*, by its white instead of rufous belly, and from the southern typical form by its rufous ears instead of white, and the usual lack of black color, though rarely entirely black individuals occur.

The eastern fox squirrel probably in former times just reached southwestern Connecticut but has long since gone. Linsley (1842), in his list of the mammals of that State, knew of it only from Northford, a century ago. In New York State it was formerly found in the southern parts in some numbers, as attested by Bachman in 1839. He mentions several lately received from Orange County but adds that in northern New York it is exceedingly rare, as he "only saw two pair during fifteen years of close observation." Merriam (1884) called it a rare or accidental straggler in the Adirondacks region and mentions a specimen or two at Lake George in 1872 or 1873 as the only recent instance he knew of, but there seems even there to be some doubt whether or not it had been brought in and escaped. In Rensselaer County he records two killed in 1854. At about the same time Dr. A. K. Fisher knew of its having been killed in Westchester County, but adds that in 1896 none had been known "of late even in that wild region." At the present time the fox squirrel is practically gone from the State. In New Jersey it was present locally at least up to about 1865 but was apparently gone by the nineties. In Pennsylvania the species was formerly common in the lower altitudes but is now much reduced. Rhoads (1903) says of its status in the early years of this century that it was "probably always rarer in Chester and Delaware counties and in southern N. J. than in south central Pa. and northern N. J. Now exterminated in N. J. but found occasionally in the Pa. counties bordering the lower Susquehanna, also yet recorded from the northwestern part of Pa." He quotes Todd that it was shot "at rare intervals in some of the northern counties" of the western border of Pennsylvania; and believed that it was destined to extermination within the entire limits of the State unless large areas of country in middle Pennsylvania "revert to a wilderness condition or become game reservations under state protection." Even in 1896 Bangs wrote that Dr. B. H. Warren informed him that "the northern fox squirrel is practically extinct in Pennsylvania except in the counties of Dauphin and Cumberland" near the south-central part of the State. In West Virginia, Kellogg (1937) reports that "it now survives in the heavily wooded and sparsely settled higher altitudes of the Allegheny Mountains" and that for many years numbers were shipped to Center Market in Washington, "from points in western Virginia and from eastern West Virginia." Apparently in all these regions the numbers have constantly and slowly dwindled in recent decades, for not only is the species constantly in demand for food, but it is less adaptable to the changing conditions of clearing and settlement than its congener, the gray squirrel. It prefers primeval stands of old timber and is much given to foraging and traveling on the ground. Hunters often employ dogs to tree the squirrels, after which they may be shot with little difficulty. At the present time it may be called locally uncommon in less settled areas from south-central Pennsylvania to the mountains of central Virginia and West Virginia.

Family CASTORIDAE: Beavers

Beavers of the genus *Castor* are the only living members of this family of rodents; they are of circumboreal distribution in the watered and forested regions of the north-temperate zone. Since prehistoric times they have been of great importance in the economy of the human race, chiefly for their fur and their meat. The Old World beavers (*Castor fiber* and races) are regarded as a species distinct from the North American species (*C. canadensis*), but the actual differences are slight, as in the proportionate depth of the rostrum (less in the Old World animal) and the length of the nasal bones (extending back of the lacrimal level more in the Old World animal). Of the New World beaver, a number of slightly marked races have been described, depending on minor differences in color or in the size or the relative shapes of some of the cranial bones. Everywhere as the country has been opened and settled the beaver has been so reduced or extirpated that its present numbers and distribution are but a fraction of their original extent. In various eastern localities reintroductions have taken place, with varying success. The literature on the American beaver is extensive, for probably few of our native mammals have been more often written about. In the following account of the various races only an outline of the main points in the history can be given, and in many cases it is hardly possible to obtain accurate details of recent date. The various races may be taken up in alphabetical sequence.

CANADIAN BEAVER; NORTHEASTERN BEAVER

CASTOR CANADENSIS CANADENSIS Kuhl

Castor canadensis Kuhl, Beiträge zur Zoologie, 1820, p. 64 (Hudson Bay).
FIGS.: Radford, 1908, 10 unnumbered pls. (col. exterior, photos, skull, works); Nelson, 1916, p. 443 (col.); Elliot, 1901, p. 115, fig. 27 (skull).

Beavers are stoutly built, the northeastern form weighing up
to 60 pounds. The short, rounded ears and broadly webbed
hind feet are adaptations to aquatic life; the coarse, brown
overfur sheds water and protects the short, dense, and plushlike underfur. The broad, flattened tail is practically bare and
covered with scales. Swimming is done with the powerful hind
feet, while the small fore feet are held against the breast or
used in transporting material. The skull is stoutly built,
rather triangular in dorsal aspect, with broad nasals that end
slightly behind the level of the upward branch of the premaxillary. In general color the eastern beaver in fresh pelage is
dark chestnut-brown above, the base of the tail and thighs
clearer tawny; below, the throat is buff, the rest of the under
side drab. In this, the typical race, the tail is over twice as
long as broad, a character distinguishing it from the Carolina
beaver, which has a relatively broader tail. Total length, about
1,100 mm. (about 35 inches); tail, 410; hind foot, 175.

The range of this race formerly extended from about New
Jersey northward to southern Labrador and Hudson Bay
(Churchill region) and westward across Canada and Alaska,
as far northward as the limit of trees, in well-watered country.
Over all this area its numbers are now greatly reduced, or in
places it is quite gone. Of the progress of this destruction only
the merest outline can be given here. At the time when the
first white settlers arrived in Massachusetts Bay and the Hudson River region, beavers were plentiful along the streams, even
near the coast. The earlier accounts contain many references
to them and their works. Thus, Governor John Winthrop, in
his "History of New England," tells how on January 27, 1631,
he set out with a small company from Boston and "went up by
Charles River about eight miles above Watertown, and named
the first brook, on the north side of the river, (being a fair
stream, and coming from a pond a mile from the river,) Beaver
Brook, because the beavers had shorn down divers great
trees there, and made divers dams across the brook." The
name still persists, though the beavers have long since gone.
Remains of beavers are common in the Indian kitchen middens
all along our eastern coast, as in Connecticut, on Block Island,
and the coast of Maine. In the earlier years of the Colonies
beaver skins were one of the most important trade products
of the country. These were obtained largely from the Indians

who exchanged them for various trifles. Traders gathered together large quantities of beaver pelts, which were sent back to England. The magnitude of this industry may be gathered when we read in Winthrop's account that in April 1633 a vessel from Massachusetts, bound out for London, was wrecked on the Virginia coast with the loss among other things of four hogsheads of beaver weighing 900 pounds; and again, in the same year, he tells of a Mr. Graves sailing with between five and six thousand weight of beaver. Bradford's "History of the Plimmoth Plantation" lists seven sailings between 1631 and 1636, in which a total of over 12,500 pounds of beaver was exported from the colony, with a total value of about £10,000 sterling. Soon after this time, John Pynchon, of what is now Springfield, Mass., was the chief one to handle the furs brought in by the Indians from the surrounding region of the Connecticut Valley. His old account books show that in the six years between 1652 and 1657 he packed for England 47 hogsheads containing 8,992 beaver skins, weighing over 13,000 pounds, with an additional 663 pounds sent in bundles. From 1658 to 1674 he packed 6,480 beaver skins. Many of these skins were from the country to the north and west of Springfield. Other furs also appear in the inventories, but in lesser quantities. At that time a beaver skin was sold at a standard value per pound, about 8 shillings; and in lieu of currency beaver skins were accepted at standard rates, which varied somewhat from time to time. The traditional "beaver hats" were made from the felted fur of this animal, and although these were mostly manufactured in England there were in later years some among the colonists who were skilled at this trade. For example, Deacon Ebenezer Hunt, of Northampton, Mass., manufactured hats extensively for 40 years following 1734, buying his furs chiefly in Boston or Albany. After 1750, beaver hats sold at from 20 to 42 shillings each (Judd, S., "History of Hadley, Mass.," p. 355, 1863). At this time beavers were already becoming scarce in the southern part of New England. Albany, N. Y., then known as Beaverwyck, and New York City itself, then New Amsterdam, were the centers from which the Dutch East India Company's posts gathered in rich harvests of furs, while in the north the Hudson's Bay Company, chartered in 1670, formed the outlet for the fur catch in that region.

After a century and a half of constant trapping and with the spread of settlements into the eastern part of the country, the beaver was extirpated from the coastal regions of New England and greatly reduced in numbers elsewhere in the eastern United States. It is said that the Indians were careful to leave a certain proportion of the beavers to continue the stock, or to kill adult animals and leave the younger ones to mature, but the insatiate white trappers killed old and young indiscriminately and took as many as possible for their immediate gain, with the result that the animals, bit by bit, were killed out from the more accessible parts of their eastern range. Yet the remains of their dams lasted for many years after the beavers had gone and often were mentioned as monuments in land conveyances, while the old beaver ponds silted up and became grassy meadows, where frequently the earlier settlers, pushing their way up the streams into the interior, found the only available pasturage for their cattle. In southern New Hampshire the last beaver in the town of Rindge is said to have been killed about 1780 (Stearns, E. S., "History of the Town of Rindge, N. H.," 1875); and the last one in the town of Peterborough about 1790 (Smith, A., "History of the Town of Peterborough, N. H.," 1876). In the town of Pawlet, southern Vermont, the "last" beaver was killed about 1800 by one Ansel Whedon, who came upon it in his cornfield and slew it with a hoe (Hollister, H., Vermont Hist. Mag., vol. 3, p. 890, 1877). On the Maine coast near Wells, the local historian records that a trapper took 17 beavers there in 1755, but they seem to have quite gone before many years after. In northern New England, the beaver, though greatly reduced, has never been quite exterminated. Zadock Thompson, writing in 1842 ("History of Vermont," p. 39, 1842), believed that they were then nearly if not quite gone and mentions that the last one that he knew of was killed in Essex County, about 1830. Probably a few lingered in this northeastern corner of the State until much later, for at that time this region was nearly a primeval wilderness. Indeed, F. S. Hoag in 1909, after having made many inquiries among the trappers of Vermont, was credibly informed by a W. E. Balch that the last beaver he knew of in the State lived at Neale's Pond, north of Lunenburg, Essex County, about 20 years before (about 1890). He believed that it was completely extinct in Vermont by 1909.

In the adjacent part of New Hampshire there were beavers in the Connecticut lakes at least down to 1884, according to Ned Norton (Forest and Stream, vol. 24, p. 457, 1885). Beavers in small numbers continued in the remoter parts of Maine till the middle decades of the last century. At about that time the fashion for beaver hats abated in favor of silk hats, and the demand for fur was also lessened by the substitution of nutria fur from South America. Thoreau, in 1853, on his memorable journey to the Maine woods, relates that they were getting to be numerous again in the Lake Chesuncook region, but their skins brought so little that it hardly paid then to hunt them. J. G. Rich, an old trapper of those days and a correspondent of Agassiz, wrote ten years later that the fur of beavers commanded only $2.50 a skin, whereas formerly as much as a dollar an ounce was paid. In 1866, legal protection was first given the beaver in Maine. Its numbers slowly increased until during the first decade of the present century it seems to have become locally common in the remoter townships, where it was not allowed to be killed at any time. Increasing complaints of timber owners that beavers were damaging their trees by cutting and flooding resulted in 1910 in the establishment of a short open season for two years in Somerset and Franklin Counties. In 1911 the area on which beavers could be trapped was extended to other counties. At the present time there seems to be no reason why a fair number of beavers can not be maintained in the wilder areas of the State.

The history of the beaver in New York State has been reviewed by Radford (1908), particularly its status in the Adirondacks. "As early as 1623 the importance of the beaver to the Dutch colony was so well recognized as to lead to its incorporation in the seal of New Netherlands." In those times Indians from the St. Lawrence Valley trapped beavers in northern New York and traded them to the French companies at Quebec. Merriam adduces evidence to show that in the 1830's beavers in the Adirondacks were at a very low ebb, and DeKay, who traversed the height of land between the sources of the Hudson and the St. Lawrence Rivers in 1840, believed them nearly extirpated, though reported in 1841 "on Indian and Cedar Rivers, and at Paskungameh or Tupper's lake" and in scattered families in parts of Hamilton, St. Lawrence, and Essex Counties. Radford believes that by 1860 there

could have been hardly more than 50 beavers remaining in New
York State, chiefly along the Raquette and St. Regis Rivers
and in the well-watered region northwest of Upper Saranac
Lake in Franklin County. Here a slowly dwindling remnant
remained for the next 30 years, their numbers gradually reduced by occasional trappers in spite of efforts to protect them
by a local inn-keeper on or near whose lands they lived. In
the winter of 1894–95 probably not more than ten remained.
In the latter year a law was passed removing an open season
for beavers in the State, and in 1904 this was given added force
by increasing the fine for taking beavers to $100 and making it
an offense to set traps for them or to molest their dams or
houses. From the beginning of this century for a number of
years beavers showed a slight increase, and at the same time
small numbers were introduced at favorable localities. Some
of this stock came apparently from Canada; 30 or more others
were obtained in 1906 from Yellowstone Park. Under protection, and through this addition of new breeding stock, beavers
have so greatly increased in New York State that during the
season of 1924, when trapping was allowed, no less than 2,478
pelts were taken, valued at $39,548, and the following year
yielded 3,573 pelts, which brought in all $71,460 (Couch, 1937).
Under the present law, the Conservation Department of New
York may declare an open season in the month of March only.
Of late years a two-week period has been given in counties that
seem to have a good supply of the animals. The population,
however, is so unevenly distributed that in some regions more
beavers are desirable, while in others, which they are invading
rapidly, it is doubtful if a beaver population can be maintained.
Since 1924 to 1939, seven open seasons of two weeks each have
been permitted. Each trapper is limited to six pelts to be
taken in the two weeks, and these must be tagged by a game
protector. In its practical application it is found that the
protective law can be best enforced when blocks of counties
are governed by like seasons, so that granting open seasons
becomes in good part a problem of law enforcement. In 1939
"there are not more than a half-dozen counties in the State,
aside from those comprising Greater New York City, in which
beaver colonies were not established. Even in Rockland
County, whose border is but a half-hour's motor trip from
Broadway, an open trapping season has been permitted for

several years" (Dr. G. Bump, *in litt.*). The following statistics have been obligingly furnished by Dr. Gardiner Bump,
Superintendent of the Bureau of Game, concerning recent
beaver catches in New York State. In 1935, 2,498 pelts were
taken in eleven counties; in 1936 there was no open season; in
1937, a total of 2,014 pelts was taken in thirteen counties; and
in 1938, in twelve counties, 2,629. It is thus clear that under
wise management and intelligent supervision the beaver may
become a considerable asset in regions where conditions are
suitable for the maintenance of a breeding population.

The story in Pennsylvania is much like that in New York
State. Rhoads (1903), after giving in detail such older records
as he could find concerning their former abundance and gradual
extirpation in the State, summarizes these as follows: "It is
evident that this interesting animal was practically exterminated in the eastern half of its Canadian habitat in Pa. about
1830; that some remained in the headwaters of the west branch
of the Susquehanna till about 1840, and that almost the last
stragglers of their race were killed in Elk, Clarion, and Centre
Cos., between the years 1850 and 1865." Beavers killed in
Clinton County in 1884 and one seen in Cambria County in
1899 may have been escapes. It seems safe to say that beavers
had been practically exterminated in Pennsylvania for 60 years
when in 1917 a pair was imported from Wisconsin. From then
until 1924, 94 beavers "were imported and set free in certain
sections of the State at a cost of about $50 each. The animals
increased so rapidly that it soon became necessary to transfer
some of them to other sections. A survey by the State Board
of Game Commissioners of the streams in Pennsylvania in
1931 revealed 899 beaver dams with an estimated beaver
population of 4,377, which by 1934 had increased to 15,000.
During the 1934 trapping season, 6,455 beavers were legally
taken, which, at the average price of $15 a pelt, brought the
trappers a total of $96,825. In 1936, under increased trapping
restrictions, 2,261 pelts were taken which brought a total
return to the trappers of $22,610, an average price of $10 each
. . . These financial returns demonstrate that the beaver
constitutes a natural resource of great importance" (Couch,
1937).

Profiting in part by the experience of New York and Pennsylvania, beavers have in recent years been introduced into

Vermont, central New Hampshire, and Mount Desert, Maine, and at the present time they seem well established in several localities.

From west of the Alleghenies to the edge of the Plains, beavers seem at the present time to be quite gone over most of their former range. For Ohio, Brayton (1882) mentions their former abundance but implies that they had practically gone by the middle of the last century. In Indiana, Hahn (1909) gives 1840 as about the last authentic record, and both he and Lyon (1936) believe that the beaver of this State may have represented the southeastern race, while the latter adduces what seems a reliable recent record of the animal from Wells County in the northeastern part of the State and implies that it may have come in from adjacent parts of Michigan, where a few beavers still exist. Possibly, however, it was introduced, for in 1935 small "plants" of beavers were made in three counties, Jasper, Pulaski, and Starke, on game preserves, and these have so multiplied that in 1939 they had spread into ten other counties of northern Indiana, and additional "plants" have been made in Jennings and Clark Counties in the southern portion, where, however, the conditions of sufficient food and water are less favorable for them. Strict protective laws are in force, but in general land owners are interested in the encouragement of the beaver, in part from the benefit to water control and in part on account of the interesting habits of the animals (from *Outdoor Indiana*, Nov. 1939).

Still farther west, Cory (1912) writes: "Beavers were formerly common throughout Illinois and Wisconsin but at the present time they are practically exterminated in the former State," although "it is probable that a very few individuals may exist in the extreme southern portion," in Alexander County, whence fresh cuttings were obtained in 1900. In 1854, Kennicott wrote of beaver dams still existing at various points in Illinois, as if the animals had practically gone even by that day. In northern Wisconsin, however, they are now common.

North of the United States, beavers still occur plentifully in the more remote parts of western Canada but have been largely reduced in the more accessible regions and, of course, extirpated in the settled areas. G. G. Goodwin (1924), writing of the mammals of the Gaspé Peninsula, Quebec, tells of finding a skull at the forks of the Ste. Anne River and adds that according to his guide "there were a few beavers left above the forks of the river and that they live in holes in the river bank." Dr. R. M. Anderson (1939a) states that though formerly common in the wooded parts of the Province of Quebec it is trapped out in most localities. However, "some projects for restoration of the beaver by setting aside preserves have been gratifyingly successful, particularly in the regions south and east of James Bay." Although beavers have been trapped in this region for nearly three centuries, since the establishment of the posts of the Hudson's Bay Company, they appear to exist in reduced numbers to this day. Preble (1902) writes, however, that owing to persistent trapping they were "becoming scarce throughout the region" over 30 years ago, although skins were annually traded at the Company's posts on the coasts of Hudson Bay. He noted "the remains of a beaver house between Pine and Windy lakes and a comparatively recent dam on a small stream which empties into Hayes River about 15 miles above York Factory. A number of skins were seen at Fort Churchill. These had been taken on the Lower Churchill River. Several black pelts were among the furs at Norway House." He mentions further that "Dr. Bell reports that a family of beavers was found by Indians on North River, a stream that flows into the Bay about 15 miles above Fort Churchill"; and that according to Hearne's account of his explorations in this region, published in 1795, the Indians accompanying him killed beavers on Seal River, the mouth of which is about 40 miles north of Churchill. This marks perhaps nearly the northern limit of the beaver on the west side of Hudson Bay; of its northward limits on the east side of the Bay no recent information is at hand. Low, writing in 1895, after traversing parts of northern Labrador, says that it is common in the wooded regions and extends into the semibarrens where food is available.

As to the recent status of beavers in the Athabaska-Mackenzie region still farther west, Preble (1908) has given a brief review. He quotes J. Alden Loring that in 1896 evidence was obtained of the former abundance of the beaver in suitable localities in western Alberta, but at that time it was nearly exterminated; tracks were seen on a small stream between Jasper House and Smoky River, but no other recent traces of the animals were found. Farther north it was formerly abundant nearly to the limit of trees; but on his journey in 1903–4, to the Great Slave Lake and Mackenzie region, he found it largely gone in many parts, and nowhere common, "though skins are received annually by all the posts throughout the region . . . The vast region which stretches from Great Slave Lake to the Rocky Mountains at present seems to be the best beaver country in the north. Many skins are brought from the upper reaches of Hay River by the Beaver Indians, and from Trout Lake by the Indians who frequent that locality. The Horn Mountain country also furnishes many skins. Along my route between Great Slave and Great Bear Lakes, the beaver has now become scarce, owing to constant hunting, but my guide intimated that in certain localities off the main route which we were following he knew of small colonies of beavers. About Great Bear Lake the best beaver ground seemed to be to the northward of Fort Franklin, and I saw several skins, some quite dark, just brought from the hunting grounds about two days' travel to the northward. During the winter of 1903–4 several beavers were killed by Indians in the region about Fort Simpson. In the spring the animals often descend the smaller streams to the main river and follow it to the mouth of the next tributary. A young one was shot near the mouth of the Liard in May, and several adults and young ones have been killed in recent years near the mouth of Bluefish Creek, opposite Fort Simpson, as a result of this habit.

"While descending the Mackenzie in the summer of 1904 I saw no beavers, but obtained information regarding the traffic in skins. About 700 skins were said to have been traded during the preceding winter at Fort Norman, which receives the fur of a very large extent of country. Skins from the country toward the Barren Grounds, according to the testimony of C. P. Gaudet, of that place, are smaller and average darker than those from the vicinity of the post. Fort Anderson, according to the fur returns, never received more than five skins annually during the few years of its existence."

In the Yukon River Valley beavers are nearly extirpated Dr. W. H. Osgood, who traversed the region in 1899, wrote (1900): "It hardly seems possible that half a million or more beaver skins have been secured in the Territory of Alaska. The animal is now almost as rare as it is in the United States, the inevitable result of continued pursuit by both whites and natives, which has so many parallels that it is useless to emphasize it here. At Fort Selkirk I saw several beaver skins taken on a small tributary of Stewart River and at St. Michael I found a very few in the warehouses of the trading companies. Beyond this I saw or heard nothing of them."

Dr. Francis Harper states that under recent protective laws beavérs are increasing in Alberta at the present time, and it seems likely that proper restrictions, if they can be enforced in all this region, will result in an increase of beavers, so that they may in time prove a regular and profitable source of revenue.

Concerning the habits of the beaver a great deal has been written. Their general activities center around, first, the dams constructed solidly of sticks, branches, and larger pieces of wood, together with stones, mud, and other material from the pond bottom; then with the resulting formation of a pond, the construction of a house which serves as a shelter for young and adults, and has entrances under water into the pond. In the pond, aspen logs are sunk for a winter food supply, for the bark of this tree is a favorite food. An older colony will in time connect various pools with canals and the dams may be extended to works of great magnitude. A single litter of from two to six young is produced in the course of a year, so that the increase of a colony may be fairly rapid and the young when of adult size move off to found new colonies. Extensive accounts of the habits may be found in the following works:

DUGMORE, A. RADCLYFFE.
ca. 1913. The romance of the beaver: Being the history of the beaver in the western hemisphere. xvi + 225 pp., illustr. Philadelphia and London.
BAILEY, VERNON.
1922. Beaver habits, beaver control, and possibilities in beaver farming. U. S. Dept. Agric. Dept. Bull. 1078, 29 pp., 7 figs., 7 pls.
1927. How beavers build their houses. Smithsonian Inst. Rept. for 1926, pp. 357–360, pls. 1–6.
CHAPMAN, WENDELL and LUCIE.
1937. Beaver pioneers. xiv + 153 pp., illustr. New York and London.
MARTIN, HORACE T.
1892. Castorologia, or the history and traditions of the Canadian beaver. xvi + 238 pp., illustr. Montreal and London.
MILLS, ENOS A.
1913. In beaver world. xiv + 228 pp., illustr. Boston and New York.
WARREN, E. R.
1922. The life of the Yellowstone beaver. Roosevelt Wild Life Bull., vol. 1, pp. 187–221.

WARREN, E. R.
  1926. A study of the beaver in the Yancey region of Yellowstone National
         Park. Roosevelt Wild Life Annals, vol. 1, pp. 13–191, illustr., maps.
  1926. Notes on the beaver colonies in the Longs Peak region of Estes Park,
         Colorado. Roosevelt Wild Life Annals, vol. 1, pp. 193–234, illustr.
  1927. The beaver: Its work and its ways. Amer. Soc. Mammal. Monogr. 2,
         177 pp., illustr. Baltimore.

BAILEY'S BEAVER

CASTOR CANADENSIS BAILEYI Nelson

Castor canadensis baileyi Nelson, Proc. Biol. Soc. Washington, vol. 40, p. 125, Sept. 26,
    1927 (Humboldt River, 4 miles above Winnemucca, Nevada).

This race of the beaver is darker than *frondator* and has a slenderer skull. From *C. c. pacificus* from the Columbia River drainage in eastern Washington and Oregon it differs in its distinctly paler color and slenderer skull. The narrow skull and especially the rostrum of the Humboldt River beaver contrast strongly with the massive skull and broad heavy rostrum of *subauratus* (Nelson, *loc. cit.*). The upper parts are described as "dull rusty chestnut, brightest on crown with a dull yellowish shade on the cheeks; ears dark brown; base of tail all around uniform with adjacent parts of body; tops of hind feet dark chestnut; underparts of body dull drab brown." Total length of type, 1,064 mm.; tail, 254 by 135; hind foot, 183.

Concerning this race of the beaver little seems to be in print. Dr. Nelson had specimens from Winnemucca, Iron Point, Golconda, and Deeth in Nevada. It is presumably confined to the region of the Humboldt River Basin of Nevada. Borell and Ellis (1934) wrote of it a few years ago: "Beavers are found in limited numbers along the main branches of the Humboldt River, but have been almost completely exterminated along the smaller streams which flow out of the Ruby Mountains. Mr. August Rohwer and Mr. William Toyn reported that there were still a few beaver in one or two of the canyons on the west slope of the Ruby Mountains. Characteristic beaver gnawings found by us on some partly decayed aspen stumps at about 7,000 feet altitude along Toyn Creek, near the summit of Harrison Pass, indicated the former presence of beaver there."

Still more recently, Vernon Bailey (1936) has reported that "these desert-valley beavers are still found in the Great Basin drainage of northern Nevada along the Humboldt River, and its tributaries and in the Malheur Lake and Steens Mountains drainage of southeastern Oregon . . . There are a few beaver all along the Blitzen from its headwaters down to near Malheur Lake, and George Benson reports one shot at the edge of Malheur Lake in 1909. In 1916 they were found in Big Fish Creek, McCoy Creek, and Kiger Creek. It is fair to assume in the absence of specimens that the beaver in the Silvies River and its branches on the north of Malheur Lake are also of this subspecies. In 1920 they were still common in many places along the Silvies and Blitzen Rivers, and while in places they were doing some damage by flooding the meadows, more often they were merely holding up the water to a better depth and improving the meadows by subirrigation." Concerning their former abundance in this last region, Bailey quotes from older records to show that a little over a hundred years ago, in 1826 and 1828, beavers were so numerous that a party of trappers took over 300 in a month.

On occasion, Bailey adds, they may dam up irrigation ditches or locate in the banks of streams near fields and orchards where they do serious mischief and have to be removed, driven away, or destroyed. With intelligent handling, "however, they could become a valuable asset on many of the eastern Oregon ranches."

COOK INLET BEAVER

CASTOR CANADENSIS BELUGAE Taylor

Castor canadensis belugae Taylor, Univ. California Publ. Zool., vol. 12, p. 429, Mar. 20, 1916 ("Beluga River, Cook Inlet region, Alaska").

According to its describer, this race of beaver is the one found from central British Columbia northward along the coast of the mainland to the mountains of Alaska. Specimens referred to the race are mentioned from Stuart Lake, British Columbia, and from various localities on the shores of Cook Inlet, Alaska. In color the single skin available to the describer was said to be slightly paler than in the neighboring races, *phaeus* and *leucodonta*. The skull, in comparison with that of the latter, is "immediately distinguishable through the narrower blades of the hamular processes of the pterygoids," with a tendency for the maxillary tooth row and ratio of this to the basilar length to be greater.

In the region of the type locality, beavers were becoming scarce 40 years ago. Osgood (1901) mentions three secured by trappers near the mouth of Turnagain Arm in 1899 and adds that a few were taken every season along streams in the mountains about 60 miles inland from Tyonek. "A trading station on the lower Sushitna River also obtains a small quota annually. Compared with former receipts, however, the number now obtained is lamentably small." In a later report Osgood (1904) adds that a little farther to the westward on the Chulitna River he found evidence of a few scattered small colonies of beavers. "The extensive area of low land about the sources of the Chulitna River is covered with hundreds of small lakes and ponds connected in most cases by small, sluggish streams eminently suitable for beavers, and no doubt a great many are still scattered throughout this area." A small number of skins were annually brought in to the trader at Nushagak at the mouth of the river of the same name. Farther south, in the Atlin region of northwestern British Columbia, Swarth (1936) writes that "as everywhere, beavers hereabout are trapped to the verge of extinction. They in all likelihood were originally abundant and generally distributed throughout the lowland lakes."

NEWFOUNDLAND BEAVER

CASTOR CANADENSIS CAECATOR Bangs

Castor caecator Bangs, Bull. Mus. Comp. Zool., vol. 54, p. 513, July, 1913 ("Near Bay St. George, Newfoundland").
FIGS.: Bangs, 1913, figure on p. 514 (skull).

Although the Newfoundland beaver was first described as a species distinct from typical *C. canadensis* of the neighboring mainland, it can scarcely be considered as more than the local representative of that animal, which through a long period of isolation has become slightly different in certain cranial characters. The color has not been accurately described on account of the lack of specimens in museum collections, but Bangs, in naming it, mentions that he had seen two in the flesh, which, though showing nothing distinctive in external appearance, nevertheless appeared "rather small" and were of an "exceptionally fine rich color." The distinctive characters of the skull are: the slightly smaller size as compared with the mainland beaver, typical *canadensis;* the wider, "more roundish" interparietal; and the lighter, less flaring zygomata, the outer side of which is more nearly straight, thus giving a much more triangular outline to the skull as seen from above. The nasals are also said to be shorter and wider.

Concerning the present status of the beaver in Newfoundland, little accurate information is at hand. Bangs, in 1913, wrote that "though much trapped for its fur, it still occurs in fair numbers in the remoter parts of the island," and probably this still holds true. It doubtless finds the more barren portions of· the country less suitable to its needs and hence can be expected to thrive best in the western and central parts of the island. Dugmore, in his "Romance of the Beaver," published about 1913, writes that when he first visited Newfoundland about 1900 and in annual visits during the three succeeding years, he never saw but one beaver colony, and that a very small one in a remote and rather inaccessible part of the country. Under governmental protection, however, beavers multiplied in following years so that on visiting the same region in 1912 he counted no less than 27 lodges within a short day of walking and canoeing. As elsewhere, this illustrates how readily beavers will breed up to the carrying capacity of the land if free from persecution, for their natural enemies are few.

For a comment on the recent status of beavers in Newfoundland I am indebted to Frank Strickland, who is familiar with conditions there. He says that previous to the declaration of a close time on beavers, about 1917, they were plentiful in Grand Lake and Red Indian Lake, but today they are very scarce in that section. What beavers are left in Newfoundland are mostly to be found between Port Saunders north to White Bay and between Gander River east to the bottom of Bay d'Espoir, including thus the central districts of the island.

CAROLINA BEAVER; SOUTHEASTERN BEAVER

CASTOR CANADENSIS CAROLINENSIS Rhoads

Castor canadensis carolinensis Rhoads, Trans. Amer. Phil. Soc., new ser., vol. 19, p. 420, Sept. 1898 ("Dan River, near Danbury, Stokes County, North Carolina"). FIGS.: Rhoads, 1898, pl. 23, figs. 1, 2 (skull).

The beaver of the southeastern United States is broadertailed than typical *canadensis*, and in this respect it resembles the southwestern race *frondator*, which, however, is paler in color. Rhoads describes the type as bright hazel above, with seal-brown underfur, the hinder back shading into bright hazel to cinnamon-rufous and tawny-olive; ears blackish, feet bister. Below, dark broccoli brown, the tips of the longer hairs wood brown. Total length, 1,130 mm.; tail, 279 by 158; hind foot, 184. The skull is characterized by its short, broad nasals and short rostrum, with the former scarcely or not extending back of the level of the orbits.

The limits of the range of this race, though in general from northern Florida to the Mississippi and northward to the lowlands of New Jersey and Ohio, Indiana, and Illinois, will probably never be exactly definable since it is now extinct over the greater part of the area and but few complete specimens are extant. Rhoads believed that it intergraded with typical *C. canadensis* in southern New Jersey and the lower parts of Pennsylvania, and Cory (1912), in his map of the range, included southern Ohio, Indiana, and Illinois in the area of presumed intergradation. Lyon (1936), who figures an imperfect skull as the only one extant from Indiana, assumes that it was probably the form occurring in that State.

Rhoads believed that by 1700 beavers had been practically exterminated from the lowlands of the Delaware, Schuylkill, and Susquehanna Valleys, which were the regions first settled; while by the time of the American Revolution, they were practically wiped out from all the lowland valleys of Pennsylvania except the northern tributaries of the Ohio; but of this there is almost no definite record. In New Jersey, owing to the inaccessible and unproductive character of the lands in the southern part of the State, beavers persisted longer, in the most retired swamps of Atlantic and Cape May Counties, but were probably quite gone by 1830, or earlier. Traces of their old dams persisted for many years later, and Dr. Witmer Stone, writing in 1908, mentions remains of a very large one that he had visited on the Nescochaque branch of Mullica River. In 1900, according to Dr. Stone (1908), there was a colony of beavers in Sussex County, N. J., due apparently to individuals that had escaped from a private preserve where they had been introduced.

Atwater's "History of Ohio," published in 1838, speaks of beavers as formerly common on the headwaters of the larger streams in that State but adds that "they have long since disappeared." For Indiana much the same story is true; Dr. Lyon (1936) quotes the Prince of Wied's statement, in 1832 and 1833, that beavers were then abundant along the lower Wabash, but with the opening up of the country to settlement in succeeding decades, they must have disappeared rapidly. Nevertheless, he adduces some evidence for the belief that in Wells County, Ind., beavers were present only a few years since, possibly introduced; while similarly, Cory (1912), although he writes that beavers are practically extinct in Illinois, believes it "probable that a very few individuals may exist in the extreme southern portion of the state."

To the southward of this tier of States that may have marked the northern limits of this beaver's range, information is meager, but it indicates that the animals still hold on in a few widely separated localities, where with real protection there is some hope that they may continue and even increase considerably.

Within the memory of men now living beavers were present in small numbers in the counties a short distance south of Richmond, Va. A writer in *Forest and Stream* (vol. 7, p. 197) for November 2, 1876, states that for the two years previous to that time trappers had been taking beavers in Dinwiddie, Nottoway, Brunswick, Cumberland, and other counties, some making good returns on these and other furs. At that time the pelts of beavers sold for a dollar apiece. Here, too, the correspondent mentions having seen in some of these localities places where beavers had totally destroyed acres of corn, causing serious loss. At the present time, I have no information of any beavers remaining in the State. Possibly, however, a few may have persisted in the mountainous parts of this State and of West Virginia. F. E. Brooks (1911) mentions what he believes to be a well-authenticated case of a beaver having been killed in Pocahontas County, W. Va., about 1907, although this was possibly brought in from elsewhere. Still later, A. B. Brooks (1923) published a note on the reappearance of beavers in West Virginia. He writes: "A few of the older trappers and hunters still living state that beaver work was observed by them many years ago on the headwaters of the Williams and Greenbrier Rivers," but they had been "counted as extinct in West Virginia for fifty years or more" until the early fall of 1922, when a farmer in Hampshire County reported finding fresh beaver work on a creek tributary to North River. Subsequent investigation disclosed a colony of beavers here. They had "built a dam and done much cutting along both banks of the stream." All efforts to learn of the origin of this colony were unsuccessful.

Beavers persisted in North Carolina until recent years. The series of specimens from Dan River, near Danbury, Stokes County, on which the race *carolinensis* was based, was collected between 1897 and 1899. C. S. Brimley, writing in 1905, says that it occurs sparingly there and is also reported from Bertie County. A specimen taken 15 or 20 years previously at Weldon is in the State Museum at Raleigh. These localities are all on the Roanoke River or its tributaries. He adds that "Mr. J. H. Armfield reports a few occurring in Beaver Swamp in the northern part of Guilford County and southern part of Rockingham, and Mr. K. E. Shore reports them from the Yadkin River, between Yadkin and Forsyth Counties." At the present time, 1939, the beavers seem to have quite disappeared.

No recent record of the beaver in South Carolina is known to me. In Georgia, however, a few still remain and are carefully protected, in the Flint River section in the southwestern part of the State and at the headwaters of the Chattahoochee. Dr. Francis Harper (1927) in his account of the mammals of Okefenokee Swamp, Ga., adduces evidence that they were formerly present there. He was shown an incisor tooth taken from a beaver killed about 1890 by an old Negro woman a mile or so east of Lloyd's Island. "The story goes that the woman came upon the animal in the road and clubbed it to death." Dr. Harper suggests that the southward range of the beaver may have been to a large extent limited by the presence of the alligator. He doubts if it ever regularly inhabited the interior of Okefenokee Swamp, else it would probably have survived there or left some tradition of its earlier presence. In former times there were beavers in extreme northern Florida (Bartram mentions them), but little or nothing is known of the time of their disappearance. An unmistakable molar tooth was lately found in an Indian mound on Indian River by J. H. Rowe.

To the westward of the Alleghenies, the Carolina beaver is

believed to have extended to the Mississippi, perhaps as far
north as Iowa. In this State, according to J. A. Allen (1870a),
they had been nearly or quite exterminated in most of the
eastern and southern portions by 1870, although at that time
a few were reported still to exist on the South Raccoon River.
Kellogg (1939) has lately summarized its history in Tennessee,
where it was originally well distributed in former times and
apparently did not begin to show much depletion until after
the middle of the eighteenth century. About 1788 the salaries
of the county clerks and others were paid in beaver skins, 300
for the county clerk, 200 for the clerk of the House of Com-
mons, and three for members of the Assembly. The latest
records for beavers seem to be those of Rhoads (1896) for the
extreme western part of the State. He examined a beaver
house in the cypress swamp bordering Reelfoot Lake, Obion
County, about 1895 and was told that there were then about
20 beavers in that district. Another colony was reported to
him from Haywood County. Beavers still exist in Alabama,
and according to A. H. Howell (1921) have held their own in
some localities remarkably well, even in settled farming regions.
He says that "apparently they are more numerous at present
[1920] in the central part of the State, in Montgomery and
Lowndes Counties, than in either the wild hill country of the
northern part or the big swamps of the south." Old residents
of Montgomery County assured him that although abundant
there in early times, they had entirely disappeared from the
region, but about 1908 reappeared, coming up from the lower
stretches of Catoma Creek. In Lowndes County, L. J. Goldman found beavers in numbers along Big Swamp Creek and in
Jones Lakes, where they do considerable damage to the corn
patches. They are little trapped for fur, although their meat
is much sought after. They now have protection either locally
by the planters or in general by State law, from March to
November. "In the northern part of the State beavers seem
almost to have been exterminated; they formerly occurred in
small numbers in the Tennessee River at Muscle Shoals, but
disappeared about 1895; they lived about the 'towheads'
(small islands) in the river and burrowed into the banks, but
did not build dams. A few were reported in 1916 in Big Wills
Creek, near Collinsville. They disappeared from Talladega
Creek, near Dean, about 1896."

These southern beavers attain a large size; Howell speaks of one killed on Pintlala Creek that weighed 65 pounds. Another from Catoma Creek weighed 38.5 pounds and measured 1,035 mm. in total length; tail, 290 by 163; hind foot, 170. Compared with a specimen of the typical race from Canada, its skull is shorter and relatively broader, with wider brain case and interorbital region.

In Kentucky, which should come within the western range of this race, Funkhouser (1925) writes: "We can find no record of its having been seen . . . within the past twenty years." In earlier times it was occasionally mentioned by the pioneers, but "was probably never very abundant in Kentucky."

Colorado Beaver

Castor canadensis concisor Warren and Hall

Castor canadensis concisor Warren and Hall, Journ. Mamm., vol. 20, p. 358, Aug. 14, 1939 ("Monument Creek, southwest of Monument, El Paso County, Colorado"). Figs.: Warren, 1910, p. 141, figs. 46–48 (photographs; skull).

Until recently the beaver of Colorado was believed to be the same as the race *frondator*, typical on the Mexican boundary of Sonora. Now, however, the above authors, after a minute study of a series of skulls, believe that it represents a recognizable subspecies, of dark color, but with a skull resembling that of *mexicanus*, yet on the average differing in the size and shape of the angular process of the mandible, which is longer and more produced posteriorly and sharp-pointed rather than short and posteriorly rounded. Other slight differences seem to separate the Colorado beavers from adjacent races. Greatest occipitonasal length of skull, to 145.2 mm.; length of nasals, 50–54.4.

Warren (1910) writes that although the beaver "was no doubt at one time found in every county in Colorado which contained streams with sufficient water for its needs, and to-day, in spite of the persecution to which it was at one time subjected from the trappers, nearly resulting in its extinction, it is found over a large area of the State, and thanks to the protection accorded it by law, is on the increase. We have records of it from Larimer, Weld, Morgan, Grand, Routt, Arapahoe, Gunnison, Delta, Garfield, Eagle, El Paso, Teller, and Mineral counties," thus covering much of the west-central mountainous region of the State. The same author (Warren, 1926) has given a detailed account of beaver colonies in Estes Park, Colo., with descriptions and photographs of their haunts and works, as well as maps illustrating their engineering enterprises. Under protection the beaver seems for the present fairly safe in Colorado.

SOUTHWESTERN BEAVER; BROAD-TAILED BEAVER; SONORAN BEAVER

CASTOR CANADENSIS FRONDATOR Mearns

Castor canadensis frondator Mearns, Preliminary Diagnoses of New Mammals of the Genera *Sciurus, Castor, Neotoma* and *Sigmodon*, p. 2, 1897; reprinted in Proc. U. S. Nat. Mus., vol. 20, p. 502, Jan. 19, 1898 (San Pedro River, Sonora, Mexico, near monument No. 98 of the Mexican boundary line).

FIG.: Mearns, 1907, p. 351, fig. 57 (skull).

Like the southeastern beaver (*C. c. carolinensis*), this is a broad-tailed race, but its color is paler and brighter. Vernon Bailey (1931) describes it as light chestnut above; middle of the belly reddish chestnut; hind feet dark chestnut; colors slightly darker in winter. Total length, 1,070 mm.; tail from anus, 360; hind foot, 185; skull length, 133, its width 99. Weight of type (a female), 62 pounds. Old males are slightly larger than females and may measure up to 1,130 mm. in length.

This race of beaver extends slightly to the south of the Mexico-United States boundary in northern Sonora and is found in Arizona along the Colorado River and in the extreme western part of New Mexico on branches of the Gila and San Juan Rivers. According to Bailey (1931) it is the form found from all points whence specimens were examined along the Colorado River system, but although formerly numerous, it is now everywhere much reduced in numbers. "There are still a few beavers in the headwaters of the Gila . . . also some in the San Juan River and its tributaries" in western New Mexico. Mearns (1907) has also given many details of its presence during the latter part of the last century along the Mexican boundary of Arizona. Within the rather restricted range at present assigned to this race, it is evidently rare and likely to be further reduced in the future.

VANCOUVER ISLAND BEAVER

CASTOR CANADENSIS LEUCODONTA Gray

Castor canadensis leucodonta Gray, Ann. Mag. Nat. Hist., ser. 4, vol. 4, p. 293, Oct.
    1869 (Vancouver Island, British Columbia).
FIGS.: Taylor, 1916, p. 450, fig. J, *a;* p. 451, fig. K, *a;* p. 452, fig. L, *a* (views of skull).

Dr. W. P. Taylor (1916) has briefly summarized some of the
characters that he believes distinguish the Vancouver beaver.
Externally it closely resembles typical *C. canadensis* from New
Brunswick in color above, but the under side is "about hair
brown in *leucodonta*, near bone brown, dark grayish brown,
dark vinaceous-drab or natal brown in *canadensis*." Cranially,
the external outline of the nasals is different, "tending to be
more parallel in *leucodonta* than in *canadensis*, in which there
is a dilation in the outline anteriorly; foramen magnum slightly
broader . . . ; hamular processes . . . definitely
broader bladed." There are other slight cranial differences
between this and neighboring races.

In the middle of the last century beavers were common on
Vancouver Island, to which this race is now regarded as restricted. Robert Brown (*in* Green, A. H., 1869), who collected
the original specimens for the British Museum, spoke of them
near Victoria, and especially in the interior, where "they are
almost everywhere abundant and on the increase. In a swampy
lake near the mouth of the Cowichan Lake we found many;
and an extensive swamp near the entrance of the Puntledge
Lake was a great stronghold . . . In the spring of 1866,
when crossing the island from Fort Rupert to the head of
Quatseeno Sound with some Indians, a great portion of our
route lay among these beaver ponds and dams. All through
this district beavers swarm."

Swarth (1912) has presented some measurements and cranial
dimensions from a series of this beaver trapped in 1910 on
Vancouver Island. The external appearance, he says, differs
from that of beavers from southeastern Alaska principally in
slightly paler color. He found that "as a result of a number
of years of protection beavers have multiplied on Vancouver
Island so as to be really abundant in many places . . .
There was a small colony at a point near Errington, but we
found them in far greater numbers at Beaver Creek, near
Alberni . . . There was old beaver work along the streams

throughout this valley, and from the size of some of the old
dams they must have existed here in immense numbers at one
time, but at present, though there are a good many left still,
they are more scattered, apparently not more than one or two
families at any one point, and such groups separated by intervals, sometimes of several miles. Nearly all the smaller streams
were obstructed by their dams, and most of the adjoining low
lying land flooded as a consequence . . . We saw no
beavers at Nootka Sound, but were told that there were many
at Vernon Lake, some eight or ten miles inland from the head
of Tahsis Canal" and a few at Central Lake.

In response to inquiry, Maj. Allan Brooks writes me under
date of July 8, 1939: "Beavers still exist in some numbers on
Vancouver Island. There are few localities where the trapping
is not in the hands of licensed trappers, who pay $10 a year for
a defined area where no other trappers are allowed. By this
method they can conserve their furbearers. There are locally
closed areas also, as at Comox, Vancouver Island, where no
beavers are allowed to be trapped and they are numerous.
Over the whole northern third of this island the beavers of late
years have been decimated by cougars; it will take them many
years to recover."

RIO GRANDE BEAVER

CASTOR CANADENSIS MEXICANUS Bailey

Castor canadensis mexicanus Bailey, Proc. Biol. Soc. Washington, vol. 26, p. 191,
Oct. 23, 1913 ("Ruidoso Creek, 6 miles below Ruidoso, New Mexico").

The Rio Grande beaver is closely related to the race *frondator*
with which it had been associated until Bailey distinguished it
in 1913 as slightly different in its duller and paler colors, with
very little chestnut at any season. He gives the weight of an
adult as 47 pounds and the total length of an adult female as
1,070 mm.

The geographic range of this race is believed to be only the
Pecos and Rio Grande drainage in New Mexico and Texas. In
northern New Mexico it shows a tendency to intergrade with
the darker *frondator*. The most comprehensive account of it is
that of Bailey (1931), who has gathered what information is
available as to its habits and status. In earlier times the beaver
was a source of food and fur for the Indians in the region and
its remains may be found in their kitchen middens. Bailey

mentions that in 1826 Pattie and a party of trappers took beavers all along the Pecos River from 20 miles above its mouth to the first Spanish settlement (probably Anton Chico). From 1881 to 1884 L. L. Dyche collected on the headwaters of the Pecos and found at that time "a considerable number of beavers about 15 miles from the head of the Pecos River"; there were many beaver dams and, he adds, "in the pools which were caused by these dams I found the best trout fishing of any locality I have ever visited in the Rocky Mountains," an interesting comment on the effect of such dams in making pools where trout may live. In 1898, C. M. Barber found a large colony on Ruidoso Creek, below the town of the same name, and there he secured the series of specimens on which Bailey later founded the name *mexicanus*. At that time the beavers were feeding on corn, which they cut and dragged to the stream and floated to their dens. Very few were being killed by the Mexicans on the ranches, since they lacked the technique for trapping. In 1902 Bailey visited Ruidoso Creek "and found that there were still a few beavers along this stream, which, with its sections of deep water and steep banks, is peculiarly adapted to the habits of beavers." In the following year he also found some of the streams inhabited by them on the headwaters of the Pecos. "There were old cuttings along many of the other streams, but in most cases the beavers had been entirely trapped out . . . In the deep water of the larger valley streams they are not so easily caught, and fortunately enough have escaped in spite of persistent trapping to prevent the complete extermination of the species . . .

"In many places along the canyons of the Rio Grande above Santa Fe there were still some of the animals in 1903-4, and trappers were then catching them in considerable numbers . . . and in 1909, E. A. Goldman saw some old beaver cuttings near Socorro and was told that there were still a few along the river. He also saw signs of them at Garfield and found them common in the Rio Grande near Las Palomas, and they were reported near Las Cruces . . . In 1915, J. S. Ligon reported them as becoming abundant in places along the Rio Grande above and below San Marcial, where there were some complaints of their felling trees across the fences.

"In such localities beavers live entirely in the banks of the rivers and select the deepest water for their operations. They are not easily trapped and usually remain the longest where they do real damage, while in the higher mountains where they can do no damage they are easily caught and quickly destroyed."

While from an economic standpoint beavers may do some damage to forest growth and even to crops, as in the case just noted, by feeding on cornstalks, nevertheless this is easily controlled. Bailey mentions that in 1910 the water company of Santa Fe was offering $50 a pair for live beavers to be placed in the upper part of the Santa Fe Canyon to aid in conserving the city's water supply. He adds: "On almost all the mountain streams they should be protected and encouraged. A series of beaver ponds and dams along the headwaters of a mountain stream would hold back large quantities of mountain water during the dangerous flood season and equalize the flow of the streams so that during the driest seasons the water supply would be greatly increased in the valleys. Beaver ponds not only hold water but distribute it through the surrounding soil for long distances, acting as enormous sponges as well as reservoirs. A series of ponds also increases the fishing capacity and furnishes a safe retreat for the smaller trout and protection from their enemies . . . A legitimate amount of trapping should eventually yield large annual returns over extensive areas of the country from which they have been almost exterminated."

MICHIGAN BEAVER; WOODS BEAVER

CASTOR CANADENSIS MICHIGANENSIS Bailey

Castor canadensis michiganensis Bailey, Proc. Biol. Soc. Washington, vol. 26, p. 192, Oct. 23, 1913 (Tahquamenaw River, 5 miles above falls, Luce County, Michigan).

This is a very dark race of beaver, with a short, broad skull. According to its describer, it is dark umber-brown above, brighter on head and cheeks; ears, feet, and nose black. Under side darker than back, with blackish on the breast and flanks. The skull has the rostrum shorter and the nasals more quadrate than in typical *canadensis*, the zygomata abruptly spreading, the occiput with an upright crest, giving a short, "sawed-off" appearance. Though said to be of small or medium size, the measurements given do not show this: Total length, 1,170 mm.; tail, 470; hind foot, 185; skull, condylobasal length, 129; zygomatic width, 96.4; nasals, 46 by 24 (type skull).

Although described from the northeastern (or "upper") peninsula of Michigan, between Lake Superior and Lake Michigan, the range of this race is believed to include much of the "Lower Peninsula," now or in the recent past. While at the present time beavers are regarded as extinct in southern Michigan, they still occur locally in northern parts of the State. According to Dice, they were found up to about 1920 along Boyne River in Charlevoix County but are now rare or extinct there except that beavers have been reintroduced on Spring Branch. In the neighboring counties, Cheboygan and Montmorency of the Lower Peninsula, they are scarce but seem to be increasing. Presumably intergradation of this race with neighboring races takes place in Wisconsin or to the northward, but the exact limits of the range of this form remain to be worked out.

Because of the rich dark color of its fur, this race of beaver is especially recommended by Vernon Bailey for introduction into other and now depleted localities. It has been much used in restocking areas in Michigan that seemed suitable, and Ruhl and Lovejoy (1930) have published a summary of such introductions carried out in various counties in southwestern, central, and northern parts of the Lower Peninsula in recent years. In most cases only one or two animals at a time were available for this purpose, yet these authors conclude that "there seems to be no difficulty in getting beaver to settle and winter even if planted as late as November 1," but there is no assurance that they will remain in any particular locality nor was the number necessary for efficient colonization determined. Where large streams are available, these introduced beavers were found usually to make burrows in banks rather than to construct lodges. According to Vernon Bailey (1922), choice skins of this dark form from northern Wisconsin have in recent years brought as much as $50 each. He writes further: "So far as at present known, the darkest, richest-colored, and handsomest beaver fur is found native along the south shore of Lake Superior, in northern Michigan and Wisconsin [and is of the race here under discussion]. In this region of heavy forest and deep snows the outer hairs of the animals are very dark brown and the under fur is almost black. When tanned and plucked the skins are very beautiful, and when made up into wearing apparel they almost equal sea otter in depth of fur and richness of color. They are decidedly superior to the Canadian and Alaskan skins . . . For many years the beavers of the region south of Lake Superior have been carefully protected . . . They are now fairly abundant in the region."

MISSOURI BASIN BEAVER

CASTOR CANADENSIS MISSOURIENSIS Bailey

Castor canadensis missouriensis Bailey, Journ. Mammalogy, vol. 1, p. 32, Nov. 28, 1919 ("Apple Creek, 7 miles east of Bismarck, North Dakota").

This race is said to be "slightly smaller than *canadensis* and much paler and duller brown. Skull more triangular in outline, not so massive and heavy; much like that of *mexicanus*, shorter and heavier than that of *frondator*. From *mexicanus* the colors differ in being noticeably duller and darker; from *frondator*, duller, and not so rusty." The total length of the type (probably not fully grown) was 900 mm. "Specimens show closer affinity with those of the Rio Grande drainage, than with those in the same State [North Dakota] in the streams flowing into Hudson Bay."

The range of this form of beaver is believed to be the drainage system of the Missouri River, typically in western North Dakota, but further study is needed to settle this. Provisionally, South Dakota, Nebraska, and possibly Kansas may be included in its present or former range. Vernon Bailey (1926) has given an excellent account of the recent status of the beaver in North Dakota. He writes that in 1804–5, Lewis and Clark found beavers abundant along the Missouri, even near long-established Indian settlements. At that time trappers were just beginning to find the region a source of pelts, and in the three decades following they reaped a large harvest. In,1833 Maximilian reported that 25,000 beaver skins had been bought during the year at Fort Union (now Buford); by the next decade, however, Audubon found them already scarce. Nevertheless, Bailey writes, where "the beavers had the protection of the deep water and high banks of the larger rivers" they persisted and "with characteristic tenacity they still cling to their old haunts or merely scatter out to establish new colonies in tributary streams." As late as 1913, he and others found small numbers as at Buford, Fort Clark, and near Williston. At this time also they were present on the Little Missouri and

its tributaries.   In 1919, after two years of open season on
beavers, many of the small colonies were reduced or wiped out;
"a few traces of their work were found along the Missouri
River at Sanish and Bismarck, and there were said to be a few
beavers still in Apple Creek and Burnt Creek.   Near the mouth
of the Cannonball River they were very scarce, although they
had been fairly common up to 1916."   Where cutting of trees
seems too evident, the local residents often become exasperated
and demand the killing-off of the animals, although the loss of
the trees and at times that of the grain growing near at hand
is less than the value of the beavers.

It is perhaps this form of beaver that was formerly common
on some of the rivers of northern and western Kansas.   Hibbard
(1933, p. 241) writes of its recent status, that although once
common throughout the State, along the large streams, it was
exterminated from many parts by early trappers; a few, referred to this race, are still "found in small scattered colonies
along the Republican, and the Kaw east into Douglas County,"
of eastern Kansas, while a few colonies are reported along the
Arkansas River in the western part of the State.

NORTHWEST COAST BEAVER

CASTOR CANADENSIS PACIFICUS Rhoads

Castor canadensis pacificus Rhoads, Trans. Amer. Philos. Soc., ser. 2, vol. 19, p. 422,
Sept. 1898 (Lake Keechelus, Cascade Mountains, Kittitas County, Washington).

CASTOR CANADENSIS IDONEUS Jewett and Hall

Castor canadensis idoneus Jewett and Hall, Journ. Mammalogy, vol. 21, p. 87, fig. 1a,
Feb. 1940 (Foley Creek, Nehalem River, Tillamook County, Oregon).

The beaver of the northwest coast from most of Oregon
northward into southern British Columbia was described by
Rhoads as a distinct race in 1898, but for many years thereafter
this name was considered a synonym of *leucodonta*, the Vancouver Island race.   In 1916, however, Taylor in his review of
the western beavers, reestablished it as a distinct subspecies.
Its characters are slight and relate principally to the form of
the nasal bones, which "in *pacificus* have their outlines somewhat more invaded laterally by the backward-extending
tongues of the premaxillaries," beyond which their lateral outlines again become somewhat more parallel.   This posterior

parallel part is longer than in *leucodonta*. Externally, the color of the fur is "remarkably close" to that of the Californian race, *subauratus*.

Bailey (1936) includes in the range of this beaver in Oregon the coastal area west of the Cascade divide and the whole drainage of the lower Columbia River basin and (in eastern Oregon) the basin of the Snake River. Specimens from the headwaters of the Deschutes, La Grande, Pine Creek near Pine in Baker County, Oreg., and from 5 miles south of Walla Walla, Wash., and from Boise River west of Boise, Idaho, are, according to this author, "typical *pacificus*," but to the southeast intergradation takes place with the Nevada race, *baileyi;* while in south-central Oregon, in the Klamath section, it is believed that the beaver is identical with the form *shastensis* of northeastern California.

Very recently Jewett and Hall have further divided this coastal beaver by describing as a separate race *Castor c. idoneus*, a smaller darker subspecies than its immediate neighbors, with a relatively broad skull and short nasals that do not extend much, if any, back of the premaxillae. Although definitely known only from the type locality (Foley Creek) and Blaine, both in Tillamook County, Oreg., the range is believed to include probably the humid coastal area in Oregon, west of the Willamette drainage. For convenience the two may be treated together here.

Quoting again from Bailey's account, "a century ago beavers were abundant in almost every lake and stream in Oregon, so abundant that the first trapping expeditions brought back rich returns in fur from the least-inhabited parts of the State. In the vicinity of extensive Indian settlements beavers were less numerous, or even scarce, in those days, and in a comparatively few years of vigorous trapping they became scarce over the whole State, and later while unrestricted trapping was allowed, they were reduced to the verge of extermination." As an example of their abundance, Ogden's trappers from October 1826 till the end of the following March took over 2,200 beavers in the State. West of the Cascades, the Willamette Valley was considered at one time the finest hunting ground for beavers in the United States west of the Rocky Mountains, but by 1824 they had already become scarce, and Ogden in 1827, when he reached the Rogue River, was informed that

Indian trappers from the Willamette had already visited the river and taken all the beavers. Even down to 1860, Lord, traveling along the headwaters of the Deschutes River, reported beavers abundant there. Beavers were gradually reduced in number over all this region. Even "at their lowest ebb a few remained in the larger rivers, however, and during the past quarter century under the awakened interest in wildlife and the most rigid legal protection that could be given them in an area of extensive wilderness, they have come back to some of their old haunts and increased locally until they now may be found in many of the streams and lakes of the State. In fact, they are apparently more common now in the Grand Ronde and Walla Walla Valleys than they were a hundred years ago when these valleys were occupied by settlements of Indians who depended largely on the native animals for food and clothing." In recent years they are reported as more or less common in a number of counties both east and west of the Cascade Mountains.

The district forester for Oregon reported in 1930 that the law providing an open season on beavers had proved to be a mistake. The eagerness of trappers to be first in the field had resulted in the greater part of the catch being taken before the fur was prime, while at the same time the number of beavers had been very greatly reduced. The effect of their dams in storing and holding back water during dry seasons was gone, with much resulting loss. Another observer in 1931 states that "the removal of beaver has been a large factor in the shortage of water during the drought through which we are passing. Streams have dried up below former beaver dams to an alarming extent and water for stock has been reduced." On a stream where previous to the advent of beavers in 1920 even a bridge was unnecessary, their dams had since increased so that in the 1931 drought, the driest season on record, "water was plentiful for a distance of a quarter of a mile below the beaver dams . . . and at least 20 acres of land that were dry in the very wet season of 1914 are kept fairly moist." Such observations indicate the value of beavers in water storage at the heads of streams during critical seasons.

In southern British Columbia beavers, though "fast disappearing" 40 years ago, are still found in small numbers in remoter districts.

ADMIRALTY BEAVER

CASTOR CANADENSIS PHAEUS Heller

Castor canadensis phaeus Heller, Univ. California Publ. Zool., vol. 5, p. 250, Feb. 18,
   1909 (Pleasant Bay, Admiralty Island, Alaska).
FIG.: Taylor, 1916, p. 431, fig. *c* (tail outline).

The beaver of Admiralty Island was at first believed to be a
very dark race, but Taylor (1916) shows that of six specimens
from Admiralty Island two are hardly different in color from
two New Brunswick examples of typical *canadensis*, although
others are very dark.   The type is described as having the long
hair of the upper parts almost black, with a slight chestnut
tint at the tips; shoulders deep russet, lightening to chestnut-
brown on the head; underfur very dark seal brown or blackish;
ears black.   On the under side, the longer hairs are seal brown,
becoming slightly reddish at the base of the tail.   The ratio of
length to width of tail is even greater than in the southern
broad-tailed beaver, *frondator*, but the widest part is located
more proximally.   The skull is chiefly notable for its narrower
interorbital region, longer and narrower nasals, broader foramen magnum, and longer tooth row as compared with typical
canadensis.

This is an island race of beaver, hitherto known only from
Admiralty Island, Alaska, although probably it was present
also at one time on some of the adjacent islands.   Heller regarded a specimen from Prince of Wales Island as intermediate
toward the race *pacificus* of the mainland to the south.   He
quotes Dixon that there were said to be no beavers on any of
the islands between Sitka and Juneau, so that their discovery
on Admiralty Island was of particular interest.   Here they
lived in the lakes, which with their irregular shore line and
quiet little bays made an ideal home.   They were seldom
disturbed, although at intervals Indians from the mainland
would come over and take a few.   Their main food supply was
found to be spruce bark, although that of willow where obtainable was preferred.   Four miles to the south of Wide Harbor
it was reported that beavers had been lately exterminated.
On the adjacent Chichagof Island, some old and dilapidated
beaver dams were found, but the beavers seemed to have been
cleared out.   Presumably they were of this race.

Concerning the status of the beaver on Admiralty Island in

the years since its description by Heller in 1909, no recent information is at hand.

COLORADO RIVER BEAVER

CASTOR CANADENSIS REPENTINUS Goldman

Castor canadensis repentinus Goldman, Journ. Mammalogy, vol. 13, p. 266, Aug., 1932 ("Bright Angel Creek, Grand Canyon of the Colorado River, Arizona").

This is said to be a "light-colored subspecies closely allied to *Castor canadensis frondator*, of southeastern Arizona and northeastern Sonora, but upper parts paler, yellowish cinnamon, instead of near pecan brown (Ridgway, 1912) as in the type; cranial characters, especially the long nasals, distinctive. Similar to *C. c. baileyi*, of Nevada, but slightly paler, upper parts more yellowish, less rufescent; skull decidedly broader. Differing from *C. c. mexicanus*, of New Mexico, in slightly yellower coloration (duller brownish in *mexicanus*) and in cranial details, especially the longer, less expanded nasals."

Goldman lists specimens from Bright Angel Creek and Yuma, Ariz.; those from the latter locality with shorter nasals "probably grade toward *frondator*," but in the massive jugal and other respects seem "nearer to *repentinus*." He adds: "At the type locality the beavers inhabit Bright Angel Creek which in short reaches descends the terraced north side, below the outer rim, of the Grand Canyon. None are known from the Colorado River in that vicinity, and a measure of isolation would seem to be due to the rapids and heavy current through rock-bound gorges extending for many miles, and affording very few places suitable for beavers to establish homes." According to Dr. Joseph Grinnell (1933) it was "originally and recurrently numerous along those parts of this river's course where willow and cottonwood grow abundantly . . . Since 1911, beavers have invaded Imperial Valley north of Mexican line following Alamo River and larger distributary canals."

CASTOR CANADENSIS SAGITTATUS Benson

Castor canadensis sagittatus Benson, Journ. Mammalogy, vol. 14, p. 320, Nov., 1933 ("Indianpoint Creek, 3200 feet, 16 miles northeast of Barkerville, British Columbia").
FIG.: Benson, 1933, fig. *c*, p. 321 (skull).

This local race of beaver is described as dark colored, with the ventral underfur dark grayish; "skull with narrow, pointed rostrum; angle between side of rostrum and zygomatic arch obtuse, so much so as closely to approach a straight line; nasals anteriorly narrow and pointed." The slight cranial peculiarities on which this form is mainly based are not very striking, but are shown in comparison with skulls of five other races in the figures accompanying the paper by Benson cited above; he also makes brief comparisons of its characters with those of the surrounding western races, and presents tables of cranial measurements.

This race is "known only from the Cariboo Range, in east-central British Columbia." It is supposed, however, that it meets the range of typical *C. canadensis* in the mountains, while in south-central British Columbia it probably intergrades with the race *pacificus*, and Davis has lately identified as of this race a skull from northern Idaho. Presumably, too, its range meets that of *belugae* "in the northern portion of the Fraser River drainage system." Concerning its general status in the east-central part of British Columbia little information is at hand, but according to Benson it apparently exists in considerable numbers in the mountains of this region. Cowan (1939) in his recent account of the vertebrates of the Peace River district, British Columbia, writes of the beaver, which evidently represents this race, that it is "rare over most of the district but according to reports of trappers increasing on certain areas thanks to the combined efforts of the game wardens and certain of the more intelligent trappers." He mentions that a large female from South Pine, British Columbia, and a yearling male from Pine River are typical of *canadensis* and exhibit no trace of intergradation with *sagittatus*, the race to the west of the mountains.

Shasta Beaver

Castor canadensis shastensis Taylor

Castor subauratus shastensis Taylor, Univ. California Publ. Zool., vol. 12, p. 433, Mar. 20, 1916 ("Cassel [Hat Creek], Pit River, Shasta County, California").

This race is based on cranial characters of relatively slight significance. It is closely similar to the race *subauratus* but although occurring in the same drainage basin, is found on the eastern or Great Basin side of the Sierra Nevada. The distinction is based mainly on the outline of the nasal bones, which show an indentation in the outer margin posteriorly, due to the premaxillary bone; the interorbital constriction is less than in *subauratus*, while the temporal ridges tend to unite to form a distinct sagittal crest posteriorly and show a "higher degree of approximation anteriorly." The interparietal also is somewhat broader.

The type locality "is situated on Hat Creek, a tributary of the Pit River, which is in turn a tributary of the Sacramento River." Thus, although living in the same hydrographic basin as the form *subauratus*, its range on the eastern side of the Sierra Nevada is probably bounded by the Pit River Narrows, "a barrier not regularly crossed by beavers." It is possible, according to Benson, that the beavers of the Great Basin may be identical with this form, but the eastern range is not definitely worked out. Grinnell (1933) gives its area of distribution as the Pit River basin in the northeastern corner of California and adds that it is recorded from "Pit River, above Narrows, north to Willow Creek and Steele Meadow, near Clear Lake, and east to Lassen Creek, east of Goose Lake, and to North Fork of Pit River above Alturas—these localities being in Modoc County." Its present status is not altogether clear, but Grinnell, Dixon, and Linsdale (1937) have summarized all the information they could obtain as to the status of this beaver in northeastern California and the adjacent region up to late 1931, as follows: In September of that year three colonies were known on Fletcher Creek, one consisting of 6 animals at Willow Creek Ranch, another of 10 or 12 individuals somewhat farther up Fletcher Creek, and the third and largest in the entire section comprising between 20 and 25 beavers near the "Mulkey place." Another colony, consisting of about 15 beavers, lived on South Willow Creek, but a colony formerly living on the North Fork of Willow Creek had apparently been destroyed by trapping. About 8 miles north of Canby lived a colony of half a dozen beavers. The largest colony in the county was on Lassen Creek and comprised about 50 animals. It extended from a point about 2 miles above where the creek enters Goose Lake for a distance of 2½ miles. Four or five individuals lived on Davis Creek where it runs into Goose Lake, and another group of the same size was known on the north fork of the Pit River 16 miles north of Alturas. They formerly (1898) occurred in the Shasta River and Scott River, Siskiyou County, flowing into the Klamath River, and there is evidence that beavers "were present in the Klamath River above Requa at least during the years 1915, 1916, and 1917" and were probably of this race. From the figures given, the approximate population of this beaver in California in 1931 must have been about 120 individuals.

The range extends into extreme south-central Oregon along the Klamath River drainage to Goose Lake, a region to the east of the Cascade Mountains, and Bailey (1936) believes that the beavers of the Klamath section, Lost River, Sprague River, and the Yamsay Mountains, are also of this form. As late as 1860 beavers were very abundant in this district. There are still a few here, where they seem to be holding their own or even increasing in recent years (Bailey, 1936).

GOLDEN BEAVER

CASTOR CANADENSIS SUBAURATUS Taylor

Castor subauratus Taylor, Univ. California Publ. Zool., vol. 10, p. 167, May 21, 1912 ("Grayson, Stanislaus County, San Joaquin River, California").

FIGS.: Taylor, 1916, fig. H, *a*, p. 431 (tail outline); fig. J, *b*, p. 450; fig. K, *b*, p. 451; fig. L, *b*, p. 452 (skull); Grinnell, Dixon, and Linsdale, 1937, vol. 2, pl. 8 (colored fig. of exterior).

Fur with a golden sheen dorsally and ventrally; size largest of the western beavers. Skull with the nasal bones more expanded and foramen magnum wider in proportion to its height than in any other western beaver. The average proportion of width of tail to length is about 42 percent, in the race *leucodonta* about the same, but in *frondator* greater, nearly half (49.1 percent). The type measured: Total length, 1,171 mm.; scaled part of tail, 320; hind foot, 196.

This is the beaver of the "lower courses of San Joaquin and Sacramento Rivers and lower portions of larger tributaries of these main rivers" below 1,000 feet altitude in western California. Grinnell (1933) gives its former range as "from Tulare Lake (formerly), Kings County, and from Kings River, near Sanger (formerly), and at Mendota in Fresno County, north to Sacramento River and Butte Creek, north of Marysville Buttes, and at one time to McCloud and upper Sacramento rivers, in Shasta County." In 1912 Taylor wrote that this beaver was then "approaching extinction, although the enforcement of the present protective law may enable it to

regain a foothold." Twelve years later Grinnell and Storer
(1924) reported that the protection thus accorded was effective "and the prospects for their perpetuation are now bright."
Indeed, by 1920 they had so increased as to become troublesome
at Snelling, through interfering with irrigation works. In the
river basins of western California, these beavers feed principally on the bark of willow and cottonwood. At the present
time they are found in some numbers in the extreme western
end of the Yosemite section, along the lower courses of the
Merced and Tuolumne Rivers west of the foothills. With
proper management it is expected that this population may be
maintained in localities where it does not interfere with human
activities. This seems especially desirable, since the golden
beaver is one of the better-marked races of North American
beavers.

A very thorough account of this beaver in California has
been published by Grinnell, Dixon, and Linsdale (1937, vol. 2,
pp. 629–721) in their recent work on the "Fur-bearing Mammals of California." They find that it is more a "bank"
beaver than most of its relatives, adapting its habits to life
along sluggish lowland streams. The largest specimen of
which there is authentic record weighed no less than 82 pounds.
They indicate that because of individual variation the shape
of the tail is of less diagnostic value in the discrimination of
races than had hitherto been supposed, and further it appears
from measurements of a series of fresh specimens that in males
its width is proportionally greater than in females. The
period of gestation is about three months, and two to four
young is the usual number per litter. Beavers in California
are now "just about free from any natural enemy," with the
reduction of bears, mountain lions, and river otters. Although
the number of beavers in a given locality is often overestimated,
these authors believe that in 1920 there were about 250 inhabiting 15 square miles of river bottom in the vicinity of Snelling.
Trapping on the San Joaquin River near Mendota in the same
year indicated about 12 animals to the square mile. On this
basis it was calculated that in 1921 there were about a thousand
golden beavers in California. Much of the area formerly
inhabited by beavers is now reclaimed and in use for agricultural purposes in the delta region, so that the beaver's range
has become more and more restricted, and by 1911 very few

were left in that district. With total legal protection given them in 1911, however, "they had bred up and had become numerous enough to endanger the levees along Cache Slough, and in that year seventeen beavers were trapped there, under special permit." Ten years later beavers had greatly increased in the Merced River bottom in the region about Snelling and became something of a nuisance to ranchers by stopping up irrigation canals. In 1925 legal protection of the golden beaver was removed, and during the two years following the population was severely reduced. From that time until 1931 the "decrease has continued until it seems possible that eventually this species may be eliminated entirely from the Great Valley of California . . . if protection is not restored."

In agricultural areas in California the damage done by beavers is summed up by the authors quoted under six heads: Burrowing into levees or dikes of reclamation work; burrowing into banks of irrigation canals; obstruction of drainage canals by dams; flooding and waterlogging of land; gnawing at head gates of irrigation canals; and cutting down of fence posts and fruit trees. They also mention the complaints of certain ranchers that beavers damage alfalfa fields and fruit trees in their use of these products as food. On the other hand they may, in regions not under immediate use, be of much value in the activities of storing water, and instances are mentioned in which the water held in beaver ponds has saved crops from drought,.or their ponds may be utilized by installing pumps to distribute water for irrigation. "One rancher states that beavers have saved him several hundred dollars each season in this way . . . In several known instances, beavers have lived in streams and ponds of pasture lands among cattle and hogs . . . with little or no competition with" the stock. "There appears to be no good reason why beavers, through their fur value, could not be made to yield a regular income on such ranches." The authors of the "Fur-bearing Mammals of California" "believe that much of the waste, dredged-over land along the Merced, Tuolomne, and American rivers, wherever these animals are not already reestablished, could be used to support beavers and thus be made an asset to the entire State."

SNAKE RIVER BEAVER

CASTOR CANADENSIS TAYLORI Davis

Castor canadensis taylori Davis, The Recent Mammals of Idaho, p. 273, Apr. 5, 1939 ("Big Wood River, near Bellevue, Blaine County, Idaho").

The beaver of the Snake River drainage basin in southern Idaho and northern Nevada has lately been distinguished on the ground of its "averaging darker" than the race *baileyi;* "nasals long and narrow (breadth averaging 46 percent of their length); anterolateral rim of orbit narrow (near 7.0 mm.); occiput nearly vertical."

No details are at hand concerning the past or present status of this beaver. Davis based his description on 11 specimens from Ada, Lemhi, Blaine, and Bannock Counties in Idaho and four from Goose Creek, Elko County, Nev.

TEXAS BEAVER

CASTOR CANADENSIS TEXENSIS Bailey

Castor canadensis texensis Bailey, North Amer. Fauna, no. 25, p. 122, Oct. 24, 1905 ("Cummings Creek, Colorado County, Texas").

FIGS.: Davis, 1940, pp. 85–86, figs. 1, A, and 2, D.

This seems to be a slightly marked form, described as resembling *frondator* in its pallid coloring, but distinguished by the skull, in which the sagittal crest is short and the lateral ridges lyrate or spreading even in old age; supraoccipital crest doubly curved, nasals long, spatulate, and tapering to a narrow point posteriorly. These characters shown in the three specimens studied by the describer "are so well marked and uniform as to justify describing the subspecies, even on so scanty material." The localities given are on the Colorado River of east-central Texas, but "whether the beaver of other streams north and south" of this valley are the same "can be settled only by specimens." More recently the matter was reviewed by Dr. W. B. Davis (1940) with additional specimens, and he concludes that the distinctive characters of *texensis* are its "relatively darker color; posteriorly pointed nasals, with an expanded area near middle of rostrum; dorsal outline of skull nearly flat, except for the distal portion of the rostrum which is *abruptly* depressed; tail relatively long and narrow, ratio of width to length, 48 (39–55)" as compared with the race *mexicanus*. His specimens were from Blanco, Kimble, and Edwards Counties.

To the eastward, intergradation with the race *carolinensis* may be expected, if specimens become available; while to the westward the beavers of the Rio Grande and Pecos Rivers probably represent the race *mexicanus*.

Writing in 1905, Bailey states that "beaver are still found in many of the streams of eastern Texas, especially in the larger rivers, where deep water and steep banks afford protection against relentless trapping. In 1892, at Arthur, in northeastern Texas, I was informed that they were fairly common along the Red River and that trappers caught a few each year. In 1902, at Texarkana, Oberholser was told that a few were still found in the Red River, and in 1901, at Mobeetie, was informed that they were common in Sweetwater Creek, a branch of the North Fork of the Red River." A few were found at this time in scattered colonies along the Colorado River and in the Brazos and Trinity Rivers. In 1904, Bailey was told that in Polk County, in eastern Texas, beavers were abundant only a few years before. In northeastern Texas, on the upper Sabine River, trappers annually obtained them.

A. H. Cook (1940), in a study of live Texas beavers captured in the summer of 1939, describes an infestation, of three out of 40 animals examined, by the screw-worm fly (*Cochliomyia americana*), which had deposited eggs in wounds on sides, back, or hind limbs. He suggests that such wounds were due to fighting as a result of overcrowding. One of the infected animals seemed unable to control movements of the hind legs and died; while another, treated with "bone oil" (a fly repellent), recovered.

Family CRICETIDAE: Hamsterlike Rats and Mice

JAMAICAN RICE RAT

ORYZOMYS ANTILLARUM Thomas

Oryzomys antillarum Thomas, Ann. Mag. Nat. Hist., ser. 7, vol. 1, p. 177, 1898 ("Jamaica").

The Jamaican rice rat is believed now to be extinct, although it lived up till about the 1880's. Probably the introduced mongoose had a large share in its disappearance, for the last known examples were taken about 1877, only five years after the introduction of that carnivore into the island. These specimens are in the United States National Museum. An earlier example preserved in the British Museum was made, in 1898, the type of the present species by Thomas, who describes its color briefly as dull rufous above, rather richer on the rump and grayer on the head, with a slight lining of black on the back; under side dull yellowish, not sharply defined, the hairs slaty gray basally; tail about as long as head and body, nearly naked, hands and feet dull whitish. Total length about 10 inches (252 mm.) of which the tail is slightly more than half; hind foot, 29.2; length of skull, 30.5 (Goldman, 1918).

This rice rat, as Thomas pointed out in his original description, is very similar to the mainland *O. couesi* or some of its Central American races. Indeed, it seems doubtful if it should not be regarded as identical with some one of them, for, as the only cricetine rodent known from the Greater Antillean islands, it is obviously a recent intrusion in a rodent fauna otherwise of a hystricoid type. In his review of the North American rice rats, Goldman (1918) compares the skull with that of typical *couesi* of Yucatan and Honduras but finds relatively few points of difference, namely, that the nasals reach slightly farther back beyond the premaxillaries, the maxillary arm of the zygoma is heavier, and the anterior palatine foramina are shorter than usual in *couesi*. Since, however, only the two specimens in the U. S. National Museum (from Metcalfe Parish and Spanish Town, respectively) were available for comparison, it seems likely that these differences may not be very significant. Without further evidence to the contrary the name may for the present be retained, but at the same time the possibility is recognized that the animal may have been a rather recent introduction through human agency. That it nevertheless thrived and multiplied is evident from the fact that Dr. H. E. Anthony (1920a) in exploring caves along the seacoast of Jamaica found none of the subfossil types of hystricoid rodents in them, though they often did yield "remains of the extinct rice rat, thus showing that at no very remote period this small rodent had a widespread distribution and was so common that it formed an important part of the diet of the barn owl," by which evidently they were brought in to the caves. "The reason for its disappearance obviously

NORTH AMERICA AND THE WEST INDIES89

lies in the advent of the ubiquitous Norway rat and the blood-
thirsty mongoose."
Doubtless this is the field mouse described by P. H. Gosse
in his "Naturalist's Sojourn in Jamaica" (Gosse and Hill, 1851)
as of a "beautiful reddish colour, with a milk-white belly."
"It takes up its habitation chiefly about the hollow roots of
large trees, and the rocky acclivities of gullies and river banks.
It is far from numerous." The type specimen in the British
Museum was collected by Gosse in 1845.

ST. VINCENT RICE RAT

ORYZOMYS VICTUS Thomas

Oryzomys victus Thomas, Ann. Mag. Nat. Hist., ser. 7, vol. 1, p. 178, Feb., 1898 ("St.
Vincent, Lesser Antilles").

Thomas, in describing this species, wrote: "It is difficult to
say to what species this mouse is most nearly allied." At that
time he compared it with the South American *Oryzomys longicaudatus*, giving it the following characters: Size and proportions about as in *O. longicaudatus;* color dark rufous, but this
probably affected by the alcohol in which the type is preserved;
below, buffy white, the hairs with slate-colored bases. Length
of head and body, 96 mm.; tail, 121; hind foot without claw, 25;
basal length of skull, 23.8.

The type and only known specimen was presented to the
British Museum by F. DuCane Godman in 1897. Since that
time no further attempt to determine the nearer affinities of
the specimen has been made, nor have any additional examples
been taken. It therefore still remains problematical whether
it is a native or an introduced animal, what its continental
relatives are, and whether it still exists on the island. Since
no representative of the genus is known from any other of the
Lesser Antilles, it may prove to have been introduced in St.
Vincent through local trade from some adjacent part of South
America; on the other hand, the type specimen collected by
H. H. Smith was marked by him "forest rat," implying its
existence in wooded areas on the island. Goldman (1918, p. 87)
in speaking of it, says: "This rice rat seems likely to be endangered by the presence of the mongoose, if it has not already
been exterminated since the introduction of that indiscriminately destructive animal."

Martinique Musk-rat; "Pilorie"

Megalomys desmarestii (J. B. Fischer)

Mus desmarestii J. B. Fischer, Synopsis Mammalium, p. 316, 1829 ("In Insula Martinica").

Synonyms: *Mus pilorides* Desmarest, Dict. Sci. Nat., vol. 44, p. 483, 1826 (not of Pallas, 1778); *Hesperomys* (*Megalomys*) *pilorides* Trouessart, Le Naturaliste, no. 45, p. 5, 1881; *Oryzomys piloris* Forsyth Major, Ann. Mag. Nat. Hist., ser. 7, vol. 7, p. 205, 1901 (based on Castor Piloris of Zimmermann, not a technical name).

Figs.: Geoffroy and Cuvier, 1830, vol. 4, pl. 258 ("Le Pilori"); Trouessart, 1885.

St. Lucia Musk-rat

Megalomys luciae (Forsyth Major)

Oryzomys luciae Forsyth Major, Ann. Mag. Nat. Hist., ser. 7, vol. 7, p. 206, Feb., 1901 ("Santa Lucia," Lesser Antilles).

Barbuda Musk-rat

Megalomys audreyae Hopwood

Megalomys audreyae Hopwood, Ann. Mag. Nat. Hist., ser. 9, vol. 17, pp. 328–330, Mar., 1926 (Barbuda, Lesser Antilles).

Synonym: *Megalomys majori* Trouessart, Cat. Mamm. Viv. Foss., ed. 2, pt. 2, p. 415, 1904 (nomen nudum).

Fig.: Hopwood, 1926, pl. 12.

The so-called "Musk-rat of the Antilles" may formerly have occurred on most of the islands of the Lesser Antilles, but it has by now probably been quite exterminated. Although its range may once have been more extensive, it is certainly known only from the islands of Martinique (the typical form, *M. desmarestii*), St. Lucia (the smaller form, *M. luciae*), and from the little island of Barbuda, where a subfossil jaw was found. These were rather large rodents, with a head and body length up to 360 mm. (14.5 inches) and tail only a little shorter, and belong to the group of sigmodont species, abundantly represented in South and Central America.

Th Martinique form was the one first named and is the larger of the two known from complete specimens. Trouessart describes a specimen in the Paris Museum as having the head and body 360 mm. long, the tail 330 mm. The head was rather short in appearance and rounded, the muzzle more obtuse than in a house rat, and the upper lip with a deep vertical furrow. The ears were well developed and nearly naked. The fur was long and harsh but not spiny and of a dark reddish brown, both above and below. The tail was black at the base, with a white intermediate area and a black tip. Desmarest, however, speaks of the color as lustrous black except for the chin, throat, and base of the tail, which are white. The skull as figured by Trouessart (1885) is provided with a conspicuous bony ridge on each side from the upper anterior edge of the orbit back over the brain case to the lateral corner of the cranium behind. The skull is rather squarely truncate posteriorly; 70 mm. long.

The St. Lucia musk-rat was slightly smaller, with the greatest length of the skull fron tip of nasals to foramen magnum about 49 mm. The color was apparently much the same as in the St. Vincent form, but the belly was nearly wholly brown instead of largely white.

That the musk-rat occurred on Barbuda to the northward is interesting, for in this extension to the northern Lesser Antilles, there is a certain parallelism in distribution with the agoutis. The Barbuda species, *M. audreyae*, is based on a lower jaw and an upper incisor tooth found in a cave breccia, which, though presumed to be of Pleistocene age, may not be of any great antiquity. The jaw seems slightly smaller still than that of the St. Lucia musk-rat, and in certain slight details of the last two molars that are preserved shows a less development of the small accessory cusps, or paraconids.

The Martinique musk-rat was first mentioned in literature by Du Tertre in 1654, in his "Histoire Générale des Isles de S. Christophe, de la Guadéloupe, de la Martinique, et Autres dans l'Amérique." He did not know of it from any of the French islands except Martinique, where, he relates, it was commonly eaten by the people, who, after first singeing off the hair, exposed the body overnight to the air, and then boiled it, throwing off the first water in order to get rid of the strong musky odor. It was said to live in burrows in the ground and against it the colonists waged war on account of its destructive habits in their plantations. In addition to human enemies, the large serpents of Martinique also attacked it. Du Tertre mentions killing a large snake in the stomach of which was one of these rats "almost as big as a cat." Of preserved specimens, there appear to be scarcely above half a dozen. The specimen figured by Geoffroy and Cuvier is a mounted one in the Paris

Museum, one of two or three collected by M. Plée, who lived
at Martinique from 1821–26. Another from the same collector
is said to be in the Leiden Museum. The Paris Museum has
another mounted one brought back by a M. Le Prieur (?date)
with no other locality but "des Antilles." The teeth of this
last specimen, but little worn, and the skull and worn dentition
of another are figured by Trouessart (1885). Exactly when the
Martinique musk-rat became extinct is difficult to say, but
that it may have existed up to the end of the nineteenth
century is indicated by the following statement communicated
to me by the late Dr. G. Kinsley Noble, who in 1914 visited
Guadeloupe and was told by a Mr. Delphin Duchamp, a
former resident of Martinique, that "about five years before
the eruption of Mount Pelée [1902] there used to exist in great
numbers among the cocoanut plantations along the Rivière
Blanche, close to St. Pierre, a species of rat which was black
as coal on the back and white as milk below. When adult
this creature was some 40 cm. long without the tail. I killed
many of them, for their flesh is very delicate. The negroes
call this rat the pilorie. It lives almost entirely in [?among]
the cocoanut trees but will take to water when driven from
shelter. I never heard of it occurring in any other part of the
island except on these plantations, and since this whole region
was destroyed by the great eruption of 1902, it is very probable
that the rat is now extinct." Inquiries among the hunters on
Guadeloupe showed that it was unknown to any of them as
occurring there, though they knew of its former presence on
Martinique. No doubt the devastating eruption of Pelée
accompanied by clouds of poisonous gas completed its destruction.

Of the St. Lucia musk-rat, Trouessart (1885) records a specimen preserved in the Paris Museum and calls attention to
its smaller size and less amount of white below as compared
with the "pilorie" of Martinique. This individual was
brought back by Bonnecour some time previous to 1881. The
only other specimen extant seems to be the one now in the
British Museum, which served as the type of Forsyth Major's
"*Oryzomys*" *luciae*. This in turn was doubtless the one mentioned as received from St. Lucia by the Zoological Society
of London in 1849 (see Proc. Zool. Soc. London, 1849, p. 105).
It was sent by Lieutenant Tyler and may have lived in London

for three years, since the accession date as shown by its number in the register of the British Museum was 1852. Possibly this species was exterminated prior to the final destruction of the Martinique species.

There is nothing to indicate when the Barbuda musk-rat was living, but probably it disappeared soon after the occupation of the island by Europeans and consequent destruction of cover. Even in Du Tertre's time the musk-rat was not known from any of the other islands, for De Rochefort's assertion that it was one of the five species of mammals native to Tobago may be received with caution.

MUSKEGET ISLAND BEACH MOUSE

MICROTUS BREWERI (Baird)

Arvicola breweri Baird, Mammals North Amer., Pacific Railway Repts., vol. 8, p. 525, 1857 (Muskeget Island, Massachusetts).
FIGS.: Miller, 1896, pl. 1, figs. 1, 1a (skull).

The Brewer's beach mouse of Muskeget Island, lying between Marthas Vineyard and Nantucket Island off southeastern Massachusetts, is of special interest on account of the characters it has developed of large size and pallid coloration, differing in the latter respect particularly from all the other island meadow mice of our coast. It is generally supposed that these traits have resulted from isolation and inbreeding on the confines of this small sandy island. On the other hand, it may be that the beach mouse is a relict species that was formerly an inhabitant of the now-vanished sandplain, which extended coastwise from New Jersey to Newfoundland, and forms a case parallel with that of the Ipswich sparrow of Sable Island, Nova Scotia, a pallid form of that sandy spot, not found elsewhere at the present day.

In addition to its somewhat larger size when adult, as compared with the common *Microtus pennsylvanicus* of the neighboring mainland and the island of Nantucket, the beach mouse is strikingly pale, a "light gray throughout, purest (almost white) on the belly and tinged with wood-brown on the sides and back, the latter somewhat darkened by a sprinkling of longer blackish hairs . . . Tail indistinctly bicolor, brownish dorsally, whitish ventrally" (Miller, 1896). A large percentage of these mice have a white mark in the forehead. The skull in adults is larger than that of typical *M. pennsylvanicus*, with somewhat longer and narrower brain case, more abruptly flaring zygomatic arches, and the outline of the interparietal is longer and narrower. Average adult length, about 200 mm. (8 inches).

Muskeget is distant only 6 miles from the western end of Nantucket. The intervening waters are shallow and on the south side it is partly protected by some small islands and long beaches. In his account of this mouse and its island, Miller (1896) writes that in 1887 the United States Coast Survey found the southern point extending out much farther to the southwest than in later years, during which the sea washed away all but the tip of the point, which remained as South Point Island. He found about a dozen species of birds breeding there and the white-footed mouse occurred in the clumps of beach plum, or about the numerous small houses along the south shore of the island. The beach mice seem to have had various ups and downs. In 1869 they were recorded as "excessively abundant"; in 1890, however, only a few were found by two naturalists visiting the island, while in 1891, William Brewster was unable to find any trace of them. Miller records that the warden, Mr. Sandsbury, who was stationed there in summer to protect the tern colony and who had been familiar with the mice for many years, believes that they had actually been exterminated by cats that ran wild on the island after the burning of the Life Saving Station a few years before. Since the mice can burrow but little in the loose sand, they may have been the more easily exterminated in this way. When Miller visited the locality in 1892, he found, however, that there were large and thriving colonies on South Point Island and the adjacent Adams Island, which had been cut off from Muskeget previous to the burning of the Life Saving Station. This accident had therefore saved the mice from total extinction. Of the further history of this interesting population, Miller (1896) writes: "The 28th of December, 1892, I spent on Muskeget and the neighboring islands. The mice were as numerous as before on South Point Island, but the colony on Adams Island had greatly diminished. In June, 1893, I again visited Muskeget, this time in company with Mr. Outram Bangs and Mr. Chas. F. Batchelder. We found that the Microtus colony on Adams Island had entirely disappeared.

On South Point Island, however, the mice were so abundant that in less than two hours we caught forty-three. After selecting as many as we wanted for specimens, we turned out twenty-six on Muskeget. Although I have not been at Muskeget since 1893, I have heard that the mice on the main island are increasing rapidly. Mr. Sandsbury has written several times to this effect, and Mr. W. K. Fisher collected two dozen specimens for the U. S. Department of Agriculture during July, 1895. Mr. Fisher found two colonies—both in clumps of beach plum bushes—one at the east end of the island, near the place where we liberated the mice in 1893, the other about a mile farther west. He also found that the species was extinct on South Point Island." The Muskeget colonies have apparently continued to flourish since their reintroduction, for as lately as the summer of 1937 Donald R. Griffin obtained a few specimens there. The island is now a reservation for nesting terns and other birds and is provided with warden service through part of the year. To this end, also, the chance introduction of cats is especially guarded against, so that for the present the outlook is bright that the mice will continue to survive. But it is obvious that any important change in the living conditions, the introduction of parasites or disease, or the lessening of human guardianship may again imperil them.

Concerning the special habits of these mice, Miller (1896) writes further that they have been "modified to meet the needs of a life among coarse, loose sand, in which no extensive burrows can be made except during the brief and irregular periods in winter, when the surface is frozen. Throughout the greater part of the year the animals are exposed to the full force of the elements, their only natural protection being that furnished by the scant beach vegetation or by fragments of drift wood and wreckage. Where the mice are abundant, a labyrinth of well beaten paths crosses the sand in every direction, and when one of the animals is chased, he follows these runways aimlessly and helplessly, until exhausted or until he finds some place of refuge, perhaps in a tuft of Ammophila, or beneath the stalks of a beach golden rod. Occasionally a mouse tries to escape by entering a burrow among the roots of the beach grass, but these tunnels always afford a very insecure protection as they are close to the surface and seldom extend more than a few inches, or at most a few feet. The mice apparently make these short tunnels with the sole object of reaching the soft parts of the beach grass stems. They are in no way connected with the nesting burrows. Another means of shelter is, so far as I know, peculiar to the Muskeget mice. They construct frail nests or forms which may be seen scattered about everywhere. The forms are usually open at the top and made of the finer shreds torn off from the beach grass. Each is large enough to contain one animal only. The walls are much thinner than those of the breeding nests, being a mere film of grass fiber, through which the occupant can be distinctly seen. The forms may be built on the bare sand or under some shelter indifferently. Often one partly arches a beaten path.

"The breeding nests, which resemble those of *Microtus pennsylvanicus*, are sometimes made under the protecting stalks of the luxuriant *Solidago sempervirens* or under cover of a fragment of wreckage. When no such convenient shelter can be found the mice construct short nesting burrows. These are from one to two feet in length and penetrate the sand at an angle of about 45°. In this way the tunnel descends quickly through the dry crumbling sand at the surface to the more compact layers beneath, where the walls are less likely to cave in and smother the helpless young. At the end of the tunnel is a hollow, completely filled by the bulky nest . . . Four or five young is the usual number in a litter . . . The food of *Microtus breweri* consists chiefly of the tender bases of the beach grass stalks . . . As the supply of Ammophila on Muskeget is practically unlimited the beach mice never suffer from hunger, but the struggle for existence must be fierce, notwithstanding, for few small mammals live in as exposed situations."

DESERT VOLE; AMARGOSA MEADOW MOUSE

MICROTUS CALIFORNICUS SCIRPENSIS Bailey

Microtus scirpensis Bailey, North Amer. Fauna, no. 17, p. 38, 1900 ("Amargosa River, near Nevada line, Inyo County, California").

This is a desert-living race of the widespread *M. californicus*, from which it differs in being slightly brighter in color, a pallid neutral gray above, but not so black as in the neighboring race *mariposa* of the western foothill belt of the Sierra Nevada; belly smoky gray; tail indistinctly bicolor, brown above, grayish below; feet brownish gray, not dusky. Six adults averaged in total length, 203 mm., about 8 inches; tail, 65; hind foot, 25.1. Skull, basal length, 31 mm.; zygomatic breadth, 19; upper molar series, 8.7.

When first described by Bailey this race was known only from the type locality, where it lived in wet ground under tall tules (*Scirpus olneyi*), in a little marsh surrounding a warm spring. Here the mice had made extensive runways through the mud and water. Kellogg (1918), in reviewing the meadow mice of the *californicus* group, points out that it is an outlying, isolated form, a relict of what was doubtless in former times a more or less continuously distributed species. "It is a remarkable race because of its occurrence away from the main mountain axes and in an area of extremely high summer temperature" in southeastern California. Since assiduous trapping at the original locality in May, 1917, failed to yield a single specimen, Kellogg believed that it had "been exterminated within recent years, as the type locality, a small tule marsh near Shoshone, Inyo County, has been burnt over for several consecutive years and is now being used as a hog pasture." Nevertheless, it seems that a remnant persists, for Dr. Joseph Grinnell writes in response to Dr. Francis Harper's inquiries, in 1937, that it has been "rediscovered within the last few years, not to be sure, at the type locality, but within a few miles' radius, as a result of intensive search. This is to be credited to Miss Annie M. Alexander, who found them in exceedingly small numbers at two desert seepages, where, however, the favoring conditions might at any time be wiped out." On account of its living in such very localized swamps, where a series of dry years or drainage and fire might at any time destroy its habitat, the race is in a precarious state much like that of an animal living on a few small islands where the environment may become unsuitable through slight changes.

GULL ISLAND VOLE

MICROTUS PENNSYLVANICUS NESOPHILUS Bailey

Microtus nesophilus Bailey, Science, new ser., vol. 8, p. 782, Dec. 2, 1898 (Great Gull Island, at entrance to Long Island Sound, New York).
SYNONYM: *Microtus insularis* Bailey, Proc. Biol. Soc. Washington, vol. 12, p. 86, Apr. 30, 1898 [not *Lemmus insularis* Nilsson = *Microtus agrestis* (Linnaeus)].

This meadow mouse is an island race of the common *Microtus pennsylvanicus* of eastern United States, from which it differs only in minor characters. At the present time it is believed to be extinct.

Bailey describes this as darker than typical *M. pennsylvanicus*, the upper parts dark yellowish bister, heavily mixed with black hairs, darkest on nose and face; belly dusky, washed with cinnamon; feet blackish; tail blackish above, dark brown below. The skull is characterized by its shorter, wider brain case and its wider and more abruptly spreading zygomatic arches. In the last upper molar the anterior inner and outer triangles are confluent and nearly opposite instead of being separated by enamel walls. Basal length of skull, 26 mm.; zygomatic breadth, 16.2.

Beyond the original and supplementary descriptions of this meadow mouse by Bailey (1900, p. 26), nothing seems to be known of it. That author remarks: "*Microtus nesophilus* needs no comparison with *breweri* or *terraenovae*, the other two insular forms from the Atlantic coast. In general appearance it more nearly resembles *pennsylvanicus*, but in cranial characters it is as distinctly different as either of the other island species. During the month of August, 1898, Mr. A. H. Howell visited Great Gull Island for the purpose of getting specimens of *Microtus*, but he found their old haunts covered by the earth moved in grading the island for fortifications, while no trace of the animals remained. He thinks they are completely exterminated." Fifteen specimens are listed in the collection of the United States Fish and Wildlife Service, but apart from these and Bailey's account there seems to be no further record of the race. It is a good example of the precariousness of the status of an island form, which with some unusual modification of its habitat is exposed to new dangers,

Since Bailey's account of this race (for such it may best be considered), the meadow-mouse of Block Island, R. I., has been described as an insular race by Bangs (1908, p. 20) under the name *Microtus provectus*. The differential characters seem slight but perhaps sufficient to warrant this action. There is nothing to indicate that it is in any present danger, though conceivably changing conditions on Block Island might alter its habitat sufficiently to imperil it. Of the supposed race *M. pennsylvanicus shattucki* Howe, of Tumbledown Dick Island,

Penobscot Bay, Maine, it has been shown by Wyman (1922, p. 163) that it is identical with the mainland species. Meadow mice are excellent swimmers and may be expected to occur on most of the small coastwise islands where conditions are suitable and where the distances between such islands and the nearest land are not too great to be crossed at intervals by them.

Family ECHIMYIDAE: Spiny Rats and Their Relatives

HISPANIOLAN SPINY RAT; "MOHUY"

BROTOMYS VORATUS Miller

Brotomys voratus Miller, Smithsonian Misc. Coll., vol. 66, no. 12, p. 7, 1916 ("Kitchen midden at San Pedro de Macoris, Santo Domingo").
FIGS.: Miller, 1916b, pl., fig. 1 (four views of type rostrum); 1929c, pl. 2, fig. 1 (rostrum); 1930, pl. 1, figs. 2, 2a, 2b; pl. 2, fig. 5 (femur).

BROTOMYS CONTRACTUS Miller

Brotomys (?) *contractus* Miller, Smithsonian Misc. Coll., vol. 81, no. 9, p. 13, Mar. 30, 1929 ("Small cave near St. Michel, Haiti").
FIG.: Miller, 1929a, pl. 2, fig. 2 (palate).

These two species of Hispaniola, the second with peculiarly narrowed palate, may, as Miller remarks, represent even distinct genera, but with the fragmentary material at present known, this is still uncertain, though they evidently are related rather closely.

Brotomys represents a spiny rat, about the size of the South American *Proechimys canicollis*, remarkable for its "robust skull with weak teeth." The antorbital opening is very large and lacks a secondary canal at the lower corner for the passage of the facial branch of the fifth nerve, a character readily distinguishing it from *Boromys*. The upper cheek teeth are four on each side, with three short roots each. There is a deep enamel infolding from about the middle of each side of each cheek tooth, meeting or slightly overlapping at the center. Probably a shallower infold is present in the crown of a fresh tooth, which soon wears down to leave a small island of enamel in at least the posterior half of each upper molar. Length of four upper alveoli, 10.8 mm. The palate is slightly emarginate. In the toothless palate representing *B. contractus* the very narrow space between the molar rows is a most striking character.

This spiny-rat genus is known only from Hispaniola, where Miller (1916b, 1929a, 1929c, 1930) has recorded it as relatively common not only in the cave deposits, doubtless made in large part by owls, but also in kitchen-middens of the aborigines. Thus he secured two imperfect skulls and more than 50 mandibles from caves near St. Michel, in central Haiti, while in the region about Samaná Bay in northeastern Dominican Republic it occurred in every one of the various Indian sites investigated. He writes (1929c): "The frequency with which the bones of this animal occur in the Indian deposits indicates that *Brotomys* must have been abundant and generally distributed in pre-Columbian days. It was probably much like the living South American spiny-rats in size and general form, but with heavier, less elongated head. I have little doubt that this animal was the Mohuy described by Oviedo as . . . somewhat smaller than the hutia [*Plagiodontia*], its color is paler and likewise gray. This was the food most valued and esteemed by the caciques and chief of this island; and the character of the animal was much like the hutia except that the hair was denser and coarser (or more stiff), and very pointed and standing erect or straight above."

Nothing is known of *B. contractus* except the type palate. No doubt the two were contemporaneous and were early exterminated after the discovery of the island. It seems unlikely, however, that hunting for food was the main cause of extinction. Possibly the introduced rats became a menacing factor, or the actual extinction may have been the result of several causes.

LARGER CUBAN SPINY RAT

BOROMYS OFFELLA Miller

Boromys offella Miller, Smithsonian Misc. Coll., vol. 66, no. 12, p. 8, 1916 ("Village site at Maisi, Baracoa, Cuba").
FIG.: Allen, G. M., 1918, pl. 1, fig. 6 (mandible).

LESSER CUBAN SPINY RAT

BOROMYS TORREI G. M. Allen

Boromys torrei G. M. Allen, Bull. Mus. Comp. Zool., vol. 61, no. 1, p. 6, Jan., 1917 ("Cavern in the Sierra of Hato-Nuevo, Province of Matanzas, Cuba").
FIGS.: Allen, G. M., 1917, pl., figs. 10–13; 1918, pl. 1, figs. 11–13 (skull and teeth).

Remains of these two supposed spiny rats differ chiefly in size, and both occur together in cave deposits; hence they may be considered under a common grouping. The genus is related to *Brotomys* of Hispaniola, but the skulls differ in that the latter shows no external swelling of the bone over the posterior termination of the root of the upper incisor, nor is there a definitely marked channel for the passage of the fifth nerve on the floor of the antorbital foramen; in *Boromys*, on the other hand, the posterior termination of the incisor root is marked by an obvious external swelling, and the floor of the antorbital canal is provided with a groove for the nerve.

So far as known from parts of the skeleton, the two species were alike in structure. There were four cheek teeth in each of the tooth rows. Each tooth had a deep inner and outer reentrant of enamel extending to the center of the tooth, the inner slightly in advance of the outer in each jaw. A smaller reentrant of less vertical depth was present in both the anterior and the posterior halves of the premolar and in the posterior half only of the three molars, penetrating from the outer side. With wear these smaller inlets are soon cut off and appear as little circular islands of enamel in the center of their respective sections and with still further wearing down, disappear. The enamel wall at this stage has nearly the outline of a figure 8. The alveoli of the molars are squarish in outline with shallow cavities for short roots. The incisors were orange-yellow in color. In the larger species, *B. offella*, the alveoli of the upper teeth have a combined length of 11.5 mm., against 7.6 mm. in the smaller animal, *B. torrei;* while the crown area of a single molar in the former is about three times that in the latter.

In former times both these species seem to have been well distributed not only in Cuba, but in the Isle of Pines as well. The larger animal was first discovered in excavations of an old village site at Maisi, Baracoa; hence it was probably used as a food animal by the Indians. Shortly after this discovery, a number of maxillae and mandibles were found in a cave at Limones, Cuba, and in similar situations in the Sierra de Casas, Isle of Pines, by Dr. Thomas Barbour and his associates. These remains may have been brought in by the now extinct giant barn owl. Other but "scanty material" representing the same animal was found at about the same time by Dr. H. E. Anthony (1919) in the course of excavations in caves at Daiquiri, in eastern Cuba, brought in probably by owls.

Of the lesser Cuban spiny rat, remains seem more numerous in the caves, perhaps because the animals were more easily taken by the owls. The species was first found in a breccia solidly cemented by infiltrated lime deposits in a cave in the Sierra de Hato Nuevo, Matanzas Province. Anthony found it abundantly represented in the cave deposits at Daiquiri, while on the Isle of Pines additional remains were unearthed in caves in the Sierra de Casas by Messrs. Barbour, Brooks, and Warner and at another cave deposit in the same island by the Messrs. Link (Peterson, 1917). Nothing further is known of either species, which must both have become extinct within the past century from causes not altogether clear. Neither Gundlach nor Poey seems to have known of the animals, yet some of the bones recovered, such as the nearly perfect skull figured in my paper of 1918, are so fresh that they can be of no very great age. Anthony (1919) writes concerning the bones he collected in the Cueva de los Indios, at Daiquiri: "Some idea of the abundance of the members of this genus is shown by the fact that I have cleaned and examined over five hundred mandibular rami, while nearly as many fragments have been ignored as too badly broken up. The small *torrei* seems to have been the dominant form, as only about five percent of this series represents the larger" one. That the smaller species was ignored as a food animal by the natives may be indicated by the absence of its remains in kitchen middens.

Although in the general structure of the teeth the genus is strongly reminiscent of the continental spiny rats of South America, it has relatively broader nasals. Miller points out a close resemblance of the enamel pattern to that of the extinct *Stichomys* of the Santa Cruz formation of the South American Miocene. The fact that the related *Brotomys* of Hispaniola is nevertheless unknown elsewhere, and the lack of similar forms on the mainland, point to long isolation. Miller regards the two genera as relatives of the Puerto Rican *Heteropsomys*, which, if this surmise proves to be substantiated, would imply some common origin of the three types now regarded as generically distinct. Anthony, however, believes that *Heteropsomys* is a near ally of the agoutis.

True (1885) records a large spiny rat taken on Martinique by Ober in 1878. It was sent to the United States National Museum and there identified as "*Loncheres*" (= *Echimys*) *armatus* of South America, whence it may have been introduced. There seems to be no recent evidence of its continued presence on the island, although Austin H. Clark in 1904 was told by the natives that it still occurred.

BLACK-TAILED HUTIA; "ANDARAZ"

CAPROMYS MELANURUS Poey

Capromys melanura Poey, Monatsber. preuss. Akad. Wiss. Berlin, 1864, p. 384
   (Manzanillo, southeastern Cuba).
FIGS.: Dobson, 1884, pls. 18–21 (colored figure of exterior; anatomy); Bucher, 1937,
   pls. 10–12 (photographs of captives).

So far as known, the black-tailed hutia is confined to extreme eastern Cuba in the wooded mountains. Its circumscribed range places it in a somewhat dangerous position, and although it may continue to exist there for years to come, changes incident to human influence, the clearing of forest, the introduction of the mongoose, and hunting for food are likely to reduce its numbers more and more.

This is a slightly smaller animal than the common hutia of Cuba, *Capromys pilorides*, less clumsily built, and of more arboreal habits. With a body slightly larger than that of a muskrat, and with a bushy tail about as long as the body without the head, the general color is a mixed blackish or brownish and buffy, due to the presence of scattered all-black hairs and more abundant hairs having smoky-brown bases and pale-buffy or ochraceous tips. The forehead and cheeks are nearly clear dark brown or clearer brown, as are the hands and the central area of the hind feet. The under side is similar but paler, mixed grayish and brown, clearer brown on the throat. There is a varying amount of clear white, which may include only the axillae and inside of the thighs, or, as in one specimen examined, the white may include the entire upper throat, the under side of the arms, and continue over the entire midventral surface to the inner side of the thighs, the ankles, and the outer margins of the hind feet. The tail is thickly haired, tapering, with abundant somewhat-stiff blackish to maroon hairs from one-half to three-quarters of an inch long. Total length about 26 inches, of which the tail constitutes about 11 or 12 inches. The claws are slender and sharply curved for climbing, and the soles are granular for better holding.

Although somewhat resembling *Capromys prehensilis*, the longer-tailed and prehensile-tailed species of western Cuba, this seems to be a quite distinct species. Although its tail is prehensile, the hair is not worn away through use of the tail in holding as it is in the former. Moreover, as is well known to those accustomed to hunt it, the tail readily breaks away near the base if strain is placed upon it. For this reason the hunter does not attempt to drag the animal out from a hole by the tail. As with spiny rats, the point of weakness is close to the base of the tail and is marked externally by a sudden change in the character of the hair from that of the body to the more shaggy type of the rest of that member. It comes away easily without bleeding, leaving a rosette of muscle fibers. The details of the anatomy and external appearance are illustrated in the paper by Dobson (1884).

First clearly described by Poey in 1864, the species continues to be little known and rare in collections. Those in the Museum of Comparative Zoology were secured in the foothills of the Sierra Maestra of extreme southeastern Cuba in 1913, and again others were obtained in the mountains north of Imias in 1936. This species replaces *C. prehensilis* in the eastern tip of Cuba and is closely related to it. The only good account of its habits is the recent one of Bucher (1937), who kept several of this and the other larger Cuban species in captivity and found them interesting pets. Of *C. melanurus* he writes that they are active and feed late in the evening and at night. In a wild state they apparently live in pairs together, and the females produce one or two young at a birth. The males fight one another for possession of a female but otherwise seem good-natured. Unlike *C. pilorides*, they do not enjoy being petted and can not be trusted not to snap at one's finger at times. They chatter their teeth when approached and at mating time use a short, low birdlike whistle. In captivity the gestation period seems to be about 17 or 18 weeks. In actions they are said by Bucher to be very squirrellike, running along branches or leaping from tree to tree, using the tail as a balance or in a prehensile manner. Bucher fed his *C. melanurus* at first on fruit of "yagruma" (*Cecropia*), and later they became adapted to a diet of sweetpotato vine, prunings of guava, any citrus fruit and grapevine leaves, buds, and bark. Unlike *C. pilorides*, they will not eat bread or cracker. Probably their arboreal life and nocturnal habits will help to keep them from extermination for a considerable time to come.

So far as known the genus *Capromys* is confined to Cuba and
the Isle of Pines. No fossil species are to be found on any of
the other West Indian Islands, which seems a significant fact
in the distribution. The two other large species, *C. prehensilis*
and *C. pilorides*, are represented by only slightly differing
races on the Isle of Pines, *relictus* and *gundlachi*, respectively.
Bucher (1937) has brought out some interesting details in
which their habits differ. Since, however, neither species
seems in immediate danger of extermination, they may be
omitted here.

DWARF CUBAN HUTIA

CAPROMYS NANA G. M. Allen

Capromys nana G. M. Allen, Proc. New England Zool. Club, vol. 6, p. 54, 1917 ("Cave
deposit in the Sierra de Hato Nuevo, Province of Matanzas, Cuba").
FIGS.: Allen, G. M., 1918, pl., figs. 1–5; Morrison-Scott, 1939, pls. 5–7 (skull and teeth).

This small *Capromys* was first made known from jaws found
in recent cave deposits at two localities in Cuba. Subsequently
it was found living in the great Zapata Swamp, on the southern
coast of middle-western Cuba, south of the original locality.

About the size of a Norway rat, this is typical *Capromys*,
with a rather coarse pelage of all-black hairs mixed with others
having a buffy or ochraceous tip, except that on the muzzle
and in front of the ear the particolored hairs have whitish tips
instead. The fingers and sides of the hind feet are whitish,
but the latter have the central area darkened. The tail,
which is slightly shorter than the combined length of head and
body, has the long hair of the back continued to its basal
three-quarters of an inch, beyond which the hairs become
suddenly shorter and somewhat sparse, so that the scaling of
the tail shows through. The upper side of the tail and the
terminal inch of its under side are black; the lower side is
sharply marked off and ochraceous-buff. Total length, about
375 mm.; tail, 176; hind foot, 45.

When first described this dwarf hutia was supposedly
extinct. It was described on the basis of ten small jaws from
cave deposits probably made by barn owls, in the Sierra de
Hato Nuevo and near Limones in western-central Cuba.
Soon after, Dr. H. E. Anthony (1919) procured no less than

300 mandibles and 60 cranial fragments from caves at Daiquiri, on the eastern tip of Cuba, indicating that in former times it inhabited suitable areas in the length and breadth of the island and probably was regularly preyed upon by barn owls, which had brought these remains into the caverns where the birds rested by day.   None of these fragments appeared to be "at all recent and since this mammal formed such a large part of the owl diet in times gone by, it would almost certainly appear in recent owl pellets" were it still living in eastern Cuba.   In the meantime, through the efforts of Dr. Thomas Barbour, living specimens had been secured in 1917 and sent to the Museum of Comparative Zoology by Don José García.   These were obtained in the great Zapata Swamp, on the southern coast of west-central Cuba, an area that is ordinarily nearly impenetrable but can be entered at times of unusual drought.   So far as known, no other examples have since been obtained, until November 1937, when Dr. Hans Böker collected a live pair in the same swamp, south of the town of Jaguey.   As previously stated by Señor García, these had been found living on small, dry, bush-covered islands in the swamp, where they are probably at most times fairly well protected against invading mongooses or other enemies.   Señor García told Dr. Barbour that the dwarf hutias are sometimes routed out when the sawgrass of these marshes is burned.   Morrison-Scott (1939) records that the pair secured by Dr. Böker were brought alive to the Berlin zoo, where on December 1, 1937, the female gave birth to a single young one, but it as well as its mother died within the next two weeks.   These two are now preserved in the British Museum, while the adult male, which survived until the following February, is now in the Berlin Museum.   The dentition of the young one, which Morrison-Scott figures, already consisted of a premolar and the first molar.

While it seems likely that the species may survive for a good many years in the Zapata refuge, it must elsewhere in Cuba have succumbed before the introduced mongoose and probably the roof rats.

JAMAICAN HUTIA; "INDIAN CONY"; BROWNE'S HUTIA

GEOCAPROMYS BROWNII (J. B. Fischer)

Capromys brownii J. B. Fischer, Synopsis Mamm., Addenda, p. 389 [= 589], 1830
("In Jamaica").
SYNONYM: *Capromys brachyurus* Hill, in Gosse and Hill's Naturalist in Jamaica, p.
471, 1857.
FIG.: Anthony, H. E., 1920a, p. 163 (photograph).

This is the first of the short-tailed hutias to be described, based by Fischer on the account of the "Large brown Indian coney" in Patrick Browne's "Civil and natural history of Jamaica," 1789. Originally placed in the same genus as the long-tailed hutias of Cuba, it was later included in a separate subgenus, *Geocapromys* Chapman, now regarded as a group of generic rank. The characters of the genus in comparison with *Capromys* have been defined by Miller (1929b), of which the more important are: First lower cheek tooth with a small additional reentrant of the enamel wall on the inner side of the first space, making three instead of two indentations; upper tooth rows convergent anteriorly, so that the bases of the two premolars of opposite sides are in contact instead of widely separated; root capsule of the upper incisors passing slightly outside of and beyond the premolar instead of stopping in contact with its base; bony bar in front of the eye nearly vertical or sloping backward instead of forward. Externally, it is distinguished by the very short tail.

This hutia is about the size of a cottontail rabbit but more stoutly built, with short legs and a stumpy tail. Above, the color is a general dark brown, resulting from abundant parti-colored hairs with dark-gray bases and ochraceous tips, mixed with all-black hairs, which are most abundant in the middle of the back. The lower surface is paler, with a buffy-gray throat and lower belly, while the chest and upper part of the belly are more thickly clothed with ochraceous-tipped hairs. The tail and backs of the feet are nearly clear brown. The ears are very short, rounded, and clothed with minute hairs. Total length, 425 mm.; tail, 50; hind foot, 60.

This was doubtless a common species on Jamaica in former times and was confined to that island. It formed an important article of food for the aborigines as attested by the fact that its bones were commonly found with ashes of their camp sites. It is said that the name Indian cony is from this association.

Though evidently now much restricted in habitat and abundance, through hunting and probably through ravages of the Burmese mongoose, introduced in 1872, it nevertheless still occurs in some numbers in the John Crow Mountains at the eastern end of the island where Dr. H. E. Anthony found it in 1919. All his efforts to discover a trace of it in the Blue Mountains, however, were unsuccessful. In the former region the native Negro population often hunt them with small dogs, specially trained for the purpose. These dogs find the dens of the hutias by scent, under large tree roots, or among loose rocks. They at once give tongue to their excitement and try to enlarge the opening and force their way in a few feet to the chamber where the quarry lives by day. Dr. Anthony (1920a) recounts a day's hunt of this nature in the course of which a few specimens were secured. When the dog has penetrated to the den, the hutia voices its alarm in "faint birdlike chirpings" but is soon dragged out by the dog and at once seized by the hunters lest the dogs devour it. "The cony possesses sufficient vitality to withstand a great deal of mauling, and can put up a good fight." One of them bit a small piece out of a dog's nose. "Not infrequently several animals are taken from the one hole," perhaps, as with other hutias, representing an adult pair and their grown young. In his day's hunt, however, Dr. Anthony found but a single animal in each den.

Jamaican hutia (*Geocapromys brownii*)

It is said to live on grasses and the leaves of low shrubs, whence comes its local name of "grazee" in use among the Negroes. It would be worth while to restrict, if possible, the hunting of the species in its mountain habitat in order to protect it from extinction as long as may be. Since 1922 it has been accorded full legal protection (Journ. Soc. Pres. Fauna Empire, pt. 2, p. 15, 1922).

Whether any other species of this genus or of the allied *Capromys* ever occurred on Jamaica is uncertain. However, Miller (1916a) reports that, in examining a few bones recovered from ancient burial sites near Salt River, jaws of two sizes of hutia were found. Although without teeth, the larger of these seemed identical with the living *Geocapromys brownii*, while the smaller, with obviously reduced last molar, was indistinguishable from the mandible of *Geocapromys thoracatus* of Swan Island.

SWAN ISLAND HUTIA

GEOCAPROMYS THORACATUS (True)

Capromys brachyurus thoracatus True, Proc. U. S. Nat. Mus., vol. 11, p. 469, 1888 ("Little Swan Island . . . entrance of the Gulf of Honduras").

This is a slightly smaller and grayer species than the Jamaican animal and was first discovered by Dr. C. H. Townsend, when as naturalist on the U. S. Fish Commission steamer *Albatross*, more than 50 years ago he secured specimens on Little Swan Island, which lies about 110 miles off northeastern Honduras, and at about a quarter the distance separating that country from Jamaica.

While resembling in general appearance the *Geocapromys brownii* of Jamaica, to which it is probably closest allied of the known species, this is somewhat smaller and in correlation with its drier island habitat is less darkened. The general color of the entire upper side is a very even mixture of blackish and pale ochraceous, resulting in a rather yellowish-gray appearance. The backs of the hands and feet are a nearly uniform dusky, minutely punctate with ochraceous. On the under side, the most conspicuous feature is a dull whitish half-collar extending across the lower throat between the arm pits. Elsewhere the color is like that of the upper side but with very little darkening, producing a smoky-buff shade. Size less than in the Jamaican animal, with a total length of some 15.5

inches (390 mm.) of which the tail is about 2.25 (57 mm.); hind foot, 2.50 (65 mm.). In both these species, the auditory bullae do not extend below the level of the basioccipital bones.

There is very little on record as to the habits of this hutia. Lowe (1911), who visited the Swan Islands in 1908, gives an excellent picture of the conditions there in his book "A Naturalist on Desert Islands." The two islands comprise a larger one, which is inhabited and serves as a signal station, and a smaller lying about a quarter of a mile to the eastward, which is untenanted except by wildlife and seldom visited on account of the difficulty of making a landing. The latter island is the home of many sea birds, which nest on the tops of the scrubby bush growth or among its rocks, and is the only place where this hutia is found. It is about a mile and a quarter long and rises abruptly from the sea with low cliffs on all but a part of its northwesterly side. "The plateau formed by the top of the island is densely overgrown with trees and bushes, which form a closely matted dome of vegetation above its wind-swept surface." On the occasion of Lowe's visit it was entirely undisturbed and could be reached from Big Swan Island only on very calm days. It appears to be a "big 'stack' of solid coral limestone which has been thrust bodily up from the sea bottom." In the central portion the surface is somewhat more even, with vegetable mould and a dense canopy of trees. Here Lowe and his party captured several of the hutias. They are diurnal in habits and were seen running about or "bolting into the big crevasses with which the island is seamed." One individual ran over some rocks and tried to escape under the spreading roots of a large undermined tree but allowed itself to be carefully drawn out and placed alive in a fishing creel. It was surprisingly mild-mannered and showed not the slightest fear or suspicion, when later it was taken alive to England and brought face to face with King Edward's favorite dog, which it quietly inspected. The two taken captive became very tame and were allowed the freedom of the yacht's deck, "drank milk with avidity, and ate any form of vegetable or fruit that was offered them." In 1912 George Nelson visited Little Swan Island and secured specimens for the Museum of Comparative Zoology.

At the present time the species seems safe enough in the narrow limits of its island home, but should any important changes take place there, such as clearing, or the introduction of goats or mongooses, its future would at once be in danger. How it originally reached this isolated little spot, whether through introduction by aborigines or by rafting at some pre-historic time from elsewhere, is still an unanswered question.

CUBAN SHORT-TAILED HUTIA

GEOCAPROMYS COLUMBIANUS (Chapman)

Capromys columbianus Chapman, Bull. Amer. Mus. Nat. Hist., vol. 4, p. 314, 1892 ("Cave near Trinidad," Cuba).

SYNONYMS: *Synodontomys columbianus* G. M. Allen, Bull. Mus. Comp. Zool., vol. 61, p. 5, 1917; *Geocapromys cubanus* G. M. Allen, *ibid.*, p. 9.

FIGS.: Chapman, 1892, fig. 3 (type, maxillary bone, and tooth); Allen, G. M., 1917, pl., figs. 7–9 (teeth).

This short-tailed hutia is not known from living specimens, yet it must have been common in Cuba up till relatively recent times. It was first made known by Dr. Frank M. Chapman from a half-palate lacking the teeth and from a few other fragments discovered in a cave near Trinidad, Cuba, "associated with the remains of birds and bats, and also fragmentary pieces of the bones of *Capromys*." "The cave is situated in the southern slope of the coral limestone coast range at an altitude of about seven hundred feet, and within two hundred feet of the summit of this part of the range . . . The floor of the cave was covered to the depth of several feet with a red, ferruginous earth, and on this was a layer four or five inches in depth of a dark earth in which the bones" were found.

On account of the fragmentary nature of the original specimens and of other later-discovered remains, satisfactory comparisons of this Cuban hutia with other forms of the genus are yet to be made. It would be important to know the relations of the audital bullae to the level of the basioccipital bone, which might indicate a relationship with the Bahaman *Geocapromys* on the one hand or to the Jamaican and Swan Island species on the other. Dr. Chapman notices the strongly converging upper tooth rows, which, however, as later finds showed, do not actually touch in front on the palatal aspect. The Cuban animal was evidently as large as the Jamaican *G. brownii*. A median bony ridge on the roof of the palate ends abruptly at the palatal margin in the latter and in *G. thoracatus* is continued as a short median projection at that point. In both *G. columbianus* and *G. ingrahami*, however, the ridge fades out before reaching the palatal margin, while the opening of the posterior nares seems more narrowed. In the former, too, the enamel folds are more nearly at right angles to the long axis of the tooth than in *Capromys*. Toothless jaws may often be identified by the indication of the extra small reentrant on the inner side of the tip of the anteriormost cheek tooth. It is obvious that until better-preserved skulls of this species are found, its distinctive characters in comparison with other forms of the genus are not very well ascertained.

This was evidently a common and well-distributed species not only throughout Cuba in former days but also on the adjacent Isle of Pines. On Cuba, in addition to the original locality, Dr. Thomas Barbour secured numerous remains from caves in Matanzas Province, as well as from the Isle of Pines, and Dr. H. E. Anthony obtained an abundance of jaws and palates from owl deposits in a cave at Daiquiri, in eastern Cuba. In the latter instance the fragments seemed to be mostly of immature and hence small animals, indicating that the adults were too large to be managed by the barn owls that evidently were the cause of the deposits. Why a species apparently so common should have died out before any modern specimens were obtained, and in so well populated an island as Cuba, is not at all clear, for apparently they disappeared before mongooses were introduced. Possibly the larger size and arboreal habits of *Capromys* were factors in their survival, whereas *Geocapromys* was ground-living and less able to escape.

BAHAMAN HUTIA

GEOCAPROMYS INGRAHAMI (J. A. Allen)

Capromys ingrahami J. A. Allen, Bull. Amer. Mus. Nat. Hist., vol. 3, p. 329, Dec., 1891 ("Plana [or Frenchman's] Keys, Bahamas").
FIGS.: Allen, J. A., 1891, p. 335, figs. 1, 3, 5–9 (skull and teeth).

Except for the Jamaican and Swan Island hutias, no living member of this short-tailed genus is known other than this small species now confined to the Plana Keys between the island of Mariguana and Acklins Island in the southern part of the Bahama Archipelago.

The general color is a mixed "yellowish brown, gray and black, giving the general effect of grayish brown . . .

Below, nearly uniform pale yellowish brown, barely a little more yellowish posteriorly . . . some are quite strongly suffused with yellowish and have less black; others are faintly suffused, giving the general effect above of pale yellowish gray mixed with black." A notable feature of the skull is the great development of the audital bullae, which in this and the other Bahaman races project conspicuously beyond the level of the basioccipital bone instead of ending at the same level with this bone. In the lower molars, the two reentrant loops of enamel from the inner side are relatively short and straight, barely reaching the center of the tooth. In size this is slightly smaller than the other living species.

The discovery of this hutia still living in one of the Plana Keys is due to D. P. Ingraham, who in mid-February, 1891, landed there on several occasions while weatherbound under the lee of the island. This key he describes as a small rocky islet, the highest point probably not more than 50 feet above sea level, "with crevices and caves worn in the rocks by the action of water, and in many places broken strata of rocks, piled upon each other." It is about half a mile wide and 4 or 5 miles long, quite without permanent fresh water. In the course of two weeks he secured a small series of specimens for the American Museum of Natural History. In none of these were fetuses found. There appeared to be a concentration of individuals at places where conditions were favorable in affording many hiding places. He once saw a number of them together at a distance from the rocks among palmettos, but later concluded that this was a result of the beginning of the rutting season. They fed mostly at night, though occasionally foraging by day, were not shy, and with caution could be approached within 25 or 30 feet before dashing to the shelter of the rocks. They fed on the leaves, twigs, and bark of the bushes, "especially the black buttonwood, and the succulent growth of the cactus plants," which doubtless supplied the necessary moisture. They seemed "very fond of the fruit of the paw-paw, and even of the body of the tree itself," for in some instances trunks were found nearly as large as a man's body "so nearly eaten off that they would not sustain their own weight. A sweet potato left on the shore was eaten up, while the body of a bird, left to tempt them, was untouched."

So far as the writer knows, no other naturalist visited East

Plana Key after 1891 until James C. Greenway, Jr., landed there in February 1933. He found the hutias still present in some numbers and brought back a few specimens for the Museum of Comparative Zoology. They frequented especially small clumps of bushes and would dash out if disturbed, seeking the shelter of an adjacent clump.

It seems evident that at some former time these or similar hutias were more widely distributed in the Bahama group. Catesby mentions a *Cuniculus bahamensis* and presents a figure of what may have been one of the Cuban species of *Capromys*, though no locality is given. According to J. A. Allen (1891), the narrators of Columbus's voyage "make frequent mention of their abundance not only in the Bahamas and at Jamaica, but also in Cuba and Hispaniola." In recent years remains of this genus have been brought to light in the investigation of caves and aboriginal sites in some of the Bahamas, and these prove to be allied but slightly distinct forms, a brief account of which may be included here.

CROOKED ISLAND HUTIA

GEOCAPROMYS INGRAHAMI IRRECTUS Lawrence

Geocapromys ingrahami irrectus Lawrence, Occas. Papers Boston Soc. Nat. Hist., vol. 8, p. 190, Nov. 7, 1934 ("Gordon Hill Caves, Crooked Island, Bahamas").
FIG.: Lawrence, 1934, fig. 2 (rostrum).

GREAT ABACO HUTIA

GEOCAPROMYS INGRAHAMI ABACONIS Lawrence

Geocapromys ingrahami abaconis Lawrence, *op. cit.*, p. 191, Nov. 7, 1934 ("Imperial Lighthouse Caves, Hole in the Wall, Great Abaco Island, Bahamas").
FIG.: Lawrence, 1934, fig. 3 (rostrum).

These two forms are very nearly related and may be treated together. Both are known from skeletal remains, including rostra and some other parts of the skull, secured in the course of archeological investigations in the Bahamas in 1933–34, by Froelich Rainey. The points of distinction thus far made out lie mainly in the details of the rostral bones and in the teeth. *G. ingrahami irrectus* seems to have been slightly larger than the Plana Keys animal, still living, with longer tooth row, wider individual teeth, and longer zygomatic arch. The two enamel loops on the inner side of the three lower molars are much longer than in the latter animal, extending as long finger-like folds nearly to the enamel wall of the opposite side of the tooth instead of about to the center of the tooth. The audital bullae, however, were large, as in typical *G. ingrahami*, extending well below the level of the basioccipital. The lower tooth row attained a maximum length of up to 17.5 mm. (alveoli); upper tooth row, 16.5; humerus, 50; femur, 67; tibia, 64. Remains of this form are known from four of the central islands of the Bahama group: Crooked Island, Eleuthera, Long Island, and Exuma. Those from the first three islands mentioned were in more or less close association with aboriginal sites in caves and hence may have been contemporaneous with early Indian occupation. Those from Exuma Island, however, though undoubtedly of the same form, may have been earlier, for the deposit in which they occurred abundantly (see G. M. Allen, 1937) showed no sign of human influence, and furthermore contained remains of three genera of extinct hawks and owls. To what extent the aborigines may have utilized these animals as food, or transported them from one island to another, is not now possible to make out.

The Abaco hutia, described from palates and other cranial fragments, was closely similar to that on the Crooked Island group, but with the anterior lower premolar "slightly more tapering anteriorly with the anterior lobe somewhat smaller and more slender" and with longer frontal bones, which ended in a pointed projection "reaching anteriorly between the nasals and the premaxillaries." The postorbital processes in available specimens are more reduced than in the two other forms of the species.

Nothing further is known about these Bahaman hutias. Possibly they were still living in Catesby's day, but the species he figures as a Bahaman cony, about 1750, appears to be a Cuban *Capromys*. Their extinction can not be wholly due to the extinct eagle and giant barn owl, which must have preyed upon them, but more likely was a result of clearing and burning the cover during the earlier centuries of white occupation, of which unfortunately there is practically no record.

HEXOLOBODON PHENAX Miller

Hexolobodon phenax Miller, Smithsonian Misc. Coll., vol. 81, no. 9, p. 19, Mar. 30, 1929 ("Small cave near St. Michel," central plain of Haiti).

FIGS.: Miller, 1929a, pl. 3, figs. 1, 1a, 1b (palate and jaw).

This is an interesting genus, closely related to *Geocapromys* and apparently taking its place on Hispaniola, where it was contemporary with other species of the recent cave fauna, such as *Isolobodon*, *Aphaetreus*, and the still-living *Plagiodontia*. At first glance the tooth pattern in the lower jaw is very similar to that in *Geocapromys ingrahami irrectus* in having the long enamel reentrants of the two last molars extend well beyond the center of the tooth. The anteriormost tooth, the premolar, however, differs from that of *Geocapromys* and agrees with *Capromys* in lacking the additional small inner reentrant to the first section. In the palate the convergence of the tooth rows anteriorly is similar to their appearance in *Geocapromys*, and the relation of the incisor roots to the first premolar is likewise the same, but, as Miller points out, the root of the premolar is "thrown conspicuously forward away from that of the first molar." Other characters are the less specialized roots of the cheek teeth, which appear to close with age instead of continually growing, and "the extension of the lower incisor root to the outer side of the mandibular tooth row." Size probably about as in the Cuban *Capromys pilorides* but perhaps with a shorter rostrum. Maxillary tooth row (alveoli), 22 mm.

This animal is known from a palate, six mandibles, and four isolated cheek teeth, collected by Miller from caves in central Haiti near St. Michel and l'Atalaye. At first sight it might easily be taken for a *Geocapromys*, which is as yet unknown from Hispaniola. The characters pointed out by Miller, however, appear to be distinctive. It was presumably exterminated soon after white occupation.

HISPANIOLAN HUTIA; "RAT-CAYES"

PLAGIODONTIA AEDIUM F. Cuvier

Plagiodontia aedium F. Cuvier, Ann. Sci. Nat., zool., ser. 2, vol. 6, p. 347, 1836 ("Saint-Domingue," taken as Haiti by Miller).
FIGS.: Cuvier, 1836, pl. 17 (exterior and skull); Miller, 1927, pl. 1, fig. 2.

PLAGIODONTIA HYLAEUM Miller

Plagiodontia hylaeum Miller, Proc. U. S. Nat. Mus., vol. 72, art. 16, p. 4, 1927 ("Guarabo, 10 miles east of Jovero, Samaná Province, Dominican Republic").
FIGS.: Miller, 1927, pl. 1, figs. 1, 1a–1c (skull).

Described and figured by Cuvier over a century ago, from a specimen brought by Alexander Ricord from Hispaniola in about 1826, no additional specimens of the genus had since been found living until Dr. W. L. Abbott secured a series of ten adults and three young at Guarabo, Dominican Republic, about 10 miles east of Jovero, Samaná Bay. These he sent to the U. S. National Museum, where Miller (1927), on subsequent study, decided that they represented a species distinct from *aedium* and proposed to call it *P. hylaeum.*

Both these species were of similar appearance in life. Cuvier describes *P. aedium* as of rather stout build, the head and body about a foot in length, the tail 5 inches and naked. In a general way these animals resemble a medium-sized *Capromys pilorides,* but the teeth in both species are very different, with the enamel folds extending diagonally instead of transversely across each molar. In this respect also they recall the teeth of *Isolobodon,* the Puerto Rican hutia, but the enamel reentrants are much more nearly longitudinal in direction, and the upper tooth rows are more nearly parallel instead of converging strongly in front. There were five claws on all four feet, although that of the thumb was a short, blunt nail. The pelage in *P. aedium* is described as thick, of fine silky hairs above, which were gray in the basal three-quarters, tipped with tawny and intermixed with longer all-black hairs. The under surfaces were paler and clearer, probably nearly buff. The mustachial hairs, as usual in this group, were long and abundant. Miller, who examined the type in Paris, adds that the tail was naked and smooth, its small scales not overlapping but tending to be rounded-pentagonal and scarcely a millimeter in diameter at 30 mm. from the base of the tail. "Ears naked internally, thickly furred along edge and apparently on outer side also . . . hind foot with claws, 74 mm."

The distinguishing features of *P. hylaeum* are given by Miller (1927, p. 4) as follows: Anteroposterior diameter of the first and second true molars in the lower jaw, each less than the transverse diameter instead of equaling or exceeding it, as in *P. aedium;* reentrant enamel folds relatively narrower and longer; and the size smaller with the length of the mandibular tooth row (alveoli) in adults less than 21 mm., instead of about 24 mm. as in *P. aedium.* The color throughout is "nearly wood-brown" darkening to buffy brown on chest and belly.

On the under parts the light brown is uniform, but, above, it is "finely intermingled with dark brown." It is thus probably a somewhat darker-colored animal than *P. aedium*, the original specimen of which is, however, much faded at the present time. The largest specimen of Dr. Abbott's series measured 405 mm. in length of head and body; the tail 130; foot, 74.

It seems likely that at the present time *P. aedium*, the older-known species of Hispaniola, is quite gone and that the smaller *P. hylaeum* is now confined to forested areas in the Samaná Bay region of northeastern Dominican Republic. Dr. W. L. Abbott, who discovered it here in 1923, wrote that his specimens were obtained for him by an old man who "caught them with dogs in hollow trees down near a lagoon near sea shore." The four adult females were all pregnant, each containing, in early December, a single young, indicating a slow rate of breeding, which he observes, "will probably help their extinction." He supposes that they may still have been abundant in the region and at that time were little hunted for food. They can climb to some extent, but their short tail and general stout appearance indicate that terrestrial habits are more typical. For this reason they are the more liable to attack by the introduced Burmese mongoose. Since Dr. Abbott's visit in 1923, William J. Clench, of the Museum of Comparative Zoology, secured two other specimens for that institution, in the same general region, in August 1937. These were an adult male and a half-grown animal of the same sex, doubtless born earlier in the same year.

Nothing is known of the habits and haunts of *P. aedium* beyond the few statements of Cuvier, to whom Ricord reported that in "Santo Domingo" the animal was known a century ago as "Rat-Cayes," or house rat, because it frequented settled areas. It was active only by night, hiding during the day. The male and female of a pair remained usually together. Its principal food consisted of roots and fruits; hence its flesh was good to eat, and the Haitians hunted it with such zeal that even at that time it had become very rare. From the fact that Miller unearthed six lower jaws from a cave in the interior of Haiti in 1925 and de Booy had previously secured a jaw from old kitchen middens at San Pedro de Macoris on the south coast of the island about 60 kilometers east of San Domingo City, it may have been that *P. aedium* was the animal of western and southern Hispaniola, and *P. hylaeum* that of the northeastern parts of the island. Even so, the ranges could hardly have been entirely separate, for in a later paper, Miller (1930), reporting on mammal remains from Indian kitchen middens on the valley floor near Constanza in the mountainous interior of Dominican Republic, identifies both species as present. Evidently both were used as food by the aborigines.

It is significant that this well-distinguished genus is as yet unknown in either fossil or recent state from any other Antillean islands or from the mainland.

LEAST HISPANIOLAN HUTIA

PLAGIODONTIA SPELAEUM Miller

Plagiodontia spelaeum Miller, Smithsonian Misc. Coll., vol. 81, no. 9, p. 18, Mar. 10, 1929 ("The crooked cave near the Atalaye plantation, Haiti").

Nothing is known of this supposed third species of Hispaniolan *Plagiodontia* beyond the account given by Miller, who found 15 mandibles, four in the group of caves near St. Michel in north-central Haiti, and the others in the "crooked cave" near the Atalaye plantation in the same region. Its main point of difference from *P. aedium*, remains of which occurred in the same caves, lies in its smaller size, as indicated by the mandibular tooth row of 15.6–16.2 mm., as against 23.6 in the former. Compared with *P. hylaeum*, the discrepancy is less, for the latter has a tooth row of 18.6 mm.

PUERTO RICAN ISOLOBODON

ISOLOBODON PORTORICENSIS J. A. Allen

Isolobodon portoricensis J. A. Allen, Ann. New York Acad. Sci., vol. 27, p. 19, 1916 ("Cueva de la Ceiba, near Utuado, Puerto Rico").

FIGS.: Allen, J. A., 1916a, pls. 1–5; Anthony, H. E., 1918, pl. 62, figs. 1a–6b; pl. 63, figs. 1a–b, 4–12c; pl. 74, figs. 6a–c; text-fig. 39, A–H (skeletal parts).

This well-marked genus is as yet unknown in the living state and is undoubtedly extinct, although abundantly represented in kitchen middens of the Indians in Puerto Rico, the Dominican Republic, and the Virgin Islands.

The skeletal characters, which alone are available, show that it was an animal of about the size of the Hispaniolan hutias, to which it is somewhat closely related. Its teeth, however, are very different. The upper tooth rows converge strongly forward instead of being nearly parallel, while the pattern of the enamel folding is simpler. Each of the upper molars has a shallow outer and a much deeper inner reentrant loop, the latter of which extends inward and forward, diagonally, to touch the smaller outer one. The first tooth of the four, the premolar, has in addition a second small outer reentrant in advance of the one that meets the inner loop. In the lower tooth row there are two shallow reentrants of enamel on the inner side of each molar, the posterior of which meets the single outer reentrant nearly at the center of the tooth. In *Plagiodontia* the inner reentrant is much deeper, runs more diagonally forward, and does not meet the smaller fold of the outer side. The teeth of young animals have the same pattern as do those of adults, for they are continuously growing; but the size of the individual teeth increases with age and wear.

This must have been a common species on Puerto Rico up till the period of white occupation. Both Dr. H. E. Anthony and I found its bones on the surface in undisturbed caves on the island, and they are abundant in kitchen middens, mingled with broken pottery and ashes, indicating that they formed a staple article of diet for the Indian aborigines. Shortly after the discovery of its bones in cave deposits probably of human origin in Puerto Rico, Miller (1916b) announced the finding of additional jaws and other parts of the skeleton in the course of excavating Indian sites at Macoris and San Lorenzo, in the Dominican Republic. He was unable, however, to distinguish these remains from those found on Puerto Rico. Again, in a later paper he (Miller, 1918a), reports the discovery of many other bones of this hutia, secured by Theodoor de Booy in the course of excavating two Indian sites in the Virgin Islands, one at Magens Bay, St. Thomas, the other at Salt River, St. Croix. The wide distribution of the species—Puerto Rico, Hispaniola, and the Virgin Islands—the complete lack of differentiation on these three areas, and finally the frequent occurrence of the remains in deposits of human origin, all point to the fact that it was a regular source of food for the aborigines and that they carried it about by canoe from island to island, to serve their needs. Whether its original home was on Puerto Rico or on Hispaniola must remain uncertain, but Anthony (1918) inclines to the view that judged from its apparently wide distribution on the former it was indigenous there and that "it is unlikely that its primitive range included both Santo Domingo and Porto Rico because no differentiation between specimens from the two places is seen." The fact that its bones may here be found near or at the surface in some deposits is evidence for his further belief that it was the last native mammal to become extinct on Puerto Rico. This must have been soon after the discovery by whites.

If we assume that the Indians used this as a staple food animal, the implication of its presence on these three different island habitats is that they kept it in a state of semidomestication and perhaps bred it in captivity for food. This they apparently did with the guineapig (the cori), remains of which also occur in shell heaps in the Dominican Republic and Cuba. Possibly, too, this was a particularly docile and tractable species, as some of the hystricomorphs are known to be.

HAITIAN ISOLOBODON

ISOLOBODON LEVIR (Miller)

Ithydontia levir Miller, Smithsonian Misc. Coll., vol. 74, no. 3, p. 5, Oct. 16, 1922 (Cave "northeast of St. Michel de l'Atalaye, northwest end of the central plain of Haiti").

Isolobodon levir Miller, Smithsonian Misc. Coll., vol. 81, no. 9, p. 14, Mar. 30, 1929.

FIGS.: Miller, 1929a, pl. 2, figs. 3, 3a.

Originally based on a single molar tooth from cave deposits in Haiti, further excavations in the same region disclosed that this species was after all an *Isolobodon* and that the original tooth was an upper premolar and not a lower molar as was at first supposed.

From the abundant remains secured in the later work in the St. Michel area, which lies at the northwest end of the central plain of Haiti, Miller (1929a) was able to show that this is the most abundantly represented of the vertebrates found in the bone-bearing deposits. The fragments of palates and jaws are constantly smaller than are those of the Puerto Rican isolobodon, the eight largest among 600 mandibles having tooth rows 16.2–17.2 mm. in length, while in the latter animal the range is from 17.6 to 19.2 mm. Such other measurements as can be obtained from crania of the Haitian animal confirm its slightly smaller size.

The evidence now available, as Miller brings out (1929a,

1929c), suggests that the remains of this genus identified as
I. portoricensis, occurring abundantly in the Indian cultural
deposits in the region of Samaná Bay, Dominican Republic,
were probably brought in originally by the Indians, if not
directly from Puerto Rico, at least as domesticated stock from
that island, for food. The smaller form native to Haiti and
doubtless extending to other parts of Hispaniola was found
sparingly in kitchen middens but is the sole one represented in
the great number of remains from the caves near St. Michel in
the central part of Haiti. Imperfect skulls also were found in
a small deposit at San Gabriel near Samaná Bay, a deposit
which, like that at St. Michel, was probably due to the giant
barn owl, *Tyto ostolaga*, now extinct, which must have sub-
sisted largely on these animals and died out when they became too few to sustain it. At what time the animal vanished
is, of course, indeterminate, but the implication is that the
aborigines about Samaná Bay, at least, found it easier to
subsist on *I. portoricensis*, which they may have domesticated,
than to hunt the smaller Haitian animal, which may already
have become scarce or restricted in distribution at about the
time of the discovery.

NARROW-TOOTHED HUTIA

APHAETREUS MONTANUS Miller

Aphaetreus montanus Miller, Smithsonian Misc. Coll., vol. 74, no. 3, pp. 3, 4, Oct. 16,
1922; also vol. 81, no. 9, p. 16, 1929 ("Larger of the two caves northeast of St.
Michel de l'Atalaye, northwest end of Central Plain," Haiti).
FIGS.: Miller, 1929a, pl. 2, figs. 4, 4a, 4b.

This is another remarkable octodont rodent, of about the
size of *Isolobodon* and closely related to it, but so far as known
confined to the island of Hispaniola and now apparently too
exterminated.

It was first described by Miller from mandibles from the
cave deposit northeast of St. Michel, Haiti, among the mountains. The teeth differ conspicuously from those of *Isolobodon*
and *Plagiodontia*, which they somewhat resemble in their
diagonally placed enamel plates, through a further development of these folds, so that the posterior of the two inner
folds extends across and fuses with the outer, thus cutting off
a posterior transverse space. In addition the teeth are re-

markably compressed anteroposteriorly, so that they are much narrower than wide. In these characters it represents a more advanced stage of development than *Plagiodontia* and *Isolobodon*, in which the reentrant folds are still separate.

In the excavations at the type locality carried on after the preliminary work had disclosed the two jaws on which the original account was based, a more extended search brought to light abundant remains of this animal, permitting the more detailed description in Miller's (1929a) second paper. Judged from the material recovered this was the second most common species brought in to the caves supposedly by the now extinct giant barn owl. In a later report Miller (1929c) remarks that no remains of this animal have as yet been discovered in the various kitchen middens and cultural deposits in the Samaná Bay region; hence there is no real evidence that the species was utilized by the aborigines as a food animal, though they may have hunted it. In addition to the collection of 17 skulls and more than 200 mandibles recovered from the cave deposit at St. Michel, other fragments were secured at San Gabriel near Samaná Bay, from a deposit evidently made by owls, as in the case of the former. Equally interesting is the discovery of six mandibles, all of immature individuals, in cave deposits on Gonave Island off southern Haiti, indicating its wide dispersal in Hispaniola in older times (Miller, 1930). The animal was apparently unknown to the early Spanish explorers, nor is it possible to tell whether it survived later than the early years of white occcupation.

HETEROPSOMYS INSULANS Anthony

Heteropsomys insulans Anthony, Ann. New York Acad. Sci., vol. 27, p. 202, Aug. 9, 1916 ("Cueva de la Ceiba, near Utuado, Porto Rico").
FIGS.: Anthony, 1916, pl. 11, figs. 2–3; pl. 12, figs. 1–5 (skull); 1918, p. 407, fig. 40, A-D (skull), p. 410, fig. 41 (vertebrae).

HOMOPSOMYS ANTILLENSIS Anthony

Homopsomys antillensis Anthony, Bull. Amer. Mus. Nat. Hist., vol. 37, p. 187, Jan. 29, 1917 ("Cave . . . near Utuado, Porto Rico").
FIGS.: Anthony, H. E., 1917a, pl. 5, fig. 8 (rostrum); 1918, p. 407, fig. 40, E (skull).

These two species are known from cranial parts chiefly excavated, with remains of other animals, in caves of Puerto Rico. In all likelihood they were contemporaneous with these latter and may have survived up till relatively recent times. They are believed to represent genera closely akin to the agoutis of South and Central America but present certain differences in cranial and dental characters. They are included here for the sake of completeness.

Both were perhaps slightly smaller than the typical agouti of Trinidad or Brazil, representing the genus *Dasyprocta*. Anthony (1916, 1918) describes *Heteropsomys* as having a skull smaller than that of an agouti, with a total length of about 70 mm. There are four molars in each jaw, of nearly equal size, each with a prominent infolding of enamel on the middle of the inner side in the upper teeth and on the outer side in the lower teeth. In the few known specimens there are three small transverse islands of enamel in the first upper tooth, and two in the second (and probably two succeeding true molars). An unworn tooth would doubtless show that these are the result of wearing away the summits of shallow transverse depressions in the enamel covering. The molars are each provided with two short conical roots. The posterior narial passage or interpterygoid fossa extends forward in a V-shape to the level of the second molar. In general the skull is less elongate and relatively wider than in typical agoutis. Anthony writes that judged from the position of the remains discovered "this rodent is doubtless of a later age" than either the small ground sloth *Acratocnus* or the large rodent *Elasmodontomys* found in the same cave deposits.

Concerning *Homopsomys*, only a few broken crania are known from which to determine its relationships. The dentition is missing from these, except for a few fragments, but the skull shows a similar broad, flattened, frontal area, with bluntly pointed postorbital projections. In his later paper Anthony (1918) writes: "*Homopsomys* is very closely related to *Heteropsomys*. Indeed it now appears that the two forms are probably congeneric, and I would make them so but for the fact that the material at hand is rather inadequate." The differences between the two, such as the length of palate, smaller size of *Heteropsomys*, its lighter incisors, and more convex frontals, may be characters due to age rather than specific or generic characters, so that future specimens, if obtained, may throw additional light on the relationship of the supposed species. Although Miller compares his *Brotomys* with these, Anthony insists that they resemble agoutis rather than spiny rats and would even make a separate subfamily, Heteropsomyinae, for their inclusion.

Hitherto these genera have not been found in any of the West Indies except Puerto Rico.

Family HEPTAXODONTIDAE

HEPTAXODON BIDENS Anthony

Heptaxodon bidens Anthony, Bull. Amer. Mus. Nat. Hist., vol. 37, p. 183, Jan. 29, 1917 ("Cave . . . near Utuado, Porto Rico").
FIGS.: Anthony, 1917a, pl. 5, figs. 1–6 (palate, jaw, teeth).

This must have been a remarkable hystricomorph, and it adds another to the peculiar mammals of this type known from Puerto Rico. It is known only from fragments of the jaws secured in cave excavation at Utuado and near Morovis and Ciales and hence was probably well distributed in the forested parts of the island at no very distant period. Its few remains seem to have occurred in much the same manner as those of other mammals in these deposits; hence it may be assumed that it lived up till about the time of discovery by whites.

Of about the size of a woodchuck, this animal was notable not only for the laminated pattern of its upper and lower grinding teeth, but also for the fact that these seem to have been reduced to but two in each series. The upper premolar was of seven "distinct and separate parallel laminae of strong enamel . . . oblique to the main axis of the toothrow," while the lower premolar was similar but reversed. In the former, however, the last enamel space is not quite completely cut off from the one in front. In the type fragment a space is present for a molar, and the palatal notch extends forward to the level of the hind margin of the premolar. In a lower mandible there are apparently only the premolar and first molar present. The length of the premolar is 11.5 mm.

According to Dr. Anthony, its discoverer, the affinities of *Heptaxodon* are with the Puerto Rican *Elasmodontomys*, but on the other hand it is so different that both may be regarded as representing distinct subfamilies of the Chinchillidae, or it may be relegated to a distinct family of its own (Miller and Gidley). What relationship if any it may have to the genera discovered by the same investigator in Jamaica, and named by him *Clidomys*, *Speoxenus*, and *Spirodontomys*, is still to be made out. These three are represented by teeth and a few other fragments almost all of which were in a hard breccia and may be of greater age than the cave material of Puerto Rico. The teeth indicate stages of development that may be ancestral to such a condition as found in *Heptaxodon*, but as yet only a preliminary account has been published (Anthony, 1920b).

Family DINOMYIDAE: Giant Rodents

"QUEMI" OF OVIEDO

QUEMISIA GRAVIS Miller

Quemisia gravis Miller, Smithsonian Misc. Coll., vol. 81, no. 9, p. 23, Mar. 30, 1929 ("The crooked cave near the Atalaye plantation," St. Michel, Haiti).
FIGS.: Miller, 1929a, pl. 4, figs. 2, 3.

ELASMODONTOMYS OBLIQŪUS Anthony

Elasmodontomys obliquus Anthony, Ann. New York Acad. Sci., vol. 27, p. 199, Aug. 9, 1916 ("Cueva de la Ceiba, near Utuado, Porto Rico").
FIGS.: Anthony, 1916, pls. 13, 14 (skull and teeth); 1918, figs. 25–37 (skull and other skeletal parts).

Since almost nothing beyond skeletal remains of these two species is known, and because they stand evidently in close relationship, they may be considered together. In general size they were about alike and probably were nearly as big as a paca, *Quemisia*, inhabiting Hispaniola, and *Elasmodontomys*, the adjacent island of Puerto Rico. Miller, in describing the former, expresses his conviction that it is the animal called "Quemi" by Oviedo in his account of the animals of Hispaniola, published slightly more than a quarter of a century after the discovery.

These two mammals, the largest of the extinct rodents known from their respective islands, are hystricomorphs with relationships to the South American Dinomyidae and Chinchillidae, but since there is no evidence that they had developed leaping modifications, it may be better to regard them as members of the former, as proposed by Miller and Gidley. In both, the enamel pattern of the cheek teeth consists of diagonally transverse folds running nearly across each tooth, so as to present a laminate appearance, with five enamel ridges to each. In *Quemisia*, according to Miller (1929a), the main points of difference in contrast to *Elasmodontomys* are: Reentrant enamel folds less nearly transverse, slanting forward at an angle of about 21° instead of about 50°; the mandibular symphysis longer, extending back beyond the middle of the first molar instead of barely to the middle of the premolar; shaft of the lower incisor not extending behind the symphysis instead of far beyond it to terminate beneath the middle of the second molar. The incisors show a shallow depression on their front face, slightly more marked in the lower than in the upper pair. The skull of *Elasmodontomys* was about 5 inches long and proportionately broader than in the Cuban *Capromys pilorides*. Anthony (1918) has well illustrated the principal bones of the skeleton. He shows that the sacrum consists of four well-fused vertebrae and that the tail was probably short. It seems to have been a heavy-bodied animal, and its short phalanges indicate terrestrial rather than climbing habits.

According to the brief description of Oviedo, the "Quemi" resembled the hutia in color but was larger. That it was utilized by the natives of Hispaniola as a food animal is indicated by the presence of its limb bones at a depth of about 4 feet in a kitchen midden near the entrance of a cave at Boca del Infierno, in the Samaná Bay region, Dominican Republic (Miller, 1929c). It must have become extinct soon after the coming of the Spaniards, probably about the first half of the sixteenth century. As to its representative on Puerto Rico, *Elasmodontomys*, nothing is known. Anthony found its bones "well bedded in the red stalactite formation, the deeper layers of the cave deposit," so that it may have died out at an earlier time.

Here may be mentioned appropriately a third but much larger member of the same group, a rodent almost as large as a black bear, to which Cope (1868) gave the name *Amblyrhiza inundata* and later synonyms based on single teeth of the same animal. These teeth were discovered in a cargo of cave earth sent to Philadelphia from the island of Anguilla at the extreme northeastern point of the Antillean chain. Additional fragments were later discovered in a cave on the adjacent island of St. Martin. More recently several fragments, including a large part of a skull and portions of the palate and incisors, have come to light in the museums at Leiden and Delft, collected over 50 years ago. These supply additional facts concerning the structure and indicate that the animal was closely allied to the "Quemi" of Santo Domingo, with essentially the same enamel pattern of the molars but with a relatively longer rostrum. A full account of these has been published by Schreuder (1933) with figures. The complete skull is estimated to have been about 400 mm. (16 inches) in length, and hence the animal must have been a giant in comparison with the "Quemi". How long ago this species lived, how it reached the two neighboring small islands on which its remains are found, and why it should have perished there are questions still impossible to answer. That it lived well after glacial times is probable, but whether it was a contemporary of the aboriginal Indians there is uncertain.

If Miller is correct in identifying his *Quemisia gravis* with the "Quemi" of Oviedo, the name should stand as *Quemisia quemi* (J. B. Fischer), since this name was given in 1830 by Fischer [Synopsis Mamm., Addenda, p. 389 (= 589)], who quotes Oviedo and Latinizes his description. He includes as synonymous, however, the account of the "Spanish Racoon" from Browne's "Civil and Natural History of Jamaica," an unidentified animal that was probably the larger Cuban hutia, *Capromys pilorides*.

Family DASYPROCTIDAE: Agoutis

St. Vincent Agouti

Dasyprocta albida Gray

Dasyprocta albida Gray, Ann. Nat. Hist., ser. 1, vol. 10, p. 264, 1842 ("St. Vincent's," West Indies).

In former times agoutis were doubtless present in most of the Lesser Antilles, and they still occur or did so until modern times on at least the following (named in order from south to north): Tobago, Grenada, St. Vincent, Barbados, St. Lucia, Dominica, Guadeloupe, Montserrat, and St. Kitts. This carries them all the way, practically, from Trinidad and South America, north throughout the chain to the northeast corner of the Antilles, a point where the distribution of some other Lesser Antillean animals stops, and beyond which to the westward the distribution of certain Greater Antillean species begins (such as that of *Amblyrhiza* on Anguilla and its relatives on Puerto Rico). It is difficult to say whether this is a natural distribution, owing to the species having succeeded in crossing from island to island northward, or whether it is due to human agency whereby they were introduced and successfully colonized. Their flesh is considered excellent food, and they are not difficult to keep in captivity; hence it is reasonable to believe that the aborigines may have been responsible for their introduction from the continent or Trinidad to the various islands to the northward. Du Tertre, writing in 1654, says that among the French islands—implying St. Kitts, Guadeloupe, and Martinique—they were well known at that time and were much hunted for their flesh, dogs being trained to run them. When pursued, they seek shelter in a hollow log or tree whence the hunters smoke them out. The female was said to bring forth two young at a time, in a nest made on the ground under a bush. In early days, too, it was said that their sharp incisor teeth were used as blades, probably set in some kind of a handle, by the Caribs for cutting their skin all over their bodies to draw blood in their religious ceremonies. A later French missionary, Labat, writing in 1742, said that he believed it was found on all the islands, although he acknowledged that he did not know of its presence on Martinique. It was then common on Dominica, Guadeloupe, and St. Kitts. Its absence, even at the present day, on Martinique is interesting and requires explanation. Possibly the introduction of so poisonous a snake as the bushmaster in early times may have exterminated it there if it previously had been present. Perhaps, too, volcanic eruptions, with their discharge of poison gas, may have had an occasional disastrous effect in the past, as when Mount Pelee went into action a generation ago. Agoutis are more or less diurnal in habit, feeding on vegetable matter, and are especially fond of certain forest fruits, so that hunters sometimes resort to the expedient of sitting in such a tree and attracting the agoutis by throwing a stone from time to time through the leafy branches. The agoutis evidently mistaking the noise of the stone crashing through the leaves to the ground for the fall of one of the fruits may sometimes be seen cautiously coming from the thicket where they have hidden, to seek the fruit, and thus expose themselves to a shot.

In external appearance this agouti does not differ essentially from the *Dasyprocta rubatra* of Trinidad. The forehead, back, flanks, chest, and belly are a mixture of blackish with small tickings, which vary in color from ochraceous or buff on forehead and shoulders to orange-rufous on the lower back, ochraceous-buff on the flanks and belly, and whitish on the lower throat. The chin is nearly clear whitish to buffy; the inner sides of the thighs are bright buff; the nape, limbs, and feet are uniform brownish black, and the central part of the back may vary to a darker blackish tone. The hind feet have but three toes, the front feet four, with stout short claws for digging. There is a short, naked, stumplike tail. Ears short and rounded. Length of head and body up to 18 inches.

It is perhaps uncertain how far the agoutis on the different Leeward Islands have become differentiated into island races. No comparisons have yet been made with sufficient series of adults from them to be very significant. Nevertheless, as long ago as 1842, J. E. Gray named as a new species an agouti from St. Vincent, calling it *Dasyprocta albida*, on account of its being "whitish grey, nearly uniform, the hair of the back elongated, white at the base." This specimen must have been somewhat albinistic, and probably young, for it is said to have been the size of a guineapig. On this basis alone the St. Vincent agouti is not distinguishable, for other specimens from there prove to be of normal coloring. Nevertheless, scanty material seems to indicate a smaller size as compared with *D. rubatra* of Trinidad, with a shorter hind foot (about 95 mm. instead of 110), and a smaller skull, having a shorter and more sharply tapering rostrum and shorter nasals. In view of these apparent differences the St. Vincent agouti may be regarded as distinct and Gray's name will apply to it.

As to the present status of this race, for such it seems best regarded, little is known. Sclater, in 1874, recorded two specimens sent to the Zoological Society of London in August, 1868. In February, 1904, Austin H. Clark procured an adult female there in the forest behind Barrouallie, where probably it may still be found in small numbers. A similar dearth of recent information exists in regard to the status of agoutis on the other Leeward Islands. However, where large stretches of forest still remain, there the animals may be expected to survive until further clearing or the introduction of such predacious animals as mongooses takes place. That on some of these islands apparently local races differing in slight characters of size or proportion are recognizable, points to an introduction of agoutis at a long-distant period or else they reached their present localities by occasional accident at equally remote times. On a visit to Grenada in 1910, I inquired of native hunters, who agreed that an agouti still occurred in the mountain forests of the interior, but I was unable to secure a specimen. In the nearby group of small islands known as the Grenadines, Austin H. Clark tells me that an agouti has been introduced at the southeastern end of the island of Bequia, but apparently it has not thrived, perhaps on account of the lack of water. The Museum of Comparative Zoology has a skin of the Antillean agouti from Grenada that was received about 1879. Another specimen, collected on Barbados about 1870, came from Governor Rawson and presumably was of local origin, though the agouti is not mentioned in Hughes's account of the natural history of Barbados in 1750. With the gradual clearing of wooded areas on any of these islands and the introduction of the mongoose (already common for a number of years past on Grenada) it is to be expected that agoutis will eventually be extirpated from all the Lesser Antilles, perhaps before specimens can be had sufficient to determine the extent of their local variation.

St. Vincent agouti (*Dasyprocta albida*)

St. Lucia Agouti

Dasyprocta antillensis Sclater

Dasyprocta antillensis Sclater, Proc. Zool. Soc. London, 1874, p. 666 (St. Lucia, West Indies).

Fig.: Sclater, 1874, pl. 82 (colored).

In November 1874, two agoutis from the island of St. Lucia, West Indies, were presented alive to the Zoological Society of London and were shortly afterward described as a new species by Sclater, who, however, compared them only with the very different *Dasyprocta punctata* of Central America. His colored plate shows an animal of closely similar appearance to the *D. rubatra* of Trinidad or the *D. albida* of St. Vincent, so that there can be no doubt of the near relationship of these two. That the name may stand for the island animal as a valid race, however, is indicated by a comparison of two skulls from skins in the Museum of Comparative Zoology, taken on St. Lucia probably about 1880.

This agouti is nearly the same in size and appearance as *D. rubatra*, but in the skulls available it has shorter nasals, which seem more narrow and tapering distally. The rostrum is shorter, and the incisive foramina are prolonged posteriorly to the meeting of the premaxillary with the maxillary, instead of ending in advance of that point. How far these characters will hold with a larger series remains to be seen. Nor is it certain whether agoutis from other islands of the Lesser Antilles are locally different.

No recent information is at hand as to the status of the agouti in St. Lucia at the present time. On the neighboring island of Dominica Allen and Chapman (1897) recorded a specimen from the forested part, and it was said to be still common in the interior. On Montserrat it occurred also until at least very recent years, for the United States National Museum has a specimen received in 1902 from that island. The skull of this individual shows a number of peculiarities, which if borne out by additional skulls might warrant naming the agouti of this island as a distinct local race. Agoutis of this type must once have been common on St. Kitts, for Du Tertre (1654) and Labat (1742) both mention them two or three centuries ago. Two skins from this island are recorded in the catalogue of mammals in the Museum of Comparative Zoology as having been received about 1881, but they have since been lost sight of. There is another in the United States National Museum. Presumably the species may still be present there. St. Kitts is thus the most northern of the Lesser Antilles from which it has been reported. It may be added that the South American *Dasyprocta aguti*, characterized by its bright ochraceous or rufous rump, is the one introduced on St. Thomas. Miller (1911) reported the identity of this agouti through a specimen received by the National Museum, while in 1917 the Museum of Comparative Zoology received one from the same island. In the island of Guadeloupe an agouti has long been known, and in 1914 I named it on the basis of two specimens secured by Dr. G. K. Noble.

GUADELOUPE AGOUTI

DASYPROCTA NOBLEI G. M. Allen

Dasyprocta noblei G. M. Allen, Proc. New England Zool. Club, vol. 5, p. 69, 1914 ("Goyave, Guadeloupe Island, West Indies").

Two specimens secured in 1914 by Dr. G. K. Noble differ notably from available skins of the neighboring islands in their darker appearance, due to extensive blackening of the head, neck, shoulders, and back, with a suppression of the reddish or ochraceous ticking, which becomes confined to the lower flanks. In a third specimen, later obtained, however, the opposite effect is seen, through the concentration of rusty tips to the hairs of the entire back, perhaps an individual and erythristic condition. If the agouti of Guadeloupe thus proves to be distinct from those on the other islands, it may eventually be better to regard it as merely an insular race of *Dasyprocta rubatra*.

As to the status of this animal on Guadeloupe, Dr. Noble reported that at the time of his visit in 1914 it was difficult to secure and was confined to a limited area of uncleared country. The animals make runways and are occasionally obtained by waiting nearby for a shot as one may chance to appear.

Order CARNIVORA: Dogs, Cats, and Their Relatives

The larger carnivorous mammals that compete with man for food, destroy domestic animals, or threaten man's security, have been exterminated or greatly reduced in settled areas. Seven families of true carnivores are recognized:

(1) Canidae, the dog family, includes wolves, jackals, foxes, and some less familiar types. Representatives of this family are found throughout the world, except in New Zealand and some of the oceanic islands.

(2) Ursidae, the bear family, formerly occurred throughout Europe, Asia, and North America and in the East Indies, the Atlas Mountains of North Africa, and in the South American Andes.

(3) Procyonidae, the raccoon family, includes the pandas, the coati, the kinkajou, and the cacomistle or ring-tailed cat. Except for the Asiatic pandas this group is confined to the New World.

(4) Mustelidae, the weasel family, includes the small fur bearers—weasels, minks, otters—forms that suffer persecution chiefly for the sake of their valuable pelts. The weasels and their relatives occur in all regions except the Australian and the oceanic islands.

(5) Hyaenidae, the hyaenas and the aard-wolf, are restricted in Recent times to Africa and southern Asia. The African aard-wolf is a termite-eating mammal with degenerate teeth and jaws; it is rare everywhere in its range.

(6) Viverridae, the genets, civets, and their allies, are catlike or weasellike carnivores with partially retractile claws and with numerous cheek teeth. Representatives are found in the Ethiopian, Oriental, and parts of the Palearctic regions.

(7) Felidae, the cat family, is world wide in distribution, except for the Australian and polar Regions and the oceanic islands. Except for the fossane (*Cryptoprocta*) of Madagascar, which is genetlike, the cats are a very uniform group, differing in little except size, length of tail, and color pattern.

Four families are considered in the present volume:

(1) Ursidae: Three races of the black bear, all the grizzlies, and Alaskan brown bears.

(2) Mustelidae, weasels, martens, mink, and wolverene: 20 species and subspecies, belonging to three genera, are discussed here; all are valuable fur bearers.

(3) Canidae, foxes and wolves: 22 forms, representing two genera, have been exterminated or endangered.

(4) Felidae, the cat family: 10 races of the puma and two of the jaguar are treated here.—J. E. H.

Family URSIDAE: Bears

THE BLACK BEARS

The black bears are much smaller than the grizzlies, with shorter claws and usually with black coloration, although in western North America several local color phases occur. The skull is characterized by its relatively short snout and short nasals in comparison with the grizzly bears; the length of nasals is equal to, instead of being more than, the width across the front of the first upper molars, and the two posterior cusps of the first lower molar instead of being in approximately the same transverse plane are arranged so that the outer is slightly in advance of the inner. The black bears were formerly found all over the wooded parts of North America south into northern Mexico, but at the present time this range has been locally restricted through killing them out in the more settled areas. Nevertheless so wary and intelligent are these animals that they have in many regions been able to survive in spite of persecution, and hence only a brief consideration is here needed. Hitherto, in addition to the typical form of the eastern parts of North America, no less than 13 local forms have been described. The value of these can not be fully estimated until a general study is made of the entire group with adequate material. However, in a recent paper, Dr. E. R. Hall (1928) has reviewed the bears of this group inhabiting the Northwest coast and concludes that the seven forms described from the region are all subspecies of the typical black bear. In the western United States and on the Pacific coast, a cinnamon phase occurs as far north as Taku River, Alaska, and young in the same litter may be either black or cinnamon in color. A gray or bluish phase is found in the region between Lynn Canal and Cape St. Elias, and this has been described as *Ursus emmonsii*, the glacier bear. Hall (1928) points out cranial characters that may serve to distinguish these bears as a local race apart from color, for black individuals occur within the same range.

Finally, on Gribble and Princess Royal Islands, British Columbia, three color phases occur, the lightest of which is nearly white and has been named *Ursus kermodei*. But "the light phase is not always pure white and may include yellowish rufous and bright golden rufous bands and spots." Since the color characters of Kermode's bear offer but slight grounds for distinction, Hall recognizes this as a valid race chiefly on the basis of minor cranial characters.

In the following account only a bare outline of the present status of some of the forms seems necessary.

EASTERN BLACK BEAR

EUARCTOS AMERICANUS AMERICANUS (Pallas)

Ursus americanus Pallas, Spicilegia Zoologica, pt. 14, p. 5, 1780 (eastern North America).
FIGS.: Elliot, 1901, pl. 34 (three views of skull); Nelson, 1916, p. 440 (col. figs.).

Since the settlement of eastern North America by whites, the black bear has retreated from the more populous or cleared sections, but, given a reasonable area of forest, it will readily adapt itself to contact and persist in wild areas. In eastern United States a few bears still exist in western Massachusetts, they are common in the less settled parts of Maine, and are present in small numbers in the White Mountains of New Hampshire and the mountainous parts of Vermont. They no longer are found in Rhode Island or Connecticut but remain in some numbers in the Adirondacks of New York State and in the Pennsylvania mountains. According to recent census estimates of the U. S. Fish and Wildlife Service, the approximate bear population of these States is: Maine, 1,400; New Hampshire, 650; Vermont, 400; Massachusetts, 10; New York 1,000. Rhoads in 1903 said that at that time it was almost exterminated in New Jersey; however, a few seem to have persisted in the cedar swamps of the southern part of the State and in the adjacent parts of Delaware. A bear was reported to have been killed in Johnsonburg, N. J., in 1920. Pennsylvania, with its large areas of mountain forests, is estimated to have a bear population of 3,300; Maryland, 150; and West Virginia, 2,100, in the mountainous regions. Virginia has fewer, an estimated 600; North Carolina nearly twice that number, South Carolina 230, and Georgia 400. West of the Alleghenies bears are still present in numbers in the wilder parts of Michigan and Wisconsin, but they were exterminated from Illinois by 1860 and from Indiana by the middle eighties. Tennessee still harbors a good number in the mountains, but Kentucky, which never was very good bear country, holds only a few at the present time. There are a few in Mississippi, and formerly they were no doubt present in Missouri, but the census quoted includes none from the latter State. Hibbard (1933) writes that though once common in eastern Kansas, the black bear is now extinct in that State.

Northward of the United States, black bears range through New Brunswick into southern Canada and as far northward as Ungava. They occur also in Newfoundland but are said now to be scarce. In the wilder regions they extend across to Alaska in timbered country. Bears of this species avoided the open plains country but formerly extended into the valleys of North Dakota. At present they are probably very scarce or nearly gone in that State.

Whether the black bear of Florida and Alabama, known as *Euarctos floridanus*, and the so-called yellow bear of Louisiana, *Euarctos luteolus*, are to be regarded as races of *Euarctos americanus* or as separate species is still uncertain. At all events, the former is now rare in Florida, though in some sections it still occurs and the Wildlife Census credits the State with 350 and Georgia to the north with 400. In Alabama, according to A. H. Howell (1921), bears are at present exterminated everywhere except in the swamps of the southern part. Skulls from this region are intermediate between the two forms noted above. The census mentioned gives the State a population of 300 bears. Westward bears are present over suitable country to central California. In this State they seem to have increased in abundance with the disappearance of the grizzly. They formerly extended to northern Mexico and no doubt still occur there, but no estimates of status are at hand.

GLACIER BEAR; BLUE BEAR

EUARCTOS AMERICANUS EMMONSII (Dall)

[*Ursus americanus*] var. *emmonsii* Dall, Science, new ser., vol. 2, p. 87, 1895 (St. Elias Alps, near Yakutat Bay, Alaska).

FIG.: Nelson, 1916, p. 440 (left col. fig.).

This is a race of the black bear, distinguished from the typical form by slight cranial characters. As might be expected it is in these characters most like the race *perniger*, of the Kenai Peninsula, but "has the rostrum decidedly longer and inflated anteriorly over the canines. Also the upper molars are smaller and the mastoid and zygomatic breadths are greater" (Hall, 1928). The name will apply to the black bears of the mainland of southern Alaska. In this race a dilute color phase occurs, which is blue-gray in appearance, but not all the bears of the region are thus colored, so that this peculiarity, which first led to its recognition in nomenclature, is not characteristic of all the individuals.

The blue bear, or perhaps in particular those individuals showing the "blue" phase, is supposed to be "threatened with extinction" because of over-hunting and because this phase has a circumscribed distribution, in the vicinity of the Glacier Bay National Monument. However, since this latter is now a reserve, adequate patrolling of the region to prevent poaching should insure its perpetuation.

KERMODE'S BEAR; WHITE BEAR

EUARCTOS AMERICANUS KERMODEI (Hornaday)

Ursus kermodei Hornaday, 9th Ann. Rept. New York Zool. Soc., for 1904, pp. 81–86, Jan., 1905 (Gribble Island, British Columbia).

FIGS.: Hornaday, 1905, 2 pls.; Allen, J. A., 1909, p. 234, fig. 1 (skin); p. 236, figs. 2, 3 (skull); Anthony, H. E., 1928, pl. 4, opp. p. 76 (colored).

Kermode's bear (*Euarctos americanus kermodei*)

Originally believed to be a species distinct from the black bear and characterized as clear creamy white to the roots of the hairs, further specimens of this bear from the type locality show that this coloring is not constant but skins may have the top of the head "yellowish rufous, with the back . . . conspicuously varied with bands and irregular patches of bright golden rufous" (J. A. Allen, 1909). The skull presents distinctive characters that warrant its recognition as "a strongly marked form"; however, according to Hall (1928), the latest writer to consider its status, it is best regarded as a local race of the black bear. The known range extends "from the lower part of South Bentinck Arm, Bella Coola River (lat. 52°), and from Aristazable, Princess Royal, Gribble, and Pitt Islands, on the coast, to a considerable distance into the interior" of British Columbia. A list of specimens and localities up to 1909 is given in the paper of J. A. Allen (1909).

Because of its circumscribed range, and its relative conspicuousness, it might be thought that this type of bear would be a special object of pursuit and thus be in danger of early extermination. However, I. M. Cowan, in a verbal communication to Dr. Francis Harper in 1937, regards it for the present as "safe enough." It may be thought of as a geographical race of the black bear, with in some cases a white color phase.

THE GRIZZLY BEARS

In the early settlement of western North America, the grizzly bear was about the only really dangerous carnivore to be found; its size and strength as well as its rather truculent nature combined to make it a formidable beast against which the rifles of earlier days were often ineffective, and many a hunter has owed his life to the fact that the grizzly is too large and heavy to climb a tree that afforded the hunter a refuge. Because of these traits and its uncertain temper, as well as on account of its depredations among the rancher's cattle and sheep, the grizzly bear has been persistently hunted and killed wherever possible for upward of a century, with the result that at the present day it has been largely exterminated over a great part of the former range.

Merriam (1896) in his preliminary review of the North American bears wrote: "The Grizzly bears (including the

Barren Ground bear) may be separated into 4 more or less well-
marked forms, as follows: (a) the true Grizzly, *Ursus horribilis*
Ord, from the northern Rocky Mountains; (b) the Sonoran
Grizzly, 'var. *horriaeus*' Baird, probably only a subspecies; (c)
the Norton Sound, Alaska, grizzly, probably another subspecies; (d) the very distinct Barren Ground bear, *Ursus
richardsoni* Mayne Reid. Whether or not the large Grizzly
from southern California deserves subspecific separation from
the Sonoran animal (*horriaeus*) has not been determined."
Following this preliminary statement of the case, Dr. Merriam
in succeeding years brought together an enormous series of
specimens from the larger part of the range of the grizzly, and
after intensive study of this material he came to the conclusion
that no less than 86 species of grizzly and big brown bears
could be distinguished as inhabiting western North America!
The main points of difference lie in cranial peculiarities, and
it is uncertain how far the species may be distinguished by
external characters. To many, Dr. Merriam writes, this number of species of grizzly bears will appear "preposterous," yet
the differences in cranial details are evident on close study.
It becomes then a matter of interpretation as to their significance. Thus we do not yet know whether the five species of
grizzly supposed to live together on Admiralty Island will
actually interbreed, or whether the 15 that Dr. Merriam has
described as occurring in British Columbia maintain pure lines
of descent or hybridize. He adds: "Cranial and dental characters among the big bears are very subtle. As a rule comparison of any two skulls of essentially the same size brings to
light so many resemblances that one is likely to infer a far
closer relationship than actually exists. This is because the
big bears of the genus *Ursus* are such a closely interrelated
group that the resemblances far outnumber the differences.
Hence the greatest caution is necessary to avoid misleading
conclusions." Under these circumstances a conservative
course of treatment may be adopted and Dr. Merriam's
original inclusive groups of grizzly bears be considered first in
a very general sense; then the various forms that he since distinguished may be listed with a brief statement of supposed
range and status.

In a general way the more typical grizzlies inhabited the
West from the edge of the Plains to the Pacific, south into

northern Mexico, and north into Alaska and Canada. The barren-ground grizzly is the type of subarctic western Canada; the big brown bears are found along the coast from northern British Columbia to and including the entire Alaskan Peninsula, but not to the exclusion of the grizzly-bear forms. From an economic point of view the grizzly bear is regarded as a destroyer of game and more especially is disliked on account of its depredations against livestock, or, recently in northern Alaska, against the reindeer herds. On the other hand, it helps keep down the increase of certain burrowing ground squirrels, and in parts of the North its intestines are used in making clothing. Its present value to human beings may well be largely an esthetic and recreational one. To an increasing number of persons who enjoy the sight of large wild animals or the thrill of photographing them, these bears can not fail to give much pleasure, while to the naturalist and to the sportsman they are a source of interest. The money brought in to the parts of the country where they are pursued is a substantial help to the local population.

GRIZZLY BEAR

URSUS HORRIBILIS HORRIBILIS Ord

Ursus horribilis Ord, Guthrie's Geography, 2d Amer. ed., pp. 291, 300, 1815 ("Missouri River, a little above mouth of Poplar River, northeastern Montana," *fide* Merriam).

SYNONYMS: For a full list of the names applied to grizzly bears see Merriam, 1918.

FIGS.: Audubon and Bachman, 1854, Quadrupeds of North America, vol. 3, pl. 131; Baird, 1857, pls. 41, 42 (skull and teeth); Nelson, 1916, p. 442 (col. fig.); Merriam, 1918, pls. 1–16 (living animal and skulls).

Merriam (1918) writes that "the differences between the grizzlies on the one hand and the big brown bears on the other are neither so great nor so constant as at one time believed . . . The typical brown bears differ from the typical grizzlies in peculiarities of color, claws, skull, and teeth. The color of the former is more uniform, with less of the surface grizzling due to admixture of pale-tipped hairs; the claws are shorter, more curved, darker, and scurfy instead of smooth; the skull is more massive; the fourth lower premolar is conical, lacking the sulcate heel of the true grizzlies. But these are average differences, not one of which holds true throughout the group."

Baird describes the general color of grizzly bears as varying from a nearly uniform dark brown with the tips of the hairs lighter, or brownish yellow, to a condition in which there is a dark blackish dorsal stripe, and the sides of the body are pale brownish yellow, bordered by a dark stripe along the flanks. The limbs are generally black or dark brown; head and belly yellowish, and a tinge of hoary over the shoulders and sides. Claws long and nearly straight, those on the fore feet about 4 inches or more long. Skull long, the length of nasals exceeding the width across last premolars. First lower molar with the two posterior cusps on about the same transverse plane, and with a small accessory cusp or two on the inner side between the anterior and posterior cusps. Weight upward of 1,200 pounds, but males are larger than females; "in some the disparity in size is very remarkable . . . in a few cases the difference is slight" (Merriam). Bear skulls undergo a series of changes from early life to old age and in most species do not attain their mature form until seven or more years of age (Merriam). Baird states that the largest specimens are "from six to seven feet" in total length. The total length of skull runs to 14 or 15 inches.

In a general way the former range of the grizzly extended from the eastern edge of the Great Plains in about the longitude of the one-hundredth meridian, westward to the Pacific coast in northern Lower California, thence south to Durango, Mexico, and northward to the southern and central parts of the Alaskan Peninsula and the Arctic coast. In the barren-ground region west of Hudson Bay it is represented by the so-called barren-ground grizzly. Baird, in 1857, wrote that "it appears first to occur on the Missouri, above Fort Pierre [in South Dakota], and becomes more and more abundant higher up on the Missouri, and especially on the Yellowstone; thence to the Rocky Mountains, which it inhabits throughout its entire extent in the United States . . . To the north it extends far into the British possessions, and southward into Mexico." It is safe to say that at the present time the grizzly bear is extinct over much of this area and survives only in some of the national parks or in wilderness regions.

In their general habits grizzly bears like somewhat open, rugged country with scattering thick growth where they may take shelter. Their food includes a wide range of both animal and vegetable matter.   In early times they preyed partly upon the larger game and animals, such as deer, wapiti, or, on the plains country, the bison, and later found an easier prey in the introduced livestock of the settlers.   In the Southwest, Bailey mentions their fondness for acorns, pinyons, cedar berries, various succulent roots, the sweet mesquite berries, bulbs, and tubers of various kinds.   They also turn over logs and stones for the insects to be found underneath.   In more northern parts of the range they dig out the burrows of small rodents, especially of ground squirrels, for their occupants.   Fish too are very much relished, and when salmon are running in the Alaskan waters the grizzlies and brown bears feast upon them, wading in and scooping out the fish.

The grizzly bear hibernates in the northern part of its range from late September to April, more or less, seeking a shelter among rock crevices or in the hollow base of a large tree or under its upturned roots.   In the southern latitudes, as in New Mexico, however, Bailey says that hibernation is less regular, and the bears may be found active at various times in winter. The young are born in these winter dens and may be two or three in number, more commonly twins.

In various papers Vernon Bailey has much to say concerning the grizzly's former range and abundance.   In his "Mammals of North Dakota" (1926) he presents a number of early records of its occurrence along the eastern border of its range here. "At the coming of the white man these large grizzlies were apparently common over practically all of North Dakota." Alexander Henry while in the Red River Valley in 1800 found them not so numerous as in the Hair Hills and Devils Lake region, where they were said to be "very malicious."   He also reported one skin in the catch from the Sandhill River, Minn., in 1807, and one from Portage la Prairie, Manitoba, localities from near the limit of its eastward range.   In 1833, Maximilian found them more common the farther up the Missouri he went.   Generally bears were found feeding here on buffalo carcasses, which were often plentifully distributed in the quicksands or along the river banks by floods and breaking ice.   "Apparently the Missouri River Valley with its great abundance and variety of large game, wild fruit, and berries, bulbs, tubers, roots, and underground beans, was a paradise for these bears before the days of the rifle."   Here, too, Audubon, in 1843,

found them common, and in 1856 F. V. Hayden of the transcontinental surveys collected specimens. Bailey quotes an old
resident that in 1867 there were many grizzlies in the river
bottoms about Fort Buford and farther west in Montana.
Old hunters told of killing grizzlies in the Killdeer Mountains
between 1864 and 1870. In the late eighties they were still
to be found in smaller numbers along the Little Missouri, but
they were constantly hunted down, so that "at the present
time there is certainly not a grizzly bear left in the State of
North Dakota, and it is doubtful if there is anywhere a living
representative of this original species of the grizzly group that
was first given a scientific name and status in literature . . .
Like some of the savage tribes with which it was associated, it
has in passing left behind a thrilling record of savage bravery
of surpassing interest to red-blooded Americans."

In the middle of the last century grizzly bears were found in
some numbers in Nebraska and Kansas. Baird (1857) lists
specimens in the United States National Museum from several
localities in the former State, and Hibbard (1933) notes that
in earlier years it was common in Kansas west of the Flint Hills.
It has long been extinct in these States and probably in Texas
as well, where, Vernon Bailey (1905) writes, "The only specimen of grizzly bear that I have seen or heard of from Texas
was killed in the Davis Mountains in October, 1890" and was
found to agree in all essential characters of the skull with the
so-called Sonoran grizzly. Merriam, however, made it the
type of a special subspecies, *Ursus horriaeus texensis*, in 1914,
later according it specific rank; he believed it identical with
bears from the adjacent mountains of southern Colorado,
a region where Cary (1911) found grizzlies rare in the wilder
parts over 30 years ago, though occasionally seen in the San
Juan, San Miguel, and La Plata Ranges. In northern Colorado, according to the best information he could obtain, in
1905–6 it was already rare. Along the eastern slopes of the
Front Range, however, where grizzlies were still found in the
early seventies, they were by 1907 apparently quite gone.
He gives a number of recent records of the grizzly in the
southern mountains of Colorado up to 1907, and no doubt a
few still remain in the more inaccessible mountainous regions
of the central and western parts of the State, for a 1939 census
issued by the U. S. Fish and Wildlife Service placed the

estimated number of grizzlies in Colorado at only 10 individuals.

In recent decades grizzlies have become all but extinct in New Mexico and Arizona and probably in the adjacent parts of northern Mexico as well, where a century ago they were common. A skull collected about 1852 near Coppermines (now the site of Santa Rita, Grant County, N. Mex.) was regarded by Baird (1857) as representing a smaller brown race, which he named *horriaeus*, but Bailey (1931) says that specimens collected in that region in later years are not identical with it, so that an immigration of grizzlies into this area from elsewhere is assumed. He quotes the journals of Pattie who hunted in this region in 1824 and 1825 and wrote that it "abounds with these fierce and terrible animals." Bailey (1931) writes that in 1894 Dr. A. K. Fisher was told that grizzly bears were then common in the mountains about 80 miles north of Silver City, N. Mex. In 1905 a large female was killed in the Tularosa Mountains and a large male was said to be still at large in that range. In 1908, there were said to be a few still in the Mimbres, Mogollon, and San Francisco Ranges. Since then the numbers seem to have decreased still further for in 1939 the U. S. Biological Survey estimated that only three grizzlies remained in New Mexico, so that the species soon no doubt will no longer exist there. Much the same story is probably true of Arizona, for which the same report fails to include any bears at all. It may be doubted, too, if any remain in the adjacent parts of Mexico, although Merriam lists specimens in the National collection as follows: Arizona, 1856, 1913; Chihuahua, 1899. A grizzly killed on Mount Taylor, northern New Mexico, in 1916, may well be among the last from that State.

A century and more ago grizzly bears were common in California and extended a short distance farther south into the mountains of northern Lower California. From the latter region, however, it must soon have been exterminated, for Dr. E. W. Nelson (1921) states that the early account by Pattie of his journey in these regions gives the only Lower Californian record, namely, that there were grizzlies in the Sierra Juarez near Santa Catarina Mission. In their work on the "Fur-bearing Mammals of California," Grinnell, Dixon, and Linsdale (1937) have given a very full account of the grizzly bears in that State. Dr. Merriam from a study of available skulls believes that seven specific types are represented among them. In the coastal counties, Humboldt and Mendocino, grizzlies were commoner in the river valleys where settlements were first made, so that on account of their depredations upon stock and the threat to the lives of children and others passing along roads, they were soon exterminated, within a short time after the first settlers arrived, about 1850. According to one informant the last grizzly taken in Humboldt County was killed in the Mattole section in 1868. The same person tells that his father in the early days had once counted 40 bears in sight at one time from a high point in the Mattole section that afforded a wide outlook over open country. In Mendocino County the authors quoted found on inquiry among old residents that the last grizzlies there were killed in the fall of 1875, when an old female, a yearling, and a large male were shot. Various fragments concerning the killing of these bears or incidents of narrow escapes from them are brought together in the work mentioned, from which one may gather an impression of the abundance of grizzlies in the third quarter of the last century, their boldness and occasional depredations, as well as the continual warfare waged against them by the settlers. As a result of constant hunting, bears became scarcer by the beginning of the last quarter of the century, but they still persisted in some localities. In the nineties there were still grizzlies "in the near ranges of the San Gabriel Mountains due north of Pasadena," even as late as 1897. "In the heavily chaparral-covered Santa Ana (or Trabuco) Mountains of Orange and extreme northwestern San Diego counties" they persisted "until well along in the 1900's," and the latest record of one being killed there is given as January 5, 1908. One of the last grizzlies killed in the Yosemite region was in 1887. "The last known southern California grizzly" was killed October 28, 1916, near Sunland, Los Angeles County, while so far as the writers above quoted are able to ascertain, the last certain record of a grizzly killed in California was of one shot in Tulare County in August, 1922. A few later reports were unverifiable.

In the State of Oregon these bears are perhaps already gone. Bailey (1936) has brought together many notes on their earlier abundance and gradual diminution. In the days of muzzle-loading rifles, grizzlies were bolder, and hunters might well hesitate to risk coming to close quarters with them. In the Lake of the Woods region the last grizzly is said to have been shot in 1868. In the last quarter century these bears have slowly diminished in numbers even in national forests. Bailey writes that in 1910 the supervisor of the Siskiyou National Forest reported grizzlies as very scarce; one was said to have been killed in the Yamsay Mountains about 1911, and there were possibly a few in the Mount Pitt section at about that time. In 1924 and 1925, the United States Forest Service reported one grizzly on each of the Cascade and Siskiyou National Forests, and in 1931 two and in 1932 one on the Wallowa Forest, while in 1933 it reported one on the Willamette. The last (1939) report of the U. S. Fish and Wildlife Service does not include it in a game census of the State; in the State of Washington, however, it gives a surviving remnant of nine.

At the present time the main population of grizzly bears in the United States outside of Alaska centers in the Rocky Mountain region in the States of Wyoming and Montana. This is partly a result of their protection from usual hunting in Yellowstone and Glacier National Parks, though others apparently frequent the wilder parts of these States. In the Yellowstone Park some grizzlies even come to the garbage piles near the hotel, but in Glacier Park, writes Vernon Bailey (1918), few have learned to do this, but most of them are shy and live in the less frequented portions of the park. A few are killed around the edges of the park annually. At times, too, the forest ranger in these parks finds it necessary to eliminate a particular grizzly that has developed troublesome ways. According to the 1939 census issued by the U. S. Fish and Wildlife Service (in December, 1940) the following estimates of the grizzly-bear population by States give at least an approximation of its present status: Arizona, 7; Colorado, 10; Idaho, 44; Montana, 620; New Mexico, 3; Washington, 9; Wyoming, 480. There is thus an estimated total of approximately 1,100 grizzlies in the United States, excluding Alaska.

Northward of the United States, grizzly bears are not uncommon in the Rocky Mountain region of British Columbia and Alaska. Cowan (1939) writes that they are now restricted to the mountainous parts of the country and are fairly com-

mon in the mountains bordering the Pine River in British
Columbia and in the Rockies north and south of the Peace
River. Still farther north, grizzly bears are well known to
occur in some numbers in the wilder parts of these regions to
central Alaska. Preble (1908), writing of the Athabasca-
Mackenzie area, says that they are found "throughout the
Rocky Mountain range and its eastern spurs west of the Mackenzie, north to the Arctic coast." Although annually some
are killed, it seems likely they will long hold out here. A report
of the U. S. Biological Survey in December 1938 states that
"the large brown and grizzly bears in Alaska are holding their
own as an outstanding wildlife resource of the Territory."
In parts of Alaska they appear to be more plentiful than for
many years, owing, it is believed, to the favorable attitude of
Territorial residents, to protective regulations under the
Alaska Game Law of 1925, and to sanctuary areas that total
more than 8,500,000 acres. Some three-fourths of these
sanctuary areas are comprised in Mount McKinley National
Park and Katmai and Glacier Bay National Monuments.
In addition, certain areas are now closed to hunting and elsewhere regulations afford a closed season from June 20 to
September 1. The bag limit for large brown and grizzly bears
is two a year, except on Admiralty Island, where a limit of one
has been made, to induce nonresident hunters to visit other
areas. The sale of bear hides is now prohibited in Alaska, a
regulation considered as an outstanding factor in permitting
the increase of these big bears, while of equal importance is
the development of a better feeling by the residents, who now
"thoroughly appreciate this source of income and have no
desire to jeopardize it by killing off this attraction at no profit
to themselves." Along the Arctic coast bears may still be
regarded as a nuisance by certain interests, as miners and
trappers, but the Survey's agent at Nome reported that in his
district grizzlies are fairly numerous with no definite increase
or decrease. The few animals that are killed are those slain
by natives working with reindeer herds, and he believes their
actual damage is slight. In these regions that may long serve
as hunting areas it seems likely that these interesting and
remarkable carnivores will continue indefinitely under wise
management.

BARREN-GROUND BEAR

URSUS RICHARDSONI Swainson

Ursus richardsoni Swainson, Animals in Menageries, p. 54, 1838 (shore of the Arctic Ocean, on west side of Bathurst Inlet near mouth of Hood River, Mackenzie, Canada).

FIGS.: Merriam, 1896, pl. 4, fig. 6; pl. 5, fig. 5; pl. 6, fig. 3 (skull).

This grizzly is believed to range over the barren-grounds from west of Hudson Bay to the Mackenzie River, and northward to the shores of the Arctic Ocean. The color varies from yellowish to grizzly brown. Size rather small for a grizzly, and the skull distinguished by its broadly spreading zygomata and the sagittal crest, which runs far forward and divides dichotomously with a branch running to each postorbital process so far anteriorly that the two ridges are nearly transverse. Dr. Merriam (1918) regards the animal from the mouth of the Mackenzie as a related but distinct species, which he has called *Ursus russelli*, and in his paper he gives a series of cranial measurements of the two.

Preble (1908) has summarized various bits of information concerning this little-known type of grizzly. Apparently the first white man to come in contact with it was Samuel Hearne, who in his famous journey (1770–1772) to the mouth of the Coppermine River saw a skin of an enormous grizzled bear at the Eskimo tents there. Franklin also observed it several times along the Arctic coast from near Fort Enterprise to Bathurst Inlet and mentions seeing a female with three cubs. The stomach of a bear killed at Bathurst Inlet contained the remains of a seal, a marmot, roots, berries, and grass. In another case a bear had been feeding on a caribou. Bell met with the species in 1900 "quite often" along the west and north shores of Great Bear Lake.

As to its present status, Dr. R. M. Anderson (1939b) writes: "A few grizzlies of the Barren Ground group, a typical form being *Ursus richardsoni*, ranging eastward in the Arctic Zone as far as Bathurst Inlet, and perhaps a little beyond, have until the past few years escaped hunting by the Eskimos, who formerly kept off the bear's range in summer. As these interesting bears do not have the shelter of mountains, it is feared that with the recent spread of trapping operations and mining developments in the Far North, and particularly the extension

of domestic reindeer herding into the Arctic portion of the
Northwest Territories with the effect of patrolling the range
throughout the year, some of these rare species will become
extinct within a few years."

The persistent reports of a grizzly bear existing in the barrens
of northern Labrador have from time to time been investigated
as far as such tales may, but no real evidence that such an
animal is found there has been elicited. Even though the tale
were true that a skin of a grizzly had once been brought in,
this might have been traded from still farther west. In that
way one might account for the origin of the reports. Dr. E.
Stirling (1884) sums up the evidence in a brief statement to the
effect that John McLean in his notes of 25 years' service in
Hudson Bay Territory reports that skins from Ungava had
several times been sent to Europe and that a factor named
Mittleberger said he had known of the animal in Labrador.

KODIAK BEAR; BIG BROWN BEAR

URSUS MIDDENDORFFI Merriam

Ursus middendorffi Merriam, Proc. Biol. Soc. Washington, vol. 10, p. 69, Apr. 13, 1896
  ("Kadiak Island, Alaska").
FIGS.: Merriam, 1896, pl. 4, figs. 2, 3; pl. 5, fig. 2; pl. 6, fig. 2 (skull); 1918, pl. 3
  (skull); Holzworth, 1930 (frontispiece in color and other photographic figures).

This animal is rated by Merriam as the "largest of living
bears, though only slightly larger than *Ursus beringiana* Mid-
dendorff, from Kamschatka; frontal region in male enormously
elevated, highly arched, and relatively narrow; zygomata
bowed outward to an extraordinary degree; postzygomatic part
of skull very short." Distinctive features are the contact of
the forepart of the jugal with the lachrymal bone and the
small size of the first upper and last lower molars. The claws
are shorter and more curved than in the usual type of grizzly,
measuring about 100 mm. on the curve.

The Kodiak bear is found on Kodiak Island and the adjacent
Afognak and Shuyak Islands, but it may be taken as a type
of the so-called big brown bears, of which closely allied forms
are found on the nearby mainland, such as *Ursus gyas* from
Cook Inlet to the entire length of the Alaska Peninsula.
Merriam (1918) writes that "the differences between the
grizzlies on the one hand and the big brown bears on the other

are neither so great nor so constant as at one time believed. And there are species which in the present state of knowledge can not be positively referred to either group." The color of the brown bears is more uniform with less of the surface grizzling, the shorter claws are scurfy instead of smooth, the skull more massive. The brown bears are in general confined to the southern Alaskan coast and peninsula and the adjacent islands. (See Dufresne, 1942, for distribution map.)

In 1912 Sheldon wrote that "the grand bear of Kadiak Island . . . is rarely seen." Osgood (1904), writing of the big brown bears of the base of the Alaska Peninsula, says that though formerly abundant persistent hunting by the natives has much reduced their numbers. They still occur in many localities but have become extremely shy. Fifteen years previously it was not uncommon to see "from eight to fifteen bears scattered about on one mountain side." Their period of activity varies, but they usually come out from hibernation late in March or early in April, depending on the season, and are not seen after early November. The young are brought forth usually in January and may number as many as four at a birth, though, as with the other grizzlies, two is the usual number and three not uncommon. Ground squirrels are much sought after by digging up their burrows, but when salmon are entering the rivers in spring they become a main object of pursuit. Small fruits, roots, and grasses also form part of their fare.

Although these bears a few years ago seemed in much danger of extirpation, present reports indicate that under the game laws that went into effect in 1925, and with the creation of sanctuaries, the outlook is bright that they will remain an asset to Alaska for a long while to come. Dufresne, the executive officer of the Alaska Game Commission, reported in 1938 that they are holding their own and that "information from Kodiak Island and the Alaska peninsula . . . leaves no question as to the plenitude of the huge brown bears." A favorable attitude on the part of Alaskan residents, who are beginning to realize the value of the bears to themselves through bringing in a certain number of hunters and photographers, is doing much to insure proper protection and regulation of the numbers killed. For the present it appears that these splendid bears are no longer in danger of being exterminated.

In order to coordinate the account of the grizzly and brown
bears with the nomenclature proposed by Merriam (1918) in
his review of these animals, the following synopsis of the names
used in his paper and their grouping is added, with a few words
on the status of these forms where information is at hand.

HORRIBILIS GROUP

Ursus horribilis horribilis Ord. BIG PLAINS GRIZZLY
Range: Plains of Montana, Wyoming, Colorado, Dakotas.
Nearly or quite extinct.

Ursus horribilis bairdi Merriam. BAIRD'S GRIZZLY
Range: "Southern Rocky Mountain region from San Juan
Mountains, southwestern Colorado, northward through Wyoming to Montana, and perhaps to southeastern British Columbia." Supposed to be a mountain form; nearly extinct.

Ursus horribilis imperator Merriam. YELLOWSTONE PARK
  BIG GRIZZLY
Range: "Yellowstone National Park, Wyoming; limits unknown." A small number live in the Park and perhaps the
nearby country.

Ursus chelidonias Merriam. JERVIS INLET GRIZZLY
Range: "Head of Jervis Inlet, British Columbia." Status
unknown.

Ursus atnarko Merriam. ATNARKO GRIZZLY
Range: Region of Atnarko River, upper Bella Coola, British
Columbia. Status unknown.

Ursus kwakiutl Merriam. KWAKIUTL GRIZZLY
Range: "Coast region of British Columbia from southwestern corner (Burrard Inlet, Howe Sound, Jervis Inlet)
northwesterly to or beyond the lower Bella Coola." Probably
a few left.

Ursus nortoni Merriam. YAKUTAT GRIZZLY
Range: "Limited apparently to coastal plain on southeastern
side of Yakutat Bay." Probably still found; specimens collected in 1910.

Ursus warburtoni Merriam. WARBURTON PIKE GRIZZLY
Range: "Coast region . . . of southeastern Alaska and

adjacent parts of British Columbia from Chilkat River south-easterly to Atnarko River." Probably still occurs; specimen collected 1915.

Ursus neglectus Merriam. ADMIRALTY ISLAND GRIZZLY

Range: Admiralty Island. Restricted but probably not in immediate danger.

Ursus californicus Merriam. CALIFORNIA COAST GRIZZLY

Rânge: "Humid coast region of California from San Francisco Bay south about to San Luis Obispo." Probably extinct since 1908.

Ursus tularensis Merriam. TEJON GRIZZLY

Range: "Dry chaparral hills of interior coast ranges between the San Joaquin Valley and Los Angeles plain," California. Extinct in 1916.

Ursus colusus Merriam. SACRAMENTO VALLEY GRIZZLY

Range: "Sacramento (and perhaps also San Joaquin) Valley and adjacent foothills; westerly . . . to Dobbins Creek canyon on the boundary between southeastern Humboldt and southwestern Trinity Counties." Extinct.

Ursus dusorgus Merriam. RINDSFOOS'S GRIZZLY

Range: "Head of Jack Pine River near Mount Bess, Alberta." Status unknown; type collected in 1916.

PLANICEPS GROUP

Ursus nelsoni Merriam. NELSON'S GRIZZLY

Range: "Sierra Madre of Mexico from northwestern Chihuahua and northeastern Sonora south to southern Durango." Probably a few remain.

Ursus texensis texensis Merriam. TEXAS GRIZZLY

Range: Davis Mountains, Texas, and mountains of southern Colorado. Probably nearly or quite extinct.

Ursus texensis navaho Merriam. NAVAHO GRIZZLY

Range: "Probably restricted to the isolated Chuska Mountains" between northeastern Arizona and northwestern New Mexico. Extinct.

Ursus planiceps Merriam. FLAT-HEADED GRIZZLY
Range: Foothills along the western edge of the plains in
Colorado and Wyoming. Nearly if not quite extinct.

Ursus macrodon Merriam. TWIN LAKES GRIZZLY
Range: Twin Lakes region of Colorado. Probably nearly
extinct.

Ursus mirus Merriam. YELLOWSTONE PARK GRIZZLY
Range: Yellowstone Park region. Probably now uncommon;
specimen (the type) killed in 1915.

Ursus eltonclarki Merriam. SITKA GRIZZLY
Range: "The Sitka Islands, Baranof and Chichagof,"
Alaska. Probably still occurs.

Ursus tahltanicus Merriam. TAHLTAN GRIZZLY
Range: "Middle and upper Stikine-Skeena region, limits
uncertain," in British Columbia. Probably still present in
small numbers.

Ursus insularis Merriam. ISLAND BEAR
Range: Admiralty Island, Alaska. Probably not now in
immediate danger.

Ursus orgilos Merriam. GLACIER BAY GRIZZLY
Range: Bartlett Bay and east side of Glacier Bay, Alaska.
Probably still occurs; collected by Hasselborg in 1912.

Ursus orgiloides Merriam. ALSEK GRIZZLY
Range: Italio River region, Alaska; in coast strip southeast
of Yakutat Bay. Probably present in small numbers; type
collected in 1916.

Ursus pallasi Merriam. PALLAS'S GRIZZLY
Range: "Southwest corner of Yukon Territory, east of the
St. Elias Range . . . and adjacent eastern border of
Alaska; easterly to McConnell River and Teslin Lake and
south into northern British Columbia." Probably not in
immediate danger.

Ursus rungiusi rungiusi Merriam. RUNGIUS'S GRIZZLY
Range: Region about the head of Athabaska River and
Kootenay Pass, Alberta, and adjacent parts of British Colum-
bia (Indian Point Creek). Probably still in small numbers.

Ursus rungiusi sagittalis Merriam.   CRESTED GRIZZLY
Range: Southwestern Yukon, Canada.   Probably still occurs in small numbers and is in no immediate danger.   Type collected in 1915.

Ursus macfarlani Merriam.   MACFARLANE'S BEAR
Range: Region of Anderson River, Mackenzie; limits unknown.   Specimens from Franklin Bay, Stapylton Bay. Status unknown; probably still to be found in small numbers.

Ursus canadensis Merriam.   CANADA GRIZZLY
Range: "Eastern British Columbia; limits unknown (type from near Mount Robson; and an adult female from Kootenay Lake)."   Not known to be in danger.

ARIZONAE GROUP

Ursus arizonae Merriam.   ARIZONA GRIZZLY
Range: Known from Escudilla Mountains, Apache County, Arizona.   Status unknown, perhaps extinct.

Ursus idahoensis Merriam.   IDAHO GRIZZLY
Range: Eastern Idaho (North Fork Teton River) to Wallowa Mountains, Oreg.   Probably still present in small numbers.

Ursus pulchellus pulchellus Merriam.   UPPER YUKON GRIZZLY
Range: Ross River, Ross Mountains and McConnell River, Yukon, Canada.   Probably still present in small numbers; type collected in 1916.

Ursus pulchellus ereunetes Merriam.   KOOTENAY GRIZZLY
Range: Kootenay District, British Columbia.   Status unknown; collected in 1916.

Ursus oribasus Merriam.   LIARD RIVER GRIZZLY
Range: Upper Liard River, Yukon, near British Columbia boundary.   Collected in 1916; probably present in small numbers.

Ursus chelan Merriam.   CHELAN GRIZZLY
Range: "Cascade and Cassiar Mountains from northern Washington to upper Stikine River and Dease Lake, British Columbia."   Nearly extinct.

Ursus shoshone Merriam.   SHOSHONE GRIZZLY
Range: "Mountains of Colorado and Wyoming."   Probably very few left in Colorado but more in Wyoming.

Ursus kennerlyi Merriam. SONORA GRIZZLY

Range: "Nothing is known of the range of *kennerlyi* except that the type specimen came from mountains near Nogales, Sonora," Mexico. "Its affinities with *utahensis* suggest that formerly it may have had a disconnected distribution northward in the mountains of central Arizona." Extinct. Type skull dated 1855.

Ursus utahensis Merriam. UTAH GRIZZLY

Range: "Southern Wasatch and Pine Valley Mountains [Utah]; limits unknown." Must be now nearly gone, though specimens have been collected as lately as 1911.

Ursus perturbans Merriam. MOUNT TAYLOR GRIZZLY

Range: Mount Taylor and Datil Mountains, New Mexico; limits unknown. Now practically extinct.

Ursus rogersi rogersi Merriam. ROGERS'S GRIZZLY

Range: Absaroka Mountains, Wyoming; limits unknown. The considerable grizzly-bear population of Wyoming must include a number of this form.

Ursus rogersi bisonophagus Merriam. BLACK HILLS GRIZZLY

Range: "Black Hills of South Dakota and adjacent northeast corner of Wyoming." Probably extinct; type collected in 1887.

Ursus pervagor Merriam. LILLOOET GRIZZLY

Range: "Interior of southwestern British Columbia; known only from Lillooet Lake and Bridge River." Probably extinct; type taken in 1883.

Ursus caurinus Merriam. LYNN CANAL GRIZZLY

Range: "Coast of mainland of southeastern Alaska from Chilkat River Valley and Lynn Canal south an unknown distance." Probably rare; type collected in 1911.

Ursus eulophus Merriam. ADMIRALTY ISLAND CRESTED BEAR

Range: Admiralty Island, Alaska. Probably not now in immediate danger.

Ursus klamathensis Merriam. KLAMATH GRIZZLY

Range: "Siskiyou Mountains of northern California and southern Oregon, ranging north in recent times to Fort Klamath region and Rogue River valley; in early days to lower

Willamette Valley (presumably same species); south in Sierra Nevada an unknown distance." Now about extinct; last ones killed perhaps about 1911. Bailey (1936) states that according to Forest Service reports, there were in 1924 and 1925 one grizzly bear on each of the Cascade and Siskiyou National Forests, in 1931 two and in 1932 one on the Wallowa Forest, and in 1933 one on the Willamette.

Ursus mendocinensis Merriam. MENDOCINO GRIZZLY
Range: Known only from Mendocino County, California, along the northwest coast of the State. Extinct. The last grizzlies were killed in the county in the autumn of 1875, a female, a yearling, and a large male, all killed at the same place on Eel River south of Covelo (Grinnell, Dixon, and Linsdale, 1937, p. 70).

Ursus magister Merriam. SOUTHERN CALIFORNIA GRIZZLY
Range: Santa Ana or Trabuco Mountains, Cuyamaca and Santa Rosa Mountains, and probably San Jacinto Mountains of California. Now extinct; last one killed October 28, 1916, near Sunland, Los Angeles County, California (Grinnell, Dixon, and Linsdale, 1937).

HYLODROMUS GROUP

Ursus hylodromus Elliot. FOREST GRIZZLY
Range: "Rocky Mountain region of western Alberta and eastern British Columbia, including Selkirk Range." Probably a few still remain.

Ursus kluane kluane Merriam. KLUANE GRIZZLY
Range: "Southwest corner of Yukon Territory east of the St. Elias Range, extending northwesterly in Alaska to Mount McKinley region (head of Toklat), easterly in Yukon Territory to McConnell River . . . and probably south into northwest corner of British Columbia" (Merriam). Not believed to be in present danger.

Ursus kluane impiger Merriam. INDUSTRIOUS GRIZZLY
Range: Merriam gives the following localities as indicative of the range: Brisco, Columbia Valley, in British Columbia; Morley and Jasper, Alberta; and headwaters of North Fork Blackfoot River, western Montana. Hollister (1912a) wrote that "the grizzly bear is still a common animal throughout the

Robson region" of Alberta, a statement which doubtless still applies to this animal.

Ursus pellyensis Merriam. PELLY GRIZZLY

Range: Pelly Mountains, Yukon. Grizzlies are still found in small numbers in the Yukon region, but since it is not possible to identify animals without killing them and examining their skulls, it is unknown whether this form is represented or not.

Ursus andersoni Merriam. ANDERSON'S GRIZZLY

Range: The type specimen is from Dease River, near Great Bear Lake, Mackenzie; limits of range unknown. Grizzly bears, according to Preble's (1908) summary, are not uncommon in the region.

HORRIAEUS GROUP

Ursus apache Merriam. APACHE GRIZZLY

Range: White Mountains of eastern Arizona. The type was collected in 1913, but at the present time the predatory-animal campaigns have resulted in reducing the numbers to so low an ebb that already this form may have been extirpated.

Ursus horriaeus Baird. NEW MEXICO GRIZZLY

Range: "Parts of New Mexico, south to Casas Grandes, Chihuahua, Mexico; probably extending into eastern Arizona" (Merriam). Probably now extinct.

Ursus henshawi Merriam. HENSHAW'S GRIZZLY

Range: "Lower slopes of southern part of Sierra Nevada; limits unknown" (Merriam). The type specimen was from near Havilah, Kern County, California, and Grinnell, Dixon, and Linsdale (1937) mention as representing probably the same sort of animal, skins from Madera County. They provisionally refer to this form the grizzly population of the Yosemite region and the central and northern Sierra Nevada generally. In the Yosemite region, according to Grinnell and Storer (1924) the grizzly bear was rare already by 1887, when the capture of one was considered "an unusual event." The last one known to have been killed in the Yosemite Park was shot "'about 1895' at Crescent Lake." Possibly a few individuals persisted longer, for the authors mentioned tell of one whose tracks were frequently seen on Bullion Mountain between the years 1908 until 1911. Undoubtedly this form of bear is now extinct.

STIKEENENSIS GROUP

Ursus stikeenensis Merriam. STIKINE GRIZZLY

Range: Region about head of Finlay River and Dease Lake region,- northern British Columbia (Merriam). Grizzlies in this region seem in no immediate danger.

Ursus crassodon Merriam. BIG-TOOTH GRIZZLY

Range: Merriam refers to this form, skulls from Klappan Creek (third south fork of Stikine River); White River, Yukon; Wolf Lake, Yukon; Tatletuey Lake, upper Finlay River; Glen- lyon Mountains and Quiet Lake, southern Yukon. Since other supposed forms of grizzlies also inhabit this general region, they may only be identified by killing them and studying the skull. At present the grizzly bear is in no danger in this region, for no cattle are raised, human population is small, and the occasional hunter is their only enemy.

Ursus crassus Merriam. THICK-SET GRIZZLY

Range: Merriam records skulls from upper Macmillan River, Yukon; and Anderson River, Horton River, and Lang- ton Bay, on the Barren-grounds. The type specimen was collected in 1916. No immediate danger for it is seen.

Ursus mirabilis Merriam. STRANGE GRIZZLY

Range: Admiralty Island, Alaska. With the present re- ported favorable attitude of the local population and the recent game regulations, it would seem that this grizzly will not be hunted beyond a reasonable limit.

Ursus absarokus Merriam. ABSAROKA GRIZZLY

Range: "Laramie and Bighorn Mountains, eastern Wyo- ming, Black Hills region, South Dakota, and northward along Little Missouri to Missouri and Yellowstone Rivers." Prob- ably extinct in the Black Hills and eastern Wyoming. The latter State still has a relatively large population of grizzly bears but these center in the Yellowstone Park region, and are regarded by Merriam as a special type. The type specimen from near head of Little Bighorn River, northern part of Big- horn Mountains, Montana, was killed in 1893, and the animal may still occur in that region.

ALASCENSIS GROUP

Ursus alascensis Merriam. ALASKA GRIZZLY

Range: Norton Sound region, Alaska, south to Chinitna, on Cook Inlet; limits unknown. Osgood (1901, p. 68) at the beginning of this century wrote that "large bears are still very often seen both on the Alaska Peninsula side of Cook Inlet and on the mountainous Kenai Peninsula. According to report they were very abundant about ten years ago, but in the short time since have been so constantly pursued that their numbers have been greatly reduced." Probably this local form requires protection if it is to survive, but no recent report is at hand.

Ursus toklat Merriam. TOKLAT GRIZZLY

Range: "So far as known, restricted to Alaska Range" (Merriam). The type specimen came from the head of Toklat River, north base of Alaska Range, near Mount Mc-Kinley, Alaska. Since this region is now a national part, there seems to be no immediate cause for anxiety for the continued existence of these bears in their range.

Ursus latifrons Merriam. BROAD-FRONTED GRIZZLY

Range: Rocky Mountains of western Alberta and eastern British Columbia from Jasper House northwesterly to head-waters of Stikine River. Probably the same remarks apply to the status of this bear as to that of *Ursus crassodon*. Some numbers may still occur.

RICHARDSONI GROUP

Ursus richardsoni Swainson. BARREN-GROUND BEAR

Range: The type came from the shore of the Arctic Ocean on the west side of Bathurst Inlet, near the mouth of Hood River, and probably is representative of the animal of northern and northeastern Mackenzie. Anderson notes that of late years with the extension of reindeer herding by the natives, these regions, which previously were but little hunted, may now be more often patrolled and these bears are likely to be in a much more precarious situation than formerly.

Ursus russelli Merriam. MACKENZIE DELTA GRIZZLY

Range: Lower Mackenzie region; limits unknown. Of the barren-ground bear in general, Preble (1908) states that it is rare over the greater part of its range. Probably it is not likely to persist about the mouth of the Mackenzie for any great length of time.

Ursus phaeonyx Merriam. TANANA GRIZZLY

Range: "Tanana Mountains between Tanana and Yukon Rivers," Alaska. Dr. W. H. Osgood, who obtained the type specimen in 1903, wrote that "very little accurate information is obtainable in regard to the grizzly in the Yukon region," and this state of affairs seems to continue. However, with the development of mining interests and settlement, it is not likely that this form of the middle Yukon will resist encroachment for many years.

Ursus internationalis Merriam. ALASKA BOUNDARY GRIZZLY

Range: "Region bordering Arctic coast along international boundary, and doubtless adjacent mountains, between the coast and the Yukon-Porcupine; limits unknown." Status not determined.

Ursus ophrus Merriam. HIGH-BROWED GRIZZLY

Range: The type, collected in 1915, came from an unknown locality in eastern British Columbia. Nothing further is known of its status.

Ursus washake Merriam. WASHAKIE GRIZZLY

Range: The type came from the north fork of the Shoshone River, Absaroka Mountains, in western Wyoming, between Bighorn Basin and Yellowstone National Park. Since the characters distinguishing the form are to be found in the skull and teeth it is not possible to say what portion of the many grizzlies found living in western Wyoming are like it.

KIDDERI GROUP

Ursus kidderi kidderi Merriam. KIDDER'S BEAR

Range: "Alaska peninsula for its entire length." According to the report on Alaska bear sanctuaries issued by the U. S. Department of Agriculture in December 1939, "information from . . . the Alaska Peninsula . . . leaves no question as to the plenitude of the huge brown bears," so that with the continuance of protective legislation no fears are felt for them.

Ursus kidderi tundrensis Merriam. TUNDRA BEAR

Range: "Tundra region of northwestern Alaska from Shak-
tolik River on Norton Sound, southerly across the lower
Yukon, Kuskokwim, and Nushagak Rivers to Bristol Bay and
north side of base of Alaska Peninsula" (Merriam). The
Government report above quoted states that "the grizzlies of
the interior seemed to be on the increase during the last year"
(1938). The agent at Nome reports that "the Alaska grizzly
is fairly numerous all through my district, and no increase or
decrease is definitely known. Very few animals are killed and
these by natives working with reindeer herds. Bears are
reported by all reindeer men as destructive to deer, but I
believe that the extent of damage is not important."

Ursus eximius Merriam. KNIK BEAR

Range: Nothing seems to be known of the range of this bear
beyond its occurrence at the head of Knik Arm, Cook Inlet,
Alaska. Probably, like Kidder's bear of the Alaska Peninsula,
it is "holding its own."

INNUITUS GROUP

Ursus innuitus Merriam. INNUIT BEAR

Range: "Coastal region of Norton Sound, Alaska, from
Unalaklik northward and westward; limits unknown" (Merriam). The range of the grizzly bear probably does not reach
the sea to the northward of the region inhabited by this form.
The report of the Nome agent, previously quoted, seems to
indicate that grizzly bears are in no immediate danger of
extermination in this area.

Ursus cressonus Merriam. CHITINA BEAR

Range: "Chitina River valley and adjacent slopes of Skolai
and Wrangell Mountains, westerly doubtless through the
Chugach Mountains to the west side of Cook Inlet; occurs as
far south as the Iliamna region" (Merriam). This local type
may be thought of as present in small numbers, but exact
information is not at hand.

Ursus alexandrae Merriam. MISS ALEXANDER'S GRIZZLY

Range: Kenai Peninsula, Alaska. This is notable as the
largest of the grizzly bears. No recent information of a definite
nature is at hand as to its present numbers.

TOWNSENDI GROUP

Ursus townsendi Merriam. TOWNSEND'S BEAR

Range: Mainland of southeastern Alaska. The type came from Sitka in 1889. No information as to status is at hand.

DALLI GROUP

Ursus dalli Merriam. DALL'S BROWN BEAR

Range: Malaspina Glacier and region northwest of Yakutat Bay, Alaska. Osgood (1904) writes of the general region about the base of the Alaska Peninsula that "Brown Bears were formerly abundant in much of the country . . . but the persistent hunting by the natives since the introduction of modern repeating rifles has reduced their numbers greatly. They still occur in many localities, but have become extremely shy and are seldom obtained unless a special campaign for them is conducted."

Ursus hoots Merriam. STIKINE BROWN BEAR

Range: Stikine River region, British Columbia. This is believed to be a small race of the brown bear, perhaps closely related to the form *sitkensis*. Merriam mentions but three specimens from the Stikine River. Its present status is unknown but is perhaps little likely to have altered much recently.

Ursus sitkensis Merriam. SITKA BROWN BEAR

Range: Sitka Islands (Baranof and Chichagof), Alaska. In the press notice of the U. S. Department of Agriculture for December 18, 1938, Wildlife Agent Douglas Gray of Juneau reports that the large brown bear continues to be "the greatest attraction to the trophy hunter that this district offers. Their numbers seem to be as plentiful as ever, notably on the Baranof-Chichagof-Admiralty Island group." With proper regulation of hunting, therefore, this form seems in no danger.

Ursus shirasi Merriam. SHIRAS'S BROWN BEAR

Range: Restricted to Admiralty Island. This is "a very large member of the brown bear group," but whether it is always black like the type specimen is unknown. Its "exceptionally broad skull with broad short rostrum, excessively broad and short frontal shield, and huge massive postorbital processes," though obviously different in comparison with the "long narrow skull with slender elongate rostrum, long and narrow frontal shield, and insignificant postorbital processes" of the form *eulophus* living on the same island, may not be as distinctive in life. Hence its status on Admiralty Island is not made out. With the closing of two areas totaling 52,000 acres on Admiralty Island, it is presumed that the brown bears present in some numbers there must include a proportion of this type.

Ursus nuchek Merriam. NUCHEK BROWN BEAR
Range: Prince William Sound easterly to Mount St. Elias; limits unknown. The range continues that of the Yakutat bear on the Alaskan coast. No late information is at hand as to its status there, but under present regulations the existing conditions are at least favorable.

GYAS GROUP

Ursus gyas Merriam. PENINSULA GIANT BEAR
Range: "Entire length of Alaska peninsula from Cook Inlet to Isanotski Strait and adjacent Unimak Island." This is "either the largest living bear or second only to the great Kadiak bear (*middendorffi*)," according to Merriam. Skulls of adult males show "a surprisingly wide range in size and form," so that Merriam distinguishes four types among them. On account of its large size this bear might form an especial attraction to hunters and thus be in more danger from this

Barren-ground bear (*Ursus richardsoni*)

source than other "species" having the same range. Present information from the Alaska Peninsula, issued by the U. S. Department of Agriculture, "leaves no question as to the plenitude of the huge brown bears."

Ursus middendorffi Merriam. KODIAK BEAR

Range: Confined to Kodiak and the adjacent islands Afognak and Shuyak. This bear shares with *gyas* the distinction of being the largest of living bears. The two are closely allied. Present information indicates that its numbers are being maintained.

KENAIENSIS GROUP

Ursus kenaiensis Merriam. KENAI GIANT BEAR

Range: Kenai Peninsula, Alaska. No recent statistics are at hand. With the passage of the Alaska game law in 1925, however, the conditions are probably as favorable as may be expected. According to the 1938 press information of the U. S. Department of Agriculture, "there has been a perceptible change for the better in the brown and grizzly bear population."

Ursus sheldoni Merriam. MONTAGUE ISLAND BEAR

Range: Believed to be confined to Montague Island, Prince William Sound, Alaska. The name is based on specimens of the brown bear type taken in 1905. No recent information as to the bear of this island is at hand.

INOPINATUS GROUP

Vetularctos inopinatus Merriam. PATRIARCHAL BEAR

This genus and species were based on a skull from Rendezvous Lake, northeast of Fort Anderson, Mackenzie, but the genus is currently regarded as inseparable from *Ursus*, while the species is not further known beyond the original specimen collected in 1864. Its peculiarities would ordinarily be ascribed to individual variation.

Family MUSTELIDAE: Weasels and Martens

THE PINE MARTENS

Among the northern fur bearers the martens, because of their soft, handsome fur, are much sought after, and their pelts bring high prices in the markets. They are characteristic of the evergreen forest belt of the northern United States northward into Canada and extend their range southward

along the higher parts of the Alleghenies in the East and the
Rocky and Sierra Nevada Mountains of western North
America. Like many carnivorous animals they occur in small
numbers relative to the abundance of the rodents and other
animals on which they prey and are given to traveling over
rather wide circuits in their search for food.

In general appearance pine martens are about the size of a
large slender squirrel, with a rather short cylindrical and well-
furred tail, short legs, and erect, rather prominent ears.
Males are larger than females and when adult develop more
prominent median crests on the skull. The general coloring is
yellowish to light brown on the head and forepart of the body,
darkening to a warm brown posteriorly and on the tail and
legs. The under side is cinnamon, darkening posteriorly, and
often with a tinge of brighter ochraceous-orange on the chest.
Adult males weigh about 2.5 pounds, females about a quarter
less. Total length, about 25 inches, of which the tail is 7 or 8
inches.

Over their wide range across the northern part of the continent pine martens show a slight degree of geographic variation,
both in shades of color and in details of the skull and teeth.
These have been made a basis for recognizing at least two
species, the typical eastern marten and the darker animal of
the Northwest coast, each with sundry races. While at present
it seems still uncertain whether only a single species is actually
represented, with more or less well-marked subspecies, these
may be listed with their type localities in accordance with
current usage, as follows:

Martes americana americana (Turton). EASTERN PINE MARTEN
  Mustela americanus Turton, Turton's ed. of Linnaeus's Systema Naturae, vol. 1,
  p. 60, 1806 (eastern North America).

Martes americana abieticola (Preble). KEEWATIN MARTEN
  Mustela americana abieticola Preble, North Amer. Fauna, no. 22, p. 68, Oct. 31,
  1902 (Cumberland House, Saskatchewan, Canada).

Martes americana abietinoides Gray. NORTHWESTERN MARTEN
  Martes americana var. *abietinoides* Gray, Proc. Zool. Soc. London, 1865, p. 106
  (Rocky Mountains between Kicking Horse Pass and Columbia River).

Martes americana actuosa (Osgood). ALASKAN PINE MARTEN
  Mustela americana actuosa Osgood, North Amer. Fauna, no. 19, p. 43, 1900 (Fort
  Yukon, Alaska).

Martes americana atrata (Bangs). NEWFOUNDLAND MARTEN
  Mustela atrata Bangs, Amer. Nat., vol. 31, p. 162, Feb., 1897 (Bay St. George,
  Newfoundland).

Martes americana boria (Elliot). MACKENZIE MARTEN
  Mustela boria Elliot, Proc. Biol. Soc. Washington, vol. 18, p. 139, Apr. 18, 1905
  (Lower Mackenzie River district; probably same as *M. a. actuosa*).

Martes americana brumalis (Bangs). LABRADOR MARTEN
  Mustela brumalis Bangs, Amer. Nat., vol. 32, p. 502, July, 1898 (Okak, Labrador)

Martes caurina caurina (Merriam). PACIFIC MARTEN
  Mustela caurina Merriam, North Amer. Fauna, no. 4, p. 27, Oct. 8, 1890 (near
  Grays Harbor, Chehalis County, Washington).

Martes caurina humboldtensis Grinnell and Dixon. HUMBOLDT MAR-
  TEN ▪
  Martes caurina humboldtensis Grinnell and Dixon, Univ. California Publ. Zool.,
  vol. 21, p. 411, Mar. 17, 1926 (5 miles northeast of Cuddeback = Carlotta, Humboldt County, California).

Martes caurina origenes (Rhoads). ROCKY MOUNTAIN MARTEN
  Mustela caurina origenes Rhoads, Proc. Acad. Nat. Sci. Philadelphia, 1902, p.
  458, Sept. 30 (Marvine Mountain, Garfield County, Colorado).

Martes caurina nesophila (Osgood). QUEEN CHARLOTTE ISLANDS
  MARTEN
  Mustela nesophila Osgood, North Amer. Fauna, no. 21, p. 33, Sept. 26, 1901
  (Massett, Graham Island, Queen Charlotte Islands, British Columbia).

Martes caurina sierrae Grinnell and Storer. SIERRA MARTEN
  Martes caurina sierrae Grinnell and Storer, Univ. California Publ. Zool., vol. 17,
  p. 2, Aug. 23, 1916 (Lyell Canyon, Yosemite National Park, California).

Martes caurina vancouverensis Grinnell and Dixon. VANCOUVER
  MARTEN
  Martes caurina vancouverensis Grinnell and Dixon, Univ. California Publ. Zool.,
  vol. 21, p. 414, Mar. 17, 1926 (20 miles south of Alberni, Vancouver Island,
  British Columbia).

FIGS.: Grinnell, Dixon, and Linsdale, 1937, vol. 2, pl. 4 (col.), of *M. c. sierrae;* Nelson,
  1918, p. 453, upper fig. (col.), of *M. americana;* Elliot, 1901, p. 334, fig. 66 (skull
  of *M. americana*); Elliott, C., 1942, col. pl. facing p. 75, of *M. americana.*

A brief survey of the status of the pine marten shows that
although once common in Nova Scotia, New Brunswick, the
northern New England States, New York, Pennsylvania, and
even New Jersey, it is now through much trapping greatly
reduced, though in places where there are large tracts of
forested country small numbers may remain. In New Brunswick, Chamberlain reported it as common 60 years ago, and
probably it is still to be found in wilder areas. Anderson
(1939a) writes that it was fairly common in the wooded parts
of Quebec in earlier days but has been overtrapped and is
"now rare, found only in areas remote from settlement." Of
the large dark Labrador race no recent statistics are at hand,
but there are many skulls in the Museum of Comparative

Zoology secured from trappers by J. D. Sornborger about 1900.
The Labrador wilderness is not much penetrated by outside
trappers, and the supply of fur is likely to hold out for a long
time to come. The Newfoundland race, however, is said now
to be very much reduced. In northern New England martens
were formerly much trapped in the Maine Woods and the
White Mountains and are still found but in smaller numbers.
A century ago Emmons (1840) wrote that the pine marten was
to be found in the mountainous parts of the Berkshires, in
Massachusetts, especially in beech woods, and describes the
method of trapping it in deadfalls. At that time, he states,
the pelts were worth 90 cents to $1.12½. Probably martens
have been extinct in Massachusetts for many years, but they
still are found in the Vermont forests. Merriam regarded them
as common in the Adirondacks in 1882 and said that hundreds
were trapped for fur every winter; they still persist in smaller
numbers. The fur is prime early in November. Rhoads,
writing in 1903, makes the general statement that the marten
was "once abundant over all the mountain regions" of Pennsylvania and New Jersey, invading even the foothills of the
Alleghenies, but was early exterminated from the latter
regions, was probably extinct in New Jersey about 1850, and
at the beginning of this century was to be found only in the
forested parts of the mountains in Pennsylvania. South of
this area there seems to be no recent report of the marten's
presence. Rhoads (1903) in his account of the species in Pennsylvania states that there it was partial to hardwood forests
rather than evergreens. Reports from various of the counties
are nearly unanimous in telling of its former occurrence and its
later decline, and in most cases tell of none having been found
for a number of years. Rhoads points to the effect of forest
fires as bearing on the depletion of the stock. In Ohio, Brayton
(1882) mentions the marten as already extinct, and there is
apparently no evidence of its occurrence in Indiana within
recent years. Dr. H. H. T. Jackson (1908) regarded it as
practically extinct in Wisconsin 30 years ago and mentions one
taken in Vilas County as lately as 1904–5, but Cory (1912)
wrote that although "steadily declining in numbers" and then
"a comparatively rare animal" in Wisconsin it was still to be
found in the northern part of that State. It seems to be gone
from Illinois, though earlier recorded from Cook County by

Kennicott. Northern Minnesota was once good marten country, and Herrick (1892) mentions that many dark pelts, especially prized, formerly came from this area. As to its recent status along the northern border of Minnesota and in the adjacent part of Canada, areas now forming national reservations, Cahn (1937) writes: "The marten is now practically if not completely extinct in the Quetico country. It has been exterminated from the Superior National Forest on the American side of the boundary. Trappers report seeing an occasional track in winter in the larger timber north of Saganaga and Saganagonse lakes, and I found one skull at a trapper's cabin up the Wawiag River in 1930. With the removal of the larger timber and their constant pursuit by trappers, the marten has retreated to the north." Still farther west, toward the edge of the Plains, martens were common in northeastern North Dakota a century and more ago. Bailey (1926) quotes Wied's early account of the number of furs brought in from local and more western points, including 500 or 600 marten skins. More particular numbers of martens taken in this region are quoted from records of Alexander Henry in 1801–7, and range from three to as many as 75 in a season at the Pembina River. "At present," says Bailey, "there are probably no martens in North Dakota," nor is it probable that they would return "even with careful protection" to the limited forest areas of the State.

The vast region north and west of the Great Lakes in Canada is probably now the main producing ground for marten fur. Concerning the species there Preble (1908) writes: "The marten is rather common throughout the forest belt of the Athabaska and Mackenzie regions. It varies greatly in color, being more or less subject to melanism throughout this area. The 'dark' martens are more highly prized than the lighter ones, and bring a higher price, sometimes as much as four or five times the value of ordinary skins . . . Martens are common along the Athabaska, Slave, and Peace Rivers, and large numbers are traded at all the posts on their banks. Skins taken in these valleys average rather dark in color and furnish a good grade of fur. The valley of the Athabaska below Grand Rapid is said to be especially good trapping ground. The number annually taken by each trapper varies from a few to a hundred or more. James MacKinlay informed me that three hunters working in the Caribou Mountains, southwest of Great Slave Lake, trapped in one season nearly 500 martens, an unusually large catch. The lower Liard River region and the Horn Mountains also are good trapping grounds. Upward of 3,000 skins are said to be usually traded at Fort Norman. Fort Good Hope also receives a large number, and as many as 6,000 have been collected at Fort McPherson during an unusually good season . . . Martens vary greatly in abundance in the same locality in different years, and to some extent this increase and decrease are periodic. The winter of 1903–4 was marked by a great scarcity of martens over much of the upper Mackenzie Valley, though in other sections the catch was about normal." At Fort McPherson, A. J. Stone was told in 1900 that martens were then as numerous as they had been 50 years before when the post was first established.

In Keewatin and the Hudson Bay region Preble (1902) found the marten (subspecies *abieticola*) "fairly common" north to the tree limit but most abundant in the heavy spruce forests of the southern part. Many skins come in to the posts at Norway House, Oxford House, and York Factory, and a few at Fort Churchill that come from the lower Churchill River."

Osgood (1900, p. 44), in describing the large marten (*M. a. actuosa*) of the Yukon region, Alaska, wrote at the time that it "is still the commonest fur-bearing animal of Alaska, notwithstanding the hundreds of thousands that have already been taken. Trappers are always confident of a harvest of martens whether other animals are abundant or not." To the westward, however, in the Cook Inlet region at the base of the Alaskan Peninsula, Dr. Osgood (1901) found it only moderately common. One trapper had taken but 15 martens in a season of two and a half months in 1899 near the mouth of Turnagain Arm. The martens of this area seem to be the typical subspecies. The latest report (July 16, 1939) of the Biological Survey credits Alaska with having shipped in 1938 no less than 9,200 pelts of this animal, surely a large number.

In the western United States and along the Pacific coast the numbers are much less, though it is still fairly plentiful in British Columbia. Of the insular race, *nesophila*, of the Queen Charlotte Islands, British Columbia, Dr. Osgood (1901) reports that it evidently is not abundant. The Haida Indians trap more or less every winter for them, but the annual catch seldom exceeds 40 skins. According to the fur traders these martens are short-haired and light-colored and do not command so high a price as do those from the mainland. On Vancouver Island they seem to be "fairly common in the higher mountains" (Swarth, 1912).

While martens are absent from the treeless parts of western United States, they are common in many areas of forest, in spite of much trapping. Vernon Bailey (1918) wrote two decades ago that in the Glacier National Park region of northwestern Montana "they are probably as common in the park as anywhere in the country, but no animal with the price on its skin that they have long maintained could well be numerous or very common. For at least half a century the park region has been famous for the number of martens caught each year by trappers . . . The animals are reported to be more common on the west slope of the mountains than on the east, but this is probably because the timber there is more dense and extensive and it has not been possible to trap them out so thoroughly . . . Steel traps are generally employed, but many deadfalls of the ordinary type are used." He recommends that "special permits to reliable parties for trapping them in the park during a limited season when they become too numerous would probably control their numbers here, while outside the park there is no danger of their ever becoming too abundant." They were reported common in the nineties in the Salmon River and Saw Tooth Mountains of Idaho by Merriam, who says that prospectors even complained that martens would carry off their meat from camp. Southward, the Rocky Mountain marten (subspecies *origenes*) seems to be still fairly common throughout the forested areas into northern Colorado and in smaller numbers into the higher mountain forests of the northern part of New Mexico. Cary (1911) writes that from 1900 to 1905 the best regions for martens in Colorado were the mountain ranges surrounding Middle and North Parks, the Williams River Mountains, and the mountains south of Aspen, Pitkin County. They were reported common on the Park Range but very rare on the Medicine Bow Range. "A conservative estimate of the annual catch in the Middle and North Park region would be 100 skins." Fur buyers at Aspen estimated about the same for their district. Cary was informed that 30 years before (about 1875) a trapper had taken a great many martens in the mountains of Gunnison County, central Colorado. Farther south the marten is much less common and reaches the southern limits of its range in northern New Mexico. Bailey (1931) adduces a few older records for this region and concludes that "the animals occur, but are by no means common in the Canadian Zone forests of the Sangre de Cristo and San Juan Mountains. It is very doubtful if they occur in any of the ranges farther south." According to this author (Bailey, 1936, p. 296) it is this race of the marten that extends into the extreme northeastern part of Oregon in the Blue Mountains, where, however, they seem to be uncommon and decreasing in numbers. In the Wallowa Mountains a few are still taken, but recent reports indicate that the numbers are small.

In the Coast Ranges of Oregon the resident animal is regarded as typical *M. caurina*, grading in the southern districts into the race *sierrae* of California. Bailey (1936) quotes returns for the season November 1, 1913, to February 28, 1914, of 518 martens taken in that State by registered trappers, indicating that the species is still well represented there. These at prices then current were worth in the neighborhood of $13,000. In California two races occur, *sierrae* of the Sierra Nevada, and *humboldtensis* of the northern Coast Range. They are confined to the Boreal Zone and are regularly trapped, especially in the northern parts of the State. Grinnell, Dixon, and Linsdale (1937) have published an extended account of the species in California and show that particularly in summer it haunts slide-rock areas among the crannies of which it pursues small rodents, especially mouse-hares and white-footed mice. The southern limit of range seems to be Tulare County, in the southern Sierra Nevada; on the coast, however, the marten extends only to the northwestern part of the State in the higher mountains. The authors quoted say that "at least three-fourths of the martens trapped in California are taken by a few professional trappers who specialize in this animal." One of these men took as many as 96 in a single season. However, reports from the trappers show "a marked decline, amounting to fully 75 per cent, in the number of martens trapped in a 4-year period," from 452 in 1920 to 121 in 1924, a decrease believed to be independent of any cyclic decline. The authors

believe this is due to overtrapping and that unless more adequate protection is given the species it will in a short time become scarce or absent except in such protected areas as the
national parks. A year-round closed season is recommended.
Concerning the marten of the Coast Range (race *humboldtensis*)
the authors above quoted regard it now as of "rather sparse
occurrence" in the redwood belt, "though in earlier years it
was more generally distributed and fairly numerous." Its
southernmost occurrence was in Sonoma County. In 1926
and 1927 two trappers were said to have worked a somewhat
inaccessible pocket within ten miles of Carlotta and to have
caught in all 25 martens, which is considered a remarkable
record.

In general it may be said that while the pine marten is still
plentiful in the most favorable parts of its range, as in the
northwest of Canada and in parts of the Rocky Mountains and
Alaska, its outpost areas in the east and south have been so
very much depleted in recent decades that it is in need of
careful protection if it is to maintain anything like former
numbers or to survive at all. They require a large stretch of
territory to range over and a sufficient food supply in the way
of small rodents. Factors that seriously affect them are the
burning by forest fires of parts of their forest range, clearing
through extensive lumbering operations, overtrapping, and

Eastern pine marten (*Martes americana americana*)

killing of females. The fact that they are more or less subject
to a periodic cycle of decline, probably due to disease or failure
of food supply through dying off of certain rodents that form
a staple diet, or to both factors combined, probably would
have an influence on the numbers of a small population, and
when these factors coincide with other unfavorable circumstances a danger point is reached. Martens are relatively easy
to trap, so that this trait adds to the hazard of their lives.
Finally, an important factor in their decline from a peak of
numbers lies in the fact that their gestation period is long, so
that killing of females often involves the death of a potential
litter. At the present time there have been various attempts
made to raise martens in captivity, but with only moderate
success. Young are born in March and April and are independent by some three months later. Further experiments being
carried on by the U. S. Fish and Wildlife Service will doubtless
provide a better knowledge of the best methods of management.

In 1936 a five-year closed season on martens in the United
States was urged by the Chief of the Biological Survey and en-
dorsed by the American Wildlife Conference. Some idea of the
number annually killed in western Canada may be gained from
the statement of Cameron (1936, p. 625) that the fur yield of
the Northwest Territories for the year 1933–34 included no
less than 5,580 marten pelts.

FISHER; PENNANT'S MARTEN; "PEKAN"; "BLACK CAT"

MARTES PENNANTI (Erxleben)

Mustela pennanti Erxleben, Syst. Regni Anim., vol. 1, p. 470, 1777 (eastern Canada).
SYNONYMS: *Mustela canadensis* Schreber, Säugthiere, vol. 3, p. 492, pl. 134, 1778
(eastern Canada); *Mustela melanorhyncha* Boddaert, Elenchus Anim., p. 88, 1784
(eastern Canada, based on Pennant); *Viverra piscator* Shaw, General Zool., vol.
1, p. 414, 1800 (eastern Canada, based on Pennant); *Mustela nigra* Turton,
Turton's ed. Linnaeus's Systema Naturae, vol. 1, p. 60, 1806 (eastern Canada,
based on Pennant); *Mustela godmani* J. B. Fischer, Synopsis Mamm., p. 217, 1829
(Pennsylvania); *Mustela canadensis pacifica* Rhoads, Trans. Amer. Phil. Soc.,
new ser., vol. 19, p. 435, Sept. 1898 (Lake Keechelus, Kittitas County, Washington).

A possibly valid race lately distinguished is

Martes pennanti columbiana Goldman, Proc. Biol. Soc. Washington, vol. 48, p. 176,
Nov. 15, 1935 (Stuart Lake, near headwaters of Fraser River, British Columbia).
FIGS.: Nelson, 1916, p. 446. upper fig. (col.); Grinnell, Dixon, and Linsdale, 1937,
vol. 2, pl. 5 (col.); figs. 72–81 (details, skull, habitat).

This larger relative of the pine marten has a range in North America nearly coextensive with that of its smaller cousin and covers mainly the coniferous forests from eastern Canada and Maine across to Hudson Bay, southeastern Alaska and British Columbia, and southward on the higher parts of the mountain country to Tennessee in the East, the Rocky Mountains to Wyoming, and the Sierra Nevada in California. Although Rhoads in 1898 described as a separate race the fisher of the Pacific coast, Grinnell, Dixon, and Linsdale (1937) have lately demonstrated that there are no clear distinctions setting off the animals of that region, but that only a single recognizable form covers the immense range indicated. Goldman, however, believes the British Columbian animal is distinguishable. The fisher is much larger than the pine marten, measuring about 40 inches in length, of which the tail vertebrae comprise about 16 inches. The ears are shorter, hardly projecting above the head. Females are smaller than males. Males may weigh up to about 10 pounds, females to about 5.5 pounds. The general color is ashy brown on the head, gradually darkening posteriorly to black on the legs and tail. There may be irregular white areas on the throat and chest or on the abdomen.

This large marten is highly prized for its handsome and durable fur and is much trapped and sought after. The pelts bring a high price. Not many years ago a prime skin might fetch as much as $100. Fishers, like martens, inhabit the heavy woods, subsisting on large and small mammals, such as hares and even the porcupines, which they seem to attack successfully; squirrels, wood rats, and mice of various kinds are also taken. Though hunting and traveling much on the ground, they are also expert climbers and possessed of great strength and agility; like the marten they have the habit of passing at intervals over a somewhat definite course, and are said to go often in pairs. Two or three young are the usual number, born late in spring (late in May in California).

On account of the value of its fur, the fisher has everywhere been relentlessly hunted and trapped, yet it is remarkable that it has persisted in some areas in spite of persecution. In the East there are still a few fishers left in northern and central Maine, northern New Hampshire and the White Mountains, and in northern Vermont and the Green Mountains. Probably a few are to be found in southwestern New Hampshire in the

Mount Monadnock region; at all events, the late Abbott Thayer obtained one or two specimens there 20 or more years ago. Formerly there were fishers in western Massachusetts, as attested by Emmons (1840) a century ago, but it is safe to say that they are no longer to be found in that State. Nevertheless they are still taken in some numbers in the Adirondack region of New York, and according to the 1939 report of the Biological Survey that State leads in the total number of fishers taken in 1938, no less than 117, exceeding even Alaska! Dr. Francis Harper (1929) quotes from the reports of the New York State Conservation Department the numbers of fishers caught, presumably all in the Adirondack counties, for the years 1920–25, as follows: for 1920, 132; for 1921, 186; for 1922, 563; for 1923, 112; for 1924, 144; for 1925, 61. The total for 1922 of 563 animals seems very remarkable. Apparently in spite of these large catches the animals are still holding their own. This area must be one of the most favorable for them in the country.

In Pennsylvania the fisher was formerly found in some numbers, especially in the beech forests of the more mountainous portions, but it had much declined by the middle of the last century. Rhoads (1903) has assembled many notes on its former occurrence, most of which attest its presence in the fifties and seventies, with a few instances of its more recent capture, as in Lancaster County in 1896; but most of the reports speak of it as gone by the beginning of the present century. In summary he says: "At the present time [1903] about the only counties where these animals are to be found are Clearfield, Cameron, Elk and probably Clinton, Potter, and Sullivan, and in all of these they are reported to be very rare." Reports of fur dealers, Rhoads further states, indicate that probably not over half a dozen fishers were annually killed in Pennsylvania at that time. In a more recent survey of the mammals of Pennsylvania by Williams (1930) the animal is not mentioned at all. Southward of Pennsylvania the fisher in former times extended along the Alleghenies of West Virginia to North Carolina and Tennessee, but seems to have long ago been extirpated from these regions. Dr. Remington Kellogg (1937, 1939) states that the authentic records for West Virginia are few; according to Surber (1909) it formerly occurred in the black-spruce region, but F. E. Brooks (1911) gives no specific records later than 1873. In 1888 Dr. C. Hart Merriam, after a journey of several hundred miles through "the Great Smoky Mountains of Tennessee and North Carolina, reported that the pekan was unknown" to local residents, but "reliable information exists that this animal formerly occurred in that area" (Kellogg, 1939). Audubon and Bachman (1846) mention skins from eastern Tennessee and the capture of an individual near Flat Rock.

West of the Alleghenies the fisher seems to have been rare even in early days, south of the Great Lakes. Brayton (1882) includes it in his list of Ohio mammals but cites no specific records. For Indiana, Dr. Lyon (1936) states that there is considerable evidence of its former presence, "either as a regular resident or as a wanderer from the north," but specific instances are perhaps three, which he gives as (1) the statement of Plummer in 1844 that it was not uncommon at an earlier period, but had not been seen since 1820; (2) the listing of a skin purchased of local trappers near Noblesville in 1859; and (3) the testimony of Wied as to its former occurrence at New Harmony. Evidently it has been gone from this region for well nigh a century. Cory in 1912 believed it by no means improbable "that a few individuals may still exist in some of the extreme northern counties" of Wisconsin, and he was informed "that it is occasionally taken in the wilder portions of the Michigan peninsula." He instanced three from the latter region, taken in Iron County in 1898 and 1900. The latest record for this region that he gives is of one killed in November 1900, between Iron Mountain and Pembine, Wis. Kennicott, half a century before, mentioned it as rather frequently seen in the heavy timber along Lake Michigan. Evidently it is now practically gone from the lake region. As to its present status still farther northwest, along the border of Minnesota and the adjacent Quetico Park, Canada, Cahn (1937) writes: "The removal of the large timber has profoundly affected the distribution of the fisher, as it has that of the marten, and it is now to be regarded as extremely rare in the Quetico, although some still are to be found there . . . I have in my collection 17 skulls of fisher which I collected from about the camps of trappers up the Wawiag River." In former days the range of the fisher extended to northeastern North Dakota, where judged from the data presented by Bailey (1926) it was fairly common at the beginning of the last century, for Alexander

Henry records a total of 1,118 skins brought in from the surrounding region during the years 1801–7. In 1833 Maximilian zu Wied stated that the approximate number of skins annually brought in to Fort Union (now Buford), N. Dak., was 500 or 600, but a large part of these doubtless came from still farther west. "At the present time," Bailey says, "there are certainly no fishers within the State and there seem to be no authentic records of their occurrence since the early trapping days."

In eastern Canada the numbers of fishers have been sadly depleted in recent years. Although formerly found in Nova Scotia, there seems to be no evidence of its presence there since Gilpin's time (1868) when he included it among the mammals of that province. In New Brunswick a few are found in remoter parts, as in the mountains of the Gaspé region, whence Goodwin in 1924 records a few taken by local trappers. In Quebec it is now "one of the most rare and valuable fur-bearing mammals of Canada . . . According to Low (1889) the fisher does not occur east of Mingan nor north of Mistassini [central Labrador]. It is still found in small numbers around the southern end of James Bay but is extremely rare near any white settlements. With a consistently high price paid for its fur, the fisher is pursued relentlessly and has steadily decreased in numbers in all parts of its former range" (Anderson, 1939a). West of Hudson Bay Preble (1902) found it "sparingly throughout the southern part" of Keewatin and saw many skins at Norway House and Oxford House. Near York Factory it was rare, but "farther south more are taken; about thirty or forty are annually traded at Trout Lake and a few at Severn River."

The same author (Preble, 1908) states that in the Athabaska and Mackenzie region it is found throughout the country north to Great Slave Lake and Liard River. "It seems to be nowhere abundant, and becomes rare toward the northern limits of its range. Along the Athabaska and Slave rivers a limited number of skins are collected at all the posts north to Fort Resolution, and I was informed that the animal was rather common in the region about the mouth of Peace River." Although according to Osgood (1900), "there is little doubt that the animal occurs along the upper Yukon" no Alaskan specimens could be adduced in proof, nor does Coues (1877) mention any localities in his statement that its range includes Alaska.

Fishers apparently are present in some numbers in the forests

of British Columbia, and Goldman (1935) has recently distinguished as *Martes pennanti columbiana* the animal from the
headwaters of Fraser River. The species seems to be absent
from Vancouver Island but is found in small numbers in the
States of Washington and Oregon, particularly in the national
forest reserves. Scheffer (1938), in some recent notes on the
species in the State of Washington, says that it occurs in the
Cascade and Olympic Mountains and on the Olympic peninsula
north to Skagit Valley and Cascade River. In 1937, however,
the U. S. Forest Service estimated that the total number in
the national forests of Washington was about 230 individuals.
In Oregon fishers are found in the cool humid coast ranges, and
probably also in the Blue Mountains section (Bailey, 1936),
but the number taken for fur seems to be small. Thus in the
trapping season of 1913–14, nine fishers were reported to the
State Game Commission by registered trappers as taken in
Washington. At that time skins were quoted at $25 each, but
in 1920–25 the price advanced to as much as $100 to $150
apiece! Fewer numbers are found in the northern Rocky
Mountain region. Bailey (1918), writing of the mammals of
Glacier National Park in Montana, speaks of it as rare, but the
few remaining in the park are now, with proper protection,
"likely to hold their own" for some time to come. "In many
years of trapping in the park region in the early days, Walter S.
Gibb has caught three of these animals, but some of the old
trappers have not secured a skin. Donald Stevenson reports
two skins that were taken by trappers on the Upper Swift current in 1910, and tracks which he saw on Swan River and
South Fork as late as 1912." Merriam in 1891 reported fishers
as already rare in Idaho and mentions a large adult male caught
the previous year near Alturas Lake that weighed 10 pounds 2
ounces. Formerly at least it extended its range to Wyoming,
but no recent report of its presence there is available, nor is
there according to Cary (1911) any evidence of its being found
in Colorado, although in 1874 it was said to occur (J. A. Allen).

Grinnell, Dixon, and Linsdale (1937) have given an excellent
account of the fisher, its habits and range, as known at the
present time in California. It is found still "in the northwestern part of the State south from the Oregon line to Lake
and Marin Counties and east to and including Mount Shasta;
not often in the immediate coastal region (redwood belt) nor,

so far as known at present, in the Warner Mountains, Modoc County; south from Mount Shasta and Lassen Peak throughout the main Sierra Nevada to Greenhorn Mountain in north central Kern County." It is found mainly at middle altitudes, from 2,000 to 5,000 feet in northern California and 4,000 to 8,000 feet in the Mount Whitney region to the southward. At the present time the fisher is found in the Sierra Nevada mainly on the west side of the range. On the coast range it formerly reached Marin County as the southward extension of its area of distribution. Fishers are nowhere abundant in California, and at best "it is unusual to find more than one or two to the township" in suitable country. These authors believe "it is doubtful if there is one fisher to each 100 square miles" of its range in California, and in 1926 estimated the entire population in the State at about 300. Forty years before 1909 they were found all along the ridges of Mendocino County, but owing to excessive trapping very few were then left. From 1920 to 1924 the annual catch dropped from 102 to 34, or a loss of 67 percent in five years. This decrease has involved the entire State and is not merely local. Since 1925 the fisher has received total protection in the national parks of California. The authors mentioned believe that a long-term closed season is much need-

Fisher (*Martes pennanti*)

ed if the species is to continue in the State. They put forth as major causes in the decrease of the species the following facts: (1) The fisher is by nature a solitary animal; (2) it requires a large area of forage territory in order to live; (3) the areas suitable for it are limited; (4) the rate of reproduction is relatively low; (5) the forests on which it depends are being constantly reduced. To these factors may be added the hazard of forest fires, and, finally, the fact that the gestation period is 11 months, so that trapping operations in winter, through destroying pregnant females, inevitably double or triple the potential loss of individuals.

The beauty and rarity of fisher fur as well as the high price it brings make it an attractive proposition for breeding under artificial conditions. Ashbrook (1928) points out, however, that the breeding of fishers in captivity for fur has not expanded to any great extent since 1912, when there were but two fisher "farms" on this continent. The difficulty seems to lie in getting them to breed under these conditions even with seemingly proper food. In the case of an animal naturally so shy and nervous, breeding seems to be accomplished with difficulty where there is the least disturbance. At present "little authentic information is available on handling fishers in captivity," but no doubt the difficulties will in time be solved.

Dr. Francis Harper has contributed notes as to the number of fisher pelts yielded in recent years. Thus in the London fur market in 1927 one dealer offered 1,700 skins; at another sale 2,729 were offered (Journ. Soc. Preservation Fauna Emp., pt. 9, p. 75, 1929). According to Cameron (1936) the fur yield of the Northwest Territories, Canada, included in 1934 the pelts of 21 fishers.

SHELL-HEAP MINK; "SEA MINK"

MUSTELA MACRODON (Prentiss)

Lutreola macrodon Prentiss, Proc. U. S. Nat. Mus., vol. 26, p. 887, July 6, 1903 ("Brooklin, Hancock County, Maine," from Indian shell-heaps).
SYNONYM: *Lutreola vison antiquus* Loomis, Amer. Journ. Sci., ser. 4, vol. 31, p. 228, Mar., 1911 ("Flagg Island, Casco Bay, Maine").
FIGS.: Prentiss, 1903, fig. a (rostrum); Loomis, 1911, figs. 1, 2 (rostrum and jaws).

Remains of a very large mink occur commonly in Indian shell-heaps along the shores of the mainland and islands of the coast of Maine, as independently described by Prentiss in 1903 and by Loomis eight years later. The upper tooth row (front of middle incisor to back of molar) in the type specimen measured 30 mm., and in Loomis's type 29.5, which is larger even than in the large Alaskan mink. Rostra are infrequent among the shell-heap fragments obtained, but jaws are fairly common in kitchen middens along the coast and islands of Penobscot Bay and Mount Desert Island. Two sizes, evidently representing males and females, occur.

No other type of mink is found in these Indian kitchen middens, and since there is an absence of European artifacts it is believed that these shell-heaps date from previous to, or perhaps up to, the time of European occupation. Remains are at present known from such sites as far as Casco Bay in the south, and northeastward to Mount Desert and Frenchmans Bay, and Roques Island, Washington County, Maine. Soon after the description of these bony fragments, the late Manly Hardy published a note (Forest and Stream, vol. 61, p. 125, 1903) recalling that his father, himself, and other fur-buyers had in former years "recognized as a distinct form a very large mink, skins of which were received from islands and coast of Maine until about 1860. By reason of their large size they commanded a higher price than did the skins of other minks . . . To this animal the name of 'sea mink' was given by the fur buyers" of Maine. "According to Hardy, the animal was large, very fat, and possessed of an odor entirely different from that of" the smaller inland animal (see Norton, 1930). Furthermore, the fur was said to be coarser and of a more reddish color than that of the latter. There seems no reason to doubt that the sea mink is the one that inhabited the Maine coasts in Indian days and persisted up to the latter part of the last century. With a limited range and on account of eager pursuit by the trappers, it probably became extinct about the sixties or seventies. Norton (1930) tells of a very large mink skin handled about 1880 by fur buyers at Jonesport, Maine, which without the tail measured over 26 inches long and may have been one of the last of this race. It was taken on one of the islands in the township of Jonesport. Norton mentions also a large mounted specimen of a mink taken at Campobello Island, New Brunswick, about 1894, and then in the collection of Clarence H. Clark, of Lubec, Maine. He speaks of its light color (possibly a result of fading) and regards it as "probably of this species." No measurements are given.

It seems probable that this big animal was the only form of mink to be found in the eastern part of the Gulf of Maine in earlier times. That it also ranged to Nova Scotia seems likely from the account by J. B. Gilpin (1867) of large skins from that region that measured as much as 32.5 inches in total length, though perhaps slightly stretched. At the present day the mink occurring along the Maine coast represents *Mustela vison mink*, the more southern race, of which a large male will seldom measure over 23 inches. Evidently this latter race, which has somewhat of a liking for seacoasts, has taken the place formerly held by the now extinct sea mink. Possibly, too, circumstances favorable to this eastward spread within the last century contributed to the driving out of the larger animal.

BLACK-FOOTED FERRET

MUSTELA NIGRIPES (Audubon and Bachman)

Putorius nigripes Audubon and Bachman, Quadrupeds of North America, vol. 2, p. 297, 1851 (Fort Laramie, Laramie County, Wyoming).
FIGS.: Audubon and Bachman, 1851, pl. 93; Coues, 1877, pl. 7 (skull); Nelson, 1918, p. 449, lower fig., col.

This ferret is of special interest on account of its being in North America the only representative of the Old World group of black-bellied weasels to which the polecats and their relatives of eastern and northern Asia belong. On account of its angular heavy skull and robust premolar teeth, as well as the color pattern, it is placed in a special subgenus with these, *Putorius*, sometimes regarded as a distinct genus. The American representative, however, has only the feet and facial mask and the end of the tail blackish; the upper parts are elsewhere creamy, with a wash of brown over the back, the lower surfaces whitish. An adult male is about 20.5 inches (529 mm.) long; the tail relatively short, about 5 inches (130 mm.) (Osgood).

The black-footed ferret is an animal of the interior plains of North America, east of the Rocky Mountain foothills, from western North Dakota to northern Montana and Alberta (?) and thence southward to Texas and central New Mexico. Its range is practically coextensive with that of the prairie-dogs, in the colonies of which it lives and upon which it preys. Its relations with these little burrowers is thus a close one and is like that obtaining in Mongolia between its relative the black-bellied weasel, *Mustela eversmanni*, and the bobac marmot in the "towns" of which it lives, preying on these rodents. The black-footed ferret is believed to rely chiefly upon the prairie-dogs for sustenance as an abundant and dependable source of food, yet it doubtless captures other small animals, and Roosevelt has even recorded a case of one killed in the act of attacking a small antelope fawn. It is surprising that in view of the abundance and accessibility of its natural prey, the prairie-dogs, this ferret should be nevertheless relatively rare, for specimens are rather uncommon in collections, and individuals are seldom seen in life even by those living in its habitat. Bailey (1926) has even suggested "that this very abundance [of the prairie-dogs] has in some way pauperized the species until reproduction is restricted," but adds that "apparently nothing is known of the breeding habits or of the number of young at a birth." Since there are three pairs of mammae the size of a litter probably does not exceed this number and may normally be less. It is obvious that in a case of such specialized food preference it would be disastrous for the species to become so common as seriously to deplete the numbers of its host, so that undoubtedly some sort of adjustment has been evolved, but its nature remains uncertain. Possibly enemies as yet unrecognized are a factor, such as rattlesnakes that might devour the young, or the hibernating habits of the prairie-dogs, although not well marked in the southern parts of the range, may affect the ferret's abundance. In its habits it is believed to be in large part nocturnal, but it has been seen active by day.

In view of the damage done to range vegetation or to cultivated crops, the hand of the agriculturist is against the prairie-dog, and of late years poisoning campaigns on a large scale have been carried on that in some localities have largely exterminated these rodents. Undoubtedly a further result of these activities will be to eliminate or at least to reduce considerably the numbers of the weasel so that the reason for its inclusion among the vanishing mammals is clear.

Writing of North Dakota, the eastward extension of its range, Bailey (1926) says that a few have been taken in the western part of the State and adduces four instances in the years 1910 to 1915; he quotes Jewett, who killed a specimen near Quinion in 1913, that none of the old residents to whom he showed it were acquainted with the species. Coues (1877) in

his account of the history of this animal mentions single specimens obtained after special enquiries, in Wyoming, Montana,
Colorado, and Kansas. Hibbard (1933) speaks of it as of
former occurrence in the western part of Kansas, from which
probably it is now largely gone. In eastern Colorado it seems
to be best known, though as elsewhere it is rare. Cary (1911)
mentions that it was reported to Streator in 1894 from three
localities in the Arkansas Valley; Lantz heard of a few in 1905
about Hugo, where they are known as prairie-dog ferrets, and
he had himself heard of it in Baca and Prowers Counties,
"where it seems to be more generally known . . .   than in
other sections on the plains." Southward of Colorado black-
footed ferrets "are found over the Staked Plains country of
western Texas and undoubtedly occupy the plains region of all
eastern and northern New Mexico, but few specimens have
been taken" (V. Bailey, 1931); a number of specific records are
given for this part of the State, to which Bailey (1905) adds a
few more from east and south of the Staked Plains of Texas.
Although the range may be expected to overlap slightly the
borders of southeastern Arizona and the adjacent parts of
Mexico, where prairie-dogs occur, specific records are not at
hand.

Nelson (1918) is inclined to attribute to its activities the
occasional deserted prairie-dog "towns," which "are not infrequently observed on the plains with no apparent reason for the
absence of the habitants." He mentions one case, however,
where a black-footed ferret lived for several days under a
wooden sidewalk in the border town of Hays, Kansas, "where

Black-footed ferret (*Mustela nigripes*)

it killed the rats harboring there." As to its prospects for the future he writes: "With the occupation of the country and the inevitable extinction of the prairie-dog over nearly or quite all of its range, the black-footed ferret is practically certain to disappear with its host species," a sad prophecy for this remarkable and useful animal!

WOLVERENE; GLUTTON; "CARCAJOU"

GULO LUSCUS LUSCUS (Linnaeus)

Ursus luscus Linnaeus, Systema Naturae, ed. 12, vol. 1, p. 71, 1766 (Hudson Bay).
Gulo auduboni Matschie, Sitzb. Ges. Naturf. Freunde Berlin, 1918, p. 153 (Rensselaer County, New York).
Gulo bairdi Matschie, *op. cit.*, p. 153, 1918 (Fort Union, North Dakota).
Figs.: Elliot, 1901, pl. 36 (photographs of skull); Nelson, 1916, p. 428 (col.); Anderson, 1935, p. 87 (photograph).

The wolverene is the largest of the weasel family and an animal of boreal evergreen forests and barrens. It is represented by closely similar races in the northern parts of the Old World, and although several forms have been named from North America it is very doubtful if their validity can be maintained, or if at best some of them are more than slight subspecies of the Hudson Bay animal.

Audubon and Bachman describe a specimen from New York State as blackish brown, with a pale reddish brown band extending from behind the shoulder to the rump on each side. These two bands join across the rump, and form a contrasting though not sharply defined light stripe. There is another pale brownish-white band from the eye to the ear on each side. The fur is long and rather shaggy. The head and body measure some two feet nine inches in length, the short tail eight inches. The animal stands about a foot high at the shoulders, and weighs 25 to 36 pounds.

Much has been written of the wolverene in the North, of its great strength in proportion to its size, and of its habit of breaking into the caches of hunters or trappers and spoiling what part of the provisions it can not eat. Vernon Bailey (1926) writes: "Wolverenes are found mainly within timbered sections of the country, but are great wanderers and at times may strike out over open country in search of new hunting grounds. They are omnivorous hunters and scavengers and have the reputation of being gorging gluttons, a fact which has given them one of their common names   .   .   .   They are said to have from two to four young."

The fur of the wolverene is much in demand among the Eskimo and other northern people for trimming their parkas, especially the sides of the hood, for it has the peculiar characteristic that the moisture from one's breath does not readily freeze and cake on it. Bailey (1936) writes that the fur has never brought high prices; the quotation for prime skins in 1923 was but $6 to $8, yet at this same time California trappers received an average of $25 each for wolverene pelts.

The wolverene is an animal of solitudes, usually found singly and shunning the vicinity of human occupation, so that it quickly vanishes with the spread of "civilization." It is therefore a species that has already gone from a large part of its former range in the United States and may be expected to survive only in the more remote wilderness areas of the North. Of its occurrence in the northeastern States, very little record remains. Audubon and Bachman (1846) nearly a century ago, wrote that they had heard of its existence, "although very sparingly," in Maine, and about 1810 "we" (probably Bachman) had examined three skins in the possession of a merchant in Lansingburg, N. Y., that were said to have come from the Green Mountains of Vermont. While these do not constitute certain evidence of the occurrence of the wolverene in New England, it is possible that it was formerly found, as these authors say, "very sparingly." It should be recalled, however, that the Canada lynx was sometimes called "wolverene" in this region, so that hearsay reports have questionable value. Nor can much credence be placed in a recent (1918) report of wolverenes in northern New Hampshire (C. F. Jackson, 1922). Even in New York State the wolverene must have been rare over a century ago. The only records seem to be those of Audubon and Bachman (based probably on the latter's observations), who give a circumstantial account of the pursuit and capture of one in Rensselaer County in 1810, the description and measurements of which are detailed and form the basis of Matschie's (1918) Gulo "auduboni"; and of a second examined in 1827 that had been killed near Sacketts Harbor, Jefferson County, near Lake Ontario. The most southerly record in the East is that given by Rhoads, of a wolverene killed about 1858 near Great Salt Lick in Portage Township, Pennsylvania.

Surprising as this seems, Rhoads (1903, p. 165), from his knowledge of the men who told it to him, had faith in the truth of this occurrence. The animal was said to have been caught in a wolf trap. Wolverenes formerly were found in the forests of New Brunswick but seem to have disappeared quickly. Chamberlain (1884) mentions in his "Mammals of New Brunswick" that about 1850 "it was occasionally met with; but no recent instance of its occurrence is known." In the Province of Quebec the wolverene "has become extinct or very rare in the more southern districts, but is found in small numbers in northern Quebec. It is more commonly found in wooded districts, but frequently wanders far into the Barren Grounds of the north and even occasionally to the Arctic islands" where, Dr. Anderson (1935, 1939) writes, it has been recorded from Victoria, King William, and Melville Islands, and it occurs fairly commonly in the region of Repulse Bay. Several times it has been taken within 30 miles of Pond Inlet. "The comparative scarcity of the Wolverene in the southern half of Baffin Island, and the relative frequency at the northern end of the island, is good evidence that they come to Baffin island by way of Melville peninsula." It still is found in small numbers in the Labrador Peninsula but probably seldom now in the southern part where Cartwright found it a century and a half ago. Audubon and Bachman (1846) mention having seen specimens "procured at Newfoundland," but it may well be doubted if they were trapped there. At all events there seems to be no evidence that wolverenes occurred on that island within the memory of living men.

Westward along the northern border of the United States wolverenes were formerly present in small numbers. Cory (1912) writes that "old trappers living in the vicinity of Champion, Michigan, claim that wolverines were occasionally killed in that locality, 30 or 35 years ago" but quotes Edward G. Kingsford, of Iron Mountain, Mich., who was much in the woods of northern Michigan, Wisconsin, and Minnesota between 1880 and 1900, to the effect that the Rainey Lake district in the last-named State was the nearest to Michigan he had ever known of one being killed. Schorger (1939) has lately unearthed, however, what seems a "satisfactory record" of one trapped on February 15, 1860, by a man living at Marquette, Lake Superior, in the northern peninsula of Michigan. In earlier times there were a few in Wisconsin, and Hoy mentions one killed in La Crosse County in 1870. Rather surprising, however, is the evidence adduced by Hahn (1909) of a wolverene having been killed in 1840 in Noble County, Ind., and a second in 1852 in Knox County of the same State. The records probably mark nearly the southern limit of range in the east in historic times. In Minnesota, Herrick, writing in 1892, says he has no recent knowledge of it, so that it doubtless was rare there at that time, but Kingsford, quoted by Cory (1912), says that "about 1895 to 1897 they were quite plentiful in northern Minnesota." More recent records indicate that a few individuals were found in Minnesota up to a much later time, for Dr. H. H. T. Jackson (1922) has recorded a skull in the collection of the U. S. Biological Survey from an animal killed in Itasca County, January 11, 1899; and C. E. Johnson (1923), who made special efforts to learn of the wolverene's former status, records that a fur trader of long experience in northern Minnesota told him in 1922 that in 30 years of buying furs in the region he would not average more than one wolverene pelt a year and had bought none during the previous three years along the Canadian border. He specifically mentions a pelt bought by this trader that was taken in 1918 in the northern part of St. Louis County, Minn. It seems to be the last definite record for that State.

In the early years of the last century these animals were found at least in the northeastern part of North Dakota and were taken in small numbers with the fur catch of those days (see V. Bailey, 1926). It seems to have been present in the State till about 1850, but there are no later records. According to Baird (1857) it occurred in "the Black Hills of the Missouri" at about the same time.

While in the eastern United States and southeastern Canada the wolverene is doubtless now to be regarded as extinct, it still is found in some numbers in the wilder and more mountainous parts of the western United States and more frequently in the Canadian Northwest, although on account of its solitary habits it can not be accounted a "common" species at any time. Writing of the mammals of the Athabaska-Mackenzie district Preble (1908) states that it is found throughout that region "but is nowhere common, though a few skins are collected at all the posts we visited. During our trip in 1901

more skins were seen at Fort Rae than at any other post, and
these had been brought mainly from the Barren Grounds,
where the animal occurs more commonly than in the wooded
country. . . In the semibarren country along the southern
shore of Great Bear Lake, tracks of wolverenes were common.
. . . A large proportion of the wolverene skins which are
obtained from the Indians of the Mackenzie are shipped to
Fort McPherson and traded to the Eskimo, who prize this fur
highly for trimming their clothing." Pike and other travelers
mention it as being met with across the Barren Grounds.
Trappers in the Yukon region secure a few annually. A. J.
Stone (1900) in the Canadian Northwest found them in timber
and on the barrens and mentions seeing them "far out on the
ice of the deep bays along the coast." Osgood (1901) speaks of
them as "apparently rather common" in the Yukon and also
in the Cook Inlet region of Alaska, whence a number of skins
annually are sent via St. Michael to trading posts on the
Yukon.

In British Columbia, on the other hand, wolverenes seem to
be diminishing in numbers. Cowan, in 1939, writes that they
are "rare in the Peace River district, but according to certain
reports are more plentiful in the Rocky Mountains." He
mentions one trapped on Pine River in 1936. On Vancouver
Island a few wolverenes still exist, according to Swarth (1912),
but are confined to the higher mountains and are seldom
trapped, except by the Indians, who bring in "one or two every
year."

In the Rocky Mountains south of the Canadian border a
small number of these mammals remain. Fifty years or more
ago Merriam (1891) wrote that wolverenes were "tolerably
common in the Saw Tooth Mountains" of Idaho, where in the
previous winter a trapper had caught five. Another had been
taken a few years before 1891 in the Blackfeet Mountains.
No doubt their numbers have since diminished, for Vernon
Bailey in 1918, writing of the mammals of Glacier National
Park in northwestern Montana, says that although in 1895 he
was told by trappers in the St. Mary Lake region that a few
existed there and one was occasionally caught, and that a few
were trapped each year before the park was made a reserve,
there were thought to be none left in the park at the time of
writing. In the high forests of the wilder parts of Colorado

wolverenes were still to be found in 1911, but although in former times generally distributed, they were then apparently restricted "largely to the San Juan and La Plata Mountains, the mountains of northern Gunnison County, and the ranges surrounding North and Middle Parks" (Cary, 1911). A number of specific records are given by Cary, which prove that the species was much commoner in the latter part of the last century. To the southward there is some evidence that wolverenes extended into the higher mountain forests of northern New Mexico. Of this Coues (1877) was assured by hunters there in 1864, but no definite records exist (Bailey, 1931), and it must have soon been extirpated from this southern outpost of its range. Confirmatory evidence, however, is given by Seton (1931), who was told by an Acoma Indian in 1930 of an animal known formerly to the people of that part of New Mexico as the Ho-hö-an or Ko-kö-an, somewhat like a small bear with a bushy tail, and the Indian then produced from his medicine bag a small carving of the creature's head, an excellent likeness of a wolverene's. He said it "was formerly found in all these mountains but had disappeared. None of the present generation had seen one." Baird mentions a specimen from the basin of the Great Salt Lake in Utah previous to 1857, but it has long been gone from this region.

The status of wolverenes on the Pacific coast still requires investigation as to numbers and racial relationships. Elliot in 1905 distinguished specimens from Mount McKinley, Alaska (type from Sushitna River), as *Gulo hylaeus* on the basis of their darker instead of gray heads and larger audital bullae as compared with specimens from eastern Canada. It is perhaps a recognizable race. In 1918, Matschie named as a distinct species on very slight basis, *Gulo katschemakensis*, from the Kenai Peninsula, Alaska, but it is doubtful if this is really different. In the same paper he described *Gulo niediecki* from a skull from Dease Lake, British Columbia, but here again the validity of the race is questionable. Very likely, however, the animal of the coastal ranges is a recognizable form, described by Elliot as *Gulo luteus*, and is accorded subspecific rank by Dr. Grinnell (see postea).

Recent information gathered by Dr. Francis Harper indicates that wolverenes are still taken in some numbers in northwestern Canada and a few in northeastern Canada. In 1931–32, 536 wolverene skins were produced, according to returns from Canada (Journ. Soc. Preserv. Fauna Empire, p. 75, pl. 21, 1934). In 1934 the fur yield of the Northwest Territories included 98 wolverenes (Cameron, 1936, p. 625).

In 1936, the Chief of the U. S. Biological Survey urged a five-year closed season on wolverenes in the United States and a resolution to the same effect was adopted by the North American Wildlife Conference at Washington, D. C., shortly after, in the hope of saving the species from complete extermination within the United States. That Alaska is nearly the center of the wolverene's abundance at the present time is indicated by the fact that according to the report of the Biological Survey, 248 skins were taken in Alaska in 1938. No reports of it are given for other States.

WEST COAST WOLVERENE; SOUTHERN WOLVERENE

GULO LUSCUS LUTEUS Elliot

Gulo luteus Elliot, Field Columbian Mus. Publ., zool. ser., vol. 3, p. 260, Dec., 1903 (27 miles south of Mount Whitney, Tulare County, California).
FIGS.: Grinnell, Dixon, and Linsdale, 1937, vol. 1, pl. 6 (col.), text-figs. 91–97.

An excellent account of the characters and habits of this race is that given by Grinnell, Dixon, and Linsdale (1937), summing up present knowledge of the wolverene in California. It was named by Elliot in 1903 as a separate species differing in its supposedly paler coloration as compared with eastern animals. The authors quoted show, however, that this was "merely a feature of a young stage of pelage" and that in the original description not a single character given is diagnostic of the race, which may only be distinguished by skull characters, namely, "skulls from California are slightly smaller than skulls of corresponding ages from Hudson Bay, Alberta, British Columbia, and Alaska, and the dentition is noticeably and uniformly lighter—in particular the carnassials are decidedly less massive. Three examples from Idaho and one from Utah, in the National Museum, are small-toothed like the California skulls." A Montana and a Minnesota skull are said to be of intermediate size, while one from Chelan, Wash., is "nearer the average of Sierran *luteus*."

The range of this race may thus be taken to include the Sierras of California northward to Washington, merging by

imperceptible degrees with that of the typical form in Utah
and Idaho. Although formerly the range was more extensive,
over the higher parts of the California mountains, it has, since
at least about 1900, become restricted to the central and
southern Sierra Nevada above 8,000 feet "from the vicinity of
Lake Tahoe south through the Mount Whitney region" to
Kern County. Though the altitudinal range varies from 5,000
to 13,000 feet, the animals are most frequent at about timberline. Probably this restricted range has resulted in making
the population of Californian wolverenes never very large.
The first to mention the species in this State was Cooper,
who in 1868 wrote that at that time a few were killed every
winter in the northern Sierras. There is some evidence, adduced by the above authors, that in the middle of the last
century wolverenes occurred in the coastal mountains of Marin
and Sonoma Counties, but no specimens are extant. Slightly
farther north, however, these animals seem to have occurred
down to about 1873, as on the higher peaks of Mount San-
hedrin, Mount Linn, and Yolla Bolly. Merriam is quoted
concerning a specimen killed about 1893 between Mounts
Shasta and Lassen.

At the present time there are probably few wolverenes left in
California. "From 1920 through 1924, the average number
reported captured by the trappers of California was less than
three a year. After considering all the available data, the
authors [Grinnell, Dixon, and Linsdale, 1937] believe that at
the present time (1933) there are at most not more than 15
pairs of wolverenes left in the State. This animal is thus one
of the rarest furbearers now living in California." "At present
the main hope" of protecting the species from extinction
within the State is its preservation within the guarded areas of
Yosemite and Sequoia National Parks, but the animals are
likely at times to wander outside the limits of these areas and
are caught or killed by trappers who may legally take fur outside the park boundaries.

How far north the characters of the southern wolverene may
hold is tentatively intimated by the above authors as perhaps
extending to the State of Washington. Bailey, in 1936, believed that they are not yet extinct in the Cascades and
Sierra Nevada and mentions one taken in the upper McKenzie
Valley west of the Three Sisters Peaks, Oregon, in 1912; how-

ever, at the present time their numbers must be few indeed. Still later, Scheffer (1938) notes that the U. S. Forest Service estimates that in the national-forest areas of the State of Washington, the wolverene population is about 20.

Family CANIDAE: Wolves, Dogs, Foxes
THE KIT FOXES

These small foxes are about half the size of a red fox and live in the open plains country or sandy deserts of western North America. The upper side of head and body is some shade of buff overlain with gray; the sides of neck, shoulders, and body are clear buff, the ears and legs usually brighter buff, the tail gray with black-tipped hairs, which terminally concentrate to form a black tip. Two species are found, the more eastern, ranging over the Great Plains, *Vulpes velox*, and the more western, centering in the Great Basin and southern California, *V. macrotis*. The former is a slightly larger animal with shorter ears than the latter, and comprises two races; the latter is more an animal of sandy desert regions and is at present divided into eight races.

SWIFT; KIT FOX
VULPES VELOX VELOX (Say)

Canis velox Say, Long's Exped. to Rocky Mts., vol. 1, p. 487, 1823 (South Platte River (? Logan County), Colorado).

SYNONYM: *Canis microtus* Reichenbach, Regnum animale . . . , vol. 1, pt. 1, p. 10, 1836, as quoted by Wiegmann in Wiegmann's Archiv für Naturg., Jahrg. 3, Bd. 2, p. 162, 1837.

FIGS.: Audubon and Bachman, 1851, The Viviparous Quadrupeds of North America, vol. 2, pl. 13.

NORTHERN KIT FOX
VULPES VELOX HEBES Merriam

Vulpes velox hebes Merriam, Proc. Biol. Soc. Washington, vol. 15, p. 73, Mar. 22, 1902 (Calgary, Alberta, Canada).

The range of the typical race is from the Staked Plains of northwestern Texas northward over the Great Plains to probably South Dakota. The northern race, *V. v. hebes*, is larger and slightly grayer, "dark patches on sides of nose darker, skull larger and heavier; palate much longer; underjaw longer, heavier, more bellied under sectorial tooth" (Merriam).

Average of four males: Total length, 844 mm., tail, 280; foot, 131; ear, about 50. Weight, 4.5 pounds.

"These little foxes," Bailey (1931) writes, "live in burrows in the open plains country, usually selecting side hills or the sunny slope of a bank in which to make their dens. They are mainly nocturnal, are wonderfully swift and graceful in their motions, but, unlike the red foxes, are so unsuspecting in their natures as to be readily caught in traps . . . and are so unable to cope with the advanced civilization that they are rapidly disappearing from the face of the earth." Cary in 1902 was told that in the Staked Plains of Texas they were at that time scarce in comparison with former years, for in the winter they come readily to poisoned bait put out for coyotes and wolves. This bait the kit foxes will take the first night it is set out, but coyotes wait till later (V. Bailey, 1905). Formerly this was a common species over the plains of eastern Colorado, but by 1911 had "become rare in most sections" (Cary, 1911). It is found still in the western part of Kansas and has been taken as far east as Douglas County (Hibbard, 1933). In 1870 Dr. J. A. Allen reported its occurrence "more or less frequently" in western Iowa, but at the present time it is probably gone from this eastern outpost of its range.

It is probable that the range of the northern race may be considered as from about North Dakota north to the Saskatchewan River. Bailey (1926) refers those of North Dakota to this race and states that "apparently the kit foxes of the northern Plains at one time covered the whole of the prairies of North Dakota, but at present they are restricted to the western part of the State, and even there they have become very scarce, although a century ago they were one of the common fur animals of the Red River Valley." With the settling of the country they have easily succumbed to trapping, poisoning, and capture by dogs, and reports from various localities in that State indicate that of recent years they have been reduced nearly to the point of extermination. In northwestern Montana, Bailey (1918) speaks of this fox as common over the plains along the eastern edge of Glacier National Park, which it probably enters in the open area at the lower end of St. Mary Lake. There is thus apparently no immediate danger of its extermination in this region, yet on account of its less wary nature it is likely to suffer gradual reduction with the encroachment of settlements and especially with trapping and poisoning campaigns carried on against coyotes or wolves. Baird records the usual stomach contents as "fragments of skin, leather with hair, berries, remnants of mice, and grasshoppers" so that economically the kit fox is an asset through its destruction of small rodents and grasshoppers and deserves whatever protection may be accorded it.

This race of the kit fox formerly extended in range as far north as the Saskatchewan River in western Canada but is now gone from many parts of this area. Specimens in the Museum of Comparative Zoology from Calgary and Buffalo Lake, Alberta, were received in 1897, and others from Assiniboia were obtained in the following year. Fowler (1937), however, writing of changes in the fauna of the High River district, Alberta, states that it became extinct there shortly after those dates; "in fact, only those people who were here before 1900 can recall having seen a kit-fox. My father states that the last bunch of kit-foxes he saw was in the summer of 1897. These had their den in a sandy knoll about a mile north of High River."

LONG-EARED KIT FOX; DESERT KIT FOX

VULPES MACROTIS MACROTIS Merriam

Vulpes macrotis Merriam, Proc. Biol. Soc. Washington, vol. 4, p. 136, Feb. 18, 1888 ("Riverside, Riverside County, California," vicinity of Box Springs, western margin of San Jacinto Plain, about 10 miles southeast of Riverside).

FIGS.: Grinnell, Dixon, and Linsdale, 1937, pl. 9, bottom fig. in color; and (other races) figs. 154–162 (skull, live animal, habitat).

The long-eared kit fox resembles *V. velox* but has longer ears (about 80 mm.), smaller hind foot, and slightly brighter coloring, but otherwise it has a similar appearance. As a species its range extends from Riverside County in southern California eastward across the Great Basin into extreme western Texas and south into Lower California and northern Mexico. Over this range it divides into a number of slightly marked local races, of which no less than nine, including the typical form, are described. These with their type localities are: *arizonensis*, from 2 miles south of Tule Tanks near the Mexican border of Yuma County, Ariz.; *arsipus*, from Daggett, San Bernardino County, Calif.; *devia*, from Llano de Yrais, opposite Magdalena Island, Lower California; *mutica*, from Tracy, San Joaquin

County, Calif.; *neomexicana*, from San Andreas Range, Dona Ana County, N. Mex., about 50 miles north of El Paso; *nevadensis*, from Willow Creek Ranch, near Jungo, Humboldt County, Nev.; *tenuirostris*, from Trinidad Valley, northwest base of San Pedro Martir Mountains, Lower California, Mexico; and *zinseri*, from San Antonio de Jaral, southeastern Coahuila, Mexico. In a recent study of the group, Benson (1938) shows that *arizonensis* is synonymous with the older-described race *arsipus*, so that the number of recognized races is now eight. This author writes that "kit foxes are now as a rule few in number even in the areas which seem suitable to them. They are so unsuspicious that they are easily trapped and even more easily poisoned. Consequently, wherever trappers are active, and especially wherever control campaigns involving the use of poison have been carried out against predatory animals on areas inhabited by kit foxes, the foxes have been greatly reduced in number or entirely eliminated. Unfortunately, there are few kit fox habitats in the United States that escape visitation by these agencies." Benson comments that the race *mutica* of the San Joaquin Valley and Walker Basin in California is a well-marked form, while the race *arsipus*, ranging east of the Pacific slope drainage, though also easily distinguishable, clearly extends into southern Nevada and may have to include *nevadensis* as a synonym.

The numbers of all these various races seem to be rapidly decreasing, but the only one which is rather certainly now extinct is the typical one, *V. macrotis macrotis*. This form once ranged over parts of California in the "San Diegan sub-faunal district, from Riverside County, northwest . . . to Los Angeles County" in the Lower Sonoran Life Zone. It formerly occurred in the Allessandro, Perris, and San Jacinto Valleys, westward along the plain at the southwest of the San Gabriel Range to San Fernando Valley, where in the early nineties local residents trapped them. The last one known to have been taken in the San Jacinto Plain was trapped near Moreno in 1903 (Grinnell, Dixon, and Linsdale, 1937). At the present time the race *mutica* is still to be found in the San Joaquin Valley of California, but the authors just quoted indicate that its range has shrunk to about half of what it was not so many years ago, so that it is now restricted to the driest plains of the southern and western parts of the valley.

"Open level sandy ground is the preferred habitat of the kit fox," for here it can easily excavate its burrows, and this type of ground is likewise preferred by numerous small rodents, such as kangaroo rats and pocket mice, which form the chief food of this little fox. "These special adaptations may account for the rather sharp limitation observable in the general distribution of this type of fox, which man's presence further restricts." Their shallow burrows are dug in open ground and may have one to four entrances. Grinnell, Dixon, and Linsdale (1937), from whose account these details are taken, found that the breeding season is early. Young are found newly born late in February, and the number to the litter may average four or five but in one case was as many as seven. It seems to have few natural enemies. There is a close correlation between the areas inhabited by the kit fox and the range of the large kangaroo rats *Dipodomys deserti* and *D. spectabilis*, on which with other smaller rodents the fox largely feeds, although insects, occasionally rabbits and snakes, and rarely poultry are also items in its diet.

Of the race *mutica* of the San Joaquin Valley, Calif., the authors quoted say that of recent years large numbers have been killed for fur. Thus, in 1919, one trapper caught 100 foxes in a single week on an area 20 miles long by 2 miles wide on the west side of the valley. But "probably the greatest number of kit foxes has been destroyed by poison campaigns directed against coyotes . . . Hundreds of kit foxes were

Long-eared kit fox (*Vulpes macrotis macrotis*)

doubtless thus destroyed in a single season." Some unusual condition added to these efforts at "control" might conceivably wipe out the remnant of these foxes in the San Joaquin Valley. However, "in the Mohave and Colorado deserts, which are now remote from human activity and where the conditions of the soil and the lack of water will long prevent future settlement, it is probable that" the race *arsipus* will endure indefinitely.

The most northerly ranging race of the desert fox is *nevadensis*, concerning which Vernon Bailey (1936) writes: "These graceful little foxes have been found in the valleys of northern Nevada, southwestern Idaho, and southeastern Oregon, not far beyond the limits of Lower Sonoran Zone valleys, where the species generally ranges." Specimens are mentioned from the Owyhee Valley as the only ones available from Oregon, but it "may be looked for in the Alvord and adjoining valleys that open out into northern Nevada." He says nothing of their present status there but surmises that they will soon be gone. He further testifies to their adaptability as pets, on account of their gentleness, their intelligence and affectionate behavior, and their ready confidence and alertness. "Why not," he asks, "keep such animals instead of cats and dogs and save a few from extermination?"

THE AMERICAN WOLVES

Wolves are of boreal distribution in both the Old World and the New, originally ranging without interruption from western Europe eastward to the Pacific Ocean in the former and from Alaska to the Atlantic coast of eastern North America in the latter area. Pocock (1935) in a recent paper regards them as of a single species with local races, which appears to be a logical course, since all are much alike. Even the narrow Bering Straits, closed by ice during part of the year, probably form no insuperable barrier to an occasional crossing. In North America wolves are found from the Arctic regions southward to the Gulf of Mexico and the Mexican tableland, but in a recent review Goldman (1937) regards the most southern or red wolf as a separate species. Exclusive of this and its two subspecies, there are at present recognized no less than 20 local races in this area, distinguished for the most part by minor characters of the skull and teeth; all these are treated as subspecies of *Canis lupus* of Europe. It is often said that the European wolf is the ancestor of the domestic dog, but the evidence for this is merely inferential. Usually wolves of any race may be distinguished from even the largest dogs by their proportionally larger teeth, shorter ears, and less elevated forehead due to the smaller development of the frontal sinuses. In dogs the length of the lower first molar or carnassial tooth is usually less (and in medium-sized and smaller breeds much less) than 22 mm., whereas in wolves it is in excess of this measurement. In their general proportions and a certain "plumpness," however, the teeth of wolves are exceedingly like those of domestic dogs and differ from the narrower more bladelike teeth of coyotes, which some have thought ancestral to dogs.

Everywhere in North America that wolves have come into competition with white men, in settlements or in agricultural communities, they have been regarded as a common enemy and killed whenever possible. The inevitable result has been their greater or less reduction in the thinly settled regions and complete extermination from larger areas where white population is denser or agricultural and pastoral use of the land makes it impossible to tolerate their presence on account of their depredations against livestock. While this is more or less to be deplored, it is unavoidable, for the rancher can not be expected to view with complacency the resulting loss. The outlook for the preservation of a remnant of this interesting species is therefore bright only in the wilder and more inaccessible regions or in large public reservations where the numbers can be controlled and where, conceivably, a small number of wolves might serve a useful purpose not only in preventing too great an increase in wild deer or mountain sheep but also in actually improving or keeping up a standard of quality by eliminating sickly or stupid individuals. It is remarkable that even in parts of Europe to this day as in Spain and France a few wolves have remained in spite of long occupation by white races. Furthermore, if one may believe the mass of published accounts, wolves under the stress of hunger have been known to pursue and kill human beings in Europe and Asia, whereas at least in eastern North America there seem to be few or no authentic cases of such bold actions on the part of wolves here in early days, although there are instances of wolves having followed and frightened many of our early settlers.

Like other large carnivores, wolves require food in larger amounts, so that in addition to what smaller game they may pick up, it is the larger ungulates that they specially hunt. In the North the caribou, and on the plains the mule deer, and even the young or sickly bison were objects of pursuit, while in the wooded regions of eastern North America the white-tailed deer was a staple food species. In the case of the last-named the wolf in areas of deep winter snows was doubtless a main factor in preventing the spread of this deer to the northward into regions where now it is abundant.

In recent years a more intensive campaign has been carried on under the U. S. Biological Survey to eliminate the wolf entirely from stock-raising regions of the West. This has resulted in the accumulation by the Survey of sufficient specimens to "afford a fairly satisfactory basis for determining specific and subspecific relationships" of the American races, as worked out in Goldman's (1937) paper. Some of these are already extinct, others nearly so. In the following brief survey, the races are taken up alphabetically, giving a condensed statement of the general status so far as at present known. A final account of the genus and its natural history is to be desired.

In a general way, the various races of wolves are much alike, about the size of a modern "police dog" but shaggier, with short ears and bushy tail, carried usually with a slight hump near the root. The usual color is a mixed black, white, and gray, giving a grizzled appearance. The long hairs of the coat are usually white for the greater part of their length, with more or less black tipping or white, producing this mixed appearance. Often the white portion of the hairs is greater than the black tipping, resulting in a pale coat, and in the Arctic parts of the range the black may be eliminated almost altogether, so that the pelage is white. On the other hand, black may predominate and the pelage in that case is blackish to entirely black. This wide variation may occur within the same family group of animals, so that color characters are often of little avail for the separation of geographic races. These are therefore in large part based on cranial characters and on size differences where they are significant. While wolves must often travel over considerable areas in their hunting, and thus tend to segregate less than more sedentary species, they must nevertheless keep to more or less definite regions where under varying conditions of environment slight differences have developed. Intergradation through individual variation often makes the exact definition of races difficult, and series are needed in working out the status of animals from different parts of the range.

According to a useful pamphlet by Vernon Bailey (1907) wolves enter very little into the national forests of the western United States but favor foothill regions for breeding and hunting. In some areas there is evidence of a certain amount of seasonal migration, in the course of which the wolves of a district follow the cattle herds into the mountains in spring, and again in autumn accompany them into lowland areas, much as in former times they followed the bison. The same paper has some account of the abundance of wolves in the West and South up to the early years of this century, with instructions for trapping and poisoning.

AMERICAN ARCTIC WOLF

CANIS LUPUS ARCTOS Pocock

Canis lupus arctos Pocock, Proc. Zool. Soc. London, 1935, p. 682, Sept. 12 ("Melville Island, Arctic America").
FIG.: Nelson, 1916, p. 421.

According to Pocock the skull of a specimen of Arctic wolf from Melville Island "may be distinguished at a glance by the great elevation of the frontal region and the resulting much more strongly convex curvature of the frontorostral line. It is also broader . . . in the muzzle and palate . . . The bulla also is noticeably more inflated" as compared with a skull regarded as representing *C. l. tundrarum.* This is a white wolf.

In addition to the skull of the type from Melville Island, Pocock lists a second in the British Museum from Discovery Bay, Ellesmere Land. The former was secured in 1853–54, the second about 1878. Parry seems to have been the first to mention this wolf, which he noticed was smaller than the white wolf of the mainland (*tundrarum*).

The present status of this wolf in Ellesmere Land and adjoining islands to the west is uncertain. There are few human inhabitants, either Eskimo or white. However, since it would

be expected that the numbers of caribou in the region would
attract a small permanent population of wolves, it seems
strange that they should be so rarely observed. Peary, who
was familiar with the region from his various polar expeditions,
wrote ("The North Pole," p. 61, 1910) that in the northern
part of the island there might be "perhaps once in a generation
a stray wolf," implying that it was almost unknown a generation ago. Had it been of regular occurrence following the
caribou herds, the Eskimo would surely have reported it.
Possibly these stray Arctic wolves may have come from farther
south on rare occasions. However, the more recent testimony
of Macmillan is rather at variance with Peary's statements.
In his book "Four Years in the White North" (1918) he has a
good deal to say about the Arctic wolves met with in Ellesmere
Land and Axel Heiberg Land. Late in March, 1916, two were
started at Bay Fiord, near Etah, but they dashed away and
finally disappeared over the rough ice of Smith Sound; later
one was killed near Eureka Sound, and another was started
from the ice foot and also ran off over the ice. "Axel Heiberg
Land is infested with them," he wrote, after seeing a pack of 12,
all white. In April of that year two others appeared and when
pursued by the sledge dogs ran off over the sea ice toward
North Cornwall. In October, 1916, the local Eskimos returned
from their annual caribou hunt, which covers the region from
Etah to the Humboldt Glacier on the Greenland coast. They
reported no young caribou, but tracks of wolves everywhere,
implying that the young caribou find it difficult to survive on
account of the wolves. Macmillan believes that a large band of
white wolves had crossed Smith Sound and was following the
herds on the North Greenland coast. They also probably
capture a few seals along the ice foot, which would account for
their presence in that place, while muskoxen too must frequently fall a prey. If this explorer is correct in his belief that
wolves cross Smith Sound, from Ellesmere Land to North
Greenland, as seems likely, there appears no reason to suppose
that their wanderings in search of game might not take them
across the northern part of that country or even to the east
coast, so that the supposed distinction of the wolves of the
two regions may prove to be unfounded.

MEXICAN WOLF

CANIS LUPUS BAILEYI Nelson and Goldman

Canis nubilus baileyi Nelson and Goldman, Journ. Mamm., vol. 10, p. 165, May, 1929
("Colonia Garcia (about 60 miles southwest of Casas Grandes), Chihuahua, Mexico").
FIG.: Bailey, 1931, pl. 18 (photograph).

This is the wolf of "southern and western Arizona, southern New Mexico, and the Sierra Madre and adjoining tableland of Mexico as far south, at least, as southern Durango," and according to its describers it is most nearly allied to the plains wolf (*C. l. nubilus*) but is smaller and darker, more brownish or rufescent, with a more slender and depressed rostrum. Its greater size and other cranial characters indicate "no close relationship" to *C. rufus*. Total length, 1,570 mm.; tail, 410; skull, condylobasal length, 262.

The authors quoted list various specimens from Chihuahua, one from Sonora, and one from Durango, Mexico, as well as a number from Arizona and New Mexico. "According to old residents wolves that formerly inhabited the southern end of the tableland, near the valley of Mexico, became extinct many years ago. Wolves are still numerous, however, in the Sierra Madre as far south at least as Durango." Specimens from southwestern New Mexico show indications of intergradation toward the plains wolf (Bailey, 1931, p. 303). "Their greatest abundance has long been in the open grazing country of the Gila National Forest" in the open yellow-pine forests and the orchardlike growth of juniper, nut pine, and oak. "Apparently they are not known in the Lower Sonoran valleys of this region." Bailey (1931) has given an excellent account of the habits of wolves in this area. He states that they persistently cling to certain localities in their range for raising their young. "Dens are always placed in the most out-of-the-way places, with seemingly little regard for convenience as to water or food." In rough country the dens are generally in a crevice or natural cavity "usually in the rim of a mesa"; badger holes are often enlarged, or the burrow may be worked out beneath a mesquite or other bush that serves as a blind.

Bailey (1931) tells further of trapping wolves in this region and records that J. S. Ligon with a corps of trappers began a trap line in 1916 for the purpose of reducing the number of wolves. He estimated that in May, 1917, there were 103 adult wolves in New Mexico and 45 in July, 1918. "In 1927 he said that they were practically eliminated from New Mexico and that he was then concerned only with reinfestation from Mexico." Thus it appears that continued and skillful effort will at length succeed in exterminating even these wily animals, but that with their tendency to range wide and far, there is a constant opportunity for new individuals to come in from outside.

NEWFOUNDLAND WOLF

CANIS LUPUS BEOTHUCUS G. M. Allen and T. Barbour

Canis lupus beothucus G. M. Allen and T. Barbour, Journ. Mamm., vol. 18, p. 230, May, 1937 ("Newfoundland").

FIG.: Allen and Barbour, 1937, p. 231, fig. (upper carnassial).

In the Newfoundland wolf the skull is relatively slender, and the nasal bones are long in contrast to the short ascending branches of the premaxillaries; the upper carnassial is characteristic in its shortness and in the size and sharp inward turn of the anterointernal cusp in contrast to the condition in other wolves. The color is white, but occasional black individuals are said to have been known. The largest of four skulls measured in greatest length, 276 mm.; outer length of nasals, 103; tip of nasal to point of premaxillary, 47; length of upper carnassial, 25.5; length of first lower molar, 28.7.

In the large size and slender proportions of the skull, as well as in its white coat, this wolf resembled the white Arctic wolf. At the present time it is apparently extinct in Newfoundland, where in former days it followed the herds of Newfoundland caribou. Bonnycastle in 1842 spoke of it as large in size and as frequently seen in the neighborhood of St. John's. On account of its depredations against young cattle, a bounty was declared on wolves. A writer in *Forest and Stream* (vol. 4, p. 390) in 1875 spoke of these wolves as then common in the island, often prowling near the houses of settlers or seen near settlements in chase. In winter when the caribou were feeding in the bogs, the wolves cooperated in hunting them. While some lay in wait along the border of coniferous trees, others went around to windward, when the caribou, scenting them, turned and ran directly into the ambush. The same writer mentions an instance where a Micmac Indian in April, 1866, was standing by the side of a small lake formed by the River Exploits, when he saw an old wolf coming toward him on the ice, to be followed presently by five or six more. The Indian ran for his "tilt" and his gun, but the wolves, following him, gained so rapidly that he sought safety by climbing into a tree beyond their reach; otherwise, he felt certain, they would have attacked and killed him. But after remaining about for nearly an hour they departed. The skin of a white wolf killed north of Grand Lake, Newfoundland, about 1896, by Dr. Elwood Worcester, was presented by him to the Museum of Comparative Zoology. It was shot as it came over the side of a hill where Dr. Worcester was waiting, gun in hand, for a chance at a caribou. Two others, which he saw at about the same time, were running along the shore of a lake above River of Ponds in pursuit of a caribou. One of these looked very dark in color. Bangs (1913) wrote that when Doane was collecting for him about 1894 one was killed, but neither Millais, writing about 1906, nor Dugmore in his book on the Newfoundland caribou in 1913, mentions seeing anything of the wolf, which by that time must have been greatly reduced in numbers. The last record known to me is of one reported to have been killed about 1911. The late Dr. John C. Phillips, who contributed this note, endeavored to obtain the specimen but was unsuccessful.

While Newfoundland at its nearest point is hardly 10 miles distant from the mainland of Labrador, it seems that this wolf, like so many other animals of the island, must have been isolated here for a long period and gradually developed the slight cranial differences that distinguish it. At the present time the Newfoundland wolf is believed to be extinct.

VANCOUVER ISLAND WOLF

CANIS LUPUS CRASSODON Hall

Canis occidentalis crassodon Hall, Univ. California Publ. Zool., vol. 38, p. 420, Nov. 8, 1932 ("Tahsis Canal, Nootka Sound, Vancouver Island, British Columbia").

Skulls of the Vancouver Island wolf differ from those of the adjacent mainland and southern Alaska in their smaller size, shortened preorbital region, less elevated tip of rostrum, and greater shallowness of the lower jaw through the coronoid process. The color is gray to black. Condylobasal length of skull, 240 mm.

Five specimens are mentioned by Hall in his original description of this wolf. Concerning the status of the race, Swarth (1912) writes that a quarter of a century ago wolves were still fairly common "in the wilder parts of at least the northern two-thirds of Vancouver Island, sufficiently so as to be a serious menace to the deer in many places." At Beaver Creek he heard one howl and was told that they were occasionally seen in the valley during the winter but very seldom in summer. At Nootka they were said to be abundant. "On the Tahsis Canal we stayed at the camp of a trapper who made it his principal occupation during the winter to hunt wolves and panthers." With the bounty of $15 a head added to the value of the fur, the trapper evidently secured enough to make it pay. This trapper used poison exclusively and seemed to have had no trouble in killing the animals, but in several years' hunting he had actually seen but two or three alive, so cunning are they in keeping out of sight. Swarth stated that wolves had been so common at Friendly Cove during the years immediately preceding 1912 that deer had been almost completely driven out of the neighborhood. Of the status of this wolf at the present day no further information is at hand.

NORTHWEST COAST WOLF; "BROWN WOLF"

CANIS LUPUS FUSCUS Richardson

Canis lupus var. *fusca* Richardson, Zool. Beechey's Voyage of the *Blossom*, Mammals, p. 5, 1839 ("California and the Banks of the Columbia River").

SYNONYM: *Lupus gigas* Townsend, Journ. Acad. Nat. Sci., Philadelphia, ser. 1, vol. 2, p. 75, Nov., 1850 (near Vancouver, Columbia River, Washington).

The wolf formerly occurring from northern California to the Puget Sound region, and probably southwestern British Columbia west of the Cascades, was regarded as a valid form by Miller (1912) in notes on the names of the large wolves of North America. He states that a skull from the Puget Sound region "indicates an animal differing from the timber-wolf of the interior region in less great size and in less enlarged teeth." Hall (1932) contrasts specimens from Oregon with the race *crassodon* of Vancouver Island and says that they differ noticeably in "the markedly less inflated tympanic bullae, much smaller teeth," in the more convex lower profile of the jaw and other minor skull characters. The color is "much darker" than in the Plains wolf (Bailey).

This race, which was perhaps characteristic of the saturate region of forest along the Northwest coast, is doubtless now extinct in California (Grinnell, 1933). In Oregon, Bailey (1936) writes, "a few of these large, dark gray wolves are still found in the timbered country west of the Cascades . . . and locally northward to British Columbia and Alaska. In recent years they have been found mainly along the west slope of the Cascade Range, but before extensive white settlements were made in the State they seem to have been common in the Willamette Valley and west to the coast . . . In 1897 Captain Applegate reported them as formerly common, but at that time extremely rare in the southern Cascade region." In 1913–14 bounties were paid on 30 wolves taken in Oregon, but in later years they seem to have been largely exterminated within the State. Bailey mentions one taken in 1930 on the Umpqua National Forest, where it had killed several sheep. It was very old with much worn teeth. A second old male was killed the same winter in Klamath County, while in Douglas County and Lane County one each was killed in 1930 and 1931. At the present time, he writes, their numbers are so nearly under control that their damage is negligible. This probably applies also to Washington, but no recent statistics are available. In the remoter regions of western British Columbia they are probably still present in some numbers.

NORTHERN ROCKY MOUNTAIN WOLF

CANIS LUPUS IRREMOTUS Goldman

Canis lupus irremotus Goldman, Journ. Mamm., vol. 18, p. 41, Feb., 1937 ("Red Lodge, Carbon County, southwestern Montana").

This is the wolf of the northern Rocky Mountain region and high adjoining plains, from northwestern Wyoming northward through western Montana and eastern Idaho at least to Lethbridge in southern Alberta. Intergradation with neighboring races is presumed and makes the precise definition of the range difficult. It is a light-colored race with narrow but flattened frontal region, in these characters differing from the race *youngi* of the southern Rocky Mountains. It is larger and paler than *nubilus* of Nebraska or *fuscus* of Washington, and smaller than the form *occidentalis* to the northward of its range.

The race is based on more than 30 specimens from Montana and Idaho; hence its characters seem well established. Probably this is the form of eastern Oregon concerning which Bailey (1936) has a few interesting notes (under *Canis lycaon nubilus*). In this region wolves were numerous in the middle of the last century and were plentiful even up till the nineties. At the present time they are largely gone from all this region, but doubtless still remain in small numbers in Montana and Wyoming.

LABRADOR WOLF

CANIS LUPUS LABRADORIUS Goldman

Canis lupus labradorius Goldman, Journ. Mamm., vol. 18, p. 38, Feb., 1937 ("Vicinity of Fort Chimo, Quebec" northern Labrador).

In color this wolf of northern Labrador varies from "dark somewhat grizzly gray to almost white." It is larger than the eastern wolf, with heavier dentition and minor cranial differences, and seems to be only slightly differentiated. Its geographic range is not at present determined but is presumed to be the Labrador Peninsula north of the forest region.

Concerning the status of these wolves in Labrador but little information is available. They are, however, not uncommon and follow the herds of barren-ground caribou. William B. Cabot, in his account of travels into the eastern interior of the peninsula, speaks of them as occasionally to be heard, and in 1905 he saw tracks of perhaps as many as 200. They are occasionally killed by hunters near the coastal settlements in winter, but since the interior of the country is rarely penetrated by white men it seems unlikely that they will be much disturbed there for a long period to come.

ALEXANDER ARCHIPELAGO WOLF

CANIS LUPUS LIGONI Goldman

Canis lupus ligoni Goldman, Journ. Mamm., vol. 18, p. 39, Feb., 1937 ("Head of Duncan Canal, Kupreanof Island, Alexander Archipelago, Alaska").

This wolf is believed to be the race characteristic of the Alexander Archipelago and adjacent mainland of southeastern Alaska. It is a race of medium size, "much smaller than *Canis lupus pambasileus* of the Mount McKinley region, Alaska, or *Canis lupus occidentalis* of the Fort Simpson region, . . .

Mackenzie." It is similar to the race *C. l. fuscus* of the coast
districts to the south, but a larger percentage of black or
blackish individuals is normal, while it is less suffused with
buffy in the gray phase. The small auditory bullae distinguish
it from the race *crassodon* of Vancouver Island, while its longer
rostrum and palate and the longer narrower nasals separate it
from *fuscus*. None of these characteristics seems very trench-
ant, taken alone, but Goldman considers it a "well-marked
form,"· closest related to the last.

Swarth (1936), commenting on the distribution of this wolf,
says that it is "found upon the same islands as the Red Squirrel
[i. e., Mitkof, Kupreanof, and Kuiu], and also upon the large
Prince of Wales and Dall Islands with some others of this
southern group that the squirrel has never reached. Evidently
the wolf did not come directly from the north" but reached
those of the inner islands that formed a series of stepping-
stones most easily crossed from the adjacent southeastern
coast. I have no recent information concerning its present
status, but apparently it still occurs on these islands in small
numbers.

EASTERN TIMBER WOLF

CANIS LUPUS LYCAON Schreber

Canis lycaon Schreber, Säugthiere, vol. 3, p. 353, pl. 89, 1776 ("Vicinity of Quebec,
     Canada," as selected by Goldman, 1937, p. 37).
FIGS.: Stone and Cram, 1902, pl. opposite p. 278; Nelson, 1916, p. 423, upper figs.
     (color phases).

The eastern timber wolf is slightly smaller than the wolf of
northern Labrador, and usually of a grizzled black, white, and
gray. As long ago pointed out by Baird, it differs from the
Plains wolf and the neighboring northern races in its weaker
rostrum. Weight upwards of 100 pounds.

Three hundred years ago this wolf ranged over the wooded
and open areas of eastern North America from southern Quebec to probably the southern States and westward to the
Plains. With the coming of white men and the occupation of
the country, it has been gradually extirpated from the settled
regions until at the present time wolves are gone from practically all the eastern United States and probably none are now
to be found south of the St. Lawrence and east of Michigan.

When the first English colonists landed on the shores of New
England they found wolves plentiful and troublesome and were

obliged at once to take active measures to prevent them from seriously depleting their precious cattle and sheep brought with so much labor from England. No doubt too they feared the attack of wolves in packs against themselves, particularly if traveling alone or at night, yet there seems to be no authentic instance of anyone actually being killed by wolves, though many a person going after dark to a neighbor's hurried his footsteps on hearing a wolf howl. Apparently the Indians along these coasts were little afraid of wolves (for they had no livestock), but occasionally they caught them in traps, and wolf bones in small amount occur in the Indian shell heaps. The early settlers often kept their sheep on the smaller outer islands where they were comparatively safe and unable to stray. But flocks or cattle in pasture were in constant danger even when in pens near the houses. The early records of Plymouth and Massachusetts Bay colonies show that a determined campaign was waged against wolves. Bounties were offered for adult wolves and lesser ones for whelps, and the heads of wolves brought in for the reward were publicly exposed on hooks at the meetinghouse. The Indians were active in this campaign and secured their share of the bounties. Yet for nearly a century wolves continued to be a menace to stock. In the "History of Cape Cod" Freeman relates that in 1717, the early settlers discussed a project for erecting a high fence of palisades or boards between Sandwich and Wareham to shut off the outer Cape completely as a safe pasture for the livestock against the wolves. But the scheme finally was abandoned, since the several towns involved could not agree on their proportionate share of the expense, while those outside the Cape did not see why the wolves should be retained on their side of the fence! Many of the towns maintained "wolf pits," dug deep enough so that a wolf could not jump out, the inwardly sloping sides sometimes smoothly faced with stone, and the whole baited with fresh meat. Wolves jumping in for the bait were unable to leap out and were later killed. The remains of such a trap are said still to exist in the Lynn Woods park in Massachusetts. The idea was doubtless taken from the Indians.

Even down to the time of the American Revolution wolves were fairly frequent in or near the settled parts of New England, but soon after, the unremitting fight against them had so reduced their numbers that they were no longer a serious menace. Occasional small packs or single cunning survivors were systematically hunted down by companies of men who would track them to deep woods or swamps which were surrounded and the animals driven out and often shot. In 1774, Connecticut repealed the law that formerly offered a bounty on wolves. But if wolves were then no longer dangerous to stock in Connecticut, they continued to be so in the less settled regions of southern New Hampshire and Maine. Bounties were increased and hunting wolves became a regular occupation of some of the Indians or white hunters. The constant war of extermination at length began to tell, and by the early years of the last century few wolves were left in southern New Hampshire and Vermont. In his history of the town of Gilsum, near the present Keene, N. H., Hayward in 1879 tells that in March or April, 1828, took place what was then still remembered as "the wolf hunt," when a lone individual that had killed a number of sheep was finally hunted down, twice surrounded by a party of determined farmers, and shot as it slunk out from an old spruce top. Many similar tales may be found in the local histories. The "last wolf" in Lancaster, N. H., was trapped about 1840 according to local account, but I have reason to believe that an occasional one or two came into the White Mountain region till a much later date. Zadock Thompson mentions a specimen in the University of Vermont that was killed in Addison County about 1830, but probably they occasionally were found well after that time. Merriam in his "Mammals of the Adirondacks" (in 1882) lists wolves on which bounties had been paid that were taken in St. Lawrence and Washington Counties, N. Y., even up to the latter date. When the last wolf was taken in Maine is perhaps uncertain. The only specimen known to me from that State is a skin now in the Boston Museum of Natural History, killed near Moosehead Lake in 1863. The late Manly Hardy, who traveled all over Maine as a trapper and fur buyer, and whose authority is unquestioned, wrote in 1884 (*Forest and Stream*, vol. 22, p. 141) that "in 1853 wolves were very plenty, and for the next five years were not scarce; plenty could be found within sixteen miles of Bangor in 1857 and 1858. They seemed to leave quite suddenly. The last I know of positively being taken was . . . in 1860, at Munsengun . . . There were rumors of occasional wolves being seen from 1875 to '80, but the first real proof I can give is that in 1880 I bought the skin of a freshly killed wolf, taken at Union River. The one who brought it said it had a mate, and they had been heard at times for several years in that vicinity." A few later reports of wolves or their tracks seen in northern Maine bordering New Brunswick may have been authentic, but evidently they were practically gone by that time, not only from Maine but from New Brunswick as well. Indeed, Chamberlain (1884) writes that although common until about 1860 in the latter region they had since "entirely disappeared."

In the wilder regions of the Adirondacks of New York, wolves in small numbers continued till a much later time. Miller (1899) has published a table showing by counties the bounties paid on wolves by New York State, incorporating and continuing the earlier one of Merriam (1882). From this it appears that between 1871, when a bounty was declared, and 1897, no less than 98 wolves were killed on which a total of $2,910 in bounties was paid. Further, in the decade preceding 1880, six was the most killed in any year, but 12 were brought in in 1881 and no less than 21 in 1882! In 1883 nine were killed, in the next three years two in each, one in 1887, and two in 1888. Thereafter appears a blank in the record, and some have believed the animal was then extinct in New York, but in each of the years 1895, 1896, 1897, bounties were paid on six wolves! One can not help the thought that something is strange about this. Of the 98 wolves on which the State paid bounties between 1871 and 1897, 45 or nearly half came from St. Lawrence County, which borders the river of that name, suggesting that there may have been occasional immigrants from the Ontario side. For the Toronto region, however, Fleming, in 1913, writes as if they had long since been extinct and states that "according to the late Dr. Brodie, wolves occasionally drove deer into Markham as late as 1840."

The status of the wolf in Pennsylvania and New Jersey has been carefully investigated by S. N. Rhoads, and the results of his search for records are summarized in his book on the "Mammals of Pennsylvania and New Jersey" (1903). From the latter State they were so early extirpated that little record remains to indicate for how long they were present there, but perhaps till early in the nineteenth century. Pennsylvania, however, with its mountains and extensive wilderness areas, continued to harbor them up to comparatively recent years. The last record for New Jersey is given as of one killed in Wayne County in 1887, which was driven in from New York State by dogs, but its ultimate source may be questionable. Wolves seem to have remained common in the less settled and wilder parts of Pennsylvania until about the middle of the last century. Thus, Rhoads quotes Warren as authority for the statement that "about the year 1845 wolves were abundant in Tomhickon Valley" while between 1808 and 1820 Lucerne County paid $2,872 in bounties for wolf scalps at about $5 each. As many as 273 wolves were killed in one of these years. Another correspondent informed him that he saw many as late as 1857 on the head waters of Pine Creek and Sinnemahonig in Potter County, where the last one he knew of was killed about 1875. Tomkins (1931) records a "last" wolf near Williamsport in 1867 and one near Ralston, in 1872, in the north-central part of the State. Many records are quoted for the middle part of the nineteenth century, and Rhoads makes the summary statement that they finally became "apparently exterminated in Pennsylvania within the last 10 or 15 years," that is, in the middle or late eighties. More recent reports lack authenticity, while of various cases investigated in which bounties had been paid in later years some proved to be deliberate frauds. In another it turned out that a wolf had been brought from the West and had later escaped. In Elk County, Pa., the last wolf is said to have been shot in 1891. Probably the actual extinction of native eastern wolves in the State may be set at about that date. A few seem to have remained still in West Virginia wildernesses, where, according to Fred E. Brooks, "what is supposed to have been the last gray wolf in West Virginia was killed in Randolph county by Stofer Hamrick in January 1900."

Apparently wolves were found in North Carolina up to about the beginning of the present century. At all events, C. S. Brimley, writing in 1905, states that it was then "found sparingly throughout the mountains. Dr. Donald Wilson reports it from Graham County, Mr. R. W. Collett says it is growing very scarce in Cherokee, Mr. Fain says there are a very few in Buncombe [County]. Mr. H. H. Brimley, Curator of the State Museum, informs me it has been taken in recent

years in Yancey, Caldwell and Watauga." Dr. C. Hart Merriam states that during one of his visits to Roan Mountain, in
1887 or 1892, a den of wolves was discovered and the young
were captured. In the last quarter of the eighteenth century
wolves were spoken of as abundant in South Carolina, but by
Audubon's day they were much fewer. The last one known to
have been killed in the State was shot in Berkeley County,
near St. Stephens, between 1856 and 1860. E. B. Chamberlain,
of the Charleston Museum, who kindly supplied this record,
had reports of other wolves in the Santee section at about the
same time.

How far to the south the gray or timber wolf extended its
range may never be certainly made out, for the black or
Florida wolf of extreme southern United States is now regarded
as a race of the species *Canis rufus* by Goldman in his recent
review. Dr. Francis Harper (1927) refers to this form the
wolves formerly found in Okefenokee Swamp, southern Georgia,
where according to his investigations the last one killed was
about 1908.

West of New York State and the Allegheny Mountains, the
timber wolf was formerly common and is believed to have
intergraded with the Plains wolf in the more open region west
of the Mississippi. The story of its original abundance and
gradual extermination is much the same as elsewhere in the
East, except that in the more remote and wilder regions, as in
northern Wisconsin, some still remain. In northern Minnesota
wolves were common till at least the late years of the last
century. Herrick (1892) has an interesting note in his "Mammals of Minnesota" indicating, as in some other instances, an
occasional influx of numbers in certain districts: "During the
winter of 1884–85, wolves became very abundant and insolent
in Wright county, and were seen about the outskirts of Monticello in broad daylight almost daily, though they were sufficiently wary to escape capture." Cory (1912) writes that this
wolf was still "common in northern Wisconsin and possibly
occurs occasionally in other parts of the State," but although
stragglers may at times appear in Illinois, all efforts to secure a
specimen have failed, and most of the reports of wolves prove
on investigation to be based on coyotes. In Wisconsin, recent
records are available from as far south as Buffalo County.

In the region of the Ohio Valley wolves were formerly plenti-

ful but with the settling of the country a century ago were
soon reduced to innocuous numbers, and in Ohio had become
very rare by 1838 and "nearly extinct" a decade later. Audubon, while living at Henderson, Ky., early in the second decade
of that period found black wolves abundant. He recounts that
one morning he found a black wolf in one of his wild-turkey
pens and shot it in the act of devouring one of the birds of
which it had already killed several. Whether these wolves
were of the timber wolf type or the red wolf type is indetermi-
nable. In Tennessee wolves were exterminated many years
ago (Kellogg, 1939), and but few records exist. Merriam in
1887 found that a few still were present in the Smoky Mountains and in middle Tennessee they were reported as occasionally found in Van Buren County. Late records of wolves
killed, Kellogg gives as: A female and her pups at Waynesboro,
about 1917; and one in 1919 on North Fork River, Cumberland
County. In western Tennessee the last available record is
given as about December 10, 1895, when two were killed near
Brownsville, Haywood County.

In the region to the southward of South Carolina and Tennessee, the black race of the red wolf is believed to be the form
found.

At the present time the timber wolf is still to be found in
limited numbers in eastern Canada, as in the less settled portions of Quebec along the north shore of the Gulf of St. Lawrence, where near Matamek I was shown in 1929 the skin of a
large one killed the winter before. Doubtless there are many
more between the Gulf and James Bay. At least until recent
years, wolves were present in the Algonquin National Park,
while farther to the west, in Quetico National Park, along the
international boundary from Lake of the Woods to the western
end of Lake Superior, and in the adjacent Superior National
Forest contiguous with it on the United States side in northeastern Minnesota, Cahn (1937) writes that "wolves are still
common" and cross back and forth freely between the two areas.
Here numerous and spasmodic drives have been made to rid
the area of these predators but have resulted mainly "in the
killing of about everything *except* wolves, which usually elude
most cleverly the clumsy efforts to trap them. Late in fall
their call is to be heard frequently all over the Quetico, but in
all my travels I have seen but 2 live wolves . . . Their

persecution is to be regretted, for they form a perfectly natural and normal check on other species." In this last statement is to be found the key to the preservation of the species in regions where it comes in contact with white men. Under the nearly natural conditions of a large national preserve for game, wolves in these northern regions will be useful in preventing too great an increase of deer, and to a less extent of moose, which in the absence of such natural predators may easily become unduly abundant to the impairment of their range as in the case of the Kaibab deer or those of the Murderers Creek Game Refuge in eastern Oregon. Even in such situations, however, the game ranger has a special problem in determining how many wolves may safely be allowed on refuge areas, and how best this number may be maintained through occasional destruction of young or of adults that become too bold or range outside the preserve to kill cattle or sheep in adjacent districts.

MOGOLLON MOUNTAIN WOLF

CANIS LUPUS MOGOLLONENSIS Goldman

Canis lupus mogollonensis Goldman, Journ. Mamm., vol. 18, p. 43, Feb., 1937 ("S. A. Creek, 10 miles southwest of Luna, Catron County, New Mexico").

This is a "rather small, usually dark-colored subspecies. Similar in general to *Canis lupus youngi* of the Rocky Mountain region . . . but smaller and usually darker in color. Decidedly larger and usually lighter in color than *Canis lupus baileyi* of the Sierra Madre of Mexico. Closely allied to *Canis lupus monstrabilis* of Texas, but smaller" and the skull with "zygomata more widely spreading; frontal region less elevated and inflated; auditory bullae smaller."

The distribution of this form is said by Goldman to include the Mogollon Plateau region of central Arizona, extending eastward through the Mogollon Mountains to the Sacramento Mountains of New Mexico, and though rather circumscribed this seems nevertheless to be well borne out by a series of 120 specimens studied by its describer. Vernon Bailey (1931) writes that "in 1908 he was again over the Gila National Forest and Mogollon Mountain region and found the wolves still common." They were feeding on nothing but fresh meat of their own killing, for "stock was abundant, and they had no trouble in finding cattle of any age or condition they preferred, but they seemed to show little choice in their selection of beef. Cows, steers, or calves seemed to be killed indiscriminately as the wolves happened to come upon them when hungry. Cattle are killed throughout the year and seem to be preferred to deer, which are more nimble and not so easily caught. In the wolf droppings along the trails cattle hair was almost the only recognizable constituent, but occasionally some jack-rabbit fur could be detected."

On account of their constant depredations against stock, a determined warfare has been carried on in this region during recent years with the result that in 1937, Goldman writes that this form is now "nearly if not quite extinct." There is some evidence, however, that if the campaign of extermination is relaxed for a time, other wolves keep coming across the border from the adjacent parts of Mexico into southern New Mexico and Arizona, so that if in later years specimens are taken in the former range of the Mogollon Mountain wolf, they may be of some other race.

TEXAS GRAY WOLF; "LOAFER"; "LOBO"

CANIS LUPUS MONSTRABILIS Goldman

Canis lupus monstrabilis Goldman, Journ. Mamm., vol. 18, p. 42, Feb., 1937 ("10 miles south of Rankin, Upton County, Texas").

This is a slightly marked race averaging darker than the wolves to the north and with a more highly arched frontal region. Its range formerly included southern and western Texas and northeastern Mexico, but because of systematic persecution its numbers are at present greatly reduced.

Vernon Bailey's (1905) account of this wolf furnishes much valuable information. At that time they were abundant in and about the Davis and Guadalupe Mountains and over the Staked Plains and open country east of the Pecos River. He writes: "When opportunity offers, the 'loafer' not only kills sheep but often kills a large number, apparently for the pleasure of killing. His regular and most serious depredations, however, are on the scattered and unguarded cattle of the range. Two or three wolves usually hunt together and sometimes pull down a steer, but most of their meat is procured from yearlings or cows. Occasionally a colt is killed but not often. Where two or three wolves take up their residence on a ranch and kill one or more head of cattle almost every day, the ranchmen become so seriously alarmed that they frequently offer a reward of $50 or $100 apiece for scalps." Bounties have been tried, and in some cases several smaller ranches combine to offer a large reward in addition to that paid by the county, but the danger is that the hunters are tempted "to save the breeding females and dig out the young each year for the bounty, thus making their business not only profitable but permanent." A better method seems to be to employ professional hunters who are well paid by the month to keep down wolves or other noxious animals.

PLAINS WOLF; BUFFALO WOLF

CANIS LUPUS NUBILUS Say

Canis nubilus Say, Long's Exped. Rocky Mountains, vol. 1, p. 160, 1823 (Engineer Cantonment, near present town of Blair, Nebraska).

SYNONYM: *Canis variabilis* Wied, Reise in das Innere Nord-Amer., vol. 2, p. 95, 1841 (Fort Clark, near Stanton, Mercer County, North Dakota).

This was the wolf found on the Great Plains of the United States from the Dakotas, Nebraska, and Kansas west to the Rocky Mountains and eastward possibly to the western parts of Iowa and Missouri. Though not so pale as the races to the north, it was less dark than *C. l. lycaon* to the east. The skull was similar in size to that of the adjacent races *monstrabilis* and *youngi*, but the frontal region was more flattened than in the former, with wider rostrum.

In the middle of the last century and earlier these wolves were common on the Central Plains, following the herds of bison and picking off young or disabled individuals, but at the present time they are extinct over the greater part of the area once occupied. With the pushing of the railroads out across the country, the coming of settlers, and the development of stock grazing, the buffalo were reduced or exterminated and the wolves for a time devoted their attention to cattle, with the result that the ranchers and hunters pursued them relentlessly until now only a few remain in the remoter regions, where the roughness or barrenness of the country makes agriculture impracticable.

Vernon Bailey (1926) has gathered together many interesting notes on their former presence in the Dakotas, where in the days of the early explorers they were abundant. With the passing of the buffalo, however, they were poisoned and trapped in such numbers that they rapidly disappeared from their old haunts. They remained abundant up to the time of Wied (1833) and of Audubon (1843), but by 1870 J. A. Allen wrote that in Iowa "although rather common twenty years since, they are now scarce, especially in the more settled districts." Coues says that in 1873 they did not appear to be numerous in the Dakotas, while by 1887 they were practically gone from most of the country across North Dakota. Bailey states that in 1913 they were numerous enough to be troublesome in the Badlands along the Little Missouri, though rare elsewhere. A few were reported in 1916 west of Cannon Ball, and in 1922 one was killed near Fargo. At the time of writing, in 1926, Bailey believed there were still a few wolves left in the least-settled parts of the rough Badlands region west of the Missouri.

Dr. M. W. Lyon, Jr. (1936), records the former abundance of this wolf in Indiana. "About the middle of the last century they were practically exterminated although a few fairly authentic records date back as recently as 25 years ago," i. e., about 1911. The pioneer's method of hunting them in the Wabash Valley about 1830 was a sort of round-up, with lines of hunters converging on a central point. Often two to ten wolves would be taken in a day at these hunts, while the bounty provided an added stimulus for their destruction.

In Kentucky this type of wolf may once have existed, but Funkhauser (1925) believes it doubtful if at the present time any are to be found in the State. On the other hand, it is surprising that in Missouri it still occurs in some numbers. In their recent survey of the game and fur animals of that State, Bennitt and Nagel (1937) believe that on the basis of careful investigation lately made "the maximum density of wolves is about one per 10 square miles and the minimum about one per township (36 square miles)." They estimate the total wolf population of Missouri as in the neighborhood of 3,500 wolves, with the maximum concentration in the ten west-central counties south of the Missouri River (a portion may be *C. rufus gregoryi*). The State paid bounties on 249 wolves between July 1, 1923, and July 1, 1925, but it is likely that a good part of these were for large feral dogs of which there are many, perhaps exceeding the wolf population. Wolves and coyotes probably furnish a most effective check on the undue increase of woodchucks and ground squirrels, but the part played by each is uncertain. Wolves also kill some deer. With the diminution of good wolf cover in recent years, there has probably been a concentration of the animals proportionately where cover is good, and it is even believed that their numbers have shown an actual increase in later times. If they become really numerous, these authors observe, they must be controlled, but under usual wild conditions they are a natural element of the fauna and their presence may even have a beneficial effect on the species that they prey upon in improving the quality of the race through their elimination of the less able animals.

Farther west, the Plains wolf is apparently quite gone from Kansas (Hibbard, 1933), though it was common in that State in the sixties or later, and the same is probably true for Nebraska where they remained in some numbers till about 1890. In Montana, Bailey (1918) writing of the fauna of Glacier National Park, says: "Along the eastern edge of the park, in the open country, are still found the large, light-colored plains wolves . . . and a few occasionally range up through the valleys and over the high parts of the mountains . . . Along the trails in the Belly River valley in August, 1917, I saw wolf signs that were not very old. The wolves had evidently been down in the cattle country as the sign was composed mostly of cattle hair. Don Stevenson reports them in the country about Chief Mountain for the past 20 years, where they have ranged up and down the edge of the Plains killing cattle and some horses, and in 1914 he saw their tracks on St. Mary Ridge at the park line. There are said to be some in the North Fork valley, where it is probable they are attracted by the abundance of deer, as they are on the eastern border by the abundance of stock. In 1895 they seemed to be no more common than at the present time, as I saw then only a few tracks on the prairie below St. Mary Lake, and some fine skins among the Indians on the Blackfeet Reservation. As the valleys settle up, more vigorous hunting and trapping is likely to crowd the wolves back into the park at any time and make them more numerous than they are at present. If so, their destruction of game will be correspondingly increased . . .

If unmolested they seem to prefer the domestic stock where it is abundant and easily accessible." With the demands of the cattle interests for their destruction, their only possibility of long surviving is in large preserved areas such as the national parks.

NORTHERN PLAINS WOLF

CANIS LUPUS OCCIDENTALIS Richardson

Canis lupus occidentalis Richardson, Fauna Boreali-Americana, vol. 1, p. 60, 1829
  (Simpson, near mouth of Liard River, Mackenzie).
SYNONYM: Canis lupus griseus Sabine, Franklin's Narr. Journ. Polar Sea, p. 654, 1823
  (Cumberland House, Keewatin, Canada).

This is the wolf of the northern interior plains east of the Rocky Mountains and north of the United States, northward to the Arctic tundra. It is still paler than the Plains wolf, C. l. nubilus, and larger.

Writing of the Athabaska-Mackenzie region in 1908, Preble says: "Gray or Timber wolves are found throughout the wooded parts of the region, and are fairly abundant and apparently increasing in some sections. In 1901 we saw numerous skins at nearly all the posts visited, and found a skull at a trapper's cabin on Slave River, 10 miles below the mouth of the Peace. Among a number of skins seen at Fort Rae, most of which were in the normal or gray phase, was one the color of which was mainly dark bluish gray, the throat and back were nearly black, the latter flecked with a few white hairs; the chest had a white patch; the belly and tail were bluish gray, the latter blackish toward the tip.

"During the season of 1903 we heard that wolves had been rather abundant for several years past in the region west of Smith Landing, in the Birch Mountains, and in the vicinity of Athabasca Landing." In the same winter a black one was killed at Fort Simpson. Tyrrell says that this wolf occurs in the country between Athabaska Lake and Churchill River, but not plentifully. Preble quotes the record of skins of this wolf received by the Hudson's Bay Company as follows: From 1858 to 1884, from the Athabaska district, 2,119; from 1885 to 1889, a further 339 skins. For the district of Mackenzie, between 1863 and 1884, a total of 1,880 skins; in 1889 only 49 skins; Fort Resolution and Great Slave Lake, between 1862

and 1887, 193 skins. Dr. Francis Harper (1932) traversing
this region in 1914 noted seeing a number of skins and other
evidences of wolves. No doubt they will continue in the general
region in slowly decreasing numbers for a long time, though
annually trapped and poisoned.

GREENLAND WOLF

CANIS LUPUS ORION Pocock

Canis lupus orion Pocock, Proc. Zool. Soc. London, 1935, p. 683, Sept. 12 ("Cape
    York, on Baffin Bay, Greenland").
FIGS.: Manniche, 1910, figs. 18, 19 (animal), fig. 20 (skull); Jensen, 1928, p. 322, fig. 2
    (mounted specimen).

The Greenland wolf is described as of "a uniform whitish
grey, except for the tolerably extensive marbling and streaking
of the black-tipped contour hairs of the upper side, but the
ears are pale buff, turning to drab towards the point; the top
of the head as far as the angle of the eye, and of the muzzle,
apart from its white tip, is very pale brownish grey . . .
the tail has a black tip, but the rest of its upper side is not so
conspicuously black and white as the back." The skull is said
to be small and with smaller teeth than those of the races arctos
of Ellesmere Land or tundrarum of the Arctic coast of Canada.
"In the fore feet, the digital pads are greatly reduced in size
and there is no trace of the pollical or carpal pads."

Professor Jensen (1928) states that this wolf "has at the
present time the same distribution as the musk-ox, in that it
occurs on the north coast and the northern part of the east
coast, as far as the region round Scoresby Sound . . .
Even in the regions where the wolf now occurs, it is by no
means frequent; it is only found scattered and is comparatively
rarely seen. Before 1899, when Nathorst, on his expedition to
northern East Greenland, observed several polar wolves, this
animal had not been seen in those parts, although they had
been visited by various travellers; this caused Nathorst to set
forth the view that the wolf had only quite recently immigrated
to the east coast from the north." The caribou or reindeer on
which these wolves must have preyed are now gone from the
east coast, but the muskox still remains in small numbers, and
presumably furnishes a major part of the wolf's sustenance.
Manniche (1910) could find no evidence that the Arctic hare

or the fox formed any part of the prey. In his account of the mammals observed by the Denmark Expedition to East Greenland, during which the ship of the expedition wintered near Hvalrossodden, he states that the party found evidence of wolves between latitudes 75° and 83° 10′ N. He believes that they have been derived from the North American regions by way of northern Greenland. At all events they are few in number and, curiously, seemed very wary, though one would have expected the contrary from their very slight contact with man. In the last of August, 1906, he saw a large white wolf and at length succeeded in shooting it by lying in ambush wrapped in the skin of a muskox he had killed, the meat of which served as bait. This female was in excellent condition, "almost fat," and weighed 35 kilograms. Its total length was about 1500 mm.; tail, 420; ear, 100 long by 100 wide. Two others were seen and tracks were found among the mountains inland from Hvalrossodden and slightly to the west and north. During the winter of 1906–7, while the expedition was frozen in near this place, a group of three Arctic wolves came about the ship from time to time, but were very wary, and in the dim polar night offered no good chance for a shot. Several sledge dogs were once set upon them, but they were driven back by the wolves, which eventually succeeded in killing four of their animals and wounding others. If a sledge journey were made to the meteorological station or elsewhere in the neighborhood one or more of the wolves would follow at a distance, but eventually they became bolder, so that by the end of the winter all three had been shot or trapped. Of these the largest was a male weighing 29 kilograms, very thin and emaciated.

It thus appears that the Greenland wolf at the present time is confined to the narrow strip of country between the inland ice and the sea from northern Greenland to about the region of Scoresby Sound, following the muskox. That in former times it ranged much farther south can hardly be doubted, and it probably followed the caribou now largely extinct in Greenland. It seems probable that the wolf, like the lemming and the muskox, spread across northern Greenland and down the east coast rather than the west coast, on account of the great ice barriers in the region of Inglefield Gulf. The wolf seems to have been gone from southern and western Greenland long ago, though mentioned by early historians. Even Egede's "Description of Greenland" in 1745 mentions them as a thing of the past. Hence it was a notable circumstance that in the winter of 1868–69 one was killed near Unamak and is now mounted in the Museum at Copenhagen. It was one of a pair seen together, but where they could have come from is difficult to tell. At the present time the wolf population of northeastern Greenland must be limited, and whether there is occasional immigration from Ellesmere Land over the ice is also uncertain. The slight basis on which *orion* was described makes necessary a further comparison between wolves of the two areas when a sufficient number of skulls can be assembled.

ALASKAN WOLF; "AUTOCRAT TIMBER WOLF"

CANIS LUPUS PAMBASILEUS Elliot

Canis pambasileus Elliot, Proc. Biol. Soc. Washington, vol. 18, p. 79, Feb. 21, 1905 ("Sushitna River, region of Mt. McKinley, Alaska").

Skull and teeth larger than in the neighboring races; "ridge of sagittal and occipital crest nearly on a level with frontal and with only a very slight descent at occiput and very deep at that point; maxillae very broad . . . premaxillae extending considerably over one-half the length of the nasals . . . Color from nearly uniform black to white and black in various mixtures." The total length of the type skull is 263 mm.; length of carnassial tooth, 27.

Elliot describes these wolves from the upper waters of the Sushitna River in the region of Mount McKinley as "remarkable for their large size and black color." He believes their skull characters are distinctive, and Goldman in his paper of 1937 lists this as a valid race, without attempting to define its range. Evidently, however, it is larger than the race *ligoni* of the Alexander Archipelago and somewhere intergrades to the south with the northern Plains wolf, *C. l. occidentalis*. Its very dark color is in contrast with the usual paleness of the latter.

The late Charles Sheldon (1930) has left a vivid account of his hunting experiences during a year spent in the "Wilderness of Denali" (the Indian name for Mount McKinley). He saw little of these wolves, though on nine occasions he found in the snow the tracks of wolves that had attempted to catch mountain sheep by dashing upon them from above from a distance of a hundred yards cr so. In each case the wolf was unsuccess-

ful; nevertheless this danger to the sheep caused them to be
very wary and to keep to the high ridges. The wolves seemed
to find the caribou at lower levels a more dependable source of
food. Just to the north of Mount McKinley, Sheldon found
wolves along the upper Toklat River very abundant, always
hovering about the feeding herds of caribou and following them
as they roamed, usually in a fairly well-defined circuit. Late
in September the caribou frequent ridges more than the low
country and would be fairly conspicuous to a wolf. He remarks also on the innate caution of the wolf, which, though
rarely pursued in this region, is so wary that he never saw or
trapped one. Living as they do, in McKinley National Park,
it seems likely that the wolves of this area will continue for a
long time to harry the caribou of the outer ranges and less
often penetrate the upper slopes for sheep.

BARREN-GROUND WOLF

CANIS LUPUS TUNDRARUM Miller

Canis tundrarum Miller, Smithsonian Misc. Coll., vol. 59, no. 15, p. 1, June 8, 1912
("Point Barrow, Alaska").

SYNONYM: *Canis lupus albus* Sabine, Franklin's Narr. Journ. Polar Sea, p. 655, 1823
(Fort Enterprise, Mackenzie, Canada). (Not *Canis lupus albus* Kerr, from
Siberia.)

The tundra wolf has a narrower palate and slender rostrum
in comparison with the Plains wolves and the northern timber
wolves. It is decidedly larger than the eastern timber wolf
and in color is "said to be frequently white or whitish." It is
the form found in the barren-grounds of the Arctic coast region
from near Point Barrow eastward toward Hudson Bay, and
perhaps too in the Arctic Archipelago north of those shores.

Little recent information concerning this wolf is at hand.
In the middle of the last century and earlier, explorers found
them in some numbers about the Isthmus of Boothia, and
Back's expedition saw white wolves near Artillery Lake.
Preble (1908) has summarized some of these later observations
as follows: "Armstrong states that a wolf was seen near Princess Royal Islands in February, 1851; and that many were seen
at Mercy Bay, Banks Land, during the winter of 1851–52.
McDougall states that a pack of wolves was seen on Melville
Island near Cape Russell in June, 1853; one was seen on May
27, 1854, near Cape Hotham, Cornwallis Island; McClintock

reports that wolves were observed in October, 1858, at Port Kennedy, and in May, 1859, by Lieutenant Hobson on King William Land. Kennedy records one seen in the central part of Prince of Wales Land in April, 1852. While in the Barren Grounds to the northeast of Fort Rae in the early spring of 1894, Russell found wolves rather common. Of a band of six, two were snow white, the others a light gray. During his exploring trip between Great Slave Lake and Hudson Bay in 1900, J. W. Tyrrell found large wolves on the east side of Artillery Lake. J. M. Bell informs me that during the same season he occasionally saw wolves near . . . the eastern end of Great Bear Lake. Hanbury, while traveling overland between Baker Lake and the Arctic coast in the early spring of 1902, noted an occasional wolf. On April 30, when the party was near latitude 67° between Lake Garry and Ogden Bay, Darrell, his companion, encountered a band of 16 large wolves. Darrell writes me that of this band 13 were of the ordinary dirty white color, 2 were nearly black, and 1 pied. He states that though these wolves live largely on caribou they are not very successful in killing these animals unless they can separate one from the herd, and that they always seem to be starving . . . The band of 16 was the largest pack seen, the animals usually being found singly or in pairs, though occasionally half a dozen were observed together."

It seems clear that this race of wolf is nowhere very common but is found in small companies or more often singly or in pairs scattered over a large area and is not likely to become exterminated for a long time. How great an area the animals may cover in their search for food may not be possible to find out, but it must be considerable, extending as it does to the Arctic Archipelago. With the accumulation of specimens in later years, a critical comparison is needed to demonstrate the validity of the Ellesmere Land and Greenland races in comparison with that of this area.

SOUTHERN ROCKY MOUNTAIN WOLF

CANIS LUPUS YOUNGI Goldman

Canis lupus youngi Goldman, Journ. Mamm., vol. 18, p. 40, Feb., 1937 ("Harts Draw, north slope of Blue Mountains, 20 miles northwest of Monticello, San Juan County, Utah").

FIGS.: Grinnell, Dixon, and Lindsale, 1937, vol. 2, figs. 208–214 (as *C. l. nubilus*).

The wolf of the southern Rocky Mountain region is described as a rather light-colored race of medium size, resembling the Plains wolf, *C. l. nubilus*, but larger, its upper side more blackish and suffused with buff and its frontal region rising less steeply. It is larger and paler than *C. l. baileyi* of Chihuahua, with a broader, less depressed rostrum.

This wolf takes the place of *C. l. nubilus*, the Plains wolf, west of the prairie region of Nebraska and Kansas and was formerly found over "southeastern Idaho, southwestern Wyoming, northeastern Nevada, Utah, western and central Colorado, northwestern Arizona (north of Grand Canyon), and northwestern New Mexico." Over most of this range it has been exterminated within recent decades by persecution of hunters and of ranchers with whose cattle interests it interfered. Bailey (1931) writes that through such efforts wolves were practically eliminated from New Mexico by 1927. Goldman (1937) states that at the present time it is mainly restricted to northwestern Colorado. Warren (1910), in his account of the mammals of the latter State, tells of one wolf, whose track was identifiable through its having lost two toes in a trap, that became so bold that special measures had to be taken for its destruction. Its tracks with those of others were in a short period found about the carcasses of 75 head of cattle and horses. He quotes the figures of wolves killed in 1907 (from U. S. Biological Survey Circular no. 63) as follows: In Colorado, 69; in Wyoming, 1,009; in Idaho, 14. In 1910, Warren believed there was not a county in the State of Colorado that did not harbor some wolves. Cary (1911) wrote at about the same time that wolves were still found in considerable numbers in North Park and in Routt and Rio Blanco Counties, where they kill a great many range cattle, and they were similarly destructive in Baca and eastern Las Animas Counties, in spite of much trapping. Cary was told by professional trappers that so persistently have wolves been hunted, trapped, and poisoned that they would rarely come to a scent of any kind and seldom to a baited trap, while poisoning was no longer successful. Traps set blind in trails or near water holes were most successful. In the Lily Park region on the lower Bear River wolves were numerous until 1902, but in the two years following a trapper killed 61, which nearly put a stop to their local depredations. By 1907 they had become uncommon over most of southern

Colorado. Such constant persecution is gradually reducing the wolf population in all this region. Whether this form of wolf originally occurred in the extreme eastern parts of California may never be known. Grinnell, Dixon, and Linsdale (1937) report the wolf as having been practically exterminated from California for many years. No specimen of wolf from the State had been preserved in any museum up to 1922, while the two since taken on the eastern border these authors identify as "clearly of the plains wolf type" referring them to the race *nubilus*.

RED WOLF

CANIS RUFUS RUFUS Audubon and Bachman

Canis lupus var. *rufus* Audubon and Bachman, Quadrupeds of North America, vol. 2, p. 240, 1851 (Texas; fixed as 15 miles west of Austin).
FIG.: Audubon and Bachman, 1851, pl. 82.

FLORIDA WOLF

CANIS RUFUS FLORIDANUS Miller

Canis floridanus Miller, Proc. Biol. Soc. Washington, vol. 25, p. 95, May 4, 1912 ("Horse Landing, St. Johns River, Florida").
SYNONYMS: *Canis lycaon* β *americana* Hamilton Smith, Griffith's Cuvier, Anim. Kingdom, vol. 5, p. 144, 1827 (not *Canis alopex americanus* Kerr, 1795); *Canis ater* Richardson, Fauna Bor.-Amer., pp. 70–72, 1829 (in part).

MISSISSIPPI VALLEY WOLF

CANIS RUFUS GREGORYI Goldman

Canis rufus gregoryi Goldman, Journ. Mamm., vol. 18, p. 44, Feb., 1937 ("Macks Bayou, 3 miles east of Tensas River, 18 miles southwest of Tallulah, Madison County, Louisiana").
FIG.: Arthur, 1931, fig., p. 147 (photograph of captive animal).

In his review of the American wolves, Goldman (1937) states that the red wolf, *Canis rufus*, "usually regarded as a wolf . . . , exhibits a departure from the true wolves, and in cranial and dental characters approaches the coyotes." He therefore gives it full specific rank and relegates to it as subspecies the Florida black wolf and the wolf of the lower Mississippi Valley which he describes as *C. r. gregoryi*. This course may be tentatively accepted and the three treated together. The typical form of red wolf was slightly the smallest of the three races and the most southwestern, with a range extending from central Texas southwestward to the Mexican tableland. In central Texas its range meets that of the Texas gray wolf, *Canis lupus monstrabilis*, "but the two are not closely allied." The latter has a much more massive and highly arched skull, its dentition is simpler, the upper carnassial with a smaller (often obsolete) anterointernal cusp, and the large upper molar with less prominent cusp development on the internal lobe; the posterior upper molars are relatively smaller than in *rufus*. The color is reddish mixed with gray.

Bailey, writing in 1905, believed that the ranges of the red and the gray wolves, though contiguous, did not overlap, but whether there is overlapping or intermingling future studies will perhaps show. As a result of special attempts to secure specimens of *C. rufus* from Texas, Bailey reported that at the time mentioned there were 14 skulls and 4 skins in the U. S. Biological Survey collection on the basis of which he outlined the range as "the whole of southern Texas north to the mouth of the Pecos and the mouth of the Colorado and still farther north along the strip of mesquite country east of the plains, approximately covering the semiarid part of the Lower Sonoran zone." He mentions a specimen from Matamoras, Mexico. In this area these wolves are destroyed by the ranchmen, since they kill young cattle, goats, and colts. The result is that at the present time this, the typical race, may now be extinct (Goldman).

In Audubon's day "wolves" were common in Kentucky and were usually black. They may or may not have represented a race of the red wolf, but in his paper of 1937 Goldman definitely names the wolf of the lower Mississippi region a race of it, *Canis rufus gregoryi*. He characterizes it as a "large but slender form of a small species . . . decidedly larger and grayer, less tawny" than *C. r. rufus*, with a more slender skull and lighter dentition than the Florida race. The middle and sides of the face are mixed black and gray, changing to black and cinnamon-buff on top of head; upper parts from nape to rump light buff, heavily mixed or overlain with black; outer surface of legs between cinnamon and cinnamon-buff, paling on the feet. Black individuals occasionally occur.

Of this race, Goldman has examined over 150 individuals from the lower part of the Mississippi Valley. He states that it is found mainly on the western side of the river in south-eastern Missouri, Arkansas, southeastern Oklahoma, eastern Texas, and Louisiana. It grades into the typical form in Texas and apparently into the eastern race *floridanus* in northern Alabama. Arthur (1931) publishes a photograph of a captive Louisiana individual which was black and shows the relatively long coyotelike ears. He says that it is found in the prairie and marsh sections of Louisiana, preying on rabbits, native rats and mice, squirrels, ground-nesting birds, and fawns, as well as on domestic calves, sheep, and hogs. The young are born in January and February and number from three to a dozen to a litter, averaging about half a dozen, so that the rate of increase may be fairly rapid. "While the wolf has been persistently hunted by man in Louisiana . . . it appears to be on the increase, and, slowly but surely, extending its range in the state . . . In La Salle parish . . . the wolves have become very obnoxious because of their depredations on live stock, and cattle men in West Feliciana parish now fear an increase of their number as the cattle and sheep raising business in this former cottonraising territory is growing in importance . . . It is not unlikely, therefore, that in a few years stringent and systematic campaigns against wolves in this state will have to be planned." Similar reports of increased numbers are credited by Dellinger and Black (1940), who write that "wolves are becoming rather common in the Ozarks" with records of several, including two black wolves, taken in late years in the northwestern and western part of Arkansas. Stanley P. Young (1940) finds that in eastern Texas the red wolf is abundant; more than 800 were caught during the previous year (1939) on account of livestock depredations. He believes that on account of its habit of living in thickets it will not easily be exterminated.

The Florida wolf is now regarded as a race of the red rather than of the gray wolf, from which it differs presumably in much the same characters as does *C. rufus gregoryi*, but it has apparently a much stouter skull and dentition. Black was the usual color, but no doubt a mixed phase also occurred. At the present time this wolf is probably extinct in Florida, as well as in southern Georgia, which formerly perhaps marked its northward range. Dr. Francis Harper (1927) has reviewed its status in the region of the Okefenokee Swamp, where the last one actually killed was about 1908, some 10 miles north of Fargo. Later accounts of what may very likely have been wolves in this region point to its survival there perhaps as late as 1918. In peninsular Florida, wolves were present in the Everglades, according to Cory (1896), up to the middle nineties. Miller in his original description of the race makes as the type a specimen obtained by the U. S. National Museum on the St. Johns River, August 12, 1890. This and a skull taken by Dr. Henry Bryant many years before, and now in the Museum of Comparative Zoology, seem to be the only extant specimens from the State. In Bradford County they were reported up to 1895 (V. Bailey, 1907).

A. H. Howell, writing in 1921, says that in former times wolves probably ranged over the entire State of Alabama, but are now on the verge of extinction. In Bartram's time, late in the eighteenth century, they were common, roaming the mountainous areas in small packs and preying considerably on the smaller domestic animals, sheep, goats, pigs, and sometimes calves. On the Gulf coast, "strangely enough, in the big swamp country in Baldwin and Mobile counties, where deer are still numerous, wolves were apparently exterminated many years ago; the last one of which there is record was reported killed near Carlton about 1894." During the second decade of the present century wolves were still present in small numbers in northwestern Alabama in the "rough, hilly country stretching from Walker County northwestward to Colbert County." Here three or four were killed in 1912 near South Lowell, while in 1915 wolves were destructive to stock in western Cullman County, afterward moving westward into Winston and Marion Counties, killing "thousands of dollars' worth of sheep and goats" and some calves. In 1917, a wolf was killed in Colbert County and is described by Howell in some detail. It is the latest record mentioned by him. Goldman says of this specimen that it is somewhat intermediate between typical *floridanus* and *gregoryi*, but in its heavy dentition is nearer the former.

There is some evidence that this small type of wolf formerly ranged northward into Tennessee. Kellogg (1939) refers to the race *floridanus* a right mandible excavated from an Indian mound near Citico Creek, Hamilton County, and thinks it quite likely that this form ranged over southeastern Tennessee at the time of the first white traders. Possibly, too, the form *gregoryi* was the wolf formerly found in the extreme western part of the State. At all events, he quotes Benjamin C. Miles that the small black wolf was exterminated about 1870 in Haywood and Lauderdale Counties, while Major Shaw is authority for the statement that it had been replaced in later times by the larger and fiercer gray wolf.

Family FELIDAE: Cats

The Pumas

The pumas, or mountain lions, are typically American and constitute a single species having a wide latitudinal range from the northern United States and southern Canada southward in forested country to Patagonia. In South America they are spoken of by people of Spanish descent as "león" in contradistinction to the "tigre," or jaguar. Other names are "puma," used in Perú, and "couguar," said to be a corruption of a Tupi word signifying an animal of the same color as a deer. For pumas are associated with deer, on several species of which they prey in different parts of their vast range. In disposition, these cats are not especially fierce in spite of many tales told by frightened persons, and very seldom indeed do they attack human beings. In South America they are not feared, the jaguar being held in high respect. Slightly smaller than the latter, the pumas are characterized by a uniform coloration of tawny shades above, whitish lips and eye-stripes, and a black spot on each side of the muzzle. With a total length of about 8 feet for an adult male, and a weight ranging up to some 200 pounds, there is a wide local variation in size, shade of color, and in cranial details, which has led to the distinction by Nelson and Goldman (1929), the last to review the matter, of no less than 19 subspecies, of which 9 are South American, including the typical race of southern Brazil, and 10 are found in North and Central America. The tropical races tend to be smaller and brighter in color, becoming a distinct reddish in tone. The southernmost races are paler, the race *pearsoni* of Patagonia being a silvery gray. In the United States, at the more northerly part of their range, pumas may show two color phases, a redder and a grayish brown, sometimes spoken of as red and blue, corresponding to the color phases of deer, though not seasonal as in the latter.

While in South America there seems as yet little to indicate a widespread reduction in numbers of any of these races, except in the more settled regions, in North America pumas have been exterminated over most of their range in the eastern United States; in the West, where ranching interests are paramount, they are locally gone, and will doubtless ere many years become few and restricted to large areas of forest country or to national parks, where with proper measures their numbers can be kept under control. Nevertheless, in other areas a good many yet remain and probably will continue for a long time to come. The North American races are here considered in order.

EASTERN MOUNTAIN LION; "CATAMOUNT"; "PANTHER"

FELIS CONCOLOR COUGUAR Kerr

Felis couguar Kerr, Linnaeus's Anim. Kingdom, p. 151, 1792 ("Pennsylvania").
FIG.: Nelson, 1916, p. 413, upper fig. (colored).

Originally the range of the eastern mountain lion extended from central New England westward to the edge of the Plains and southward through the forested country to Georgia and northern Alabama, where presumably it merged with that of the Florida puma. Over this region it is at the present time probably extinct, with the possibility, however, that a very few may remain in the southern Alleghenies. Its range coincided more or less with that of the Virginia deer, which formed its main object of prey.

The eastern mountain lion is described as dark reddish brown, darker along the middle of the back, the tail similar, becoming blackish at the tip, and the feet dark also. The muzzle is whitish, with a black marking just back of the white and in advance of the eye; a small white line in front of the eye; under side paler, yellowish white. A grayer phase probably occurred as well. Length of body when full grown, about 6 feet, tail about 3 feet; weight about 175 pounds for a Vermont specimen. Smaller animals, perhaps females, measure less, about 7 feet over all, with a weight of 118 pounds (Vermont specimen).

The catamount, or panther, as these big cats were usually called in New England, was not especially common even in early days but was nevertheless evidently troublesome to the first white settlers on our shores, for bounties were offered and many were killed though with little record. At first they were thought to be young lions, and one is so reported by John Josselyn at Cape Ann in earlier times. As early as 1694 Connecticut offered a bounty of 20 shillings apiece for catamounts and as late as 1769 paid for four or five. Massachusetts first offered a reward of 40 shillings for killing these animals in 1742. In 1753 this was increased to £4. Probably by the time of the Revolution panthers were fairly well gone from the three southern States of New England. Wood, in his early account of New England, tells that "Plymouth men have traded for Lyons' skins in former times," but they seem to have been few in eastern Massachusetts and were early driven back. In the Boston *Gazette* of April 20, 1741, is a notice of a strange animal exhibited at the Greyhound Tavern in Roxbury that had been "caught in the woods about 80 miles to the westward," hence in western Massachusetts. "It has a tail like a Lyon, its legs are like Bears, its claws like an Eagle, its Eyes like a tyger." It was "called a Cattamount." Judd, in his "History of Hadley, Massachusetts," 1863, mentions that one was killed by some Northampton hunters in 1764, and others were said to have been shot in later years in Hampshire. Emmons in 1840 regarded the species as then extirpated in Massachusetts, yet one was killed in 1847 or 1848 in West Greenwich, R. I., was mounted and for many years was preserved in the museum of the Providence Franklin Society, and then was secured by the Boston Society of Natural History, in whose museum it still is. This seems to be the last record for the State. In Connecticut it disappeared at about the same time, for Linsley (1842), writing of the mammals of Connecticut a century ago, had no later record of it than of one he saw some years previously that had been killed in the northern part of the State. Panthers were occasional in the southern half of Maine during the early days of settlement but were practically gone by 1815, although what may have been the last one killed in the State was shot about 1845 at Sebago (Norton, 1930). From time to time there have been rumors of panthers in the wilder parts of Maine even down to the present day, but it seems safe to say that these reports deserve little credence. In southern New Hampshire panthers were occasionally killed, and there are

several accounts in local histories of such events in the latter
part of the eighteenth century, but the last one actually captured and still preserved seems to be the specimen now in the
possession of the Woodman Institute, Dover, N. H., which was
shot on November 1, 1853, in the town of Lee. I have one or
two later accounts of panthers seen at short range in the
White Mountains as lately as about 1880, the details of which
are so circumstantial that they seem quite credible. Vermont,
however, was the best country for these animals, and in the
days of settlement previous to the American Revolution they
were often hunted and killed. At the present time there are
extant perhaps three specimens, possibly four, that were killed
in the State. The last one was taken in the town of Barnard
in 1881 and is in the State Museum at Montpelier. Since then
there have been a few other reports, some of which seem
credible, but probably the species has ceased to exist in Vermont for nearly 50 years

The wilder parts of New York State were formerly good
country for panthers. In DeKay's time, a century ago, there
were still a few in the Catskills, and in his book of the mammals
of New York he mentions that as a boy he recalled the appearance of one in Westchester County within 25 miles of the city
of New York and was also informed of one that had been killed
in Warren County. Merriam has given an account of the
species in the Adirondacks in the latter part of the last century.
Here they were then present in some numbers, and when in
1871 a bounty was offered on them no less than 46 were reported killed in the succeeding decade, about half of them in
St. Lawrence County. Merriam (1882) comments that in
1882, owing to the incentive of the bounty, they had been
killed down to nearly the point of extermination, yet Miller
(1899) continues the bounty tabulation down to 1890, with an
additional 107 panthers on which $20 each had been paid.
Since the last date no further bounties were claimed up to
1897, when a panther, now mounted at Albany, was killed on
Sumner Stream. The last bounty was paid on one killed
December 27, 1899. Since that date, however, there were occasional reports of panthers from the Adirondacks, the last in
1903, said to have been seen at Big Moose, though it seems
safe to say that they were virtually extinct in the State by
about the close of the century.

To the westward there were formerly a few panthers in southern Ontario and to the northward they extended into extreme southern Quebec. But the Quebec records, according to Seton, were long ago: Sherbrooke, about 1840; and near Sorel, October 3, 1863; and there is one old record for the Toronto region of Ontario. Ohio never seems to have had many of these animals, or else they were early killed out. Kirtland, in the Ohio Geological Survey for 1838, wrote that they had already'disappeared but that there were Ohio specimens in the museum of a Mr. Dorfeuille at Cincinnati. The bounty of $4 for a grown panther killed in Ohio was discontinued in 1818. The last record for the State is perhaps of one killed in 1805 near Newark (Brayton, 1882). For Indiana, Lyon (1936) writes that they were gone from the southern part of the State at the time of the Prince of Wied's sojourn there in 1832–33 but that they persisted a little longer in the northern part. A few final records take the panther to about 1838, with additional vague reports up to about 1850, when Hahn believed it had become extinct in Indiana. Cory (1912) lists several later occurrences in Illinois: the last one killed in Macoupin County about 1840; one killed in Alexander County about 1862; one in Daviess County in 1840. In Wisconsin one was shot on the headwaters of Black River in December 1863, and one was killed in Vernon County, near Westly, about 1870. Possibly a few remained into the next decade. What is perhaps the only extant specimen from this State is one recorded by Schorger (1938) that was killed at Appleton, Wis., November 22, 1857, and is preserved at Lawrence College. The last record of panther in Minnesota is of one killed at Sunrise, Chisago County, in 1875 (Herrick).

According to Bailey (1926) this species must once have ranged over much of the Dakotas, but it is not mentioned by Alexander Henry and his trappers in the early years of the last century. After detailing a few records for western North Dakota up to the late years of the nineteenth century, Bailey mentions a report of a pair seen at Sullys Lake in 1907, and comments: "It is not improbable that a few may still lurk in the very rough Badlands country in the western part of the State, but it is more probable that the last record for the State has been made." He refers the Dakota panther to "*Felis hippolestes*," the type locality of which is Wyoming in the

Wind River Mountains, but it seems likely that those formerly believed to occur in the eastern parts of the Dakotas were of the race *couguar*.

Summarizing the former presence of the mountain lion in New Jersey and Pennsylvania, Rhoads (1903) says that though originally found in every part of both States it was always more plentiful in the Allegheny Mountains. As early as 1697, on account of its destructiveness to stock, a bounty was placed on this animal in New Jersey, amounting to 20 shillings for "whatsoever Christian shall kill and bring" in the head, or half that sum to a Negro or an Indian. In 1730, this bounty was reduced to 15 shillings, and evidently it had been effective, for the species seems to have been extirpated by about 1830 or 1840. In the wilder parts of Pennsylvania, however, the mountain lion persisted till much later. In Audubon and Bachman's time, about the middle of the last century, it was so common "among the mountains of the headwaters of the Juniata River . . . that one man has killed for some years from 2 to 5, and one very hard winter, 7." The latest date when one was killed in Pennsylvania was, according to Rhoads, about 1871, although later reports of two panthers killed in Treaster Valley take the date down to 1893, and may be trustworthy. Three subsequent reports of tracks and even an animal seen are as recent as 1913 (Shoemaker, 1914). It is not at all impossible that panthers may still survive in the wilder parts of the West Virginia and Tennessee Alleghenies. Kellogg (1937, 1939) has summarized the available information on this matter and finds that although numerous enough at the time of settlement to give the pioneers some trouble, their numbers had been much reduced by the middle of the last century. He cites statistics showing that in West Virginia 11 were killed in 1853, 14 in 1856, 11 in 1858, and 6 in 1859. The last record for Lewis County was in 1855, and there is a skeleton in the U. S. National Museum from Hampshire County, taken in 1850. Although no record of any having since been killed is given, Kellogg includes various reports of late date, such as "tracks of a panther in the snow on Black Mountain during the winter of 1935 and also in 1936"; but all such reports should be received with caution, even though made by persons who might be capable of correctly identifying the species. Shoemaker (1914), however, states that one was killed in November, 1913, several miles north of Washington, D. C. The panther records assembled for Tennessee relate mostly to earlier days, with some evidence that they persisted up till about 1875, or slightly after. Merriam, who traveled through the Great Smoky Mountains in 1888, concluded as a result of his inquiries that it was at that time unknown to the local inhabitants. Nevertheless, Kellogg accepts a report of one said to have been killed in 1929 in the Holston Mountains, Johnson County, and another of one "seen crossing the trail on Roan Mountain on September 18, 1937," without adducing further evidence. C. S. Brimley (1905) records that the last authentic report for North Carolina is of one killed near Rose Bay, Hyde County, some years before the Civil War. Probably the range extended slightly farther south into the northern parts of Georgia and Alabama and then merged with that of the lowland Florida race. Howell (1921) writes that in the latter State (Alabama), although it is now "nearly, if not quite, exterminated . . . recent reports, although rather indefinite, indicate that a very few may still remain in the big swamps of the southern counties." If these reports may be credited, it is likely that they refer to the Florida form, and Dr. Francis Harper regards the animal of southern Georgia as the same, giving records of its presence up till at least the early years of the present century.

From the foregoing brief survey, it is clear that the eastern panther, though fairly common for so large a beast of prey, was exterminated from the more settled parts along the Atlantic coast in the colonial days, while in the wilder and more mountainous regions, as in Vermont and New Hampshire, the Adirondacks, and the Alleghenies, it persisted in some numbers till about the middle of the last century, after which the last surviving scattered individuals were gradually shot or trapped until they were exterminated, or practically so, by the last years of the nineteenth century. Later reports, though in some cases perhaps credible, must nevertheless be received with skepticism for, as shown by Cory in his (1912) account of the animal, even a trained eye and a person familiar with the appearance of the animal may sometimes be deceived. The testimony of those who report "tracks" requires careful substantiation, since few hunters or trappers in the East have ever had opportunity to examine these, much less to recognize the animal in the wild.

FLORIDA COUGAR

FELIS CONCOLOR CORYI Bangs

Felis coryi Bangs, Proc. Biol. Soc. Washington, vol. 13, p. 15, Jan. 31, 1899 ("Wilderness back of Sebastian, Brevard County, Florida").

SYNONYMS: *Felis concolor floridana* Cory, Hunting and Fishing in Florida, p. 109, 1896 (not *Felis floridana* Desmarest, 1820); *Felis arundivaga* Hollister, Proc. Biol. Soc. Washington, vol. 24, p. 176, June 16, 1911 ("12 miles south of Vidalia, Concordia Parish, Louisiana").

The puma of the Florida Peninsula and the adjacent parts of southern Georgia, Alabama, and Louisiana is a brighter-colored animal and smaller than the eastern puma, of a "rich ferruginous or intense rusty red" above, with smaller feet. Hollister, in describing the Louisiana puma as distinct, separated it partly on the basis of its color, which is a "grayish fawn . . . with a decided cast of ecru drab," especially on flanks and legs. Since, however, Nelson and Goldman (1929) have relegated this name to the synonymy of the Florida puma, it seems evident that his description applies to the grayer color phase of the same animal. Hollister describes the skull as "much larger than the skulls of *F. couguar*, with well developed crest and much larger nasals" and ear bullae. The condylobasal length of the skull in an adult male described by this author was 193.5 mm.; greatest length of nasals, 63.

The Florida puma, though fairly common in many parts of Florida and the adjacent States at the end of the last century, has apparently become much reduced in numbers of late years. Cory (1896), in his book "Hunting and Fishing in Florida," has much to say of his experiences with this animal. He speaks of it as "still not uncommon in the more unsettled portions of the State" on both the east and the west coasts. He himself had found tracks of seven in one week within 30 miles of Lake Worth in southern Florida and mentions that one John Davis had killed six in that region in the season of 1895. The Indians reported to him that they were also "numerous" in the vicinity of the Big Cypress south of Fort Myers on the western side of the peninsula. Farther north they were even then less common and were "scarce" on the peninsula east of the Indian River, "but were common there a few years ago." He recounts that in the eighties a hunter named Quarterman killed several in the vicinity of Canaveral, once making a double shot at two old males that he discovered fighting. Outram Bangs, in 1898, secured several through a hunter who obtained them in the wilderness back of Sebastian and in his paper on Florida mammals writes (1898) that though the exact range could not then be given, "the puma is extinct in all the region directly northeast of Florida, and I believe in northern Florida as well." At the present time there are still a number of pumas in the Everglades, where they live largely on deer, but probably they have been extirpated from most other parts of the State.

Dr. Francis Harper (1927) has gathered a mass of notes as to the presence of the puma in the region of the Okefenokee Swamp in southern Georgia and refers the animal to this form. Here he says "it is now very nearly if not entirely extinct. Yet it lingered well into the present century, and it is perhaps not beyond the bounds of possibility that some solitary survivor may yet be taken." At all events, he records one killed about 1883 and one seen alive about 1903. Older residents of the region supplied other instances of animals killed about 1885. Most of the later reports are of tracks seen or other signs, with a final record of one said to have been killed about 1925 on the southern edge of the Swamp. The residents in that region universally speak of it as the "Tiger." Hunting is usually done in Florida with dogs. When started, the puma usually runs a short distance and then takes to a tree. The dogs keep it at bay until the hunters come up and shoot it.

While probably now quite gone from northern Florida and Georgia, this race doubtless still occurs in parts of southern Alabama and the canebrakes of Louisiana. Writing of the former State, Howell (1921) speaks of it as now "nearly, if not quite, exterminated"; recent reports, however, "although rather indefinite, indicate that a very few may still remain in the big swamps of the southern counties." Tracks were seen near Seale about 1912 by an old trapper, and another was reported as actually seen about 1905 in Baldwin County, but these are rather questionable bits of evidence. In 1911 Hollister wrote that pumas "are still fairly common in the wilder parts of the cane brake region of eastern Louisiana," and he himself while hunting in the Bear Lake Cane in February, 1904, several times heard panthers "crying."

Panthers formerly were found in somewhat similar country in Arkansas, and True (1889) reports a few killed or seen up to the late eighties, but it is not certain that they were of this race.

At the present time what few may remain are probably to be found in the Florida Everglades and in southern Louisiana.

TEXAS COUGAR

FELIS CONCOLOR STANLEYANA Goldman

Felis concolor stanleyana Goldman, Proc. Biol. Soc. Washington, vol. 51, p. 633, Mar. 18, 1938 ("Bruni Ranch, near Bruni, southeastern Webb County, Texas").

SYNONYM: *Felis concolor youngi* Goldman, Proc. Biol. Soc. Washington, vol. 49, p. 137, Aug. 22, 1936. (Preoccupied by *Felis youngi* Pei, for a fossil Chinese species.)

Goldman has lately distinguished the cougar of southern and central Texas and northeastern Mexico as larger than *azteca*, with lighter upper parts of a more grayish tint, black on tail usually more restricted, the dentition heavier, the nasals depressed. It is smaller and paler than *hippolestes* to the north. Total length of the type, 2,134 mm.; greatest length of skull, 220 mm. A series of specimens examined by Goldman represents 16 localities in Texas, and there were also two from Matamoros, Tamaulipas, across the border in northeastern Mexico. On the east it presumably intergrades with the race *coryi* of Louisiana and Florida. Its general status may be considered together with that of its near ally:

MEXICAN COUGAR

FELIS CONCOLOR AZTECA Merriam

Felis hippolestes aztecus Merriam, Proc. Washington Acad. Sci., vol. 3, p. 592, Dec. 11, 1901 ("Colonia Garcia, Chihuahua, Mexico").

The characters claimed for this cougar are its large size, though slightly smaller than the Montana *hippolestes*, "general color dull fulvous [as in the latter] . . . but tail darker, browner, with longer black tip and no white underneath"; ears almost wholly black. The skull is large and massive, though not equalling that of *hippolestes*, but shorter and the teeth somewhat smaller. The total length of an adult male, the type, was 2,268 mm.; tail vertebrae, 731; basal length of skull, 171.5. It is thus a somewhat larger, duller animal than *browni*.

The range of this race is believed to extend from the southern border of the United States in Arizona and New Mexico, south into Mexico for an undetermined distance, but probably over the tableland in at least the northern half. Of its present status in Mexico and Arizona, little information is at hand.

Bailey, writing in 1905, says: "In most of eastern Texas panthers are reported as formerly common, but now as very rare or entirely extinct. Individuals have been killed, however, within a few years in the swamps not far from Jefferson in the northeastern part and Sour Lake in the southeastern part of the State. At Tarkington Prairie Mr. A. W. Carter says there were a few panthers when he was a boy in 1860, but he has not seen one since. In the Big Thicket of Hardin County a few panthers have been killed in past years, and Dan Griffin, who lives 7 miles northeast of Sour Lake, says a very large one occasionally passes his place. He saw its tracks in the winter of 1903–4 . . . In the rough and sparsely settled western part of the State mountain lions are still fairly common in certain sections, where they often lay a heavy tribute on colts, calves, and sheep." In the region about Langtry they were reported as common a few years previously, but in 1903 were become already scarce; and there were a few at that time in the Franklin Mountains, where they annually killed numbers of colts. "In the Davis Mountains these cougars have been hunted with hounds till scarce, but in the Santiago Range, in the Chisos Mountains, and along the canyons of the Rio Grande and Pecos they" were still common in 1905 (Bailey). Even at the present day a few cougars still trouble the cattle ranchers in this region, but are constantly being hunted down. Of their future prospects, Bailey writes: "The rough desert ranges, full of canyons, cliffs, and caves, are the favorite haunts of the panthers, and will be their last strongholds, not only because of the advantages they offer for foraging but because of the protection they afford from hounds and hunters." In extreme southern Texas they were, according to Attwater in 1896, "not as scarce as the Jaguar in the country west of San Antonio, but they are fast becoming killed out" (J. A. Allen, 1896). He knew of but two records in recent times that he considered trustworthy; these, in Bexar and Kerr Counties, respectively, were sight records made in 1893 and 1894.

Mountain lions probably referable to the race *azteca* "are or have been common over practically all of New Mexico, but they are rapidly decreasing in numbers and in 1931, writes Bailey, "are rare or absent from most of the open plains country, but are still found in many of the rough or timbered mountain ranges, which afford them cover and game." In a report for 1917, J. S. Ligon had killed during the year 84 and estimates that there were still about 400 left alive in New Mexico. "At the present time they are probably most common in the Mogollon Mountain region, and in the Animas, San Luis, and Sacramento Mountain Ranges, with a few scattered through some of the small desert ranges over the southern and western parts of the State." The continual hunting down of these animals by ranchers and by government-paid hunters can not fail within a few years more to reduce their numbers to very small proportions. Bailey (1931) quotes the following figures for panthers killed by hunters in government employ in New Mexico: In 1917, 17; in 1918, 14; in 1919, 41; in 1920, 63; and in 1921, 29, a total of 164 in five years. With such a determined campaign waged against them, it seems likely that the species will soon be largely wiped out over much of the State. When one locality is rid of them, they may come in from surrounding territory, for they are great travelers. Bailey mentions a case where a hunter followed a track for two days and estimated that the animal had covered 30 miles without making a kill or stopping for any length of time. They may have as many as six young at a litter but usually four or even two; the gestation period was 96 days in the case of a captive individual (J. A. Allen, 1896). Hence animals killed in early or mid winter have probably not yet bred, but with females shot late in winter the potential increase is likewise destroyed.

YUMA MOUNTAIN LION; COLORADO DESERT PUMA

FELIS CONCOLOR BROWNI Merriam

Felis aztecus browni Merriam, Proc. Biol. Soc. Washington, vol. 16, p. 73, May 29, 1903 ("Lower Colorado River 12 miles south of Yuma, Arizona").

Very little is known concerning this puma. Grinnell, Dixon, and Linsdale (1937) describe it as "closely similar to the California Mountain Lion but with shorter pelage, paler tone of coloration, and smaller skull and teeth." Merriam (*loc. cit.*) in describing the original specimen emphasized similar characters in comparison with the more eastern race, *azteca*, calling attention further to the smaller and lower audital bullae, small canines and carnassials. Merriam suggested that the slender canines indicated that the animal fed upon smaller game than do the larger neighboring races. The type specimen was said to have measured in the flesh 7 feet 4 inches from tip of nose to tip of tail, of which the latter was 28.5 inches. It weighed 170 pounds (perhaps an estimate). Greatest length of skull, 198 mm.

This small race of the puma was probably confined to the desert regions of the lower Colorado River in southeastern California and the adjacent parts of Arizona, where, according to the authors above quoted, it "is now rare, perhaps even near to extinction." They add that in the "spring of 1910, while exploring the Colorado River from Needles to Yuma," they obtained evidence, both direct and through report, of the presence of mountain lions about Riverside Mountain in the extreme northeastern part of Riverside County, California. The animals here "appeared to range chiefly through the densely wooded bottom lands, though one was reliably reported to have been seen among the rough desert hills which constitute 'Riverside Mountain'." They saw a fresh track on May 1, 1910, four miles below Potholes, on the California side of the River, and had further reports from Ehrenberg, Cibola, and Potholes; and secured two hides and skulls from a rancher 18 miles north of Picacho who had shot the animals the previous autumn. These pumas had appeared in the region where none had been seen for ten years, and one by one killed off eight of the rancher's hogs. Finally one was hunted down and shot. "Meanwhile the hogs had become thoroughly frightened and had taken to swimming the river twice daily to forage for mesquite beans on the Arizona side, where they appeared to feel safer." A second lion continued the depredations and was eventually shot. Inquiry of the rancher 12 years later brought out the fact that he had seen no more pumas since that event. In 1909, a pair of mountain lions appeared near Calexico and were occasionally seen by the ditch tender swimming the main Imperial Canal at that point. These lions lived on pigs that had gone wild. Since 1910 no information is available from California as to the status of this race, and it is doubtful if it still exists.

Outside of the immediate delta region of the Colorado, it is likely that this subspecies was found in northern Lower California. Nelson (1921) includes it without comment in his lists of the fauna of the region. Probably it was closely similar to the race *improcera* of the central and southern parts of the peninsula. How far it may have ranged into the adjacent part of Sonora is also unknown, but it may have already become nearly extirpated.

LOWER CALIFORNIA PUMA

FELIS CONCOLOR IMPROCERA Phillips

Felis improcera Phillips, Proc. Biol. Soc. Washington, vol. 25, p. 85, May 4, 1912 ("Calmalli, Lower California").
FIG.: Phillips, 1912, pl. 5 (skull).

Little seems to be known of this puma. The adult male upon which the subspecies was founded is small, with a skull of only 150 mm. in basal length, and of a rounder, less elongate form than in neighboring races. The color is "dark fawn," darker along the back, the general hue less reddish than in *F. c. azteca.*

This small puma is believed to be characteristic of central and southern Lower California. Calmalli, the type locality, lies in the Vizcaino Desert district, which occupies the middle third of the peninsula and includes the great lava plateau, with scattered mountains, low ridges, and groups of granite mountains. Two remarkable plants are largely characteristic of this region, the "cirio," which forms polelike forests, and the "elephantwood," with fantastic massive trunks and small branches. There is abundance also of giant and other cactuses. In this arid region of the Lower Sonoran desert and in the Arid Tropical area of southern Lower California, this little puma is found. Practically nothing is recorded of it. Dr. Phillips believed it "probably a rare animal throughout the entire length of the peninsula," for he adds that he is informed by W. W. Brown, Jr., that it occurs "even south to the vicinity of Cape St. Lucas." On account of its restricted habitat and the barren country in which it lives, its numbers can not be large and are not likely to increase. Unless changes come in this habitat, it is likely to remain as it is except as it comes in contact with the scattered ranches and interferes with stock raising. At the present time there is no evidence at hand.

ROCKY MOUNTAIN PANTHER OR COUGAR

FELIS CONCOLOR HIPPOLESTES Merriam

Felis hippolestes Merriam, Proc. Biol. Soc. Washington, vol. 11, p. 219, July 15, 1897 ("Wind River Mountains, Wyoming").

OREGON COUGAR

FELIS CONCOLOR OREGONENSIS Rafinesque

Felix (sic) *oregonensis* Rafinesque, Atlantic Journ., vol. 1, p. 62, 1832 (Northwest coast of United States).
SYNONYM: *Felis hippolestes olympus* Merriam, Proc. Biol. Soc. Washington, vol. 11, p. 220, July 15, 1897 (Lake Cushman, Mason County, Washington).
FIGS.: Elliot, 1904, pt. 2, pls. 44, 45 (skull).

CALIFORNIA COUGAR

FELIS CONCOLOR CALIFORNICA May

Felis californica May, California Game "marked down," p. 22, 1896 (Upper Kern River, Kern County, California).
FIGS.: Grinnell, Dixon, and Linsdale, 1937, pl. 11, col. (showing red and gray phases), figs. 215–239 (skull, photographs of old, young, habitat, etc.).

VANCOUVER COUGAR

FELIS CONCOLOR VANCOUVERENSIS Nelson and Goldman

Felis concolor vancouverensis Nelson and Goldman, Proc. Biol. Soc. Washington, vol. 45, p. 105, July 15, 1932 (Campbell Lake, Vancouver Island, British Columbia).

The present status of these races may be considered briefly together, for although none of them seems now in actual danger of extermination, nevertheless in the years to come, with the constant encroachment of human occupation, with hunting for sport or for bounties, and with forest fires and other causes, it is likely that their ranks will eventually dwindle, and that they can survive in any numbers only in large reserves or in country that remains in a more or less primeval condition, with shelter of forests and food in the shape of larger game, meaning chiefly deer. The fallacy of completely killing out these larger predators in deer reserves has been several times demonstrated. In the case of the Kaibab Forest, from which panthers and wolves were eliminated by purposeful hunting and trapping, and from which deer hunters were excluded, the mule deer in the course of a few years became so abundant that not only did the animals destroy all the available food but also permanently injured the sparse forest of the area so that hundreds died from starvation. A nearly similar state of affairs took place in the Murderers Creek Game Refuge of eastern Oregon, which was established in 1929 in the belief that the deer there needed protection (Englis, 1939). In the course of some years the mule deer so increased that in one section 12,000 deer were trying to exist "where even 6,000 would have gone hungry." Bitterbush, mountain mahogany, and juniper, the chief winter food plants, were so overbrowsed that bitterbush became mere stubs, and the junipers were trimmed as high as a deer could reach. Many deer starved to death and the others were small and undernourished. In 1935 the area was reopened to hunting and the refuge given up. In such cases it is clear that a proper proportion (to be determined) of panthers would not only keep the deer down to a number commensurate with the carrying capacity of the range, but also afford a certain return from fur, besides adding to the human interest of the situation, in hunting or observation. This view of the value of predators has only in recent years been brought out forcibly as a result of the experiments in "control" that have been more or less intentionally carried out by federal and other agencies in our West during the past 60 or 70 years. It now becomes clear that "predatory animals are to be considered as an integral part of the wild life protected within national parks, and no widespread campaigns of destruction are to be countenanced," but native predators may be allowed to continue their normal utilization of other park animals, unless in special cases where the need for some regulation becomes obvious (Cahalane, 1939b). This logical and scientific policy, based on an accurate knowledge of the various species concerned, should become increasingly established over all the larger areas of unsettled country.

Of the four races listed above, *Felis c. hippolestes* is the largest member of the species; it is of a dull fulvous color and has a large massive skull with a highly developed sagittal crest. A large male measured 8 feet in total length and weighed 227 pounds (Merriam, 1901, p. 586). The skull measured 196 mm. in basal length. Young are born in January and February in Colorado. This race ranges from extreme northern New Mexico (probably) northward through Colorado and the adjacent parts to Wyoming, Montana, and British Columbia.

Bailey (1931) refers to this race a large specimen in the collection of the U. S. Biological Survey from the Jemez Mountains of northern New Mexico and believes that other dark-brown skins from Taos and Pecos River Mountains of that region are the same. In the latter district they were "common" in 1903, and a few were killed every year in the Taos Mountains. "In 1910 officials of the Forest Service reported mountain lions as fairly abundant on the Carson National Forest and as still very common in the Jemez Mountains. In 1914 they reported 3 killed on the Carson, 3 on the Pecos, and 2 in the Jemez National Forest; in 1915, 4 on the Carson and 4 on the Santa Fe National Forests; and in 1916, 4 on the Carson and 7 on the Santa Fe National Forests." These large cougars could and did kill even elk, as well as deer, but as these and "other native game animals become scarce, the mountain lions turn their attention to domestic stock and seem especially to relish colts, but if these are not to be found, they take horse meat of any kind. In spite of the bounty usually paid for their destruction and the efforts of stockmen and hunters, they have until recently held their own in the rougher parts of the country, but with the present organized effort it will not be long before they are sufficiently reduced in numbers to prevent any great losses" (Bailey, 1931).

In Colorado the range of this race, which formerly inhabited all the "rough parts of the State, and in early times" was occasionally seen "even well out on the plains along the more heavily brush-fringed streams," has now become much more circumscribed. In 1911 Cary wrote that it was already rare east of the Continental Divide, though holding its own fairly well in the rough canyon and mesa country of the western and southwestern parts of the State, where locally the animals were still sufficiently numerous to be very destructive to stock, especially young colts. Cary (1911) lists eight regions in the northern mountains of Colorado in all but one of which they were said to be from uncommon to "common"; in the Snake River region where formerly they were common, none remain. Reports from southern Colorado for ten regions where they are found indicate that they are much less numerous, though a few still occur. They may be found locally up as high as 10,000 feet in some of the mountain ranges. At least until recent years the cougar was of local occurrence in the mountainous parts of Utah and Idaho, but its numbers can not be very great, as a result in part of determined efforts of stockmen and professional hunters.

Bailey (1918) writes that they were still common in Glacier Park, northwestern Montana, 20 years ago but were confined for the most part to the western slopes, where dense forest cover and abundance of deer offered excellent living conditions. "Apparently they are still almost as numerous as they were in 1895," when he first went through the region. "In this region," he adds, "their food consists mainly of the white-tail deer, which abound on the west slope of the park." Although Bailey advocates their destruction, as contributing little to the tourist interest of the park, since they are seldom seen, nevertheless their value as a check on the over-increase of deer might well justify the maintenance of a proper number.

In southern British Columbia the cougar is uncommon but extends into the Peace River district. Cowan in a recent report (1939) writes of a female killed in March 1937 by Ted Strand of Little Prairie, and quotes Seton ("Lives of Game Animals") as to a specimen shot in November, 1921, near the junction of Cypress Creek and Halfway River. This latter "seems to be the northernmost record for North America."

On Vancouver Island the panther still occurs in some numbers in wilder areas and has lately been distinguished as a separate race, characterized by its darker, more rufescent upper parts and the more elevated frontal region of the skull, in comparison with the Rocky Mountain and Oregon races. Swarth, in his paper of 1912, wrote that for an animal of this type it was abundant "throughout the wilder parts of Vancouver Island, and frequently seen near many of the smaller towns also." They are shy and secretive but are often hunted successfully with dogs. One farmer in the Beaver Creek Valley, near Alberni, had killed as many as 13 during the previous winter. In a letter dated July 8, 1939, Maj. Allan Brooks writes me that "over the whole northern third of this island beavers have been decimated by cougars of late years, and they will take many years to recover if they ever do." Cougars have also been an active agent in the destruction of deer, concentrating on the more healthy upland population, on account of the dying off of deer in the lowlands from infection by liver flukes. At the present time, therefore, the Vancouver cougar seems in

no danger, unless more intensive operations for its destruction
are undertaken to preserve the deer.

Farther south, along the coasts of southern British Columbia,
Washington, and Oregon, occurs the race *oregonensis*, which is
nearly as large as the Rocky Mountain subspecies but darker
and richer in color, with more black on the tail. A large one
was said to have weighed 150 pounds. Concerning its status
in the State of Washington, Taylor and Shaw (1929) write
that it is "probably more common in the Olympic Mountains
than elsewhere, but present also in the Cascades and Blue
Mountains. Predatory-animal control campaigns are markedly
reducing its numbers." In Oregon cougars were common in
the forests west of the Cascade Mountains up till recently but
at the present time have been so reduced by professional
hunters over the State "that they are no longer a serious
menace to livestock industries" (Bailey, 1936). Some idea of
their numbers in recent years may be gained from the figures
given by Bailey (1936), who states that for the period from
October 1, 1913, to December 31, 1914, bounties totalling
$4,035 were paid on 269 mountain lions killed in Oregon. In
Curry County alone no less than 60 were killed, and smaller
numbers in 19 other counties. In the fiscal year 1930, Jewett
reported 17 killed by U. S. Biological Survey hunters in Oregon,
"where they had been reported killing stock or game. While
the number is insignificant, it shows a marked decrease in these
big cats during recent years and that their destruction of livestock and game is being well curbed." It seems clear from these
figures that mountain lions will ere long become uncommon in
the State if this policy is continued. In the wilder sections, it
may be that a certain number of these predators will be valuable in keeping down too great an increase of deer.

Grinnell, Dixon, and Linsdale (1937) have published an excellent summary of our knowledge of the race *californica* as it
occurs in California. The race is less dark and richly colored
than the Oregon cougar. Both red and gray phases occur,
with an intermediate condition, all three in about equal proportions. Adult males weigh upwards of 165 pounds, with an
average of about 140. It occurs in forested and chaparral-
covered areas mainly in the mountains west of the Great Basin
and desert divides from Oregon to the Mexican line. For the
most part it lives at middle altitudes in the mountains between

2,000 and 5,000 feet. Young seem to be born in almost any month of the year, but with a peak in April. The usual number seems to be two young to a litter in California. The chief prey is deer, on the increase of which it forms a natural check. Some valuable data on the abundance and feeding habits of cougars, based on much field experience, give perhaps for the first time a fairly accurate picture of the economic status of mountain lions, at least in California. In good lion and deer country 'there is on an average about one lion to a township (36 square miles), and in a few very favored localities about one to each 10 square miles. Where deer are most plentiful, as in national parks and game reserves, there also the mountain lions tend to be most concentrated. A careful study indicates that at the time of writing, according to the authors quoted, the mountain-lion population of California was about 600 and that the annual toll of these animals upon the deer was roughly 21,600. Yet in spite of this, and of a nearly equal number annually taken by hunters in the State, deer are actually increasing. From 1908 to 1921 the annual kill of mountain lions averaged 258, and the State even employs a professional hunter for their reduction. Yet it seems that the species is about holding its numbers in spite of this toll and a natural mortality. In regard to stock-killing propensities, it appears that usually those lions that have learned by experience that this sort of prey is easily secured are the main ones to be feared, and with their elimination in grazing areas the trouble is much abated. The present prospect for the California mountain lion is that although inevitably it must retreat before the spread of settlement and agriculture, nevertheless in wilder areas it will persist for many years to come and continue to be a source of slight revenue for hunters and perhaps in places a real asset in the natural control of deer populations in protected areas. Its situation is perhaps more favorable than is that of the other three races of the West, the Rocky Mountain, the Vancouver, and the Oregon cougars.

The Jaguars

In a recent paper Nelson and Goldman (1933) have reviewed the systematic relationships of the local races of jaguars in America. These, the largest of American cats, constitute but a single species, which inhabits the tropical and subtropical regions from south-central Argentina northward to southern United States. With the general appearance of a leopard, having a yellowish ground color marked with black spots or circles of spots, the jaguar is slightly heavier of build than a leopard, with a more massive head and relatively shorter tail. The color pattern is variable, but usually at least some of the rosettes of black spots have a central spot in the jaguar, which is absent in the leopard. The authors mentioned have given descriptions of no less than 16 local races of jaguar over the wide range covered by the species as a whole. The characters on which these are based are usually not striking and depend largely on slight peculiarities in the skull. Of the 16 races, five occur in North America, the others in South America. Concerning most of these, information is rather scanty and in general, although jaguars are frequently hunted wherever they come into proximity of man, there is little to indicate that they have been effectively depleted in numbers except perhaps in the regions of thickest settlement. Since the two forms that occur along the southwestern border of the United States have probably become much reduced in numbers and in the extent of the country they occupy, they may be included together here.

ARIZONA JAGUAR

FELIS ONCA ARIZONENSIS Goldman

Felis onca arizonensis Goldman, Proc. Biol. Soc. Washington, vol. 45, p. 144, Sept. 9, 1932 ("Near Cibecue, Navajo County, Arizona").

NORTHEASTERN JAGUAR

FELIS ONCA VERAECRUCIS Nelson and Goldman

Felis onca veraecrucis Nelson and Goldman, Journ. Mammalogy, vol. 14, p. 236, Aug., 1933 ("San Andres, Tuxtla, Vera Cruz, Mexico").
FIG.: Nelson, 1916, colored fig. on p. 413.

These two races of the jaguar are characteristic, respectively, of the subtropical areas of the "mountainous parts of eastern Arizona north to the Grand Canyon, southern half of western New Mexico, and northeastern Sonora," and the "Gulf slope of eastern and southeastern Mexico from the coast region of Tabasco north through Vera Cruz and Tamaulipas to central Texas." Their ranges are therefore separated by the high tableland of north-central Mexico. The race *arizonensis* is a large northern form distinguished by its flatter, more depressed nasal bones from other subspecies; it differs additionally from the race *hernandesii* to the south by its more massive skull with broader rostrum, wide anterior nares, and narrower posterior nares. The race *veraecrucis* is the largest of the North American races and has the nasals more arched. A tanned skin of *arizonensis* measures in total length, 2,145 mm.; tail, 660; the skull has a condylobasal length of 237 mm. An adult male of *veraecrucis* has a total length of 1,993 mm., the skull a condylobasal length of 247 mm. (Nelson and Goldman, 1933).

The northeastern jaguar just reaches the southern border of the United States in Texas but apparently has never been known to be common, and by now it is doubtless nearly extirpated in this area. J. A. Allen in 1894 wrote that in Aransas County, Texas, on the Gulf of Mexico, it was then already gone from the region. He mentions a skin formerly owned by a Captain Bailey that was killed in 1858 on Live Oak Peninsula, but Attwater who contributed the note had heard of none since in that region. The same collector, quoted by J. A. Allen (1896), speaks of it as formerly present in Bexar County, southern Texas, but adds that it was then (1896) "rare east of the Nueces River, but still taken occasionally in the chaparral thickets in the counties bordering the Rio Grande." How far to the eastward it may once have extended is uncertain. True, in 1885, in his provisional list of the mammals of North and Central America and the West India Islands, even stated that it ranged from Louisiana to Patagonia, but the basis of the Louisiana report is not given. Seton (1920) has called attention to an account of what seems to have been the jaguar in an old book on "Rocky Mountain Life," by Rufus B. Sage, who while encamped on Soublets Creek, headwaters of the Platte within 30 or 40 miles of Longs Peak, Colo., mentions a "strange looking animal" encountered by one of his party. He believed it to have been "of the Leopard family" and adds that they (meaning jaguars) "are not infrequently met in some parts of the Cumanche country, and their skins furnish to the natives a favorite material for arrow-cases." If this refers to the jaguar, as seems likely, it furnishes the most northeasterly record. Possibly, however, the ocelot was the animal meant. Bailey (1931) mentions a jaguar killed near Center City, Texas, as lately as 1903. It was treed by some dogs and after being wounded with a revolver shot was finally driven into some brush, surrounded, and shot, but not before it had killed a dog and a horse. Nelson and Goldman mention a specimen examined from Goldthwaite, Mills County, Texas.

Concerning the Arizona jaguar, the latter authors write that at the present time its range marks the most northern point where the species is known. Formerly, according to old records, it ranged into extreme southern California, and in recent years, "while not very abundant, it appears to be a regular resident of southeastern Arizona." They examined specimens from Cibecue, Greaterville, and Nogales in that State. That jaguars occurred in southern California in the first half of the last century is attested by Merriam (1919), who quotes several older accounts: that of Langsdorff, 1814, who mentions it as among the species of the Monterey region; Beechey (Narrative, 1831), who in 1826 says it was reported to be found in the country between San Francisco and Monterey; and Saint-Amant, who included it in 1854 as a California species. He further calls attention to a circumstantial account of the finding of a jaguar family in the Tehachapi Mountains by the famous James Capen Adams about the middle of the last century, as detailed in Hittell's (1860) account of the adventures of this old hunter. The Indians of a former generation living in southern California apparently were well acquainted with this jaguar, and Merriam (1919) was told by an old chief of the Kammei tribe that in the Cuyamaca Mountain region in San Diego County it was there known as "big-spotted lion" in their native tongue. Another early writer, Pattie, mentions one killed on an island at the mouth of the Colorado River about 1822. Other Indian records, as gathered by William D. Strong (1926) in this region, indicate that the jaguar formerly occurred in the mountains bordering the Mohave Desert and that the "old people made a practice of following jaguar and mountain lion trails in order to uncover and eat the deer remains the animals buried. The last jaguar that his informant could remember as having been killed in the region was near Palm Springs, Calif., about 1860. In New Mexico the jaguar is now rare if not quite extirpated. Bailey (1931) has summarized a number of later occurrences of jaguars in the southern part of the State: Grafton, in 1900; Ute Creek, San Miguel County, 1902–3; near Fulton, 1903; Datil Mountains, 1902; Clanton

Creek ranch, 1903; and Sierra de los Caballos, in about 1904 or 1905. Since these dates, no later instances are mentioned, and probably the species has been reduced to near the vanishing point in the United States. It has been found to kill cattle on the ranches in these regions and hence is regarded as a menace by the ranchers, to be killed wherever found. Probably it still occurs in small numbers in northeastern Mexico. According to Nelson (1916) the jaguar has little of the truculent disposition of the leopard. In parts of Mexico he made careful inquiry without hearing of a single case where one had attacked human beings, although the natives everywhere fear it on account of its size and strength. He writes: "Jaguars are very destructive to the larger game birds and mammals of their domain and to horses and cattle on ranches. On many large tropical ranches a 'tigrero,' or tiger hunter, is maintained, whose duty it is immediately to take up the trail when a 'tigre' makes its presence known, usually by killing cattle. The hunter steadily continues the pursuit" in which dogs are ordinarily used, until the animal is killed or driven far away. He mentions that along the Mexican coast in spring, when sea turtles come ashore to lay eggs, fresh tracks of jaguars may be found showing where they have traveled along the beach for miles in search of the eggs. In the province of Guerrero, Mexico, the hunters have a way of imitating the call of the jaguar during the mating period and thus enticing it within shot.

Order ARTIODACTYLA: Even-toed Ungulates

The cloven-hoofed herbivores form a large and complex group. About a hundred genera are usually recognized from the Holarctic, Oriental, Ethiopian, and Neotropical Regions. The artiodactyls do not occur in Australia, but the deer reach Celebes, and the pig family is found on most of the oceanic islands, probably carried by man to the islands west of Celebes. European and American deer have been introduced into New Zealand and some of the other islands, where they are doing well.

Since these herbivores are everywhere hunted for food and sport, many forms have become greatly reduced in numbers. There are three major groups:

(1) Suina, the hippopotamuses, pigs, and peccaries.

(2) Tylopoda, the camels and their South American relatives, the huanaco and vicuña.

(3) Pecora, the ruminants, to which belong the three families treated herein:

(1) Cervidae, the deer. Six forms of wapiti, 11 forms of the American deer, and 13 forms of caribou are considered to come within the scope of this work.

(2) Antilocapridae, the North American pronghorn antelope. Four races of the single Recent species are here recognized. The family is the only endemic group of the Artiodactyla in the New World.

(3) Bovidae, the cattle and their relatives. All the American representatives of this group, except the Rocky Mountain goat (19 forms, 3 genera), are included here as vanishing mammals.—J. E. H.

Family CERVIDAE: Deer

THE WAPITI, OR AMERICAN ELK

These large deer, although almost universally called elk in America, should more properly be termed by the American Indian name wapiti, since elk in the Old World was originally applied to the species resembling our moose, found across northern Europe and Asia. In general appearance this animal is much like the familiar red deer of Europe but is much larger and of a darker color, without the whitish eye ring of the latter. The antlers, too, in addition to their larger size, seldom show the "cup" of the Old World species, in which the three terminal tines tend to come off together. Originally found over most of temperate North America, this species has become very greatly restricted in range within the three centuries since active settlement by Europeans. At present some half dozen geographic races are recognized, which may be taken up in detail, as follows:

EASTERN WAPITI, OR ELK

CERVUS CANADENSIS CANADENSIS Erxleben

Cervus elaphus canadensis Erxleben, Syst. Regni Animal., vol. 1, p. 305, 1777 (Eastern Canada; as later restricted, "near Montreal," Quebec).

FIGS.: Audubon and Bachman, 1851, vol. 2, pl. 62 (colored figure of animals caught when young in western Pennsylvania).

The general appearance of the eastern wapiti is described by
Audubon and Bachman (1851), the latter of whom kept on his
grounds near New York City a pair that were obtained as
young animals in western Pennsylvania and that later served
as the originals from which their plate was drawn by Audubon.
Head dark brown, neck darker, blackish; a white patch on
each side of the under jaw, with a black stripe between, passing
down on to the throat.   No pale eye-ring.   General color dark
gray all over except for the prominent white rump-patch.
The male in winter develops a heavy fringe of long hair on the
throat and back of the neck.   Under surface of body, brown.
The winter pelage is somewhat grayer than that of summer
which is redder, and the young are spotted with white.   The
large antlers have a rounded beam and extend back, giving off
a brow tine and two others, the bez and trez, before the longest
is reached, beyond which is another fork, its tines in the same
anteroposterior plane.   Although there are a number of antlers
in existence, there is apparently but a single skin of the eastern
wapiti preserved, namely, one in the possession of the Academy
of Natural Sciences of Philadelphia.   Bailey (1937), on the
basis of the slender evidence available, believes that the
eastern animal was not so large and heavy as the Rocky Mountain race and was brighter brown and more richly colored than
any of the western forms.

Three hundred years ago the eastern wapiti ranged from
southern Quebec to the edge of the Plains and southward
through extreme western New England and western New
York, perhaps as far south as North Carolina on the Atlantic
seaboard, and through the Allegheny Mountains to northern
Alabama.   Such a large animal could not fail to have been
useful to the early settlers on account of its meat and hide;
hence it is not surprising that localities the elk haunted or
where they were killed became commemorated and distinguished from other wilderness spots by appropriate place-
names.   A fairly accurate map of the former range of this
animal in the eastern United States might be made by plotting
the cities, counties, creeks, and rivers named after it.   Thus in
western New York we have Elkcreek (town) and Elk Creek
(stream), Elkdale; in Pennsylvania, Elk City, Elk County,
Elk Creek, Elk Grove, Elk Hill, Elk Horn, Elk Lake, Elkrun;
in Maryland, Elk Neck and Elkton; in Virginia, Elk Creek,

Elk Garden, Elk Hill, Elkton, Elkwood; in West Virginia, Elk Garden, Elk Horn; in North Carolina, Elkville; in Tennessee, Elk Horn, Elk Mills, Elk River, Elkton; in Kentucky, Elkfork, Elk Horn, Elkton; in Alabama, Elk and Elk River. Other place names of a similar sort are on the maps of Ohio, Indiana, Michigan, and Iowa. But the native elk has long since gone, although in a few places as in Corbin Park, N. H., western stock has been imported and maintained under fence.

In the northeastern part of its range the animal was known to the French explorers of the St. Lawrence River, but Dr. R. M. Anderson (1939a) writes that although found in the province of Quebec south of the St. Lawrence in early days it has been gone from there for at least a century. He quotes W. P. Lett that about a hundred years prior to 1884 elk were present in small numbers in Carleton County, Ontario, and the antlers are frequently turned up by the plow in the vicinity of Ottawa. Presumably elk were present at that time on the Quebec side of the Ottawa River. In New England there is no record of the wapiti in historic times, yet it must occasionally have reached western Vermont, for antlers have been found in bogs in that region. Western New York was a part of the wapiti's range at one time. DeKay, in 1842, after correcting a few erroneous conceptions concerning this species, writes that they were at that time found in "the northwestern counties of Pennsylvania, and the adjoining counties of New-York. In 1834, I am informed by Mr. Philip Church, a stag was killed at Bolivar, Allegany county. My informant saw the animal, and his description corresponds exactly with this species." He also quotes a certain "Mr. Beach, an intelligent hunter," that he had shot at one in 1836 on the north branch of the Saranac and another hunter, Vaughan, who had actually killed one at nearly the same place. Merriam (1884), however, is inclined to doubt these last records on the ground that no old hunter with whom he had talked in the Adirondack region had ever seen or heard of one; nevertheless he admits that they must once have been common in the Adirondacks, since a number of antlers have been discovered, the best preserved of which that he had seen was found in a bog on Third Lake of Fulton Chain, in Herkimer County. The largest of several discovered at Steels Corners in St. Lawrence County measured 12½ inches in circumference at the burr and 10 inches immediately above it. Thus, in spite of Merriam's doubts, it is clear that the eastern wapiti formerly occurred in the northwestern part of the State and probably became extinct a century or more ago.

For Pennsylvania the record is much fuller, and Rhoads (1903) in particular has gathered what evidence he could find of their former presence. Early accounts tell of their abundance in that State, especially in the vicinity of salt licks, to which they had, with other large mammals, worn broad trails. Peter Kalm related how in the winter of 1705 great numbers came off the mountains because of the deep snows and were killed. Barton in 1806, a century later, implies the reduction of the herds: "In the memory of many persons now living, the droves of elks which used to frequent the salines near the river Susquehanna in Pennsylvania were so great that for 5 or 6 miles leading to the licks the paths of these animals were as large as many of the great public roads of our country. Eighty elks have sometimes been seen in one herd upon their march to the salines." In the vicinity of these congregating places they were apparently much hunted and killed, which may in part explain their early extermination. Rhoads says: "In the northeastern Alleghenies of Sullivan, Luzerne and Wyoming counties they seem to have totally disappeared in the second decade of the 19th century, although a few remained in a favorite haunt called 'Elk Forest' in the Pocono range of Wayne Co. until exterminated between 1830 and '40. In Tioga, Lycoming and Potter counties they haunted the headwaters of Pine Creek and the Black Forest until 1862, when the last was killed. In Somerset and Bedford counties, where the mountain glades and saline or sulphur springs were sought out by numerous bands of wapiti and buffalo in early colonial times, their extermination must have been of very early date . . . Even more obscure is the evidence of their former occurrence in the southwestern counties of Pennsylvania, and in the parts of New Jersey pertaining to the valley of the upper Delaware."

Stragglers, however, driven from the Pennsylvania mountains are believed occasionally to have been taken in northern New Jersey in former days. A writer in 1835 (R. C. Taylor, in London's Mag. Nat. Hist., vol. 8, p. 536) says that at that time elk were almost extinct in Pennsylvania; nevertheless a few continued for a number of years and were shot by hunters

at the salt licks, or were tracked down with the help of dogs
and shot. It was not thought unusual for a hunter to follow a
stag 40 miles before finally bringing it to bay. Shoemaker
(1915) writes of these final captures: "Taken by sections, the
last elk in the Blue Mountains was killed about 1800; in the
Pocono Mountains in 1845; in Lackawanna County five or ten
years earlier. Caleb Mitchell killed the last elk of the Seven
Mountains at the head of Treaster Valley, Mifflin County, in
1857; James David killed the last elk in Clearfield County in
May, 1865. It was brought to Lock Haven on a raft from the
mouth of Medix Run, where it was killed . . . Jim Jacobson, a half-breed Indian, killed an elk in Elk County in 1867,"
which according to Rhoads is the last to have been shot in the
State. Shoemaker (1915), however, says that this same
Jacobson killed others "annually until Nov. 19, 1875, when he
killed his last near Roulette, Potter County," and adds that
the very last Pennsylvania elk was shot on September 1, 1877.
Up to the middle of the last century "there was quite a thriving
business of catching elks alive in northern Pennsylvania."

In the adjacent State of West Virginia wapiti were common
till about the middle of the eighteenth century and thereafter
dwindled in numbers up to about the time of the Civil War.
Kellogg (1937), in summing up their brief history, notes that
"between 1830 and 1835, elk were killed at a deer lick near
'The Sinks' on Gandy Creek . . . Three elk were killed
on the Black Fork of Cheat River near Davis, Tucker County,
in 1843 . . . During 1845, seven elk were seen near
Durbin, Pocahontas County." McWhorter in a historical
account of the region states that an elk was killed in 1867 at
Elk Lick on Middle River, in the same county, and tracks were
said to have been seen even in 1873. At the present time a few
elk, escaped from an enclosure in Marlinton, are said to be at
large on the ridges of the eastern part of the State, but these
were imported.

Still farther south, C. S. Brimley (1905) states that this
animal doubtless occurred in North Carolina a century and a
half previously, and it seems also to have been present in
Virginia in the years after early settlement, up to about 1847
(Audubon and Bachman, 1846–54). For Tennessee, Kellogg
(1939) has assembled evidence to show that "elk at one
time were plentiful . . . occurring not only in the high

passes and narrow valleys of the mountainous sections but also in association with the buffalo visited the licks of middle Tennessee, browsed along the rivers and creeks in the southern counties, and wandered through the canebrakes of the Mississippi bottomlands." Crockett refers to them repeatedly between the years 1820 and 1830 as then present in the bottomlands of Obion and Dyer Counties. The last records as given by Rhoads (1896) seem to be: About 1849 one killed at Reelfoot Lake by David Merriwether and one reported killed in 1865 in Obion County. Doubtless a few must have reached the mountains of northern Alabama as evidenced by the place-names, previously mentioned, and may have wandered into the adjacent part of Georgia, but no contemporary record is known to me.

West of the Alleghenies to the edge of the Plains this race of elk was formerly common. Historical accounts of Ohio tell of its presence in the pioneer days of settlement, but it seems to have been much reduced by the end of the eighteenth century. Kirtland, however, writing in 1838, says it was "frequently to be met with in Ashtabula county until within the last six years. I learn from Col. Harper, of that county, that one was killed there as recently as October of the present season." There were elk in Kentucky in pioneer days, affording the early settlers a desirable source of meat and leather but they were early reduced in numbers. Audubon wrote that when he first settled in that State (in 1808) there were still some to be found and a few in Illinois across the Ohio River, but by 1847 they seem to have been pretty well gone. Cory has assembled many older accounts for Wisconsin and Illinois. In 1818 they were no longer to be found east of the Illinois River, in Illinois, though a few seem to have remained in the northern part of the State. In southern Illinois they are said to have been common up to about 1820; the last records in Indiana are of one killed in Knox County in 1829 and another in the following year. In Wisconsin they apparently held on till much later. Hoy wrote in 1882 that they were found on Hay River in that State in 1863, but Brayton, in 1882, said they were still found in the vicinity of Green Bay, Wis. They seem to have been "numerous" in eastern Michigan as late as 1860 in Huron and Sanilac Counties about the headwaters of Cass River, but so relentlessly were they being hunted with rifle and trap pens that their early extermination was foreseen by Miles. In 1856 they were not uncommonly seen at Saginaw Bay. Elk were formerly abundant in Minnesota, and according to Herrick (1892) they were occasionally killed by the Indians to the north of Lake Superior as late as 1885, and he was informed of their presence in that year at Red Lake. Although Cory (1912) stated that a few individuals were said still to remain in the extreme northern part of Minnesota, no evidence of this is given. Cahn (1937) says that in Quetico Park, adjoining the Superior National Forest in that region, elk have long been extinct, but that in 1914 or 1915 they were introduced into the latter reserve, and on at least one occasion "some members of this herd were seen in the Quetico Park" on the Canadian side of the common boundary. At the present time, according to a Department of Agriculture press statement dated January 29, 1939, there are in Minnesota some 45 elk, and in Michigan 5, but what part of these, if any, represents the native stock is uncertain. From the same source it appears that estimates of elk populations show the following figures: In New Hampshire, 250; in New York, 100; in Virginia, 140. Presumably these are all from stock introduced from the West.

How far to the westward the typical eastern elk ranged may perhaps never be demonstrated. From analogy with climatic conditions and from what is known concerning other animals of wide distribution, it may be presumed that somewhere along the eastern edge of the Great Plains the characters showed intergradation with those of the Rocky Mountain elk, so that available notes from the States of the eastern Plains may be grouped under that race. In North Dakota, where this transition may have been found, Bailey (1926) writes of the former abundance of elk all over the State, where they were equally at home in the timber and on the open prairie. Explorers and others tell of the numbers found at the beginning of the last century, but they rapidly disappeared before on-coming settlement. A few remained into the early eighties, one of the last reports being that of six killed in 1883 near Elkton in Cavalier County. In former times the valleys seemed to be their wintering grounds, where they found a dense cover of timber and abundant food. The antlers were shed by the males mainly during March and April, and quantities of these might be picked up. "Next to the buffalo," says Bailey, "the elk at the height of their abundance were the easiest to hunt and hence the most rapidly killed of the large game, but when much hunted they became very wild, and it is probable that besides the vast numbers killed in the State, many were driven out of its borders." Running down elk on horseback was a favorite form of plains sport. The meat was in great demand as about the best of game animals, while the hides were much used as leather not only by the Indians for moccasins but by the whites for various purposes. The upper canine teeth were a prized decoration of Indian women, and in later times were in great demand as watch charms among the whites, a demand that for a time led to much ruthless slaughter.

The possibility of raising elk commercially under fence has been somewhat developed and is the subject of more recent

Eastern wapiti (*Cervus canadensis canadensis*)

experiment. Bailey (1926) says that "in domestication elk have proved more hardy and prolific than other stock and almost as easily handled under well-fenced range. If in the future the production of elk meat proves as profitable an industry as it promises, there will be found ideal conditions for elk pastures in many parts of western North Dakota, where rough and steep slopes lie close to brushy bottomlands, and winter browse and summer grass can be inclosed in single or adjoining areas. The severe winter weather which means suffering and loss to domestic stock without shelter is a joy to these native born and bred deer if a suitable and adequate food supply be available. Along many of the stream valleys with Badlands borders, which now lie idle or are of little use for stock, elk would find an abundance of their favorite food and choice living conditions. The time seems ripe for adding this industry to the many resources of the State."

ROCKY MOUNTAIN WAPITI; NELSON'S WAPITI

CERVUS CANADENSIS NELSONI Bailey

Cervus canadensis nelsoni Bailey, Proc. Biol. Soc. Washington, vol. 48, p. 188, Nov. 15, 1935 ("Yellowstone National Park," Montana).
FIGS.: Elliot, 1901, pl. 12 (skull and antlers); Nelson, 1916, p. 454 (col. fig.).

The wapiti of the Rocky Mountain region, from northern New Mexico northward into Canada, and including formerly perhaps the Great Plains area, is regarded as a race larger in size of body and in antlers than that of the eastern woodlands, and in color it is the palest of the races except the dwarf elk (*C. c. nannodes*). Bailey describes the type as light buffy fawn in summer, fading to creamy buff; rump-patch creamy buff or whitish; head, neck, legs, and belly dull rusty brown to dark umber and blackish; eye-rings buffy. In winter, the body color is buffy gray over lavender, with dusky tips that wear off leaving a creamy or soiled-whitish appearance; large rump-patch, including the tail, whitish or clear white; head and neck dull rusty brown with dark-brown manes, darkest on lower throat; ears dull light brown, lined with pale buff. The basal length of the skull of the type (male) was 430 mm.; length of antler over the beam, 1,250–1,260 mm.

It may now be impossible to ascertain where this race intergraded with the eastern form or whether the range of the

Rocky Mountain wapiti should be regarded as extending eastward to the edge of the Great Plains. At all events, the species
formerly was found over much of this region. Thus, in 1804–5,
Lewis and Clark recorded elk along the Missouri River all the
way through North Dakota, and 40 years later Audubon
found them abundant along the Missouri and Little Missouri
Rivers. Bailey (1926) mentions being told of "thousands"
seen along the Lower Yellowstone in 1864 and they remained
common in the Dakotas till about 1880, but "as the country
filled up with settlers they rapidly disappeared," and were
practically gone from the State by the middle eighties. The
late J. A. Allen (1870) wrote of their occurrence in Iowa, that
though formerly numerous, they were by 1879 "extinct in
most of the region." An old resident with whom he talked in
1867, at New Jefferson, Greene County, told him that only
seven years before "the elk were abundant in some parts of
that county. Prior to this date he used to see herds nearly
every day, and sometimes several in a day, some of them of
very large size. During the early settlement of this part of
Iowa they were of great value to the settlers, furnishing them
with an abundance of excellent food when there was a scarcity
of swine and other meat-yielding domestic animals. But, as
has been the case too often in the history of the noblest game
animals of this continent, they were frequently most ruthlessly
and improvidently destroyed. In the severer weather of winter
they were often driven to seek shelter and food in the vicinity
of the settlements. At such times the people, not satisfied with
killing enough for their present need, mercilessly engaged in an
exterminating butchery. Rendered bold by their extremity,
the elk were easily dispatched with such implements as axes
and corn-knives. For years they were so numerous that the
settlers could kill them whenever they desired to, but several
severe winters and indiscriminate slaughter soon greatly reduced their numbers, and now only a few linger where formerly
thousands lived, and these are rapidly disappearing. Their
home here being chiefly the open country, they much sooner
fall a prey to the 'westward march of civilization', through the
most merciless treatment they receive at the hands of the emi-
grant, than does the deer."

On the plains of Kansas the elk was formerly abundant but
has long been extinct. In these open regions elk were con-

spicuous because of their large size, while the excellence of their meat made them an object of pursuit by the pioneers. Add to these points their gregarious habits, the dangers to which they were exposed through severe winters, prairie fires, and diseases, and it becomes obvious that they would be among the first to go in the face of these perils. Shortly after the Civil War, with the increase of settlers over the prairie country, elk became reduced in numbers on the Plains until they were left only in the more rugged country in the foothills of the Rocky Mountains.

This race of elk reached its southern limits in the mountains of extreme northern New Mexico. In the San Juan Mountains they were reported as abundant by Pike in 1807 and by Cope as not uncommon in 1874, but in succeeding years these numbers seem to have quickly dwindled, although they were still to be found in 1892. In September, 1909, forest rangers reported *two elk* in these mountains. Bailey (1931), who records these facts, was unable to learn of elk in the Jemez Mountains when he was there in 1906. Nelson, who in 1883 was staying near the head of Pecos River, had a few reports of elk in the nearby mountains at that time, but the last record that Bailey could obtain was of one killed in 1902. While probably the native stock was by then wiped out, several attempts at restocking have since taken place, by importing animals from Colorado and Wyoming, as in 1911, when small numbers were "planted" in Potato Canyon, Cimarron Canyon, Gallinas Canyon, and later in San Miguel County. These introductions, in part under fence, were reported as doing well and increasing slowly. With the setting aside of several game reserves, it seems likely that a stock may eventually be built up.

In Colorado, elk were early exterminated in the eastern parts and in 1871 were already rare even in Park County in the eastern hills. Cary, writing in 1911, says that they were then exterminated over much of their former range in Colorado, and "the few bands which remain in the wildest parts of the western plateaus and mountains are small and widely scattered . . . Estimates in 1898 placed the number of elk in Colorado at 7,000; in 1902 at 3,000. In 1909 their numbers were reduced to considerably less, and were divided about equally between northern and southern Colorado . . .

Careful estimates made by the Forest Service officers in the spring of 1911 show a total of about 2,100." Since Cary's report in 1911, the herds seem to have been built up very greatly, for the U. S. Biological Survey in its census published in 1939 gave an estimated total of 23,000 elk for Colorado.

At the present time, owing to adequate protection in recent decades, the elk herds of Wyoming, Idaho, and Montana have increased to such large proportions that they are no longer in danger. The chief centers of abundance are in such national parks as the Yellowstone, where formerly hundreds were slaughtered by hunters; another famous place is the Jackson Hole region, Wyoming, a regular wintering area for elk coming down off the surrounding mountains where they spend the summers. In Glacier Park, Montana, there are smaller numbers, but these are apparently increasing. One difficulty in maintaining elk in large preserves is, as Bailey points out, the problem of providing upland mountainous areas for their summer range and suitable lowland places where food is available for wintering them. The 1939 wildlife census provides the following figures for elk populations in the Rocky Mountain States, from south to north: New Mexico, 5,000; Colorado, 23,000; Utah, 3,800; Wyoming, 40,700; Idaho, 24,400; Montana, 26,700; Nevada, about 200.

In addition to these there are a good many elk in other States that have been introduced from the Rocky Mountain area. Some of these are living under fence, and others may be free. Thus the report above quoted gives the following: Arizona, 4,400; California (in several places in the northern part); Michigan, 5; Nebraska, 31; New Hampshire, 250; New York, 100; Oklahoma, 230; South Dakota, 3,400; Texas, 350; Virginia, 140. The Rocky Mountain elk is obviously in no present danger. The feasibility of restoring elk to regions from which they have been extirpated is evident from the following quotations (gathered by Dr. Francis Harper). According to Barker (1936, p. 177), in New Mexico, "elk, completely exterminated about 1900, have been restored so that we now have about 5,000 animals." "Prior to 1912, elk had disappeared from the ranges of the State of Utah. Since 1912 there have been planted within our State, a few at a time, 193 head in seven different areas. These plantings were made during the period from 1912 to 1925, and the elk were imported

from Jackson Hole and Yellowstone Park . . . We now
have approximately 3,500 head on the ranges" (Cook, 1936,
p. 187). In Wyoming, Montana, and Idaho they have been
completely saved from extinction through adequate protective
measures. In 1932 there were, in national parks of the United
States, an estimated total of 15,420 and in national forests
over 96,800 (Phillips, 1935).

In a recent survey of the elk situation, it is shown by Skinner
(1928) that in the Yellowstone region, for example, any adequate plan for maintaining the elk population should consider
providing a sufficient food supply for winter as well as summer.
This seems to consist under natural conditions of "browse"
as well as grass, so that the hay supplied in recent years for the
Jackson Hole herd in winter is probably not an adequate
diet. He gives a partial list of food plants used from month
to month. Protection against unusually heavy snows and cold
is another problem, for when elk are forced out from Yellowstone Park into the surrounding low country in winter, thousands are killed by hunters, without supervision or restraint.
There is the further problem of competition with bison herds
of the region for food, the depredations of coyotes, wolves,
and mountain lions, though these are less important. Finally
diseases, some of which may be introduced through domestic
stock, and parasites are as yet insufficiently known. Murie
(1930) has made a special study of winter losses among the
elk at Jackson Hole, Wyoming, and attributes a large portion
of them to necrobacillosis, the symptoms and general etiology
of which he describes and illustrates. The sharp awns of the
squirreltail grass, which produce lesions in the skin of mouth,
tongue, or throat and so afford entrance for the disease organ-
isms, seem to be a contributory factor in this. The elimination
of this grass, if that is possible, might aid in preventing the
trouble. All these problems are matters of importance in
maintaining the elk herds and increasingly demand careful
consideration. A beginning in this had already been made by
the U. S. Biological Survey, in concert with the Forest Service
and a program of management laid 30 years ago (see Graves
and Nelson, 1919). The present excellent condition of the
herds in Yellowstone Park reflects the wisdom of the policies
pursued.

A decade ago, during prohibition days, a number of elk

were imported into eastern Massachusetts and ostensibly maintained for breeding and experimental purposes, until it developed that the pine grove in their spacious and well-guarded paddock concealed a large illicit still!

North of the United States-Canadian Boundary this race of elk extended its range in former times to about latitude 60° nearly to Lake Athabaska but was driven back in the last century. Nevertheless there are still "some numbers in East Kootenay district, British Columbia, where they are hunted to some extent . . . Some small herds of typical Rocky Mountain elk have within the past few years been demonstrated to occur on some of the southern tributaries of Nelson River in northeastern British Columbia" (Anderson, 1939b). They are, however, apparently now gone from the Peace River region where they formerly occurred. In a manuscript report of Harry Snyder to the Canadian Secretary of the Interior, as communicated by Dr. Francis Harper, the former tells of the discovery of a herd of 150 to 200 wapiti on the Prairie and Henry River watersheds of northern British Columbia, an area comprising 750 to 800 [?square] miles, about 500 miles north of the nearest known area now inhabited by elk.

MANITOBA WAPITI

CERVUS CANADENSIS MANITOBENSIS J. G. Millais

C[ervus] c[anadensis] manitobensis J. G. Millais, The Gun at Home and Abroad, vol. 4, p. 281, 1915 ("Manitoba and eastern Saskatchewan," Canada).

The elk in the most northerly part of its range in North America are "apparently larger and duller colored than typical *canadensis;* not so large or light colored as *nelsoni* of the Rocky Mountains. In summer rich chestnut brown, darker on head and neck and belly; in winter somewhat lighter. The name *manitobensis*, applied to this northern animal by Millais in 1915, is regarded as valid by Bailey (1935) for the race found in Manitoba and Saskatchewan and presumably still farther to the westward. Its precise area of distribution, however, is somewhat uncertain. In former times the wapiti, whether of this race or *nelsoni*, ranged to the Rocky Mountains on the west and northwestward, to the plains of Peace River, where Alexander Mackenzie found it in abundance near the trading post that he established at the mouth of Smoky River in the autumn of 1792 (see Preble, 1908). In that day it ranged as far north as Fort Nelson River, according to Richardson, but the nineteenth century saw its numbers so depleted that in 1894 Caspar Whitney placed its northern outpost as on the Saskatchewan, between Edmonton and Lac la Biche. Loring, in 1896, reported that a few were said still to exist near the head of Pembina River, where, however, they had been nearly exterminated by Indians through "crusting." Preble (1908), whose account summarizes these facts, adds that a few were seen on the south side of the Athabaska River in 1897. The most recent account of the status of this race is that of Dr. R. M. Anderson (1939b), who writes that in 1923 there were estimated to be 400 or 500 elk at Riding Mountain, Manitoba, and other bands on Duck Mountain Forest Reserve, but none elsewhere in Manitoba. The Riding Mountain herd in seven years under careful protection had by 1930 increased to about 8,000 head, but in the severe winter of 1934 the heavy mortality cut this down to about 6,000, with an estimated 300 in Duck Mountain Reserve, 250 in Porcupine Reserve, and 600 in the Inter-Lake district. In 1923 the Provincial Game Guardian of Saskatchewan estimated that in the Moose Mountain Reserve in that province there were about 100 elk, and in the region north and east of Prince Albert about 1,200 more. In 1927 a short open season was allowed here in the second half of November. The Prince Albert National Park, established that same year, "now shelters numbers of elk, but the exact figures are not known, and there are several bands outside the Park." It thus appears that in these two provinces, to which this race may be considered restricted at present, there are something over 8,000 head, largely in government reserves under careful supervision, so that in these areas there is as yet no fear for the elk's extinction.

MERRIAM'S ELK, OR WAPITI

CERVUS CANADENSIS MERRIAMI Nelson

Cervus merriami Nelson, Bull. Amer. Mus. Nat. Hist., vol. 16, p. 7, Jan. 16, 1902 ("Head of Black River, White Mountains, Arizona").
FIGS.: Nelson, 1902, figs. 1, 3, 5 (skull); Bailey, 1931, pl. 3 (antlers).

Equaling in size the Rocky Mountain elk, this race is described as paler and more reddish in color, with more massive skull and more erect antlers; the nasal bones are remarkably broad and flattened, with a well-marked constriction in the middle.

Fifty years ago this elk was common in the Sacramento, White, and Guadalupe Mountains east of the Rio Grande River and in the Mogollon group of mountains west of it, in southern New Mexico, as well as in the White Mountains of Arizona. There are old records for the Datil and Gallina Mountains of Socorro County, New Mexico, and a doubtful record for the Manzano Mountains. At the present time this race, with a restricted range in the mountains of southern New Mexico and Arizona, is believed to be extinct (Bailey, 1931).

Bailey has summarized the history of this deer. He surmises that it was antlers of this race that Montezuma showed to the followers of Cortez. That it was once common in southern New Mexico is inferred from the statement published by J. A. Allen in 1874 that a trapper and guide in the Rocky Mountain region had met with droves of 2,000 individuals as far south as the Mexican boundary. In the White Mountains and the Blue Range of Arizona, "more particularly on the head of Black River," according to D. B. Rudd, a forest ranger, they were present in large bands in 1876 when his father moved to that part of the country. "As late as 1890 elk could be found but not so plentifully. Since the year 1895 I cannot find that any have been seen." Nevertheless, another ranger had seen "bedding signs" of a small band between Black River and the higher plateau of the Blue Range, about 1904, which seems to be the latest report of them for that region. In the Mogollon Mountains H. W. Henshaw found tracks of these elk in 1873, and in 1882 Nelson heard reports of their presence near the extreme headwaters of the Gila River. In 1886 he collected specimens in the White Mountains of Arizona. Reports of the forest rangers indicate that these elk became scarce in the Mogollon Mountains about 1888, although up to that time they seem not to have shown any alarming decline. Bailey adduces a few instances of animals shot in the Mogollon Mountains up to 1890, when a cow and a bull were killed. The last record, however, seems to have been in 1894, when a fine male was reported seen on Lily Mountain, north of the main peaks of the Mogollons and tracks of three later in the same year.

In the Mimbres Range Bailey was unable to find any tradition of elk, nor in the Datil Mountains could Hollister in 1905 find any ranchers who remembered seeing them, although old antlers were occasionally discovered. A similar story of traces of their former presence was told in the Bear Spring and Indian Spring Mountains, which probably once formed the northern boundary of this elk's range. In the Sacramento Mountains elk were said to have been killed up to 1898, but Bailey himself, in 1902, could get no record of elk killed or even seen there later than 1893.

Concerning these elk in the White Mountain region of Arizona, Nelson (1902) wrote that their main range covered an area about 30 by 50 miles in extent, at an elevation 8,000 to 10,000 feet above sea level. At that time, between 1885 and 1888, "elk were far from numerous" but seemed to be most often found "about some beautiful damp meadows in the midst of the dense fir forest on the rolling summit of the Prieto Plateau, between the Blue and the Black Rivers." W. W. Price, who collected in this region in 1894, saw several and shot a male at 9,000 feet elevation. The report of tracks seen here in 1901 by a local hunter, who followed them unsuccessfully for two days, indicates that a few survived until that time, perhaps till about 1904, as previously noted. The fact that this survivor was trailed for two days shows that elk were still hunted in spite of legal prohibition.

In the Chiricahua Mountains of southeastern Arizona these elk in early times were numerous, but with the extension of grazing interests in the latter part of the last century there came "a long slow reduction in numbers due chiefly to the elks' inability to compete with cattle on the over-grazed range." Hunting accomplished their final extermination in the region, for the last small band was killed in the vicinity of Fly and Chiricahua Peaks about 1906 (Cahalane, 1939a).

DWARF ELK; CALIFORNIA WAPITI; TULE ELK

CERVUS CANADENSIS NANNODES Merriam

Cervus nannodes Merriam, Proc. Biol. Soc. Washington, vol. 18, p. 23, Feb. 2, 1905 ("Buttonwillow, Kern County, California").
FIG.: Merriam, 1905, p. 23, fig. (from photograph of a male).

Although called "dwarf elk," this race of southern Cali-

fornia is after all only slightly smaller than the form of the
Rocky Mountains. Compared with the latter it is paler, with
a smaller and narrower rump-patch. The legs are shorter,
and the skull is slightly smaller but has longer palatal bones
in proportion. Premolar and molar teeth are of the same length
in both, hence relatively larger in *nannodes*. Antlers in general
similar to those of the Rocky Mountain form but smaller and
with the posterior terminal prong less developed. "Front of
legs and feet bright golden fulvous; back and flanks varying
from buffy gray, slightly washed with fulvous, to grizzled
buffy whitish"; inner side of the ears "buffy white, the white,
particularly at posterior base, much more extensive than in the
other" races. The type specimen, a two-year old male, had a
total length of 2,030 mm.; tail, 140; hind foot, 620; basilar
length of skull, 358 mm. as against 388 in a male of same age
representing the Rocky Mountain form.

Prior to 1860 this form of elk was common in nearly the
entire San Joaquin and Sacramento Valleys, California,
especially in their lower parts. It was found at least as far
north as Butte Creek, in Butte County, and south to near
Bakersfield, Kern County, and westward through the southern
inner coast ranges as far as the plains of the Cuyama Valley,
San Luis Obispo County, and extreme northern Santa Barbara
County, and to the south end of San Francisco Bay, Santa
Clara County (Grinnell, 1933). "The encroachments of civilization have resulted in the gradual extermination of this elk
over the greater part of its former range, until" by the end of
the last century it had become "restricted to a small area
between Tulare and Buena Vista lakes, where at present
[i. e. in 1905] the survivors are confined almost exclusively to
lands included in an extensive cattle ranch (Buttonwillow
Ranch) owned by Miller and Lux." About 1903 these owners
presented the herd to the United States Government and a
park for its reception was constructed on Kaweah River in
the Sequoia National Park. In November, 1904, an attempt
was made to round up and corral this herd and move the
animals to the new area, but it was not a success, for "the elk
refused to be driven and escaped to the adjacent foothills of the
Temploa Mountains." During the process several were roped,
with fatal results, but the skins and skulls were preserved for the
U. S. Biological Survey collection (Merriam, 1905). Since

then, apparently, the remnant of this herd has continued, wild or in part under fence, in "western Kern County between Tulare and Buena Vista lake basins and at times in adjacent hills to westward. In 1932, about 170 individuals remained" (Grinnell, 1933). "Many transplantings of Dwarf Elk from the remaining 'herd' in the Buttonwillow district to other parts of the State have been made, first to Sequoia National Park, Tulare County, in 1904 and 1905, and more recently to Yosemite Valley, to Monterey County, etc. None of these has resulted in establishment under conditions of really wild freedom. The Sequoia animals had entirely disappeared by 1926" (Grinnell, 1933). With the protection now accorded them, unless local requirements change, it seems likely that this remnant in the Buttonwillow district may continue for a long time.

ROOSEVELT'S ELK; OLYMPIC ELK OR WAPITI

CERVUS CANADENSIS ROOSEVELTI Merriam

Cervus roosevelti Merriam, Proc. Biol. Soc. Washington, vol. 11, p. 271, Dec. 17, 1897 ("Mt. Elaine (on ridge between heads of Hoh, Elwah, and Soleduc rivers) near Mt. Olympus, Olympic Mts., State of Washington").

SYNONYM: ? *Cervus occidentalis* Hamilton Smith, Griffith's Cuvier, Animal Kingdom, vol. 4, p. 101, 1827. [Not certainly applicable to any American deer (Bailey)].

FIGS.: Bailey, 1936, pl. 20 (photographs of wild individual and a herd).

This elk of the Northwest coast is perhaps the largest of the races, the males with massive skull and antlers that are often "cupped," that is, the three terminal tines tend to come off together. The beam of the antler is relatively short and straight, with the terminal prong reduced. The body color in summer is a rich cinnamon-buff; head, neck, and belly dark brown with much black; in winter the body is dark gray with a dusky dorsal stripe and with dusky on the face, mane, and belly. In the skull, the frontals are broad and much flattened, and the preorbital cavity is small, as compared with the Rocky Mountain race. Total length of an adult male, 2,490 mm.; tail, 80; spread of antlers, 990 (3 feet 3 inches); length of left beam (in type), 1,050 (41.25 inches). The length of antler is about 500 mm. (20 inches) shorter than in a Rocky Mountain elk of comparable development.

The range of this race is confined to the humid forest belt along the Pacific coast from northern Vancouver Island south through the coast ranges of Washington, Oregon, and California to (formerly) about San Francisco Bay. Eastward in California the range included Mount Shasta. Altitudinally the area inhabited extended in California to about 7,000 feet (Grinnell). On Vancouver Island, its northward limit, it was, according to Swarth (1912), formerly abundant everywhere in the forests, decreasing in numbers southward to within 30 miles of Victoria. "They keep well back from the settled districts and are quite scarce near the east coast and the adjacent woods. They are most abundant in the north end of the island, particularly in the northwestern section and the vicinity of Kuyuquot Sound . . . The wapiti are seldom hunted by. the Indians, who prefer the more easy task of killing deer on the beaches." In the interior of Vancouver Island the wapiti are still fairly safe, since the forests are relatively unexplored and the animals are little disturbed (Sheldon, 1912). The Government took active steps to stop the killing of these wapiti for their canine teeth when, about 30 years ago, they were in active demand. Dr. I. M. Cowan, in 1937, told Dr. Francis Harper that there were supposed to be only about 700 elk left on Vancouver, this decimation being due in part to the ravages of wolves and cougars, but possibly also to disease that may have come among them, as in the Rocky Mountains.

This elk is not found on the mainland of British Columbia opposite Vancouver but appears again across the Strait of San Juan de Fuca in the mountains of the Olympic Peninsula and in scattered bands in the coast ranges of Washington and southward. Not many years ago its numbers seemed to have reached a low level in this State. Taylor and Shaw, in 1929, reported that in addition to the small groups found south to Pacific County, a small herd was said to be living on the headwaters of the Cispus River, south of Mount Rainier. It was at one time feared that this remnant might be even further reduced, but recent reports indicate that it is at present thriving under protection and is in no present danger. It should be borne in mind, however, that according to these authors Rocky Mountain elk have been introduced into several counties of Washington: Stevens, Garfield, and Walla Walla in the eastern part and Skagit, Snohomish, King, and Yakima in the central part. It is believed that in former times the ranges of these two forms did not overlap in the Northwest.

In Oregon the status of this deer has been summarized by

Vernon Bailey (1936), who reports that there are still considerable numbers of them in the coast ranges to which they are confined, from the Columbia River to the California border. Originally they inhabited the western slope of the Cascade Mountains and thence to the coast over all western Oregon. In 1841 Wilkes found them plentiful in the Willamette Valley, and Peale reported them from the mountains south of the Columbia River. Suckley and Gibbs about 1854 met with them abundantly in the mountains west of Astoria. "Later as the country was settled, elk were reported from almost every valley and mountain range of western Oregon, including the west slope of the Cascade Mountains, but there seems to be no record from the east [drier] slope of the range. In recent years, under rigid protection, apparently they have been holding their own, while in some localities actually increasing. The continual spread of settlement, though, is restricting their range, and the greater number of hunters each year makes it more difficult to prevent poaching in out-of-the-way places" (Bailey, 1936). In 1926 there was an estimated total population of 436 elk on the national forests of western Oregon, a figure that, says Bailey, covers the greater part of the Roosevelt's elk in the State. This is a slight increase (of about 40) over the estimate for 1933, but less than those for 1930 and 1931. It may be pointed out that the 17,000 elk estimated in 1939 as inhabiting the State of Oregon (Federal census), are doubtless mostly the Rocky Mountain elk, native and imported, in eastern parts of the State.

Still farther south this elk formerly occurred in abundance all the way to San Francisco Bay in the humid coast belt of northwestern California and eastward to the nearer inner coast ranges and to Mount Shasta. Of recent years, however, its numbers have dwindled, until by 1933, according to Grinnell (1933), it was to be found only in Del Norte and northern Humboldt Counties, while the total population was believed not to exceed 400 head. Its vertical range extended originally from sea level up to at least 7,000 feet, as formerly in the Scott Mountains, Trinity County. Its usual habitat was in and about openings in forest.

While the population of this elk is small, with a few hundred in Vancouver Island, and in each of these three northwestern States, nevertheless with the protection now given it there seems no reason to be apprehensive for its survival for a long time to come. Nevertheless, in order to preserve the race in its purity, care should be exercised that introductions of the Rocky Mountain elk are avoided within the range of this coastal form.

EASTERN MULE DEER; PLAINS MULE DEER

ODOCOILEUS HEMIONUS HEMIONUS (Rafinesque)

Cervus hemionus Rafinesque, Amer. Monthly Mag., vol. 1, p. 436, Oct., 1817 (Sioux River, South Dakota).
SYNONYM: *Cariacus virgultus* Hallock, Forest and Stream, vol. 52, p. 404, May 27, 1899 (Near Hallock, Kittson County, Minnesota).
FIG.: Nelson, 1916, col. fig. on p. 455.

Unlike the white-tailed deer, this is more a species of open or rough brushy country, so that where its range meets that of the former it is found in a different type of habitat. The antlers, while often having a basal prong, are usually characterized by the dichotomous forking of the main beam. The ears are longer than in the white-tailed group; the tail is short and either black-tipped or largely black above (black-tailed deer of the Pacific coast). The metatarsal gland is much longer and higher up on the foot. Both these types of deer are characterized by the extension of the vomer backward to form a complete longitudinal division of the posterior nasal passage; both also belong to the group Telemetacarpalia, in which the lateral digits of the forefeet are represented by the outer instead of the inner ends of the metacarpals.

As a species the mule deer and its west coast forms, the black-tailed deer, are or originally were found from the eastern edge of the Plains to the Pacific Ocean. While most of the western races are still abundant locally, the eastern form is largely extinct and may therefore be mentioned here. Baird describes its color as "ashy brown, pointed or varied with gray, and without any rusty tinge whatever. There is a distinctly marked stripe from the crown of the head to the root of the tail, the hairs in which are much darker throughout their extent than elsewhere. The under parts generally appear to be ashy brown, like the back, but without annulation of the hairs. The only whitish portion of the inferior surface is seen beneath the head, around the axillae, and in the groin. On each side of the tail, on the end of the rump, is a dull white patch, crossing above the tail and involving its entire basal half or two-thirds. The tail itself is quite slender and cylindrical on the basal two-thirds; the hair there being compact and close and then expanding into a dense tuft, which is entirely black" (Baird, 1857). Total length from tip of nose to tip of tail vertebrae, about 6 feet 6 inches.

Formerly the eastern mule deer was found in the Plains country from northern Oklahoma, Kansas, Nebraska, the Dakotas, and extreme northwestern Minnesota northward into southern Manitoba and westward to the foothills of the Rocky Mountains, where it is believed to have intergraded with the Rocky Mountain mule deer, *O. h. macrotis*, which is still common in the region from northern New Mexico northward into southern British Columbia. In the Dakotas this was a common species in the early days, and Bailey (1926) has brought together many notes of their presence from the accounts of early travelers in the region. In the seventies of the last century they were more abundant than the white-tailed deer on the upper Missouri, but in the succeeding decade the increasing influx of settlers and hunters had greatly reduced their numbers. J. S. Weiser, quoted by Bailey, reported them so common in the vicinity of Valley City in 1878 "that one could not travel 5 miles without seeing them," and John Hailand stated that though common at that time the last one was shot in 1885 or 1886. The latter adds: "There was so much venison in camp during the first years that visitors' ponies were usually loaded down with it before they returned. There was no sale for venison nor for skins, they were so plentiful. Skins were used for mattresses; they would get damp and deteriorate during summer and a new supply was provided each fall for the winter's sleeping." In 1896, Seton (1909) in a 15-mile ride across the Badlands of the Little Missouri, counted only three where ten years before he and his companion had counted 160 over the same ground. The numbers seem to have declined rapidly in the early years of the present century. Bailey states further that in 1912 they were reported rare in the Turtle Mountains of North Dakota, but just across the line in Manitoba they were more common and a number were killed each year. In 1913 Jewett found them "still fairly common" in the Badlands along the Little Missouri, but in the Killdeer Mountains he found that all had been killed off near settlements. He was told that at that time they were found only in the rougher parts of the Badlands, where a few may still persist, "but, if not already extinct, this finest of all native species of the smaller deer will soon have vanished from the State" (Bailey, 1926). They are apparently rare also in South Dakota.

There were mule deer in Nebraska in the seventies, but their numbers have been much reduced, and from Kansas they are quite gone. At the end of the last century a few existed in the open northwest corner of Minnesota, from Red Lake to Lake of the Woods, but they were exterminated soon after. In 1911 Cary wrote that "apparently none remain on the plains east of the mountains" in Colorado, "where they were common in early times." The mule deer of the mountainous areas here are perhaps of the race *macrotis*, although, as Bailey says, so few specimens of the typical plains form are in existence that we may never know its precise characters.

In the 1939 estimate of game animals by the U. S. Biological Survey, the following figures are given for the mule deer in the States east of the Rockies where it formerly was found: Oklahoma, none; Kansas, none; [eastern Colorado, gone;] Nebraska, 350; South Dakota, 4,900; North Dakota, 100; Minnesota, none. Although the basis of the figures for South Dakota is not given, it is likely that their center is in the Black Hills region, now a national park. Here Dr. Walter Granger reported them "numerous" in 1895 although "about extinct in the Bad Lands" (see J. A. Allen, 1895). With strict protection it seems likely that they might be permanently preserved in such areas as parts of the Badlands afford, with due consideration of the fact that they are wont to move down from the higher hills in autumn to winter in the more sheltered places of the lowlands.

WHITE-TAILED DEER; VIRGINIA DEER

ODOCOILEUS VIRGINIANUS VIRGINIANUS (Zimmermann)

Dama virginiana Zimmermann, Specimen Zoologiae Geogr., p. 351, 1777 ("America," assumed to be Virginia).

FIGS.: Elliot, 1901, pl. 15 (skull), as *O. americanus;* Nelson, 1916, p. 458, upper fig. (col.).

The white-tailed deer is found in woodlands of the temperate

zone quite across the United States, barely entering southern
Canada; to the southward it extends to Central America and
northern South America. Over this wide range it develops
several local races, some of which are in danger of being unduly reduced. A brief survey of these is here given, since this
animal is one of our most important game species.

The total length from nose to tail is given by Baird as 59
inches for a doe from Virginia; tail about 9 inches. Males are
slightly larger and heavier, weighing up to 200 pounds. In
winter coat, "pale grayish chestnut, faintly annulated"; in
summer "bright uniform rufous"—the "blue" and the "red"
coats of hunters. Under parts of body and tail, inside of the
limbs, the area between the jaws, and lining of ears, white;
a pale eye-ring. Tips of ears and a spot at the angle of the
mouth black. Antlers with a basal prong, the beam curving
up, out, and then slightly inward and forward, usually with
three erect prongs, but often with additional small points.

The typical race of Virginia deer is believed to range from
central or southern Pennsylvania south to the region of Palm
Beach in eastern Florida; westward it extends at least to the
Mississippi basin in Ohio and Kentucky, and formerly to the
edge of the Plains. Over most of this range it still is found in
woodland regions and survives in spite of persistent hunting,
even in fairly well-inhabited areas.

In New Jersey and southern Pennsylvania the white-tailed
deer formerly abounded, but Rhoads (1903) in the early years
of this century writes of it as confined to limited areas in
southern New Jersey, while from the lowlands of the Susquehanna, Allegheny, Monongahela, and Delaware River Valleys
it was exterminated. In New Jersey it was found then in
Burlington, Atlantic, Cape May, and Ocean Counties in small
numbers. At the same time in West Virginia deer were "still
rather plentiful" though much less abundant than in earlier
times (F. E. Brooks, 1911), and this is generally true for other
nearby States. Thus C. S. Brimley (1905) reports it rare or
absent in the more thickly settled parts of North Carolina
but "not uncommon" in the eastern section of the State and
in the mountains. Dr. Francis Harper (1937) notes that in
the Okefinokee Swamp region of southern Georgia it was
"abundant in former times" but "had become greatly reduced
in numbers through excessive hunting in late years, even before

the cutting of the timber and the great increase of the human population" of the area. On account of its ready adaptability it can maintain itself in varied cover and persist even in proximity to settled districts if given a reasonable chance. With two young at a birth its numbers readily come up with protection, so that even where much hunted it will continue in the face of considerable persecution. In the Great Smoky Mountains National Park it is said that there were believed to be "not more than a score of deer" remaining in this region when it was established in 1931, but already they show some evidence of coming back (Campbell, 1939). Kellogg (1939) summarizes records showing the "incredible number" of deer formerly found in parts of Tennessee and the importance of their meat and hides to the early settlers. By the latter part of the last century they had been so reduced in many areas of the State that the "Cumberland Mountain range has been almost entirely depleted of its stock of deer." Action of the legislature in 1895 prohibiting their killing for five years in five of the counties of Tennessee and the later prohibition of their hunting in the Great Smoky park will doubtless save the remnant. In 1882, according to Brayton, the deer was then "rarely met with in Ohio," and the same story holds elsewhere of its great depletion in the eastern States. Even in Alabama, Howell (1921) tells that they "once ranged in large numbers over all" parts of the State but are "now exterminated in all but the wilder and more inaccessible" districts.

As a good example of what may be done, however, is the result reported by F. B. Chapman (mimeographed report of the Ohio Wildlife Research Station, release 105, 1939). Deer, almost if not quite extirpated from Ohio by 1904, were reintroduced in 1922–30, and under protection they have so increased that by 1939 they numbered more than 2,000, distributed in 31 counties, in spite of a certain amount of poaching and occasional accidents and disease. The sex ratio is found to be about four or five does to one buck. As might be expected, the abundance of deer is roughly proportionate to the amount of forest cover.

Estimates of the deer population of the States in which this race occurs were given by the U. S. Biological Survey in January, 1939, as follows: New Jersey, 8,000; Indiana, 400; Ohio, 2,000; Iowa, 450; Virginia, 15,000; Kentucky, about 700;

Missouri, 700; West Virginia, 17,500; Tennessee, 1,700; North Carolina, 51,000; South Carolina, 23,000; Georgia, 16,400; Alabama, 20,200; Arkansas, 8,400; and Mississippi, 4,600. A comparison of these figures with the statements given above indicates that under recent legal protection the numbers have probably increased very greatly over what they were a few decades ago, so that a certain amount of hunting will become warranted.

At the present time the white-tailed deer is the largest and most valuable of our game animals in the eastern United States. As an object of interest to the increasing numbers of persons who delight in seeing wildlife, as an important item of food for those living in rural or wilderness areas, and as a chief object of pursuit by the many who enjoy hunting in the invigorating autumnal season, this deer may be reckoned as one of our most important species in the regions where it is found. The readiness with which it adapts itself to the proximity of man and the rapidity with which its ranks may build up if given proper protection should make its continuance in reasonable abundance a matter easily managed by any efficient game department.

Northern Virginia Deer

Odocoileus virginianus borealis Miller

Odocoileus americanus borealis Miller, Bull. New York State Mus., vol. 8, p. 83, Nov. 21, 1900 ("Bucksport, Hancock County, Maine").

Figs.: Stone and Cram, 1902, pl. opposite p. 42; Barbour and Allen, 1922, pl. 4, fig. 2 (antlers).

The northern Virginia deer is a slightly larger animal than the more southern race, weighing when full grown up to 250 pounds or even more. In winter coat the pelage is slightly longer and thicker, and the antlers of the males tend to be wider, more spreading, and less bent in at the tips.

The northern Virginia deer probably did not range farther north in early times than the coastal regions of Maine and adjacent parts of New Brunswick and Nova Scotia, avoiding the central parts of Maine, northern New Hampshire, and northern Vermont and southern Canada. The northern and central parts of New England and New Brunswick are regions of heavy and lasting snowfall, in which the movements of deer become much restricted in winter, while in times of crust formation, wolves would probably get most of the deer in such regions. A hundred years ago, says Dr. R. M. Anderson (1939a), "deer were said to be very seldom seen north of the Ottawa River." Within the past 50 or 75 years, however, considerable changes have taken place. Wolves are gone south of the St. Lawrence River, and even to the northward are much reduced in Quebec, so that they hardly form a deterrent to the spread of deer. Furthermore, with the intensive lumbering industry in New Brunswick, northern Maine, Michigan, and Wisconsin, areas of primeval spruce and white-pine forest have been cleared, with a consequent springing up of a great sprout growth of deciduous trees, which afforded cover and abundant food. These two factors have probably contributed in great part to the spread northward of this deer over Nova Scotia, New Brunswick, northern Maine, and southern Quebec, until "in 1930 a deer was taken in Abitibi River district within one hundred miles of James Bay" (R. M. Anderson, 1939a). Deer have been introduced and are thriving on Anticosti Island. They are common in northern Michigan, northern Wisconsin, northern Minnesota and the adjacent parts of Canada as in Quetico Park (Cahn, 1937), where, though some are killed by wolves during winter, "such depredations are not at all serious."

In his map of the distribution of eastern races of the Virginia deer, Cory (1912, p. 66) shows as blank areas from which the deer is "now practically extinct," western New York, northwestern Pennsylvania, practically all of Ohio, Indiana, and Illinois, the southern third of Michigan and Wisconsin, all of Iowa, the southern third of Minnesota, and a part of northern Missouri. Over much of this area it has in recent years come back. According to Dr. M. W. Lyon, Jr. (1936), deer at the present time are extinct in Indiana, where in pioneer days they were abundant. "The last stand of the deer in the state was in the northwest in the Kankakee region and in Knox County," where the last wild deer were seen near Red Cloud in 1893. Probably the estimate of 400 deer in the State given by the Government census in 1939 requires confirmation, but indicates a very recent return. Hollister, writing in 1908, says that the last wild deer were exterminated in southeastern Wisconsin nearly 60 years before. In Walworth County, where they were abundant a century ago, they rapidly

decreased after 1842, and the last one was seen near Delavan
in 1852. "Probably the most southern limit of their range in
Wisconsin at the present time is Sauk County" (Cory, 1912).
Although formerly abundant in Illinois, deer seem to have
been greatly reduced by the last decade or so of the last century,
and by 1900 were regarded as practically exterminated within
the State, although even as late as 1910 Cory had reliable
reports of a very few in Alexander County in the southern
portion of the State. Possibly this remnant has increased in
the succeeding quarter century enough to justify the figure
given in the 1939 Federal estimate of 250 animals.

The way in which this deer will "come back" if depleted
numbers are allowed to breed up for a period of years is well
illustrated by the experience of the three southern States of
New England. Before the settlement of the country deer were
a staple source of food for the Indians. From deer skins they
prepared clothing, and from the straight metapodial bones
they skilfully cut out portions for use as implements. The
first settlers also depended in part on these animals for sustenance and buckskin, and there was a large trade in the hides.
As early as 1646 Rhode Island had a closed season on deer
from May 1 till November 1. In 1698 Connecticut ordered
that deer should not be killed between January 15 and July 15,
and this period was soon after extended to include the remainder of these two months. Massachusetts soon followed
suit, and deer reeves were appointed to enforce the law. For
nearly a century the numbers continued without notable depletion, but by the close of the eighteenth century deer had
become scarce or nearly exterminated over much of southern
New England, until in 1842 Linsley, in his account of the mammals of Connecticut, makes mention only of one killed the
previous year in Waterbury. In 1869 J. A. Allen wrote that
in Massachusetts they were gone except for a few in Plymouth,
Barnstable, and Berkshire Counties, where they were "strin-
gently protected by law." Much of southern New Hampshire
and parts of Massachusetts were in the middle of the nineteenth
century cleared and used as grazing country, supplying the
nearby markets until the opening of the more extensive areas
of the Middle West, after which these regions gradually re-
verted to woodlands. Toward the end of the century the
remnant of deer that had hung on in the Berkshires of the

western part of Massachusetts and in the Plymouth region of the eastern section gradually built up a small population, which overflowed into the surrounding regions and, helped by a few introductions, began at length to attract notice. Under protective laws the numbers have increased so greatly that by 1910 Massachusetts declared an open season of six days late in November. Since then there has been an annual open season with few exceptions, and of about the same length. The number killed each year has varied from as low as 832 to over 2,000 (in 1924). There seems no reason to believe that with proper regulation the deer may not continue to be a game animal not only in Massachusetts but also in the other New England States where a somewhat similar increase also took place, in Connecticut, Rhode Island, and Vermont (in the last-named as a result in part of introduction). A similar wise administration has brought about a like result in Pennsylvania, where in early days it abounded, but by the end of the last century, Rhoads (1903) said, it had become "sparsely scattered or locally exterminated" though most often found in the Pocono and South Mountain regions. At the present time, the estimate published (in 1939) by the U. S. Biological Survey, places the white-tailed deer population of Pennsylvania at 793,000! The success of these eastern States in the replenishment of their forest covers with deer, and the asset which this game may be to the commonwealths, should prove an example to other States, in which the deer have been greatly depleted, to encourage an attempt at restocking.

FLORIDA DEER

ODOCOILEUS VIRGINIANUS OSCEOLA (Bangs)

Cariacus osceola Bangs, Proc. Biol. Soc. Washington, vol. 10, p. 26, Feb. 25, 1896 ("Citronelle, Citrus County, Florida").
SYNONYM: *Odocoileus virginianus mcilhennyi* F. W. Miller, Journ. Mamm., vol. 9, p. 57, Feb. 9, 1928 ("Near Avery Island, Louisiana").
FIGS.: Barbour and Allen, 1922, pl. 5, figs. 5-7 (antlered skulls).

In the southern part of the Florida Peninsula, and extending up on the western side and along the Gulf coast to Louisiana, the representative of the Virginia deer is a small animal, with notably smaller antlers than the typical race. Although the type locality is in the intergrading area of the two races, the name may for the present be retained. Of these small Florida deer, Cory (1896) states that he has killed full-grown bucks that did not weigh over 110 pounds, although they average larger. Apparently the recently described small deer from the coast marshes of Louisiana may be considered the same and is here included as a synonym.

The exact status of the small Florida deer is not well ascertained. It is apparently common in southern Florida and was considered to be "of very general distribution" over much of the peninsula in 1898 by Bangs, although "in the more thickly settled and accessible parts of the State it has been much reduced in numbers." This reduction has of late been accelerated, because of the killing of deer on account of their being hosts to ticks that spread disease. On the Gulf coast they are said to be no longer found in western Florida, but in extreme southwestern Alabama what may possibly be this same race still exists. In this State, according to A. H. Howell (1921), deer are now practically exterminated except in a few areas in the northern part (presumably typical *virginianus*) and in "the big wooded swamps of the lower Tensaw and Mobile Rivers" (presumably *osceola*). Here a number are killed during the open season every fall. They are hunted with dogs that drive the deer past the waiting hunter at some favorable "stand." "The deer take readily to the water and swim easily from one island to another in this great swamp; in this way they are able to keep ahead of the dogs, but are often shot while swimming a creek or river or when crossing an opening in the timber. Deer are still found in moderate numbers in the sandhills and swamps of southern Baldwin County . . . Twenty years ago or more they were common in the sandhills and small swamps of Mobile County, but now apparently all have been exterminated from that region." Both these counties border the Gulf of Mexico in extreme southwestern Alabama. No data are at hand concerning the deer in coastal Mississippi, but it seems probable that the small deer with large toothrows of south-central Louisiana described as a race, *mcilhennyi*, are the same and are of local distribution in the coastal region.

Probably some restriction on the killing of deer in these areas is desirable.

KEY DEER; "SPANISH DEER"

ODOCOILEUS VIRGINIANUS CLAVIUM Barbour and Allen

Odocoileus virginianus clavium Barbour and Allen, Journ. Mammalogy, vol. 3, p. 73,
    May, 1922 ("Big Pine Key, Florida").
FIG.: Barbour and Allen, 1922, pl. 5, fig. 4 (antlered skull).

This is the smallest of the eastern races of this deer, characterized by its pale colors, very small antlers, and small teeth (upper cheek teeth 67 mm. in combined length). It is short-coated at all seasons and somewhat buffier in color than the mainland form.

This small deer is confined to a few of the outer keys off the southeast coast of the Florida Peninsula, at the present time being found only on the chain of islands from Big Pine Key southwestward to Boca Chica, a small island 7 or 8 miles from Key West; on the latter there were deer in the early nineties. "Deer were killed on Stock Island, a small key adjoining Key West," about 1910, but none has since been known there. There were deer on Boca Chica until about the same time, when they disappeared and were not again noticed there until late in 1920, when two were seen. "Deer have always been found from time to time on Ramrod Key, all three of the Torch Keys, and probably Newfound Harbor. They swim readily from key to key and if hunted on the smaller islands they leave and go back to Big Pine Key," the largest of the "lower keys." On this island and some of the others the dense thorny thickets of pricklypear and other growth offer them a safe refuge, and in 1922 they were said to be more plentiful than they had been a few years previously.

On account of its restricted range and the assiduity with which it is hunted, even by parties coming over from Cuba, this small deer may be considered to maintain a rather precarious existence, but unless its stronghold of thorny growth is burned or destroyed in some other way it is likely to hold out in small numbers for a long time.

TEXAS WHITE-TAILED DEER

ODOCOILEUS VIRGINIANUS TEXANUS (Mearns)

Dorcelaphus texanus Mearns, Proc. Biol. Soc. Washington, vol. 12, p. 23, Jan. 27, 1898
    (Fort Clark, Kinney County, Texas).

This is the race of the semiarid part of southern and middle Texas, but the exact limits of its range remain to be defined. It is said to be of small size, with relatively short legs, small ears, and with small and strongly incurved antlers. The molar and premolar teeth are relatively very large, the colors pale. Total length, 1,585 mm. Weight of bucks up to 100 pounds females 75 pounds (Mearns, 1907).

The range of this race extends into Mexico from southern Texas at least as far as San Luis Potosí. Mearns (1907) wrote of it that in the early years of this century it was abundant in the bottomlands and low mountain ranges of southern Texas, notwithstanding the fact that the Seminoles kill numbers of them every year. He had seen them in great bands in Devils River Valley. Bailey (1905) says that "on many of the large ranches between Corpus Christi and Brownsville, where the oak and mesquite thickets are interspersed with prairie and grassy openings, deer find ideal conditions, with abundant food and cover. The nature of the ground is such as to protect them from wolves and other natural enemies; but it is well suited to either hunting on horseback or still hunting, which, if freely allowed, would soon exterminate them. With protection, however, they increase rapidly, and in many places are abundant . . . On certain large ranches they are still numerous, while on others they have become extremely scarce and would be entirely exterminated but for the recruits from surrounding and better protected ranches . . . In spite of the protection of State laws and ranch owners there are still remote sections of rough, uncontrolled range where every year hunters kill wagonloads of deer for the market, or worse, kill the deer for the hides only, leaving the carcasses to rot. I was told that in the winter of 1901–2 hundreds of deer skins were brought out of the country west of Kerrville." Bailey attributes much of the present abundance of this deer to the enlightened attitude of the ranch owners who give it reasonable protection.

LOUISIANA DEER

ODOCOILEUS VIRGINIANUS LOUISIANAE G. M. Allen

Odocoelus [sic] *virginianus louisianae* G. M. Allen, Amer. Nat., vol. 35, p. 449, June, 1901 (Mer Rouge, Morehouse Parish, Louisiana).
FIG.: Allen, 1901, fig. on p. 453 (antlered skull).

The status of this form is imperfectly known. It is a large, rather pale animal, not very different apparently from *virginianus*. Its range is believed to be the northeastern part of Louisiana, northeastward into the adjacent region. No statistics of its numbers or notes on its status are at hand. Probably, however, the 2,000 deer credited to Louisiana by the 1939 Federal census of big game are largely of this race.

Plains White-tailed Deer

Odocoileus virginianus macrourus (Rafinesque)

Corvus (i. e. *Cervus*) *macrourus* Rafinesque, Amer. Monthly Mag., vol. 1, p. 436, 1817
(Plains of Kansas River, eastern Kansas).
Fig.: Bailey, 1931, pl. 2, fig. D (antlered skull).

This race of the mountains and plains of the western United States is described by Bailey as large for a white-tailed deer, color in winter pale gray, yellowish red in summer; tail long and bushy, ears small. He describes a doe from Texas as lacking the black tips on the ears, and in general brighter colored than the race *texanus*. It is larger and paler than typical *virginianus*.

Originally well distributed in wooded and brush-grown areas in valley bottoms and along streams from the Dakotas west to the Rocky Mountains and south to eastern New Mexico, it is naturally restricted in these regions to the local habitats it favors, avoiding open country, but seeking the protection of thickets along the streams. In North Dakota, Bailey (1926) writes that though much reduced in numbers locally, this deer, because of its secretive habits has hung on and is even in places common in spite of settlement. It may even be farmed with profit, like domestic stock, so readily does it respond to careful handling. Elsewhere its numbers vary. Thus in Kansas, where it was originally described, it is now extinct (Hibbard, 1933). In early days, wrote Cary (1911), it was found generally over the Plains region of Colorado, but it is at present uncommon in the State and largely restricted to the foothills and eastern slopes of the front ranges, where it occurs sparingly across the entire width of the State. In recent years deer are reported as locally common in the mountains of eastern New Mexico, although much hunted. They especially frequent the willow thickets along stream bottoms. Bailey (1931) writes that "this white-tailed deer will soon become exterminated from the open country in New Mexico, and the only possible hope of keeping it from entirely disappearing from the State will be to give it a permanently protected breeding ground where conditions are suitable for food and shelter. Within its present range these conditions could be obtained in great perfection on the eastern slope of the Sacramento Mountains and along the southern and eastern slopes of the Sangre de Cristo Range."

In recent years, according to Seton, this deer has extended its range into parts of Utah.

NORTHWESTERN WHITE-TAILED DEER; YELLOW-TAILED DEER; "PEND OREILLE DEER"

ODOCOILEUS VIRGINIANUS OCHROURUS Bailey

Odocoileus virginianus ochrourus Bailey, Proc. Biol. Soc. Washington, vol. 45, p. 43,
  Apr. 2, 1932 ("Coolin, south end of Priest Lake, Idaho").
FIGS.: Bailey, V., 1918, pl. 7, fig. 2 (photograph of doe), fig. 3 (head).

This race is found from Idaho and Montana to the eastern slopes of the Cascade Mountains, Oregon, and a short distance into northern Nevada and the extreme northeastern corner of California, and extends northward into the southeastern corner of British Columbia (Cowan).

Equaling the Plains white-tailed deer in size, it differs in being darker with less black and more ochraceous on the upper side of the tail. In winter coat it is dark buffy gray above, becoming bright ochraceous on top of tail, on the legs, and on the edges of the belly. Forehead and top of head dark brown, brisket dusky; sides of nose and eye-ring light gray. In summer the upper parts are bright tawny or light bay, legs but little paler, not yellowish as in the race *macrourus*. Antlers large and heavy when well developed, and frequently having the brow tine and the proximal long tine slightly forked.

Concerning this race Bailey (1936) writes: "There is very little on record of the habits of this deer in Oregon, except that they are found mainly in thickets and willow bottoms along the streams and valleys. In recent years they are sometimes found back in the hills, crowded back probably by settlements. Like most of their group they are secretive and would rather hide than run. In the more extensive thickets and forests of Idaho and Montana they are still abundant in favorable locations but over much of their ranges they are doomed to be crowded out by settlements, or killed by predatory animals as they gather on winter ranges and are easily pulled down by coyotes and dogs in the deep snows." Bailey (1918) has given a further account of this deer in Glacier National Park (under *O. v. macrourus*) where it is abundant and protected. In extreme northeastern California, it was evidently at one time common in Modoc County but apparently now is no longer so. Grinnell (1933) gives as "a late definite record" one taken in extreme eastern Lassen County in January, 1922. On the eastern slopes of the Cascade Mountains in Oregon and Washington this race seems still to be common.

Estimates of white-tailed deer populations for the States in which this race occurs are given by the U. S. Biological Survey for 1939 as follows: Idaho, 10,000; Montana, 24,000; Oregon, not given; Washington, 7,500.

By Executive Order in 1939 a Federal refuge for this deer and other forms of wildlife was established in Stevens and Pend Oreille Counties, Washington. It will contain eventually about 65,000 acres and is well adapted to the management of these deer, since they spend the spring and summer in the mountains and the autumn and winter in the lowlands of the area. The need for such a refuge has for some time been urged because the deer have become locally much limited through the operations of farming and logging.

PACIFIC WHITE-TAILED DEER; COASTAL WHITE-TAILED DEER; "TIDELAND DEER"; "COTTONTAIL DEER"

ODOCOILEUS VIRGINIANUS LEUCURUS (Douglas)

Cervus leucurus Douglas, Zool. Journ., vol. 4, p. 330, 1829 (Lower Columbia River, Oregon; description based on examples from Falls of the Willamette and mouth of the Columbia).

FIGS.: Bailey, V., 1936, pl. 23, fig. A (antlered skull); Scheffer, 1940, p. 275 (photographs of a doe).

This is the only race of white-tailed deer to reach the Pacific coast of the United States.

Small in size, standing about 3 feet 5 inches at the shoulder, and characterized by its small delicate antlers, this is likewise a darker race than *ochrourus*, its nearest neighbor, an appearance due to the narrowness of the pale subterminal rings of the hairs. There is a poorly defined median dark dorsal line on neck and shoulders; upper side of tail light ochraceous-buff at base, more dusky toward tip; brow patch with prominent suffusion of chestnut; white of under parts not reaching the axillae. Summer coat redder.

Formerly this deer was found "at least in the Cowlitz and lower Columbia River Valleys of western Washington, possibly also eastward for some distance along the Columbia, there being one report from Pasco" but at present is much restricted and has even been supposed to be extinct in that State (Taylor and Shaw, 1929). South of the Columbia River it formerly ranged along the coast west of the Cascades nearly to the California line. It was typically an animal of the river bottoms. In 1826 Douglas reported this as the commonest deer in the districts adjoining the Columbia River and in the fertile prairies of the Cowlitz and Willamette Rivers. He found it also near the head of tidewater on the Umpqua River. There are no positive records of its occurrence farther south in the Coast Range valleys but northward these deer extend to the Puget Sound country of Washington. In 1872–75 they were still of regular occurrence in the Willamette Valley, though less common than 20 years before, but after that time they rapidly disappeared. According to the report of a reliable hunter in that valley, the last whitetail he knew of was killed about 1898 near Sweet Home, Linn County (Bailey, 1936). These deer were said to be common in the foothills about Beaverton, Washington County, Oreg., from 1860 to 1875.

Until very recently the only remaining deer of this race were supposedly to be found in Douglas County, Oregon, where, according to Vernon Bailey (1936), Stanley G. Jewett in 1915 reported a few still inhabiting the Long Tom Swamp west of Eugene and a few on the oak-covered hills along the Umpqua River, some miles northeast of Roseburg. In this latter region, according to Scheffer (1940), the "herd" is now believed to number 200 to 300 animals, upon which the State Game Commission enforces a strict closed season. Curiously, however, Scheffer reports that this deer is still to be found in some numbers on both sides of the mouth of the Columbia River, a fact that had previously quite escaped notice. According to his detailed account (Scheffer, 1940), the present range of these deer includes chiefly low brushy islands and tidelands, below the 100-foot contour; above this the hills rise sharply from the river valley and the whitetails give place to the black-tailed deer. In the State of Washington the area inhabited by the former includes chiefly Skamokawa, Elokomin, and Cathlamet Islands, Puget Island, Tenasillahe Island, and Price Island, a total area of over 12,000 acres, with an estimated whitetail-deer population of between 400 and 500. On the Oregon side of the river's mouth the area inhabited is slightly greater (nearly 14,800 acres), but the deer population is less than half that in Washington, since the bulk of it is confined to the less cleared Webb and Westland districts. "As far as the main-land is concerned, the four corners of the range are fixed by steep bluffs that rise from the water's edge on both the Oregon and Washington shores." With practically no competition from blacktail deer, and with nearly complete freedom from large predatory mammals, the danger to this group seems small. Nevertheless in some of the islands as on Puget Island, the deer "have increased to the point where their depredations were distinctly annoying to the farmers." A few are annually killed in spite of legal protection, but with the gradual clearing and settlement of their restricted range, this remnant, Scheffer believes, will be in danger of extermination. "The obvious solution," he writes, "is to move one or more breeding stocks of the deer to nonagricultural areas," if suitable ones can be found, or to make a sanctuary of some tideland area already occupied by them and as yet only slightly devoted to farming, as on Skamokawa Island. This deer is well known to the farmers and fishermen of this region as "tideland deer" or "cottontail deer."

Sonora Deer; Fantail

Odocoileus couesi (Coues and Yarrow)

Cariacus virginianus var. *couesi* Coues and Yarrow, Rept. Geogr. and Geol. Explor. and Surv. west of 100th Meridian (Wheeler), vol. 5, p. 72, 1875 (Camp Crittenden, Pima County, Arizona).

Fig.: Nelson, 1916, p. 458, lower fig. (colored).

Though possibly to be considered a race of the Virginia deer, Bailey (1931) believes the Sonora deer are best regarded as a distinct though closely allied species. About half the size and weight of a Virginia deer, they are extremely pale in color, a light gray, somewhat more rusty in summer, but in pattern much the same as their larger relative. Old bucks reach a maximum weight of about 100 pounds, does 75 pounds. Total length of a large buck, 1,530 mm.; tail, 270; ear, 203.

This small deer is still common on many of the wooded mountains "of middle and southern Arizona, southern New Mexico, western Texas, and in the Sierra Madre of Chihuahua and Sonora, Mexico," which constitute its range, but "with the growing occupation of their territory by cattle and sheep and the increase in the number of hunters, these once abundant deer are rapidly diminishing" (Nelson, 1916). In winter, if snows became deep on the upper levels of their mountain haunts, these little deer would move down into the valleys, and it was not uncommon to see bands of 20 to 100 in the White Mountains of Arizona in the nineties of the last century (Nelson). Concerning their status in New Mexico, Bailey (1931) writes that they occupy the mountain ranges "west of the Rio Grande as far north as the Datils and possibly to the Zuni Mountains . . . In 1908 Goldman reported them as formerly abundant in the Burro Mountains, but at that time apparently all gone. In 1909 he was told by residents that there were a very few of them in the Zuni Mountains, but in previous years" others had failed to find them. In the Mimbres Range, Bailey reports that Goldman in 1909 found them in limited numbers and that same year the Forest Service reported them in the Datil, Gallinas, Magdalena, and San Mateo Mountains. In the Animas Mountains they were found common by Bailey in 1906, but he believes that their numbers are a result of the protective natural features of their haunts, and that "a few persistent hunters could easily exterminate them." This deer probably reaches its eastern limit in the Chisos Mountains of western Texas, where according to Bailey (1905) it ranges from 5,000 to 9,000 feet in the oak, juniper, and nut-pine cover. Where undisturbed they may often be seen feeding by day.

As to the future outlook for this deer, Bailey writes of it in New Mexico: "In September, 1915, J. S. Ligon reported Sonora deer still common in parts of the Mogollon Mountains, but much less so than formerly, owing to unrestricted hunting in season and out. On December 31, he wrote: 'The number of deer killed in New Mexico during the season just closed far outnumbers the increase for the year, I am quite sure.' These mountains now form the principal range of the species in New Mexico, but as the country fills up with settlers the deer will entirely disappear unless given better protection than they have received in the past . . . The many game refuges in these mountains will now doubtless insure the perpetuity of this interesting little deer." In the Chiricahua Mountains of southeastern Arizona, Cahalane (1939a) has lately reported them as numerous "from the tops of the highest peaks to the lower limit of the upper Sonoran Zone." Owing to their aversion to leaving the shelter of forest cover, they are practically "marooned" on these isolated ranges and in 1933 were found to be increasing so rapidly that already they "were too abundant for the carrying capacity of the range . . . The depletion of food was becoming a serious problem at this time" and reduction of their numbers by hunting was insufficient on account of the rugged nature of the country they inhabit. "A check on this undesirable increase would be effected by dropping control of mountain lions," the reduction of which during the previous decade by the "predatory-animal control" "has been followed by a too rapid growth of the deer population."

The Caribou

Two types of caribou are found in the northern parts of the New World, the barren-ground and the woodland. Both are divided into several geographic races, not very sharply defined. The barren-ground caribou, as its name implies, inhabits the Arctic tundra. It is shorter of limb but often longer in its antlers than the woodland caribou, which is found slightly to the southward of the barrens, in regions where open bogs alternate with evergreen forest. The term "caribou," almost universally applied to these animals in America, is from a Micmac word meaning "a shoveler," in allusion to the way in which these animals paw away the snow in winter to get at the reindeer moss on which they feed. In contrast to other members of the deer family, the females as well as the males may have antlers, although less often in the woodland than in the barren-ground species; when present, however, they are smaller in the females and in the woodland species are generally spike-like. The hoofs are broad and spreading as an adaptation to living on boggy or snow-covered ground, and the body is stocky

for a deer. Because of their gregarious habits, their manner of
living in more or less open country, and a sort of stupid curiosity they may often be closely approached or attracted and
so in former days were easily brought within gunshot and
several killed before the herd could escape. In many parts of
their range they have become greatly reduced in numbers and
merit protection wherever found. As a source of food and
clothing they are a mainstay of Eskimo and Indians in the
parts of their range where these primitive people live.

BARREN-GROUND CARIBOU

RANGIFER ARCTICUS ARCTICUS (Richardson)

Cervus tarandus var. *arctica* Richardson, Fauna Boreali-Americana, vol. 1, p. 241, 1829
  (Fort Enterprise, Mackenzie, Canada).
FIGS.: Grant, 1902, pls. [18, 19] (antlers and skull).

As Murie (1935) points out, the characters distinguishing
the barren-ground type from the woodland type of caribou
are sometimes "confusing." In general, however, the former
is shorter of limb and lighter in color, the antlers tend to have
the main beam more nearly cylindrical rather than flattened,
and the antlers themselves are less compact, with long, backward
then forward curved beam, branching dichotomously at the
summit. The two brow tines tend to show a wide triangular
expansion or palm. So great is the variation in these structures,
however, that scarcely any two are alike, and the opposite
antlers of the same individual may be considerably different.
Hollister (1912a) states that in the barren-ground type the
lower incisors (which in both are small and weak) decrease in
size from the middle to the outer pair by conspicuous steps,
with the outer pairs very small, whereas in the woodland type
the gradation from the middle to the outer pair is more uniform.
General color in summer "clove-brown, mingled with reddish
and yellowish brown, under-parts white; in winter entire coat
dirty white" (Lydekker, 1915). In size this is one of the smaller
American races, standing about 46 inches in height at the
shoulder. The basal length of skull averages about 365 mm.,
the maxillary tooth row about 89, but there is a slight overlapping with the larger Alaskan race (Murie, 1935). The
antlers of the male are "very long, slender, and rounded, with
few points on the expanded portion of the beam, which is

separated by a long interval from the third tine, . . . back
tine usually, if not always, wanting; female antlers much
smaller, simpler, and scarcely curved at all" (Lydekker). In
the few specimens available the antlers seem to be less spreading
than in other races, but, as Murie has shown, there is great
individual variation in their form.

The range of this subspecies is believed to be continental
North America from the west side of Hudson Bay to the Mackenzie River and northeastward to include Boothia, Southampton Island, and Baffin Island. The migratory habit so
characteristic of caribou leads to more or less irregular wandering, apparently in search of better feeding areas, and the animals often congregate and pass through certain sections in
great numbers, while in other seasons they may hardly be
found at all. This uncertainty leads at times to much hardship
on the part of Indians and Eskimos who depend upon them as
a source of food. Preble (1902) states that the southern limit
of the barren-ground caribou on the west coast of Hudson Bay
is Churchill River. "Even in former years these caribou were
seldom known to cross that river, and they are still killed within
a few miles of Fort Churchill. Farther inland they reach the
south end of Reindeer Lake." In his later paper on the
Athabaska-Mackenzie region, Preble (1908) has given a detailed account of the presence of this animal as recorded by
various travelers along the western part of the barren grounds,
the shores of the Arctic Ocean, and the outlying large islands
as Banks Land and Victoria Land. "As winter approaches,
the caribou which have summered on the Barren Grounds
move southward in herds, many of which enter the wooded
country. Their movements are more or less irregular." Few
persons traverse the inland barrens so that this race probably
remains, as Dr. R. M. Anderson says (1939b), "the most
numerous of all the caribou, although now very rare or missing
from much of its fairly recent former range along the Arctic
coast." Nevertheless, he adds, it "has perhaps not been
greatly reduced in total numbers, as where it has disappeared
many of the natives have not followed the caribou. The
caribou have also retreated farther from the shores of Hudson
Bay, and there have been many reports of large concentrations
of caribou in the interior east of Great Slave Lake and south of
Bathurst Inlet. In some cases shifting of range is due to human

crowding and in others the destruction of winter forage of lichens by fire may have been the prime cause of extended movement . . . Within the past few years more caribou than usual have come into parts of northern Manitoba and Saskatchewan, in winter, and quite recently barren ground caribou have crossed the Slave River into the Wood Buffalo Park and still farther south of the Park in northeastern Alberta where the species was never known before. This southward trend of the barren ground caribou of course brings them out of the comparative protection of the large native hunting reserves and restrictive regulation of white trappers in the Northwest Territories into the northern parts of the Prairie Provinces where white trappers abound. Reduced killing of caribou in parts of the north has perhaps been counterbalanced by increased slaughter in parts of the winter range. Recent expert investigators inform the writer that there has not been much new evidence to change his estimate [of 1930] of about three million caribou in Canada."

On Southampton Island in northern Hudson Bay there is a local herd of which Sutton and Hamilton, in 1932, saw a few animals. They write that this caribou was "once a very abundant animal all over Southampton Island. At the present time it appears to have disappeared almost altogether from the southern part and to be restricted principally to the region of the high country between East Bay and Duke of York Bay, and to the more or less unknown country inland from the coast and north of Cape Kendall." The Eskimos evidently hunt them only occasionally, and there is no evidence that they are greatly depleted. In Baffin Land both Hantzsch and Soper report the barren-ground caribou as local in occurrence and irregular in its appearance about the misson settlements of Cumberland Sound. Almost nothing is known of their numbers or their migrations, but it seems likely that they keep mainly to their archipelago, which they must have originally reached by way of Boothia.

LABRADOR BARREN-GROUND CARIBOU

RANGIFER ARCTICUS CABOTI G. M. Allen

Rangifer arcticus caboti G. M. Allen, Proc. New England Zool. Club, vol. 4, p. 104,
Mar. 24, 1914 (30 miles north of Nachvak, eastern Labrador, Canada).
SYNONYM: *Tarandus rangifer labradorensis* Millais, The Gun at Home and Abroad,
vol. 4, p. 259, 1915 ("Nain, Davis Inlet, and Fort Chimo").
FIGS.: Grant, 1902, pls. [8, 9] (skull and antlers).

This is the race of the Labrador Peninsula north of its
forested base. It is believed to be characterized by the wide
antlers, with very sweeping backward and forward curve, and
the great palmation of the brow and bez tines. If other differences occur, as in color, these have not been made out.

Dr. R. M. Anderson (1934b) writes that this caribou "is
found in more or less scattered bands over the treeless Arctic
Zone area and through parts of the scantily timbered Hud-
sonian Zone of the peninsula. In most of the districts near the
coast they have been greatly reduced in numbers, but considerable numbers are still found in the more isolated inland
districts." These are regions seldom penetrated by white
hunters, and accurate information as to the status of this
animal is difficult to obtain. Low, at the beginning of this
century, was told by the Nascopie Indians that there were
three main herds or stocks: One near the coast on the highlands between Nachvak and Nain; one in the hinterland of
Ungava Bay that crosses the lower Koksoak and passes the
summer on the tundra along Ungava Bay and Hudson Strait;
and one on the east coast of Hudson Bay, south to Clearwater
Lake. Before 1886 the last herd was said to have fallen off
greatly. Of the second, W. B. Cabot (1912) and others have
witnessed something of the migrations and mention the hunting
of the migrating animals by the Indians who rely partly on the
caribou for sustenance. Prichard (1910) states that these
animals often work out to the coast by November, and at
that time a good many may be taken, but their appearance is
not to be counted on, and they may come out at different
points in different seasons. There is some evidence that extensive fires have destroyed the available food in parts of their
range, thus excluding them from return to such districts.

There is every reason to believe that this caribou never
crosses the rough water and ice of Hudson Strait to Baffin
Land but is isolated on the Labrador Peninsula. To the south-

ward its range is limited by the forest country of the base of the peninsula, where the woodland caribou is found.

STONE'S CARIBOU

RANGIFER ARCTICUS STONEI J. A. Allen

Rangifer stonei J. A. Allen, Bull. Amer. Mus. Nat. Hist., vol. 14, p. 143, May 28, 1901 ("Kenai Peninsula, Alaska").

SYNONYMS: *Rangifer excelsifrons* Hollister, Smithsonian Misc. Coll., vol. 56, no. 35, p. 5, Feb. 7, 1912 ("Meade River, near Point Barrow, Alaska"); *Tarandus rangifer ogilvyensis* Millais, The Gun at Home and Abroad, vol. 4, p. 263, 1915 (Ogilvie Mountains, north of Dawson, Yukon, Canada); *Rangifer mcguirei* Figgins, Proc. Colorado Mus. Nat. Hist., vol. 3, no. 1, p. 1, Dec. 28, 1919 (Kletson Creek, a tributary of White River, Yukon, Canada).

FIGS.: Allen, J. A. 1901, figs. 1–4 (head, skull, antlers).

In his recent review of the Alaska–Yukon barren-ground caribou, Murie (1935) has shown that only one race is recognizable over most of central and northern Alaska (exclusive of the Alaska Peninsula and Unimak Island), ranging to the western part of Yukon, Canada. This is recognizable by its large size, with an upper maxillary tooth row averaging 94 mm. The large cheek teeth, large size, maximum for the *arcticus* type, dark color, with well-developed white fringe on the throat, and large, heavy, and "rangy" antlers are given as diagnostic characters.

Murie states that this caribou has now disappeared from the Kenai Peninsula, whence it was first described, but the form of the interior of Alaska is the same, and it is probable that the Kenai animals simply represented those remaining from a periodic overflow of the herds of the interior.

Stone's caribou, named in honor of Andrew J. Stone, who collected the type, is at present represented by four herds, which Murie (1935) briefly characterizes as follows:

(1) The Bering seacoast group, consisting of scattered bands distributed over a wide area of lowland bordering Bering Sea from Bristol Bay to Bering Strait, but which even by the early eighties had begun to decline. Residents agree that at the beginning of this century caribou were much commoner in the country north of the lower Yukon and inland from Norton Sound and may still be found in the hills of that region particularly at the head of Unalakleet, but at the present time are "entirely absent or occur only as stragglers on the Bering

Sea coast, in most of the Kuskokwim region, along the lower
Yukon, and in the vicinity of Norton Sound, and much of this
area is now occupied by domestic reindeer" (Murie, 1935).

(2) The Alaska Range herds, consisting of scattered bands
along the entire length of the Alaska Range. Murie believes
that an approximate estimate of this group would be between
25,000 and 30,000 animals, of which the principal aggregation
is included in Mount McKinley National Park.

(3) Northern herds, including the scattered remnants on
the Arctic slope, comprise the animals "ranging along the
Endicott Mountains, through the upper Koyukuk and Chanda-
lar watershed, across the Porcupine into Yukon Territory."
An estimate of 60,000 for the animals of this area is "probably
conservative." In early times caribou were plentiful along
the Arctic coast, but "in later years they largely disappeared
in this area, owing no doubt partly to the activities of whalers,
fur traders, and natives."

(4) The Yukon–Tanana herds, which comprise the largest
numbers of all, occupy the country west of the Mackenzie
River, on the uplands between the Yukon and Tanana Rivers.
Migrations of these herds, often numbering many thousands
of animals, are described by Murie from accounts gathered.
Except locally, their numbers show no depletion of importance.

GRANT'S CARIBOU

RANGIFER ARCTICUS GRANTI J. A. Allen

Rangifer granti J. A. Allen, Bull. Amer. Mus. Nat. Hist., vol. 16, p. 122, Mar. 31,
1902 ("Western end of Alaska peninsula, opposite Popoff Island").
FIGS.: Allen, J. A., 1902a, figs. 1–6 (skulls and antlers).

The caribou of the Alaska Peninsula and Unimak Island is
distinguished by "averaging somewhat smaller and paler than
R. a. stonei, many antlers diverging widely and with sharply
recurving beams, although these antler characters may not
hold uniformly in a large series." The average length of the
maxillary tooth row is 94.5 mm., or about as in *stonei*.

"In their present depleted numbers" the caribou of the
peninsula are "isolated from the interior herds" but appear
to have been "sufficiently isolated to form a local race"
(Murie, 1935). The antlers show a "tendency toward wide
divergence of the beams," which "average lighter in weight

than those of *stonei.*" At one time these caribou were abundant throughout the length of the Alaska Peninsula from a point nearly opposite Kodiak Island west to the island of Unimak and thence all around the Alaskan shore of Bering Sea (Nelson, 1887), as well as on Nunivak Island. At present, writes Murie (1935), "the numbers on the peninsula have dwindled greatly, but a few herds are still holding their own. One herd, numbering possibly 2,500, ranges from Morzhovoi Bay to Herendeen Bay, with the center of abundance in the vicinity of Pavlof Valley. The other herd, apparently a little larger, ranges from Moller Bay to the vicinity of Black Lake. The latter herd appears to be less molested by hunters than the others, but as a whole the caribou of the peninsula have been and are rapidly dwindling . . . Caribou are scarce to the eastward of Port Heiden, but a few have been recorded as far east as Becharof Lake in comparatively recent years. Several islands adjacent to the peninsula were inhabited at one time. Caribou occurred in considerable numbers on Unga Island, according to A. J. Stone, and Deer Island is also said to have had caribou, but today none are found on either. In July 1925 a caribou skeleton was found on Amak Island, 12 or 14 miles off the Bering Sea shore . . . This island cannot be much over 2 miles square. Unimak Island, roughly 30 by 75 miles in extent, represents the westernmost point of distribution for caribou and harbors a group that has been estimated at from 7,000 to 10,000 animals; a visit to the island in 1925 inclines the writer to favor the lower figure." According to reports of Donald H. Stevenson, quoted by Murie, the caribou here were decreasing rapidly in the eighties and early nineties, when it was thought many caribou were killed for food by men hunting sea otter. With the cessation of these activities the caribou commenced to increase until "by 1905 the island held all that the range could carry. About 1908 they again began to decline in numbers, but soon were able to hold their own and later increased once more." At intervals these island animals have been known to cross to the mainland of the peninsula, and there is some evidence of migratory movements lengthwise up and down the country.

From the evidence brought together by Murie it seems that in spite of a depletion that has restricted these caribou to parts of the peninsula and islands, and cut them off from the herds of interior Alaska, they are at present in no danger of extinction and with proper regulation of hunting should hold their numbers for a long period.

OSBORN'S CARIBOU

RANGIFER ARCTICUS OSBORNI J. A. Allen

Rangifer osborni J. A. Allen, Bull. Amer. Mus. Nat. Hist., vol. 16, p. 149, Apr. 16, 1902 ("Cassiar Mountains (60 miles southeast of Dease Lake), British Columbia").

FIGS.: Grant, 1902, pls. 18–21 (unnumbered) (head with antlers).

This race of the barren-ground caribou is darker than *R. a. stonei* with the dusky tipping of the white throat fringe more pronounced and the maxillary tooth row longer, averaging about 100.5 mm., according to Murie. The differences are, however, actually slight, and it is hard to find any very tangible distinctions between the two, beyond these average ones of size and color. The antlers sometimes show the flattened form of beam characteristic of the woodland caribou.

The geographic range of *R. a. osborni* includes southern Yukon and northern British Columbia, where according to late information it is still "reasonably common" (R. M. Anderson, 1939b). This race is believed to be much less migratory than the others.

PEARY'S CARIBOU; ELLESMERE LAND CARIBOU

RANGIFER ARCTICUS PEARYI J. A. Allen

Rangifer pearyi J. A. Allen, Bull. Amer. Mus. Nat. Hist., vol. 16, p. 409, Oct. 31, 1902 ("Ellesmere Land, N. Lat. 79°").

FIGS.: Allen, J. A., 1908, figs. 1–6 (antlered skulls); Nelson, 1916, p. 421 (col. fig.).

The caribou of Ellesmere Land, Grinnell Land, and Grant Land is smaller than the Greenland caribou or the typical *R. a. arcticus*, its nearest neighbors, and is nearly pure white in color, with, however, a slight admixture of gray to gray-brown in the middle area of the back. The maxillary tooth row ranges from 83 to 95 mm. The antlers "have a much greater upward curvature than in *arcticus*, in proportion to their length," and the main beam has an average length of about 1,019 mm.

From Peary's notes on these caribou, which range the Arctic islands mentioned, it appears that they live in small scattered groups of up to a dozen individuals of both sexes, and penetrate as far as latitude 83° N. on the northern coasts of these areas. They are not known to show any distinct mass migrations but remain the year round thriving on the lichen, moss, and other dwarf and scanty Arctic vegetation. Their chief enemies are the Arctic wolf and, of course, man, particularly the native Eskimo, who hunts them for food and clothing. "In these northern wilds, amid the most intense cold, the caribou passes from three to five months of continuous night, its wanderings lighted only by the moon, stars, and the marvelous displays of waving northern lights" (Nelson, 1916). According to Anderson these caribou are not very numerous, although Sverdrup found them in abundance on the west coast of Ellesmere Land. Since there are rather few human inhabitants it is likely that the caribou will persist for a long time to come.

GREENLAND CARIBOU

RANGIFER ARCTICUS GROENLANDICUS (Gmelin)

[*Cervus tarandus*] *groenlandicus* Gmelin, Linnaeus's Systema Naturae, ed. 13, vol. 1, pt. 1, p. 177, 1788 (Greenland).
FIGS.: Grant, 1902, two unnumbered plates (4, 5) (skull with antlers).

Lydekker (1915) describes the Greenland caribou as "closely allied to *R. t. arcticus*, with a broad sharply defined white ring round each eye, and distinct broad white bands above the hoofs; skull with an elevated frontal region." Whether or not these color characters are really distinctive, J. A. Allen (1908) states that it is darker in color than typical *arcticus* and much darker than *pearyi*, resembling greatly the coloration of the Woodland caribou in its dark-brown body, with neck and ventral area much lighter. Three male skulls average in condylobasal length, 368 mm., which is greater than in *arcticus* and considerably more than in the little *pearyi*. The upper maxillary tooth row is also greater, 81–99 mm. Antlers of adult males are large and spreading; the brow tines are not greatly palmate, the main beam is bent sharply forward at near a right angle at the most posterior point, at which there is a small but well-developed backward tine. Although the Greenland caribou has by some naturalists been associated with the Old World reindeer as a subspecies, and by others is regarded as a derivative of the New World barren-ground caribou, it seems quite as likely that Jacobi (1931) is correct in calling the forms of both merely races of a single circumboreal species, *Rangifer tarandus*.

The Greenland caribou, or reindeer, is believed to be derived from North America by way of the islands lying to the westward, and in that way to have reached the Greenland coast. Since, however, Peary's caribou now occupies the northern Arctic Archipelago, one must assume either that both have since differentiated from a common stock or that the Greenland animal arrived in some other way.

Formerly the Greenland caribou was found over the whole outer land fringing the ice cap of this country, except, apparently, the northern part of the coast. During the last century and a half constant hunting on the part of both Eskimo and white population has greatly reduced their numbers, so that at the present time they are found only locally in the areas most suitable to their needs on the southwest and west coasts but are gone from the eastern coast. Jensen (1928) has given some interesting data on the past and present distribution. These caribou were frequent on the southernmost part of the west coast even as late as the end of the eighteenth century, but they disappeared from this southern tip of the peninsula during the early part of the nineteenth century. Nevertheless, a good many still remain not far to the northward, near Narssalik (south of Frederikshaab). The best hunting district is a little farther to the northwest, Sukkertoppen, at latitude 65° N., where "even now" about a thousand animals are killed annually. The Godthaab district, slightly to the south, is also a favored habitat, where Jensen says about 600 are taken yearly. The present distribution of these caribou extends still farther northwestward to the southern part of the Upernavik district, in about latitude 73°, so that the range of the animal now is mainly limited to the stretch of coast covering about 800 miles from the southern Frederikshaab district to the Upernavik area. They no longer occur, however, on Disko Island about in the center of this stretch. Jensen states that in former times these animals extended their range still farther north to the Thule district, "at least as far north as Rensselaer Bay (lat. 78° 40′ N.)," where now they have "practically disappeared." Nevertheless, a remnant still persists here and apparently forms the dependence of the Eskimo of the Etah and Smith Sound area. Macmillan (1918), in his account of experiences here, tells of the Eskimo setting forth on their annual hunt for the caribou, about 50 miles north of Etah, on September 10, 1914, and returning on the 23rd with "forty-two warm skins, invaluable for bed-robes, coats, and sleeping-bags for the extreme temperatures to come." At another time the Eskimos reported killing 19 in two weeks. In February, 1916, Macmillan noticed the wandering of the caribou herd southward to the vicinity of Etah, because of deep snows covering their feeding grounds between there and Humboldt Glacier, which forms a natural barrier to the northward extension of their range. Of six killed near Etah, the heaviest weighed but 120 pounds. It is believed that this northern herd is much preyed upon by wolves, for in 1916, Macmillan writes, the Eskimos returning late in October from the annual caribou hunt throughout the region extending from Etah to Humboldt Glacier, reported "no young caribou whatever and tracks of wolves everywhere." It was his belief that the wolves had crossed over Smith Sound on the ice from Ellesmere Land and had accounted for the young caribou. The Eskimo stated that they had seen a number of caribou sleeping on the ice in the center of lakes, probably for security against attacks by wolves.

Returning to the southern tip of Greenland, Jensen notes that these caribou were in former times found at Angmagssalik but are exterminated. During recent decades they have also disappeared from the coast between Cape Dalton and Cape Brewster. In the northern part of East Greenland the Ryder expedition in 1891–92 "encountered reindeer with comparative frequency in the region round Scoresby Sound; in 1899 Nathorst only saw a few herds." The "Danmark Expedition" in 1906–8 found "innumerable traces (cast-off antlers and excrements) of the former occurrence of reindeer in great numbers, as far north as Holm Land (lat. 80° 20′ N.), but now they have entirely disappeared"; this disappearance from the northeast coast is corroborated by later reports of explorers and hunters. Coincident with this disappearance may have been the abandonment of the region by the Eskimo, whose deserted camps have been investigated in the same region. Nathorst, who in 1899 saw only a few herds in the Scoresby Sound region, attributed this disappearance to wolves, which are said to have appeared in East Greenland "rather suddenly" at about the time of the disappearance of the caribou. This, however, may be only part of the reason. Quite possibly overhunting had much to do with it, or there may have been other contributory causes.

From an economic standpoint, the Greenland caribou is an important asset to the Eskimo and white inhabitants of that country and one that should be exploited with care. For a great many years the export of caribou hides to Denmark has been going on, to an extent that was evidently unwarranted by the size of the herds. Jacobi (1931) quotes figures showing a decline in the numbers during part of last century. It is said that 37,000 caribou were killed in Greenland in 1839; from 1841 to 1850 an average of 13,900 hides were exported; from 1851 to 1860, an average of 5,667 yearly; from 1860 to 62, the average yearly number was below 1,000; and since 1862, below 100. In 1891, none was shipped. Nevertheless, there seems to be some evidence of an increase in numbers locally at the close of the last century.

"Among land mammals the reindeer is the most important object of hunting to the Eskimos. The meat is eaten, and the fat is used, for instance, as cream for coffee, and the contents of the paunch are considered a special delicacy; the skins are used as underlayers on sleeping platforms and for sleeping bags and garments, the antlers for hunting implements, the sinews for thread" (Jensen, 1928). Apparently caribou hunting is a summer occupation in South Greenland, when the Eskimo and their families seek the great plateaux in the neighborhood of the inland ice, and having selected their camp sites the men carry on the hunting till about the first of September, when they return to their dwellings on the outer coast. In the Etah region the hunting season is apparently in October. Since 1924 this pursuit has been somewhat regulated by the government in South Greenland. It has forbidden the hunting of caribou or molesting of the calves between May 20 and July 20, and during the open season no more animals may be killed than can be utilized on the spot or taken care of for future use by the hunters. Obviously these animals are of great importance in the economy of the Eskimo, to whose use it would seem they should mainly be relegated. Macmillan writes (1918, p. 74) that caribou meat "is lamentably lacking in

strength and stamina-producing properties," yet it is nevertheless more palatable than walrus or polar bear and forms a
welcome change from seal meat.

QUEEN CHARLOTTE ISLANDS CARIBOU

RANGIFER DAWSONI Seton

Rangifer dawsoni Seton, Ottawa Nat., vol. 13, p. 260, Feb., 1900 (Graham Island,
Queen Charlotte Islands, British Columbia).

FIGS.: Seton, 1900, pls. 4, 5 (type specimen, antler and skull); Sheldon, 1912, pl.
opposite p. 234.

This is supposed to be a small island form, darker in color
than the barren-ground caribou of the mainland. The single
antler of the type is peculiar in that the brow tine does not
project parallel to the forehead but turns upward and is well
separated from it. The terminal forks of the main beam turn
backward instead of extending forward. Length of type
antler following outer curve to highest point, 28¾ inches.

Very little is known of this caribou. Indeed, its very existence in the Queen Charlotte Islands was doubted by Osgood
(1901) and it was not until years after its description that
satisfactory evidence of its presence on Graham Island, the
most northerly island of the group, was obtained. Dr. G. M.
Dawson, while making a geological survey of the islands in
1878, was the first to learn of a caribou there, but from the
meager description given him by the natives he at first was
inclined to suppose the animals were wapiti. Nevertheless he
noted the use of pieces of caribou antler in the implements of
the native Haidas. After some effort the portion of cranium
with an antler that afterward served as the type was secured
through the Indians with the aid of a local trader, on Virago
Sound. In 1904, 1905, and 1906, the Rev. Charles Harrison,
a missionary stationed there, found evidence in the shape of
tracks, dung, and hair. In 1906 the late Charles Sheldon
undertook an intensive search for caribou in the country west
and southwest of Virago Sound on Graham Island but found
nothing more than old tracks and dung. In 1908 a bull and two
cows were killed, and a calf was seen by two half-breeds near
Virago Sound, and the specimens were acquired by the Provincial Museum in Victoria, B. C. (Keen, 1909). In October,
1910, Francis Kermode found two old tracks in the same district, and expressed the opinion that the form was nearly

extinct. Wharton Huber informed Dr. Francis Harper that in 1930 two prospectors again found tracks on Graham Island but saw no animals. This was on grass-covered mountains about 2,000 feet high in the northwestern part of the island. I. M. Cowan further informed Dr. Harper that in November, 1935, "Ed White reported fresh caribou tracks on Massett Island." It seems likely, then, that a few still exist in the interior mountainous parts of these islands. Since 1910 the British Columbia authorities have prohibited the killing of these animals, and because the local Haidas are more a fishing than a hunting race and do not care for caribou meat, it seems probable that the law will be observed.

There has been much speculation as to the origin of this caribou group and how it should have survived in such seemingly small numbers with no known natural enemies. The nearest point of land is about 30 miles away to the coastal archipelago, and the nearest relatives of the caribou live 150 miles distant at the present time. Dawson has suggested that the ancestral stock reached the archipelago during the Ice Age, when the islands were more easily accessible. If the race proves to be one of the barren-ground group, as seems likely, the fact will be all the more interesting.

EASTERN WOODLAND CARIBOU

RANGIFER CARIBOU CARIBOU (Gmelin)

[*Cervus tarandus*] *caribou* Gmelin, Linnaeus's Systema Naturae, ed. 13, vol. 1, pt. 1,
    p. 177, 1788 (eastern Canada).
FIGS.: Grant, 1902, 2 pls. opposite p. 18 (photographs); Nelson, 1916, p. 459 (colored
    fig.).

The woodland caribou, as its name implies, is a more southern animal than the barren-ground species, inhabiting the boreal evergreen forests and their bogs quite across North America from Newfoundland to British Columbia. It is larger of body but with less elongate antlers than the latter type; the antlers usually tend to have a more flattened beam, and the lower incisor teeth are more uniformly graded in size from middle to the outer ones. The females occasionally have small antlers, but these are ordinarily much less developed than in females of the barren-ground caribou. About five closely allied forms are at present recognized.

The eastern woodland caribou is usually darker than the

barren-ground species, with the head in front of the ears, the body from shoulders to tail, and the legs to just above the hoofs a dark brown; the lips and neck with its fringe of long hair below, and the legs just above the hoofs white or hoary. There is a narrow white area bordering the buttocks, but the upper surface of the short tail is dark. The antlers of the male are shorter than in the barren-ground type, less sweeping, and extend outward and forward, with a short tine at the bend, palmate brow tine on one or both sides and a varying number of tines on the terminal part of the main beam. Large antlers may measure in length of beam 42 inches on the outside curve.

The range of this eastern race originally extended from Nova Scotia westward across New Brunswick, northern Maine, extreme northern New Hampshire, and Vermont to southern Ontario, and on the north side of the Gulf of St. Lawrence to the wooded parts of southern Labrador west to James Bay. Westward of the latter region it grades into the race *sylvestris*. Its southward limit was the north shore of Lake Superior. It apparently did at one time reach the Adirondack region of New York. Over this range the woodland caribou is now largely gone, chiefly as a result of hunting and partly perhaps as a result of lack of reproduction on account of reduced living area and the harrying of civilization. The caribou south of the St. Lawrence have probably long been cut off from their western and northern neighbors since the settlement of southern Canada and may be thought of as a separate herd having a tendency to wander irregularly over the area. Thus during the nineteenth century at intervals of about 15 years, the records show a great influx of their numbers into northern Maine, so that they came down as far as tidewater in the eastern part of the State and to the large bogs near Bangor in the interior. For a few years there would be caribou in some numbers in the Maine woods, then they would drift away again eastward into New Brunswick and Nova Scotia and might be nearly if not quite absent from Maine for another period. New Brunswick with its greater extent of barrens and southern Quebec south of the St. Lawrence were probably more attractive feeding grounds. Caribou are easily killed on account of their gregarious habits and a curious inquisitiveness that leads them to stop their flight and approach an unfamiliar object. In former times a hunter on being discovered might lie on his back and kick his legs in the air or wave a red cloth, when presently the whole herd would turn and approach to investigate. The hunter, waiting his chance, would leap up and get in several shots before the caribou could dash off. This southern herd must have become gradually reduced by hunting and the effects of settlement without much cognizance being taken of it. The last great infiltration in Maine was in the early nineties, when they were reported for a time more numerous than deer. In 1895 and again in 1896 the Bangor and Aroostook Railroad alone shipped out about 130 caribou each year that had been killed by visiting sportsmen, but after that the number in the State began to decline, owing in part probably to the eastward movement of the animals once more and in part to summer and winter killing in both Maine and the adjacent parts of Canada. There were a few caribou in the bogs of northern New Hampshire until at least 1885. In 1899 a closed time on caribou in Maine for six years was established and on its expiration was renewed for another six years. Meanwhile, however, the animals had practically gone from the State. The last caribou in the Mount Katahdin region, formerly their favorite haunt, was seen in 1905 and a small herd remained on the northwestern border of the State near the St. Johns River until 1916, but since then there seem to be no certain records.

The history of this herd is much the same in New Brunswick and Nova Scotia—a gradual diminution and retreat. Dr. R. M. Anderson (1939b) writes that in Nova Scotia caribou were so numerous in the sixties that a certain English sportsman killed 120 in a single day in Lunenberg County. "The last caribou on the mainland of Nova Scotia was killed in Guysborough County about 1912," and they were "almost certainly gone" from the once famous caribou grounds of Victoria and Inverness Counties in northern Cape Breton Island by 1925, although in only the previous year he found recent "traces" of them. "In New Brunswick a closed season was established for caribou in 1919," but it was too late to help them, for in a few years they seem to have altogether gone. "Fairly authenticated records in the upper Tobique River in 1924" are mentioned by Dr. Anderson, and the New Brunswick Game Department is quoted as saying that "reports from wardens and woodsmen show that caribou probably remained in the Province in small quantities until about 1926, and one

warden actually reported seeing five caribou east of Bartibogue
Station during the spring of 1927." Since then, however, the
herd south of the St. Lawrence seems to have vanished, except
for a small remnant still surviving in the Gaspé region. This
remnant is chiefly confined to the Shickshock Mountains in
the northern part of the country and though small is nevertheless of sufficient size to allow a few to be shot each year.
There is a considerable barren area on the summits of some of
these mountains that is attractive to caribou, and the surrounding wilderness is at present little disturbed. As the last
remaining woodland caribou south of the St. Lawrence River,
this little group should be given careful protection until it
appears that it is numerous enough to survive. One may
believe, however, that it will not persist for a great many years,
when annually hunted. In southern Labrador "a few" woodland caribou are found "here and there in the interior north of
the St. Lawrence River and a small number scattered through
the back districts of northwestern Quebec . . . The situation in Ontario is even less hopeful. On a map prepared at
the Royal Ontario Museum of Zoology in 1935, caribou are
considered to have disappeared entirely from the east of a line
drawn from east end of Lake Superior to James Bay, the dates
of extirpation being dotted on the map here and there—1894,
1908, 1912, 1919, 1926, etc. The most southern band at present
is said to occupy Shakespeare Island in Lake Superior, with a
few about Lake Nipigon, Lake of the Woods, and the Rainy
Lake area. Local bands exist north of the Canadian National
Railway lines, but the most recent reports are to the effect
that the numbers of caribou are not large even in the more
northern parts of Ontario." The range in southern Labrador
probably extends to Hamilton Inlet and Sandwich Bay on the
east, and on the Hudson Bay side to Great Whale River or
thereabouts. According to Eidmann (1935) it has been killed
out over most of this range, but small herds are still occasionally met with, especially in the southeastern part of Labrador, where a small herd appeared in the Matamek area in 1930
and several were killed. Its extermination has been especially
hard for the native Indians, who relied on it in part for food
and clothing.

Minnesota is the only one of the eastern United States in
which caribou still exist in a wild state. C. L. Herrick (1892)

found them 50 years ago "only about the headwaters of the White-face River and along the St. Louis River near Knife Fall. There it was in 1884 not rare, though so shy as to be secured with difficulty. Along the North Shore of Lake Superior it is less shy and the animals may be seen feeding quietly in groups along the upland meadows." G. S. Miller (1897b) in 1896 found these caribou "very abundant on the north shore of Lake Superior" and saw "heads, antlers, and jaws of caribou at White River, Peninsula Harbor, Schreiber, and Nepigon. A wet pasture among the hills a mile or more northeast of Peninsula Harbor is a favorite feeding ground of these animals." At the west end of Lake Superior, in what is now Quetico Provincial Park of Ontario, caribou are extinct, "although this region was once the approximate southern limit of its winter migration. There are no records in recent years. Nash reported it as very shy but not rare in the White-face and St. Louis River country of northern Minnesota as late as 1894 . . . There is an abundance of its favorite food, the caribou moss, *Cladonia rangiferina*, throughout the region" (Cahn, 1937). A century ago there were caribou in Chippewa County, northern Michigan (Schorger, 1940). A recent report by Breckenridge (1935) shows that a last remnant of the woodland caribou still holds out "in the muskeg country lying between Upper Red Lake and Lake of the Woods in northwestern Minnesota." In company with game officers he spent from February 28 to March 3, 1935, investigating the status of these animals. Of three adults seen at close range on March 1, one retained its antlers. Evidence of at least six animals in this region was obtained, a number that is reported in the August, 1939, Biological Survey census to have been increased to 12, but the basis of this estimate is not given. The district where these caribou live is now included in the Red Lake Game Refuge, where they may be considered fairly safe except from wolves which still are found in small numbers. The refuge includes over 400,000 acres of land, "which is practically worthless, not only to the agriculturalist, but to the forester" (Swanson, 1936).

Finally, in the hope of building up the stock more rapidly, W. T. Cox (1941), in charge of the refuge, arranged to introduce new stock from Saskatchewan. With the aid of Indians, seven calves and an adult bull were captured alive and after preliminary conditioning were brought in 1938 to the refuge. Nearly a year later the bull was seen ranging with the cows. The calves, however, were kept in a corral and small pasture and later were transferred to a larger fenced area, to be liberated later. At last accounts the little group was thriving encouragingly, and every effort is being made to ensure the success of the attempt at colonization. The danger is that the animals may wander outside the reserve and fall prey to settlers or the Indians on a nearby reservation.

To sum up, the woodland caribou, once so common in the muskeg areas from Nova Scotia to western Minnesota and north to southern Labrador and James Bay, is now everywhere so greatly reduced that it is in actual danger of extermination. South of the St. Lawrence a single small group still exists in the mountains of northern Gaspé; it is gone from Nova Scotia, New Brunswick, southern Quebec and northern New England. A few scattered groups still remain in southern Labrador, but to the westward it is all but gone from Ontario, and a very small group still holds out in northern Minnesota. The main factor in its extermination has no doubt been overshooting; other factors are doubtless the animal's innate aversion to the presence of settlements, thus tending to a restriction of its range and lowered prolificness, its gregarious habits and curiosity often making easier the killing of several individuals at a time by hunters; finally forest fires may affect the food supply, and wolves, though fewer now than formerly, may be a factor. Of possible diseases nothing is known, but that deer of this group are subject to serious attack by bot flies is well ascertained, although what effect these may have in causing lowered vitality is not clear.

NEWFOUNDLAND CARIBOU

RANGIFER TERRAENOVAE Bangs

Rangifer terraenovae Bangs, Preliminary Description of the Newfoundland Caribou, p. 2, Nov. 11, 1896 (privately printed) ("Codroy, Newfoundland").
FIGS.: Grant, 1902, two pls. unnumbered (14, 15) (heads); Prichard, 1910, col. pl. opposite p. 80; Dugmore, 1913, many photographs.

The caribou of Newfoundland is not very different in general from the woodland caribou of the neighboring mainland, even though usually accorded specific status. It is said to be lighter in color, the back, sides, and legs drab, somewhat mixed with

yellowish-white hairs paling on flanks to white. Face and inner
surface of ears rich bister brown, nose and chin white; tail
short, drab above, white beneath (Bangs). The antlers are
rather distinctive, being "low, widely spread, much forked and
with the points pointing forward and inward" (Bangs). They
are, in a well-developed head, rather shorter of beam, with
large palmated brow and bez tines. The skull is said also to
be somewhat larger than in the typical woodland caribou.
An adult male stands from 46 to 49 inches at the shoulder.
Does are in about half of the cases provided with small branching antlers. Weight of a full-grown male up to about 300
pounds.

Both Prichard (1910) and Dugmore (1913) have given
excellent accounts with illustrations of this caribou. According
to the former, the population of this species in the first decade
of the present century was said to consist of three groups:
One north of the railway that crosses the island from east to
west, especially frequenting the Humber River valleys and
Birchy Lake region; the main herd, largely south of the railroad, inhabiting the central and southern parts; and a small
"herd" consisting of a few animals that still survive in the
Avalon Peninsula, south of St. John's. The last group is
believed to be nonmigratory, but the other groups perform
annual north and south migrations, with more or less regularity,
although they may not always be found at the same places in
different seasons. The first of these groups is said to be the
best known and most accessible and crosses the railway in its
southward wanderings, especially in the vicinity of Howley.
To this region resort the greater number of sportsmen in
search of trophies and of settlers who to some extent depend
on caribou meat.

In 1913 Dugmore believed that a conservative estimate of
the caribou population of the island was not less than 150,000
animals. Some estimates were much larger. It is difficult to
judge of the general status, since those visiting the hunting
grounds annually for short seasons may not find the larger
groups each time or the caribou may be for various reasons
less in evidence in different years. The interior barrens are
vast and travel is difficult. Nevertheless the consensus seems
to be that the numbers have greatly declined in the last two
decades, owing in large part to overshooting. Jacobi (1931)

writes that in February, 1899, an observer saw 550 carcasses unloaded in the harbor of St. John's and two weeks later about the same number, so that the price of meat fell to 3 cents per kilogram. However, as late as 1913 they were still common and could be seen in large bands, especially during the migrations, but large heads were more difficult to secure.

In a letter to Dr. Francis Harper, dated October 4, 1934, Greville Haslam writes that he had spent nine of the previous fourteen summers in the island, and found in 1919, 1920, and 1921 "a few caribou" each year in the region north of the railroad near the Humber River and Birchy Lake. "There was no question in anybody's mind that the caribou were disappearing, but they all claimed that this was because the animals no longer migrated, and that they would be found in large numbers in some other section, especially the country lying at the head of the Gander River and extending around Mount Cormack and west around Meelpaig Lakes. In 1929 we spent three weeks in this country but saw not a single caribou and only a few tracks made some months before. In the summer of 1934 we spent three weeks on the Serpentine River but saw no tracks." It seems that the numbers have apparently fallen off considerably in late years, but exact statistics are unavailable. At all events there was a general impression in 1934 that caribou were again increasing and in that year the Government permitted an open season, charging $50 for a license to shoot a caribou. Brooke Dolan reported that according to a Newfoundland official, 60 licenses (including two to aliens) were issued in 1936 and that some caribou were killed. One herd of about 700 was reported seen north of the railroad, but shooting was permitted to the southward of the railroad only. In 1938 John K. Howard found small numbers a little distance north of the head of White Bay. Thus it seems that there are still a good many caribou left in the country, but in order that the numbers may be maintained at an economic level some care in administration is needed.

Dugmore (1913) presents some interesting notes on habits. Summer in Newfoundland begins late in June. During this month the young caribou are born, and at this time the does seek the thick forests of spruce and fir. Usually there is a single young at a birth but twins are not rare. With the passing of wolves on the island, the lynx is about the only potential enemy. On the other hand, the swarms of black flies and mosquitoes must be a great source of annoyance to the animals as they are to human beings at this season. "During the warmer months the caribou are more or less solitary in habit, going about singly or in pairs and only rarely in small herds of half-a-dozen or more. In the day-time they keep very largely to the woods, coming out to feed at the approach of evening . . . by September their habits have completely changed and they become almost entirely diurnal," and bands gather.

An attempt is being made to introduce this caribou from Newfoundland into Nova Scotia, in the hope that it may, if the plan is successful, in time replace to a certain extent the eastern woodland caribou, which has for a number of years been extinct in this province. On April 10, 1939, nine females, of which five were "with calf," arrived in Halifax from Newfoundland. The five pregnant females were at once taken to the Liscombe Game Sanctuary in Guysboro County, while the four others were being held temporarily at Halifax pending the arrival of the three males, which were to be imported in order to start this new herd (R. W. Tufts, 1939). The result of this experiment may be awaited with interest.

WESTERN WOODLAND CARIBOU

RANGFIER CARIBOU SYLVESTRIS (Richardson)

Cervus tarandus var. β sylvestris Richardson, Fauna Boreali-Americana, vol. 1, p. 250, 1829 (southwestern shores of Hudson Bay).
FIG.: Hollister, 1912b, pl. 2, fig. 2 (skull).

The western woodland caribou is much the same as the eastern animal, but according to Hollister (1912b) it may be distinguished by its longer and slenderer skull, with a narrower rostrum and larger teeth. The tooth rows, especially the lower, are longer. The neck and head are darker, the ears, back, and sides of the neck are much darker, the hairs brown to their roots. Total length of a male skull, 417 mm.; upper tooth row, 107 mm. These characters, while not very sharply marked, are supposed to distinguish the animals west of Hudson Bay; presumably those of the Lake Superior region and James Bay are intermediate but may be referable to this rather than to the typical race.

The precise range of this race has not been well defined but is believed to have originally extended from the southwestern

shores of Hudson Bay westward across northern Manitoba to
the Anderson River, overlapping the winter range of the
barren-ground caribou to some extent and possibly reaching
the Mackenzie River region.

Dr. R. M. Anderson (1939b) writes that it is widely distributed in the timbered portions of the Northwest Territories,
but never common, ranging as far north as Great Bear Lake.
It is fairly certain that human settlement is the controlling
factor in the present range of the species. "Small numbers of
woodland caribou are found in the wooded parts of northern
Saskatchewan and Alberta, but many reports indicate that
the large number of trappers and prospectors who have
strung trap lines all along the northern parts of the Prairie
Provinces are rapidly causing the woodland caribou to disappear. Bush fires destroy their winter food of lichens which are
slow to recuperate, and the woodland caribou are shy of settlements as well as being easy to kill on the 'barren' openings in
the forest in winter." Writing of this caribou in 1902, Preble
says that he found it throughout the region he traversed between Norway House and Hudson Bay. Between York
Factory and Fort Churchill a few small bands are found
throughout the year on the "barrens." Dr. Milne, who had
resided 14 years at York Factory, told Preble that Cape
Churchill was considered a good place to hunt them at any
time of year and that he believed the small bands occurring
here formed the northern fringe of those that migrate to the
coast in spring, the great majority of which cross to the south
of Nelson River. Their return movement occurs from about
the middle of October to the last of November. "During
these semiannual movements the animals are much pursued,
especially in the fall, when the weather is usually cold enough
to preserve the meat for winter use." A resident at Oxford
House said that the species was much less common than
formerly. In his report on mammals of the Athabaska-
Mackenzie region, Preble (1908) wrote that it is found in the
"country between Lake Winnipeg and Athabaska Lake, and
though nowhere in large numbers is more abundant on the
southern than on the northern shores of this lake. Between
Athabaska and Great Slave lakes . . . the animal is
met with chiefly on the west side of Slave River, and through
all the country lying between Peace River and Great Slave

Lake." Caribou still exist in small numbers in the Peace River district, as in the vicinity of Peavine Lake and on Mount Bickford and Tuscoola Mountain (Cowan, 1939), and are presumably of this race. According to Anderson, there is some evidence that in areas visited by game officers in the winter of 1937–38, the caribou are increasing. With proper protection, they should hold their own in most of their range for the present.

Mountain Caribou

Rangifer montanus Seton

Rangifer montanus Seton, Ottawa Nat., vol. 13, p. 129, Aug., 1899 (Selkirk Range, near Revelstoke, British Columbia).

Figs.: Allen, J. A., 1902b, pp. 154, 155, 156, 157, figs. 3–6 (antlered skulls).

Rangifer fortidens Hollister

Rangifer fortidens Hollister, Smithsonian Misc. Coll., vol. 56, no. 35, p. 3, Feb. 7, 1912 ("Head of Moose Pass branch of the Smoky River, Alberta (northeast of Mount Robson)").

Fig.: Hollister, 1912a, pl. 10 (antlered skull of type).

Hollister, in 1912, described the large caribou of the woodland type from Mount Robson region as a species distinct from *R. montanus* of the Selkirk and Gold Ranges in southeastern British Columbia. The two must be closely related (the type localities are little over a hundred miles apart) and may even prove to be much the same when further study can be made with adequate specimens. Hence it is convenient to treat both together here.

Both agree in being darker in color than the more eastern forms. Dr. J. A. Allen (1902b) describes *R. montanus* in September coat as in general terms "a *black* caribou, with the neck and shoulders, especially in the males, much lighter than the body and limbs." The "whole body and legs blackish brown, varying (in different specimens) to glossy black over the middle of the dorsal area from shoulders to rump; lighter, more brownish black, on the flanks and ventral surface; inguinal region, sides and under surface of tail, a narrow band bordering the hoofs, and ventral median line of neck, grayish white; nose and edge of lips grayish white; sides of neck grayish brown varied with blackish and, in the males, tinged more or less with rusty. The females are much darker than the males, especially on the neck and shoulders, but have the grayish white areas of the males replaced by nearly pure white." The distinction between the two "species" seems to be that in *R. montanus* the size is somewhat less in skull and teeth, with shorter beams to the antlers and a more exuberant development of tines; whereas *fortidens* is said to be largest of the caribou with less branching and less shortened antlers. No doubt both should eventually be regarded as races of *R. caribou.*

The range of the more southern *montanus* was the Selkirk and Gold (or Columbia) Ranges and doubtless the adjacent country, southward to the northern border of Washington.

Newfoundland caribou (*Rangifer terraenovae*)

322 EXTINCT AND VANISHING MAMMALS

Anthony states that it formerly reached the mountains of Montana and Idaho, but certainly it has not been known in these States for a long time. In the State of Washington, Taylor and Shaw (1929) wrote that it was formerly "of occasional occurrence along the Canadian boundary in the northeastern part of the State, south to Usk, and west to Okanogan County" but that it was exterminated a decade ago (about 1920). Nevertheless the latest wildlife census by the U. S. Biological Survey credits the national forests of the State with an estimated four individuals in 1938. In a letter to Dr. Francis Harper in April, 1937, I. M. Cowan wrote that in British Columbia there are still a number of *montanus* but none now south of the main line of the Canadian Pacific Railway. In general, caribou are "definitely on the wane through overhunting," he says, "mainly by Indians."

Cowan's statement probably applies in part to the Mount Robson form, *fortidens*, as well, for he says they are "almost gone" in the Chilcotin region. Hollister in 1912 said they were not common along the line of the railroad east of the boundary line of Jasper Park but were formerly common down to the eastern foothills. Dr. R. M. Anderson wrote in 1938 that *R. montanus* "is still fairly common in the Rocky Mountains of western Alberta, but the animals are extremely scarce on most of their former range in central and southern British Columbia." In 1929 he had "fairly conclusive evidence of the presence of a small band ranging along Summit Creek on both sides of the British Columbia–Idaho border, and if these still exist they are probably the most southern representatives. At that time a few were still supposed to be in the mountains southwest of Nelson, British Columbia." Carl Rungius (in Ely et al., 1939) has lately published an account of hunting *R. fortidens* in the Mount Robson region, but he gives no dates. At the time, caribou were fairly numerous there.

Family ANTILOCAPRIDAE: Pronghorns

The Pronghorn Antelope

The pronghorns are the last surviving members of a family, the Antilocapridae, that has developed exclusively in North America. Though related to the true antelopes of the Old

World, they differ in that the horn sheaths are forked instead of simple and are shed and renewed annually instead of being permanently retained. In many of the fossil forms, the bony core of the horns was forked to correspond to the forked sheath, but in the living species this front branch of the horn core is represented by a slight bulge only. In some of the extinct species the horns showed a twisted core recalling that of the Old World bushbucks. Only a single species is known to have lived down to the Recent period, but smaller forms, such as *Capromeryx*, with a forked horn core, must have persisted to no very distant period, and have left their remains in the tar pits of Rancho La Brea, California, and elsewhere in the Southwest.

Four races of the pronghorn have been described, but they differ in such slight characters that they may be best considered together.

Pronghorn Antelope; Plains Pronghorn

Antilocapra americana americana (Ord)

Antilope americana Ord, Guthrie's Geography, 2d Amer. ed., vol. 2, pp. 292, 308, 1815 ("Plains and highlands of the Missouri").
Figs.: Stone and Cram, 1902, pl. facing p. 64 (photographs); Nelson, 1916, p. 451, upper fig. (col.); 1925, pls. 1–6 (photographs and habitat).

Mexican Pronghorn

Antilocapra americana mexicana Merriam

Antilocapra americana mexicana Merriam, Proc. Biol. Soc. Washington, vol. 14, p. 31, Apr. 5, 1901 ("Sierra en Media, Chihuahua, Mexico").

Oregon Pronghorn

Antilocapra americana oregona V. Bailey

Antilocapra americana oregona V. Bailey, Proc. Biol. Soc. Washington, vol. 45, p. 45, Apr. 2, 1932 ("Hart Mountain (Warner Mts.), Oregon").

Lower California Pronghorn

Antilocapra americana peninsularis Nelson

Antilocapra americana peninsularis Nelson, Proc. Biol. Soc. Washington, vol. 25, p. 107, 1912 ("Forty-five miles south of Calmalli, Lower California").

Light of body and limb, the pronghorn stands about 34 to 36 inches at the shoulder, with a total length of about 54 inches in adult males, females slightly less (Anthony). The forehead, nape, and upper part of the back and the outside of the limbs are rich reddish brown, with a mixture of blackish on the muzzle and in the short mane. On the throat the reddish brown of the upper parts extends as two collars, separated by a white space, around the throat, although the lower one is often incomplete in the middle line below. Under parts and flanks and a prominent rump-patch, white. Tail and a central dark line dividing this patch are colored like the back or darker. Horns erect and diverging, the posterior and longer point curving backward, the anterior point short and blunt, projecting forward.

The Mexican race is similar but paler, with a tinge of cinnamon. That of the peninsula of Lower California has the ears darker, with the facial markings dark and strongly contrasting with the pale areas. The Oregon race is slightly larger than the typical race of the plains, with relatively larger feet, longer horns, and slightly paler color. The distinctions between these races are slight and the distributional areas need more careful mapping.

Pronghorns are characteristic of open plains country of a semi-desert nature and seldom enter tree-grown areas except in winter to find shelter from storms. Their flashing of the erectile white hair of the rump-patch makes a remarkably striking semaphore visible at a great distance in sunlight and affords an automatic danger signal to others of their kind. They go in bands of varying size according to the circumstances and when once alarmed can reach a great speed, seeming fairly to fly over the ground. A curious habit seen in this and in some other animals, as gazelle in the Gobi or seabirds in open ocean, is a seeming desire to match speed with pursuers, and, attaining a sufficient lead, to cross in front. Another characteristic trait is curiosity, leading animals often to approach unfamiliar appearing objects. Nelson tells of enticing shy animals up within gunshot by donning a white sheet and approaching them on all fours.

In an important paper on the status of the pronghorned antelope, Dr. E. W. Nelson (1925) presents a careful summary of its former and recent distribution. It originally ranged over an enormous area, from the present provinces of Manitoba, Saskatchewan, and Alberta in the north to the southern part of Texas and the Mexican tableland in the south, and from the

eastern edge of the plains in Minnesota, Iowa, Kansas, and
Oklahoma westward to eastern Washington, Oregon, and the
valleys and coast of southern California and most of the peninsula of Lower California. "In Mexico it occupied the open
plains country of the tableland south almost to 20° of latitude,
nearly to the valley of Mexico" and the western part of Sonora.
Originally it was abundant and well distributed over this
territory and exceeded the bison in numbers where both
occurred together. It is estimated by Nelson that at the time
of the settlement of this continent by Europeans the pronghorn population was "not less than thirty to forty millions,
possibly more." A recent census of those still existing in the
United States, Canada and Mexico (1922–24), indicates that
of these vast numbers about 30,000 then remained, but a later
figure (1939) makes this over 180,000.

   The pronghorn just reached the prairie country of southwestern Minnesota in its northeastward distribution, but
Herrick, writing of it in 1892, speaks of it as having "long since"
gone. That it may even have penetrated farther east is
possibly indicated by the recent discovery of a horn buried in
a few inches of earth at Moline, Ill., although it may have been
brought there by Indians in earlier years (Fryxell, 1926).
Formerly abundant all over the Dakotas, it began to decline
in the late seventies, and with the encroachment of settlement
gradually disappeared. By 1924, Nelson wrote that but five
small herds aggregating 225 animals remained, and these in
the southwestern corner; in South Dakota about three times
that number were found in the western half of the State.
"Of the countless thousands of antelope which once roamed
the plains of Nebraska but 10 small bands remain, containing
a total of about 187 animals." "At one time Kansas was
inhabited by myriads of pronghorns, and for years after the
construction of the transcontinental railroads they were a
familiar sight to passengers on the trains. In 1923, however,
they had become almost exterminated throughout the State,"
and the few remaining were to be found only in the extreme
southwest corner where they wandered at times into the
adjacent parts of Oklahoma. Otherwise the species once so
common in this State was gone, but in 1910 an attempt was
made to establish a herd in the Wichita National Game Preserve in Comanche County. After several unsuccessful im-

portations of antelope from Yellowstone National Park, the difficulties were finally overcome, and in 1925 Nelson reported that the birth of three pairs of young had brought the total number of this small band up to 17.

Except for Oregon the Rocky Mountain States seem now to hold the largest antelope populations. Nelson's account shows Montana with some 44 herds and a total population of over 3,000; Wyoming leads with 27 areas in which a total of nearly 7,000 is carried; Colorado has 28 localities mostly in the eastern half of the State where over 1,200 pronghorns are found; in New Mexico the numbers were decreasing, but a total of 31 localities and nearly 1,700 animals was recorded in 1924. In Arizona the estimates were 18 bands totaling about 650 animals; they appeared to be increasing on cattle ranges but decreasing on sheep ranges in the State. In Utah the number of bands was 10, with about 670 animals; in Idaho 14 bands with about 1,500 animals. In Nevada, where once they were plentiful, they were found in only 11 limited areas, but since some of these are areas sparsely occupied by man the numbers of antelope are large, aggregating over 4,200. Southeastern Oregon, where the form *oregonus* is found, "forms part of a rough, rocky desert covering also northern Nevada and south-western Idaho, on which natural conditions have been exceedingly favorable for antelope. This region constitutes one of the few areas in the United States where large herds of these animals numbering hundreds still continue to congregate during the winter season." Here they have increased in recent years and were in 1924 estimated at over 2,000 animals. In Texas, antelope formerly abounded on the plains in the western part, "but with the occupation of the country they have decreased until it has been possible to obtain definite information of only 42 existing bands, numbering about 2,400 animals, for the entire State." While most of these are in the western third, a few hundred are also found in the southwestern tip. A few antelope remain in California, where once they were abundant; in 1923 there were six widely separated areas in the State where small bands were found totaling about 1,057.

In comparison with these estimates of 1924, the following issued by the U. S. Biological Survey are significant: South Dakota, 4,508 (large increase); Nebraska, 750 (large increase); Kansas, none (decrease); Oklahoma, 36 (increase); Montana,

6,740 (doubled); Wyoming, 24,071 (more than tripled); Colorado, 1,770 (slight increase); New Mexico, 26,564 (great increase); Arizona, 9,410 (great increase); Utah, 35,350 (great
increase); Idaho, 12,328 (great increase); Nevada, 12,700
(about tripled); Oregon, 28,550 (great increase); Texas, 9,075
(great increase); California, 14,212 (great increase). The
estimate published by Nelson in 1925 gave a total of 26,604
pronghorns in the United States; the 1939 estimate by the
U. S. Biological Survey was 186,114, or nearly a sevenfold
increase for the same States. It is clear that the animal is no
longer in danger; in fact, in some areas it is common enough to
cause resentment among the ranchers for fear that the herds
will make the grazing less available for their cattle. In several
of the States antelope refuges have been established, which,
especially in Nevada and Oregon, are well populated by the
animals.

Obviously, with the continued increase of these herds and
their tameness as a result of protection, there will come points
where the numbers are too great, and their competition for
food with domestic stock must result in measures being taken
to reduce the numbers to a reasonable proportion. It remains
to be seen whether this is best done by having brief open
seasons such as have been declared in Wyoming and Nevada
or in some other way. The natural enemies of the pronghorn
are chiefly coyotes, which kill the fawns, and bobcats, which in
winter may kill a few. Wolves formerly were doubtless a
principal enemy. With present measures against these animals, the menace seems slight. These antelope are said not to
do well under fence, for it has been found that "within such
areas" they seem "to lose their freedom of movement and become extraordinarily helpless. This is particularly the case
during heavy snowstorms, when they remain within more or
less definite areas, in which predatory animals capture them
with surprising ease."

In Canada the pronghorn formerly ranged eastward to
southwestern Manitoba but is now restricted to southwestern
Saskatchewan and southern Alberta. Nelson's (1925) estimate
for 1924 gave a total of 1,327 antelope for Canada, but Anderson (1939b) shows a figure nearly double this, about 2,400 in
1932, as a result of protection, and adds that in 1938 the Fish
and Game Commissioner of Alberta estimated the antelope

population of that province at 15,000, and there have been two short open seasons. In certain districts they have even extended their range north of the South Red Deer River, as well as into the adjacent parts of Montana and Saskatchewan. In the latter province there was an open season in 1936 during which 267 antelope were taken.

In Mexico the situation is less clear, but Nelson's (1925) report gives an estimate of about 2,400 animals, of which 500 are in Lower California, the rest being in the States of Sonora adjoining and Chihuahua, Durango, and Coahuila to the eastward. In Lower California the pronghorn was formerly found over much of this desert country nearly to the tip of the peninsula, which is mountainous and unsuitable for them. At present the range extends, according to Nelson, only to the basal half, on the plains east of the central mountain range, and on the Desert of Vizcaino west of it. With the establishment of a close season at the time of Nelson's report, he believed that their prospect of surviving in these sparsely settled desert lands was very good.

From the human viewpoint pronghorn antelope may be a source of food in some areas, and they have an esthetic and recreational value as well for those who enjoy the sight of wild game or take pleasure in hunting it with gun or camera. Large herds such as gather in winter may, on the other hand, cause some competition with grazing stock of which ranchmen are jealous. On the whole, however, it seems that the preservation of the species at least in certain large areas of our West is well assured at present and that its numbers can be readily controlled where the necessity exists. Some pertinent suggestions for the management of this antelope in the arid Southwest have been put forth by Dr. W. P. Taylor (1936), who points out that in these regions herds of pronghorns in severe winter weather are wont to come down off the mountains to lower levels where they come into competition with cattle on the ranches for winter food. Ordinarily they do not like sheep ranges but prefer those suitable for larger stock. These factors are often of critical value in the selection of reserves for their preservation. The ranchmen have often done much to encourage these animals and give them protection.

Family BOVIDAE: Sheep, Goats, Cattle

THE MUSKOXEN

Much has been written on the relationships of the muskox to other ruminants. Although many fossil skulls have been found of this and related animals, there seems to be little evidence that the type represented by the living species was derived from the Old World. It is therefore believed that it must have originated in the New World and in late geological times spread into northern parts of the Old. While some zoologists have thought it related to the sheep or the goat-antelopes, the latest suggestions favor its close affinity to the bison. The single living species is of high Arctic distribution from (until recently) Alaska to Hudson Bay and the Arctic Archipelago, and thence across northern Greenland to the eastern coast of that country. Over this area it becomes differentiated locally into three generally recognized races, for a full account of which the reader is referred to the extensive papers of J. A. Allen (1913) and Elisabeth Hone (1934).

BARREN-GROUND MUSKOX

OVIBOS MOSCHATUS MOSCHATUS (Zimmermann)

Bos moschatus Zimmermann, Geographische Geschichte, vol. 2, p. 86, 1780 (based on Pennant's description; type locality "therefore the region adjoining Hudson Bay between the Seal and Churchill rivers (about latitude 59°)", Keewatin (J. A. Allen, 1913)).

SYNONYM: *Ovibos moschatus mackenzianus* Kowarzik, Fauna Arctica, vol. 5, pt. 1, pp. 97, 116–122, 1910.

FIGS.: Allen, J. A., 1913, figs. 28, 30, 32, 39 (exterior and skull).

The typical race of the muskox is "very dark, nearly black on the head, neck, sides, and underparts, with the feet and nose white; the back is lighter (browner black), with a still lighter "saddle" behind the shoulders. There is no white area on the head in adult males, although individual white hairs may often be found on the face; in young animals and females there is sometimes quite a trace of white on the front of the head" (J. A. Allen, 1913). The long hair of the body forms a protecting fringe on the sides. The horns are characteristically dark brown and are very broad at the base in proportion to their length. They sweep downward and slightly forward, then turn upward to form a hook; the record length

of horn on the outside curve is 29 inches. A large bull killed
at Aylmer Lake was measured by Seton as follows: Total
length, 96 inches; tail, 4 inches; height at shoulder, 59 inches.
The basal length of the skull in adult males is about 466 mm.,
with a maxillary toothrow of 132 mm.

The continental range of the muskox formerly was more or
less coextensive with the barren grounds west of Hudson Bay,
extending to the Arctic coast and the adjacent islands, which
must have been reached by crossing on the ice in winter. On
account of certain characteristic habits this species became
peculiarly liable to extermination when hunted by men with
modern weapons. Lacking the speed to escape such enemies
as wolves, and having the habit of living in small groups, these
animals when attacked would form a close circle, the adults
with heads out to the enemy, the young huddled at the inner
side against their mothers' quarters. When closely approached
by wolves, one of the company would suddenly dash out from
the ring in an endeavor to rip one of the assailants with its
horns, then as quickly dart back into its place. This method
of defense, while probably efficient against wolves, its only
natural enemy, was often its undoing when attacked by men
with modern guns, for the entire group might then be killed
at close quarters. Against Eskimo and Indians, who in former
days often depended in part upon muskox for winter food, this
defense was probably more effective before the use of firearms.
During the summer season the almost impenetrable muskegs
of the north form a fairly safe retreat, and the animals' long
silky coat seems sufficient protection against cold and bliz-
zards. But against Eskimo and Indians with modern arms,
they can make little stand, while the thoughtlessness of human
pursuers in wantonly killing entire groups has in places brought
the species to the verge of extinction.

There is evidence that at no very distant time the range of
the muskox extended westward at least to Point Barrow,
Alaska, where according to Frank Russell, in 1898, the oldest
natives "say that their fathers killed muskox, which were then
abundant." The fact that skulls of muskoxen have been found
on the neighboring tundra confirms this statement. J. A.
Allen (1913), in reviewing this evidence, believes that muskoxen
existed on the tundra of northern Alaska till about the middle
of the nineteenth century. A. J. Stone, after extensive inquiry

among the Indians and Eskimo west of the Mackenzie, came
to the conclusion that the species had not inhabited that region
for a very long period. Their western limit, at the close of the
nineteenth century, he writes (1900); is "far to the east of
Anderson River and Liverpool Bay." In the region about
Artillery Lake, where the muskox was common shortly before
1901, it was practically exterminated a few years later. Continual hunting by the Eskimo from the coasts and by the
Indians from the southern borders of the barren grounds had
reduced their numbers still further in the early years of this
century, so that Dr. R. M. Anderson, in 1917, believed that
they were extinct west of the Tree River and much reduced
elsewhere, especially near the accessible regions along the
Arctic coasts,

In 1913 Dr. J. A. Allen well summed up the situation at that
time as follows: "With all its natural fitness to survive, the
muskox is doomed wherever it can be utilized by man as a
commercial asset. The history of its restriction in range and
decline in numbers over the western part of its former range
during the last quarter of a century . . . indicates clearly
its fate wherever it can be reached by the white man, either
directly or through his Eskimo or Indian allies . . . But
wherever its range is shared by the Eskimos, as many portions
are, the muskox's fate is sealed, as shown by its extermination
over the greater part of the large expanse of land known as
Victoria Island. It will also rapidly decline over the more
accessible parts of Ellesmere Land and Grinnell Land, through
intrusions of ambitious sportsmen. It is doomed throughout
the mainland of northern Canada unless the Canadian Government takes the utmost care in restricting the killing . . .
Much could be done to preserve a considerable remnant of
these unsuspicious animals if the Danish, Canadian, and other
governments would declare muskox peltries contraband and
suppress all traffic in them, while the Canadian and Danish
governments might set aside reservations within which neither
Eskimos and Indians nor white hunters should be allowed to
kill them." Fortunately the Canadian Government in 1927
established a sanctuary known as the Thelon Game Sanctuary,
with an area of 15,000 square miles, northeast of Great Slave
Lake, which so far as then known included the last important
herd of muskoxen remaining on the mainland of Canada. No

person may hunt or trap within its borders, and entry is prohibited except under permit from the Minister of the Interior. In 1929 it was estimated that there were 250 muskoxen in this sanctuary. In 1935 a representative of the department made an airplane survey and counted 180 muskoxen north of the junction of the Thelon and Hanbury Rivers (Cameron, 1936), and Dr. R. M. Anderson (1937) adds that there are a few scattered bands and individuals still farther north, although few if any animals are now known to occur very near the Arctic coast. With this protection it seems likely that the remnant of the continental muskox is safe enough at present.

HUDSON BAY MUSKOX

OVIBOS MOSCHATUS NIPHOECUS Elliot

Ovibos moschatus niphoecus Elliot, Proc. Biol. Soc. Washington, vol. 18, p. 135, Apr. 18, 1905 (type locality, head of Wager Inlet, Hudson Bay, not "600 miles north of Hudson Bay" as originally given).
FIG.: Kowarzik, 1910, vol. 5, fig. 8.

In his key, J. A. Allen (1913) characterizes this race as having "usually no coronal nor facial white areas in adult males, but traces of them (often well developed) in young males and females; horns more slender and longer in proportion to their basal breadth, and generally light-colored; toothrow relatively longer (max[illary] series, ♂, 130 [mm.]); basal length of skull in old males, 442 mm." The males are usually more intensely black than the typical race, and the horns are lighter colored. While males generally lack the white on face and crown, the females and young are much like the Greenland race. In body size it is much as in the typical race.

The range of this race, and indeed its characters, do not seem to be very well defined. The region whence came the original specimens was at the head of Wager Inlet, in the northwestern corner of Hudson Bay. According to Captain Comer, who collected them, the muskox does not now range south of Chesterfield Inlet, but it is believed that the distribution of this race extends northward from the latter point to the Arctic coast of the mainland and inland for an undetermined distance. They are not found on Melville Peninsula or in Baffin Land, nor do the natives there have any tradition of their former occurrence. North of Baker Lake the natives say that the muskoxen are larger, perhaps representing the typical race. Captain Comer states that formerly the native Eskimo hunted these animals but seldom on account of the risks involved in making the inland trips, but are encouraged to undertake their pursuit by traders who are eager for the pelts. Up till recent years at least, the remoteness of the region where these muskoxen occurred was itself a factor of safety, for few hunters would enter it unless well provisioned (J. A. Allen, 1913).

Though explorers agree that no muskoxen are now known to occur on Melville Peninsula or on Baffin Island, there is some evidence that they may formerly have been found there but have been exterminated by the Eskimos. "The Canadian commission report (1922, p. 13) notes a tradition of a Muskox once killed on Baffin island . . . ," while on Melville Peninsula Freuchen states that it has so recently been exterminated there that the Eskimos "still knew the names of men who have hunted it" (Hone, 1934). Apparently there is nothing to indicate that muskoxen ever occurred naturally on Southampton, although, as noted by Miss Hone, Freuchen "says that some teeth were found in the settlement at Kuk on the west side of York Bay, and according to the Eskimos there was a skull in a house ruin on the south shore."

WHITE-FACED MUSKOX

OVIBOS MOSCHATUS WARDI Lydekker

Ovibos moschatus wardi Lydekker, Nature (London), vol. 63, p. 157, Dec. 13, 1900 (Clavering Island, off East Greenland).

SYNONYM: *Ovibos moschatus melvillensis* Kowarzik, Fauna Arctica, vol. 5, pp. 113–116, 1910.

FIGS.: Allen, J. A., 1913, figs. 29, 31, 33, 34–38, 40–44, pls. 11–17 (exterior, live animals, skull, teeth).

This northernmost race of the muskox has "conspicuous areas of white between and behind the horns, and face and sides of the head sometimes suffused with white to a greater or less extent in old males, in which much of the original white area is obliterated by the development of the horn bases; horns long and slender in proportion to their basal breadth, very light creamy white; tooth row relatively longer than in *moschatus* (max[illary] series in males, 140 mm.); basal length of skull in old males, 442 mm." "In general coloration *wardi* is not so dark as either *moschatus* or *niphoecus;* the saddle area and especially the horns are much lighter in color" (J. A. Allen, 1913). Tables of cranial measurements for this and other races of the muskox are given by the latter author.

The range of the white-faced muskox occupies "a narrow coast belt of Greenland from about latitude 70° on the east side north as far as land extends, and thence southward along the west coast to about 81°, and within historic times as far south as Westenholme Sound (latitude 78°), where its further progress south appears to have been checked by impassable glaciers. It formerly occupied practically the whole Arctic Archipelago from Grant Land and Ellesmere Land westward to Prince Patrick Island and south to Lancaster Sound and Coronation Gulf. Thus it must have nearly met the range of *niphoecus* on the mainland west of the Gulf of Boothia, and the range of *moschatus* thence westward to Coronation Gulf and Dolphin and Union Strait . . . They have been exterminated from the greater part of Victoria Island, including Victoria Land, Wollaston Land, and part of Prince Albert Land. Hundreds have been killed on Melville Island, and thousands in northern Ellesmere Land, Grinnell Land, and Grant Land, mainly by explorers for the support of their dogs and men. They are found in winter as well as in summer on the most northern known land, being in no sense migratory" (J. A. Allen, 1913).

On Banks Island muskoxen were formerly numerous, for there was much good pasturage there. They were exterminated, however, by the Eskimos, who killed entire bands, utilizing little of the meat. The latest record given by Miss Hone (1934) is of a band killed by Eskimos in the spring of 1911. At the present time the muskox is said to be extinct on this island. On Victoria Island there were formerly "plenty" in the little-visited northern part, and there are reports of them having been killed as recently as 1924 (Hone, 1934); the stock is, however, apparently small. Prince of Wales Island, at least within a few years, held a population of muskoxen that Anderson estimated at 1,500. They were present on Somerset Island in the middle of the last century but are now gone. Melville Island was the first of the Arctic islands where muskoxen were found; Parry in 1819–20 reported them "in considerable numbers." Storkersen in 1916 estimated that there were about four thousand on this island. They occur also on

Byam Martin Island and on Bathurst Island, where Anderson estimates there are about 1,500. The numbers on Devon Island seem fewer according to recent reports. On Axel Heiberg they are plentiful, although, according to Anderson, they are found only on the east side and may number in all about 1,000. On Ellesmere Island they were common along the east coast up till the eighties, but since then they have seldom been seen there, although numbers occur in the western areas and may in these less-visited parts be still numerous.

On the short stretch of coast opposite Ellesmere Island in west Greenland muskoxen formerly occurred, as far south as Cape Alexander. South of this point the obstructing glaciers prevent further extension. A few animals were to be found northward of these points till about 1850, when the last living muskoxen in the region were reported seen by Eskimo near Cape George Russell. Macmillan (1918) mentions numerous skulls to be found from Etah north to Humboldt Glacier, but the animal no longer occurs there and is believed to have become extinct about 1860. Various expeditions have reported muskoxen in some numbers at various localities on the north coast of Greenland and Miss Hone (1934) has lately assembled many

White-faced muskox (*Ovibos moschatus wardi*)

notes on their occurrence in bands large or small along the east coast as far as the region of Scoresby Sound. Anderson, a decade ago, believed there were approximately 1,500 head in East Greenland, but others believe this figure too low. Jennov places the numbers between 6,000 and 10,000. There is some evidence that they are more abundant than they were when this region was inhabited by Eskimo. Their distribution may be sporadic, depending on the depth of winter snows and on whether the summer has been warm enough to produce pasture.

There has been some controversy as to whether muskoxen are in need of protection in Greenland. While the inhospitable nature of their habitat prevents much hunting by visitors, it is obvious that near the Eskimo settlements, as in northwestern Greenland, they will continue to dwindle, unless perhaps, as has been hinted, these Eskimo themselves may be decreasing. After four years in East Greenland, Pedersen is of the opinion that protection is more than ever needed, partly on account of the excessive use made of the animals as food by trappers from Norway, and partly on account of the trade in young animals for zoological gardens, for in order to secure the calves, the herd of adults must first be shot. Although regulations have been proposed for limiting the number of animals that may be killed as well as prohibiting hunting for sport or for the capture of calves for commercial purposes, the latest reports at hand do not indicate great progress in this direction.

An interesting experiment was undertaken a few years ago in introducing this muskox into Alaska, in order if possible to reestablish the animal over areas formerly occupied by it. In 1930, on the suggestion of the legislature of Alaska, the United States Congress appropriated $40,000 for obtaining the necessary stock. Thirty-four animals, both calves and adults, were captured in East Greenland, transported to Norway, thence to New York, and by rail to Seattle, whence they were finally brought by boat to Seward, Alaska (Bell, 1931). This herd has prospered, so that in 1936 Dr. Bell wrote to Dr. Harper in response to inquiry that the animals were doing well, had reached breeding age, and already had produced two crops of calves, five the first year and six in the second year. In 1935 two pairs of animals were transferred to Nunivak Island as an experiment and have thrived there, since food is plentiful. The herd was later placed on Nunivak National

Wildlife Refuge. At last accounts the herd was in excellent condition and had increased to 90 animals (Dufresne, 1942).

THE AMERICAN BISON

Although evidence is accumulating that at least one large species of extinct bison was contemporaneous with early man in North America, only one species was found on the continent at the time of its discovery by Europeans (see Meserve and Barbour, 1932). This species is closely related to the Old World bison, *Bison bonasus*, but differs in numerous details, as in the larger chest, smaller pelvus and shorter tail. In early days the "buffalo," as it is almost universally called, was found in great numbers over a vast range in this continent, but with the westward expansion of settlements it became an object of exploitation on a tremendous scale, so that literally millions were killed, and it was wiped out in the East and later over much of its western range. The story of this decimation has been many times told, but more especially by J. A. Allen (1876a, 1876b, 1877), Hornaday (1889), and recently by Garretson (1938). Although attempts have been made to distinguish several local races, the characters of these are for the most part imperfectly known, and the respective ranges undefined. The northern form, or wood bison, however, constitutes a fairly well marked race.

PLAINS BISON; "BUFFALO"

BISON BISON BISON (Linnaeus)

[*Bos*] *bison* Linnaeus, Systema Naturae, ed. 10, vol. 1, p. 72, 1758 (Mexico).

Bos americanus Gmelin, Linnaeus's Systema Naturae, ed. 13, vol. 1, pt. 1, p. 294, 1788.

Bison bison hanningtoni FIGGINS, Proc. Colorado Mus. Nat. Hist., vol. 12, no. 4, p. 30, pls. 8, 9, Dec. 5, 1933 ("Head of Rock Creek, northeast South Park, Park County, Colorado"). Doubtfully distinct.

Bison bison septentrionalis Figgins, *op. cit.*, p. 28, pl. 7, Dec. 5, 1933 ("Six miles northeast of Palmer, Nebraska"). Doubtfully distinct.

FIGS.: Allen, J. A., 1876a, pls. 5, 6, 9, 10, 12, fig. 1-6 (skulls and teeth); Garretson, 1938, pls. facing title page and p. 5.

EASTERN BISON

BISON BISON PENNSYLVANICUS Shoemaker

Bison americanus pennsylvanicus H. W. Shoemaker, A Pennsylvania Bison Hunt (Middleburg, Pa.), p. 9, 1915 ("Pennsylvania").

Since the first accounts of the American bison were those
brought back by the Spanish explorers of northeastern Mexico,
this is taken as the type locality of the so-called Plains bison,
the range of which is believed to have covered much of interior
North America from the tableland of Mexico and the grass-
lands of the West to the eastern Alleghenies, perhaps even
reaching the coast in the southeastern States. In a recent
history of the bison in Pennsylvania, Shoemaker has named the
animal ranging "between the east and west slopes of the
Alleghenies, migrating between the Great Lakes and the valleys
of Southern Pennsylvania, Maryland and Virginia, to Georgia,"
as a distinct eastern race, *pennsylvanicus*, but unfortunately
the description is not based on a comparison of specimens, but
upon local tradition that the bison of this region was larger
than the Plains animal, and "very dark, many of the old bulls
being coal black, with grizzly white hairs around the nose and
eyes"; the hump "was notable by its absence" (which seems
strange), while the legs were "long" without the contrast
between the height of the fore and hind quarters seen in more
western animals. It is difficult to know what value to give
such an account, but the probability that these eastern bison
were somewhat different from those of the Mexican tableland
warrants the tentative recognition of the name. The characters claimed for the bison of Colorado and of Nebraska, named
B. b. hanningtoni and *B. b. septentrionalis*, respectively, seem
more likely to be merely individual variations in tooth structure, so that I have for the present considered these names as
synonyms of *B. bison bison*.

An adult male Plains bison stands about 5½ to 6 feet at the
highest point of the shoulder, but only about 4⅔ feet at the
hip, so that the hind quarters are proportionately small and
the back is sloping. The females are somewhat smaller than
males. J. A. Allen (1876a) gives the following measurements:
Muzzle to insertion of tail, male, about 9 feet (2.75 m.); female,
about 6.5 feet (2 m.). The horns are short, thick at the base,
curving outward and upward, then somewhat inward. In the
female they are slenderer than in the male. "In winter the
head, neck, legs, tail, and whole under parts, are blackish-
brown; the upper surface of the body lighter. The color above
becomes gradually lighter towards spring; the new short hair
in autumn is soft dark umber or liver-brown. In very old

individuals the long wooly hair over the shoulders bleaches to a light yellowish-brown . . . The chin and throat are also covered with long hair, which under the chin forms an immense beard, eight or ten inches to a foot or more in length. Thick masses of long hair also arise from the inner and posterior surfaces of the fore legs, where the hair often attains a length of six or eight inches. A strip of long hair also extends along the crest of the back nearly to the tail. The tail is covered with only short soft hair till near the tip, from which arises a tuft of coarse long hair twelve to eighteen inches in length" (J. A. Allen, 1876a). Rarely, black or melanistic individuals occur, and still more rarely an albino. Many cranial measurements are tabulated in the monograph of J. A. Allen (1876a, 1876b).

Much has been written on the history, distribution, decimation, and reestablishment of this species. In the eastern part of North America the bison ("*pennsylvanicus*") occurred as far east as the western parts of New York State, but in interglacial times it probably extended to New England, as proved by the discovery of a piece of the maxilla with characteristic milk premolars found in glacial till on Cape Cod (G. M. Allen, 1920). From western New York southward small herds were found in former times in the mountains of Pennsylvania, West Virginia, and Tennessee, into the upper parts of North and South Carolina, following the valleys of the New, Holston, and French Broad Rivers. Probably the extreme southeastern limit was in Georgia, where in the southeastern part is a creek still known as Buffalo Creek. There seems to be no certainty, however, that it was found in the present limits of the State of Florida, although its occasional presence there in former times is not unlikely. It is believed that the eastward extension of the bison's range was taking place at the time of the discovery, aided in part by the clearing of forests by the Indians and in part by the attraction of salt licks as in the mountains of Pennsylvania and West Virginia. To the northward the animals reached the shores of Lake Erie in their annual migrations and thence ranged westward to Lake Winnipeg and in increasing numbers over the Great Plains, to the edge of the Great Basin, and north of that to the extreme northeastern part of California and southeastern Oregon. The bison of the latter State has recently been described as a distinct race (see below).

In its southward extent, the bison seems to have reached northern Alabama, central Mississippi, and Louisiana but attained the Gulf coast only in extreme southern Texas and northeastern Mexico (see map in J. A. Allen, 1876a).

There is but little contemporary record of buffalo in early days east of the Alleghenies, but what evidence remains indicates that they were locally common in western Pennsylvania, West Virginia, and the Carolinas, but were constantly persecuted by settlers, explorers, and to some extent by the Indians, for meat and hides, and even wantonly destroyed. In their spring migration northward and during the autumnal migration southward over a considerable extent of country, they wore deep trails following the easiest gradients and natural passes, going to better feeding grounds. Many of these paths came to be the trails and routes used later by the settlers pushing westward from the coast. This emigration received impetus after the Revolution when "thousands of officers and men who had served in the war received their pay in land script" (Garretson, 1938). Even before this, the settlers had found that numbers of bison were incompatible with their own safety, for on occasion the herds would eat and trample down their slender crops and on one occasion an early settler on Toby and Licking Creeks (now Oil and Clarion Creeks), Pennsylvania, had his cabin demolished by a herd of these animals that persisted in rubbing their backs and sides against its timbers. In his first two seasons this man and his companions killed 600 or 700 bison, the skins of which brought but 2 shillings apiece. Such continued slaughter together with the destruction of the natural food of the bison, through firing of the grass and canebrakes by the settlers, gradually reduced their numbers so that by the close of the eighteenth century the "buffalo" in Pennsylvania "had been reduced to one herd, numbering between three and four hundred animals which had sought refuge in the wilds of the Seven Mountains, where, surrounded on all sides by settlements, they survived for a short time by hiding on the most inaccessible parts of the mountains" (Garretson, 1938). According to Garretson, the last buffalo migrations from the Ohio country into Pennsylvania had ceased prior to 1783, and the year 1795 marked the disappearance of the last herds in the northwestern parts of the State. In the very severe winter of 1799–1800, what was probably the last herd in Pennsylvania was slaughtered when, huddled together in the deep snow in a great hollow known as the "Sink" in the White Mountains of Union County, they were rendered nearly helpless. In the following year a bull, a cow, and a calf were seen in the same county, and the bull was killed the following year; it was believed to be the last wild buffalo to be shot in the State. The cow and calf were hunted but eventually disappeared, and with that the bison became extinct in Pennsylvania. The story of the buffalo in West Virginia is very similar, but they persisted a little longer. According to Garretson (1938), "the last buffalo killed in Kanawha County, West Virginia, was in 1815, on the waters of the Little Sandy Creek of Elk River, about twelve miles from Charleston. It is also recorded that as late as 1825 a buffalo cow and her calf were killed at Valley Head, near the source of Tygart's River, and these are believed to be the last buffalo killed in the East." Thus by 1825, with the rapid opening up of the Middle West, and the slaughter of these animals by the settlers, the buffalo had become practically extinct east of the Mississippi, although a few stragglers were killed in Wisconsin as late as 1833 (Cory, 1912).

With the transcontinental surveys followed by the transcontinental railways in the two or three decades after 1830, added to the expansion of the fur trade in the West, the slaughter of the vast herds beyond the Mississippi began in earnest. "As early as 1840 the American Fur Company sent 67,000 robes to St. Louis and in 1848, 110,000 robes were received, also 25,000 tongues." The skins of cows only were used for robes, for those of bulls were too heavy. Hayden, of the U. S. Geological Survey, who visited "the upper Missouri country in 1850–1860, estimated the number of buffalo killed every year to be about 250,000 of which 100,000 were for robes" (Garretson). The railroad companies, advancing their lines across the western country, employed hunters to keep their camps supplied with buffalo meat, and the hunters likewise shipped back incredible quantities of tongues and hides for sale in the East.

After the Civil War the army posts on the Plains increased in number, and hunters on contract supplied the camps with meat. In the seventies bison were recklessly slaughtered by the hundreds of thousands, and for every one utilized Hornaday (1889) believes two were wasted. Only the best hides and the choicest parts of the meat were saved. South of the main transcontinental railroad lines, what came to be known as the "southern herd" centered in Kansas, Oklahoma, and Texas. In December 1877 and January 1878 the "last great slaughter" of this group took place when more than 100,000 hides were taken by an army of hunters. By the end of the latter year, this herd had been practically wiped out. A few remained in the southwestern corner of Kansas until 1879, when the last one in that State was killed west of Dodge City. In Texas, scattered herds survived later, but it is believed that a little group of four killed near Buffalo Springs were the last survivors of the southern herd. It was said that at this period, when war was still being carried on against some of the tribes of Plains Indians, the extermination of the buffalo on which they chiefly depended for food was a factor also in the destruction of the Indians. This period of the seventies marked the turn of the tide for the buffalo, and their numbers rapidly decreased both in the southern and the northern part of their range. Garretson (1938) has published some interesting pictures of the vast quantities of bones bleaching on the sites of slaughter, and for years after persons made a living by collecting these bones in cartloads and shipping them east to be made into fertilizer.

In the late eighties naturalists and others interested in wild life began to realize that the bison was approaching extermination. Apart from a few privately owned herds and a herd closely protected by the Government in Yellowstone National Park very few remained in a wild condition in the United States. It was at this time that Dr. Hornaday (1889) made his stirring protest against the extermination of the species. By 1900 there were but two herds of bison remaining in a wild state in North America: the small one in Yellowstone Park and the wood bison in Athabaska. Notwithstanding supposed protection of the former, there was for a time considerable poaching, and it was not until May 1894 that an effective law for the preservation of the bison was passed by Congress. In 1902 Congress appropriated $15,000 for the purchase of buffalo from privately owned herds to build up the small stock then remaining in Yellowstone Park. Soon after, through the efforts of the New York Zoological Society, the Wichita herd was established, following the plan that numerous small herds

NORTH AMERICA AND THE WEST INDIES

in different areas would be the wisest way to build up a stock of these animals. In 1905 the American Bison Society was founded, starting with a group of 16 public-spirited citizens who saw the need for steps being taken if the bison was not to become endangered. The story of its work in establishing at various suitable places small herds as nuclei, and thus building up a sufficient population so that the species would no longer be in danger, has been graphically told by Garretson (1938). The effectiveness of these efforts is evident from the table published by the latter, showing that in 1889 the total population of bison in existence was placed at 1,091 but by 1933 had been built up to well over 21,000, of which the greater part (17,043) were in Canada. There are now some 121 small herds in 41 States totaling 4,404 animals. Thus the species seems no longer in danger of vanishing from the face of the earth, but there is good assurance that in suitable places and under supervision sufficient numbers may be maintained under fence to make certain of its preservation.

From a practical point of view, bison were formerly the main source of meat for many of the Plains Indians, as well as for the early settlers in certain regions. Their later exploitation by hunters was no doubt largely unnecessary. yet one should not lay too great a blame upon the shoulders of those who, in the presence of seemingly unbounded stores of animals, made use of them for their own gain. For as yet the needs of "conservation" had not been made obvious.

Experiments have from time to time been made in crossing the bison with domestic cattle, but although the resulting "cattaloes" possess certain desirable qualities, it does not appear that the hybrids have proved popular with agriculturalists.

One of the largest of the protected herds has been that maintained at Buffalo National Park at Wainwright, Alberta. Its numbers were lately estimated at about 3,000 head, and in addition on the reserve were nearly half as many wapiti, as well as numbers of deer and moose, together with some imported yak from Tibet. Now, 1940, as a late development of the war in Europe, comes word that this national park must be utilized for other purposes, which according to rumor, include the training of aviators, and the animals must be cleared from the area. According to a quotation in *Science* (vol. 91, pp. 12–13, Jan. 5, 1940), the bison are to be killed and the meat and hides sold.

OREGON BISON

BISON BISON OREGONUS Bailey

Bison bison oregonus Bailey, Proc. Biol. Soc. Washington, vol. 45, p. 48, Apr. 2, 1932 ("Dry bed of Malheur Lake, Oregon").

In the extreme western extension of its range, the local bison was slightly different from the typical Plains bison of southwestern Texas, being "slightly larger, with relatively longer and straighter and less abruptly tapering horn cores, indicating wider and straighter horns of a somewhat larger animal. The rostrum or arch formed by the upper premaxillary bones is slightly longer and relatively narrower than in southern specimens; interpterygoid fossa wider and larger; auditory inflations smaller than in typical Texas skulls; molars larger." The external characters are unknown.

This race of the bison is now extinct, but a century or more ago it was found over southern Idaho and extreme northern Nevada to southeastern Oregon and northeastern California, areas that it reached from the more eastern plains through broad flat valleys such as those of the Quinn River and Alvord Valley. Vernon Bailey (1936) has gathered together what is known of its history. From the lips of older Indians of the region, he heard that these animals formerly abounded about the Cow Creek Lakes country in the early part of the last century, and Townsend in 1834 found them across southern Idaho to the Malad River. They seem to have vanished from Oregon before the arrival of the white man, and disappeared from Idaho soon after the coming of the early explorers. This disappearance Bailey attributes largely to the fact that by the beginning of the last century the Indians of this region were then well supplied with horses and thus were able to make more serious inroads into the ranks of the bison, finally exterminating them. Merriam (1926) was able to obtain definite accounts of its former presence in northeastern California where old Indians of several tribes said that their fathers had killed these animals, as in Pine Creek Valley west of Eagle Lake. The Indians believed that they came in small bands from still farther north, indicating that here as elsewhere the bison made seasonal migrations in search of better feeding grounds. Bailey learned from an old chief of the Piute Indians that in the Malheur Lake region of Oregon bison were found all over the district at a time probably about the middle of the last century. They went into the mountains in summer and came down into the valleys in winter. During dry years, Bailey writes, the waters of Malheur Lake became very low, and numerous bison skeletons were laid bare, so that a series of specimens was collected on which the new race was described. These remains were evidently of animals that "had bogged down in search of water at some dry period long ago when the water had receded; or else, in attempting to cross the lake on the ice in winter, or to get out to open water, they had broken through and drowned." There is therefore "no question that only a few generations back buffalo covered in considerable numbers many of the large valleys of southeastern Oregon, and that they disappeared after the introduction of horses among the Indians and before many firearms were obtained." According to an old chief, Yakima Jim, said in 1916 to be 110 years old, the "last of the buffalo were killed during a hard winter when the snow was so deep that they could not get grass and a good many tumbled over the high bluffs on the Owyhee River" (Bailey, 1936). Grinnell (1933) comments that although the bison evidently was sporadically distributed in the northeastern part of California in Modoc and Lassen Counties a century ago, there seems to be no good evidence that it ever reached the Sierra Nevadas. It may be that future comparisons will show, if material becomes available, where this race intergraded with the typical Plains bison.

Wood Bison; Woodland Bison

Bison bison athabascae Rhoads

Bison bison athabascae Rhoads, Proc. Acad. Nat. Sci. Philadelphia, for 1897, p. 498, Jan. 18, 1898 ("Within 50 miles southwest of Fort Resolution, Mackenzie, Canada").

Figs.: Garretson, 1938, pl. opposite p. 12 (head and refuge map).

The wood bison is a distinct northern race characterized by darker color, more dense and silky coat, somewhat larger size, and more particularly by its longer and slenderer horns and horn cores, as compared with the Plains bison to the south. The longer and more incurving horns give the animals a distinctly different look from their shorter- and stouter-horned relatives, which is obvious even in photographs of the living animals.

The range of this race is (or was) north of the United States, in northwestern Canada, east of the Rocky Mountains to about the 95th meridian, and between latitudes 55° and 63° N., approximately. According to Dr. R. M. Anderson (1937) there "is evidence that the wood bison formerly was found some little distance northwest of Great Slave Lake as far as Horn Mountains and Liard River, and for an indeterminate distance up the Peace River valley, and southward, but it is now restricted to the Wood Buffalo Park area, on both sides of the 60th parallel." Preble (1908) has assembled a large amount of data gleaned from the accounts of older travelers and explorers concerning the bison of this northern region. It appears that the animals "formerly ranged over immense areas north to Great Slave Lake and Liard River," where in 1772, Samuel Hearne found them "very plentiful." At the beginning of the last century Mackenzie recorded "numerous herds" on the plains near Vermilion Falls and in the Peace River region, which was probably close to its southern limit. There is some evidence that by 1828 it was already diminishing in numbers here, and according to Cowan (1939) the last record of its presence in the district is furnished by Dawson, who, in his report of his expedition down the Peace River in 1879 and 1880, mentions the many scattered bones and the saucershaped wallows of the buffalo, adding that "the Beaver Indians report having seen in the summer of 1879, six woodland buffaloes of which they killed one in the vicinity of Pouce Coupé." Probably they did not long persist in this part of British Columbia after that time. Their destruction in this region may not have been wholly due to man, for in 1877 J. A. Allen published a letter giving observations of two young men who had reached the Yukon through British America in which they state that in making a portage from Peace River to Hay River, they saw "thousands of buffalo skulls and old trails in some instances two or three feet deep, leading east and west. They wintered on Hay River, near its entrance into Great Slave Lake, and there found the buffalo still common, occupying a restricted territory along the southern border of the lake. This was in 1871. They made inquiry concerning the large number of skulls seen by them on the portage, and learned that about fifty years before snow fell to the estimated depth of fourteen feet, and so enveloped the animals that they perished by thousands." Such wholesale decimation must have been rather rare, yet nevertheless shows what an unusual season might so. Another danger to which these animals sometimes must have succumbed is illustrated by an account given to Preble (1908) of a herd of about 50 bison that were all drowned in attempting to cross a small lake too early in the season, before the ice would bear their weight. This was near where the Petite Rivière Bouffante enters the Athabaska.

Macfarlane, who resided at Fort Chipewyan during the years 1870–85, said that the fort hunters seldom failed to kill a few bison each winter, mainly on the north side of lower Peace River (Preble, 1908). Writing in 1888, William Ogilvie (quoted by Preble, 1908) reported that the wood bison was "nearly a thing of the past . . . In the winter of 1887–88, on the headwaters of Hay River, which flows into Great Slave Lake, and west of Battle River, a tributary of the Peace, the Indians saw three bands containing 17, 10, and 4, respectively; they killed 5 . . . The same winter three bands were seen between Salt River and Peace Point, on Peace River, numbering 50, 25, and about 25, respectively . . . During the winter of 1886–87, between the north end of Birch and the south end of Thickwood Mountains, distant about one day or 30 miles from Fort McMurray, on Athabasca River, one band of about 13 was seen. Since then 5 of this band have been killed. Below Red River, a tributary of the Athabasca, and between Birch Mountains and Athabasca River, and ranging down to Poplar Point, on the Athabasca, another band said to contain about 20 was seen. Altogether we have only about 180 head of wood buffalo in this vast extent of territory." In 1891 the same explorer estimated the wood-buffalo population as not exceeding 300 in all. He speaks of the Indian method of killing them by stampeding the animals into a bog where they soon become mired and are easily slaughtered.

In February, 1894, Caspar Whitney "estimated the total number then living as about 150" (Preble; 1908). That the numbers were indeed low is indicated by the fact that Preble on his journey through their region in 1903 and 1904 was able to obtain but few reports of their presence. In the winter of 1902–3 he found two small bands, aggregating 24 individuals, in the thickly forested region about 125 miles southwest of Fort Smith. There were apparently no young animals with this herd, and it was believed that wolves had accounted for any there may have been. In 1907 Inspector A. M. Jarvis and Ernest Thompson Seton in much the same region found two herds of 13 and 20.

Fortunately, in December, 1922, the Canadian Government set aside as Wood Buffalo Park an area of 10,500 square miles, which included the entire habitat of the known herds, as a sanctuary. This was subsequently enlarged to 17,300 square miles and placed under the charge of a dozen skilled rangers. By 1929 the number of animals had increased to about 1,500, or nearly three times the number estimated to inhabit the region in 1914 (Harper, 1932). This satisfactory increase has continued, but an undesirable element has been that since 1925 there have been transported to Wood Buffalo Park the increase of the Wainwright herd of Plains buffalo from central Alberta in at least four annual shipments totaling 6,673 animals. On account of the close relationship of the two races, it seems inevitable that they must interbreed and that the remnant of the wood buffalo will eventually be represented by a mongrel stock. From a zoological point of view this result will be highly undesirable, but on the other hand may, through the

Wood bison (*Bison bison athabascae*)

increase of the herd, tend to add to the living resources of the human population in the region. The combined herds have so increased that in 1934 the total number of buffalo in the park was estimated at about 8,500 (Anderson, 1937, p. 103).

Outside and to the northwest of the park there is said to be a small band of 20 to 30 buffalo in a place known locally as the Buffalo Mountains on the South Nahanni River, and it is not impossible that these may help to perpetuate the woodland stock, since its requirements are slightly different from those of the Plains bison (notes of Dr. Harper from manuscript report of H. M. Snyder). Thus, while the wood bison may be considered as no longer in danger of extermination by man, it remains to be seen whether its type will disappear through interbreeding with the imported Plains stock.

THE BIGHORN, OR MOUNTAIN SHEEP

Of all American game animals, probably the bighorn offers the greatest thrill to the sportsman. A dweller in open mountainous country, keenly alert to the least danger, with exceptional eyesight and hearing, it is the most difficult to approach of all American mammals, while its magnificent horns make a fine trophy for the successful hunter. The American members of this genus appear to have come in from Asia at a time when it was possible to cross from the northeastern extremity of that continent to Alaska, probably during the Pleistocene period. Thence they have spread southward through the western mountain chains to northern Mexico and eastward to the Dakotas. At the present time zoologists recognize two American species, the white, or Dall's, sheep in the northwest and the mountain sheep, or bighorn, from British Columbia south. Several races of each have been named at various times, but only recently has a comprehensive study of the group been made (Cowan, 1940), the results of which have been followed here.

WHITE SHEEP; DALL'S SHEEP

OVIS DALLI DALLI Nelson

Ovis montana dalli Nelson, Proc. U. S. Nat. Mus., vol. 7, p. 13, June 3, 1884 (mountains west of Fort Reliance, Alaska, on the divide between Tanana and Yukon Rivers).

FIGS.: Hornaday, 1901, figs. on pp. 83, 86, and pls. facing pp. 86, 92, 94; Nelson, 1916, p. 450, lower fig. (col.); Sheldon, 1930, pls. facing pp. 78, 79 (photographs).

This is slightly smaller than the other North American sheep and with its races is considered to represent a species different from the more southern *O. canadensis* and its races. In general appearance it is similar, but the horns are slenderer and the coat is white at all seasons, with sometimes a few scattered black hairs, especially near the base of the tail, where at times they may form a distinct black line. As a species distinct from *O. canadensis, Ovis dalli*, the white sheep, is smaller, with horns of greater length but of less basal circumference, "with the anterior surfaces strongly rugose, the orbital angle prominent, and often developed into a pronounced ridge overhanging the orbital surface of the horn" (Cowan, 1940). Height at shoulders, 39 inches; total length, 58.5 inches; tail, 4 inches. Record length of horn, 47.5 inches. Weight of rams about 200 pounds (Seton); of ewes 50 or more pounds less.

Originally white sheep were found in the mountain ranges of Alaska "from those bordering the Arctic coast south through the interior to the cliffs on Kenai Peninsula, but are now scarce or gone from some mountains." "Coming within a few miles of the Arctic coast south of Herschel Island," they follow the Mackenzie Mountains as far south as Nahanni River, north of the Liard River. Probably at one time their range was practically continuous over this area. Hornaday (1901) mentions the presence of this sheep in the mountains east of Nome, Alaska; it was not uncommon in the region about Cook Inlet, and extended as far eastward as about fifty miles from the Mackenzie delta. Southward it extends along the Rocky Mountains to about latitude 60° N. At the beginning of this century it was regarded by A. J. Stone as common throughout most of its range, but "not nearly so abundant as formerly. Where hundreds roamed eight years previously, we saw but sixty-four." Sheldon (1930) found them still abundant in the Mount McKinley region, and Dr. R. M. Anderson (1939b) writes that it is "holding its range in most parts of Yukon Territory and limited numbers are found along the eastern slopes of the Mackenzie Mountains in Northwest Territories from the Arctic coast south nearly to Liard River."

Thus, although on the borders of its distributional area it has undoubtedly been reduced in numbers, it is still common on the main mountain ranges of Alaska and Yukon. Various excellent accounts are in print of its habits and hunting, notably by A. J. Stone (1900), and in the Mount McKinley region by Charles Sheldon. The natural enemies are chiefly the wolf, less often the lynx (Sheldon), and Lee emphasizes particularly the depredations of grizzly bears, which ambush them and succeed often in killing them. During winter, when snowstorms cover their upland pasturage, they may lie up for days among sheltering rocks without venturing forth to feed. Their range is usually above timberline on the open slopes where they can readily detect the approach of danger from below. Two young are usually produced at a birth, some time between May 1 and August 1. "The males and females are hardly ever found together during the summer months. The males generally inhabit the roughest and highest peaks, while the ewes and lambs keep along the high plateaus" (Lee, in Hornaday, 1901).

Except for food and trophies these sheep are little hunted, for the coat even in winter is so brittle that it is not in demand. Also since their area of distribution is mainly outside tracts used for grazing domestic sheep, the bighorns of this type are relatively safe from infection with scabies, which has proved so destructive to their more southern relatives in the United States. Nevertheless, there is always danger of introducing new diseases where domestic animals are brought in. Thus Maj. Allan Brooks (1923) writes that "lumpy-jaw was very prevalent in the range of *Ovis dalli* and its subspecies (north side of Stikine River) up to 1908, but is now apparently stamped out."

KENAI SHEEP

OVIS DALLI KENAIENSIS J. A. Allen

Ovis dalli kenaiensis J. A. Allen, Bull. Amer. Mus. Nat. Hist., vol. 16, p. 145, 1902 ("Head of Sheep Creek, Kenai Peninsula," Alaska).

This race, confined to the Kenai Peninsula of Alaska, is similar externally in its white pelage to typical *O. d. dalli*. It is distinguished, however, on the basis of cranial characters: basilar length less; molar series significantly shorter (70–72 mm.); basioccipital narrower; angle between basioccipital axis and palatal axis apparently greater (Cowan, 1940).

The sheep on the Kenai Peninsula constitute a population now quite isolated from their mainland relatives and characterized by slight though significant differences in certain cranial proportions, so that Cowan believes they deserve recognition as a distinct geographical race. This fact, he comments, "probably indicates a very long period of residence there and an effective degree of isolation by the lower ground between the peninsula and the mountains of the contiguous mainland." Very little seems to be recorded as to the present status of the sheep on the Kenai Peninsula. W. T. Hornaday (1901) reproduces an account of hunting them in the Kenai Mountains by Harry Lee, who mentions their great reduction in numbers at the hands of prospectors and miners in the region forty years ago. Previous records for this race from the base of the Alaska Peninsula are regarded by Cowan (1940) as referring to typical *dalli*.

Undoubtedly on account of its limited range it should be protected if it is to be saved from eventual extermination.

Stone's Sheep; Black Sheep

Ovis dalli stonei J. A. Allen

Ovis stonei J. A. Allen, Bull. Amer. Mus. Nat. Hist., vol. 9, p. 111, Apr. 8, 1897 (headwaters of the Stikine River, British Columbia, altitude 6,500 feet).

Synonyms: *Ovis liardensis* Lydekker, Wild Oxen, Sheep, and Goats, p. 215, fig. 41, 1898 (Liard River, Canada); *Ovis fannini* Hornaday, Fifth Ann. Rept. New York Zool. Soc., p. 78, June 1, 1901 (Dawson City, Northwest Territories); *Ovis cowani* Rothschild, Proc. Zool. Soc. London, 1907, p. 238 (mountain chain near Mount Logan, British Columbia); *Ovis canadensis niger* Millais, The Gun at Home and Abroad, vol. 4, p. 324, 1915 (Skeena River, mountains at the head of, British Columbia).

Figs.: Hornaday, 1901, col. pl. opposite p. 78 (*O. 'fannini'*), pls. opposite pp. 92, 98, 100; Nelson, 1916, p. 450, upper fig. (col.).

South of the range of the typical form of the white sheep occurs a dark-colored race, with intermediate conditions shown by specimens from the mountains west of the Yukon between Selkirk and Forty-mile River (the *O. "fannini"*) while variations from the mountain ranges in northern British Columbia, though given distinct names, are now regarded as all referable to Stone's sheep.

Of the same general type as Dall's sheep, with slender, outcurving horns of triangular cross section, Stone's sheep develops a partly pigmented coat, varying from one with a gray saddle to a more gray or dark-brown condition, with a black dorsal stripe from the back of the head to the tip of the tail.

Face and midventral area white. Height at shoulders in males said to be as in *dalli*, in an adult female 32 inches. Record length of horn on front curve, 51⅜ inches, with a tip-to-tip spread of 31 inches (Muskwa River, British Columbia) (Ely et al., 1939).

The range of Stone's sheep approaches that of the Rocky Mountain bighorn south of the upper Peace River, British Columbia. It is still common about the "upper Stikine River and its tributaries; thence it extends easterly to Laurier Pass in the Rocky Mountains, north of Peace River, and south perhaps to Babine Lake. Unfortunately it seems to have become extinct in the southern border of its range" (Nelson, 1916). Cowan (1939), however, mentions the occurrence of a single young ram on the shore of Charlie Lake during the summer of 1937, in the Peace River district. It is said to be especially common east of Dease Lake. The intermediate form, the so-called Fannin's sheep, or saddleback sheep, occurs in the same groups with white animals, and there is a condition in which the white sheep show in some individuals a decidedly black tail, especially in the Nahanni Mountains. All such, however, are best regarded as connecting steps in the passage from the two extremes of coloration, rather than as distinct races.

Nelson (1916) writes that this sheep occurs in "one of the most notable big-game fields of the continent. Its home above timberline is shared with the mountain goat and in the lower open slopes with the caribou, while within the adjacent forests wander the moose and two or more species of bear. Owing to its frequenting remote and sparsely inhabited country it continues to exist in large numbers; but if its range becomes more accessible, only the most stringent protection can save this splendid animal from the extermination already accomplished on the southern border of its range."

BIGHORN, OR ROCKY MOUNTAIN SHEEP

OVIS CANADENSIS CANADENSIS Shaw

Ovis canadensis Shaw, Naturalist's Miscellany, vol. 15, text to pl. 610, 1804 (mountains on Bow River, near Calgary, Alberta, Canada).

SYNONYMS: *Ovis cervina* Desmarest, Nouv. Dict. Hist. Nat., vol. 24, pp. 5, 6, 1804 (Alberta); *Ovis montana* G. Cuvier, Règne Animal, vol. 1, p. 267, 1817 (= Dec., 1816) (Alberta).

FIGS.: Hornaday, 1901, figs. on pls. opposite pp. 102, 106, 110; Nelson, 1916, col. fig. on p. 447; Chapman, W. and L., 1937, pls. following p. 86.

The bighorn group has the facial part of the skull an inch or two longer than in the white sheep and its race, Stone's sheep; the body is larger and the horns stouter, less spreading. The pelage is coarser and in winter somewhat shorter, crinkled. In color the Rocky Mountain bighorn is a uniform gray-brown, varying much in individuals, even in the same group, and on the front of the hind legs becoming darker. The end of the muzzle, a conspicuous patch on the rump, and the backs of the limbs, white to creamy. "This dark-colored abdomen seems . . . to render this mountain animal less conspicuous from below" (Hornaday, 1901). The massive horns of the male usually make one complete turn, sometimes more, in a rather close spiral. A record head with about one and one-half turns is figured by Hornaday (1901, opp. p. 106). In females the horns are shorter, more nearly erect. There is no groove under either edge such as is seen in horns of male white sheep. Height at shoulder, 40 inches (1,018 mm.); length from nose to base of tail, 58 inches (1,476 mm.); tail, 3 inches (77 mm.). In the record head, the greatest length of horn was 52.5 inches on outer curve; the longest listed by Ely et al. (1939) is 49.5 inches. Cowan (1940) states that the short ear is additionally diagnostic of the typical race.

The range of this sheep is from the mountains of western Alberta and southeastern British Columbia to about 120 miles south of Peace River, thence southward in the Rocky Mountains to Colorado, Utah, and northern New Mexico. Over parts of this range, owing to persecution, and to some extent to other causes, it has become scarce or even extirpated. "Their wariness, their strength and agility in climbing, and the rugged mountains which they inhabit combine to render them difficult to find and difficult to kill," while the impressive horns of an adult male form a spectacular trophy, so that more perhaps than any other game mammal of North America they have a strong appeal to sportsmen. According to Dr. Hornaday, the young, usually one or more rarely two, are born late in spring, between May 15 and June 15. The young lambs are sometimes the prey of eagles, and the adults are occasionally killed by wolves in winter. The same author states that although they have been exhibited in zoological

gardens in eastern Unites States, they do not long survive
change in altitude, humidity, and food.

In the Rocky Mountains of western Alberta, Dr. R. M.
Anderson writes (1939b) that this sheep is "still fairly common
. . . and many good specimens are taken annually."
Under present conditions and with adequate legal protection,
the prospect for their survival seems excellent. In Canada
ewes are protected at all times, and the rams during about
two-thirds of the year, while in a national park created by the
Canadian Government on the boundary adjacent to Glacier
National Park in northwestern Montana, there is of course
year-round protection. In the Glacier Park, Montana, Bailey
(1918) reported that these sheep are abundant "on practically
all the high, rugged ranges . . . especially on the rocky
slopes above Two Medicine Lakes and around Chief and
Gable Mountains. In summer they scatter out over the high
and more inaccessible ridges above timberline . . . but
during the winter they come down on the lower slopes and,
especially in spring and early summer, are much in evidence."

Bailey estimated the total sheep population in the park as
about 2,000. Their chief enemy here is the large mountain
coyote, but outside the Park "the animals are not easily
protected from poachers" who hunt for meat. In the adjacent
State of Idaho, sheep were formerly plentiful and widely distributed. In 1884 "thousands of sheep were in the Lost River
area; Hornaday (1901) reports that in 1887 trappers encountered 2,000 to 2,500 head on the Middle Fork of the Salmon
River" (Davis, 1939); Merriam a few years later found them
common in the Lemhi and Pahsimeroi Mountains and in
smaller numbers in the Sawtooth Mountains. A 1939 estimate
of the bighorn population in Idaho was but 2,450, of which
the greater part were in national forests. The same source
(U. S. Dept. Interior, Wildlife Leaflet BS-142) placed the
bighorn population of Wyoming at 5,079, or nearly as great as
the number in Montana and Idaho combined. These animals
were said to be about equally divided between grazing areas
and national forests, and hence largely in the western part of
the State. The estimate given for Utah was 252, probably
mostly in the Ashley National Forest. When about 20 years
ago I accompanied Dr. Theodore Lyman to the Uinta Mountains in search of sheep, we could gather nothing but vague

reports of a few animals said to have been seen within recent years. However, Cowan (1940) reports 150 head there at present. Most of the upper parts of the range are grazed by domestic sheep in summer. In Colorado, Merritt Cary in 1911 reported that bighorns were to be found in small numbers on nearly all the high mountain ranges, especially in the northern parts of the State. Since 1885 they had been protected by law, but this apparently had not always been well enforced. With better protection and a developing public sentiment against killing them, an encouraging increase in numbers took place in the early years of this century. In 1902, Dall De Weese estimated that there were probably 200 in the State. By 1907, "sheep were reported on most of the mountain ranges of southern Colorado, and seemed to be on the increase." The 1939 census credited the State with some 2,285 sheep, of which all but about 150 were in national forests. To the southward the typical Rocky Mountain bighorn extended formerly into the northern parts of New Mexico, but at the present day there are few if any left there. Bailey gives as its former limits of distribution the Sangre de Cristo Mountains as far south as the Truchas Peaks, Pecos Baldy, and Santa Fe Baldy on the east of the Rio Grande Valley, and probably through the San Juan Mountains to the Jemez on the west of the valley. Sheep disappeared from the lower and more accessible San Juan Mountains some time toward the close of the last century for in 1904 Bailey could obtain no recent record of them from local ranchmen, while from the Jemez Mountains still farther to the south they must have gone soon after 1880. Sheep were common in the Santa Fe region in 1873, and probably a few lingered among the mountains at the head of the Pecos till the early years of the present century. Bailey (1931) believes that given adequate protection bighorns will in course of time increase in Colorado and the overflow will repopulate northern New Mexico, following the mountain chains. The future of the species seems well assured, for summing the censuses of 1939 for the five Rocky Mountain States gave an estimated total of nearly 11,000 animals, of which about half are in the State of Wyoming.

Cary (1911) as well as Warren (1910) mentions the coyote as an occasional enemy, especially in winter when, in deep snows, it is sometimes impossible for the sheep to escape, whereas with a light crust the coyotes are able to give pursuit effectively. Another danger that has developed is the introduction of scab by the grazing of domestic sheep on the upper ranges in summer, in the States where bighorn occur. Warren was told of an instance in which 75 bighorns were found dead from this cause in the West Elk Mountains. More recently the bighorn in Glacier Park have in some instances shown the development of a fatal pneumonia, to the extent in one case that 15 out of a band of a hundred had died. The primary trouble seems due to a lungworm, which opens the way for secondary bacterial infection. Most of this seemed to occur among bighorns that in a certain locality were fed with hay, where local pasturage had been overgrazed. Other cases of young lambs dying of pneumonia due to infection by *Pasteurella*, without primary infection by the lungworms, were also found. No suggestions for eradicating this danger have so far been made. The lungworms probably pass one stage in a snail and then, if the small snails are eaten by the sheep while grazing, the parasite continues its development in the new host, and invades the lung tissue (see Marsh, 1938). The late George Bird Grinnell (1928) wrote that "many years ago Col. Edward L. Munson expressed the belief that an epidemic of anthrax communicated to them from domestic sheep feeding on the plains below had exterminated the wild sheep of the Bear Paw Mountains in Montana." They were formerly common there, but in later years none has been found. Thus it seems likely that bighorn may be susceptible to various introduced diseases that are brought in by domestic sheep and against which they may need in some way to be guarded.

As a preliminary to more intelligent management and protection of this species, H. B. Mills (1937) has made an intensive study of the bighorn population of the Yellowstone National Park in the northwestern corner of Wyoming and the adjacent edge of Idaho. Here, notwithstanding Vernon Bailey's earlier estimate that the area might easily support ten times the present population, the number of bighorns has remained about 200 for the past 20 years or more and even dropped to about half that number as from 1927–33. Thus under protection from both man and natural predators, the animals show a decrease. A careful census of the bighorns in the park in 1934–35 gave a total of 240. They keep more or less in groups, each having its range, migrating in autumn to wintering areas and in spring to the extensive summer ranges. A proper winter range thus becomes essential to their well-being, but it appears that at the time when the report was made (1937), the winter range had "been so depleted by the large bands of wapiti that the bighorn were feeding on very short grass all winter . . . cropping grass so closely that plants were uprooted and the roots and adhering soil were swallowed." In addition to this competition for food, "two diseases, scabies and lungworm infection, have caused reduction of the bighorn population in this region." There is also a certain amount of infection from nematodes, which may be more or less normal. Mills believes that the conditions may be alleviated by restoring the winter range to a better condition (involving some reduction in the wapiti herd as well as a possible acquisition of additional park territory) and maintaining a proper proportion of large predators that will eliminate unhealthy individuals. The study points the way to a better understanding of the requirements of the bighorn and of methods for maintaining a normal population.

BADLANDS BIGHORN; AUDUBON'S BIGHORN

OVIS CANADENSIS AUDUBONI Merriam

Ovis canadensis auduboni Merriam, Proc. Biol. Soc. Washington, vol. 14, p. 31, Apr. 5, 1901 ("Upper Missouri," believed to be the Badlands of South Dakota).
FIG.: Audubon and Bachman, 1846–54, vol. 2, pl. 73 (col.).

This is the most eastern race of the bighorn, but it is now unhappily extinct. It seems to have been but very slightly different from the typical Rocky Mountain bighorn, but the upper tooth row averaged longer, and the tooth rows were less nearly parallel. Audubon and Bachman (1846–54) described the color as "light grayish brown," the rump and under parts grayish white; weight of an adult male 344 pounds, and of a female 240 pounds.

A century ago this sheep was abundant in the broken country or Badlands of the upper Missouri and Little Missouri in western Dakota. Bailey (1926) has summed up its history in North Dakota; its former range in that State "included all of the very rough Badlands country along and west of the Missouri River." It was found in western South Dakota, western

Nebraska, and to an undetermined distance westward probably into eastern Montana and Wyoming, where it must have intergraded with the typical form of the Rocky Mountains. At the present time it is believed to be extinct over all this region. Audubon in ascending the Missouri River in 1843 first met with the bighorn in western North Dakota above the mouth of the Little Knife River, probably, as Bailey points out, at about the same place where Maximilian ten years before had found them. Probably this was very near the northeastern limit of distribution, for Bailey quotes a resident long acquainted with that region as stating that there "never were any mountain sheep near the Missouri at Cannon Ball, but that formerly the Indians went farther west to hunt them." Dr. George Bird Grinnell (1928) pointed out that in those days sheep were far less shy than later, when the white hunter with his rifle proved a deadly enemy; it was then common to find the bighorn grazing on open prairie near the high buttes to which they could escape if threatened with danger. The Platte River in southern Nebraska marked about the southeastward extent of the range. Grinnell recalls that in earlier days, about the middle of the last century, "on that stream certain isolated buttes and pinnacles were their favorite resorts, but when the country about these high points—for example, Scottsbluff—began to settle up, the sheep were cut off from the mountains and could neither escape to other refuges nor could their numbers be added to by others of their kind from the mountains.

"In the early eighties Theodore Roosevelt . . . hunted mountain sheep in the Badlands along the Little Missouri," but their numbers were apparently not large. In 1888 three were killed near the present town of Oakdale, in the Killdeer Mountains, North Dakota. Three others were killed from a little band of five in the Badlands of the Little Missouri in 1898. The last positive record for the bighorn in North Dakota is said by Bailey to be an old ram killed about 1905 on Magpie Creek, in the Killdeer Mountains. There are later reports, however, for the Badlands of South Dakota. Apparently the sheep held out longest in the Black Hills region, where in 1895 Dr. Walter Granger was told of the presence of a small herd in the vicinity of Harney Peak. "In the Bad Lands," he wrote (in J. A. Allen, 1895), "they are quite com-

mon. Several were seen by our party, and their tracks could
be seen at any time. They live mostly in the high flat-topped
buttes, where there is good grass." Just when the last ones
disappeared from this State and from Nebraska, where they
were earlier exterminated, is difficult to say, but they must
have held out in the Black Hills region till rather recent dates.

Badlands bighorn (*Ovis canadensis auduboni*)

CALIFORNIA BIGHORN; LAVA BEDS BIGHORN;
RIMROCK SHEEP

OVIS CANADENSIS CALIFORNIANA Douglas

Ovis californianus Douglas, Zool. Journ., vol. 4, p. 332, Jan., 1829 ("Near Mt. Adams, Yakima County, Washington").

SYNONYMS: *Ovis canadensis samilkameenensis* Millais, The Gun at Home and Abroad, vol. 4, p. 324, 1915 (Similkameen Mountains, British Columbia); *Ovis cervina sierrae* Grinnell, Univ. California Publ. Zool., vol. 10, p. 144, 1912 ("East slope of Mount Baker, Sierra Nevada, Inyo County, California").

FIGS.: Bailey, V., 1936, pl. 17 (horns).

This race was believed to have been characterized by its slightly darker color than the Rocky Mountain bighorn, with heavier jaws and teeth, and especially by its horns, which were slightly more spreading and less closely coiled, as well shown in Bailey's (1936) figure. Cowan (1940), however, believes the color hardly different from that of *canadensis*.

Originally described on the basis of a specimen from Mount Adams in western Yakima County, Washington, sheep referred to this race extended northward into the mountains of south-central British Columbia, and southward through the lava-beds region of extreme northeastern California and perhaps the adjoining part of western Nevada to Tulare and Inyo Counties, California. The race at the present time is believed to be nearly extinct in California, where probably it occurred west to "include neighborhood of Mount Shasta, and to Sheep Rock . . . , east side of Scott Valley, and to Siskiyou Mountains, in Siskiyou County . . . ; also south as far at least as Observation Peak, near Nevada line in eastern Lassen County" (J. Grinnell, 1933). In their account of the vertebrate natural history of the Lassen Peak region in extreme northeastern California, Grinnell, Dixon, and Linsdale (1930) adduce a few last records of sheep in that corner of the State. A band of about 40 "that had lived on Observation Peak were thought all to have perished in the severe winter of 1922," and many skeletons were found there the following summer. In 1927 a small band thought to consist of four females and two males was located in the extreme southeastern corner of the region, close to the Nevada line. In Lassen County the last sheep of which the authors could secure information was seen in 1872, but on Lassen Peak itself there seems to be no evidence that the animal ever was found.

According to Dr. Joseph Grinnell (1933), it ranged in the high Sierra Nevada of California, from the vicinity of Sonora Peak, in Alpine County, southward to southeastern Tulare County; probably also this was the race formerly present on the upper parts of the White Mountains in Mono County, eastern California. At the date of writing this account, Dr. Grinnell said that it was still to be found from the vicinity of Mammoth Pass, Mono County, south to the vicinity of Olancha Peak and the Kaweah Peaks, Tulare County. Its altitudinal range extended from 5,000 feet (in winter) in Tulare County up to 13,000 feet on the ridge east of Whitney Pass. There was some evidence of an autumnal movement to lower altitudes in fall and winter, on the eastern slopes of the Sierra.

In a consideration of the present status of this sheep in California, Dr. J. Dixon (1936) believes it is now in a very precarious position. In various ways this is a result of human influence, the chief factors being deer hunting, in the course of which bighorns may at times be unlawfully killed though accorded full legal protection, and grazing by domestic sheep on the lower winter ranges, which results in the eating of food that should be reserved for the bighorns. Intensive human intrusion in the form of summer camps is an added disturbing factor. In September, 1935, Dr. Dixon knew of but a single band still in existence, probably numbering seven animals, near Mount Baxter. Testimony of deer hunters and others in the region is nearly unanimous that some bighorns are shot every year as camp meat and not for trophies. The critical time is only about a month in the hunting season, so that by bringing in a "roving ranger" at that period and by obtaining the active cooperation of the Forest Service, which is withdrawing domestic sheep from all parts of the bighorn's range where they might compete with the latter for food, there is still a chance for its survival. Those who have eaten it agree that no other meat that the game animals of this continent yield is equal to that of mountain sheep; hence arises the temptation to hunters to kill an occasional animal for the pot, even at considerable risk of detection.

In Oregon this was a sheep of relatively low country, occurring over most of the State east of the Cascade Mountains. Bailey (1936) has gathered much detailed information on their former presence, from which a few notes are here extracted.

"Originally mountain sheep inhabited every canyon, cliff, and lava butte as well as many of the rough lava beds of Oregon east of the Cascade Mountains. They were common until recent years in the Steens and Warner Mountains and are still found in the Wallowa Mountains and along the canyon walls of the Imhaha River . . . . There are also records of sheep seen within the memory of many now living over most of the extensive lava beds and buttes of eastern Oregon." They were formerly abundant along the Deschutes Canyon; old settlers who came to the Bridge Creek region on the John Day River in 1873 found these sheep in bands of as many as 50 or more, but they have long been extinct. In the early nineties they were numerous "on all the rimrock of the surrounding country from Burns to Bend, on the rough rim of Dry Basin, on Glass Mountain, Rams Rock, Juniper Mountain, in the Warner and Abert Mountains, around Christmas lake, and even out on the sagebrush plains where they sometimes joined the herds of domestic sheep and fought the rams. They seem to have been last seen in the Mount Warner area about 1912. Captain Louis, an old Indian, told Bailey that in former days they frequently crossed the sagebrush valleys and then were hunted on horseback with bows and arrows. His people reported them in the Wagontire and Juniper Mountains as lately as the autumn of 1915. In the Steens Mountains the last one was killed in 1911; at least a thorough search of these mountains in 1916 revealed no trace of living sheep. To the east of these mountains, they had gone at about the same time. In south-central Oregon the bighorn sheep disappeared shortly after the settlement of the country by white men. "In 1905 James H. Gaut was told by people living west of lower Klamath Lake that mountain sheep had been numerous on the lava ridges near there up to 1885 and that the last was killed in 1890." In Lake County, where formerly sheep were numerous, they had nearly disappeared by 1897. In the 1939 census of big game by the Fish and Wildlife Service, Oregon is credited with 50 Rocky Mountain bighorns, but though these may include a few referred to this race that reach the extreme northeastern part of the State (see Bailey, 1936, p. 65), the figure probably also includes the remaining few Lava Beds bighorns mentioned as still found in the Wallowa Mountains. To the southeast there are probably still small numbers in western Nevada, but their precise subspecific status is unknown.

In the State of Washington this sheep is "now nearly extirpated, though a few are reported as of irregular occurrence in the Mount Chopaka and Mount Bonaparte region." Formerly they occurred easterly in the Cascade Mountains from the Canadian boundary south to the Columbia River (Taylor and Shaw, 1929). In the 1939 census this State is credited with only ten bighorns. A few still exist also, according to Dr. R. M. Anderson (1939b), "in the southern interior of British Columbia (Okanagan, Similkameen, Lillooet, and Chilcotin districts), but apparently no sheep ever ranged in the Selkirk Mountains."

With this race now near extinction from its former range, one asks again why it should so suddenly have begun to disappear in the late eighties and nineties, and the answer is no doubt in part that its habit of frequenting lower levels, where it came in contact with the domestic sheep then on the increase, resulted in many areas in its contracting scabies and perhaps other diseases, for there is much testimony to the effect that hunting by white settlers alone did not account for the rapid decline. For example, Bailey (1936) quotes W. F. Schnabel that in the Mahogany Mountains of Oregon, where mountain sheep were plentiful,. they practically disappeared in 1885, during the winter of that year and the one before. "They did not starve but were killed by some disease. I found their carcasses everywhere and grass and feed were plentiful in those days." Nowadays, with the greater care taken by ranchers to free their domestic stock from the ravages of the scabies parasite, the danger of infecting the feeding ranges is probably lessening, but in many instances this precaution may have come too late to save the bighorns.

According to Maj. Allan Brooks (1923), the "mountain sheep of the greater part of the dry interior [of British Columbia] were wiped out forty or fifty years ago by the introduction of rifles to the Indians and the introduction of domestic sheep to their range. Scab decimated the sheep of the region east of the Fraser River about 1870. A virulent disease that affects the heart and liver is now being introduced in [the Chilcoten and Similkameen River districts] . . . by domestic sheep that are brought over to graze from the state of Washington by sheep-herders. The government veterinary at Osoyoos is unable to determine this disease . . . Ticks were very bad in 1897 and 1898. The ears of rams killed were packed to the drum with larval ticks, pale blue with sulphur-yellow legs. None were found in the ears of rams killed in 1902 and 1905." Brooks believes that coyotes and golden eagles annually kill "at least seventy-five per cent of all the lambs on two of the ranges on which" he has an opportunity to observe, which "prohibits all possibility of any increase." As corrective measures he recommends the total prohibition of grazing permits for domestic sheep on any range inhabited by mountain sheep and the appointment of wardens whose duty it should be to enforce the game laws and to reduce the predatory eagles and carnivores.

According to Cowan (1940) the largest remnant of the California bighorn is now to be found in British Columbia; a few are still living in the Ashnola and Similkameen district where they were formerly abundant. Small bands are present in the mountains near Vasseaux Lake and the northern end of Okanagan Lake.

MEXICAN BIGHORN; DESERT BIGHORN

OVIS CANADENSIS MEXICANA Merriam

Ovis mexicanus Merriam, Proc. Biol. Soc. Washington, vol. 14, p. 30, Apr. 5, 1901 ("Lake Santa Maria, Chihuahua, Mexico").

SYNONYMS: *Ovis canadensis texianus* V. Bailey, Proc. Biol. Soc. Washington, vol. 25, p. 109, June 29, 1912 ("Guadalupe Mountains, Texas"); *Ovis canadensis gaillardi* Mearns, Mamm. Mexican Boundary, U.S. Nat. Mus. Bull. 56, p. 240, 1907 ("Gila Mountains, between Tinajas Altas and the Mexican Boundary Line in Yuma County, Arizona"); *Ovis sheldoni* Merriam, Proc. Biol. Soc. Washington, vol. 29, p. 130, Sept. 6, 1916 ("El Rosario, northern Sonora, Mexico").

FIGS.: Elliot, 1904, pt. 1, pls. 24, 25 (skull of type); Mearns, 1907, figs. 35–38 (feet, skull, horns).

This is a pale desert race of the bighorn, with long ears, a short broad skull, and relatively short, moderately spreading horns. Height of ear from notch, 106 (95–120) mm. (Cowan, 1940). The latter author describes the color in September topotypes as paler than in any of the other races in comparable pelage with the possible exception of *cremnobates;* above, pale vinaceous-fawn and vinaceous-buff, tail wood brown, lower legs between avellaneous and wood brown; much white on abdomen, extending forward narrowly on to chest, and as a narrow white line down fore and hind legs. Horns pale, tapering more rapidly than in *nelsoni.*

In his recent review, Cowan (1940) regards the Texas and the Arizona bighorn as insufficiently distinguished, while *O. sheldoni* of Sonora is based on a 'runt' or dwarfed individual, as pointed out by Dr. H. H. T. Jackson (in Ely and others, 1939).

The range is from extreme southwestern Texas, southern New Mexico, and Arizona south across northwestern Chihuahua and in Sonora to Seriland opposite Tiburon Island. Northward it intergrades with neighboring races.

This race of mountain sheep was formerly found in the most arid desert ranges of western Texas in the San Andreas and Guadalupe Mountains and on the western slopes of the latter range in extreme eastern New Mexico as well as in eastern Chihuahua. Its numbers and distribution are now greatly reduced. Bailey (1905, 1931) has given a good summary of notes he obtained as to the status. In 1912–14 the number of these sheep in eastern New Mexico was estimated at 200 in the Guadalupe Mountains, but a more thorough census in 1916 resulted in a count of about 100 or less. "All the reports from the Sacramento, Capitan, and Jicarilla Mountains assert that no sheep have been known in these ranges in modern times." To the northwest of the Guadalupe Range, in the San Andreas Mountains of New Mexico, there were a very few left in 1902, according to Gaut who made a special trip in search of them and as late as 1914 located about 30. At the same time he was "informed that sheep formerly were found along the crest of the Organ Mountains, but that none had been seen there in recent years." On account of the accessibility of their range, they were much hunted over this region, and Bailey in 1931 concluded that within the limits of New Mexico this race is now to be found only on the Guadalupe and San Andreas Ranges. He believes that "with adequate protection for a term of years the mountain sheep could doubtless be brought back to its original range and abundance. The difficulty of enforcing game laws, however, in these uninhabited mountains is almost insurmountable, and wholly so without the full cooperation of the resident population. The fact that these sheep occupy land that will always remain practically worthless for stock raising or other agricultural purposes makes it doubly important that their numbers should be increased." Since now the "whole summit and eastern slope of the Guada-

lupe Mountains from Guadalupe Peak in Texas north to Dog
Canyon in New Mexico is "a permanent game refuge that
could easily support a thousand bighorns, the desirability of
reestablishing the local race is apparent. "Under wise control
and a definite plan for use of the surplus game, either for
hunting or stocking other ranges, such an area could be made
not only self-supporting but a valuable piece of property"
(Bailey, 1931).

In western Texas, in addition to the Guadalupe Mountains,
a few sheep formerly were found in the Eagle and Corozones
Mountains and on the northwest side of the Chisos Mountains.
"They come into the Grand Canyon of the Rio Grande
mainly from the Mexican side . . . The sheep are by no
means confined to isolated mountain ranges. In several
valleys I saw tracks," writes Bailey (1905) "where they had
crossed from one range to another through open Lower Sonoran
country. In this way they easily wander from range to range
over a wide expanse of country in western Texas, and might be
considered to have an almost or quite continuous distribution
between the Guadalupe Mountains and the desert ranges of
Chihuahua." Here they have more or less held their own for
many years, and in the wildlife census of 1939 were estimated
to number 280 individuals.

No data are at hand as to the status of this race in eastern
Chihuahua, Mexico, but since the time of Bailey's investigations a study of the bighorn sheep in Texas was carried out in
1938 by W. B. Davis and W. P. Taylor (1939), which affords
an excellent summary of present numbers and living conditions. This sheep is now confined in Texas to the extreme
western wing of the State west of the Pecos River, an arid
region having a scanty rainfall averaging between 9 and 17
inches annually, depending somewhat on elevation. About 1
percent of this area is under cultivation, and the rest is used
for grazing. "The present range of the Texas bighorn in Texas
is considerably more restricted than it was when Vernon Bailey
worked in trans-Pecos Texas at the turn of the century."
None occur now in the Chisos and Corozones Mountains or in
the Grand Canyon of the Rio Grande, and they seem to have
been absent in these areas for the past ten or fifteen years.
"The heaviest concentration is north of the Texas and Pacific
Railway in the Beach, Baylor, Carrizo, and Diablo mountains,

where the bighorns doubtless cross freely from one mountain range to another." The authors quoted state that "probably not more than 25 mountain sheep occur in all the Guadalupes, none of them on the top in the heavily wooded sections." The numbers here seem to be decreasing but were probably never very high. In other ranges single rams or rarely small bands appear sporadically from time to time, but in other of the 16 mountain masses for which data were gathered sheep have been absent for years. Perhaps not more than 30 occur south of the Texas and Pacific Railway. Summarizing the figures given, there are approximately 410 bighorns in western Texas, of which some 300 are found in the four mountain ranges Baylor, Beach, Carrizo, and Sierra Diablo, while the remainder are chiefly in the Apache (40), Guadalupe (25), Delaware (17), Eagle (8), and Glass (13) Mountains. The requirements of these sheep include not only craggy regions but also a particular type of vegetation, of low, shrubby, xerophytic sorts, low enough to afford an unobstructed view. In the Baylor Mountains the evidence seems to show that bighorns move into them seasonally and leave "when conditions are adverse." Young are born in March and April, usually a single one at a time, and they follow their mothers throughout at least the first summer and autumn. Davis found that in the Yellowstone National Park grass constituted nearly 60 percent of the food for Rocky Mountain bighorns, but for the Texas bighorns investigation shows that grass contributes about 3 percent only, and that the animals prefer mountain-mahogany, Mexican tea, yellow trumpetflower, mock-orange, and wild onion. Davis and Taylor consider carefully the reasons for the decrease in numbers of this bighorn and conclude that it is not due to overhunting, for the season has been closed since 1903; nor is it a result of depredations by mountain lions, for these predators have been reduced to very small numbers. Golden eagles may take toll of a few lambs, but these birds are not a very significant factor, and besides predators have always lived in the region. They conclude that "the incursion of domestic sheep possibly has been the most serious factor affecting bighorn numbers" and suggest that this is in part because of the introduction of diseases to which domestic sheep are liable, in part to direct competition for food and water, and in part perhaps to an intangible factor of psychic incompatibility, for bighorns are commonest where sheep are fewest. On account of the rather unfavorable conditions of the area, they doubt if it will ever be possible to increase the bighorn population enough to warrant an open season in western Texas.

There is little recent information at hand as to the present status of the bighorn in northern Chihuahua or the adjacent parts of New Mexico, beyond the fact of its evident depletion within the past 50 years. In extreme southwestern New Mexico Mearns in 1892 found them in some abundance in the Dog, Big Hatchet, and San Luis Mountains. In 1900 sheep were brought in and sold for meat at Deming from the mountains near the international boundary; but by 1908 there were only a few remaining in the Big Hatchet Mountains, "and probably none in the other ranges of southwestern New Mexico. In the country north of Deming there seem to be no recent records," nor could Goldman and Bailey at that time procure any records for the Burro and Carlisle Mountains or the Mogollon Mountains. In 1905 old horns were reported to Hollister as found from time to time in the little ranges from the Magdalenas to the Zunis, but no one could tell when the animals had last lived there.

In northern Chihuahua and the adjacent sierras of Sonora these sheep were found up to a few years ago on all the ranges, but now, owing to relentless hunting, and in spite of the fact that these sheep are not to be killed legally, they are in danger of becoming extinct. A reservation for this animal is contemplated in the Altar district of Sonora (Zinser, 1936, p. 9).

Bighorn sheep, presumed to be of this race, formerly inhabited the Chiricahua Mountains in the extreme southeastern corner of Arizona but are now extinct there. In former years, according to information supplied to Cahalane (1939a, p. 439), a life-long resident of the mountains recalled that they were "fairly numerous" in all the lava hills of the vicinity but were gradually shot out, though he believed that the last remnant (probably in the Rincon Mountains) succumbed to the drought of 1903–5.

During the early nineties mountain sheep were common along the international boundary and the adjacent parts of Arizona. Mearns (1907) writes that he saw many horns in the Papago Indian settlement, and the Indians reported them common in the higher ranges visible from Nariz, where they killed many, in consequence of which the animals were much scarcer than they had formerly been. The surveyors of the party saw sheep "in the rugged Tule Mountains in 1892. When my party was there, in February, 1894, no sheep were seen, but many tracks and heaps of horns were noted, as also in the neighboring Granite Mountains. During our stay at Tinajas Altas, at the foot of the Gila Mountains, from February 14 to 23, 1894, sheep were seen on four occasions, in flocks of 6, 3, 3, and perhaps as many as 20. They were feeding largely upon a *Cylindropuntia* cactus, in valleys at the base of the mountain, but tracks and beds were seen at all altitudes."

Dr. W. P. Taylor (1936, p. 653) speaks of this region as a desert of rare beauty, and one of the most arid in the United States. "There is but one small cow outfit in the entire region, at least on the American side. A few prospectors work the territory. Aside from a handful of Indians and an occasional smuggler or United States custom agent, there are no other inhabitants of the area, and no permanent residents at all. Both antelope and bighorns are at present subject to poaching on both sides of the international boundary through lack of adequate warden service."

In 1939, by Executive order, two game ranges were established in Arizona, with a view especially to protecting the sheep, mule deer, antelope, and peccaries of this region. One in central Yuma County, the Kofa Range, comprises over 660,000 acres and is at one point within 15 miles of the border of southeastern California. The other, the Cabeza Prieta Range, lies 35 miles to the south on the international border, in Yuma and Pima Counties, and includes 866,880 acres. Negotiations are still pending with the Mexican Government to set aside a corresponding adjacent area on the Mexican side of the border. It is believed that these game ranges will prove of great value in preserving the larger wild mammals of the State. "A few years ago this section abounded in game, but indiscriminate hunting and poaching came dangerously near to eliminating some of the most valuable species."

As to the present status of this sheep in Arizona, Cowan (1940) quotes A. A. Nichol, who has made it the subject of special investigation lately. He gives an approximate census for 1937 as follows: Granite Mountains, 10; Aquila Mountains, 4; Gila Mountains, not including the Tinajas Altas, 15; Kofas, 25; Trigos, 10–15; Chocolate Mountains, 6 or 7; Buckskin Mountains, 10–12; west end of Harcuvar Mountains, 7 or 8; Black Mountains, 60–75; Superstition Mountains, 47; while C. T. Vorhies adds that there were known to be at least 6 in the Tucson Mountains and about 71 in the Santa Catalina Mountains—altogether approximately 275 animals.

Nelson's Bighorn; Desert Bighorn

Ovis canadensis nelsoni Merriam

Ovis nelsoni Merriam, Proc. Biol. Soc. Washington, vol. 11, p. 218, July 15, 1897
("Grapevine Mountains, on boundary between California and Nevada").

This is a "comparatively small Bighorn, with rather slender horns somewhat triangular in cross-section near base; color very pale; white rump patch divided lengthwise to base of tail with dark line" (H. H. T. Jackson, *in* Ely and others, 1939). Molar teeth heavy, horns slender. Total length, 1,280 mm.; tail, 100; height at shoulder, 830. In its pale salmon-gray pelage, this subspecies is strikingly different from the Rocky Mountain bighorn; and its ears are noticeably longer.

This pale, small race is found in the desert mountain ranges of southeastern California east of the Sierras and in the adjacent parts of southern Nevada. Although the limits of distribution have not been carefully worked out, Dr. J. Grinnell (1933) regarded it as the form now or lately in the mountain ranges of Inyo and Mohave Desert regions, northeast to Owens Valley, Mono County, south to the Chocolate Mountains in Imperial County, and west to San Bernardino, San Gabriel, and (formerly) the Tejon Mountains and the southern end of San Joaquin Valley, California.

Recent observations on the status of this desert race are few. According to Burt (1934, p. 424) they are still common in the Sheep Mountains of southern Nevada, and he was informed of a herd of 24 at Corn Creek which watered at a cattle tank. They were formerly common in the Charleston Mountains, but few if any were left by 1934, although Burt was told of a small band seen shortly before, along the southwestern border of the mountains. In California they are somewhat more restricted than formerly but still remain in some numbers in the desert regions of the southeastern parts of the State. The

1939 estimate of their numbers by the Biological Survey credited California with 1,770 desert bighorns, and Nevada with 1,485. If these figures are approximately correct, the race is no longer in immediate danger. In both States they are protected by law throughout the year. Cowan (1940) has given a good summary of its recent history with a list of specimens examined, including one from as far west as Caliente Peak, San Luis Obispo, Calif.

LOWER CALIFORNIA BIGHORN

OVIS CANADENSIS CREMNOBATES Elliot

Ovis cervina cremnobates Elliot, Field Columbian Mus. Publ. 87, zool. ser., vol. 3, p. 239, Dec., 1903 (Matomi, San Pedro Martir Mountains, Lower California, Mexico).

FIGS.: Elliot, 1904, pt. 1, figs. 26, 27 (drawings of adult ram, immature ram, and ewe).

This race of bighorn is described as resembling *O. c. nelsoni* "but of a much lighter color, the head of a three-year-old ram being nearly white, with a very small caudal patch not divided from color of upper parts by any perceptible line; fore part of legs almost black . . . ; head very broad between orbits, from 20 to 25 mm. broader in old rams than the head of *O. c. nelsoni;* horns of adult rams very large." Length along outer curve of horns in an old ram, 850 mm. (Elliot, 1904). "Perhaps the palest" of the races.

The isolated desert mountains of the northern half of Lower California, Mexico, northward to extreme southern California, on the eastern and northeastern faces of the mountains along the west side of the Colorado Desert, and to the lower northern slopes of the San Jacinto Mountains in San Gorgonio Pass, form the range of this palest of the desert bighorns. In southern California it is not known ever to have invaded the Pacific slopes but reached the eastern edges of San Diego and Riverside Counties.

This was the first of the races of the bighorn known to Europeans, for it was briefly described as long ago as 1702, in a memoir by the Jesuit priest Francis Maria Piccolo, on the discovery of a passage by land to Lower California. The animal was called the "Taye" and was figured in 1758 by Venegas, as detailed by J. A. Allen (1912) in whose historical paper the figure is reproduced. He writes: "Sheep still exist where the first Spanish missionaries found them in 1697. Dr.

Charles H. Townsend on his recent 'Albatross' expedition to Lower California . . . obtained some imperfect skulls of mountain sheep from the natives at Conception Bay, and saw a living specimen in the low mountains at the head of that bay. He also informs me that mountain sheep are said still to inhabit the low mountains near the Gulf coast as far south as Saltillo del Rey, or to within about one hundred miles of La Paz, and that they range thence northward in all the high hills and mountains, especially on the Gulf side, nearly to the United States boundary." Mearns (1907), during the survey of the international boundary, was informed by Indians that sheep were then (1894) abundant in most of the rocky ranges of northern Lower California. In more recent years, however, the needs of miners and prospectors have jeopardized the continued existence of bighorns in the region. Dr. E. W. Nelson (1921) wrote that they were then "still widely distributed on the main mountains of the eastern half of the peninsula," but "the difficulties of transportation and the scarcity of live stock through most parts of the peninsula render the securing of food supplies so difficult that great numbers of game animals, especially mountain sheep, have been killed and the meat dried, or jerked, to supply mining camps and other communities. This deplorable and wasteful slaughter still continues and unless checked will ultimately result in the extermination of the sheep . . . Mountain sheep are peculiarly endangered by this slaughter owing to their habit of going in bands and drinking at certain watering places, where hunters lie in wait behind blinds built of loose stones and kill individuals of all ages and sexes, often in a few minutes destroying an entire band. I have been informed of one party having killed more than 100 sheep in this manner to make dried meat during a single season."

Although in 1917 the Mexican Government prohibited the hunting or exploitation of mountain sheep in Lower California, "no effective enforcement of this regulation appears to have been undertaken" (Nelson, 1921, p. 132).

Cowan (1940) regards specimens from slightly north of Calmalli, Lower California, as intermediate between this and the race *weemsi* of the lower part of the peninsula, while others from the Chuckawalla Mountains, California, are intergrades between *cremnobates* and *nelsoni*.

Weems's Bighorn

Ovis canadensis weemsi Goldman

Ovis canadensis weemsi Goldman, Proc. Biol. Soc. Washington, vol. 50, p. 30, Apr. 2, 1937 (Cajon de Tecomaja, Sierra de la Giganta, about 30 miles south of Cerro de la Giganta, southern Lower California, Mexico).

This recently named race occupies the mountainous country at the tip of the peninsula of Lower California and is remarkably dark for a desert-frequenting animal. In its "usually darker" color it seems chiefly to differ from the race *cremnobates* of the upper parts of the peninsula, "varying from very dark brown more or less mixed with black," rump patch white, almost divided by the tail stripe. Horns in the adult female are said to be remarkably long and gradually tapering; in males the lateral surface is flatter and the external ridge more prominent than in other races.

Very little information is at hand as to the status of this sheep. Major Goldman describes the country in which it lives as supporting a richer vegetation than that to the north where the race *cremnobates* is found, indicating a greater rainfall. The Sierra de la Giganta is the highest range of mountains in the southern part of the Cape, about 60 or 70 miles long and isolated by a low gap on the north and the south, close to the Gulf of Mexico. Its eastern face is much steeper and more broken than the western. The flora includes a number of subtropical species not found to the north. Here this southernmost race of mountain sheep still occurs in small numbers. Goldman mentions four specimens secured by his party at the type locality in 1936. There is a mounted head in the Museum of Comparative Zoology obtained in 1925 near La Paz, and it is of the dark-brown color characteristic of the race. Although doubtless the puma occasionally attacks this sheep, as Goldman intimates, yet this animal is probably not now common enough in Lower California to be nearly so important an enemy as man. The Mexican Government nominally gives the sheep of this area full legal protection, but, as earlier mentioned by Dr. Nelson, the law is difficult to enforce. Nevertheless it is encouraging to learn that this small remnant of mountain sheep still holds out in the isolated ranges of the tip of Lower California. Cowan (1940) regards specimens from Sierra San Borjas, 20 miles north of Calmalli, as intermediate between this race and *O. c. cremnobates*.

SOUTH AMERICA

Order EDENTATA: Edentates

THE NEW WORLD edentates are discussed elsewhere in the present volume, p. 34. The only edentate considered in this section is the Patagonian giant ground sloth, which became extinct after man reached southern South America.

Family MEGATHERIIDAE: Giant Ground Sloths

PATAGONIAN GIANT GROUND SLOTH

GRYPOTHERIUM LISTAI (Ameghino)

Neomylodon listai Ameghino, Première Notice sur le *Neomylodon listai*, un Representant Vivant des Anciens Edentes Gravigrades Fossiles de l'Argentina, La Plata, Aug. 1898; transl. in Natural Science, vol. 13, pp. 324–326, Nov., 1898 (Consuelo Cove, Last Hope Inlet, Patagonia).

SYNONYM: *Grypotherium domesticum* Hauthal, Roth, and Lehmann-Nitsche, Revista Mus. La Plata, vol. 9, pp. 409–474, 1899.

FIGS.: Hauthal, Roth, and Lehmann-Nitsche, 1899, pls. 1–5; Woodward, 1900, pls. 5–9 (piece of skin).

Much interest was aroused by the announcement in 1898 of the discovery of a large piece of skin of a ground sloth in southern Patagonia. In a preliminary notice, F. Ameghino briefly described this and, believing it to represent a new genus related to the extinct giant *Mylodon*, named it *Neomylodon listai*, after the ill-fated explorer Lista, who described what he believed to have been a living example in the region of the eastern base of the Andes. Although it is probable that he was mistaken in identifying the animal he briefly saw, nevertheless the finding soon afterward of the portion of skin with the hair intact, and with the small bony nodules imbedded in it, as characteristic of the Pleistocene Mylodons, raised at the time high hope that a living example might yet be found. With this object in view, H. Hesketh Prichard (1902a) undertook a journey to the region, an account of which he gives in his book "Through the Heart of Patagonia"; no evidence did he find, however, that this mysterious animal was still extant.

375

The piece of skin on which the accounts of the animal are based was so fresh that the hair and serum on it, though dried, were still intact. The hair was 4 or 5 cm. long, reddish tinged with gray, while in a large portion of the fragment were numerous small oblong or rounded dermal ossicles. The skin was discovered in a large cavern, where at a shortly subsequent date further investigations were made by Hauthal, geologist of the La Plata Museum. Here he found not only "another piece of skin, but also various broken bones of more than one individual of a large species of ground-sloth in a remarkably fresh state of preservation. Moreover, he discovered teeth of an extinct horse and portions of limb bones of a large feline carnivore, in association with these remains; he likewise met with traces of fire, which clearly occurred in the same deposits as the so-called *Neomylodon*. All these remains were found beneath the dry earth on the floor of an enormous chamber, which seemed to have been artificially enclosed by rude walls. In one spot they were scattered through a thick deposit of excrement of some gigantic herbivore, evidently the ground-sloth itself; in another spot they were associated with an extensive accumulation of cut hay. Dr. Hauthal and his colleagues, indeed, concluded that the cavern was an old corral in which the ground-sloths had been kept and fed by man" (Woodward, 1900).

Remains of at least three individuals were found in this cave. So fresh were these that bits of dried tissue still adhered to some of the bones, and one of the skulls showed evidence of having been cut away at the occiput by an instrument. In the lower jaw there were four cheek teeth without any evidence of a caniniform tooth in front of them. The upper jaw likewise had four cheek teeth, thus fixing the identity as *Grypotherium* instead of *Mylodon*, in which there are five, as also in other large ground sloths. Of particular interest are the masses of excrement, which have been determined to consist of grasses largely. A few pieces of stems appear sharply cut and suggest that, like the quantity of cut hay found in association with the remains, these had been fed to the animals by their human captors. Complete measurements are not available, but these ground sloths were doubtless as large as a cow, though differently and heavily proportioned.

Order RODENTIA: Gnawing Mammals

The rodents, as an order, are discussed hereinbefore (p. 41). Representatives of four family groups in South America are considered vanishing forms:

(1) Cricetidae. The rats and mice of the New World are separated from most of the Old World types by important dental characters, although frequently similar in appearance. Six species of two genera of rice rats, peculiar to the Galápagos Islands, are in danger of extinction.

(2) Myocastoridae, hystricoid water rats, or coypús. Three races are in need of protection because of persecution for their fur.

(3) Dinomyidae, hystricoid giant rats. A single species is considered here.

(4) Chinchillidae. Three races of the rare chinchilla are in need of protection.—J. E. H.

Family CRICETIDAE: Hamsterlike Rodents

THE GALÁPAGOS RICE RATS

The Galápagos group of islands, lying on the Equator nearly 600 miles due west of the western coast of Ecuador, is remarkable for the various peculiar endemic birds found there, including the flightless cormorant, the dwarf penguin, and such land birds as *Geospiza*, while among reptiles there are sundry species of giant land tortoises, large iguanas of a genus peculiar to the islands, and others. The land mammals, however, until a few years ago were believed to comprise but two species related to the continental rice rats of the genus *Oryzomys*. Later explorations have now raised the number of indigenous rodents to six, representing two related genera, *Oryzomys* and *Nesoryzomys*. Commenting on these discoveries, Osgood (1929) writes that the native rodents now "take on considerably more importance than formerly and will doubtless need serious consideration in speculation regarding the derivation of the insular fauna. Until thorough study of mainland forms is made, however, no satisfactory conclusions are to be expected. While the oryzomyine rodents are widely distributed and greatly varied in South America, they are also highly developed in Central America, and no competent study of the whole group has yet been undertaken. When such a study is made, it may be possible to determine something more than the general affinity of the insular and continental forms. At present, it can not be affirmed even that the nominal genus *Nesoryzomys* is confined to the Galápagos, for at least in some of its characters it is closely paralleled by certain forms of the mainland. However, the number and diversity of the island rodents may perhaps be taken as indicating that their existence on the islands is not an accidental matter and the view is somewhat substantiated that the present land area has been reduced from former larger proportions. Furthermore, it seems quite certain that before the introduction of house rats the native rodents were more generally distributed throughout the different islands of the group than at present." Since the various species have much general similarity in appearance, they may have been frequently confused with house rats by casual visitors, and so neglected with the result that very little is as yet known of them. The six species hitherto described are the following:

CHATHAM ISLAND RICE RAT

ORYZOMYS GALAPAGOENSIS (Waterhouse)

Mus galapagoensis Waterhouse, Zool. Voyage of the *Beagle*, Mammalia, pt. 2, p. 65, 1839 ("Chatham Island," Galápagos group).

FIGS.: Waterhouse, 1839, pl. 24 (animal in color), pl. 33, fig. 8, a–c (skull and teeth), pl. 34, fig. 14, a (lower jaw).

Slightly smaller and more delicately built than a roof rat, this species has rather large thin ears, a tail about as long as the body, and in color is brownish above, with a mixture of black hairs and others having a subterminal yellowish band; the sides are yellowish, and the under surface of the body is whitish, with a faint yellowish wash and with dark gray bases to the hairs. Feet whitish; tail distinctly bicolor, dark above, white below. Head and body about 6 inches long (150 mm.); tail, 4.75 inches (120 mm.); hind foot, 1$^1/_6$ inches (about 30 mm.); length of skull, 31 mm.

The colors and general appearance of many of the small rodents of South America are rather nondistinctive, so that cranial characters give the best clues to the genera. *Oryzomys* is characterized by the double series of enamel tubercles on the anterior molars, with narrow secondary enamel folds between them.

When Darwin visited Chatham Island in 1835 he found this
rice rat abundant. "It frequents the bushes," he wrote,
"which sparingly cover the rugged streams of basaltic lava,
near the coast, where there is no fresh water, and where the
land is extremely sterile." He seems to have made search for
it or other native rats on other islands, for he remarks that he
was unable to find it on other parts of the archipelago; nor has
any one since taken specimens. Indeed, Heller (1904), who
visited the island in 1898–99 and searched for it unsuccessfully,
believes "it is now probably extinct or else restricted to the
barren eastern part of the island where Darwin secured his
specimens." If it has really been extirpated, one may suppose
that the introduced brown and black rats have been too
active competitors.

BAUR'S RICE RAT

ORYZOMYS BAURI J. A. Allen

Oryzomys bauri J. A. Allen, Bull. Amer. Mus. Nat. Hist., vol. 4, p. 48, May, 1892
   ("Barrington Island," Galápagos group).

The rice rat of Barrington Island, in the Galápagos Archipelago, is believed to be very closely allied to *O. galapagoensis*
of Chatham Island but "differs mainly in having a somewhat
shorter tail and less yellow on the upper parts" (Heller, 1904).
The general color is said by its describer to resemble very much
that of the cotton rat, *Sigmodon hispidus*. A series of average
measurements given by Heller: Total length, 273 mm.; tail,
136; hind foot, 30–31; greatest length of skull, 31.5.

This rodent is known only from Barrington Island, about 30
miles to the east of Chatham Island. Here Dr. George Baur
obtained the three specimens that served for the description of
the species a number of years ago. As Heller points out, the
lack of actual specimens of *O. galapagoensis* makes close comparison out of the question, but there is every reason to believe
that it is distinct from the latter. Dr. Baur found it rather
common on Barrington, "between the bushes near the shore,
and also high up between grass and the lava rock." When
Heller visited the island ten years later, in 1898–99, he found
it "very abundant," inhabiting crevices among the loose lava
rocks and burrows and runways beneath bushes and brush
piles. "In habits it appears to be somewhat diurnal and was
as often seen at midday as at other times." Nothing further

seems to be known of the species, but presumably it still is to be found on its island home.

INDEFATIGABLE RICE RAT

NESORYZOMYS INDEFESSUS (Thomas)

Oryzomys indefessus Thomas, Ann. Mag. Nat. Hist., ser. 7, vol. 4, p. 280, 1899 ("Indefatigable Island," Galápagos group).
FIGS.: Orr, 1938, pl. 25, figs. 3, 3a (skull).

This and the three other remaining rodents of these islands are placed in a somewhat aberrant genus, *Nesoryzomys*, which, though thus far considered endemic, may nevertheless eventually prove to be represented on the mainland of South America, as Osgood (1929) has remarked. Compared with typical *Oryzomys*, the frontal bones are much narrower, with rounded orbital edges; the snout is more elongate, the nasals narrower and less convex in profile, and the tooth rows are shorter. Externally the fur and the tail are shorter. The present species is dull mouse gray above, heavily lined with black, and with a slight tinge of fawn on the posterior back; below, the hairs are slaty at the base, tipped with white. The tail is about as long as head and body, well haired, black above and white below. An average specimen measures: Total length, 269 mm.; tail, 108; hind foot, 29; ear, 22. Skull length, 35.3.

This species was described from a specimen taken on Indefatigable Island by the Rothschild Expedition. Later, in 1898–99, Heller found it abundant on the same island, as well as on South Seymour Island, and secured a series of specimens. He did not find it on the adjacent North Seymour Island. He writes (1904) that it "seems to be more nocturnal in habits than *Oryzomys*. It inhabits burrows or rock crevices beneath bushes." Nothing further is known of its habits. Although at present believed to be still common, it is probable that if Old World rats and mice or house cats (the latter recently introduced) should become established on these islands, as they have on some others of the group, this native rat would be in jeopardy.

NARBOROUGH RICE RAT

NESORYZOMYS NARBOROUGHI Heller

Nesoryzomys narboroughi Heller, Proc. California Acad. Sci., ser. 3, zool., vol. 3, p. 242, Aug. 31, 1904 ("Narborough Island," Galápagos group).
FIGS.: Orr, 1938, pl. 25, figs. 2, 2a (skull).

The rice rat of Narborough Island is described as similar to
N. indefessus of Indefatigable but larger, the feet and ears
especially larger, the former 31 mm. or greater in length;
coloration much darker above, chiefly blackish mixed with
some rusty brownish; below, darker gray (Heller, 1904). The
skull is wider, with longer nasals and shorter palatal foramina
than in the latter. Total length, 303 mm.; tail, 131; hind foot,
33; ear, 23. An adult male skull measured 41.5 in length.

According to Heller's account, "this species was found inhabiting the cracks and fissures in barren black lava fields near
the coast of Mangrove Point, Narborough Island. Individuals
were rather scarce at this locality, perhaps owing to the paucity
of the vegetation. The contents of several stomachs were
examined and found to contain a reddish material resembling
pulverized Crustacea." At the time of Heller's visit the European rats and house mouse apparently had not reached Narborough Island. Should they later become established there,
it is likely that this native species will suffer.

SWARTH'S RICE RAT

NESORYZOMYS SWARTHI Orr

Nesoryzomys swarthi Orr, Proc. California Acad. Sci., ser. 4, vol. 23, p. 304, Sept. 1,
    1938 ("From the vicinity of Sulivan [=Sullivan] Bay, James Island, Galápagos
    Islands").
FIGS.: Orr, 1938, pl. 25, figs. 1, 1a (skull).

This island race is evidently closely related to *N. indefessus*
of Indefatigable Island and is indistinguishable from it in
color, but the skull shows broader nasals, a larger rostrum,
greater diastema and much larger molariform teeth than any
of the other species of the genus yet known. The average
measurements of three males are given as: Total length, 312.3
mm.; tail, 133.7; hind foot, 35.7; length of skull, 40.6.

The four specimens from James Island, from which no
mammals had previously been known, were collected in 1906
by J. S. Hunter for the California Academy of Sciences and
may be regarded as the representative form on that island, of
the *indefessus* type, which is again present on Narborough
Island in the much darker *N. narboroughi*. In the 30 years and
more since the species was discovered, no other examples have
been collected by more recent expeditions, so that, as Orr
writes, "the possibility exists that this form may now be

extinct as a result of the introduction of non-native old world rats. Examples of *Rattus rattus alexandrinus* were taken during the same visit to James Island on which the specimens of *N. swarthi* were secured." Heller (1904) remarks that "leaving out of consideration Albemarle, James, Charles, and Duncan, the islands which are inhabited by introduced species, it seems remarkable that large islands like Abingdon, Bindloe, and Hood should lack indigenous species of Muridae [Cricetidae]. A careful search, however, failed to discover any mammals on these islands. It is probable that James, Duncan, and Albemarle islands, intervening between the ranges of the two species of *Nesoryzomys*, were until recently inhabited by indigenous species of this genus which became extinct upon the introduction of" the house rats. This suggested distribution is now partly substantiated through the subsequent discovery of *Nesoryzomys* of a related type on James Island. Moreover, the fact that Heller failed to find it in 1898–99, while Hunter secured four specimens in 1906, merely shows how elusive small mammals may be, even when sought for by so skilled a collector as Heller.

DARWIN'S RICE RAT

NESORYZOMYS DARWINI Osgood

Nesoryzomys darwini Osgood, Field Mus. Nat. Hist., zool. ser., vol. 17, p. 23, July 12, 1929 (Academy Bay, Indefatigable Island, Galápagos group).
FIGS.: Orr, 1938, pl. 25, figs. 4, 4a (skull).

From its nearest island relatives, *N. indefessus* and *narboroughi*, this species differs in its decidedly smaller size and in its bright fulvous coloration, which extends to the entire under parts. The skull is slender and without sharp ridges or angles. Total length, 222 mm.; tail, 89; hind foot, 27; length of skull, 30.

This small, bright-colored species is remarkable in that it furnishes the only instance known of two species of the genus occurring side by side on the same island, "indicating a distinction of long standing." Three specimens were taken at Academy Bay and a fourth at Conway Bay, Indefatigable Island, while on the same dates 12 examples of *N. indefessus* were taken at the former and 13 at the latter locality, indicating that it is probably much the less numerous. Orr (1938) records the capture of two additional specimens at Academy Bay by the California Academy's Expedition of 1905–6, making six known examples. Though this species at present may be in no danger, it is likely to disappear first if Old World murids are introduced or other unfavorable circumstances intervene.

Family MYOCASTORIDAE: Coypús

COYPÚ; "NUTRIA"; "SWAMP BEAVER"

MYOCASTOR COYPUS COYPUS (Molina)

Mus coypus Molina, Saggio Stor. Natur. Chile, p. 287, 1782 (Chile).
SYNONYM: *Guillinomys chilensis* Lesson, Nouv. Tabl. Règne Anim., p. 126, 1842.

ARGENTINE COYPÚ

MYOCASTOR COYPUS BONARIENSIS (E. Geoffroy)

Myopotamus bonariensis E. Geoffroy, Ann. Mus. Hist. Nat. Paris, vol. 6, p. 81, 1805 (Paraná River, Paraguay).

MYOCASTOR COYPUS SANTACRUZAE Hollister

Myocastor coypus santacruzae Hollister, Proc. Biol. Soc. Washington, vol. 27, p. 57, Mar. 20, 1914 ("Rio Salado, near Los Palmares, Santa Cruz, Argentina").
FIGS.: Waterhouse, 1848, pl. 15, fig. 1; pl. 16, fig. 1 (skull); Hudson, 1892, p. 12 (female and young)

The coypú, or nutria, is so important as a fur animal and has in some places become so depleted that it may be briefly considered here. With somewhat the appearance of a large muskrat, this is a dark yellowish-brown or reddish-brown animal, with longer and coarser guard hairs than a muskrat, which when plucked disclose a soft velvety coat of under fur of a dark slaty color. The tail is about as long as head and body and is covered with coarse scales, but unlike the tail of the muskrat it is round instead of compressed from side to side. The large hind feet are webbed for swimming. Tip of muzzle and chin white. Length of head and body, about 25 inches; tail, 17.5 inches; hind foot, 5.5 inches. The large incisor teeth are of a deep orange-red; the cheek teeth are four in each row, with three outer and one inner enamel fold in each of the upper and the reverse in each of the lower series set at an angle directed forward. Length of skull, 4.8 inches.

As a species this large aquatic rodent is found in the temperate parts of southern South America, from the valleys of central Chile in about latitude 33° S., southward to the Straits of Magellan and eastward across Argentina to extreme southern Brazil, Paraguay, and Uruguay. Over this wide area there is some geographic variation, so that at present three living races are recognized: the typical form of Chile at lower altitudes; the race *bonariensis* of northern Argentina, Uruguay, Paraguay, and southern Brazil, in which the notch at the posterior border of the palate is broadly arched and concave instead of strongly V-shaped as in the typical *coypus;* and lastly the Patagonian race *M. c. santacruzae*, of southeastern Argentina, in which the skull is larger with the posterior border of the palate V-shaped as in the Chilean animal, but the upper cheek teeth increase conspicuously in size from before backward, the last with nearly twice the crown area of the first, instead of being of uniform size. All three races are evidently closely related and to be distinguished only upon comparison of skins and skulls.

The coypú, like the North American muskrat, is an animal of lakes, streams, and swamps, but on the south coast of Chile it is said to frequent the coastal tide waters as well, living in the bays and channels among the small islands. Although primarily a vegetarian, it is said also to eat shellfish. According to Bennett the breeding season is in September and October, but Gay (1847) states that there are two litters, or even three, in a year, and young may be up to five or seven to a litter. Hudson (1892), however, says that the number may be as many as eight or nine, and he has published a sketch of an adult female, with her brood, swimming, some of the young being ferried along on her back, the others paddling behind. He mentions the peculiar moaning cries the animals make, but these may be given mostly at mating seasons, as with the muskrats.

The soft, plushlike underfur of this animal early attracted the notice of Europeans. At the beginning of the last century, Azara in his account of the species in Paraguay (where it was known by the native name of "quouiya") says that the fur was then beginning to be used for felt hats. Since his day this use has greatly increased, while the pelts also, after the long coarse guard hairs have been plucked, are much used in fur. They dye easily and give a soft plushlike effect. So great has

become the demand for this fur that in recent decades the
animals have in places become greatly depleted.

Hudson, writing in 1892, said that it was much more abundant in the La Plata region 50 years previously than at that
time. Its skin was largely exported to Europe. "About that
time the Dictator Rosas issued a decree prohibiting the hunting
of the coypú. The result was that the animals increased and
multiplied exceedingly, and abandoning their aquatic habits,
they became terrestrial and migratory, and swarmed everywhere in search of food. Suddenly a mysterious malady fell
on them, from which they quickly perished, and became
almost extinct." This account of a sudden and decimating
epizootic among these rodents recalls the cyclic fluctuations
known among such northern rodents as meadow mice and
snowshoe hares. No other evidence is known to me of such an
epizootic elsewhere among the coypús.

In his account of the mammals of Uruguay, Sanborn (1929)
writes: "Coypus have been so hunted for their fur that they
are now quite scarce in settled districts. I heard of many at
the Laguna Negra in Rocha but did not have a chance to
visit there. At most places the people said there were a few
left where many had been." The Argentine Government, in
1931, issued a bulletin on the nutria, remarking on the great
persecution to which it had been subjected on account of the
value of its fur and calling attention to the fact that in consequence it had now disappeared from many parts of Argentina,
while recent droughts had augmented these losses. The export
of the fur is now under governmental control, and already
there are farms for breeding it. The report adds that the
hunters are now their worst enemy. They hunt not only for
the fur but also for the meat, which is palatable and is said
even to have been served by a hotel in Goya.

Numerous breeding farms have of recent years been established in Uruguay and have given excellent results. Devincenzi (1935) states, however, that "pitiless persecution by the
professional hunters, without regard to season, sex, or size
has so decimated the numbers in many sections of Uruguay,
that where once it was abundant, it is now rare." Frank G.
Ashbrook, summing up the situation, writes to Dr. Harper
(1935): "The nutria is perhaps not in as great danger of extermination as the chinchilla, but strict conservation laws

applied to this animal are necessary." There is the added circumstance that the nutria is much more prolific than the chinchilla, so that with reasonable opportunity of breeding it should maintain its numbers better.

Live animals have also been exported to various European countries for breeding purposes and appear to have flourished. In France, where it is known as the "ragondin," the nutria was bred in captivity, at least as early as 1882, by Pays-Mellier at Champigny on Veude, and in 1888 by Edgard Roger in the park of the Château de Naudy (Seine et Marne). In the two decades preceding the World War of 1914–18, there were apparently a number of persons breeding these animals in France, but the war seems to have put a stop to such enterprises until about 1925, when the raising of this animal was again taken up, especially in southern and south-western France. The nutria seems to adapt itself readily to conditions under captivity and reproduces normally. Economic conditions during the past ten years in France appear to have been unfavorable, however, for the hopes entertained for financial profit from this source and most of these breeding colonies have been given up. Many animals have escaped and established the species as an element of the wild fauna, which may in time prove a valuable asset or the reverse. At present the capture of such wild individuals is subject to the hunting restrictions applied to other game (Bourdelle, 1939).

Family DINOMYIDAE: Giant Rats

"PACARANA"

DINOMYS BRANICKII Peters

Dinomys branickii Peters, Monatsb. Akad. Wiss. Berlin, 1873, p. 551 (Colonia Amable Maria, Montana de Vitoc, Andes of central Perú).
SYNONYMS: *Dinomys pacarana* Ribeiro, Arch. Escola Sup. Agric. Med. Veterin., vol. 2, pp. 13–15, 1919 ("Amazonas, Brazil"); *Dinomys branickii occidentalis* Lönnberg, Arkiv Zool., vol. 14, pp. 49–53, 1921 ("Gualea, Ecuador"); *Dinomys gigas* Anthony, Amer. Mus. Nov., no. 19, pp. 6–7, 1921 ("La Candela, Huila, Colombia").
FIGS.: Peters, 1873, pls. 1–4; Sanborn, 1931, pl. 5 (skull); Mohr, 1937b, figs. 1–9 (photographs).

It is remarkable that this large rodent should continue to be so rare in collections that, although first described in 1873 on the basis of a specimen captured in the Andes of central Perú, it remained practically unknown thereafter until 1904, when Goeldi (1904) published an account of two living individuals sent to him at Pará from the upper Rio Purus, Brazil. These were the first he had known of in 20 years' acquaintance with the fauna of the country. Another, perhaps from the same region, was described by Ribeiro in 1919 as *Dinomys pacarana* on the basis of its brown instead of black color; and two years later Lönnberg named as a new race, *occidentalis*, a specimen from near Gualea, Ecuador. The animal had meanwhile been taken in Colombia, near La Candela, Huila (J. A. Allen, 1916b), and this specimen was in 1921 made the type of *D. gigas* Anthony. In 1922–23, Edmund Heller secured a series of 23 specimens from the natives about Buena Vista and Vista Alegre on the Río Chinchao, and at Pozuzo, Perú, and purchased another at Manaos, Brazil. On the basis of the specimens available in North American museums, Sanborn (1931) reviewed the history of the species and showed that all the names given doubtless applied to but a single form. In 1937 Dr. Erna Mohr (1937b) published an account, with photographic illustrations, of a live one in the zoological gardens at Hamburg, with remarks on previously known specimens in Europe.

From Sanborn's account it appears that this large and heavily built rodent is found in the Andean region from "central Colombia through Ecuador to central Peru, and east to the Rio Purus region of Brazil." Attaining a length of head and body of about 730–790 mm., with a tail of about 190 mm., it is of a black or brown color, with on each side of the midline two more or less continuous, broad white stripes, and on the sides two shorter rows of white spots. Apparently older animals have the stripes broader and more conspicuously white. The ears are short and rounded, the tail stout and cylindrical; the skull measures in length some 153 mm. (about 6 inches) in the adult male, but the females are smaller, with a skull length of about 141 mm., and the bodily proportions correspondingly less. The incisors are disproportionally large, the cheek teeth small relatively, each showing three transverse enamel folds, with in the three last teeth a small additional posterior fold.

The Tupí name, pácarána, signifies "false paca," since the size and color pattern recall those of the common agouti-like paca (*Cuniculus*). The present animal, however, is extraordinarily different in its stout, heavy appearance and thick tail of about half the body length. Goeldi describes the gait as "waddling" on account of the plantigrade position of the feet and the shortness of the legs, while the whole appearance "reminds one of an immense rat well advanced in development towards a bear." Of his captive animals Goeldi (1904) writes that they are "of a peaceful, phlegmatic disposition," exhibiting as a predominant trait "a combination of leisurely movements and supreme good nature . . . It is not easily irritated, and permits one to stroke and to scratch its head and back, and only occasionally manifests its displeasure by a low guttural growl. I have never yet observed a manifest intention to bite. When let out of the cage it makes no attempt to escape, and limits its excursions to an exploration of the immediate neighborhood in search of something to eat . . . This phlegmatic disposition seems to me to be a very precarious endowment for the struggle for life; and considering the evident advantages which result to the smaller domestic rodents . . . from their nervously active constitution, it would not be strange if the species should tend to disappear. The apparent rarity of *Dinomys* may possibly find its explanation in the consequences of such a psychological endowment in a more nervous environment; but it is also possible that this rarity is because of the circumstance that the real habitat of the species has not yet been ascertained." Goeldi's captive female shortly gave birth to a young one and died in unsuccessful parturition of the second fetus, so that two young at a birth is probably normal, indicating a slow rate of increase (see also Tate, 1931). Dr. Mohr corroborates Goeldi's account of the slow and gentle behavior of the animal.

Heller, who secured the series in the Field Museum, is the first to have gleaned much information as to the habitat of the species, and owes the skulls he secured to the habit of the natives of the upper Huallaga River of preserving the skulls of the game they kill, hanging these in their huts for good luck in hunting. He states (in Sanborn, 1931): "It is not a fighter but merely fights as a last resort to save its life. It is slow in motion and can not turn about quickly, therefore it has no rear protection from alert foes like ocelots, tayras, coatis, etc. It therefore lives in rocky cliffs, or holes in the ground by

preference, where it can back up and secure rear protection."
In several months' stay in the region where it occurs he never
met with one of these animals, though he was taken to their
haunts by the natives, who use dogs to trail it.

Because of its large size the pacarana is sought out by
natives for food, while its lethargic manners and inoffensiveness
make it easily vulnerable to its enemies. In habits it is likely
to prove largely nocturnal, but captives seem to be active by
day as well. Unless in some way given protection it is likely
to be exterminated in the limited area where it occurs. A
similar fate at the hands of the natives very likely in former
days overtook its West Indian relatives, *Elasmodontomys* and
Amblyrhiza.

Family CHINCHILLIDAE: Chinchillas

SMALLER, or CHILEAN, CHINCHILLA; "COAST CHINCHILLA"; "CHINCHILLA BASTARD"

CHINCHILLA LANIGERA LANIGERA Bennett

Chinchilla lanigera Bennett, Gardens and Menagerie Zool. Soc. London, vol. 1, p. 1,
Oct., 1829 (Coquimbo, Chile).
SYNONYM: *Eriomys chinchilla* Lichtenstein, Darstellungen neue oder wenig bekannt.
Säugeth., pl. 28 and text, 1830 (Chile implied); *Chinchilla velligera* Prell, Zool.
Anz., vol. 108, p. 100, Nov. 1, 1934 (based on Bennett's description; hence Co-
quimbo, Chile).
FIGS.: Lichtenstein, 1830, pl. 28 (colored fig. of animal); Bennett, 1833, vol. 1, pl. 1,
(skeleton).

PERUVIAN CHINCHILLA; "CHINCHILLA REAL"

CHINCHILLA LANIGERA BREVICAUDATA Waterhouse

Chinchilla brevicaudata Waterhouse, Nat. Hist. Mammalia, vol. 2, Rodentia, p. 241,
1848 ("Peru").

BOLIVIAN CHINCHILLA; "CHINCHILLA CORDILLERANA"

CHINCHILLA LANIGERA BOLIVIANA Brass

Chinchilla boliviana Brass, Aus dem Reiche der Pelze, vol. 2, p. 613, 1911 (Bolivia).

The nomenclature of the chinchilla has been much confused
owing to the fact that the naturalists of over a century ago
believed that Molina's description of his *Mus laniger* applied
to it. In 1830 Lichtenstein pointed out that Molina's animal

was too small to be regarded as identical with the chinchilla, and himself proposed a new genus *Eriomys* and named the animal *Eriomys chinchilla*. However, in the year previous Bennett had already described the animal anew from specimens and given it the name *Chinchilla lanigera*, thus creating for it a special genus. Molina's name, *Mus laniger*, is now regarded as pertaining to a small, long-haired mouse, *Abrocoma*, so that Bennett's new name is not invalidated and becomes the correct term for the chinchilla. His account was based, he says, on two animals brought back to England by Surgeon Collie, who accompanied Captain Beechey on his exploring voyage around Cape Horn to the northwest coast of North America in 1825–28. On the voyage out their vessel stopped at Concepción and Valparaiso, Chile, but on the return put in for a few days at Coquimbo, a short distance to the north of these ports. Here evidently were obtained two chinchillas, one of which survived the voyage and reached England alive, while the other died and was preserved as a skin and skull to serve later as the basis of Bennett's description. In the later account by Waterhouse (1848) this specimen is mentioned as in the British Museum. The living specimen seems to have been presented by Surgeon Collie to Lady Knighton, who in turn gave it to the London Zoological Gardens, where it lived "for some time" and was "said to be from Coquimbo." It was perhaps the skeleton and internal anatomy of this individual that were described by Yarrell and Bennett. It seems clear that whatever Molina's *Mus laniger* was it could not have been a true chinchilla and that the first tenable name for the latter was applied to the animals brought back by Collie from Coquimbo.

This is a stocky, short-limbed rodent, with a head and body about 9 inches long, and a well-haired, somewhat tufted tail about 5 inches long to the end of the vertebrae, beyond which the tuft projects about two inches. The ears are broad, about two-thirds the length of the head, prominent and oval. The fur, about an inch in length and extremely soft, is a beautiful gray strongly mottled with dusky or black above, passing into an "impure yellow-white" below. Feet dull white. Tail along the middle line above and below, as well as its tuft, black, with the sides dull white. Length of cranium about 2.5 inches.

From time immemorial the thick fur of a delicate buffy-gray

tint has been used in wearing apparel, first by the Incas and other native peoples of the southern Andes and later by Europeans. The former likewise utilized the long hair for weaving into cloth and the flesh was highly regarded as food (Ashbrook). When the fur was introduced by dealers to the European trade, it became highly prized and much sought after. The price in recent decades has been so high and the animals themselves have become so reduced that naturalists have found it difficult to assemble sufficient series to determine the limits of geographic variation, so that the definition of races has been to this day unsatisfactory. A recent writer (Prell, 1934) has attempted, however, to distinguish and allot names to three races, the Chilean, the Bolivian, and the Peruvian, but it can not be said that the characters of these are as yet sufficiently defined or their respective ranges traced. The name *Eriomys chinchilla* was given by Lichtenstein to a skin of a chinchilla obtained through fur traders and is said to be still in the Berlin Museum. A careful perusal of that author's account reveals nothing of the origin of the specimen beyond the fact that it was one of others traded through Carthagena and La Guayra, Venezuela. On the other hand, he implies that Chile is the home of the species, rather than Perú, as sometimes given, for in mentioning Molina's chinchilla or *Mus laniger* from Chile, he adds, "Die Uebereinstimmung des Namens, sowie der Fundort, machen es sehr wahrscheinlich, das damit unser Thier gemeint sei" (the correspondence of the name as well as of the locality makes it very probable that our animal is the same). Moreover, the tail length of the specimen figured of half size, would be 6 inches, of the hind foot about 2.5. It was the largest of various skins at a fur dealer's. It thus seems most likely that Lichtenstein's name is a synonym of *C. lanigera*, published by Bennett very shortly before. This leaves the latter's *Chinchilla brevicaudata* as the first name applied unequivocally to the Peruvian chinchilla. Prell (1934) believes that the Bolivian chinchilla is also a distinct race and adopts for it the name *boliviana* given by Brass in a German treatise on fur. The ranges and characters of these races may be further outlined, as follows:

The Chilean chinchilla is said to occur from about the Río Chupa in latitude 32° S. northward along the western base of the Andes to the region of Copiapó in northern Chile. It is said by Gay to prefer the warmer areas along the coastal foothills and the inner valleys. It is thus somewhat of a lowland animal. In the fur trade it passes under the names of small, or coast, chinchilla, Chilean chinchilla, and bastard chinchilla, and its fur is the least valuable.

The Peruvian chinchilla is described as somewhat shorter-tailed and larger in body (length of head and body, 14 inches; tail vertebrae 3 inches). The general tint is more silvery than in the 'Chilean form, the back silvery gray with a clouding of blackish. Its range is said by Prell to be at higher altitudes on the western slopes of the coastal Cordillera of Perú at altitudes of 8,000 to 10,000 feet. In the trade this is known as the big chinchilla or royal chinchilla and is the most prized as fur.

The Bolivian chinchilla has more rounded ears than the two others and is short-tailed like the Peruvian race, but in color it is with difficulty distinguished from the coast chinchilla, even by the fur dealers among whom it passes under the names Bolivian, La Plata, or Argentine chinchilla, after the ports whence it is shipped out. The range of this race is the eastern Andes and upper plateaus of Bolivia and northern Argentina, especially the provinces of Jujuy, Salta, Catamarca, and La Rioja.

According to Ashbrook (1928) the chinchillas are very swift in movement and in the early morning and late forenoon, when they are abroad, are shy, dashing at once to the shelter of their holes at the least alarm. Their curiosity, however, often prompts them to reappear shortly after, to see the cause of their fright. They generally feed actively early in the evening, sitting on their haunches and holding the food in their fore paws. They are fond of grains, seeds, fruits of shrubs, dry and green herbs, mosses and lichens. "Of all fruits, they seem to prefer the Algarrobilla, the seed of which is sweet and nutty, although the pod is astringent. The pods are found stored in their dens."

Because of the extremely soft quality of the fur and its delicate tints of gray, the chinchilla is the most valuable and most sought after of all South American furs. Formerly so numerous that travelers in their haunts could see "thousands of them daily," they have now become so rare that in parts of the range, especially in Perú, whence the royal chinchilla comes, they are practically exterminated. Ashbrook (1928) states that till recently at least they were still common in Villenar Province, Chile, but are gone from the provinces of Antofagasta and Tacna. The countries in which these animals occur have of recent years realized the value of chinchillas as fur bearers, and not only have passed laws to safeguard them from extermination if possible but also have made some attempts to breed them in confinement for fur. Dr. Francis Harper through correspondence has assembled some notes on this subject, from which some of the following details are extracted: In the winter of 1923, M. F. Chapman succeeded in securing five male and seven female coast chinchillas and bringing them to California for breeding purposes. At the end of the third breeding season (1926) his stock had increased to 65 animals. He found them easy to handle, for they quickly become tame, but they do not thrive in a damp atmosphere. In Chile captive animals have been found to produce two litters a year and are polygamous. The gestation period is about 111 days. Females will mate and commence breeding at four months of age, but it is inadvisable to breed them so young. Those brought to the United States have, after four years in captivity, raised even three litters a year. The number of young at a birth averages two but varies from one to four (Ashbrook, 1928). Following Chapman's success with these animals, the stock was divided in order to establish other "ranches." In 1935 M. L. Weaver, who has had a share in raising this stock, wrote that "we have ranches at Logan, Utah; Idaho Falls, Idaho; Afton, Wyoming; and Madison, Wisconsin; all doing well." He knew of several later shipments of live animals from South America, but none had been successful. In Chile, the home of this chinchilla, local attempts are being made to raise the animals and to develop an improved cross-breed, but efforts to hybridize the coast chinchilla with other forms have been unsuccessful. The former, though prolific, is less valuable than the Peruvian chinchilla, has coarser and less grayish fur, and is worth about half as much in price. Hitherto most of the efforts of breeders in the United States have been directed to building up a stock, some of which has been sold for fabulous prices to prospective breeders as royal chinchillas, which strictly they are not. There are several chinchilla farms in Chile, where the coastal form is still locally common.

Concerning the Bolivian race, the so-called "Indian" or "Cordilleran" chinchilla, Carlos García-Mata, of the Argentine Embassy, wrote Dr. Harper that in April, 1933, the Argentine Government started a chinchilla farm in Abra Pampa, Jujuy, at 12,548 feet altitude in the Andes, and has been very successful with it. From a start of 9 animals, in three years the number had increased by breeding to 61, an average per pair of 3.8 a year. It was planned to start selling breeding stock to local breeders by 1937. A decade before, the Argentine Government had made a similar attempt in cooperation with local hunters at the same place, but most of the stock was lost through ignorance of proper methods of care. They prove very sensitive to humidity and quickly succumb if kept in a damp place. At the present time there are stringent laws establishing close seasons and regulating the hunting of these animals. In 1926 the hunting, exportation, transportation, and sale of chinchilla skins were prohibited by law. In Bolivia, likewise, laws have been passed for its protection, and the exportation of the fur was prohibited under laws of 1920 and 1922. The hunting of chinchillas in Bolivia is said to be in the hands of a monopoly, but because of the scarcity of the animals very few are taken. In 1931, according to the American vice-consul at La Paz, there were no chinchilla farms in Bolivia.

The royal chinchilla ("chinchilla real") of the Andes of western Perú is the most valuable of the three forms because of its longer and silkier fur and its pale "bluish" tint. The most valuable skins formerly came to market at Oruro or Tacna and Arica. This form has now been brought nearly to the verge of extinction. Not only were they persistently trapped and hunted by the natives for the fur trade, but it is said by Waterhouse (1848) on the authority of Bridges, who traveled in Perú a century ago, that they even trained a species of grison (of the weasel family) to hunt them by entering their burrows and capturing them as they endeavored to escape. Dogs also were used in hunting. In a letter to Dr. Harper in 1935, Carlos García-Mata, of the Argentine Embassy, wrote that a few still remain in the steep and inaccessible rocks of the lower Andes, but that attempts to capture a pair for breeding stock have resulted in failure. Where 30 or more years ago they were common, and the pelts brought only $6 or $7 a dozen, by 1930 they had become so scarce that pelts brought as much as $200 apiece. However, as early as 1920, hunting and the sale of pelts as well as exportation were prohibited by the Peruvian Government, except under license. There continued to be nevertheless a small amount of illicit trade, but this is now apparently reduced to a minimum, for the animals are too scarce to make the trade remunerative.

In 1931, William C. Burdett wrote to Dr. Harper, in response to inquiries, that "it is almost impossible to obtain accurate information in regard to the Peruvian chinchilla, since it is practically extinct. No one in this office (American consul-general's) has ever heard of a chinchilla ranch. As far as is known no live chinchillas have been seen in Lima for over 20 years. The Peruvian center for the traffic in wild animals and their pelts is Sicuani, a mountain town near Cuzco in southern Perú, and the Indian dealers there report that they have not seen any specimens of chinchilla for many years."

Formerly "most of the Chilean pelts were purchased by buyers in Coquimbo," and some statistics from the customs office of that city presented by Bidlingmaier (1937) are interesting. It seems that in 1905 the quantity sold amounted to 18,153 dozen valued at from $100 to $110 (? per dozen). In the following year the number sold was about half that figure, and in 1907 it was again reduced to half that of 1906. In 1909 it had dropped to 2,328 dozen, and the price had risen to $400 to $500. European markets instruct their agents "to purchase

Peruvian chinchilla (*Chinchilla lanigera brevicaudata*)

skins at any price" thus increasing the greed of the "chinchil-lero," or professional native hunter, who redoubles his efforts. The relentless and systematic methods of destruction by the latter are recounted and the difficulties of exercising any effective control by governmental agencies. Bidlingmaier suggests that perhaps the most feasible way would be to enact "stringent laws especially aimed at the traffic in contraband skins." Some attempts have been made to breed these animals in Chile, as in the vicinity of Vallemar and Copiapó, where their natural food plants are available, especially the "algarrobilla," but so far "nothing of great value has been revealed . . . Today there remain only five licensed criaderos (breeding farms), two of which are now presumed to be working in conjunction with a syndicate from the United States."

Order CARNIVORA: Dogs, Cats, and Their Relatives

The families of carnivores are discussed on page 134. Four groups occur in South America, the cats, the dogs, the raccoons and their relatives, and the bears. The bears occur only in the Andean Mountains, while the raccoon family developed in this continent. The bear and the Falkland fox, or wolf, are the only carnivores considered in this section.—J. E. H.

Family URSIDAE: Bears

SPECTACLED BEAR; "HUCAMARI"

TREMARCTOS ORNATUS ORNATUS (F. Cuvier)

[*Ursus*] *ornatus* F. Cuvier, *in* E. Geoffroy and F. Cuvier, Hist. Nat. Mammifères, vol. 3, pt. 50, p. 2 and pl., June, 1825 (Cordillera of Chile).

SYNONYM: *Ursus frugilegus* Tschudi, Fauna Peruana, pp. 11, 90, 1844 (Peru, probably near Lima).

NORTHERN SPECTACLED BEAR

TREMARCTOS ORNATUS MAJORI Thomas

Tremarctos ornatus majori Thomas, Ann. Mag. Nat. Hist., ser. 7, vol. 9, p. 216, 1902 ("Southern Ecuador, probably the province of Azuay").

SYNONYMS: *Ursus ornatus thomasi* Hornaday, Bull. New York Zool. Soc., no. 45, p. 748, 1911 ("Andes of southern Colombia"); *Tremarctos lasallei* Maria, Bol. Soc. Colombiana Cien. Nat., vol. 13, no. 76, p. 115, Aug. 1924 ("Arauca, Boyaca Province, Colombia").

FIGS.: Geoffroy and Cuvier, 1825, pl. 50; Hornaday, 1911, pp. 747–748, 4 figs. (photographs).

This is the only member of the bear family living in South America, where as a species it occurs from the Andes near the Venezuela–Colombia boundary, across Colombia and Ecuador, to Perú, northern Chile, and Bolivia. Although several names have been given to specimens of the species, the supposed differences appear to rest mainly on individual variations. Thomas (1902) found that skulls from Ecuador differed from the typical southern skulls in being larger, longer in proportion, and more slender, and the teeth "rather larger throughout." He therefore named these latter specimens as a northern race, *majori*, but even yet it is uncertain what are the limits of variation in the more northern bears, or how the ranges of the two races should be drawn. As long ago as 1844, Tschudi distinguished the Peruvian animal as *Ursus frugilegus* on account of the supposed shorter head, shorter soles of the feet, and much slenderer body, but the differences appear again to be of an individual nature, and the Peruvian animal is currently believed to be inseparable from that of Chile. In 1911 Hornaday casually bestowed the name *Ursus ornatus thomasi* on a bear of this species from the Andes of southern Colombia living in the New York Zoological Gardens, but, again, the supposed diagnostic character, the lack of white markings, is now known to be individually variable; and Maria's *Tremarctos lasallei* from Arauca, Colombia, based on a mounted skin, having longer muzzle and claws than typical *majori*, can hardly be other than a synonym of the latter.

In coloring and pattern both northern and southern races are apparently alike. The entire body is uniformly black or blackish brown, except that usually there is a narrow line of white beginning on each side about halfway between the ear and the eye, continuing forward nearly to the bridge of the muzzle in front of the eye, then turning downward across the cheek to the midline of the throat, and continuing parallel with the corresponding mark of the other side, to the chest. This marking, which from the semicircle about the eyes, gives the bear its English name, shows, however, considerable variation. Its upper part may be washed with pale yellowish; again, the muzzle may be light tan, or more extensively whitish, to include the forehead, nose, cheeks, and throat. As an opposite extreme, the white markings may be lacking altogether in animals from the same region. Cuvier mentions the total length as about 3 feet in the original specimen, height at the shoulder about 20 inches. Thomas's measurements for the type specimen of the northern race are: Head and body, 1,625 mm.; hind foot with claws, 210; ear, 75; greatest length of skull, 263 mm. (in one of the typical race, 231, a male in each case); zygomatic width, 169 mm. (in typical race, 163).

Various writers reiterate that very little is known of this bear beyond the fact that it seems to be rare throughout its range and is seldom seen or hunted. This fact and its restricted range may warrant its inclusion among species in a precarious situation. The specimen on which Frédéric Cuvier founded his description and of which he published a colored figure, was said to have been brought from the Cordillera of Chile, and it doubtless did come from that region, probably in northern Chile. It is also known in Bolivia, where as well as in Perú, it is called "hucamari" in the Quichua tongue. Krieg (1931) mentions that it is reported from the Bolivian (?) Chaco, and he obtained a skin from near Caraparisito. There it was said to be exceedingly rare and very shy of men, though occasionally accused of killing cattle. The individual exhibited in the New York Zoological Gardens in 1911 was from near Quito, Ecuador, and it seems likely that the center of abundance now lies in southern Colombia, Ecuador, and parts of Perú.

Osgood (1912, 1914), who made special efforts to learn something of the habits of this bear, writes of securing an adult female and wounding a male accompanying it, in the mountains about 10 miles northwest of Menocucho, east of Truxillo, northern Perú. The region inhabited by this bear is here extremely arid and mountainous, with a scanty vegetation consisting mainly of cacti and small thorny bushes. The mountains range from 1,000 to 5,000 feet in height and are not greatly different in character from the desert plain stretching westward to the sea. The principal food of the bears seemed to be a pear-shaped fruit with a hard outer shell enclosing numerous seeds, a species of *Capparis* locally known as "chapote." "The region is for long periods almost waterless and animal life is very limited . . . From reports received from local sources, it is evident that bears are fairly common in numerous localities in the arid region." The two seen by Osgood were feeding at midday in the full glare of the tropical sun, but the natives advised that the early morning was the best time for hunting them and they use dogs in the pursuit.

Quite different is the type of country inhabited by these bears in southwestern Ecuador, where Tate (1931) found them, and farther northeast in the Páramo de Tama near the Colombia–Venezuela boundary, where, writes Osgood (1912, p. 58), they are very seldom seen and are decidedly rare. In four weeks' hunting he found only a fragment of dung and no tracks; "natives say the bears live almost exclusively in the forest and it is only on the very rare occasions when they wander out into the cultivated clearings that they have been killed." Tate, in company with a native hunter, found traces of an adult pair in the rain forest on a large plateau in southwestern Ecuador, on the Andean slope at about 4,000 feet altitude. He followed the tracks a long distance up the slopes, and came upon six places where the bears had "bedded down." He saw also where they had broken down many trees 2 inches in diameter and "were feeding on the seeds of a palm called "pambili" trees from 80 to 100 feet high. They evidently climbed the trees and brought down the whole fruit-stalk, which looks somewhat like that of the royal palm. Numbers of the trees had been climbed, some of them several times, since they had both old and fresh claw marks. Other food was secured by breaking down young palms, tearing open the green stalk and eating the unopened leaves in the interior. According to Olalla [a skilled collector], in the region about Quijos in eastern Ecuador bears appear at a certain season of the year upon the mountain sides to feed upon the ripe fruit of a certain tree," but the statement that they make large nests of sticks in the tree tops for sleeping purposes, as Olalla told him, seems open to question.

Nearly a century ago Tschudi (1844) gathered together many notes on this bear in Perú, from which the following are culled. He transcribes a few interesting points from the accounts of the early Spanish explorers. Thus Ulloa said that the bear was common in the provinces of Guijos, Macas, and Jaen de Bracamoros. It was sometimes lassoed from horseback. It was also found in the forests east of La Paz, Bolivia. According to the account of Garcilasso de la Vega, it was rare in Perú, a fact that he attributed to the method of hunting. Great annual drives were held in which the Incas used as many as 25,000–30,000 Indians, whose lines would cover 20 to 25 leagues, converging toward a funnel into which the game of the enclosed area was driven. As the circle became smaller, the lines of Indians would become deepened by the addition of their number on the outer edge of the line, to prevent animals from breaking through. When the enclosed animals were finally penned, the carnivores were all killed, but of the deer, vicuñas, or other such game, only a certain number of males and old females were slain, the others freed. Tschudi had seen similar drives in his time, but on a smaller scale, and agrees that the number of bears thus captured or killed stands in very small proportion to the number of other large carnivores, so that their apparent scarcity is probably an actual one. He doubts if the bear that served for Cuvier's description and figure really came from the Chilean Cordillera but suggests that the only likely harbor on the west coast of South America from which such an animal might be shipped was Truxillo. In distinguishing his supposed new species, "*frugilegus*," from *ornatus*, Tschudi stresses the reports that while the latter preys upon young deer, vicuñas, and huanacos, the former is chiefly a vegetarian and often does much damage in plundering the maize fields of the natives. The available evidence does not indicate that this bear is much of a predator but finds abundant food in the way of fruits, leaves, or roots.

Family CANIDAE: Wolves, Dogs, Foxes

ANTARCTIC WOLF; FALKLAND FOX

DUSICYON AUSTRALIS (Kerr)

Canis vulpes australis Kerr, Linnaeus's Animal Kingdom, p. 144, 1792 (West Falkland Island; see Osgood, Journ. Mamm., vol. 1, p. 35, 1919).

SYNONYMS: *Canis antarcticus* Bechstein, Uebers. Vierfüss. Thiere Pennant, vol. 1, p. 271, footnote, 1799; *Dusicyon antarcticus* Thomas, Ann. Mag. Nat. Hist., ser. 8, vol. 13, p. 353, 1914.

FIGS.: Mivart, 1890, pl. 8 (col.); Pocock, 1913, figs. 70B, 71A, 73, 74B, D (skull and teeth).

The Falkland Island fox, although often called a wolf, is not a wolf at all and is not even closely related to the North American coyotes, as Huxley formerly supposed. Instead it is a near relative of the group of South American foxes, which are now regarded as distinguishable under the generic title *Dusicyon*. How this animal reached the Falkland Islands will doubtless ever remain a matter for speculation.

Foxlike in appearance, this animal stands 15 inches at the shoulder. Its coat is thick and soft, lacking coarse long hair and having a bushy tail. Pocock (1913) describes a specimen as having the prevailing color of the body brown "relieved by fine speckling due to the narrow pale band on the individual hairs." Below, the color is brownish, except that the posterior part of the belly and upper end of the throat are white, the chin and lower jaw white with a fuscous tint. There is a marked fuscous patch above the hock of the hind leg. The tail on its basal two-fifths is like the back, the middle part black and the tip white. The ears, according to Pocock, are unusually small. The skull is characterized among other things by the lyrate sagittal area and truncated instead of pointed occipital crest. In these respects it agrees with some other of the South American "foxes." Mivart (1890) gives the following measurements: Length of head and body, 970 mm.; tail, 285; hind foot, 180; ear, 65; skull length, 110. It is said that the animal formerly occurring on the East Falkland Island was smaller and redder than the one on West Falkland.

The history of the Falkland fox has been several times written, most recently by Renshaw (1931). He points out that the animal was first discovered in January, 1690, on South Falkland by Strong's party, who captured one alive and kept it for several months on their ship. Unfortunately the vessel finally had occasion to discharge its guns, which so startled the fox that it leaped overboard and perished. In his voyage of 1763-64, the French navigator Pernetty again found the species, and the discovery of it had been credited to him by writers, until Strong's earlier account was brought to notice. In 1765 Commodore Byron took possession of the islands for Great Britain, and his landing party records that several of these foxes came to meet the men, wading out toward them in curiosity at the strange apparition. The sailors, however, believing the "wolves" were actuated by ferocity, at first retreated, but later found that the animals were quite without fear. The animals were so numerous that the men set fire to the long grass and presently saw great numbers of them running to escape the flames. Byron brought a live one back to England, and this individual was later described by Pennant and thus became the basis of Kerr's name.

When Darwin during the voyage of the *Beagle* stopped at

the Falklands in 1833, the animal was still common there, but its absurdly tame habits, he foresaw, would lead to its early extermination. Indeed, he mentions that the Gauchos would capture them by holding out a bit of meat to a fox in one hand and stab the animal with a knife held in the other, when the fox came within reach.

Such an abundant and soft-furred animal, thus easily caught, attracted the notice of John Jacob Astor, then active in the fur trade, who in 1839 sent men to the Falklands to collect pelts, and great numbers of them were taken. Hamilton Smith mentions seeing quantities of them in Astor's warehouse at New York. Renshaw even says that the extermination of the species from East Falkland may date from this exploitation; at all events by 1863 they were already extinct in the eastern part of East Falkland. When, later, the Scotch settlers started raising sheep on the Falklands, the foxes seem to have developed a taste for mutton and would kill sheep by attacking one or two or three together. As a result a poisoning campaign was undertaken and many were destroyed. In 1870 Byng wrote to the Zoological Society that they were almost exterminated, and the last one is said to have been killed in 1876 at Shallow Bay, West Falkland.

Antarctic wolf (*Dusicyon australis*)

The Antarctic "wolves" were said to feed on various native birds, harrying the penguin colonies and driving the upland geese to nest on small islands off the coasts. Seals were eaten too. Their extreme tameness may have been a result of long isolation and lack of contact with man, but their failure to develop any wholesome fear of him may have been in part a result of the use of such silent weapons as bolos and knives and probably traps, rather than firearms.

Captain Fitzroy of the *Beagle* and Darwin in 1836 brought back four of these animals, two of which are still preserved as specimens in the British Museum, which has a skeleton in addition. The Royal College of Surgeons had two skulls which may now be in the British Museum, for according to Pocock (1913) there are five crania in that institution. Pocock adds that the other known material representing this animal is in Paris, but he does not tell of what it consists. Renshaw, however, states that the Leiden Museum has three specimens. It was first exhibited by the Zoological Society of London in 1845. Twenty years later, in 1868, a pair was again sent to the Society, but one only survived the journey. Again in 1870, a pair was sent by Byng, of which the male died on the voyage.

Order PERISSODACTYLA: Odd-toed Ungulates

This order is represented by three Recent families:

(1) Equidae, the horses, asses, and zebras. The wild horses are Eurasian, but all except a few individuals of the Przewalski horse of Mongolia have become extinct.

(2) Rhinocerotidae, the rhinoceroses of southern Asia and Africa.

(3) Tapiridae, the tapirs, with nose and upper lip produced into a short proboscis, are found in Central and South America, the Malay Peninsula, and part of the Malay Archipelago.

The odd-toed ungulates are represented in South America only by the tapirs. The mountain tapir is poorly known and is thought to be endangered by the agricultural development of the northern Andes.—J. E. H.

Family TAPIRIDAE: Tapirs

ROULIN'S TAPIR; MOUNTAIN TAPIR; "HAIRY TAPIR"

TAPIRUS ROULINII Fischer

Tapirus roulinii Fischer, Synopsis Mammalium, Addenda, p. 602, 1830 ("Summos montes Andes Americae australis").

SYNONYMS: *Tapirus villosus* Wagler, Syst. des Amphib., p. 17, 1830; *Tapirus pinchacus* Blainville, Ostéograph., Unguligrades, Genus *Tapirus*, pl. 3, fig., 1845; *Tapirus leucogenys* and *enigmaticus* Gray, Proc. Zool. Soc. London, 1872, pp. 488, 490 (Assuay and Suñac, Ecuador).

FIGS.: Gray, 1872a, pl. 21, fig. 1; pl. 22, fig. 1 (col. fig. of young and subadult); Sclater, 1878, pl. 39 (col., adult); Hatcher, 1896, pl. 4, figs. 2, 2a; pl. 5, fig. 2 (skull).

Very little seems to be known of the habits and present status of this tapir of the northern Andes. It was first brought to the notice of naturalists by M. Roulin, who communicated to Baron Cuvier an account of the animal, which was published by Cuvier in the Annales des Sciences Naturelles in 1829 and further elaborated by Roulin in the following year in the same journal. Roulin gave the tapir a French name, "Tapir pinchaque" from the name used by the native Indians to denote a fictitious monster, but the Latin form was not used. In 1830, both Fischer in the supplement to his Synopsis Mammalium and Wagler in his System des Amphibiens, etc., proposed new Latin names based on Roulin's description, but since it is not evident which had precedence, it seems better to follow Thomas (1880) in adopting Fischer's name, which commemorates the discoverer of the species.

This tapir does not apparently differ in size from the lowland species of the Amazon Valley, which is about as large as a pony. The hair, contrary to the usual belief, is said by Sclater (1878) to be rather short, the individual hairs about an inch long, and the color nearly uniform black, shading to brownish; outer edge of the ears and a spot at the corner of the mouth white. Iris light bluish hazel, rather than brown as in the lowland tapir. The form of the nasals is very different from that of the latter, being long, and tapering, with concave outer borders. The brain case is shorter and the sagittal crest less high. Measurements given by Roulin are: Tip of snout to tip of tail, 5.5 feet; height at shoulder 2 feet 9 inches, but these are perhaps not of a fully adult animal. Greatest length of skull (M. C. Z.), 380 mm.; median length of nasals, 95.

The home of the mountain tapir seems to include the high-level forests from central Colombia to Ecuador and possibly northern Perú. Most of the specimens seem to come from the Andes of Ecuador. Its discoverer, Dr. Roulin, obtained his specimens from the Páramos of Quindiu and Suma-Paz, during his residence at Bogotá, and it was met with by Goudot on the peak of Tolimá between 1,400 and 4,400 meters, in south-eastern Colombia. P. L. Sclater (1870) quotes a letter from Robert B. White dated from Popayan, Colombia, June 8, 1869, in which he speaks of finding this tapir on the central Cordillera, in the region of the volcano of Puracé, adding that "they are very shy, and I have not been able to get near them, but have seen them at a distance of half a mile, with a telescope, bathing themselves in a small lake. I have also seen the skins occasionally brought in by the Indians . . . It is never found at a lower elevation than 3,500 metres above sea-level . . . and it exists up to 4,200 metres. These animals are rarely killed, because the skin only sells for" 3 shillings.

In the Santa Marta region of northern Colombia, there are tapirs in the somewhat isolated Santa Marta Range, but judged from a skull from Dibulla, in that region, the species there is *T. terrestris*. Farther south, however, in the Department of Santander, M. A. Carriker, Jr., informs us that tapirs are rather common in the southern part of the area at altitudes from 8,000 to 10,000 feet, and are much hunted by the natives. Owing to clearing of the forests for cultivation, the tapirs are likely in time to become driven out or much depleted in numbers.

Thomas (1880) mentions that a Mr. Buckley secured a series of 15 specimens of this tapir at Sarayacu, Ecuador, but "unfortunately before the skins were prepared, a troop of revolutionary soldiers put in an appearance and cut off the hoofs of every specimen to make into amulets," which so vexed Mr. Buckley that he abandoned the entire lot!

Mountain tapirs were first exhibited in the London Zoological Gardens in 1878, according to Sclater (1878), who probably did not then regard as the same the two youngish ones from Ecuador that Gray in 1872 named *enigmaticus* and *leucogenys*. There is a mounted skin and a skeleton from Ecuador in the Museum of Comparative Zoology, and there are two specimens in the Academy of Natural Sciences of Philadelphia taken in the Uanganatis Mountains on the headwaters of the Curaray River, Ecuador, at 14,000 feet, in 1935–36.

Whether the range of this tapir extends to Perú, or formerly did, is uncertain. Tschudi (1844), however, wrote that the presence of this species seems almost certainly to be indicated on the testimony of the natives that a tapir is to be found in the eastern slope of the inner Andes at 7,000–8,000 feet, especially in the Ceja region. No one seems to have verified this supposition, nor is there enough available information on the species at hand to give any idea of its present abundance.

Order ARTIODACTYLA: Even-toed Ungulates

This order is represented in South America by two families, the camel group and the deer; these are discussed on page 256. The wild South American camel-like mammals, the guanaco and the two races of the vicuña, are in need of protection from hunters, chiefly natives. Four species of deer, representing three endemic genera, are rare and appear to be decreasing in numbers.

Family CAMELIDAE: Camels, Llamas

GUANACO; WILD LLAMA

LAMA GLAMA HUANACUS (Molina)

Camelus huanacus Molina, Saggio Storia Nat. Chile, vol. 1, p. 317, 1782 (probably the Chilean Andes).
SYNONYM: *Auchenia llama* Waterhouse, Zool. Voyage *Beagle*, Mamm., p. 26, 1839.
FIGS.: Prichard, 1902a, pl. opp. p. 160; Cutright, 1940, pl. opp. p. 119 (photograph).

The wild huanaco, or guanaco, is believed to be the original source of the domesticated llamas and alpacas of the Peruvian aborigines, and with the smaller vicuña it is the only living member of the camel family in America. The family seems to have originated in North America, becoming much diversified in middle and late Tertiary times and spreading to the Old World and to South America. It has since completely died out in North America.

The guanaco has somewhat the slender build and long neck of the camel, but the ears are proportionately long, the tail is short and bushy, there is no "hump," and the coat is soft and woolly. In color the wild species is a dark fawn-brown above, with a blackish face and white under surfaces. It stands about 3 feet 7 inches high at the shoulder, and the skull is about 11.5

inches in basicranial length. The upper incisor and canine are lancet-shaped and capable of inflicting a bad wound, but the lower incisors are procumbent. There are callosities on the inner side of the fore limbs.

The range is from the Andes of south-central Perú southward to Patagonia, where it comes to the lower altitudes, and thence to Tierra del Fuego. Very likely, when sufficient series of specimens are available, more than the single geographic form may be distinguished. Indeed, Lönnberg (1913) has described as *Lama huanachus cacsilensis*, an animal of small size from Cacsile, Nuñoa, Perú, which seems to be more like the vicuña and according to Osgood (1916) is "not closely related" to the common guanaco. Its status may await further study.

Osgood (1916) states that the herds he saw on the Pampa de Arrieros, between Arequipa and Puno, at the northern part of the animal's range, are "almost if not quite the northernmost now existing." Inhabiting as they do the alpine zone between 14,000 and 18,000 feet above the sea, they are perhaps also the most lofty-living of the species. Barren though these heights appear, the animals obtain pasturage sufficient to sustain existence. Though little hunted by white man, they are persecuted by the Indians, who shoot them from blinds erected at waterholes. The skins are used in making beautiful rugs or for saddle cloths, while the meat is of excellent quality. B. T. Colley, writing to Dr. Francis Harper from Oroya, Perú, in April, 1934, states that to the south of the Puno region, and beyond the Atacama Desert, the guanaco is rather plentiful, and he has seen herds of over a hundred animals on the continental divide above Santiago, while farther to the south there are many more. Here, as winter sets in, they move down from the higher regions to lower altitudes, retiring chiefly to the Argentine side because of the abruptness of the Chilean Cordillera. They have a characteristic habit of making zigzag trails in which the angles tend to be equal and regular.

In Chile, José M. B. Toro reports (in litt., 1934), the guanaco has become so much reduced in numbers in the past 20 years or more because of persecution that in 1929 a decree was passed prohibiting the hunting of it for three years, after which the close time was extended for two years more to December 1, 1935. At the present time there are still a few scattered bands to be found in the steeper parts of the Cordillera and along the Argentine border, but any close estimate of their numbers is difficult.

On the pampas of southern Argentina and over most of Patagonia the guanaco seems to be still common from the Río Colorado in about latitude 40° S., and is even said to have increased within recent years.

Darwin has given a brief account of the abundance and habits of the guanaco as he saw it a century ago in the Santa Cruz region of Patagonia. They go in small herds of from half a dozen to thirty, but he mentions one herd of "at least five hundred." He speaks of their taking readily to water and swimming to islands near the mainland. They have a certain curiosity when alone but in herds easily become bewildered and stampeded, a fact of which the Indians take advantage in killing them. Both Darwin and Prichard (1902a) mention coming upon places where great numbers seem to have perished and left bones bleaching on the ground. Prichard was told that in the winter previous enormous numbers of guanacos had sought Lake Argentino and perished there of starvation. "In the severities of winter they seek drinking-places where there are large masses of water likely to be unfrozen. The last few winters" had been so severe that great havoc had been wrought among the animals. Prichard crossed Patagonia from the Río Chubut southwesterly to the Andean foothills, and thence proceeded southward, coming out at Punta Arenas on the Straits of Magellan. Over most of this country guanacos were common, and in regions where they were not much hunted were not very shy.

Apparently the main danger to which this species may be exposed, apart from the decimating effect of severe winters, is the extension of grazing by the cattle and sheep of the settlers, and the exploitation of the guanacos for their hides and meat. As to the former, a writer in an Argentine journal (La Chacra, 1936) states that in 1913 ranchers in Santa Cruz pleaded for the destruction of the guanaco on the ground that it was a detriment to sheep raising and a national plague. Wire fences used to enclose ranges prove the ruin of many guanacos, victims of cold and hunger. On the other hand, the animal does not interfere with sheep raising in parts farther south that are unsuitable for sheep. It is much persecuted for its hide and meat. In the report of the world's fur production for 1928 (Journ. Soc. Preserv. Fauna Empire, pt. 12, p. 64, 1930) the number of guanaco skins brought to market is given as 300,000. While at present it can hardly be said that the species is in danger of extermination, nevertheless the demand for hides to be used as robes, and the encroachment of grazing and hunting, will doubtless much restrict its area and its numbers in years to come.

SOUTHERN VICUÑA

VICUGNA VICUGNA VICUGNA (Molina)

Camelus vicugna Molina, Saggio Storia Nat. Chile, vol. 1, p. 313, 1782 ("Probably Peru"—Lydekker; but Molina says in the Cordillera of the provinces Coquimbo and Copiapó).

PERUVIAN VICUÑA

VICUGNA VICUGNA MENSALIS (Thomas)

Lama vicugna mensalis Thomas, Smithsonian Misc. Coll., vol. 68, no. 4, p. 3, Apr. 10, 1917 ("Incapirra, Junin, Peru").

FIGS.: Tschudi, 1844, pl. 17 (col.); Royal Nat. Hist., vol. 2, p. 412, fig., 1894.

The vicuña resembles the guanaco in general form but is about a fourth smaller, somewhat slenderer, and paler in color, a pale fawn, without black on the face. The fore limbs have no callosities such as are present on the inner side of the "knees" of the guanaco. Although formerly placed in the same genus with the latter, Miller (1924c) regards it worthy of generic distinction, since the lower incisors are peculiar in being long, slender, and ever-growing from persistent pulps, like those of rodents, but with the enamel on the inner side. This condition is unique among living artiodactyls but recalls that of the dwarf wild goat (*Myotragus*), the remains of which are found in Pleistocene cavern deposits of the Balearic Islands. Osgood (1916) gives the following measurements of a Peruvian specimen: Length from between ears to root of tail, 1,250 mm.; base of ear to point of shoulder, 670. The height at the shoulder, according to Lydekker, is about 2 feet 9 inches; Tschudi (1844) gives 2 feet 6 inches. Length of skull, about 220 mm.

Although Lydekker says that the "typical locality is probably Peru," Molina's account, on which the name is based, states that they are found in the parts of the Cordillera belonging to the provinces Coquimbo and Copiapó, but keep to the steep summits of the mountains, minding neither snow nor ice.

Whether or not the vicuña did occur in Molina's day, 1782, as far south as the Cordillera of Coquimbo, in Chile, it apparently no longer does so, but one may regard the type locality as the latter region on Molina's authority. Northward the range extends to northern and central Bolivia, Perú at high altitudes, and southern Ecuador. Thomas has named, as a distinct race, *mensalis*, the northern animal, basing his description on specimens from Incapirra, Junin, Perú. The characters claimed are the more strongly fulvous color and slightly smaller size and smaller teeth, as compared with true *V. vicugna*, the type locality and size of which are not indicated. The range of this race is given as "Peru and Bolivia" and is assumed to include also southern Ecuador at high altitudes. This would leave typical *V. vicugna* as the form of Chile, where it is possibly now extinct. The two races may be considered together. An adult male measured from "between ears to root of tail," 1,250 mm.; base of ear to point of shoulder, 670, or more than in the guanaco. The skull of the type of *mensalis*, a male, had a greatest length of 240 mm.; length of molars, 45.

The vicuña is apparently at the present time gone from Chile, but the British Museum has a mounted skin from Catamarca, northwestern Argentina. In Bolivia it is found in a restricted area in the north-central part. In Perú, its chief centers of abundance are said by Maccagno (1932) in his recent monograph to be: Junin, Huanta, Ayacucho, Puno, Cuzco, Apurimac, Huancavelica, and Arequipa.

These animals live on the vast plains at altitudes between 11,500 and 18,500 feet in Perú, going in small droves of 10 to 15 females and an adult male. In general they are said to be easily tamed, and often one or two may be seen about ranch houses, but in confinement they do not breed readily. On the other hand, if allowed practical liberty under fence with sufficient area, they are said to breed freely and may be caught and sheared for their wool, which is much sought for its fine quality.

In Perú the vicuña was accorded legal protection as long ago as 1825, but the law apparently remained a dead letter until the animals had become much reduced through hunting. Finally, on October 8, 1920, a decree was passed prohibiting the making of goods from vicuña wool and forbidding the sale of skins. A heavy fine was provided for infractions. As a

result it is said on good authority that in Perú the vicuña is
fast recuperating and is now locally common as in the Junin
area (William C. Burdett, *in litt.*).   Nevertheless it is difficult
to enforce these laws and many of the animals are killed.
In Bolivia the exportation of vicuña wool and hides is prohibited under laws of 1920 and 1922.   Vicuña rugs are often
manufactured in Perú, but their export is forbidden except that
a person leaving the country may take one out by securing an
official permit.   The robes are made of small strips of the hide
perfectly matched in color and texture.   Several grades are
made by using the skin from different parts of the body, the
back and sides for one type, the neck for another, and the legs
and belly for a third.   The most valuable are those made from
the back and sides, and some of the best may sell for as high as
$100 (Carriker).   It is believed that it may eventually be

Vicuña (*Vicugna vicugna*)

feasible to raise vicuñas on ranches and shear them for the wool, which brings a good price, as much as $5 a pound. This would require special sanction of the government concerned. Like the llama and alpaca, this animal is subject to such parasitic infections as lungworm, scab, and flukes, particularly at lower altitudes (B. T. Colley, *in litt.*).

In earlier days the native Indians made much use of this species. Tschudi (1844) describes how they carried out extensive drives, gradually working the animals into a narrow funnel-shaped place among the rock walls, where many were captured, their wool sheared, and the captives then freed.

Family CERVIDAE: Deer

ECUADORIAN PUDU

PUDU (PUDELLA) MEPHISTOPHILES (de Winton)

Pudua mephistopheles de Winton, Proc. Zool. Soc. London, 1896, p. 508.
FIGS.: De Winton, 1896, pl. 19; Lydekker, 1898, pl. 24, fig. 1.

This small deer stands about 14 inches high at the shoulder and is peculiar in its short metapodials, very short spikelike antlers in the male, short ears, and practical absence of an external tail. Very little is known of it, but since its habitat is restricted and is likely to be further limited by various developments in the future, it may deserve mention here.

The general color is a rich brown, due to a blackish-brown ground color, sprinkled with bright rufous. Ears relatively short, with long white hairs lining them. Face and legs nearly black.

Originally made known from a specimen taken on the páramo of Papallacta, Ecuador, very few examples of this deer have since found their way into collections. The Swedish consul Söderström sent a specimen to the British Museum and one to the Royal Museum at Stockholm, the latter with antlers about 78 mm. long. All these are from an altitude of about 12,000 feet at Papallacta, outside of which the species is unknown. It is believed that even here it is uncommon.

Peruvian Guemal; "Taruga"

Hippocamelus antisiensis (d'Orbigny)

Cervus antisiensis d'Orbigny, Ann. Mus. Hist. Nat. Paris, vol. 3, p. 91, 1834 (Andes, near La Paz, Bolivia).
Synonyms: Anomalocera huamel Gray, Scientific Opinion, p. 384, 1869; Xenelaphus chilensis Gray, Ann. Mag. Nat. Hist., ser. 4, vol. 12, p. 61, 1873.
Fig.: Lydekker, 1898, pl. 23 (col.).

This small deer is confined to a rather restricted alpine habitat in the Andes and may be included here as a game animal that may need more protection. Somewhat smaller than a Virginia deer, having a coarse brittle coat and lacking metatarsal glands, this species is of a nearly uniform speckled brown and buffy, with a darker line on the forehead. Tail dark brown on base and most of the upper surface, but its tip and lower side are white. The antlers are present in males only, and consist of a short fork commencing close to the burr. Height at shoulder about 34 inches (Lydekker).

In the Andes of Ecuador, Perú, Bolivia, and northern Chile this species is found at high altitudes, mainly between 14,000 and 16,000 feet but at times lower. Lydekker in 1898 wrote that it was abundant in Ecuador on Chimborazo, Pichincha, and Cotapaxi, but Richardson in 1912–13, collecting for the American Museum of Natural History, failed to obtain specimens when he was in that region. In Perú, Tschudi gives some account of its habits and speaks of it as frequenting rocky areas, often hiding in caves by day, and coming out in the evening to feed on mosses and other vegetation, and lichens. Osgood (1914) in his journey to northern Perú in 1912 did not find even a track of one and writes that "so far as learned from inquiry, it never has been common in the region and it was only at rare intervals that we met a man who ever had seen one. A few doubtless remain in the higher parts of both the western and the eastern cordillera but at the points we were able to touch" none was found. The Peruvian Indians call it "taruga," and Tschudi mentions that he was to have named it Cervus taruga but discovered that d'Orbigny had already described it. It seems likely that the drives formerly held on a large scale by the Peruvian Indians must often have captured these small deer. On his later visit to the Arequipa region, Osgood (1916) secured a single specimen at Pampa de Arrieros, Perú. It was found up to an altitude of 13,000 feet, ranging somewhat lower

than the guanaco and vicuña. In Bolivia, Neveu-Lemaire
and Grandidier (1907) have recorded it from the Yuru district,
at 5,000 meters. On account of the limited distribution and
the hunting to which this deer is subject, it is evidently becoming uncommon and requires adequate protection.

PAMPAS DEER; "VEADO BRANCO"; "GUAZUTI"; "VEADO CAMPEIRO"

BLASTOCERUS BEZOARTICUS (Linnaeus)

Cervus bezoarticus Linnaeus, Syst. Nat., ed. 10, vol. 1, p. 175, 1758 (Brazil).
SYNONYMS: *Cervus campestris* F. Cuvier, Dict. Sci. Nat., vol. 7, p. 484, 1817; *Cervus
azarae* Wiegmann, Isis, col. 954, 1833 (Paraguay).
FIGS.: Lydekker, 1898, pl. 22 (col.); 1915, p. 190.

The pampas deer is much smaller than its congener the
marsh deer, about the size of the European roebuck, but more
delicately built. The color is a light reddish brown, the face
darker, and occasionally a black patch on the crown; "tarsal
tuft, a patch at base of backs of ears, a ring round pedicles of
antlers, another round each eye, lips, throat, chest, under-
parts, fronts and inner sides of thighs, and inner sides of buttocks and upper part of fore-legs whitish; . . . tail dark
blackish brown above and white below." The antlers of the
male are small, with a large brow tine and a posterior beam
that forks usually once; length of beam up to 14.5 inches.
Males usually have the upper canine present.

The general range of this small deer includes the open
campos of Brazil, Paraguay, and Uruguay to the pampas of
Argentina and northern Patagonia (Lydekker, 1898). Possibly the animals of the more southern part of the range may be
separable as a distinct subspecies for which, as pointed out by
Lydekker, the name *azarae* is available. It is said to inhabit
dry open plains, avoiding forests and thickets. "Formerly,
when the tussocks of tall pampas-grass were dotted more or
less thickly over all the plains, it had plenty of covert; but in
the more settled districts it now has to live almost completely
in the open, and has consequently become wary in the extreme"
(Lydekker, 1898). It may be found in small groups or pairs,
but the adult males are often solitary for most of the year.
In the evening they are active but during the daytime lie up in
concealment. They are said to have a strong and characteristic
odor. When started, they bound off at a considerable speed,

so that a good horse is necessary to overtake one. The natives sometimes capture them with the bolas. In parts of Brazil the animal goes by the native name of "guazuti," and in Uruguay it is known as "gama."

According to Lydekker (1901) it has completely disappeared from many districts of Argentina and Uruguay. As long ago as 1894, Aplin (1894) wrote that in the neighborhood of Santa Elena, Uruguay, it had been exterminated except for a small herd of about a dozen does and seven bucks preserved in a certain district. He found it rare on the Río Negro, but in some other areas it was still common. Sanborn (1929) in 1926–27 found it plentiful in one locality in Rocha, Uruguay, but in most other places rare, and this is corroborated by Devincenzi (1935), who speaks of Rocha as the district where it is now to be found, although 30 years before it was abundant in the whole country.

Dr. Roberto Dabbene, in a letter to Dr. Francis Harper in 1937, stated that though formerly common in the northern and central regions of Argentina as far as northern Patagonia, it is now very scarce as far as the Chaco, and if not protected adequately is certain to disappear from the Argentine fauna. He deplores the introduction of exotic deer into the national parks, rather than the encouragement of the native species.

While further and more precise information on the present and past status of this species is much needed, it is evident that it is much reduced in many districts and requires careful protection. In Argentina hunting this species was prohibited by presidential decree several years ago.

MARSH DEER; "VEADO GALHEIRO GRANDE"; "GUAZUPUCO"

BLASTOCERUS DICHOTOMUS (Illiger)

Cervus dichotomus Illiger, Abh. Akad. Wiss. Berlin, for 1811, pp. 108, 117, 1815 (Brazil).

SYNONYMS: *Cervus paludosus* Desmarest, Mammalogie, pt. 2, p. 443, 1822; *Cervus palustris* Desmoulins, Dict. Classique Hist. Nat., vol. 3, p. 379, 1823.

FIGS.: Lydekker, 1898, pp. 284, 285 (antlers, animals).

This is the largest South American deer, attaining about the size of the British red deer, but more slenderly built, standing about 46 inches at the shoulder (Azara). "General colour in summer bright rufous chestnut, in winter brownish red, becoming lighter on flanks, neck, and chest; legs black from knees and hocks downwards, and tarsal tuft also black; abdomen, inside of thighs, chin, and insides and bases of backs of ears white . . . a whitish line above, or a ring round eyes, most marked in females . . . tail yellowish rusty red above and black beneath . . . Fine antlers attain a length of from 21 to 24½ inches" (Lydekker, 1915); they are doubly forked, each of the two branches having a simple fork.

The range is extensive in the tropics and subtropics of South America, from probably Guiana southward through Brazil to Paraguay and Uruguay and the Chaco or wooded districts of northern Argentina. Unlike its smaller relative, the pampas deer, it inhabits dense jungle on the borders of streams or swamps and it is said to go in small parties of three to five individuals. The skin is much used for leather by the natives, but the meat is apparently not held in high esteem. Lydekker remarks on the similarity in color between this deer and the maned wolf, which is found in the same areas in parts of the range.

Although little information is at hand as to the details of distribution and relative abundance of this large deer, it is evident that in certain of the more settled regions in the southern part of the range it is becoming much reduced in numbers. Devincenzi (1935) writes that in Uruguay the Departments of Rocha and Treinta y Tres have been "considered the last refuge of the species," while Sanborn comments that it is now very rare in Uruguay but was reported to be found in small numbers in Rocha. No effort has been made to preserve them. Dr. Roberto Dabbene writes, in response to inquiry by Dr. Harper, that in Argentina it was formerly common and occurred as far as the islands of the Delta of La Plata but is now (1937) confined to the Territory of Formosa, where it is not common. By presidential decree the hunting of this deer is prohibited in Argentina.

Though no data of importance are available for Brazil, it is apparently to be found in fair numbers.

OCEANIC MAMMALS

Order CARNIVORA: Dogs, Cats, and Their Relatives

THE carnivores, considered as an order on p. 134, are represented by the sea otter (family Mustelidae) of the northern Pacific Ocean. Two races of this species are recognized; both were brought to the verge of extinction because of their valuable fur, but now they are recovering in numbers and may be an important resource in the future.

Family MUSTELIDAE: Weasels, Martens, Otters

NORTHERN SEA OTTER

ENHYDRA LUTRIS LUTRIS (Linnaeus)

[*Mustela*] *lutris* Linnaeus, Systema Naturae, ed. 10, vol. 1, p. 45, 1758 (Kamchatka).
SYNONYM: *Lutra marina* Schreber, Säugthiere, vol. 3, p. 465, pl. 128, 1778 (ex Steller);
  Nov. Comment. Petropol., vol. 2, p. 367, pl. 26, 1751.

SOUTHERN SEA OTTER

ENHYDRA LUTRIS NEREIS (Merriam)

Latax lutris nereis Merriam, Proc. Biol. Soc. Washington, vol. 17, p. 159, Oct. 6, 1904
  ("San Miguel Island, Santa Barbara Islands, California").
FIGS.: Royal Nat. Hist., vol. 2, p. 98, fig., 1894; zur Strassen, 1914, pp. 12*, 13*;
  Nelson, 1916, col. fig. p. 434.

The distinction between the northern sea otter and the southern race rests apparently upon slight cranial differences; hence it is not possible to distinguish the two without recourse to the skulls. Accordingly they may be treated together as representing but a single species, while the limits of geographical and individual variation still remain to be more precisely defined. It is believed that the southern race is the one occurring north at least to the coast of Oregon.

The sea otter is of rather heavy, robust form, about 4 feet in length, of which the tail is about a foot. The fore feet are small, with naked palms, but the hind feet are long and broad, webbed and with furry soles, recalling the flippers of a seal.

417

The color is dark brown, becoming hoary on the head.   The sparse whiskers are stout and short.   The posterior teeth are remarkably enlarged, broadened, and their cusps blunted to form low rounded knobs suitable for crushing the shellfish that form their diet.   Dr. Merriam states that the skin of the type of the southern race was 6 feet long, but it may have been stretched, or perhaps a very large individual.   Barabash-Nikiforov (1935) gives a maximum length of 1,635 mm., of which the tail was 330, and a maximum weight of 35 kilograms.

Sea otters were abundant formerly from the coasts of southern Kamchatka to the Kurile Islands in the western North Pacific and in the waters about the islands of the Bering Sea and Alaskan coasts southward following the cooler currents even to the coasts of southern California.   On the Asiatic side they ranged at one time as far south as Yezo.   On account of the richness of its fur the sea otter was ruthlessly pursued since its discovery by the Russians in about the middle of the eighteenth century, down to more modern times, until by the first decade of the present century it was very nearly exterminated.   The few skins that then came on the market sold for as much as $1,000 apiece.   Finally the United States Government in 1910 passed a law forbidding its capture in American waters and negotiated treaties with other interested nations for giving similar protection.   Now, after a lapse of little over a quarter of a century, there is encouraging evidence that the species is recovering and it has lately appeared in some numbers off the California coasts.

The history of the pursuit and exploitation of the sea otter has at various times been written.   From some of these accounts the following pertinent facts are gleaned.   Active trade in sea-otter skins seems to have begun in 1742, when Bering, after being wrecked in the sea bearing his name, returned to Petropaulovsk with about 900 skins stowed in the small boat built from the wreck of his vessel, the *St. Peter*.   These at first were chiefly traded with the Chinese, by whom they were highly valued.   Shelikof, a Russian trader, at once saw great possibilities in further trade in this fur.   He founded a colony on Kodiak Island and made plans for collecting sea-otter skins on a large scale.   He died before his object was accomplished, but his son-in-law, Nicholas P. Rezanof, carried on the work and in 1799 obtained from Emperor Paul the charter of the Russian-American Co. Shortly after, under the management of Shelikof and Baranof, the work was organized, and a fleet of bidarkas, manned by native Aleuts, started an intensive campaign. H. W. Elliott (1875) writes: "During the first few years the numbers of these animals taken all along the Aleutian chain, and down the whole northwest coast as far as Oregon, were very great . . . ; for instance, when the Prybilov Islands were first discovered, two sailors, Lukannon and Kaiekov, killed at St. Paul's Island, in the first year of occupation, *five thousand*, the next year they got less than a *thousand*, and in six years after not a single sea-otter appeared, and none have appeared since. When Shellikov's party first visited Cook's Inlet, they secured three thousand; during the second year, two thousand; in the third, only eight hundred; the season following they obtained six hundred; and finally, in 1812, less than a hundred, and since then not a tenth of that number. The first visit made by the Russians to the Gulf of Yahkutat, in 1794, two thousand sea-otters were taken, but they diminished so rapidly that in 1799 less than three hundred were taken. In 1798 a large party of Russians and Aleuts captured in Sitka Sound and neighborhood twelve hundred skins, besides those for which they traded with the natives there, fully as many more; and in the spring of 1800 a few American and English vessels came into Sitka Sound, and anchored off the small Russian settlement there, and traded with the natives for over two thousand skins, getting the trade of the Indians by giving fire-arms and powder, ball, &c., which the Russians did not dare to do, living then, as they were, in the country. In one of the early years of the Russian-American Company, 1804, Baranov went to the Okotsk from Alaska with fifteen thousand sea-otter skins, that were worth as much then as they are now [1875], viz., fully $1,000,000."

These tremendous inroads very quickly had an alarming effect. A Russian report, quoted by Elliott, tells that in 1826 the total number secured in the entire Aleutian chain was only 15, where previously more than 1,000 had been regularly taken each year. In 1835 the number from this district was 70 to 150 annually. The natives employed in collecting these furs were frequently subjected to great dangers, not only from the elements but from other native tribes who were unfriendly. When Alaska was purchased by the United States, writes H.

W. Elliott (1875), "the Russians were taking between four and five hundred sea-otters from the Aleutian Islands and south of the peninsula of Alaska, with perhaps a hundred and fifty more from Kenai, Yahkutat, and the Sitkan district; the Hudson's Bay Company and other traders getting about two hundred more from the coast of Queen Charlotte's and Vancouver's Islands, and off Gray's Harbor, Washington Territory. Now, during the last season, 1873, instead of less than seven hundred skins, as obtained by the Russians, our traders secured not much less than *four thousand skins.* This immense difference is not due to the fact of there being a proportionate increase of sea-otters, but to the organization of hunting parties in the same spirit and fashion, as in the early days . . . The keen competition of our traders will ruin the business in a comparatively short time if some action is not taken by the Government.

"Over two-thirds of all the sea-otters taken in Alaska are secured in two small areas of water, little rocky islets and reefs around the island of Saanach and the Chernobours, which proves that these animals, in spite of the incessant hunting all the year round on this ground, seem to have some particular preference for it to the practical exclusion of nearly all the rest of the coast in the Territory. This may be due to its better adaptation as a breeding ground. It is also noteworthy that all the sea-otters taken below the Straits of Fuca are shot by the Indians and white hunters off the beach in the surf at Gray's Harbor, a stretch of less than twenty miles; here some fifty to a hundred are taken every year, while not half that number can be obtained from all the rest of the Washington and Oregon coast-line; there is nothing in the external appearance of this reach to cause its selection by the sea-otters, except perhaps that it may be a little less rocky.

"As matters are now conducted by the hunting-parties, the sea-otters at Saanach and Chernobours do not have a day's rest during the whole year. Parties relieve each other in succession, and a continuous warfare is maintained. . . So the bad work goes on rapidly, though a majority of the natives and traders deprecate it." The optimum region mentioned by Elliott is described as a chain of small islets, most of them bare at low tide but with numerous reefs and rocky shoals with beds of kelp. "As the natives have never caught the mothers bringing forth their offspring on the rocks, they are disposed to believe that the birth takes place on kelp-beds, in pleasant or not over-rough weather. The female has a single pup [rarely two], born about fifteen inches in length. . . The sea-otter mother sleeps in the water on her back, with her young clasped between her fore-paws."

The methods employed in taking sea otters Elliott describes as four: Shooting them in the surf at long range with a rifle, and waiting till they drift ashore if the surf is too rough to permit of launching a boat; surrounding an otter by a party of spearers in their boats and awaiting its return to the surface after it becomes exhausted in several dives; clubbing them in winter when they may at times be stealthily approached among rocks and kelp; and using nets 16 to 18 feet long and 6 to 10 feet wide, of coarse meshes, spread out on the kelp beds. Frequently several at a time are thus taken, for when enmeshed they seem to make little or no attempt to get free. It is said that this method is preferred by the Japanese, since it permits the release of inferior animals or breeding females. The young, according to Scammon (1874), are met with at all times of the year, so that there appears to be no definite breeding season; the period of gestation is believed to be eight or nine months.

Writing in 1874, Captain Scammon speaks of the Lower California coasts as the haunt of sea otters and adds that Cerros, San Geronimo, Guadalupe, San Nicolas, and San Miguel Islands were "regarded as choice places to pursue them." Earlier, when California was part of Mexico, the pursuit of sea otters was prohibited by that Government under severe penalty. In recent years bones of the sea otter have been found in Indian shell heaps on Santa Cruz Island and near Monterey (E. M. Fisher, 1930).

Previous to the purchase of Alaska from Russia, Wrangell had already instituted somewhat more far-sighted methods of making the annual catch, allowing no part of the hunting grounds to be used for two consecutive years, and thus somewhat restricting the number killed. From 1842 to 1862 the average catch, including that of the Kurile Islands, was about 1,249, and the total for the 20 years was 25,899. The result was to restore the sea-otter population to a slightly better condition. But these careful methods were abandoned when Alaska became part of the United States, and the pursuit was followed with the greatest intensity, so that from 1881 to 1890 the take was 47,842, or nearly 5,000 a year (C. L. Andrews, 1937). The immediate reduction of the breeding stock by thus overexploiting these animals caused the Alaska Commercial Co., which had practically secured control of the Alaskan fur production, to close four or five of its posts by 1897. In 1900 the company was able to secure but 127 skins, and ten years later the entire catch of its fleet of 16 schooners was but 31 skins. Even at the price of $1,000 a skin there was no profit in this undertaking. Fortunately, in 1910, the taking of sea otters by citizens of the United States was prohibited, and by treaties of similar import with other interested nations the species was given respite just in time.

The gradual recuperation of the sea otter since 1910 from the verge of extinction to appreciable numbers during the last 30 years since protective laws were established has been most encouraging, although relatively meager data only are at hand as yet. In the Commander Islands their principal habitat is the rocky Copper Island, in the northwestern part of the group. Here from 1930 to 1932 the Russian naturalist I. Barabash-Nikiforov (1935) spent much time in an extensive study of their biology, and he concludes that the entire "herd" there then numbered between 600 and 700 animals and that the yearly increment was about 7 percent. The animals seem to be slowly building up a considerable population under careful protection. At about the same time Eyerdam (1933) published a brief report on his observations in the Aleutian Islands, where in a few localities "they seem to be on the increase." From fishermen and natives he learned that they are now frequently seen along the coasts of Afognak Island, and he himself in 1922 saw several during his stay there. In July, 1932, while staying on Atka Island, he learned that they are now becoming fairly common in the western Aleutians, adding that "among the dangerous, windswept foggy islets and reefs between Atka and Adak Islands, more properly known as the Sitkin Islands, sea otters can nearly always be seen if the weather permits." A captain of the Bureau of Fisheries vessel *Crane*, that summer, reported that "he had counted upwards of 40 sea otters between Adak and Atka Islands although the weather was unusually stormy at that time." Eyerdam also reported that sea otters seem to be increasing at the Sanakh

Islands, formerly a favorite resort for them; the residents there see them not infrequently. There is said, however, to be a small amount of poaching by Japanese vessels, for much of these coasts are uninhabited and can not readily be patrolled.

With regard to the sea otter on the coast of California Grinnell, writing in 1933, observed that, though formerly abundant about the islands and open seashore the whole length of the State, it was then rare but that nevertheless "individuals have been reported as seen almost every year off coasts of Monterey and San Luis Obispo counties. Last actual specimen" taken from near Monterey, September 9, 1915. On the Oregon coast the species was apparently exterminated half a century ago, for the last report given by Bailey (1936) is for 1876. Very recently a considerable herd appeared off Monterey, Calif., and formed the subject of interesting and valuable studies by Edna M. Fisher (1939). The animals were first noticed on March 19, 1938, off the mouth of Bixby Creek and attracted much attention. After about two weeks they moved slightly farther northward but remained in the general vicinity at least into early September. A careful count and estimate placed the number in this group as slightly less than 100, about 94 or fewer having been made out on various occasions. Miss Fisher's studies and sketches add greatly to a knowledge of the habits of the animal. The food secured by the otters was found to be red abalones, sea-urchins, and crabs; occasionally they nibble at the kelp. No evidence of their feeding on mussels was observed. These notes corroborate those of

Sea otter (*Enhydra lutris*)

Barabash-Nikiforov, who analyzed many droppings and found that in the Kurile Islands remains of sea-urchins constituted about 59 percent of their content, mollusks 23 percent, crabs about 10 percent, fish about 7 percent, and seaweeds a trace. Further details may be found in a paper by Murie (1940). Aside from man, their chief natural enemy is probably the killer whale, small groups of which haunt these seas and especially those about the more northern fur-seal rookeries.

While this recovery in numbers is encouraging, it must be evident that the building up of a considerable population will be slow. At the present time the Kurile herd must number nearly 700 or more, while information supplied by the Alaska Commercial Co. of San Francisco states that reports of substantial numbers have come to them from Atchitka and Rat Islands of the Aleutians; other estimates of the sea-otter population in the western part of this chain place the numbers at several hundreds. From southeastern Alaska there have been as yet no reports. That the numbers in the Kurile Islands are now sufficient to warrant the taking of a certain proportion for commercial purposes is indicated by the fact that according to the Fur Trade Review Weekly of May 4, 1939, 50 sea-otter skins were sold at recent London fur sales. "At about the same time The New York Auction Company offered 22 and the Fouke Fur Company of St. Louis, 10 pelts of this animal." Investigation has shown that all these were legally killed in the Kurile Islands by the Japanese Government, and "were certified in accordance with the Act of August 24, 1912" (Journ. Mammalogy, vol. 20, p. 407, 1939). If the sea otter continues to increase it may eventually with proper management be made a productive source of profit once more.

Order PINNIPEDIA: Seals, Sea-lions, Walruses

The sea-lions, seals, and walruses are related to the carnivores, differing from the latter group in the finlike structure of the feet. There are three families:

(1) Otariidae, the eared seals, sea-lions, and fur seals, or sea-bears. Representatives of this family occur on the temperate, subarctic, and austral shores of the Pacific, southern Atlantic, Indian, and northern Antarctic Oceans. Six species of the southern fur seal and three forms of the northern genus are discussed here.

(2) Phocidae, true seals or hair seals. These are more highly specialized for aquatic life than the sea-lions. The seals occur along the shores of all seas and oceans, and certain forms are found in the Caspian Sea and in Lake Baikal in central Asia. Seven species are threatened with extinction.

(3) Odobenidae, walruses. Two species of the single Recent genus are recognized; both are endangered by hunting activities, although they are still represented by large herds in the Arctic Ocean.—J. E. H.

Family OTARIIDAE: Sea-lions, Fur Seals

SOUTHERN FUR SEAL

ARCTOCEPHALUS AUSTRALIS (Zimmermann)

Phoca australis Zimmermann, Geographische Geschichte, vol. 3, p. 276, 1782 (Falkland Islands, based on Pennant's account).

SYNONYMS: For full synonymy see J. A. Allen, 1905, who gives among important synonyms the following: *Phoca falklandica* Shaw, General Zool., vol. 1, pt. 2, p. 256, 1800; *Arctocephalus ursinus* Gray, List Spec. Mamm. Brit. Mus., p. 103, 1843; *Arctocephalus nigrescens* Gray, Zool. Voy. *Erebus* and *Terror*, and Proc. Zool. Soc. London, 1859, pp. 109, 360.

FIGS.: Townsend, in Jordan et al., 1899, vol. 3, pl. 35; Allen, J. A., 1905, pl. 15, fig. 1; pl. 16, fig. 2; pl. 17, fig. 2 (skull).

The fur seals of the genus *Arctocephalus* are allied to the North Pacific species of the genus *Callorhinus* but are distinguished by having the facial portion of the skull slender, narrow, and elongated, with the upper profile sloping instead of nearly flat, the molars larger. The several isolated groups are in some cases regarded as separate species, but the differences are based largely on skull characters. All have been much hunted for their pelts and are largely depleted or even on the verge of extinction in parts of their range.

The pelage is of two kinds—a long, coarse, blackish overhair, tipped with gray or yellowish gray, giving a grizzled effect, except on the lower surface; and a thick, soft, brownish underfur, lighter at the tips and darker basally. Skull short and broad, the brain case rather squarish, the antorbital region very short, with short nasals; sagittal crest slightly developed. Unworn teeth tricuspid, with a main cusp and small anterior and posterior cusps. Teeth relatively much smaller than in *A. philippii*. Basal length of skull, 235 mm.; zygomatic width,

to 148 mm. Like other eared seals, the neck is relatively long,
the fore limbs longer than the hind, which are capable of
turning forward.

According to J. A. Allen (1905), from whose account the
foregoing details are taken, no adequate description of the
external characters of this fur seal has as yet been published.
Its breeding places "formerly included the Falkland Islands,
New Year's Island, Staten Island, Desolation Islands, and
other islands and coasts off the southern portion of South
America, and probably the more southern South Shetland,
South Georgian, and Sandwich groups. They doubtless still
resort to most of these localities, but only in small numbers in
comparison with their former abundance" (J. A. Allen, 1905).
It ranged northward along the Patagonian coast to the mouth
of the La Plata, frequenting the small islands off Maldonado,
Uruguay, and in 1887 was known to straggle as far north as
Rio de Janeiro, doubtless following the cooler northward-flowing
currents. The Straits of Magellan were a favorite resort,
while on the west coast of Chile it ranged at least to the southern part of the archipelago.

The status of the fur seal about the southern part of South
America is somewhat difficult to make out definitely, but it
still occurs in some numbers locally. Dr. Barnum Brown (in
manuscript notes published by J. A. Allen, 1905), at the beginning of this century saw "considerable numbers on the
south coast of Tierra del Fuego, but they were not observed
off the coast of Patagonia. One herd estimated to contain
1500 head, was seen near Cape Hall, west of the Strait of Le
Maire, and two smaller herds were seen south of Lenox Island,
having less than 200 individuals each. These seals are poached
by a few natives, but owing to the abrupt, rugged rocks they
are seldom found on shore and cannot be driven to a killing
ground. The Argentine Government sends a gunboat to these
waters once a month to keep off poachers."

The rugged shores of the Magellan region probably now
offer a last stronghold for this fur seal, where the very nature
of the seas and shores affords it partial security against human
predation. Elsewhere, however, the species is largely gone.
Dr. Robert Cushman Murphy (1918) has given a summary of
the history of its pursuit. "Sealing on the coast of Patagonia,
the Falklands, and the islands north and east of Cape Horn

began during the third quarter of the eighteenth century. Alexander Dalrymple, writing in 1775, reports that there was at the Falkland Islands an abundance of . . . fur seals in 'such numbers that they killed eight or nine hundred in a day with bludgeons on one small Islot.'" At present fur seals are no longer found on the Falklands, but the date of their disappearance can not have been very long after the beginning of the last century, for already soon after the American Revolution New England and British sealers were pushing their search for pelts to South Georgia, and then to the South Orkneys and the South Shetlands. The Portuguese were also according to Forster engaged in this pursuit in its earlier years. About 1800, sealing at South Georgia had already about reached its peak. In that year, the *Aspasia*, of New York, one of 18 sealing vessels at the island, "secured the season's prize catch of 57,000 fur seal skins. This record was never again equalled, although the hunting evidently continued, for when . . . Bellingshausen sailed along the blustery, uncharted south coast of the island in December, 1819, he met with two English three-masters in one of the fjords. These ships had already been there four months, or through the southern winter, and had carried on a profitable business." Five years later, in 1824, when Capt. James Weddell visited the island, he found that seals of all kinds had become almost extinct. He mentions that the American sealers traded these skins to China where they frequently brought $5 or $6 apiece. He estimates that not less than 1,200,000 of the hides had been gathered there since the opening of the sealing exploitation. Fur seals are believed to have been practically exterminated at South Georgia about 1874, "but rumor has it that a New England vessel made a small illegal catch there in 1907." In 1874 no less than 1,450 skins were taken, and in the year following 600. In 1892, according to Lönnberg (1906), 135 fur seals were killed at this island "and they may have been the very last ones," for in 1905 "a Chilenian sailing vessel visited the coasts of this island," hunting in every cove and corner for fur seals but found none. However, Dr. Murphy records that about the middle of February, 1915, some Norwegian whalers discovered a single fur seal, evidently a straggler, on the beach near the eastern end of South Georgia, and unfortunately killed it. With this exception no fur seal has been definitely known from the island since 1910, when the first sealing license was issued by the Falklands.

With the reduction of the fur seals on the Falklands and South Georgia, the hunt was pushed still farther south to the South Shetlands. Weddell writes of the success of his and other crews here: "The quantity of seals taken off these islands, by vessels from different parts, during the years 1821 and 1822, may be computed at 320,000 . . . This valuable animal, the fur seal, might . . . have been spared to render annually 100,000 furs for many years to come. This would have followed from not killing the mothers till the young were able to take the water; and even then, only those which appeared to be old, together with a proportion of the males, thereby diminishing their total number, but in slow progression." Shortly after Weddell's time, the pursuit of fur seals in this region was nearly abandoned, since the seals had been largely extirpated. Fifty years later, however, the remnant seems to have somewhat recovered, for between 1871 and 1891 at least 18,000 skins were taken from various parts of the group. "From this second catastrophe they were never allowed to recover, and their final extermination is believed to have taken place in the opening years of the present century. The last authentic capture occurred in 1902, when the Swedish expedition found a single fur seal on Nelson Island. Since then . . . none has been recorded from the group" (Marr, 1935).

The South Orkneys, lying to the northeast of the South Shetlands, seem to have yielded relatively fewer fur seals. Only three were reported by Weddell in 1823, but Dallmann 50 years afterward reported 165 seals, and he is the last to record the seal's presence there, "but it is by no means certain that it was he who exterminated it there," for these islands seem a less favorable place since they are surrounded by pack ice for a much longer period each year than are the South Shetlands (Marr, 1935, pp. 370–373). On the South Sandwich group, still more to the northeast, Rudmose Brown (1913) supposes this seal may still rarely occur for "it certainly was found there in comparatively recent years."

While thus the southern fur seal is believed to be gone from the island groups where it formerly occurred within the Falkland dependencies, a few probably remain in the Straits of Magellan region, and it may survive under some protection for a while longer. Dr. Roberto Dabbene in a letter to Dr. Francis Harper dated January, 1937, writes that it has almost vanished from the Argentine coasts because of constant persecution for its fur. Thirty years before, when he visited Punta Arenas, a single skin brought a pound sterling. He saw but two individuals during a voyage through the Fuegian canals. It has disappeared from "La Isla de los Estados" (Staten Island) and the Patagonian coast.

In striking contrast to this depletion, however, is the wise policy of Uruguay in protection and "farming" the rookeries of these fur seals on Lobos Island off its coast near Maldonado. This island is less than a mile in length, low and brush-covered, but with rocky shores. A few houses are in its center. The fur seals here have for many years been carefully protected and managed under governmental supervision so that they yield an annual return. "Commercial sealing was carried on here prior to 1820. The present lessees of the island, operating under the direction of the Government of Uruguay, placed upon the London market, from 1873 to 1897, 319,746 salted skins, or an average of over 13,000 a year" (C. H. Townsend, in Jordan and others, 1899). Here is an excellent example that should be followed by other nations of these latitudes, for under proper management and protection the fur-seal colonies might be made to yield a good return for years to come.

NEW ZEALAND FUR SEAL
ARCTOCEPHALUS FORSTERI (Lesson)

Otaria forsteri Lesson, Dict. Classique Hist. Nat., vol. 13, p. 421, 1828 (New Zealand).
SYNONYM: *Gypsophoca tropicalis* Gray, Proc. Zool. Soc. London, 1872b, p. 659.
FIGS.: Gray, 1872, figs. 5, 6; 1874, pl. 18.

SOUTH AUSTRALIAN FUR SEAL
ARCTOCEPHALUS DORIFERUS Wood Jones

Arctocephalus doriferus Wood Jones, Rec. South Australian Mus., vol. 3, no. 1, 1925 ("South Australia").
FIGS.: LeSouëf, Burrell, and Troughton, 1926, figs. 12, 13, opposite p. 101 (photographs); Wood Jones, 1925, figs. 246–248 (skull and feet).

TASMANIAN FUR SEAL
ARCTOCEPHALUS TASMANICUS Scott and Lord

Arctocephalus tasmanicus Scott and Lord, Papers and Proc. Roy. Soc. Tasmania for 1925, p. 189, 1926 ("Tasmania").

While J. A. Allen (1905) regarded the fur seals of the Australian and New Zealand seas as representing but a single form, *A. forsteri*, those of South Australia and of Tasmania have lately been given distinctive names. Whether these are really separate races or species, or whether the characters represent merely individual variations, seems as yet to be uncertain. According to Wood Jones, *A. forsteri* has the dorsal surface dark brown, grizzled with white-tipped hairs, and the ventral surface reddish brown, with a fine red-brown underfur. A distinguishing feature is said to be that the hind foot has the prolongation of the middle three digits only slightly shorter than the marginal digits, and the teeth have an accessory cusp on only the front edge instead of on both fore and hind margins as in the South Australian animal, which he describes as *A. doriferus*. In the Tasmanian fur seal the large size is apparently a supposed distinction; condylobasal length of skull 280–290 mm. against about 250 in *A. doriferus* for adult males. The three may be briefly considered as to status, for although now more or less protected, they are reduced to a small part of their former numbers; and while supposed to be distinct, are not certainly identifiable when alive so that the applicability of notes is uncertain.

Hutton and Drummond (1923) have given a brief history of the exploitation of the fur seal in New Zealand. When discovered by Capt. James Cook on his first voyage, he noted them on the south island and on his second voyage found the fresh meat of seals killed at Dusky Bay a welcome addition to the larder. It was not until 1792, however, that the first sealing crew landed there and in the course of nearly a year at Dusky Bay procured over 4,500 fur-seal skins. In the opening years of the nineteenth century, with the decline of the sealing in Bass Straits, a schooner from Sydney, New South Wales, traded a cargo of 2,000 sealskins at Dusky Bay, Breaksea Sounds, and Solander Island. Sir Joseph Banks, who had accompanied Cook on his first voyage, was much impressed by the numbers of fur seals: "The beach is encumbered with their quantities, and those who visit their haunts have less trouble in killing them than the servants of the victualling office have, who kill hogs in a pen with a mallet." In 1806 he added that on one vessel bound to London from Sydney there were 30,000 sealskins! The result of this reckless slaughter was that as early as 1810 the numbers were seriously depleted, but in that year the discovery of the Campbell and Macquarie Islands "gave new life to the trade." Nevertheless the search for seals was carried on relentlessly, and in 1824 ten vessels were said to have secured 70,000 to 80,000 on New Zealand and the adjacent islands. Two years later a vessel spent six months cruising for new sealing grounds, but obtained only 449 skins. Stewart Island was a specially favored spot.

In former times fur seals were abundant on the Tasmanian coasts, in Bass Straits, and along the islands in the bight of South Australia. Péron saw them at Kangaroo Island in 1802–3. The breeding season was from about November to April. Sealing continued in these regions until a comparatively recent date. Wood Jones, writing in 1925, states that the last large haul of skins from Kangaroo Island and its outlying rocks was made "nearly forty years ago [i. e. about 1885], and it is very doubtful if a fur seal has been seen on the Island since then." On six visits to the islands of Nuyts Archipelago and the Investigator group he had not seen a single one, although he was told of recent sealing there. He adds that "it is practically certain that the animals still live on the inner Casuarina Island, which was one of their great strongholds in the old days, and from which only 13 years ago [1912] 20 fur seals were said to have been taken." This island is now a sanctuary. The fur seals were almost exterminated from Tasmania, "but protection there has led to the re-establishment of some small herds." It is said that on the coast of Western Australia it still breeds in small numbers in the extreme southwest, off Cape Leeuwin, and perhaps rarely on the Houtmans Abrolhos, and that stray individuals have been seen as far north as Shark's Bay (Shortridge, 1936, p. 745). While spending two weeks on the Abrolhos in November, 1931, however, I saw no sign of fur seals. It is said that in 1921 an expedition to the Recherche Archipelago gathered 300 skins of a fur seal but realized very little on them. They are not protected here and no permit is required for taking them. "Doubtless on the outlying islands, which are very difficult of access, fur seals may still be found, but unless strict measures are taken for their protection they will soon disappear" (Hull, in Hanna, 1922, p. 14). It seems a pity that these remnants should not be protected and allowed to increase until the time when they can be successfully maintained as a useful asset.

KERGUELEN FUR SEAL

ARCTOCEPHALUS GAZELLA (Peters)

Arctophoca gazella Peters, Monatsb. Preuss. Akad. Wiss. Berlin, 1875, p. 396 (Kerguelen Island, southern Indian Ocean).

SYNONYM: *Arctophoca elegans* Peters, Monatsb. Preuss. Akad. Wiss. Berlin, 1876, p. 316 (St. Paul and Amsterdam Islands, Indian Ocean).

FIGS.: Turner, 1888, pl. 6, figs. 4, 6 (skull).

The fur seal of Kerguelen in the southern Indian Ocean was described by Peters on the basis of a specimen brought back by the exploring ship *Gazelle* in 1874. The back, sides of head, neck, and crown are grayish brown, this color extending forward in a triangle between the eyes and on the sides of the neck to in front of the ears. Below, the fore neck and upper chest are pale yellow, becoming rusty brown posteriorly. Lips rusty red and vibrissae white. The underfur is rusty red. The specially distinctive characters lie in the skull, which has very small auditory bullae. Turner (1888) speaks of the skeleton as slenderer than in the South American species, with nasals on the same plane as the top of the skull, and the cheek teeth without secondary cusps but with a weak cingulum. The sixth postcanine tooth is much smaller than the others. The adult male measured in total length, 1,770 mm.; ear, 40; hind foot, 305. The female showed a total length of 830 mm.; tail, 35; ear, 30. Greatest length of skull, 212 mm.; zygomatic width, 131; length of palate, 92.

Kerguelen or Desolation Island, lying in latitude 49° S., in the southern Indian Ocean, has long been known as a resort especially of the elephant seal, but it maintained also small numbers of fur seals that apparently differed slightly in cranial characters from other isolated groups in the southern hemisphere. Peters emphasizes particularly the small bullae and lack of accessory cusps on the postcanine teeth. The seal found on the St. Paul and Amsterdam Islands, not very far to the north of Kerguelen, Peters later distinguished as *Arctophoca elegans*, a name to which Trouessart (1904–5) gave subspecific status, but Dr. J. A. Allen (1905, p. 122) believed that the supposed differences were insufficiently defined to recognize more than the one form among these, and probably on the Crozet Islands as well as on Kerguelen, which seems a reasonable conclusion, for the colonies are not so far apart that they might be expected to develop peculiarities through isolation.

Apparently the fur-seal population of Kerguelen has not been large during recent times. As early as 1830 vessels in pursuit of elephant seals visited it and doubtless obtained a few fur seals as well. In 1874 there were four expeditions there to observe the transit of Venus, the German with the ship *Gazelle*, the English on the *Challenger*, and a French and an American expedition. Moseley of the *Challenger* wrote that in January, 1874, two of the whaling schooners then at the island killed over 70 fur seals in one day and upwards of 20 on another at some small islands off Howes Foreland, and he deplores the wantonness and shortsightedness of their destructive methods. At the same time J. H. Kidder (1876) who spent four months on Kerguelen, saw none of this species but notes that "sealers speak of a few scattering fur-seals upon this and Heard's Islands, but they have never been found in large numbers." The latter island, though a favorite resort of elephant seals, seems to have been less attractive to fur seals. J. A. Allen (in Jordan and others, 1899, p. 316) quotes Capt. George Comer as to the seals at Kerguelen. He spent five months there in the winter of 1883–84 and obtained only six skins. He adds, "About 1850 this island was visited by an American who practically cleaned off the seals. The captain I shipped with—Joseph Fuller—visited the island in 1880 and took 3,000 seals—practically all there were—and this was the increase for thirty years from 1850."

The St. Paul and Amsterdam Islands lie about 11° north of Kerguelen and may be taken as the northward limit of this fur seal. They were visited by Capt. Henry Cox in 1789, in May, who on landing "found the shores covered with such a multitude of seals that we were obliged to disperse them before we got out of the boat . . . We procured here a thousand skins of very superior quality, while we remained on the island of Amsterdam, besides several casks of good oil." Lord Macartney, who touched at Amsterdam in 1773, found there five men collecting seal skins for the Canton market. He says of the seals: "In the summer months they come ashore, sometimes in droves of 800 or 1,000 at a time, out of which 100 are destroyed, that number being as many as five men can skin and peg down to dry in the course of a day . . . Most of those which come ashore are females, on the proportion of more than thirty to one male." In 1874, Charles Vélain of the

French transit of Venus expedition, reported considerable herds of fur seals there (J. A. Allen, in Jordan and others, 1899), but the more recent status of these animals seems difficult to determine.

In 1924 the French Chamber of Deputies completely prohibited taking or hunting seals in the Crozet Archipelago, St. Paul and Amsterdam Islands, Howe, McMurdo, and Briant Islands in the north of the Kerguelen Archipelago, and on part of the south coast of Kerguelen, islands that together now constitute a national park.

Presumably the fur seals formerly frequenting the Prince Edward and the Crozet Islands were the same as the Kerguelen fur seal, or possibly were nearer to the form of South Africa. No precise studies of the matter seem to have been made. The former group lies some 900 miles southeast of the Cape of Good Hope, and the latter about the same distance to the east and half way between the Prince Edward and Kerguelen groups. According to J. A. Allen (in Jordan and others, 1899) fur seals formerly abounded on the Prince Edward group. About 1806, Capt. H. Fanning obtained a full cargo of fur seals there, as did other vessels at the same time, but definite statistics are unavailable. He was also the first sealer to visit the Crozet Islands (in 1805), but although he saw an abundance of seals there he passed on to the Prince Edward Islands. Later on, however, many seals were taken over a number of years at the Crozets. At Possession Island, the largest of the group, Captain Brine in 1876 found "hundreds of seals, which were resting on the damp grass bordering on the stream which at this point enters the sea." They must have been greatly depleted soon after, however, for in 1887, Captain George Comer visited the islands on the recommendation of people at Cape Town who had formerly taken great numbers there, but after five months his party succeeded in obtaining only three seals (J. A. Allen, in Jordan and others, 1899). What numbers if any now occur on these islands would be interesting to know.

CAPE FUR SEAL

ARCTOCEPHALUS PUSILLUS (Schreber)

Phoca pusilla Schreber, Säugthiere, vol. 3, p. 314, 1776; p. 584, 1777; pl. 86, 1775 ("Im indischen Meere" but assumed to be South Africa).

SYNONYMS: *Phoca antarctica* Thunberg, Mém. Acad. Sci. St. Pétersbourg, vol. 3, p. 222, 1811; *Otaria peronii* Desmarest, Encyclop. Méth., Mammalogie, p. 250, 1820; *Arctocephalus delalandii* Gray, Proc. Zool. Soc. London, 1859, p. 107 (Cape of Good Hope); *Arctocephalus nivosus* Gray, Ann. Mag. Nat. Hist., ser. 4, vol. 1, p. 219, 1868 (Cape of Good Hope); *Arcto-cephalus schist-hyperoës* Turner, Journ. Anat. and Physiol., ser. 2, vol. 2, p. 113, 1868 (Cape of Good Hope).

FIGS.: Gray, 1859, pl. 69; Sclater, W. L., 1900, vol. 1, figs. 34, 35; Shortridge, 1934, vol. 1, 4 pls. opposite p. 204.

While there seems some doubt as to the strict applicability of the name *pusilla* to this species, it is generally assumed that it was given to a South African specimen; the next available name, and the one sometimes used, is *antarctica*.

The characters of this fur seal have not been well defined. According to Gray the palate is concave, "hinder aperture narrow, with a rather acute, ovate anterior edge; teeth large; lower jaw rather short, strong." Otherwise no characters are pointed out that might distinguish it from *A. gazella*. Length of adult male, 8 feet from nose to root of tail; an average female about 4 feet 4 inches (W. L. Sclater).

This seal was formerly abundant on the islands off the coasts of South Africa, but W. L. Sclater (1900) wrote that by the beginning of this century "the number killed of late years has not been very great, as they have been nearly exterminated, and it is considered very desirable to allow them to increase." This wise course evidently resulted in their recuperation, for at the present time there are some flourishing rookeries on these coasts. The most northern breeding colony is at Cape Cross, 100 miles north of Walvis Bay, on the mainland of Southwest Africa, and is the only colony on the mainland. It is now visited annually "by a far larger breeding colony than is on any of the islands" (Shortridge, 1934). Other localities are the various islands between Walvis Bay and Lüderitz, comprising a number of small islands, though from some the seals seem to have departed. On the east coast the fur seals breed as far as Rocky and Bird Islands, in Algoa Bay, and occasionally are seen along the coast as far as East London.

At one time, Lydekker wrote, as many as 70,000 to 80,000 skins were annually imported from the Cape to London, but the number "is now much reduced." The females come ashore in November to give birth to their young. Since Sclater in 1900 did not mention the large rookery at Cape Cross, one may conclude that it has been established in later years as a result of protection.

It is believed that it was this fur seal that formerly was abundant at Tristan da Cunha and the neighboring islands. This group was first "visited for fur seals in 1790 by Captain Patten, of the American schooner *Industry*, of Philadelphia, who secured 5,000 skins. Large numbers are said to have been subsequently obtained there, probably from the smaller islands of the group, Inaccessible and Nightingale Islands. The latter is apparently still frequented by a few fur seals. Gough Island, somewhat to the southward of the Tristan group, formerly abounded with fur seals" (J. A. Allen, in Jordan and others, 1899); but according to Capt. George Comer there were practically none left by 1887, when his vessel put six men ashore there for nine months. They were able to secure only 40 or 50 skins. Nevertheless "odd specimens were killed in the Tristan group up to 1920, but now appear to have been exterminated" (Shortridge, 1934).

Whether the fur seal of the Crozet Islands was the same as the South African form or more resembled that of Kerguelen Island does not seem to have been determined. However, for the present it is included under the latter.

PHILIPPI'S FUR SEAL

ARCTOCEPHALUS PHILIPPII (Peters)

Otaria (Arctophoca) philippii Peters, Monatsb. Akad. Wiss. Berlin, 1866, p. 276 (Juan Fernandez Island, Perú).

SYNONYMS: *Otaria (Arctophoca) argentata* Philippi, Monatsb. Akad. Wiss. Berlin, 1871, p. 560, pls. 1, 2 (Juan Fernandez Island); *Otaria leucostoma* Philippi, Anal. Mus. Nac. Chile, sect. 1, zool., pp. 6, 46, 1892 (Masafuera Island); *Arctocephalus galapagoensis* Heller, Proc. California Acad. Sci., ser. 3, zool., vol. 3, pp. 245–248, 1904 (Wenman Island, Galápagos Islands, Ecuador). For additional synonymy see J. A. Allen, 1905, p. 131.

FIGS.: Allen, J. A., 1905, pl. 15, fig. 2; pl. 16, fig. 1; pl. 17, fig. 1 (skulls); Townsend, 1934, figs. 15–22 (photographs and skull).

Closely allied to the southern fur seal, this species is described as blackish gray above, becoming more yellowish gray on the head and neck; brownish black below, lips and chin rusty brown. Six rows of mustachial bristles, some all black, some all white, some particolored. The long overhair is rusty brown basally with rusty yellow tips on the back, head, and neck; on the ventral surface uniform brownish black or tipped with ferruginous. The thick underfur is rusty red. Total length of a young adult male, 1,570 mm.; tail, 35; hind foot, palm, 300; ear, 36. Basal length of skull, 260–272 mm. (The above details are from J. A. Allen, 1905.)

The skull as a whole is longer than in *A. australis*, the posterior part much longer, rostral part longer and more sloping, nasals longer and narrower, and the dentition much heavier, with the accessory cusps absent or very small. The sagittal crest is strongly developed.

The distribution of this fur seal is given by J. A. Allen (1905, p. 132) as "from the Straits of Magellan northward along the west coast of South America to the Galapagos Archipelago." "Numerous records" are mentioned of their capture "at many points on the coast of Chili, at the Chincha Islands, and in the Bay of Callao on the coast of Peru." The chief congregating places for breeding, however, seem to have been the small islands of Masafuera and Juan Fernandez off the coast of central Chile; the little group comprising St. Felix, St. Ambrose, and St. Marys Islands, about 9° of latitude farther north and on the same meridian of 80°; and the islands of the Galápagos group, especially Albemarle and Wenman Islands. Although, in 1904, Heller named the fur seal of the last group as a distinct species, it is, according to J. A. Allen (1905), indistinguishable from typical *A. philippii*, the range of which therefore includes the cooler waters of the Humboldt Current flowing northward along the west coast of South America. This current, as Dr. R. C. Murphy has at various times pointed out, is responsible for carrying far toward the Equator many marine forms that frequent cool water, and are otherwise of sub-Antarctic distribution.

A history of fur-seal hunting on these groups of islands has been published by J. A. Allen (in Jordan and others, 1899, p. 309) from which the following notes are extracted. Masafuera when first discovered in 1563, "swarmed with fur seals," but they apparently were unmolested until 1792, when the ship *Eliza* of New York secured a cargo of 38,000 skins which were taken to Canton and sold for $16,000. In 1798 Capt. Edmund Fanning, of the ship *Betsey*, also from New York, visited the island and secured the better part of 100,000 sealskins there. These also were disposed of at Canton. In leaving the island he estimated that there were still left in this rookery between 500,000 and 700,000 seals. Capt. A. Delano tells that about this time there were, on one of his visits, people from 14 ships

killing seals on the island. He estimated that in a period of
seven years more than 3,000,000 skins had been taken thence
to Canton, and he makes the statement that when first discovered the total seal population was two or three million.
This great slaughter very soon depleted the stock so that by
1807, according to Captain Morrell, "the business was scarcely
worth following," and in 1824 there were practically none left.
"In later years the island has been visited at intervals by fur-
seal hunters and small catches obtained. As late as 1891
Capt. Frank M. Gaffney states (affidavit) that on visiting the
island for fur seals he saw 300 or 400, and took 19, showing
that a few are still to be found at Mas-á-Fuero." Sealing at
Juan Fernandez, only a few miles distant, began at about the
same time. Dampier, who visited the island in 1683, speaks of
their abundance at that time, finding that "there is not a Bay or
Rock that one can get ashore on that is not full of them . . .
Here are always thousands, I might say possibly millions of
them . . . Large ships might here load themselves with
Seal Skins and Trayne Oyl. for they are extraordinary fat."
Juan Fernandez was earlier settled than Masafuera and already
had a population of 3,000 persons in 1800, so that according to
Delano there were not then any seals left on any part of it.
"Subsequently the island appears to have been visited at
intervals by sealers in search of fur seals, but always with poor
success." Nevertheless, according to Captain Gaffney, a few
were seen there in December, 1891, but "the number left is too
small to possess any commercial importance."

Formerly fur seals were abundant on the little islands of St.
Felix, St. Ambrose, and St. Marys, a group north of Masafuera off the coast of Chile. Delano in 1801 speaks of large
catches being made at the two first-mentioned while in 1816
Captain Fanning took 14,000 skins at St. Marys. This destruction seems to have gone on unabated until about the last
quarter of the nineteenth century, for in 1870, according to J.
A. Allen, a certain George Fogel saw "thousands" at Chikla-
way. By 1891, however, they were nearly gone, and in December of that year Captain Gaffney further testified to their
depletion, for he saw only two at St. Felix and St. Ambrose
where formerly they had been so abundant, while at Rees
Inlet he obtained a single one. He testified that they still bred
on the islands, but "the Chilians go there and kill all they can

obtain, as has been the case for many years at other islands off
the Chilean coast. Hence there is little opportunity for the
recuperation of the seal herds."

In the Galápagos group the story is much the same. On
these and perhaps the other groups just mentioned, the seals
were probably nonmigratory but were to be found the year
round and had an extended breeding period. Captain Fanning
in 1816 obtained here 8,000 fur seals. Wenman and Albemarle
Islands seem to have been favored resorts or possibly the animals were here more easily secured. They seem to have developed slightly different habits from those on the more
southern groups of islands, for instead of frequenting the more
accessible parts of the coast they seek shelter in the many
rocky caverns and under overhanging ledges or haunt the
roughest parts of the coastline where they are taken only with
difficulty.

Dr. C. H. Townsend (1934) has given some further records
of catches made at the Galápagos Islands in former years.
Thus in four voyages made by Capt. Charles W. Read between
1872 and 1880, about 6,000 were taken; in 1880 another vessel
secured 261 on the islands Culpepper, Albemarle, Narborough,
Tower, and Wenman; and in 1882 there were 800 taken. The
last big catches were in 1885, when 1,000 were killed, and 1887,
when 1,200 more were secured. The last lot sold at $7 each.
About the last of the sealing vessels to make catches among
these islands was the schooner *Julia E. Whalen*, of San Francisco, which in 1897–99 took 224 seals. For a time the fur seal
was believed to have been quite exterminated in the Galápagos
Archipelago, until in 1906 R. H. Beck, while collecting there
for the American Museum of Natural History, secured a specimen. A remnant seems to have survived, however, for in
1932–33 six or eight were captured alive and given to the San
Diego Zoological Gardens, California. At least three of these
died after a few months in captivity and now form part of a
group at the American Museum. Still more recent information
reported to Dr. Harper in 1937 implies that the fur seals have
somewhat increased and are now "rather common in some
bays." If adequate protection can be maintained for this
herd, it should continue to build up.

GUADALUPE FUR SEAL

ARCTOCEPHALUS TOWNSENDI Merriam

Arctocephalus townsendi Merriam, Proc. Biol. Soc. Washington, vol. 11, p. 178, 1897
(Guadalupe Island, Lower California, Mexico).
FIGS.: Allen, J. A., 1905, pls. 18, 19, 20 (skull); Townsend, 1931, figs. 345 (col.), 356
(photographs of animals and skull).

This is the only fur seal of the genus *Arctocephalus* found
north of the Equator and it may be supposed to have been
derived from ancestral forms of the South Pacific Ocean. The
differences as compared with *A. philippii* are in the skull,
which is much narrower, especially the rostral portion, with a
narrower and more depressed palate, flatter audital bullae,
and somewhat smaller size. The external characters are not
known, but probably it closely resembled its more southern
relatives. The type skull measured: Greatest length, 256 mm.;
zygomatic width, 151; canine to last molar (inclusive), 88.

The history of this species has been summarized by J. A.
Allen (1905) and by C. H. Townsend (in Jordan and others,
1899) who was the first to obtain specimens for study purposes. According to the former, large numbers were in earlier
days taken at the San Benito, Cerros, Guadalupe, Santa
Barbara, and other islands off southern and Lower California as well as on the coast of the mainland. It was resident on these coasts the year round. In 1806 and 1807 one
vessel took over 8,300 seals at Benito Island, and another in
the following year killed 3,000 off Cape San Lucas. Dr. Joseph
Grinnell (1933) wrote that up to about 1833 it occurred on the
coast of Monterey County and on the Farallon Islands, California, and there were a few still around Santa Barbara Islands
up to about 1890. North of the Mexican boundary, however,
it was then extinct or nearly so. In 1825, Capt. Benjamin
Morrell reported that on Socorro Island, in latitude 18° 53′ N.,
about 20 fur seals were seen, on May 20. In the previous
March at Guadalupe he had found and captured a number.
Cerros Island, he states, was formerly a great place for them,
but at that time it had been abandoned as a resort. Arriving
at the Farallon Islands on May 11, 1825, he wrote that "many
years ago this place was the resort of numerous fur-seal, but
the Russians have made such havoc among them that there is
scarcely a breed left." Scammon (1874) refers to their former

occurrence at San Benito Islands and the California coast, prior probably to 1850.

In May, 1892, Dr. Charles H. Townsend made a special visit to Guadalupe Island to ascertain if these seals were still present there and to secure specimens. Arriving on the 16th, he spent ten days in exploring the coastline but saw only seven fur seals, though none of them on land, as it was apparently too early for the breeding season to have started. Young are not brought forth till June. It was here that he picked up skulls on the beach that served for the description of the species.

On his return from this visit he made efforts to gather information on the former presence of this seal, as follows: In 1876–77 a few were killed on San Benito Island. These were said to be accompanied by young. In 1877 several vessels were sealing at Guadalupe, one of them having taken about 300 and another some 500 skins, then worth only $2.50 apiece. At that time one captain reported that the rookery numbered about 1,000. In 1879 about 1,550 seals were taken on these two islands and were sold in San Francisco at $10 to $15 each. In 1880 Captain Haritwen took 104 fur seals on Guadalupe in May, chiefly on the west side where the largest rookery contained 600 or 700. Another vessel secured 500 seals, staying longer than the others, and reported that the young were born in June. Other vessels also made catches. In 1880, the estimated population was between 3,000 and 4,000 seals. In 1883 Capt. George Wentworth made four trips to Guadalupe in November, December, January, and February, securing about 2,000 seals and seeing about as many more. In 1885, sealer James N. Niles made six trips to the island, finding seals present during most of the year; about 2,000 were seen and 200 were killed. The colonies seem by this time to have been fairly broken up, for in 1890 and 1891 sealers found them few and three reported only 14 taken altogether. In 1893, however, A. W. Anthony stated that 36 were taken, but in the following year only 15. Between the years 1876 and 1894, the total catch from the incomplete accounts obtained was thus about 5,575. Since then no figures are available, but it seems that a few animals still remain.

At the present time this remnant is nominally protected by the Mexican Government, and if poaching can be completely stopped it is likely that the number can be increased to form eventually a valuable source of income under proper management. For already there is some evidence that as a result of partial respite, it is beginning to show an increase. Indeed, according to Grinnell (1933) one was credibly reported near the Santa Barbara Islands in 1929. In 1930 Huey noted that two were brought to the San Diego Zoo alive in April, 1928, and that on further inquiry it developed that these had been captured on Guadalupe Island where a herd numbering about 60 was present.

That this fur seal was common in former times on the coast of southern California is attested by the discovery of abundant remains in aboriginal shell mounds at Point Mugu, Ventura County (see Gretchen M. Lyon, 1935).

Commander Islands Fur Seal

Callorhinus ursinus ursinus (Linnaeus)

Phoca ursina Linnaeus, Systema Naturae, ed. 10, vol. 1, p. 37, 1758 (Commander Islands, Bering Sea).

Kurile Islands Fur Seal

Callorhinus ursinus mimicus (Tilesius)

Phoca mimica Tilesius, Oken's Isis, Heft 8, p. 715, 1835 (Bay of Patience near Cape Patience, Sakhalin Island, Okhotsk Sea).

SYNONYMS: *Callorhinus curilensis* Jordan, Fur Seals and Fur-seal Islands of North Pacific Ocean, pt. 1, p. 45, 1898; Jordan and Clark, ibid., pt. 3, p. 3, 1899 (Robben Island, south of Cape Patience, Okhotsk Sea); *Callotaria ursina mimica* Stejneger, Georg Wilhelm Steller, p. 286, footnote 37, 1936; C[*allotaria*] *curilica* Stejneger, Georg Wilhelm Steller, p. 286, footnote 37, 1936.

Probably no other wild species has been so thoroughly studied and written of as the fur seal of the North Pacific. Three local forms have been named, each of which represents a supposedly circumscribed colony. The typical *C. ursinus*, first brought to the attention of naturalists by Steller, was found by him in 1741 on Bering Island, of the Commander group off the east coast of Kamchatka. Jordan and Clark (l. c.) overlooked the name *mimicus* applied by Tilesius (l. c.) to the fur seal of the Okhotsk Sea and proposed *Callorhinus curilensis* for the fur seal of Robben Island off Cape Patience, Sakhalin Island, in Okhotsk Sea; and at the same time distinguished that of the Pribilof Islands as *Callorhinus alascanus*

[= *Callorhinus ursinus cynocephalus*]. On account of their interest and value as fur bearers, these seals may be briefly included here.

The North Pacific fur seals are placed in a genus, *Callorhinus*, distinct from that of the southern fur seals, from which they differ in "the form of the facial portion of the skull, which in *Arctocephalus* is narrower, longer, and much less convex, with much longer nasals" (J. A. Allen, 1880). Otherwise, "in coloration, character of the pelage, size, general form, and dental formula" the two are much alike. The Commander Islands animal has the head less stout and broad, the neck slenderer, while "the females and young males are sooty, rather than brown, the light and dark shades being for the most part equally without ochraceous tints; the belly is usually rather sharply paler than the back; the gray pup is more brownish and less gray than in the Pribilof animal." The fur seal of the Kurile Islands differs from both in the whitish color of the under fur, instead of rusty brown. Probably all should rank as subspecies. Total length of an adult male from Commander Islands, 1,930 mm.; of an adult female, 1,283 mm.

At the Commander Islands the fur seals have been regularly taken for a long period of years. Stejneger (1897, 1898) has given a full account of the history of the industry there. From his figures it appears that between 1870 and 1896 a total yield of over 800,000 skins was obtained. In 1896 alone Bering Island yielded 9,526 and Copper Island 6,893 skins. In 1877 the Russian Government appointed Grebnitski as administrator of the Commander Islands, and under his wise supervision the herds of seals continued to produce an annual and well-sustained revenue. Only natives were allowed to work on the rookeries, and there were heavy fines for killing female or young seals. In the eighties, however, poaching parties made heavy raids on the islands, so that it became necessary to station a small force of soldiers there for their protection. Later the natives were organized as armed guards. Soon it became evident that the poachers had adopted new tactics, lying offshore outside the 12-mile territorial limit and killing the seals that came and went from the rookeries to the feeding grounds. Since these were chiefly females with small pups on shore, the result was a great destruction of both the breeding females and their young. On Stejneger's second visit in 1896, the result of this was plainly evident in the depletion of some of the rookeries that had formerly been well populated. It was not until pelagic sealing was stopped by international agreement in 1911 that this danger was removed. At the present time the colonies are apparently in flourishing condition on the Commander Islands, although the great yields of their palmy days are no longer taken. According to Barabash-Nikiforov (1938) the seals "spend only the summer period on the Commander Islands. They begin to arrive at the end of April or the beginning of May but are present in their greatest numbers at the beginning of August. The first new-born young appear in the middle of June, 2 or 3 days after their mothers arrive at the island. Soon after this the fertilization of mothers occurs. Moulting takes place from the middle of August until the middle of September, and about the middle of October the animals begin to leave the island. Fish is the chief food of the fur seal . . . Infection with endoparasites, chiefly *Uncinaria*, is especially great among the young fur seals."

The fur-seal rookeries of the Kurile Islands, the home of *C. ursinus mimicus*, were not discovered until 1881, or 11 years after the islands were ceded to Japan by Russia in exchange for the southern half of Sakhalin Island. There were four islands on which rookeries occurred, and these totaled a population of about 22,000 seals as then estimated. They were so speedily decimated by Japanese sealers that by 1898 Stejneger on careful inquiry concluded that a possible 30 animals might still remain. The race may already be extinct.

It is believed that both the Commander Islands and the Kurile Islands fur seals at the close of the breeding season moved southward into somewhat warmer waters for the winter season, but the extent of this migration is not clear. Sowerby (1923) writes that they are said to occur off Chefoo, in northern Shantung Province, China, and even perhaps to Shanghai, but the evidence is not very definite.

ALASKAN FUR SEAL

CALLORHINUS URSINUS CYNOCEPHALUS (Walbaum)

Siren cynocephala Walbaum,. Artedi, Genera Pisc., p. 560, 1792.
SYNONYMS: *Trichechus ? hydropithecus* Shaw, Gen. Zool., vol. 1, pt. 1, p. 247, 1800;
    Manatus ? simia Illiger, Abh. Akad. Wiss. Berlin, Phys. Kl., 1804–11, pp. 64, 68,

1815; *Callorhinus alascanus* Jordan, Fur Seals and Fur-seal Islands of North
Pacific Ocean, pt. 1, p. 45, 1898; Jordan and Clark, ibid., pt. 3, p. 2, 1899;
Callotaria ursina cynocephala Stejneger, Georg Wilhelm Steller, p. 285, 1936;
Callorhinus ursina cynocephala Hall, California Fish and Game, vol. 26, no. 1, p.
76, Jan. 1940.

FIGS.: Allen, J. A., 1870b, pl. 2, pl. 3, figs. 1–8 (skull and teeth); Nelson, 1916, col. fig.,
p. 432.

The northern or Alaskan fur seal of the Pribilof Islands in
Bering Sea is believed to differ from those on the Commander
and Kurile Islands of the Asiatic coasts in its "stouter, broader
head," the thicker neck, the "prevalence of warm brown shades
in the coloration of the female and the young males," and in
the more silvery color of the gray pups. "The fur in *alascanus*
is also of superior quality and exhibits sufficient difference to
make it possible for dealers to distinguish by this means alone
whether the skins come from the Commander or Pribilof herds"
(Jordan and Clark, 1899).

In their southward migrations from the breeding rookeries
on the Pribilof Islands, these seals are believed to trend along
the coasts of the Alaskan Peninsula and British Columbia,
going as far south as the coasts of northern California to the
vicinity of Point Conception. Grinnell (1933) quotes an
instance of its occurrence near Monterey in 1925. The usual
season of appearance on the California coast is from December
10 to April. With the coming of spring "they leave the northwest coast and many of them travel steadily across more than
two thousand miles of the North Pacific. For days at a time
they swim through a roaring gale-swept sea, under dense low-
hanging clouds, and with unerring certainty strike certain
passages in the Aleutian Islands, through which they press to
their breeding grounds, more than 100 miles beyond, on the
small, fog-hidden Pribilof Islands." The extraordinary tenacity
that the fur seals show in their return year by year to their
traditional breeding grounds explains the preservation of
slight differences in the populations of the different colonies.

The old males arrive at the islands as early as April and
establish themselves on the beaches, and they are soon followed
in May and June by the females. Each adult male gathers
around him a harem, varying in size up to as many as 40 or
even more females, and until the end of the breeding season
remains at his chosen station, driving off other neighboring
males, so that the groups become somewhat spaced. After

the birth of the young the females are ready for mating and are occupied with the care of the pup, going and coming freely to and from the feeding grounds in the adjacent seas. The nonbreeding immature males or "bachelors" consort by themselves in a separate part of the shore. It is from this group that killings are best made, since the polygamous habits of the species result in the production of many more males than are needed for propagation, assuming that the ratio of the sexes is approximately the same among the young pups. Parker (1917) records that in 1914, he found "the number of cows associated with one bull varied by actual count from 1 to 106," with an average of about 60, a number probably "somewhat too high for the best condition of the herd." In August the harems begin to break up, and the pugnacity of the adult males relaxes. By November the rookeries are nearly deserted, and the herds put to sea once more on their southward migration.

The rookeries on the Pribilof Islands were under the administration of the government of Russia until 1867, when Alaska was purchased by the United States. Up to that time the collecting of pelts was under the monopoly of the Russian-American Co. Since the discovery of the islands in 1786, more than 5,000,000 sealskins have been taken, and with proper management there is no reason why the yield should not continue indefinitely.

But the exploitation of these resources in the decades after the purchase of Alaska by the United States soon began to show in the decline of the herds. Investigations proved that the chief cause was "pelagic" sealing. For while the breeding colonies were managed with a certain degree of discretion ashore, and the poaching of sealing crews was more or less stopped, it developed during the eighties that an increasing number of sealers made a practice of lying offshore outside of territorial limits and shooting the females that came out to their feeding areas. The resulting reduction of the females thus involved the loss of their new-born young through starvation on the rookeries. This abuse was eventually stopped by international agreement in 1911 between the United States, Great Britain, Russia, and Japan. At that time, in 1912, it was estimated that the colony of fur seals on the Pribilof Islands had been reduced to some 130,000, a number far smaller than the population that can be carried by the available area. Strict protective measures over intervening years have now built up the herds to an estimated 1,500,000 in 1935, and there is an annual revenue derived from them through the killing of a certain proportion and marketing the hides under governmental supervision.

The fur seal offers an excellent example of a species once reduced in some colonies to a mere remnant of its normal numbers, which under protection and wise management has been restored to an abundance that permits an annual harvest of pelts, bringing in an excellent return. While many persons may deplore the yearly slaughter of a proportion of these interesting seals for commercial purposes, it must nevertheless be admitted that this reasonable use of a natural resource is far better than its wanton exploitation and eventual complete destruction.

For extensive accounts of these seals the reader is referred to the four-volume report by Jordan and others, 1899; J. A. Allen, 1880. A brief and readable report on the more recent conditions is that of G. H. Parker, 1917.

"No one who has seen the great seal herds will hesitate to reckon them among the chief wonders of the world, and there is no naturalist who would not think himself well repaid for a journey half around the earth by the sight of them."

Family PHOCIDAE: Hair Seals

Ribbon Seal

Phoca fasciata Zimmermann

Phoca fasciata Zimmermann, Geograph. Geschichte, vol. 3, p. 277, 1783 ("Off the Kuril Islands").
Synonym: *Phoca equestris* Pallas, Zoogr. Rosso-Asiat., vol. 1, p. 111, 1831.
Figs.: True, 1884a, pls. 11–14 (skull and skeleton); Nelson, 1916, p. 438 (col. fig.).

This is the rarest and least known of the northern seals, with a range restricted to the Bering Sea and nearby waters. It may therefore be regarded as a species to be afforded encouragement and protection if it is not to dwindle and finally disappear.

The species gets its name from the broad, yellowish-white, sharply defined bands that give its otherwise dark brown body the appearance of being wrapped with bandages. One such band encircles the neck, extending forward to the middle of the

head above; a second and broader one encircles the hinder part
of the body a short distance from the tail; while from this there
runs forward on each side a branch, the two uniting ventrally
and forward, then each forming a wide circle about the fore
shoulder. In the female the bands are less marked. The skull
has six upper and four lower incisors; cheek teeth, except the
first, double-rooted and conical, with sometimes a slight
accessory cûsp. The adult male may attain a length of 6.5 feet.

The general range of the ribbon seal is from the Kurile
Islands and Okhotsk Sea northward along the coasts of Kamchatka and in Bering Sea to Bering Straits. It is rarely seen
among the Aleutian Islands, but on the Alaskan coasts it is
most frequently found south of the Yukon Delta and from
Cape Nome to Bering Straits. Little is recorded of its habits,
but it is apparently only to a slight extent gregarious. Usually
only single ones are seen, rarely several together. True (1884a)
has figured and described the skeleton on the basis of specimens
—four in all—obtained in 1880 for the United States National
Museum at Plover Bay, eastern Siberia; he mentions also
specimens from Cape Romanzof and Cape Prince of Wales in
the same institution. The same author (True, in Jordan and
others, 1899) mentions one taken 84 miles west of St. Pauls
Island in 1896, whence he concludes that it may be an occasional visitor to the Pribilofs. A. M. Bailey and Hendee (1926)
state that these seals are rare at Cape Prince of Wales, Alaska,
"although a few are seen and one or two are usually killed each
year." During their stay there they saw but two in the course
of the spring hunt, both well out on the ice. In a later note
Dr. Bailey (1928) reports a remarkable migration of these and
the spotted seals (*Phoca vitulina richardii*) at Cape Prince of
Wales. The latter species is very common there in the lagoons,
while the ribbon seal is considered even by the Eskimos as
very rare. When caught in these lagoons by an early freeze
the seals left the lagoons and made a journey overland and
over ice to reach the sea.

Although in Pallas's time the ribbon seal was apparently
found in small numbers among the Kurile Islands, it is at
present rare among the Commander Islands and adjacent seas
(Barabash-Nikiforov, 1938). Even Scammon (1874) regarded
it as scarce in Alaskan waters, but his mention of seeing a group
ashore at Point Reyes, California, is clearly an error.

Though Dr. Nelson (1916) wrote that "the scarcity of the ribbon seal and its solitary habits will serve to safeguard it from the destructive pursuit which endangers the existence of some of its relatives," nevertheless there is a price on its head, for its attractively marked skin caused the male to be especially sought by the Eskimos, as formerly by fur traders, for use as clothes-bags! "The skin is removed entire and then tanned, the only opening left being a long slit in the abdomen, which is provided with eyelet holes and a lacing string, thus making a convenient water-proof bag to use in boat or dog-sledge trips" (Nelson, 1916). Scammon says also that in former times the Russian traders used it especially for covering trunks. Whether it should or can be specially protected is a question, although it seems unlikely that it will increase at all unless such measures are taken.

MEDITERRANEAN MONK SEAL

MONACHUS MONACHUS (Hermann)

Phoca monachus Hermann, Beschäftigungen Berlin. Ges. Naturf. Freunde, vol. 4, p. 501, pls. 12, 13, 1779 (Mediterranean Sea).

SYNONYMS: *Phoca albiventer* Boddaert, Elenchus Anim., p. 170, 1785 (Adriatic Sea); *Phoca bicolor* Shaw, General Zool., vol. 1, pt. 2, p. 254, 1800 (Adriatic seacoasts); *Phoca leucogaster* Péron, Voy. aux Terres Austr., vol. 2, p. 47, footnote, 1817 (Nîmes, France); *Phoca hermannii* Lesson, Dict. Classique d'Hist. Nat., vol. 13, p. 416, 1828 (Adriatic Sea); *Monachus mediterraneus* Nilsson, Kongl. Svenska Vet.-Akad. Handl., Stockholm, for 1837, p. 235, 1838 (Adriatic Sea and Grecian Archipelago); *Heliophoca atlantica* Gray, Ann. Mag. Nat. Hist., ser. 2, vol. 13, p. 202, Mar. 1854 (Deserta Grande Island, Madeiras).

FIGS.: Hermann, 1779, pls. 12, 13; Cabrera, 1914, col. pl. 11, opposite p. 215.

The monk seals are characterized among the Phocidae by the peculiar form of the skull, with the brain case about as long as broad and the interorbital region long and parallel-sided instead of tapering forward. The dentition is reduced in having but two instead of three upper incisors on each side, as in the lower jaw. The cheek teeth are five on each side in each jaw, behind the canine, and are set at an angle with the long axis of the skull, stout and bluntly conical, with a strongly developed cingulum. The fore feet have well-developed claws, but those of the hind feet are small. The genus is further peculiar in being restricted to warm subtropical waters of the Northern Hemisphere. Three species are known.

The adult male is blackish gray, with ill-defined paler areas on head and neck. The belly is white or tinged with yellow in variable degree, forming a contrast with the upper parts. Females and immatures are very much paler gray above, becoming soiled yellowish below. Head and body, 2,300 mm. (about 7.5 feet); tail, 80; fore limb from insertion to tip, 320. Skull, condylobasal length, 280 mm.; zygomatic width, 211; interorbital width, 30; width of brain case, 128; upper cheek teeth forming a row 86 mm. long.

The Mediterranean monk seal is chiefly confined, as its name implies, to the Mediterranean Sea, but it is found also in the Black Sea and rarely on the coasts of northwestern Africa to the Madeira and Canary Islands. Apparently nowhere common, and very little gregarious, it frequents small coastal islands in out-of-the-way places and seems to have no economic value. It is occasionally killed wantonly, and most recent records are of solitary individuals. It is apparently losing ground slowly but still maintains a small population.

In the eastern Mediterranean, it is said by Aharoni (1930, p. 337) still to occur off the coast of Palestine, well offshore, and is now and then brought in for sale by the fishermen from Askalon and Jaffa. No data are at hand as to its presence in the Black Sea beyond the fact of its occurrence there. In the Greek Archipelago small numbers haunt the outlying islands and coasts. Danford and Alston (1877) mention observing a seal off the island of Rhodes about 1877, and it is occasionally seen in the Bay of Corinth. In the Adriatic Sea it is still to be found, though rarely, on the Dalmation coasts. Prof. M. Hirtz, in reply to inquiry by Dr. Harper, states that off the coast of Jugoslavia it is now very rare in the upper Adriatic. The last remaining animals are found on isolated cliffs in the Istria, where during the past 40 years about 15 specimens have been taken, mostly by local fishermen. Because of its rarity off these coasts it is not included in the game regulations; nevertheless it is known by the common names of "morski-medo" (sea-bear) or "morski-fratar" (sea-monk). There is said to be a colony on the Illyrian Islands also. It seems to have been commoner in this part of the Adriatic in Hermann's time at the beginning of the last century. On the immediate coast of Italy it must be very rare, but recent information indicates that there are small numbers on the shores of Sardinia, and it is occasionally seen on the rocks and small islands of the Tyrrhenian Sea. The Italian Government was lately reported as studying measures to be taken for its protection. Fifty years ago it was said by Trouessart to be often taken on the Mediterranean coast of France, especially in the Gulf of Lyon, at the Îles d'Hyères, and in the roadstead of Banyûls near Port-Vendres, and is reported occasionally on the coasts of Corsica. In 1910, however, the same author speaks of it as rather rare in the waters of the French coast.

On the northern coasts of Africa, this seal still occurs locally on some of the sandy islands that are seldom visited. Formerly an individual was reported now and then near or west of Alexandria, but it is now almost never seen on the Egyptian coast (Anderson and De Winton, 1902, p. 248). Maj. S. S. Flower (1932), however, says that "seals formerly occurred in some numbers along the coast to the west of Alexandria. Admiral W. H. Smith . . . writing of the period 1810–1824, said 'between Alexandria and Benghazi . . . we found fish and seals in abundance.' Several were said to have been killed during the war (1914–1918). At least one was reported to have been still living at Sollum [western border of Egypt] in 1919. Col. R. S. Wilson . . . told me that this animal was still alive there in 1920 and that strict orders had been issued that it was not to be shot at." Slightly farther west, on the Isle of Birds in the Gulf of Gran Sirte, Cyrenaica, Moltoni (1938, p. 16) mentions seeing a splendid specimen hauled out on the sand at a distance of only 50 yards from where he landed, in August, 1938. Westward again, "it occurs on the north coast of Morocco and among the adjacent islands . . . In 1919 and 1924 there were reports of individuals killed in the Zafarines Isles (off the extreme eastern coast of Morocco), and it has occasionally been seen near Ceuta" (Cabrera, 1932, p. 197). In Spanish waters, Cabrera (1914) speaks of its presence in the Balearic Islands and says that at the beginning of this century some were still to be found on the southeastern coast of the Spanish Peninsula, from the Gulf of Almeira to the coast of Alicante, but had since completely disappeared. However, it was still to be found on the islands near the African shore.

Among the Madeira Islands there are still a few. One from there was sent alive to the London Zoological Gardens on July 16, 1894 (see Proc. Zool. Soc. London, 1894, p. 749) and another in April, 1910 (ibid., 1910, vol. 1, p. 768). Monod (1923) has summed up lately what is known of its presence on the Atlantic coast of Africa, where near Cape Blanco about 20 kilometers north of Port Etienne is an area of cliffs, rather difficult of access, the haunt of some numbers of these seals. In the transparent waters here this author was able to look down and see the seals pursuing fishes. They are seldom disturbed by the natives. These seals formerly occurred in the Canary Islands. Monod (1923) tells us that as long ago as 1341 skins of seals are mentioned among things brought from the islands. Between the islands of Lanzarote and Fuerte Ventura is an "Isla de Lobos" (Seal Island) formerly much frequented by them; and there was a fishery for the seals organized in 1749 by Gadifer de la Salle. At the present day they must be very few indeed.

WEST INDIAN SEAL

MONACHUS TROPICALIS (Gray)

Phoca tropicalis Gray, Cat. Spec. Mamm. British Mus., pt. 2, Seals, p. 28, 1850 (Jamaica).

SYNONYM: [*Phoca*] *wilkianus* Gosse, Naturalist's Sojourn in Jamaica, p. 307, 1851 (Jamaica).

FIGS.: Allen, J. A., 1887, pls. 1–4 (animal and skeletal parts); Elliot, 1904, vol. 2, pls. 56–59 (skull).

Notwithstanding the fact that the West Indian seal was known from the time of Columbus on, no specimens reached museums until the middle of the nineteenth century, when already its numbers were so depleted that it had become rather rare. For summary accounts of its history and characters we are indebted to J. A. Allen (1880, 1887) and to True and Lucas (1884).

Externally this species resembles its relative, the Mediterranean monk seal, but is a nearly uniform "brown, tinged with gray, caused by the hairs being light at the extreme tip. The color becomes lighter on the sides, and gradually passes into pale yellow or yellowish-white on the ventral surface of the body" (J. A. Allen, 1887). It therefore does not show the contrasting white belly of its eastern relative. Length of an adult from nose to end of tail, 2,410 mm., or about 7.5 feet. Adult females are but a trifle smaller than males. Skull, condylobasal length, 280 mm. For a detailed description of the cranial and dental characters and comparison with other seals, see the paper by J. A. Allen (1887).

In his paper of 1887, Dr. J. A. Allen gave a general history of
this species, from which a few particulars are extracted. What
is doubtless the first mention of this seal is in Columbus's account of the second voyage, when in 1494, near the end of
August, he came to anchor near the rocky islet of Alta Vela,
off the southern coast of Hispaniola. Here several seamen
landed and killed "eight sea wolves, which were sleeping on
the sands." According to Dampier it was, in the eighteenth
century, the basis of a profitable seal fishery, and presumably
was so persistently slaughtered for its oil that it had become
already rare by the time that Gosse gave an account of it in
1851. Its geographical range, as indicated from the scanty
records, seems to have included the Gulf of Mexico and Caribbean Sea to at least as far south as the coast of Honduras, and
eastward to Jamaica, Cuba, and Hispaniola; thence it ranged
northward throughout the Bahamas. The many Seal Keys,
or perhaps too, Sale Keys and Lobos Keys, are place names
reminiscent of the former presence of these seals. Sir Hans
Sloane in 1707 ("History of Jamaica") wrote: "The *Bahama*
Islands are filled with Seals; sometimes Fishers will catch one
hundred in a night. They try or melt them, and bring off their
Oil for Lamps to the Islands." Evidently they were then
abundant and were being rapidly destroyed. At the Alacranes
Islands, about 75 miles north of Yucatan (called Alacran Reefs
on modern maps), Dampier found them in abundance in about
1675. He adds that "the Spaniards do often come hither to
make Oyl of their Fat." Englishmen from Jamaica also came
for the same purpose, and he mentions especially one Captain
Long, who, caught in a heavy north wind, nearly lost his vessel,
which was blown ashore. He later succeeded in repairing it,
however, and "filled all his casks with oil." Gosse's account
shows that at least up to 1846 there was a small colony at a reef
known as Pedro Keys off the south coast of Jamaica, where as
many as five were seen hauled out. In 1875, two were seen
near Cape Florida, and at the same time according to J. A.
Allen (1887) seals were said "to be found in great numbers at
some islands [Anina Islands] situated between the Isle of Pines
and Yucatan." At that period they were exceedingly rare on
the coast of Florida, but still occasional in the Bahamas.
"Their presence at Salt Key Bank, between Florida and the
Bahamas, as late as 1868–69, is attested by information re-

ceived some years since from the late Count L. F. de Pourtalès."
In 1883 one was captured near Habana, Cuba. No doubt the
Seal Keys, a little southwest of Turks Island, were a former
haunt.

In December, 1886, Henry L. Ward, accompanied by Fernando Ferrari-Pérez (naturalist-in-chief of the Mexican Geographical and Exploring Commission), visited the Triangle
Keys, a group of low sandy islets to the west of Yucatan, where
seals had been reported. Bad weather prevented them from
staying more than three days, but they were successful in
finding the seals there "in considerable numbers" and killed
no less than 49, of which only 34 skins and seven skeletons
could be preserved. It was Ward's share of this spoil that
formed the basis of Dr. J. A. Allen's (1887) paper. These keys
seem to be the last stronghold of the species, but possibly a
few may be found elsewhere. Gaumer (1917) wrote that up to
1890 this seal was found in the Alacranes Islands and now and
then turned up on the neighboring coast of the peninsula. In
more recent years, however, the fishermen had not reported
seing seals in this group; but in January, 1911, some fishermen
had visited the Triangle Keys and killed about 200 seals,
leaving, as they said, "muy pocos vivos" (very few alive). In
1909, four, probably from there, were received by the New
York Aquarium (Townsend, 1909). Gaumer believes they
must have nearly exterminated the animals, yet it is likely
that a few may have escaped and that they may still resort
thither. As lately as March 15, 1922, one was killed near Key
West, Fla. (Townsend, 1923). Francis W. Taylor, president
of the Warren Fish Co., of Pensacola, Fla., wrote to Dr.
Harper in 1936 that on numerous occasions in the past fishing
vessels had brought these seals in to Pensacola alive. He
understands that they are now to be found only on the Eastern
Triangle Key, which has a protected bay inside, to which the
seals resort, so that one must land in order to discover them.
Here, he says, "the fishermen tell me that at one time there
was a tremendous colony of seals . . . but it is their
belief that the Mexicans have killed a great many, possibly all
of them, for their oil . . . I know of no seals which have
been taken from the island in recent years . . . In the
early part of 1915 our vessel the Seminole brought six of these
seals to Pensacola which were held in captivity here in one of

our bayous for quite a long period of time. The bathers here seriously objected to their presence, and I believe that they were finally turned loose and remained in the bay for a while thereafter."

From what little can be gleaned from the few observations made it appears that the young are born in the first part of December, for several of the females killed by Ward's expedition to the Triangle Keys had each a fetus nearly ready for birth. The animals themselves seem to be remarkably sluggish and unsuspicious, allowing persons to come among them without great alarm, so that numbers may easily be killed without difficulty. No doubt it is this lack of suspicion and fear that has been their undoing. Of the various stomachs examined by Ward, none contained identifiable food.

While conclusive information is at present unobtainable, it nevertheless seems very likely that there may be a few seals still resorting to the Triangle Keys, and possibly on rare occasions individuals may turn up elsewhere, but clearly the species was of restricted habitat, and within historic times has been brought nearly to the verge of extinction. It would appear to be a simple matter for the British Government to pass protective regulations for the preservation of any that may still exist in the Bahamas and for the Mexican Government to prohibit their killing on the islands off Yucatan so that they might breed up to numbers placing them less close to the danger line.

West Indian seal (*Monachus tropicalis*)

HAWAIIAN MONK SEAL

MONACHUS SCHAUINSLANDI Matschie

Monachus schauinslandi Matschie, Sitzb. Ges. Naturforsch. Freunde, Berlin, 1905,
p. 258 ("Laysan" Island, Hawaiian Islands).
FIGS.: Atkinson and Bryan, 1914, p. 1050, fig.; Bryan, 1915, p. 96, pl. 21, fig. 4; p. 294,
pl. 76.

The discovery of a species of Monachus in the Hawaiian
Islands was one of the interesting results of modern discrimina-
tive `study, for though the animal had long been known to
sealers no specimens had received attention from naturalists
until 1905, when Matschie pointed out that a skull from
Laysan, in a German museum, belonged to this genus. This
discontinuous distribution of Monachus—in the Mediterranean,
the Caribbean Sea, and Greater Antillean Islands, and finally
in the Hawaiian Islands—is one the explanation of which
forms an interesting speculation. This Pacific colony may be
presumed to have been derived from the Caribbean at some
time in the Tertiary, when, as seems well established, the
latter was in open connection with the Pacific. In late Tertiary
times the Panamanian union with South America was again
established, cutting off the Caribbean from Pacific waters.
That the seals should now be limited to the Hawaiian group
in the Pacific, however, must indicate that they are a relict
group, which once had a wider distribution, with a preference
for tropical seas.

The Hawaiian monk seal is not very different in appearance
from the West Indian seal, but Matschie points out 16 cranial
characters in which it differs from the Mediterranean species.
It is dark brown above, the sides are paler brown, and the
belly is whitish. The skull is more nearly like that of the
West Indian seal; Matschie emphasizes as obvious points that
the jugal meets the maxillary above the last molar instead of
above the next to the last cheek tooth, and that the bony
bridge forming the lower part of the antorbital foramen is
narrower. Greatest length of skull, 268 mm.; condylobasal
length, 265.

Until Schauinsland brought back to Germany a specimen of
this seal no one seems to have paid much attention to it. In
1915, however, Bryan summed up its brief history, pointing
out that as early as 1824 the brig Ainoa set out from the Hawaiian Islands on a sealing voyage, and that at different times

sealing expeditions have been made among the islands to the west of Kauai. Of these the most notable was in 1859 when the *Gambia* returned to Honolulu with 1,500 skins and 240 barrels of seal oil, thus furnishing some idea of the numbers of this seal that must then have been present. A few further details are furnished by Atkinson and Bryan (1914), who report that a J. J. Williams in 1893 found these seals at French Frigate Shoals and had heard of an expedition killing as many as 60 or 70 on Laysan. About this island, however, they are rare now and are hard to see in the water, and rest far out on the reefs. On Midway Island none was seen by Captain Miller and his crew who were shipwrecked there for 14 months. In 1913 about 35 were seen by Governor Frear on Pearl and Hermes reef. Bryan (1915) continues: "Of recent years they have been far from abundant, though seals are regularly reported from Laysan, Lisiansky, Pearl and Hermes Reef, and are occasionally seen at Midway. In January, 1912, the U. S. Revenue Cutter *Thetis* returned from a cruise to Midway and Laysan and brought a seal-skin back which was presented to the Bishop Museum. Baby seals were seen at that time, and it is quite probable that, if not interfered with, the herd will increase in numbers." In 1923 Dr. Alexander Wetmore visited these western Hawaiian Islands and saw seals at Ocean Island and at Pearl and Hermes Reef. The total population was estimated as about 400. A few were collected as specimens. It is possible that a good many of these seals have been poached in times past, as the breeding albatrosses have been by the Japanese. This has now been put an end to, and this seal is included on the list of mammals for which special protection is to be recommended.

Ross's Seal

OMMATOPHOCA ROSSII Gray

Ommatophoca rossii Gray, Zool. Voyage *Erebus* and *Terror*, pp. 7–8, pls. 7, 8, 1844 ("Antarctic Ocean").

FIGS.: Barrett-Hamilton, 1901, plate (skull); Brown, R. N. R., 1913, pl. 3, fig. 1 (photograph); Wilson, E. A., 1907, figs. 27–29, p. 44 (photographs).

Ross's seal is so rare in collections and is so little known that it may perhaps be a "vanishing" species, with restricted range and very specialized habits, traits that often go with perilous status.

Of the various seals of the Antarctic this is the smallest,

and it is not often found of a greater length than 7 or 8 feet. "It is a blackish or brownish grey above, and lighter below, with the chin and throat in some quite pale, in others black, and a number of paler streaks pass obliquely backwards along the sides of the neck to the hinder third of the body." The skull is remarkable for its very short muzzle, enormous orbit, and weak dentition. There are four upper incisors, of which the two outer are the larger, and four lower incisors. The cheek teeth are five behind the canine, and form an outwardly bent row. They are usually regarded as comprising four premolars and a molar and are two-rooted. The claws of the fore foot are reduced to two or three which are very small. Basal length of skull, to 242 mm.; zygomatic width, 176.

This seal, so far as known, is confined to the Antarctic Ocean and has not been recorded from the shores of any of the southern continents. Until the voyage of the *Belgica* at the end of the last century, it was known only from the two specimens brought back to the British Museum by the voyage of Sir John Ross, and with no more exact locality than Antarctic Seas. In 1898, the *Belgica* secured two others in latitude 70° S. and longitude 83–85° E. These were reported upon briefly by Barrett-Hamilton. Since then Marr (1935) has mentioned nine records between 1903 and 1907. Rudmose Brown (1913) writes: "We found, as all other Antarctic expeditions have found, that the Ross Seal was the rarest of these four species [of Antarctic seals] and was very infrequently seen . . . [and] despite the frequent expeditions of recent years, still remains one of the rarest of known mammals. It is the only one of the Antarctic seals that is entirely confined to Antarctic seas and which has never been recorded from extra-polar regions. During the voyage of the *Scotia* the Ross Seal was only seen on five occasions, and on four of these it was among the pack some distance from land." These localities were: Between South Orkneys and Coats Land; Scotia Bay; on the Drygalski Ice Barrier tongue in Victoria Land; Weddell Sea; and Deception Island in the South Shetlands. "Solitary individuals," this author adds, "as in the Weddell Sea, have been recorded by practically all recent expeditions from other parts of the Antarctic, but everywhere the Ross Seal is very rare . . . It is almost certain that the species does not collect in rookeries at the breeding season; probably the young are born on the pack ice." It is known to feed principally on cuttlefish, but remains of fish and small shrimps (*Euphausia*) have also been found in stomachs. It is said to be very agile in the water so that Trouessart believes it is for this reason safe from attacks of the killer whale. Possibly, too, its habit of staying in the pack ice offers further immunity.

According to Barrett-Hamilton (1901) the *Belgica* expedition found these seals fairly numerous in the pack ice. The diet of cuttlefish seems as in certain cetaceans to lead to a weakened or degenerate dentition.

While at present its peculiar habitat renders it comparatively safe from human interference, so that it is not in need of immediate protection, it may nevertheless be regarded as a rare seal and possibly a waning species.

NORTHERN ELEPHANT SEAL

MIROUNGA ANGUSTIROSTRIS (Gill)

Macrorhinus angustirostris Gill, Proc. Essex Inst., vol. 5, p. 13, 1866 (St. Bartholomews Bay, Lower California, Mexico, lat. 27° 40′ N.).

FIGS.: Allen, J. A., 1880, figs. 57–60 (skull); Elliot, 1904, pt. 2, pls. 62–66 (skull, photographs); Nelson, 1916, p. 434 (col. fig.); Huey, 1924, pls. 24–27 (photographs); Beebe, 1942, pls. 3, 4 (photographs).

The northern elephant seal, or "sea-elephant," much resembles its southern relative, *M. leonina*, but is perhaps somewhat smaller. Gill based the distinction mainly on the supposed narrower and longer snout of the adult female. Adult males reach a length of at least 14.5 feet, but apparently may attain a larger size (Scammon, 1874, says the largest he ever measured was 22 feet). The color is yellowish brown, but youngish animals have a grayer appearance. When full grown the males lose much of the hair of the throat, and the skin becomes creased. The proboscis is somewhat inflatable. Huey (1924) observed that in the process of shedding the hair seasonally, large patches of cuticle may come away with it. Females are smaller, about 9–10 feet, with very much less development of the proboscis.

The northern elephant seal was formerly found from the vicinity of Point Reyes, Calif., southward along the coast to about latitude 24° N., in the region of Cape Lazaro, Lower California. Larger or smaller numbers were "at all times found on shore upon their favorite beaches, which were about the islands of Santa Barbara, Cerros, Guadalupe, San Bonito, Natividad, San Roque, and Asuncion, and some of the most inaccessible points on the main-land between Asuncion and Cerros. When coming up out of the water, they were generally first seen near the line of surf; then crawling up by degrees, frequently reclining as if to sleep; again, moving up or along the shore, appearing not content with their last resting-place. In this manner they would ascend the ravines, or 'low-downs,' half a mile or more, congregating by hundreds . . . Notwithstanding their unwieldiness, we have sometimes found them on broken and elevated ground, fifty or sixty feet above the sea" (Scammon, 1874, p. 117). Apparently more were found ashore at times of having young and during the period of shedding fur.

In the middle of the last century the elephant seals were actively pursued by sealers for the sake of their oil, which was deemed "superior to whale oil for lubricating purposes." On approaching a rookery the sealers would get between the herd and the water; "then, raising all possible noise by shouting, and at the same time flourishing clubs, guns, and lances, the party advances slowly toward the rookery, when the animals will retreat, appearing in a state of great alarm." Those that stood their ground or showed fight were shot or dispatched with a blow on the head from a heavy oaken club or were lanced. The sealers, then rushing upon the main body, killed as many as they could before the panic-stricken animals, roaring loudly, could return to the sea. The blubber was then stripped off in long pieces, which were towed to the vessel for trying out. Scammon speaks of a large bull, 18 feet long taken at Santa Barbara Island, that yielded 210 gallons of oil. The breeding season is from February to June and as usual with seals, a single young one is born.

Their comparative helplessness when on shore and even tameness made their destruction easy, and it became evident soon after the middle of last century that their numbers were being rapidly reduced, and by the decade 1870–80 they are spoken of as already nearly exterminated on the California coast. By the end of the last century there remained a single small colony on Guadalupe Island, which though occasionally raided escaped destruction. With the passing of protective legislation this colony has slowly increased. According to the historical review by Huey (1930a), its numbers in 1892 were reduced to but nine individuals (with doubtless a few others at sea), and of these nine, seven were killed (Townsend, in Jordan and others, 1899). From this lowest ebb the herd recovered until by 1907, when Rothschild's expedition visited Guadalupe, there were about 40 lying on the beach. Of these, 14 were killed and preserved as specimens. The remoteness of their island haunt is probably what saved the species from complete annihilation. At length, in 1911, the Mexican Government passed legislation for the complete protection of this seal, of which in March of that year the population had again shown an increase to about 125. By 1922, Huey (1924) reports, this number had increased to about 264. He was able to secure a number of photographs of the animals, lying unalarmed on the beach. Townsend (1930b) visited the island again on September 27, 1929, and by careful count ascertained that no less than 469 elephant seals were lying on the beach. This number, Townsend believes, probably represented only a part, perhaps half, of the herd, since the number of breeding adults was less than in 1911. There was no evidence that the animals had been molested, for they were altogether fearless and showed no concern as Dr. Townsend's party walked among them. This increase is no doubt to be correlated with the fact that of recent years they have occasionally appeared once more off the coasts of southern California, as near Santa Cruz Island in 1921, San Miguel Island in 1923, off Santa Barbara in 1927, and off San Diego in 1929 (one killed) (Huey, 1930b).

Concerning food and natural enemies, there are apparently none of the latter except perhaps the killer whale, which may on occasion attack the young animals. The food is probably

Northern elephant seal (*Mirounga angustirostris*)

462 EXTINCT AND VANISHING MAMMALS

cuttlefish and small fishes. Townsend (1930b) mentions that
the animal killed off San Diego had been feeding on fishes for
its stomach contained, among other species, a skate.

The case of this seal is thus a happy one in which, with strict
protection over a period of years, it has shown a recuperative
power and has increased well beyond the danger point. With
further increase, it is likely that the species will gradually
enlarge its hauling grounds and spread to other adjacent parts
of its former range.

SOUTHERN ELEPHANT SEAL

MIROUNGA LEONINA (Linnaeus)

Phoca leonina Linnaeus, Systema Naturae, ed. 10, vol. 1, p. 37, 1758 (Antarctic Seas).
SYNONYMS: *Phoca elephantina* Molina, Saggio Storia Nat. Chili, p. 280, 1782 (coasts
    of southern South America); *Phoca proboscidea* Péron, Voyage aux Terres Austr.,
    vol. 2, p. 34, pl. 32, 1817 (King Island, New South Wales); *Phoca ansonii* Des-
    marest, Mammalogie, vol. 1, p. 239, 1820 (in part) (Falkland Islands); *M*[*irounga*]
    patagonica Gray, in Griffith's Cuvier, Animal Kingdom, vol. 5, p. 180, 1827
    (Patagonia). For other synonyms see also Allen, G. M., 1939, p. 249.
FIGS.: Murphy, 1914, pls. 1–7 (photographs).

The southern elephant seal is the largest of the seal family
(Phocidae), attaining a length of 25 feet (or possibly more in
the case of an adult male), with a greatest girth of 15 to 18
feet. The males have a short proboscis, which is capable of
slight inflation. The females are considerably smaller and lack
a distinct proboscis. As in the other true seals, the hind limbs
are turned permanently backward, and the animal when on
land does not use them in progression but humps itself along
with wriggling, caterpillarlike movements. The thin hairy
coat is dark yellowish brown, and in old males it wears away
about the neck, leaving the skin bare. The young animals are
described as blackish brown above and light creamy buff below.
There is some variation in color with age in adult animals.
Murphy (1914) found that the "disproportion in size between
the sexes is much greater than with the California species."
The females do not exceed 3 meters in length, while the males
measure about 5 meters when full grown. The largest male
measured by this investigator was 455 cm. from tip of snout to
tip of tail; the largest female 265 cm. He points out that the
snout is entirely different from that of the California species
in that "the whole nasal tube is narrower and shorter in the

southern species, and is only slightly pendulous even in the case of the largest and oldest males. Nine out of ten of all those . . . [seen] at South Georgia had practically no 'trunks' at all." Lydekker (1909) has discussed the cranial characters of this seal.

The "blubber" of these seals is deep and so nearly clear oil that a cask of chunks of it tries down to nearly the same amount of oil (Murphy). For this reason the animal has been much persecuted by sealing crews in the southern oceans, and immense numbers have been killed during the last century and a half, bringing it in parts of its range nearly or quite to the verge of extermination. In former times this seal occasionally came as far north in the South Atlantic as the island of St. Helena, where what must have been one of the last visitors there was killed about 1739 (see Fraser, 1935). It was at one time abundant on the island of Tristan da Cunha, on Inaccessible Island, and on Gough Island, but it has been extinct in those places for many years, with almost no record remaining. Elsewhere in the South Atlantic it has been known to appear on the coast of South Africa at rare intervals, as in 1926 when one was killed, and earlier at Algoa Bay in 1919 (Fitzsimons, 1920, vol. 4, pp. 227–229) where one was shot and later mounted for the Port Elizabeth Museum. On the east coast of South America, the late Dr. Roberto Dabbene wrote in 1937, in response to Dr. Francis Harper's inquiry, that at the breeding season a few individuals appear on the coasts of Valdes Peninsula, in the province of Chubut, but from other parts of the Argentine coast they have now quite disappeared.

Farther south it was formerly common on the Falkland Islands, but even in the nineties was already rare (Kennedy, 1892) and in recent decades has appeared but sporadically. On the island of South Georgia, however, it still remains in some numbers under a certain degree of protection. Dr. Lönnberg (1906) has published a number of notes on its habits here and reproduces some excellent photographs. Dr. R. C. Murphy has also given an account of the sealing industry in this region. The breeding season is in the southern spring. The animals then are ashore for longer periods, and though they are monogamous there is much fighting between neighboring bulls as if for adequate spacing, as well as for possession of the cows. Pairing of the adults takes place shortly after the birth of the single young. Stomachs of specimens lately come ashore contained remains of squids and small fishes of about 25 cm. length, with occasional bits of kelp, apparently swallowed incidentally, and often pebbles. While the southern elephant seal is not a strictly Antarctic species, frequenting more especially the seas between the Antarctic Circle and about 35° of south latitude, nevertheless occasional individuals wander much farther southward. It has been recorded from McMurdo Strait, in latitude 77° 50′ S., where E. A. Wilson on Scott's expedition mentions one they found asleep on a sandy beach at Cape Royds. Its stomach "was empty of food, as also were the intestines, which were contracted into firm, hard cords, and contained only a few threadworms; yet the seal was heavily blubbered, having upwards of two inches of fat under the skin all over."

A century ago the sealers were actively pursuing these and other seals in Antarctic waters. Murphy writes (1918): "At South Georgia persistent killing pushed it so near the verge of utter extinction that in 1885 the crew of a Connecticut schooner during ten weeks of the breeding season (September to January) was able to find only *two* of the animals. From before that date, however, until after the beginning of the twentieth century, the seat of the 'elephant oil' traffic was transferred from the South Atlantic to the fresher islands of the Indian Ocean, and so the species was given an opportunity partially to regain its foothold at South Georgia." In 1909, the Falkland Islands Government passed the Seal Fishery Ordinance designed to regulate the taking of these animals and other seals in the Falkland Islands and their dependencies. Under the existing regulations and with the strict limitation of the number of licenses issued, the elephant seals have so recuperated as now to be found "in large numbers," as described by Dr. Murphy, thus vindicating the government's policy. The quantity of oil taken, which in 15 months of 1914–15 is said to have been 850,000 gallons, is believed by Dr. Murphy to be more than the species can stand as an annual toll and should probably be reduced. For these seals, "slow, unsuspicious, gregarious . . . can be hunted profitably until the last one has gone." Skottsberg (1911) voiced a similar warning, and remarked that "American sealers do a good deal of poaching on the west side

of the island." More recent accounts speak of the killing of
elephant seals as now "carefully regulated" by the Falkland
Islands Government not only on South Georgia but also on
other islands within its jurisdiction, so that improvement and
perpetuation of the industry may be hoped for. This improvement in this species is apparently indicated also by the recent
conditions in the South Orkney Islands, to the southward; for
Marr (1935, pp. 373–375) writes that, though far from plentiful, it is now found there in moderate numbers. "At one time
it used to frequent the South Shetlands [to the southwest] in
vast numbers, and for the sake of the oil it yielded, perished in
thousands along with the fur seal during the wanton destruction of 1820–22. So heavy had the slaughter of elephant seal
been that when the 'Chanticleer' arrived at the South Shetlands in 1829 not one was to be seen, although no doubt the
species still survived, as did the fur seal, on various out-of-the-
way sites unfrequented by sealers. Offering a relatively small
commercial reward, it escaped extermination and is to be found
to-day in some parts of the South Shetlands, particularly on
Elephant Island where several hundred were seen by the
Shackelton-Rowett expedition in the autumn of 1922. For all
its former abundance at the South Shetlands, the early sealers
between 1821 and 1823 do not record a single elephant seal at
the South Orkneys"; the first record was in 1874, when Dallmann saw many, after which it was noted as an infrequent
visitor, although more were seen during the ice-free year of
1908. In 1914–15, Marr notes that large numbers came ashore
to bask and sleep on Signy Island. In January, 1933, he
writes, the number of elephant seals hauled out on the South
Orkneys was estimated to be about 296, but it was not definitely ascertained whether they bred there. Probably the
varying ice conditions about these islands, now as in the past,
are the determining factor, rendering the group more or less
unsuitable as a breeding ground.

In the southern Indian Ocean elephant seals formerly frequented Kerguelen Island and the Crozet Islands in large
numbers. During the first half of the nineteenth century they
were almost exterminated on Kerguelen, but after that there
came a respite during which the numbers seem to have built
up once more. With a revival of the hunt for oil at about the
beginning of the present century, sealers had again devastated

the Kerguelen rookeries. Ring (1923) has given a picture of the life of the elephant seal at Kerguelen 30 years and more ago. He states that in 1905–6, a Norwegian, Capt. C. A. Larsen, established a whale fishery at South Georgia, catching and utilizing elephant seals as a side issue. In 1907 a Norwegian steam-sealing factory was set up at the Crozet Islands, and three years later a French floating factory cleared the beaches of the remnant left by the Norwegian vessel. Meanwhile, in 1908, a Norwegian company established a whaling factory at Kerguelen, and in the four years succeeding killed such great numbers that their extinction seemed certain. Of the habits of these seals at Kerguelen, where the breeding season lasts from about the middle of October until early April, Ring has given an interesting account of the tremendous noise and confusion attending the pairing season. In 1912–13 the Kerguelen Whaling Co. would have had a disastrous season on account of the few whales taken, had it not been able to eke out its catch with elephant-seal oil. "But as a consequence, in 1913, there would only be a small remnant of Elephant Seals left to reproduce themselves. How far this remnant has succeeded in recovering—if it has been able to recover—during the decennium which has passed since the slaughter of the animals ceased, is difficult to conjecture. It is by no means improbable that the existence of these seals has been jeopardized through the strain which the stock has suffered during three seasons' intense hunting, as all the large and virile bulls would have been killed on account of the greater yield of blubber . . . It was seen by us that as much as 35 percent of the pups in a harem succumbed to the dangers of the first voyage of migration."

According to Aubert de la Rue (Terres françaises inconnues, 1930), the destruction of seals in rather recent years had been considerable there. On the Crozet Islands, too, a similar scene has been enacted. In 1930, according to an account quoted by the Journal for the Protection of the Fauna of the Empire (pt. 12, pp. 14–15, 1930), a vessel visiting these islands found the foreshores "covered with sea elephants." "Just after our arrival there a sailing vessel came in and put ashore a sealing party. The following morning when we visited American Bay it was a mass of bloody carcases." If this poaching of seals is still going on, it is in direct violation of the decree of the French

Government, in 1924, completely prohibiting the hunting of these and other seals in the French possessions comprising the Crozet Archipelago, the islands of St. Paul and Amsterdam, Howe, McMurdo, and Briant, as well as part of the south coast of Kerguelen, so far as the animals may be found on them. It is reported that the elephant seals are now chiefly to be found only on "the weather side" of Kerguelen. Heard Island, somewhat to the southeast of Kerguelen, was in past times a great resort of this seal and is said still to be frequented by considerable numbers. How far the sanctity of these reservations is preserved is not clear, but doubtless in the absence of regular patrols it will be difficult to maintain.

In the seas about southern Australian waters elephant seals were formerly present and attracted British, French, and American sealing vessels, which came first perhaps for the abundance of fur seals and secondarily for the oil obtainable from them and from the elephant and other seals. Between the years 1798 and 1826, destruction of these species went on apace (Le Souëf, 1925, p. 113). The elephant seal was at that time found in some numbers on King Island but became exterminated in 1803. At the present time it occurs only as a straggler in the waters off southeastern Australia and Tasmania. Macquarie Island was also a former resort, but the herd there was so often raided that it was reduced to the verge of extinction until with protection by the Australian Government it has in more recent years gradually built up again. In 1933 a "return to normal breeding was reported since protection, which should never be relaxed" (E. LeG. Troughton, in litt.).

Very little information is at hand as to the status of the elephant seal in the South Pacific. It is known to have occurred formerly on the island of Juan Fernandez, and in Anson's time (1740–44) it was abundant there, and according to Molina (1782) was common also on the coast of Arauco, southern Chile. At present, however, it apparently is unknown in these areas. Philippi (1892), in a brief summation of its former status, says that according to information that he gathered on the Chilean coast the last one killed was in 1840 (not 1870 as appeared by misprint in an article in the German publication "Der Zoologische Garten"), and during the next half century was likely to disappear entirely!

It is clear from this brief review that the elephant seal is a species that, if unmolested, rather quickly breeds up to considerable numbers; for in the various instances where depleted populations have been given protection, their numbers have doubled and trebled in relatively brief spaces of time. This may indicate an almost complete lack of "natural" enemies correlated with the large size of the animals. Perhaps the killer whale may occasionally attack a young animal, but the size of the young by the time it takes to sea may again be its protection. Furthermore, this rapid recuperation may indicate a normal sex proportion and a regularity in breeding.

As pointed out by Dr. R. C. Murphy (1918), the methods of killing and utilizing these seals as formerly practiced by the sealing crews are both cruel and wasteful. "After the slain 'elephant' has been allowed to bleed thoroughly, the hide is slit lengthwise down the back, and then transversely in several places from the dorsal incision to the ground. The flaps of hide are next skinned off, and the remaining investment of white blubber, which may have a maximum thickness of about eight inches, is dissected away from the underlying muscle and cut into squarish blanket pieces. The animal is then rolled over and the same process repeated on the ventral side. Thus the hide, and the considerable amount of blubber which clings to it, are lost at the start." The large blanket pieces are then towed out to the waiting vessel, and allowed to soak for about 48 hours until the red blood is washed out, after which they are hauled on board, minced very finely with hand knives, and finally tried out in the deck try-works. During this process there is considerable further loss of oil. In the more recent operations by the Norwegian whalers at South Georgia, the sea-elephant oil supplements that secured from the whales. "The chunks of sea-elephant blubber are left attached to the skin, and loaded into a steamer's hold, after which the cargo—hide, fat, blood, dirt and all—is dumped into steam try-works at the whaling station and reduced to oil and slag."

Family ODOBENIDAE: Walruses

PACIFIC WALRUS

ODOBENUS DIVERGENS (Illiger)

[*Trichechus*] *divergens* Illiger, Abhandl. Akad. Wiss. Berlin, for 1804–11, p. 68, 1815 (about 35 miles south of Icy Cape, Alaska).

SYNONYMS: *Trichechus obesus* Illiger, *op. cit.*, p. 64, 1815 (nomen nudum), and of various later authors (?North Pacific); *Trichechus cooki* Fremery, Bijdrag. tot de Natuurk. Wetensch., vol. 6, p. 385, 1831; *Rosmarus arcticus* Pallas, Zool. Rosso-Asiat., p. 269, 1831.

FIGS.: Allen, J. A., 1880, figs. 14, 17, 19, 21, 22, 24, 27, 29, 31, 33, 35, 36 (skull in comparison with Atlantic walrus); Nelson, 1916, fig. p. 430 (col.).

The Pacific walrus was first distinguished from the Atlantic walrus on the basis of Capt. James Cook's account and figure showing its converging tusks in what may have been a female. In the adult male the tusks are longer and less diverging (in spite of the specific name!) than in the Atlantic species. The tusks, when removed from their sockets, may show a length up to a yard or slightly more. Externally the two species are much alike, but the Pacific walrus has shorter and smaller mustachial bristles, and the "muzzle is relatively deeper and broader, in correlation with the greater breadth and depth of the skull anteriorly." An adult male will weigh upwards of a ton and a half, with a total length of about 10 feet for head and body. In the reference above noted, J. A. Allen (1880, p. 156) has given a minute comparison of the skeletal characters of the two species.

The Pacific walrus is found in a somewhat limited range of the Arctic coasts of eastern Asia and northwestern North America, from about Cape Chalagski (Chalakskai) or Chaun Bay in about longitude 170° E. to Banks Land, to the east of the Alaskan coasts; thence it is found south to the coasts of Kamchatka, Bering Strait, and the Pribilof Islands. At the present time it is less often seen south of the Alaska Peninsula. In autumn it migrates somewhat to the southward, reaching the mouth of the Amur and Sakhalin. Northward walruses have been found common as far as ships have penetrated, in the broken icefields.

Nelson (1916) writes: "Walruses were formerly very abundant in Bering Sea, especially about the Fur Seal Islands, and along the coast north of the Peninsula of Alaska, but few now survive there." He mentions that in July, 1881, the steamer

Corwin cruised for hours along the edge of the ice pack off the Arctic coast of Alaska, where "we saw an almost unbroken line of walruses hauled out on the ice, forming an extended herd which must have contained tens of thousands." They are still common on parts of the Arctic coast of eastern Asia but seem easily disturbed when hunted. Bernard (1923) has indicated how, at a place on the Siberian coast about 20 miles from East Cape, the Eskimos by being careful not to kill more than they needed for meat had succeeded in encouraging the walruses in increasing numbers to return to a traditional "hauling ground" near their village. Here on a beach about a mile long the natives at a given time lance the animals with as little disturbance as possible, and thereafter leave them in peace.

In early days walruses were common about the Pribilof Islands and at Walrus Island. With the coming of sealers, however, the walruses have become very rare. Hanna (1923) writes that he knows of but two breeding rookeries of walruses in Bering Sea: one in the eastern part of one of the group of Walrus Islands, off Togiak Bay, and one on Hall Island, the westernmost of the St. Matthew group. The first herd that he saw in 1911 contained over 300 animals, while the second in 1916 was estimated to be of about 500. At the present time, Townsend (in Gray, P. N., 1932, p. 175) believes that "the walrus is probably holding its own in the Pacific, largely due to the decline in commercial hunting." Madison Grant (1933) recommends that Hall Island be made a sanctuary for these animals and polar bears, as it is entirely treeless and uninhabited. In Alaska there is now a closed season at all times on both walruses and sea-lions, although a limited number may be permitted under special conditions (Rept. U. S. Comm. Fisheries, 1929). Eastward of Alaska walruses are now apparently much less numerous than formerly. Dr. R. M. Anderson (1937) quotes Macfarlane as to their one-time abundance between Point Barrow and Cape Bathurst; on several trips to Franklin Bay between 1862 and 1865 he had seen a few in the pack ice. Now, however, "records from the northern Alaskan coast and east of the Mackenzie delta during recent years are rare and doubtful. One was killed at Herschel Island in 1911, and one at King Point, Yukon Territory, in October, 1914, and there is a hearsay record of one stranded in Dolphin and Union strait some years prior to 1914."

As an example of wasteful methods of hunting the walrus, Captain Bernard (1925) tells that where 30 or 40 years before there were numerous places on the Alaskan coast where walruses used to haul out on beaches for rest, today, although the herds pass along the Alaskan coast in their migration north or south, they keep well offshore and haul out on the floating ice instead of on land. For this reason the Eskimos have to go out in their boats and hunt them as they rest on the floes, with the result that numbers are killed and not recovered, while much of the meat is wasted because it can not be landed. He adds, "During the summer of 1923, while cruising along the Alaskan coast north of Point Hope to Wainwright Inlet near Point Barrow, I examined a stretch of coast of over 200 miles from Cape Lisburne north. A westerly wind had washed ashore on that one part of the coast over a thousand bodies of walrus which had been killed among the ice floes by the Eskimos. One-third of the walrus bodies still had the ivory tusks, showing that the walrus had been shot and had slipped off the ice and sunk before the natives had reached them. These animals were a total loss as the meat was spoiled when the bodies came ashore." Captain Bernard points out that between the entrance of Maryatt Inlet and Cape Lisburne is a stretch of broken beach about 25 miles long that was formerly a very favorite hauling place for walruses and "is the only place on the coast of Alaska where today a walrus occasionally lands." This stretch, if it could be set aside as a walrus reserve, would provide an area where they would undoubtedly return in increasing numbers to spend a season, just as happened in the case of the beach near East Cape, Siberia. This protection, Captain Bernard believes, would not interfere with the hunting by the natives at Point Hope and other settlements, not far distant. "If such a reservation should be established and regulations made whereby the natives were allowed an allotment of walrus to be killed on certain days, as is the custom at Ingshong, Siberia, there would be no waste as now exists under the present custom of killing out on the ice." Bernard adds that "it seems impossible to enforce the present law to the effect that walrus are to be killed only for meat. The natives kill for the ivory or not at all. No matter how much they need the meat, they can only bring small pieces of it ashore."

Concerning the present economic uses of the Pacific walrus,

apart from its use as food by the natives of the Arctic coasts, Townsend (in Gray, P. N., 1932, p. 176) writes: "In former years, the entire walrus was used commercially. The oil brought good prices. The ivory was sold to Japan, where, in Yokohama, many ivory carvers were engaged carving the figures of Eskimos, polar bears and walruses. These were shipped to Alaska to be sold to tourists as native work. The hides of the walrus were usually shipped to England or Scotland to be tanned, as the process required several years to complete. The finished leather was used in polishing wheels and other products. However, in late years, the commercial demand has fallen off and this, together with the remote habitat and uncertain location, seems to warrant the belief that the walrus, while more rare than formerly, is not in immediate danger of becoming extinct."

In a recent article on the habits of the Pacific walrus, Collins (1940) tabulates figures for the annual kill by Eskimos on the Alaskan coasts and believes that the number taken ranges from 1,000 to 1,500, chiefly at St. Lawrence Island, King Island, Diomede Island, and Wainwright. With the decline of whaling in these waters, the walrus have been less persecuted and are now in no immediate danger of extinction. The Eskimo hunt them at the islands mentioned chiefly in the spring when great numbers pass northward. Other than man their only enemies are polar bears, which occasionally kill the young, and the killer whales, which are their worst enemy, "often killing them in great numbers." Collins relates that a few years ago "a large herd of walrus was driven ashore by killer whales in the vicinity of Panuck, St. Lawrence Island. The frightened animals piled up on top of each other in such great numbers while hauling out on the beach that over 200 of them were smothered and crushed and left dead on the beach. The carcasses were used by the Eskimos" who store the meat and blubber in caves, usually keeping from one to two years' supply ahead.

ATLANTIC WALRUS

ODOBENUS ROSMARUS (Linnaeus)

[Phoca] rosmarus Linnaeus, Systema Naturae, ed. 10, vol. 1, p. 38, 1758 (Arctic seas).
SYNONYMS: Trichechus longidens Fremery, Bijdrag. tot de Natuurk. Wetensch., vol. 6, p. 384, 1831; Rosmarus arcticus Lilljeborg, Fauna öfvers Sveriges och Norges Ryggr., p. 674, 1874.

FIGS.: Allen, J. A., 1880, figs. 1, 2, 3, 15, 16, 18, 20, 23, 25, 26, 28, 30, 32, 35 (skull); Stone and Cram, 1902, col. pl. opp. p. 222; Anderson, R. M., 1935, p. 79 (photograph).

The walruses, although not breeding in large rookeries like fur seals, are nevertheless highly social and consort together in smaller or larger groups, often "hauling out" on ice floes to rest, or on shelving beaches in certain favored localities. Like the fur seals, they still retain the power of turning the hind feet forward when on land or ice, and the feet are modified for swimming through the development of webbing between the toes and the elongation of the digits. The thick heavy body may weigh up to a ton and a half, with a well-developed neck. The short coarse hairy covering is dark yellowish brown, but it often may rub off with wear so that the back and shoulders are more or less hairless. External ears are lacking. The large canine teeth are developed as tusks, which are used in fighting, in digging on shallow bottoms for the clams on which they chiefly feed, or as aids in dragging the heavy body out on land or ice. The muzzle is narrower than in the Pacific walrus, and the tusks of males are shorter and slightly divergent outward. Well-developed tusks may be as much as 20 inches long, but the portion projection from the mouth seldom exceeds 15 inches. They are therefore shorter than in the Pacific species. The cheek teeth are soon worn down to large, flat-surfaced pegs.

In glacial times this walrus was found as far south as the coast of Virginia, as proved by fossil remains, but at the time of the discovery of America by Europeans it probably did not come farther south than Massachusetts Bay, and then only occasionally. In colonial times its most southern breeding ground was Sable Island off Nova Scotia. On the European side it occasionally occurs as a straggler as far south as the British Isles and in one instance to the coast of Holland (Nieuwediep, in November, 1926, see Van den Brink, 1931, p. 176). It rarely appears in the seas about Iceland and southern Greenland. Northward its range extends to the western side of Hudson Bay and south into James Bay, and throughout the eastern archipelago to Smith Sound in about latitude 80° N. The eastward limits are the seas about Spitsbergen and Franz Josef Land and possibly to the Lena Delta. Apparently its range at no point now meets that of the Pacific walrus.

Over all the southern parts of its Atlantic range the walrus

has been gradually exterminated during the past three centuries, so that it now is rare south of Cape Chidley, Labrador.
The influence of cold near-shore waters resulted in its ranging
farther south in the western than in the eastern Atlantic,
where the Gulf Stream swings northward. The only known
occurrence of the walrus in Massachusetts Bay is of one
captured at Plymouth, Mass., in December, 1734, apparently
a small one, 9 feet long, with 5- or 6-inch tusks. It was on
exhibition for a time in Boston. In addition, fragments of
skulls with tusks have been brought up by trawlers in the Gulf
of Maine in at least four instances of recent years (see G. M.
Allen, 1930). In colonial days these animals had as their most
southern breeding place the shelving beaches of Sable Island,
off Nova Scotia, and must occasionally have come in tc the
waters off Maine. Between 1633 and 1642 vessels from the
Massachusetts Bay Colony made a number of expeditions to
this island to secure the tusks and oil. In 1641 a vessel with
12 men spent eight months there and returned bringing "400
pair of sea horse teeth, which were esteemed worth £300.'
After about 1650 the walrus was probably exterminated or
driven away from this outpost. It remained, however, in some
numbers in the Gulf of St. Lawrence for at least another
century. The Magdalen Islands were a favorite resort with a
"hauling ground" particularly on Brion Island. An old account by Shuldham (quoted by J. A. Allen, 1880, p. 67) tells
of their repairing here early in spring "in great numbers;
formerly, when undisturbed by the Americans, to the amount
of seven or eight thousand." Here they were regularly killed
by attacking them at night, and, as Shuldham relates, "in this
manner there has been killed fifteen or sixteen hundred at one
cut," possibly an exaggeration but at least an indication of
their abundance at about 1775. Walruses have occasionally
visited the Straits of Belle Isle and the Newfoundland waters
down to recent years, but at the present time they occur there
only as rare stragglers. One is reported by Grenfell as killed
near Cape Meccatina as recently as 1909 (see also Vigneau,
1908a, 1908b). Dr. R. M. Anderson (1935) states that Maj.
L. T. Burwash, who has made a special study of the matter,
reported in 1931 that he did not know of any walruses south of
Hudson Strait. Low, in 1906, wrote that they were only rarely
killed at Cape Chidley, the most northern part of Labrador.

In Hudson Bay they were formerly found as far south as Paint Islands on the east side of James Bay, but now their southern limit is the Belcher Islands in about latitude 57° N. Low (1906) adds that there had been a rapid diminution in their numbers here during the past few years (after 1898) since the Scottish steamer *Active* had been engaged in their capture. But since only one in four or five of those killed was recovered, and the proceeds from oil, hide, and ivory were less then $50 apiece, the prospect for their early extermination seemed obvious. According to the investigations of Major Burwash, "the biggest walrus hauling ground in eastern North America was formerly at Padlei, northeast of Cumberland Sound, Baffin Island. One company took over 4,000 skins per year, and began to create a demand for walrus hides for lining of automobile tires. Walrus are still found in some numbers off Amadjuak Bay, and are more numerous farther west, especially about King Charles Cape, Mill, and Salisbury Islands. They are also found along the east coast of Baffin Island, but are scarce in Cumberland Sound. Farther north they are more abundant in Lancaster Sound, Jones Sound, and Smith Sound north to at least 80°."

In 1928, while with the Canadian Arctic Expedition, Dr. R. M. Anderson made a special effort to ascertain the westward limits of the Atlantic walrus. From information secured it appeared that in February of that year an inspector found "thousands at the edge of the floe in the northern end of Foxe basin, and smaller numbers in Fury and Hecla strait. The natives there live largely on walrus and remain on the ice nearly ten months of the year. There is open water there all winter." Walruses were abundant at Port Leopold, Somerset Island, in 1924–27, but none was seen around Prince of Wales Island to the west. They are abundant in Repulse Bay. Summing up, Anderson writes: "Apparently the western limit of range of the Atlantic Walrus in the south is Fury and Hecla strait, and in the north the upper part of Prince Regent inlet down to Bellot strait and the middle of Barrow strait, south of Cornwallis Island."

It seems then that on the western side of the Atlantic walruses have retreated to within the Arctic Circle, or nearly so, and frequent regions where some open water may be found the year around. The need for regulation of their killing is apparent, and in 1931 the Canadian Government passed an order in council prohibiting the killing of walruses in the area including Hudson Bay, Hudson Strait, and northward, except for food and not in excess of actual needs; and no one but an Eskimo may kill walrus without a license. The export of walrus tusks or ivory, except in the form of manufactured articles, is also prohibited except by permit from the Minister of Fisheries.

Summing up the situation in Greenland, Jensen (1928) writes that the walrus on the west coast "is only a permanent resident between Sukkertoppen and Egedesminde—particularly at the mouth of North Strømfiord, where in the autumn it is in the habit of appearing in great numbers and creeps up on the islands round Taseralik—as well as in Upernivik District, Melville Bay and Smith Sound. In other places its occurrence is more sporadic. On the east coast it rarely appears at the southern part, but at Scoresby Sound it is in summer of comparatively frequent occurrence out at the coast and also farther north, and it has been observed as for north as at Amdrup Land (lat. 81° 10′ N.). North of this locality it has not been met with, nor in the part of the north coast which faces the Arctic Sea proper.

"In the Thule District the walrus is of such great importance that it must be termed the chief animal of capture. It also plays a part in the newly established settlement on the east coast at Scoresby Sound. To the remaining part of Greenland it is of no great importance."

In its eastward range the walrus seems to have been always scarce about Iceland, straggling on occasion to the British Isles, but it was not regularly to be found in numbers until the colder waters are reached on the north coasts of Finmark, and about the islands to the north and east, Bear Island, Nova Zembla, and particularly Spitsbergen. Concerning their abundance here and their destruction in the course of the last three centuries, J. A. Allen (1880, p. 74) has given a summary account. Even in the early years of the seventeenth century, great numbers were regularly taken at Bear or Cherie Island by expeditions from England, and there was a certain amount of trouble and unfriendly rivalry with crews from Spain, Holland, and Denmark. The intensive slaughter of the walruses at Bear Island compassed their practical extermination by about 1617, when the visiting crews turned their attention more to whaling. About 1612 the walrus began to be intensively pursued in the Spitsbergen Archipelago, and large numbers were killed. The pursuit, however, seems to have relaxed considerably in succeeding centuries, although walruses at times eked out cargoes of whale products. Captain Scoresby in 1820 wrote that in his time "the Sea-horses range the coasts of Spitzbergen almost without molestation from the British. The Russians are their principal enemies who, by means of the hunting parties sent out to winter on the coast, capture a considerable number. The whale-fishers rarely take half a dozen in a voyage; though my Father, in the last season, procured about 130 in Magdalane Bay." Lamont in his "Seasons with Sea-horses" has given an account of his experiences in hunting walrus in Spitsbergen seas for sport in the middle of the last century. The animals seem to be still present in numbers about these islands and on the northwest coast of Nova Zembla. No recent figures or estimates of the walrus population are at hand, however. The remoteness of the regions they inhabit and the small value of their tusks and oil probably offer little inducement to their pursuit, so that for the present they may be fairly safe.

The food of the walrus is mainly clams, which they dig up in shoal bottoms and, skilfully extracting the soft parts, reject the shells. At times they will eat seals, which apparently they capture for themselves, a curious cannibalistic trait.

Order CETACEA: Whales, Porpoises, Dolphins

Whales are highly modified for a pelagic life, with fishlike bodily build, finlike front limbs, no hind limbs, and transversely expanded tail-fin, or flukes. They are completely independent of the land, although the young are usually born in shallow bays rather than on the high seas. Two Recent suborders are recognized.

Odontoceti, toothed whales. These usually have numerous, simple teeth, but some forms have very few (the male narwhal has a single tooth, while the female has none that are functional). Six families are distinguished:

(1) Platanistidae, including only the fresh-water dolphin of the Ganges River. These have a long, narrow snout, many teeth, and vestigial eyes.

(2) Iniidae, the fresh-water dolphins of the Amazon, the Plata, and the Yangtse Rivers. These are similar to the Ganges form, except for some important details of structure. The Yangtse species is discussed in this section.

(3) Delphinapteridae, the white whale, or beluga, and the narwhal.

(4) Delphinidae, the dolphins and porpoises. This is a large group, containing many diverse genera. Some of the species are rare, others are abundant. The false killer whale is considered here because for some time it was thought to be extinct.

(5) Ziphiidae, beaked whales. The beaked whales have only one or two teeth on either side of the lower jaw, and both jaws form a beaklike structure. The ten species of the genus *Mesoplodon*, all poorly represented in museum collections, are thought to be vanishing mammals.

(6) Physeteridae, sperm whales. There are two genera in this family, one a pygmy type, the other reaching 60 feet in length. The sperm whale, or cachalot, was much sought by whalers during the eighteenth and nineteenth centuries and was thereby greatly reduced in numbers; it is now thought to be on the increase.

Mystacoceti, the whale-bone whales. These have no teeth after birth; instead they have fringed plates of baleen which act as sieves to retain the small animals on which the true whales feed. Three families are recognized:

(1) Rhachianectidae, the gray whale of the northern Pacific Ocean. The unique species combines characters of the fin whales and the right whales. It is seriously threatened by the Japanese whale-fishery.

(2) Balaenidae, right whales. The right whales have neither dorsal fin nor throat-folds. Three species of as many genera are discussed here.

(3) Balaenopteridae, fin whales. These have a dorsal fin and the throat is plicated. Five species of three genera are seriously affected by modern whaling operations and will be exterminated unless protective measures are made effective.—J. E. H.

Family INIIDAE: Fresh-water Dolphins

WHITE-FLAG DOLPHIN; YANGTSE DOLPHIN

LIPOTES VEXILLIFER Miller

Lipotes vexillifer Miller, Smithsonian Misc. Coll., vol. 68, no. 9, p. 8, Mar. 30, 1918
(Tung Ting Lake, Hunan Province, China)..
FIGS.: Miller, 1918b, pls. 1, 2, 4, 6, 8, 9, 11, 12 (exterior and skeleton).

This remarkable fresh-water dolphin was discovered as recently as in 1916, when Charles M. Hoy, for some years a resident in China, secured a specimen and sent it to the U. S. National Museum, where it was studied and described two years later by Miller. The species is known only from the large fresh-water lake of Tung Ting, in the interior of southern China, and may be regarded as a relict of a group of dolphins once more widely spread, with its nearest living relative *Inia geoffrensis*, of the Amazon River.

About 2.5 meters in length, this is a long-beaked dolphin, with a low triangular adipose fin on the back. The color is "pale blue-gray above, white below." The "beak" has a slight upward curve, whereas that of *Inia* is the reverse. There is a long mandibular symphysis, and each tooth row carries 31–33 teeth. The eyes are very small. The teeth have "the form of the crown and character of the enamel-wrinkling much as in the median teeth of *Inia*, but root not thickened, the entire tooth resembling that of the Miocene '*Schizodelphis*'." Basal length of skull, 510 mm.; rostrum 350. Weight, 297 pounds.

Hoy (quoted by Miller, 1918b) writes that the local name Pei Ch'i given to this dolphin by the Chinese means "white flag" because of the dorsal fin, which they liken to a flag; it is prominent when the animal comes to the surface to breathe. "The sudden appearance of a school of these whitish dolphins close to a small boat is very startling. To the best of my knowledge this animal is found in large numbers only around the mouth of Tung Ting Lake. In winter when the water of the lake is so low that there is scarcely more than the river channel left they are easily seen and are found in great numbers in bunches usually of three or four, but occasionally of as many as 10 or 12 individuals. They are often seen in shallow water working up the mud in their search for fish. The one I killed had about two quarts of catfish in its stomach. When shot it gave a cry like that of a water-buffalo calf. In summer the

water rises to a height of 48 feet above its winter level. The
mountain streams feeding the lake are then full, and the dolphins disappear. The natives say that in the late spring when
the lake is rising the dolphins make their way up the small,
clear rivers, and that these are their breeding grounds." Beyond the fact that the British Museum and the American
Museum of Natural History have each since acquired a specimen, and that there are a skull and a jaw in the Shanghai
Museum (without data), nothing further seems to have been
ascertained concerning this remarkable animal. Hoy's specimen weighed about 297 pounds. The Chinese usually regard
this dolphin with a certain superstitious fear and seldom kill it,
but as its blubber is thought to be of medicinal value, it is not
impossible that in the future increasing numbers may be shot
as improved weapons reach these parts of China, or the demand
for specimens offers an inducement to hunters. As a sort of
"living fossil," a relict from earlier ages, and the only strictly
fresh-water dolphin in eastern Asia, the species is worth preserving.

Family DELPHINIDAE: Dolphins and Porpoises

FALSE KILLER WHALE

PSEUDORCA CRASSIDENS (Owen)

Phocaena crassidens Owen, Hist. British Fossil Mammals and Birds, p. 516, 1846
  ("In the great fen of Lincolnshire . . ." near Stamford, England).
FIGS.: True, 1889b, pl. 44 (exterior and skull); London Illustr. News, Dec. 21, 1935,
  p. 1125.

While apparently not threatened or vanishing, this large
porpoise may be included here as an example of a species that
was believed to be extinct but that later proved to be living
and in considerable numbers. It was first described in 1846
from a skull found in the great fen of Lincolnshire, England,
but in 1862 Reinhardt gave an account of it from three individuals that were thrown ashore on the Danish islands Sealand
and Funen, in that year. Since then but few specimens have
been made known, until within a few years a number of schools
have been reported as stranded in various parts of the world.
This porpoise attains a length of up to 20 feet. It is black
all over, with a large bulbous snout, which slightly overhangs
the mouth. There is a good-sized falcate fin on the lower

half of the back. The teeth are large, conical, and spaced, usually about eight to nine in each tooth row. The animal thus bears a superficial resemblance to a blackfish, but the head is less globose, and the pectoral fin is shorter, about one-eighth or a ninth instead of a fifth of the total length.

In 1927 a school of no less than 126 came ashore at Dornoch Firth, off Sutherlandshire, Scotland, and their skeletons were secured by the British Museum to form the basis of a comprehensive study. In the few years following other schools were stranded at such distant parts of the world as the Ligurian Sea, the coast of Malaga, Ceylon, Tasmania and New South Wales, Zanzibar, and the coast of South Africa near Capetown.

Instead, therefore, of being an extinct or rare species as at first believed, this large porpoise proves to be common, frequenting the temperate and tropical seas of the world. A social species, it may gather in schools of considerably over a hundred, old and young, and is believed to subsist chiefly on squid. What drives these "suicide squads" to become stranded in such numbers is uncertain. Various ideas have been advanced, but the true reason is difficult to fathom. Ordinarily they seem to keep well off from land but perhaps may at times follow in schools of their favorite food animals, whether fishes or squids, and coming too near land in shallow shelving coastal waters get panic-stricken and drive on to the beach. Hitherto they have served no economic use, for their appearance is too undependable to make it worth the effort to hunt them.

Family ZIPHIIDAE: Ziphioid Whales

BEAKED WHALES OF THE GENUS MESOPLODON

The whales of this genus are so rarely stranded or captured, or preserved in museums, that very little is known of them beyond the general appearance and anatomy of the occasional specimen that has fallen into the hands of a naturalist. It is believed that they are relatively few in numbers and represent a waning group, once more numerous but now slowly dying out. Many fossil remains have been referred to the genus. Nevertheless, more likely it is their solitary habits and pelagic life, and the infrequency of their visits to near-shore waters,

that to some extent account for our lack of knowledge about
them. Cetaceans at sea are difficult to identify if of small size
and only briefly seen from a distance. Probably the food of
this group is chiefly squids and other cephalopods, and the
habit of feeding on these soft-bodied animals has resulted in
the degeneration of practically all the teeth, although at the
same time with the loss of most of the tooth row, one or sometimes two pairs of teeth have been retained and even enlarged,
for what purpose one may only conjecture. Thus *M. bidens* is
characterized by a pair of lower teeth, one on each side, in
about the middle of the row, large and conical; *M. stejnegeri*
has this tooth much larger; in *M. mirus* the teeth are smaller
and at the tip of the jaw; while in *M. layardii* the two teeth,
although in about the middle of the jaw, are not conical but
flattened and straplike, actually curving inward and nearly
meeting above the rostrum so that the mouth is capable of
very little opening. What the use of such teeth may be is
unknown. Since none of the species of the genus is common
enough to be of any commercial or economic value, no protective measures are needed nor could they perhaps be made
effective if passed. The group needs therefore only passing
mention at most, as a possibly declining genus, of which a
number of species still remain but of which little is known.

For convenience, a list of the living species hitherto described
is given, exclusive of synonymy. Dr. F. W. True in 1910
published an account of the few specimens then available in
American museums. Notwithstanding the rather large number of species, the various dental and cranial characters seem
on the whole to show their distinctness.

SOWERBY'S TWO-TOOTHED WHALE
MESOPLODON BIDENS (Sowerby)

Physeter bidens Sowerby, British Miscellany, p. 1, pl. 1, 1804 (near Brodie-house,
Elginshire, British Isles).

Range: North Atlantic.

BOWDOIN'S BEAKED WHALE
MESOPLODON BOWDOINI Andrews

Mesoplodon bowdoini Andrews, Bull. Amer. Mus. Nat. Hist., vol. 24, p. 203, Feb. 26,
1908 (New Brighton Beach, Canterbury Province, New Zealand).

Range: Unknown except from type region.

MESOPLODON DENSIROSTRIS (Blainville)

Delphinus densirostris Blainville, Nouv. Dict. d'Hist. Nat., ed. 2, vol. 9, p. 178, 1817 (Indian Ocean).

Range: Indian Ocean, Australian Seas, and North Atlantic.

MESOPLODON EUROPAEUS (Gervais)

Dioplodon europaeus Gervais, Zool. et Paléontol. Françaises, ed. 1, vol. 2, p. 4, 1848–52 (English Channel).

Range: North Atlantic.

MESOPLODON GRAYI (Haast)

Oulodon grayi Haast, Proc. Zool. Soc. London, 1876, pp. 7, 450, pl. 26 (Chatham Islands).

Range: Australian Seas, to New Zealand.

LAYARD'S BEAKED WHALE; STRAP-TOOTHED WHALE

MESOPLODON LAYARDII (Gray)

Ziphius layardii Gray, Proc. Zool. Soc. London, 1865, p. 358, fig. (Cape of Good Hope).

Range: Southern Ocean from Cape of Good Hope to Australia and Tasmania and Patagonia.

HECTOR'S BEAKED WHALE

MESOPLODON HECTORI (Gray)

Berardius hectori Gray, Ann. Mag. Nat. Hist., ser. 4, vol. 8, p. 117, 1871 (Tatai Bay, Cook Straits, New Zealand).
FIG.: Hector, in Knox, 1871, pls. 14, 15.

Range: New Zealand Seas.

TRUE'S BEAKED WHALE

MESOPLODON MIRUS True

Mesoplodon mirum True, Smithsonian Misc. Coll., vol. 60, no. 25, p. 1, Mar. 14, 1913 (Beaufort Harbor, North Carolina).

Range: North Atlantic.

LONGMAN'S BEAKED WHALE

MESOPLODON PACIFICUS Longman

Mesoplodon pacificus Longman, Mem. Queensland Mus., vol. 3, p. 269, pl. 43 (skull), Mar. 31, 1926 (Mackay, Queensland).

Range: Australian Seas.

STEJNEGER'S BEAKED WHALE

MESOPLODON STEJNEGERI True

Mesoplodon stejnegeri True, Proc. U. S. Nat. Mus., vol. 8, p. 584, Oct. 19, 1885 (Bering Island, Commander Group, Bering Sea).

Range: Bering Sea to Oregon coast.

True, in reviewing the group in 1910, listed eight valid species, to which two have since been added, *M. mirus* True and *M. pacificus* Longman. From the evidence of the specimens hitherto reported, it seems that three of these are so far known from the North Atlantic only (*M. bidens, M. europaeus, M. mirus*), one from the North Pacific (*M. stejnegeri*), five from the southern oceans (*M. bowdoini, M. grayi, M. hectori, M. layardii, M. pacificus*), while only one, *M. densirostris*, is known from so widely separated stations as North Atlantic, Indian Ocean, and Australian Seas. Further captures may at any time add to our knowledge of the distribution of these beaked whales.

WHALING

The history of the whaling industry as developed by Europeans and Americans has been many times written. The voluminous literature of whaling would form a library in itself, covering the varied aspects of the undertaking from scattered records of earlier days to the more connected accounts of later centuries. The classic works of Zorgdrager and Martens give us some of the first reports of Arctic whaling, later followed by the well-known works of Captain Scoresby. In the last century came a series of books recounting adventures of round-the-world cruises in search of sperm whales, such as those of Bennett, Browne, Beale, Scammon, and a later host of reminiscences following the culmination of the industry in the latter half of the nineteenth century. For statistics of whaling vessels, the fine volume by Alexander Starbuck is still a standard source book. There are even many books of recent years on modern whaling, so that the human aspects of the subject are well documented. Perhaps the best summary account in print is that of Sir Sidney F. Harmer (1928) who has treated the matter from a different point of view and shows that the history of whaling may be divided into several periods according to the type of whale chiefly pursued.

Whaling history begins with the North Atlantic right whale, which seems to have been first regularly pursued by the Basques of the Biscay coasts of France and Spain. "The industry was important as early as the twelfth century, as is shown by documentary evidence. It is believed to have been going on for a considerable time before that period, probably from the 10th or 11th century, at least." This species, characterized by its arched and narrowed forepart of the skull, its narrow blades of whalebone, of which the longest in the middle of each rank measures about 7 feet, and by the lack of a dorsal fin, is found in temperate seas, more particularly coastal waters, and is migratory. Formerly on the European coasts it appeared during the winter and early spring months in the near-shore waters. Until perhaps the fifteenth or sixteenth centuries, the Basques carried on a fishery for these whales. "Some of the old watch-towers, situated on eminences overlooking the sea, from which the early whalers first sighted their prey, may still be recognized." When a whale was seen, boats would put out from shore in pursuit, with harpoons. The word "harpoon" is said to be of Basque origin. The Bay of Biscay seems to have been a favorite winter resort for this whale, but even as early as sixteenth century it apparently became less common there, and the Basque whalers went farther and farther afield in its pursuit. There is some evidence that they reached the Newfoundland waters even slightly before Columbus's discovery, but at least by the latter part of the sixteenth century they were regularly pursuing whales here. During at least the first century following the arrival of the Pilgrims, right whales were a source of revenue to the New England colonists. These whales arrived in Massachusetts Bay in autumn, and while many passed on southward to winter as far south as the Carolina coasts others seem to have wintered in the Gulf of Maine and were taken by the settlers in small numbers at that time and especially in early spring when the whales passed northward to their summering "grounds" in the latitude of Iceland. About 50 or 60 "whaling ships visited Iceland annually during the 16th century. The industry flourished specially from 1596 to 1622 between the North Cape and Bear Island, with whaling stations at Hammerfest and elsewhere, but it began to decline at this time, partly because there were fewer whales, but also owing to the fact that the attention of the whalers was becoming diverted to the Greenland Whale."

Summarizing the pursuit of this whale in the North Atlantic, Sir Sidney Harmer (1928) writes: "The Biscay Whale has thus been successively hunted in the Bay of Biscay, in the neighbourhood of Newfoundland and New England, off Iceland, and to the north of Norway during a period of at least 700 years (1100–1800). In all the localities in question its numbers diminished, the industry terminating about 1700 on the European side of the Atlantic and about 1800 on the American side. It had become excessively rare, and for many years it was believed to be extinct." Nevertheless it eventually recuperated in the next half century and a few were killed annually, about ten a year, at the Scottish whaling stations, between 1908 and 1914. However, "it does not seem to have reached anything like its former abundance."

The second phase of whaling centers about the bowhead or Greenland whale. This is a larger species than the right whale, with a more arched skull accommodating its 12-foot plates of whalebone, and the blubber encompassing its body is deeper. It is confined to Arctic waters, from the Gulf of St. Lawrence northward to the seas about Spitsbergen and Jan Mayen in the east, and to Davis Straits, Lancaster Sound, and the Alaskan and neighboring waters in the west. It was slightly migratory, keeping close to the edge of the pack ice, which it followed a short distance south in winter and north again in spring. Although known to the Icelanders in the thirteenth century, and later apparently to the Basque fishermen who reached the Gulf of St. Lawrence, it was not until 1611, when Thomas Edge was sent by the English Muscovy Company to Spitsbergen, that its intensive pursuit really began. So valuable were these whales for their yield of oil and "bone" that in later years even the capture of a single whale might cover the expenses of the voyage for a small vessel. The flocking of whalers to Spitsbergen waters made it necessary even by 1618 to allot sections of the coast to the English, Dutch, Danish, Hamburgers, and Basques. So abundant were the bowheads in the bays of Spitsbergen and Jan Mayen that the ships were anchored in some convenient situation "and generally remained at their moorings until their cargoes" of oil were completed. The whales were killed near shore and the oil was tried out at the station on shore. It was not many years, however, until (about 1630–40) the whales became scarce in the bays, and whalers went farther and farther in their pursuit, towing the carcasses back to land for rendering. Later the shore works were abandoned, and the whales were cut up at sea, the blubber packed in casks and the oil "extracted at home after the conclusion of the voyage." This pursuit reached its height about 1636–37 and declined rapidly in the Spitsbergen seas thereafter. Nevertheless for two more centuries the bowhead was relentlessly pursued, first in Davis Straits, then in the pack ice farther north. According to Eschricht and Reinhardt, in the 60 years between 1719 and 1778, the Dutch caught 6,986 whales in Davis Strait and Disco Bay, while in later years the British whalers took a much larger number in the northern parts of Baffin Bay, and in Lancaster and Barrow Straits over 3,300 in the four years from 1827 to 1830. For many years following the Arctic whaling centered from Peterhead and Dundee, but it gradually declined, until in 1912 and 1913 only one ship left Dundee and each time came back empty. Meanwhile, however, the pursuit of the bowhead began in the North Pacific, at first in the Okhotsk Sea, and by the middle of the nineteenth century extended to Bering Straits and the western Arctic Ocean. After 1851, the number of ships engaged fell gradually from 138 in that season to 16 in 1875. On a small scale the fishing has continued into the present century. As in the east, the pursuit here was at first very profitable, but the whales soon were so reduced that it no longer paid. The whales seem to be very slow in recuperating, even under lessened pursuit.

A third phase of this industry centers about the sperm whale. Unlike the right whale and the bowhead, which were easily killed and throve in colder waters, the sperm whale required more energy and skill and is a species found usually in temperate and tropical seas. Not infrequently, however, it penetrates to colder waters, and it is of practically world-wide distribution. The sperm whale was valued not only for its oil but for the spermaceti or waxy liquid contained in the "case" surmounting the enormous head. Being one of the toothed whales, it gave no whalebone yield, but the large teeth in the lower jaw were sometimes used for carving or other purposes.

Sperm whaling was a typical New England pursuit and

seems to have commenced at Nantucket about 1712. This port and New Bedford, Mass., were its main centers for over a century and a half, although a number of whalers sailed from England and France as well. The Atlantic, the Pacific, and the Indian Oceans were searched for sperm whales year by year, the vessels often making voyages of several years' duration and navigating the seas of the world. "English ships had joined in the business in 1785, and in 1788–1790 the 'Amelia' of London was the first ship to sail round Cape Horn into the Pacific, where 'the enormous cargo of 139 tons of sperm oil' was obtained. In 1789 the operations were extended to the Indian Ocean, the neighbourhood of Madagascar proving to be a rich whaling ground. Pacific whaling rapidly increased, the coasts of Chili and Peru and the Galapagos becoming favorite resorts. About 1802 the Sperm Whale began to be hunted in New Zealand waters, and vessels were visiting the Molucca Islands with the same object. New grounds were shortly afterwards discovered in the Japan seas, where there were nearly 100 whaling ships in 1835" (Harmer, 1928). The United States fleet began to decline after 1846. In 1859 came kerosene as a rival illuminant to whale oil, which had so long been supreme. This added factor contributed to lowering the profits from long whaling voyages, and a still more rapid rate of decline set in. Since the American industry had passed its zenith over 20 years before, it becomes evident that a main cause for the decline was the increasing scarcity of whales, which had been destroyed faster than their rate of reproduction. After the middle of the last century sperm whaling on a small but lessening scale continued till about 1884. On these longer voyages the whalers had discovered right whales in the southern oceans, as well as in the North Pacific, and eked out their catches of sperm oil with that of these whales. They were largely fished out, however, by the middle of the last century. The Japanese seem to have hunted the right whale in their own waters from an earlier period.

What may be termed a fourth and perhaps the final phase of whaling was introduced with the invention of a harpoon gun by Svend Foyn in 1865. Much earlier an explosive bomb had been invented to be shot from a shoulder gun; the dart carried an explosive charge, which after having been fired into the whale's body at short range, presently caused its death. This was later developed by Foyn into a cannonlike weapon, mounted at the bow of a small steamer, discharging a heavy harpoon into the whale. A hawser, attached to the harpoon and carried to steam winches on deck, enabled whalers to attack successfully the various species of rorquals (finbacks, humpbacks, blue and gray whales), most of them hitherto unmolested since, on account of their swifter and more violent actions, their thinner coating of blubber, and their short plates of whalebone, they were less valuable and also it was practically out of the question to kill them with ordinary harpoons. This fishery had been first developed on the Norwegian coasts, but at the end of the last century, with the partial depletion of these areas, "whaling factories" were set up in Newfoundland and in Antarctic waters. Capt. C. A. Larsen, who in 1901 commanded the Swedish Antarctic Expedition, on his return to Buenos Aires, founded the Compañía Argentina de Pesca, the first of modern whaling companies to operate in the sub-Antarctic seas. Larsen saw thousands of humpbacks off South Georgia in the southern summer and abundance of blue whales. He returned to South Georgia in the autumn of 1904 to begin intensive operations. In the succeeding year he was followed by two other Norwegian whalers, and the field was extended to the Straits of Magellan, the Falkland Islands, and the South Shetlands. "The new Antarctic industry was a success from the first, and it developed with great rapidity. New companies were founded and conducted their operations principally at South Georgia and the South Shetlands. The size of the whale-catchers was increased and the whaling plant was made more efficient. In 1910–11 the total number of whales captured at South Georgia alone reached the high figure of 6,529, of which 6,197 were Humpbacks." Not only are the blubber oil and the body oil tried out separately, but the flesh is then dried, ground and sacked for fertilizer or for cattle feed, the bones are ground up for lime, and other byproducts are utilized so that there is as little waste to each carcass as possible. Most of the work is now in the hands of Norwegian whalers, operating under license of the government of the Falkland Islands. The number of whales killed in the course of a year runs into large figures. In the season of 1925–26, Harmer states, the total was 26,962, which yielded an average of 43.8 barrels of oil apiece. In 1923 a new departure was undertaken by Captain Larsen, who instead of conducting a shore station for cutting up and rendering the whales, took out a "mother ship" large enough to permit of hauling a whale aboard to be there taken care of, while each such ship was accompanied by five small hunting steamers to bring in the catch. At the same time a smaller amount of whaling by this and other methods continued to be carried on elsewhere. According to Sir Sidney Harmer, in 1926 whaling operations were being carried on not only in these Antarctic waters, but also on the southern coasts of Africa, Chile, Perú, and Ecuador, as well as in Australian waters and in the North Pacific on both sides, from Japan to Kamchatka and from Mexico to Alaska; nor was the product of the North Atlantic in the same year inconsiderable. A detailed list of the catches for the year 1926 is given by this author, with the total of whales at the different places.

Clearly if such numbers of whales continue to be killed annually, the supply will ere long be so reduced that the industry will no longer be profitable. This has, of course, been foreseen, and Harmer points out that not only have whaling operations repeatedly been responsible for a very serious reduction in the number of whales, but also that "when a species of whale has been finally driven from a particular locality it may show more than a reluctance to return to it." According to James Blake (1938), in the Antarctic summer of 1930–31 no less than 42,000 whales were killed, and in the corresponding period of 1935-36 the total was about 45,000. At the same time the statistics are said to show that the average size of the whales is declining, an indication that the inroads are being too severe into the adult breeding stock.

In 1935, after several years of effort, a convention was entered into between the United States of America, Great Britain, France, and Norway and certain other members of the League of Nations for the regulation of whaling. It prohibits the killing of right whales, Greenland whales, and pygmy right whales, as well as the taking or killing of calves or suckling whales, immature whales, and female whales accompanied by young. Furthermore, the treaty provides that "the fullest possible use shall be made of the carcases of whales taken" for which adequate facilities must be prepared. Other provisions relate to the licensing of whaling ships and the keeping of records of whales taken. With this beginning an eventual adjustment may be hoped for whereby a more intelligent management of the industry will ensue, and a just balance be maintained between the normal reproduction and the numbers killed. The investigations of the *Discovery*, especially assigned by the British Government to study all matters relating to the habits and reproductive capacities of the commercial species, have already provided some basis for such knowledge.

Commercial products.—With the substitution of gas and electricity for oil in lighting requirements, and the use of stainless steel for whalebone, one might suppose that the draft upon the whale supply would abate. This, however, does not seem to be the case. There is a large demand for the oil in making the finer grades of soap, especially glycerine soaps. During the World War of 1914–18, the blue whale especially was in demand at the whaling stations, since it yields from its blubber about 17 percent of glycerine, an important ingredient of certain high explosives. According to Salvesen (1914), "Whale oil is usually graded into four qualities, . . . though some companies add a fifth." The two best grades, Nos. O and I, are made entirely from blubber; No. II from the tongues and kidney fat and from the residue of the blubber boilings; No. III from the flesh and bones; and No. IV from refuse." In 1914 the best grade brought about £24 a ton net weight; No. II was worth £22 a ton; No. III, £20; and No. IV, £18 a ton.

The baleen of the southern right whale in 1914 was said to be worth only about £750 a ton; that of the finwhales very much less, so that the marketing might be more costly than the value received. The fresh whale meat converted into a meal is a nutritious and wholesome food for cattle, with about 17.5 percent proteid; while guano made from the remaining flesh and a third of bone is high in ammonia (8.5 percent) and tribasic phosphates (about 21 percent). Bone meal, made exclusively from the bones, contains about 4 percent ammonia and about 50 percent of phosphates. The prices for the various products are much less than formerly.

Ambergris is a concretion found in the intestines of occasional sperm whales and is still a desideratum among perfume makers, for which no substitute has yet been found. It has the peculiar property of holding delicate scents.

Family PHYSETERIDAE: Sperm Whales

SPERM WHALE

PHYSETER CATODON Linnaeus

Physeter catodon Linnaeus, Systema Naturae, ed. 10, vol. 1, p. 76, 1758 ("In Oceano septentrionali," i. e., Kairsten, Orkney Islands).
SYNONYMS: *Physeter macrocephalus* Linnaeus, Systema Naturae, ed. 10, vol. 1, p. 76, 1758 ("In Oceano Europaeo"); *Catodon (Meganeuron) krefftii* Gray, Proc. Zool. Soc. London, 1865, p. 440 (Australian seas).
FIGS.: Townsend, 1930a, p. 16 (drawing); Matthews, 1938a, pls. 3–11 (drawings and photographs).

The sperm whale is the only one of the whales in which there is a great disparity in size between males and females. The adult male may measure up to 17.5 meters, or nearly 60 feet, while the female goes to about 10 meters, or about 33 feet, and is much slenderer with a proportionally smaller head. The male's enormous head forms nearly a third of the total length; it is full and bulbous, the snout slightly rounded in front and slightly overhanging the jaw. The single blow-hole is asymmetrically placed on the left side near the tip of the rounded snout. There is a low hump in the center of the back slightly past the midlength, and it is succeeded by a few irregular and smaller humps. The long, narrow jaw carries about 25 or 27 pairs of large blunt teeth, but the few often present in the upper gum are very small and functionless. The general color is dark bluish gray, often paling considerably below, with white marbling about the lips.

This whale, which was the chief object of pursuit during the height of the American whaling period, was not hunted until the early part of the eighteenth century, but from about 1712, for a century and a half, the ships from Nantucket and New Bedford and smaller numbers from France and Great Britain followed it relentlessly in all the Seven Seas. It is a species particularly of the tropical waters, but recent studies show that "in summer there is a movement towards the temperate seas of the hemisphere concerned. Pairing mainly takes place during this migration and the females give birth to their young in subtropical and temperate waters. A small proportion of the males, though fully active sexually, leave the females at the height of the pairing season and migrate alone into high latitudes, later returning to temperate waters and joining the general movement of the schools towards the equator during winter" (Matthews, 1938a). The species is polygamous, with many more adult females than males in the mating herds. The main pairing season is from August to December, with its peak in October. The period of gestation is about 16 months, and the young one when born is about 4 meters long.

The food of the sperm whale is largely squids, especially of the smaller species, but the males may devour larger species and are said even to attack and eat the giant squids. Sometimes the marks of the large sucking disks of the squids and the scratches from their claws may be seen on the skin. Fish, too, are sometimes found in their stomachs, and Dr. R. C. Murphy has even recorded the presence of a seal's mustachial bristle in the ambergris recovered from a sperm whale.

While found in all the oceans, there were nevertheless favored regions, or "grounds," well known to the whalers of a former period, where these whales congregated, doubtless drawn by abundant food. In a recent account, Dr. Charles H. Townsend (1935) has plotted the localities where, in old logbooks, sperm whales were recorded as killed. The records show that among these "grounds" those off Charleston, S. C., off the Azores, off Brazil, in the western Indian Ocean, east of Japan, and about the Hawaiian Islands and off Perú were famous resorts for sperm whales. The beginning of the decline of this species in the last century came about 1837, or 20 years or more prior to the use of kerosene; hence it is believed that the persistent hunting of the previous hundred or more years had by then seriously depleted the numbers. The substitution of kerosene and later of electricity for lighting purposes undoubtedly saved the species from very serious diminution, yet it was not for a number of years after the introduction of the new illuminants that the numbers recuperated to a visible extent.

The present situation is summed up by L. H. Matthews (1938a) as follows: The sperm whale is taken in numbers at the present time mainly on the Natal, Chile, and Japan "grounds," whereas elsewhere the whalebone whales are those chiefly sought. Yet the total catch for 1934–35 was 2,238, a rather large number, although as Matthews points out, less than the annual catch in the days of American whaling of the last century. Sperm-whale oil and spermaceti are no longer handled separately in utilizing this whale; furthermore sperm oil is not suitable for the purposes of hardening by which the oil from "other (whalebone) whales is converted into margarine or edible fat. Even a small proportion of sperm oil will contaminate that from whalebone whales so as to render it unusable for this purpose. The result is that stations concerned chiefly with catching the latter sorts of whales find the sperm whale a source of embarrassment." The demand for sperm oil is small so that the present whaling industry is not specially tempted to hunt these whales intensively. Since the species is polygamous, and the sex ratio about equal, it would nevertheless be possible to confine the capture to surplus bulls, thus allowing the females to breed and so keep up the stock. Since the larger bulls "segregate themselves during their solitary migration into high latitudes, the unrestricted capture of sperm whales north and south of latitudes 40° N. and 40° S. respectively would be unlikely to affect adversely the world stock of sperm whales, provided all sperm whales between those latitudes were protected." It is the species thus most suitable for such "rational exploitation," but at this time is of relatively small economic importance.

Ambergris is the product of this whale and is sometimes found floating on the sea or cast up on shore, or it may be discovered in the intestines of sperm whales. It is usually in the form of a concretion, perhaps started in the first place by some obstruction, as a squid beak becoming lodged in the intestinal wall. Small squid beaks are found in these lumps, and the mass itself may attain a size large enough to block the intestine and, apparently, cause death. For this reason, in older days, the whalers always opened and examined dead sperm whales found afloat, in the hopes of finding ambergris. The substance may be identified by its minutely layered appearance in fresh section, by the pale chocolate color (poorer grades are black), the presence of minute opaque granules in the section or by occasional squid beaks, by the fecal odor, and by the fact that when burned, as with a hot needle, it gives off a sweetish odor. Its value lies in the fact that it is used by makers of perfumes to hold delicate scents, a property in which it excels other known substances. Frequently persons walking the seabeach in summer find and mistake for ambergris such things as lumps of sewer grease, varnish waste, and wax.

In 1937, by international agreement among those nations

chiefly interested in whaling, it was made illegal to take sperm whales of less than 35 feet in length, so that "cows" will (or should) thus be practically eliminated from the annual catch. The toll will therefore fall upon the bulls, but on account of their polygamous habit, this will permit a large catch without reducing the total males below breeding requisites. It is said also that the sperm whale will receive further protection "by the imposition of close seasons on the various whaling grounds" (Matthews, 1938a).

Family RHACHIANECTIDAE: Gray Whales

CALIFORNIA GRAY WHALE; "DEVILFISH"

RHACHIANECTES GLAUCUS (Cope)

Agaphelus glaucus Cope, Proc. Acad. Nat. Sci. Philadelphia, 1868, p. 160 (Monterey Bay, California coast).

FIGS.: Scammon, 1874, pl. 2 (upper fig.); Andrews, R. C., 1914, pls. 19–27, figs. 1–22 (photographs and skeleton).

In his monograph on this species, Dr. R. C. Andrews (1914) assigns it the rank of a family, intermediate in some respects between the right whales and the fin whales, and recalling in its long straight humerus the extinct *Plesiocetus*. Females are slightly larger than males, attaining as much as 45 feet (1,371 cm.), the males 43 feet. There is no dorsal fin. The throat has two large grooves, one on each side, with sometimes a shorter median one between. The whalebone plates are yellowish white, sometimes with a touch of grayish in the posterior ones, and the frayed portion is the same. They are coarse and thick and relatively fewer than in other large baleen whales, about 138–174 in each rank. There is much individual variation in color, but in general "the head, throat, back, and the dorsal and ventral ridges of the peduncle are black, or very dark slate, and are usually unmarked. On the dorsal and lateral surfaces of the distal half of the rostrum there is considerable white and light gray in flecks and small spots . . . The throat and sides to the pectorals are usually unmarked. From the fins to a point opposite the anus, on the sides, breast and belly, are many roughly elliptical and circular markings with irregular edges." The pectoral fins are dark slate like the body.

This interesting species is apparently at present confined to the North Pacific Ocean. In summer it is found in Bering Sea and in the Okhotsk Sea. Scammon (1874, pl. 5) has pictured them "emerging between scattered floes, and even forcing themselves through the field of ice, rising midway above the surface, and blowing in the same attitude in which they are frequently seen in the southern lagoons." With the coming of autumn they start migrating southward again. At the whaling station in southeastern Korea, Ulsan, Dr. Andrews found them beginning to appear on their southward passage, about the end of November. "Single pregnant females come first and a little later both males and females are seen but the latter considerably outnumber the former. About January 1, schools of from ten to fifteen males, with perhaps one or two females, appear, the female always leading. From the 7th to the 25th of January, when the migration is completed, only males are present, the females all having passed." The young are probably born among the islands at the extreme southern end of the Korean Peninsula. On their passage northward, these whales arrive at Ulsan about the middle of March and by the middle of May have all passed northward. On the American side a corresponding migration takes place, but it is not known whether the herds of the opposite coasts mingle in the northern waters. During October and November they appear off the coasts of Oregon and northern California and from November till February are to be found wintering off the coasts of southern and Lower California, where the young are born in the early part of the year. According to Scammon the bearing season is December to March, and the young are brought forth in quiet lagoons, while the males remain outside offshore. In May or somewhat earlier the whales are passing north again, accompanied by the young.

From an economic standpoint this species seems to have been of some importance in earlier days and was killed with harpoons from small boats, beginning about 1846. Scammon, writing of his experiences in the fifties, tells that the boats' crews pursued these whales in the shallow lagoons of southern California where often the females were very close inshore. Having once got "fast" with a harpoon, the officer in charge went forward in an endeavor to discharge a bomb lance, which, if it did not kill the whale at once, usually paralyzed it sufficiently to allow the boat to come up and lance it. At other times the whalers lay in wait for the gray whales on their passage offshore along the kelp beds and shot them at close range with bomb lances (this was "kelp whaling"). The whale sinks when dead, but after about 24 hours it is buoyed to the surface by the gases of decomposition. The pursuit of the females in the narrow confines of the lagoons and passages was considered much more dangerous than that offshore. The Indians of the Northwest coast also took toll of these whales on their passage northward or southward, and the Eskimo, according to Scammon, killed them farther north. So great became the slaughter that in his day he questioned if the species would not ere long become exterminated.

Dr. C. H. Townsend, in 1886, wrote that of the 11 whaling stations mentioned by Scammon as earlier established along the coast of California only five then remained. From an elevated lookout about 40 whales were seen passing southward in December, 1885, at the San Simeon station. Allowing as many more to have passed by night, and an equal number for January, gave an estimate of 160 whales that might be seen from one point on the shore. Those nearer shore were believed to be largely females seeking lagoons farther south for bringing forth their young, while those farther offshore were probably mostly males. The lagoon whaling, in Lower California described by Scammon, had already been given up as no longer profitable. In the following years, however, this must have worked to the advantage of the species, allowing the remnant to breed up in small numbers, for while in 1880 it had not been possible to kill any gray whales, in 1883–84 the total catch of the southern California stations was 58, in 1884–85, 68, but in 1885–86, as a result of bad weather, only 41. The numbers seem, however, to have been later reduced to nearly the vanishing point. In recent years a very few have occurred on the Californian coast, so that there may be still some chance that if unmolested in its breeding area, the lagoons of Lower California, its numbers may in time recuperate. Grinnell (1933) notes the following recent records: During a period of three and a half years, from 1918 on, five were captured at Moss Landing whaling station on Monterey Bay; two were seen off San Diego on March 5, 1921; one was killed near Crescent City in July, 1926; and finally one was captured off the coast in 1928. A. B. Howell and Huey (1930) believe it "doubtful whether more than a few dozen individuals survive in the eastern Pacific" and add that the individual killed in July, 1926, "was in company with four others and was the only individual of this species ever secured at this station" (Trinidad).

Very little recent information is at hand as to the status of the gray whale in the western Pacific, beyond that supplied by Dr. R. C. Andrews (1914). In 1910 he learned that a Japanese whaling company operated at Ulsan on the southeastern shore of the peninsula of Korea, and on visiting it during the winter of 1911–12 he found that the gray whale formed the basis of its winter fishery. During the months of January and February while he was at the station, 50 or more gray whales were taken. According to C. H. Townsend (1930a) a total of 1,051 were taken from 1910 to 1920 off Japan. Further statistics are given by Harmer (1928, p. 83), who notes that the largest number of this species recorded for the eight years 1919–1926 from the Japanese stations is 78 in 1921; but 114 were taken in 1915, and 105 in 1918. "It is the general opinion of Japanese whalers that the industry is declining, and that the fall is most marked in the case of the Gray Whale, of which an annual average of 81 is recorded for the period 1915–1919, but of only 21 for 1922 to 1926." The figures do not give much encouragement to the belief that the gray whale is slowly gaining ground. It may be necessary to prohibit its killing altogether for a term of years if it is to be maintained at all. In the Convention between the United States and other Powers for the Regulation of Whaling, proclaimed in 1935, no mention of the species is made, but a certain amount of good may ensue if strict adherence can be obtained from the whalers to Article 5, which prohibits "the taking or killing of calves or suckling whales, immature whales, and female whales which are accompanied by calves (or suckling whales)." Since the young are brought forth in midwinter on the coasts of Lower California and southern California and among the islands just south of Korea, and would be accompanying their mothers on the northward migration in spring (April and May), such a prohibition would be effective in preserving a certain proportion, while in the Arctic waters frequented by these whales in summer the amount of hunting is probably negligible. Unfortunately, Japan is not a signatory to this treaty. With the expiration of the 1935 agreement a similar one was entered into in June, 1937, by which the gray whale was given complete protection by the nations signing the treaty; again Japan, the nation most affected, was not included among these. The killer whale is the chief natural enemy apart from various parasites. Dr. Andrews has described how, when a school of these voracious whales appears, the gray whales become at times paralyzed with fear, and lie at the surface belly up, often to have their tongues and lips bitten by the killers.

That this whale may formerly have occurred in the North Atlantic is indicated by the recent discovery of parts of a skull identified as of *Rhachianectes*, in beds of the Glacial period in Holland (Junge, 1936). In modern times, however, it is unknown outside of the North Pacific.

Family BALAENIDAE: Right Whales

PYGMY RIGHT WHALE

NEOBALAENA MARGINATA (Gray)

Balaena marginata Gray, Zool. Voyage *Erebus* and *Terror*, p. 48, 1846 (off Western Australia).

SYNONYM: *Balaena antipodarum* Gray, Proc. Zool. Soc. London, 1864, p. 203 (Jackson Bay, New Zealand).

FIGS.: Beddard, 1901, pls. 7–9 (skeleton); ? Wilson, E. A., 1907, fig. 2, opposite p. 4 (blowing); Hale, 1931, figs. 1–4.

Very little is known of this whale, for on account of its small size and perhaps actual fewness of numbers it does not enter into commercial catches. As a species possibly decadent, however, it may deserve mention here.

The pygmy right whale resembles the other members of the right whale family in the arched and narrowed forepart of the cranium, in the absence of a coronoid process on the lower jaw, the complete fusion of the seven neck vertebrae, and in the absence of throat folds. On the other hand, it is like the fin whales in having a small dorsal fin of fibrous tissue, in the elongated form of the shoulder blade, and in having but four instead of five fingers in the hand. Peculiar to it are the extremely broad ribs, the few (two) lumbar vertebrae, the long narrow plates of whalebone which are whitish, with a dark outer margin. Total length when adult, about 20 feet, of which the head forms about one-fifth.

Beyond the few specimens captured in fishing nets or stranded on the shores of Western and South Australia, New South Wales, Tasmania, and New Zealand, almost nothing is known of the habits and distribution of this remarkable little whale, which in some ways seems to combine characters of both right whales and fin whales, though evidently most nearly allied to the former. Hale (1931) has given details of the measurements of three individuals reported many years before from South Australian waters, and adds record of a fourth. These are: One stranded at Brounslow, Kangaroo Island, October 21, 1884, the skeleton of which is in the South Australian Museum; a second tangled in a fishnet, at Victor Harbor, Encounter Bay, September 13, 1887, and now in the same museum; a third from Kangaroo Island, October 21, 1889, and now in the Museum at Cambridge, England; and a fourth of which a photograph is given, from West Sister Island, Bass Strait, June, 1929. Lord and Scott (1924) mention one washed ashore at Kelso Bay, Tasmania, "many years ago." Oliver (1922) mentions that a very few specimens have been stranded on the New Zealand coast and that there are skeletons in the Dominion Museum at Wellington. There is a mounted skeleton in the Australian Museum at Sydney, New South Wales, from Canterbury coast, New Zealand, and there are two in the British Museum, one of them from Stewart Island, New Zealand; a second skeleton from this island is in the Dominion Museum, as well a skull from Kawau. Finally a skeleton from probably Stewart Island is in the Paris Museum. It is evident that the present known range of the species is limited to the seas about New Zealand and the southern parts of Australia. E. A. Wilson (1907), however, believed that this was the whale he saw commonly in the Ross Sea where he met with it constantly "wherever there is loose pack ice. It is a black or dark grey whale of from 20 to 30 feet in length, with a very rounded back, and a small hook-like dorsal fin which slopes well backwards . . . As a rule this whale was solitary; occasionally two or three, but never more were seen together." While such identifications made at sea may not always be relied on, Wilson's observation may be quoted for what it is worth. At all events, the species does not enter into recent whaling statistics for the Ross Sea, and while at present it is probably exempt from capture on account of its small size, it may nevertheless someday be pursued in Australian waters if it is found to occur regularly.

North Atlantic Right Whale; "Nordcaper"; "Black Whale"

Eubalaena glacialis (Borowski)

Balaena glacialis Borowski, Gemeinnüzzige Naturgesch. Thierreichs, vol. 2, pt. 1, p. 18, 1781 (North Cape, etc.).

Synonyms: *Balaena nordcaper* Lacepède, Hist. Nat. des Cétacées, 4to ed., p. 103, 1804 (North Atlantic, between Spitsbergen, Norway, and Iceland); *Balaena biscayensis* Eschricht, Rev. et Mag. Zool., ser. 2, vol. 12, p. 229, 1860 (San Sebastian, Bay of Biscay, Spain); *Balaena cisarctica* Cope, Proc. Acad. Nat. Sci. Philadelphia, 1865, p. 168 (opposite Philadelphia, Pennsylvania).

Figs.: True, 1904, pls. 42–46 (exterior and skeleton); Collett, 1909, pls. 25–27 (photographs).

Southern Right Whale

Eubalaena australis (Desmoulins)

Balaena australis Desmoulins, Dict. Classique Hist. Nat., vol. 2, p. 161, 1822 (Algoa Bay, Cape of Good Hope).

Synonyms: *Balaena mysticetus antarctica* Schlegel, Abth. Gebiete Zool., pt. 1, p. 37, 1841 (in part) (Cape of Good Hope); *Hunterius temminckii* Gray, Ann. Mag. Nat. Hist., ser. 3, vol. 14, p. 349, 1864 (Cape of Good Hope).

Figs.: Matthews, 1938c, pls. 12–17 (photographs and drawings).

North Pacific Right Whale

Eubalaena sieboldii (Gray)

Balaena sieboldii Gray, Ann. Mag. Nat. Hist., ser. 3, vol. 14, p. 349, 1864 (North Pacific Ocean).

Synonyms: *Balaena aleoutiensis* Van Beneden, Bull. Acad. Belg., Bruxelles, ser. 2, vol. 20, p. 854, 1865 (Aleutian Islands); *Balaena japonica* Gray, Zool. Voy. *Erebus* and *Terror*, pp. 15, 47, 1846 (not of Lacepède).

Fig.: Scammon, 1874, pl. 12 (drawing).

Although the right whale of the southern oceans and that of the North Pacific are believed to be probably racially distinct from the North Atlantic right whale, the diagnostic characters, if any, are not well made out. Lönnberg (1923) has compared skeletons of the latter with a skeleton of the southern right whale from South Georgia and regards the differences as of taxonomic importance. Further comparisons in series are needed to establish the validity of the supposed races or species. Since all are essentially similar in general appearance, they may be considered together here, as separate populations.

The right whales are of stout, massive proportions, the head forming about a quarter of the total length and having the rostrum much narrowed and strongly arched to accommodate

the longest plates of whalebone, which are black and measure
up to 7 feet or slightly more in length. There is no dorsal fin,
and the throat is without grooves. The fore limb is nearly
squarish in outline. Lower lip very deep, the lower jaw bones
much bowed outward. Fingers of the hand five. Color black,
often with a certain amount of white on the lower surface.
Length of the North Atlantic right whale seldom exceeds 50
feet over all; the longest measurement, from tip of snout to
notch of flukes, in five southern right whales was 15.23 meters
(about 49.5 feet); longest whalebone plate, 2.05 meters.

On account of its relatively slow movements and its predi-
lection for coastal waters, this whale had since early times been
the chief object of pursuit with simple hand apparatus in boats
putting out from shore. This was probably the whale taken
by the Norwegians off the Tromsö coast as early at least as the
ninth century; hence "the history of whaling naturally begins
with this species, which was hunted by the Basque inhabitants
of the Biscay coasts of France and Spain. The industry was
important as early as the twelfth century, as is shown by documentary evidence . . . The Biscay Whale is a migratory
animal, and it formerly appeared close inshore on the Basque
coasts during the winter and early spring months . . .
Even this limited hunting seems to have produced the effect
of driving the whales from the coast, a conclusion which is
supported by the fact that the Basque sailors found it necessary
to undertake long voyages, in pursuit of whales, about the
middle of the 17th century, or even earlier." As early as the
fifteenth century these people had reached the Newfoundland
waters. After 1800 the species was nearly exterminated in
European seas. Meanwhile the Pilgrims, on reaching New
England in 1620, found right whales in abundance, and it
seems likely that, as on the European coast, the animals arrived early in autumn and passed southward to the Carolina
coasts in part, and in part wintered northward to Massachusetts Bay. In spring came a general northward movement to
the seas about southern Greenland and Iceland for the summer.
The New Englanders pursued these whales eagerly for over a
century, when, as the numbers declined and voyages were
made to sea, the industry of shore whaling was gradually given
up, "terminating about 1700 on the European side of the Atlantic and about 1800 on the American side. [The right

whale] had become excessively rare, and for many years it was believed to be extinct" (Harmer, 1928). "About 1850 the Biscay Whale began to re-appear . . . and by 1880 it had become the object of a moderate whaling industry off the Eastern United States. Some ten years later a few individuals began to be caught by Norwegian vessels off Iceland and the Faeroe Islands; and since that time an appreciable number have been taken by whaling stations off the West of Ireland and the Outer Hebrides." Catches made at the Scottish stations from 1908 to 1914 totaled 67, or an average of about 10 a year, and 18 were taken by Irish stations between 1908 and 1910. The Scottish catch was made chiefly in June. Thus there is evidence that the North Atlantic population had recovered slightly after about a century of comparative immunity from pursuit, but it has certainly not again reached its former abundance nor does the right whale now frequent the old wintering area on the Biscay coast.

In the first half of the last century, when whaling ships from Massachusetts made round-the-world voyages of several years in pursuit of whales, they took right whales on the coasts of South Africa and again in the North Pacific, although most of their hunting was in warmer waters for sperm whales. The North Pacific population seems likewise to have been migratory, for according to Scammon (1874) some were taken as far south as "the Bay of San Sebastian Viscaino, and about Cedros or Cerros Island, both places being near the parallel of 29° north latitiude" in northern Lower California, from February to April, after which they were taken from April to September on the "North-west Coast." "In former years," Scammon wrote, "the Right Whales were found on the coast of Oregon, and occasionally in large numbers; but their chief resort was upon what is termed the 'Kodiak Ground,' the limits of which extended from Vancouver's Island northwestward to the Aleutian chain, and from the coast westward to longitude 150°. In the southern portion of Behring Sea, also upon the coast of Kamschatka, and in the Okhotsk Sea, they congregated in large numbers." On the western side of the Pacific they came southward at least to the seas about Japan. Scammon states that the average yield of oil of the North Pacific right whale is 130 barrels, but in earlier days individuals of large size might give twice that amount. So vigorous was the hunting for this species in the early half of the last century that according to Bolau, between 1846 and 1851 there were 300 or 400 whaling ships engaged in its pursuit on the Kodiak grounds from April to September. At that time, too, the use of the bomb lance had just come in, and its deadly effect was that the right whale was soon practically exterminated from these waters. According to Harmer (1928) "the Japanese appear to have formerly hunted this Right Whale, in their own waters, from an early period, but it seems to have become rare in the North Pacific, and it is not mentioned in recent returns from that area." On the California coast, Grinnell (1933) gives the last report known to him as of one found near San Simeon, about 1885. While few recent figures for the capture of this whale at the Japanese stations are available, Townsend (1930a) has compiled statistics for the years 1910 to 1920 (both inclusive), from which it appears that right whales formed a very small percentage of the catch, varying from none to as many as seven or eight annually, with an average of three and a fraction. In the 11 years the total number taken was but 35 in a grand total of 17,862, or 0.002 per cent. From 1928 to 1936, other statistics show a total of 36 right whales taken. Evidently the North Pacific stock has been depleted to nearly the vanishing point.

The intensive pursuit of the southern right whale hardly began until the opening decade of the last century, when it was found in large numbers in the southern oceans mainly between latitudes 30° and 60° S. It was "particularly numerous in coastal waters of the southern part of the African and American Continents, Australia and New Zealand . . . It was the subject of a large fishery which, by the destruction of the females and young on the breeding grounds, reduced the numbers of the species to so low an ebb that its capture was abandoned. • According to Harmer (1928), 193,522 Southern Right Whales were captured from 1804 to 1817, an average of 13,823 annually." The charts compiled by Townsend (1935) from old log-books show the position of capture of over 6,000 of these whales by American whalers between 1785 and 1913. From these it is evident that most of the positions lie between latitudes 30° and 50° S. In June and July (the southern winter) these whales were on there wintering and breeding grounds in the northern part of this area. A favorite place was Walvis Bay on the southwestern coast of Africa. With the coming of the southern spring and summer, the right whales moved southward toward polar waters "in a well-defined band right across the oceans of the world between" latitudes 30° and 40° S. "Later in the season, from January to March, hunting was carried on farther south and was particularly intensive around the Crozets and Kerguelen" (Matthews, 1938c). There was thus a wide tropical belt between latitudes 30° S. and 30° N. in which practically no right whales were taken. The fact that the southern stock was moving southward at a time when the northern stocks were retreating to north temperate latitudes tended to continue this separation, and it is believed that for a long period there has been little if any mingling of northern and southern populations. This supposition, if true, would give some ground for the belief that racial differences between the stocks might have developed through practical isolation at least within Recent times.

With the recommencement of intensive whaling in the Antarctic waters and with the use of modern methods, a few southern right whales were taken in the earlier years of the present century. The statistics given by Townsend (1930a) for the nine seasons 1909–10 to 1917–18 show an annual catch of from 6 to as many as 82 right whales, but after the latter date no more in the next four seasons. At the South Shetlands in these years smaller numbers were taken (less than 60 in nine years). Only three were captured in the five seasons 1923–27 in the Natal waters. In all, Townsend records 410 right whales taken in the southern waters between 1909 and 1927, out of a total of over 122,000 for all large whales. There is some evidence, however, that the abundance of rorquals led to the capture of these latter as easier than making any special effort to take right whales. Nevertheless, it is clear that the former abundance of the latter has already been reduced to well beyond the danger point and that from the first they have formed a very inconsiderable percentage of the total whales destroyed. Whether the species will ever recuperate sufficiently to become commercially important again seems at present doubtful. Under the new International Agreement for the Regulation of Whaling, of 1937, the right whales of all species are given complete protection, thus extending the protection given them by the Norwegian Whaling Act of 1929.

As with other large whales there is normally but a single young one at a birth. According to Millais, the northern right whale bears a young one every two years, and suckles it for 12 months, but precise information on these matters is still a desideratum. The adult whales feed chiefly on "krill," or small pelagic crustaceans particularly of the genus *Euphausia*, like other whalebone whales.

Greenland Whale; Bowhead

Balaena mysticetus Linnaeus

Balaena mysticetus Linnaeus, Systema Naturae, ed. 10, vol. 1, p. 75, 1758 (Greenland seas).

SYNONYMS: *Balaena mysticetus* var. *roysii* Dall, in Scammon, Marine Mamm. Northwestern Coast, p. 304, 1874 (Okhotsk Sea); *Balaena mysticetus* forma *pitlekajensis* Malm, Bihang til Kongl. Svensk. Vet.-Akad. Handl., Stockholm, vol. 8, no. 4, p. 37, figs., 1883.

FIGS.: Scoresby, 1820, vol. 2, pls. 12, 12 (bis); Roy. Nat. Hist., vol. 3, p. 7, fig.; col. pl. opposite p. 8, 1894-95.

The bowhead, or Greenland whale, attains a length of up to about 60 feet, but Captain Scoresby in his account of the species gave credence to a report of up to 67 feet. The enormous head forms about a third of the length, and thus is larger in proportion than in the right whales. The skull differs from that of the latter in having its narrow rostrum much more arched, to accommodate the longer whalebone plates, of which the longest usually measured about 12 feet or slightly less, and were from 10 to 12 inches wide at the base. The inner edge frays out into fine brownish fibers. As in the right whales, there is no dorsal fin, and the throat is without folds. The large pectoral limbs are short and squarish and have five fingers in the skeleton. The general coloration is velvety black on the back, most of the upper jaw, and part of the lower jaw, as well as on the fore limbs and tail. The fore part of the under jaw and lips, sometimes the tip of the upper jaw, and a varying portion of the belly are white. The details of the pale areas vary individually, and Scoresby mentions having seen whales that "were all over piebald." The same author, whose personal experience was wide, states that the yield of a large whale would be upwards of 21 tons of oil or approximately 5,300 gallons; yet this might vary a great deal according to the condition of the animal. The weight of a 60-foot whale is said by Scoresby to be 70 tons.

In the seventeenth and eighteenth centuries this was the most valuable of the various whales that were hunted. The large yield of oil and the value of whalebone at that time often made a profit if even one whale were taken during a cruise. The bowhead is remarkable on account of its distribution, for it is a wholly Arctic species, found most of the year close upon the edge of the ice pack in Arctic waters, following it northward in spring, and retreating a short distance to the southward with the coming of winter. The food of the bowhead is said to be plankton in the form of small pelagic crustaceans, such as copepods and shrimps, as well as the small mollusks of the pteropod type, all of which swarm in Arctic seas.

Three groups or populations of these whales were recognized by the whalers. The first inhabited the waters in the neighborhood of East Greenland, Jan Mayen, and eastward to the Spitsbergen Archipelago, where they were especially abundant. The second centered in Davis Straits and Baffin Bay, migrating in winter as far south as the Gulf of St. Lawrence and in summer penetrating northward to Lancaster Sound and Barrow Strait to Melville Sound; and into Hudson Bay with the breaking up of the ice. The third population was found in the seas about Point Barrow, Alaska. In winter the whales of this group migrated through Bering Straits to the Okhotsk Sea and Bering Sea, and in spring returned, passing Point Barrow to the eastward as soon as the ice pack opened there. It is uncertain how far to the westward on the Asiatic side they penetrated. These three groups seem to have been kept more or less apart by their geographic isolation, yet it is likely that there was occasionally some intermingling, particularly of the two latter populations, in proof of which is often mentioned the case of a whale killed in the Bering Strait region, with a Dutch harpoon embedded in it, that was thrown at it by the whalers about Spitsbergen.

Although the Basque whalers are believed to have taken this whale on the south coast of Newfoundland at Grand Bay at an earlier date, its intensive pursuit began about 1611. In this year the Dutch discovered Jan Mayen Land, while in the same year Thomas Edge of England was sent by the English Muscovy Co. on a whaling expedition to Spitsbergen. Here the bowhead was found in such abundance that in the following years Dutch, Danish, Hamburger, and Basque vessels were actively killing them. The unsuspicious whales at first were

easily taken, and their blubber was tried out on shore while
the vessel remained at anchor in some bay where operations
centered. The crews of the nations whaling here frequently
engaged in hostilities, so that it became necessary for a time to
divide the Spitsbergen coast among the several nationalities.
Meanwhile the Dutch whalers were busy at Jan Mayen pursuing this species there. In the course of two decades of this
slaughter the whales became scarce in the bays of Spitsbergen
though still for a time plentiful in the adjacent seas, so that
the carcasses could still be towed into some harbor and the oil
tried out on shore. "But as the whales increased their distance it became necessary to take the blubber on board, and
the ships could enter port only occasionally. The blubber had
to be packed in casks and the oil was extracted at home, after
the conclusion of the voyage. The factory buildings in Spitsbergen had become useless, and Scoresby remarks that several
of them were still to be found in 1671" (Harmer, 1928). With
the opening decades of the eighteenth century, the fishery in
these seas, which had begun to decline even by 1640 or thereabouts, was now almost unprofitable. The few whales still to
be found were sought along the borders of the ice pack in
places difficult of access and at a distance from land.

At about this time the Dutch in 1719 began whaling in
Davis Strait, and the activities thereafter centered on the west
coast of Greenland. The pursuit eventually was chiefly carried on by whalers from England and Scotland and continued
actively for nearly two centuries. Some idea of its magnitude
may be gained from the figures given by Scoresby (1820, vol.
2, pp. 128–131), who presents a table showing that in the four
years ending with 1817 a total of 586 vessels was sent out to
the fishery from British ports alone, and their total catch was
5,030 whales, practically all of which were bowheads. The
Dutch between 1719 and 1778, took nearly 7,000 in Davis
Strait and Disco Bay. Nevertheless, as Harmer points out,
this slaughter was small compared to that lately carried out in
the Antarctic waters against the fin whales. In 1851, vessels
began wintering over in Cumberland Sound, Baffin Island, in
order to be on hand at the breaking up of the ice in spring.
Vessels equipped with steam penetrated through Lancaster
Sound to Pond Inlet, and other waters where whales still could
be found following open water along the edge of the ice pack.

After 1840 the diminishing number of whales caused a gradual falling off in the industry, but a few whalers continued to sail annually from Dundee and Peterhead. "From 1887 there were not more than 10 ships in any year, and with this number the catch generally averaged less than 2 whales a ship. The largest total after 1887 was 29, obtained in 1893 by 5 ships. In 1910, 18 whales were caught by 10 ships; and in 1911 only 7 by 8 ships. The discouraging results of that year are indicated by the fact that only 1 ship left Dundee in 1912 and 1913, and that the total catch in each of those years is returned as 0" (Harmer, 1928).

With the practical extermination of the Davis Strait population, attention was next directed to the Bering Sea stock. "In 1848 Captain Roys was the first whaler to pass through Bering Strait to the Arctic Ocean, where he found whales innumerable, some of which yielded two hundred and eighty barrels of oil" (Harmer, 1928). Most of the whaling here was carried on by American whalemen, in increasing numbers. "The first whaling ship to venture east of Point Barrow to Herschel island was the *Newport* in 1888. It returned west without wintering. The *Newport* and other ships lured by the new whaling ground came to winter in 1889, and by 1893 one-fourth of the vessels whaling in the North Pacific and Arctic spent the winter around the mouth of the Mackenzie River. In 1894–1895 fifteen vessels, with about 800 men, wintered at Herschel Island, Yukon Territory. Ships occasionally spent the winter at Cape Bathurst and on two occasions as far east as Langton Bay. As the ice in this part of the Arctic presses in close to the land and is never far away, the whaling season varied from six weeks to a maximum of three months for ships which wintered. During the latter years of the whaling business in the Western Arctic, whales were hunted chiefly for the baleen or 'whalebone,' and the oil and other products were largely disregarded. This was inherently an extravagant and wasteful exploitation of one of the few natural resources of the region, but with whalebone selling at $4 or $5 per pound, high profits might be made, in spite of lean years and casualties. Catches of 64, 67, and 69 whales per ship in a two-year voyage were recorded. The season of 1893 was the high year of the Western Arctic whaling fleet, with 309 whales taken . . . The whaling industry in the Western Arctic lasted only about

25 years.   One ship and one gasoline schooner, the only vessels
which whaled in Beaufort Sea, killed twelve whales apiece
during the summer of 1912, but the voyages were considered
unprofitable on account of the unsaleability of whalebone"
(R. M. Anderson, 1937).   As Dr. Anderson in the excellent
summary just quoted has pointed out, the short era of whaling
was a great moment to the local Eskimos through developing
their interest in trapping and offering them a market for fur.
He concludes his account by calling attention to the encouraging fact that "the suspension of whaling operations for many
years seems to be bringing the number of Bowheads up again
to some extent and their future is assured until such time as the
increase in numbers is sufficient to arouse commercial interest
again.   Fortunately for them, highly organized methods of
pursuit are restricted by the difficult ice conditions and any
great reduction in numbers of whales automatically renders
whaling operations unprofitable.   The most valuable use of
this species of whale seems to be as a subsidiary food and fuel
supply for the Eskimo people."

How far Eskimo may become dependent upon this species
of whale for food and fuel is an interesting speculation.   For
example, R. W. Gray (1935, pp. 75–77) in calling attention to
various earlier records (1696, 1812, 1813, 1866) of Eskimo
harpoons of East Greenland type found in whales killed in
Spitsbergen seas, suggests that the Eskimo of that region may
have died out because they depended too largely on Greenland
whales for their flesh, oil, and whalebone.

As to the present status of the bowhead, it has been believed
that the herd between East Greenland and Spitsbergen was
quite extinct.   However, Ruud (1937) has lately adduced evidence that may indicate the existence of a very few within
recent years.   Thus he is inclined to credit a report of a whaler
who is positive that he saw one in 1917 in the ice between
latitude 64° and 65° N., off East Greenland.   A still later report
is given of four bowheads shot "by mistake" in 1932 near the
edge of the ice pack north of Spitsbergen.   A slab of whalebone
from one of these whales measuring 3.85 meters in length was
preserved in the Marine Museum in Norway and thus established the identity.   Probably then a very few bowheads are
still in existence in the Spitsbergen seas.   They were probably
never quite exterminated in the Davis Strait and Baffin Bay

region, and the few that still remain may in time increase. Dr. R. M. Anderson (1935) has reported one that was driven by killer whales into an ice lead near Pond Inlet in 1922 and shot by a native; and two were reported to him as seen near Kingua, Cumberland Sound, in 1928. The population centering in Baffin Bay must, however, be reduced to very small numbers. Nevertheless bowheads still come into the northern part of Hudson Bay annually, though probably not now do they go so far south as formerly, when they were found at least to Churchill. Dr. Sutton and Dr. Hamilton (1932) in their report on mammals of Southampton at the north end of Hudson Bay record a number of bowheads seen or killed: two in November, 1924; one in 1926; five seen and one killed in October, 1926; a young one seen by Eskimos in 1927; a large one killed at Seahorse Point, September 17, 1928; in 1929 a large one killed near Leyson Point, and half a dozen were seen together on September 25. Since the killing of these whales (as being "right whales") was abandoned by the Norwegian whalers in 1929, and is prohibited by the International Agreement for the Regulation of Whaling of 1937, they are likely to have a long respite except for the occasional killing of one by Eskimos, so that the gradual recuperation of the stock is to be looked for. There are small numbers left in the western Arctic Ocean, which may be expected to increase, as noted by Dr. Anderson. Indeed, in a recent note, F. Rainey (1940) has given a graphic account of the pursuit and capture of bowheads off Point Hope, Alaska, by the local Eskimos using a hand harpoon with a bomb in its "nose" as well as an old model "shoulder gun." The season lasts there from early April until June 10. He adds, exuberantly, "There are scores of them, all bowhead . . . The number is simply unbelievable. We have seen at least 20 every day." Evidently the stock is responding well to the reduced persecution.

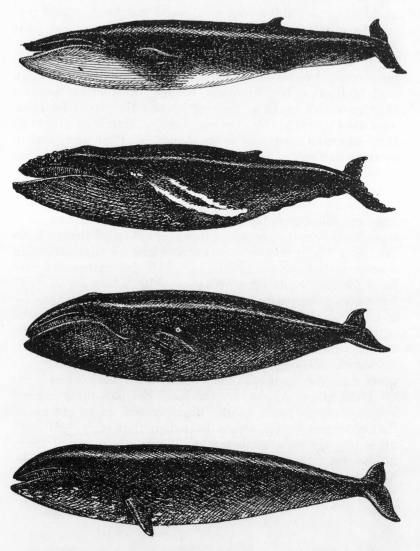

From top to bottom: Lesser rorqual (*Balaenoptera borealis*); humpback whale (*Megaptera novaeangliae*); Greenland whale (*Balaena mysticetus*); California gray whale (*Rhachianectes glaucus*).

Family BALAENOPTERIDAE: Fin Whales

COMMON FINBACK WHALE

BALAENOPTERA PHYSALUS (Linnaeus)

Balaena physalus Linnaeus, Systema Naturae, ed. 10, vol. 1, p. 75, 1758 (European seas).
SYNONYMS: See Allen, G. M., 1939, p. 265, for list.
FIGS.: True, 1904, pls. 1–6, 8–12 (photographs of exterior and skeleton); Mackintosh and Wheeler, 1929, pl. 25, fig. 2 (col.), pls. 32–34 (photographs).

The finback whale is found the world over in all oceans and with the blue whale forms the mainstay of the modern whaling industry. Although it can hardly be said that it is in present danger of extermination, nevertheless the enormous numbers annually destroyed make it imperative that whaling be conducted with proper regard for the reproduction and perpetuation of the species.

This is the second largest of living whales, attaining a length of about 65 feet, or even up to 82 feet in the female. The long, slender body is a dull brownish gray in life, except that in the middle of the under side it is pure white. There is a large falcate fin in the middle of the after part of the back. The throat is thrown into a number of branching lengthwise folds, of which there may be 70 to 80 between the pectoral limbs. The whalebone plates are more or less variegated in stripes of purplish or yellow, and the anterior third or so of those on the right-hand side are all white, a remarkable case of asymmetry.

The finback whale is found in all the seas but is most abundant in those of the Temperate Zone, or in special regions where its favorite food of small shrimps (*Euphausia*) and other pelagic crustaceans and small fish is to be had in quantities. It is somewhat social, often gathering in small schools or larger associations where attracted by abundant food.

In former times the finback was very rarely attacked by whalemen, for occasional attempts usually resulted disastrously because of the strength and swiftness of the animal. It was not until the invention of the more deadly bomb lance by Svend Foyn in 1865 that the attention of whalers was seriously turned to the rorquals, while the growing scarcity of the more valuable right and sperm whales proved an added stimulus. Soon the bomb lance was improved, and in the latter decades of the nineteenth century the Norwegians began using small staunch iron steamers fitted with a whale-cannon in the bow and steam winches for handling the "line," a stout hawser attached by an iron ring in the slot of the harpoon shank. The whales when shot were then "fast" to the steamer, and if not very soon killed they could be played until they were exhausted, and then lanced from a boat. Since the rorquals usually sink when dead, there was an immediate advantage over the earlier method of awaiting the return of the carcass to the surface buoyed up by gases of decomposition; for the dead whale could be towed at once to the shore station, to be there disposed of. This method of whaling was at first carried on extensively on the Norwegian coast, then extended to Spitsbergen waters. In the last decade of the nineteenth century several stations sprang up on the south coast of Newfoundland. Here finback and blue whales were at first abundant, and additional "factories" were set up on the east coast and along the coast of southern Labrador. However, the supply of whales soon became scarcer, and most of the stations closed, although a number of others have continued in operation on the Irish coast and in British Columbia and Alaska. In the early years of the present century, with the discovery that fin whales abounded in the seas near South Georgia, the South Shetlands, and South Orkneys, activities became in large part transferred to the Southern Hemisphere. Here the industry has flourished, so that in recent years more than half the whales annually killed are taken in this region. According to the figures compiled by Sir Sidney F. Harmer (1931) for the year 1928–29, the total kill of finback whales for the world was 9,132, of which 6,689 were taken in the Antarctic. Statistics for the years from 1925 to 1929 in the general regions of South Georgia and neighboring seas show that there was a marked decline in sexually mature females amounting to 20 per cent in the last over the first year. It seems very likely on further study that "whales do not wander at random throughout the Antarctic area, but are to some extent separated into assemblages which have preferences for particular localities." The result of singling out the largest animals in hunting is to reduce the number of mature whales in any given assemblage, so that a gradual decline is noticed among this class.

There is accumulating evidence that in the Southern Hemisphere, as presumably also in the Northern, there is a migration of these whales into higher latitudes with the coming of summer. A certain number of adults seem to spend the winter in the Antarctic, but the number declines to a low point in August or September. After the end of December there is a distinct increase, and the whales push farther south. In the North Atlantic a similar movement probably takes place. At least on the New England coasts finbacks are commoner in summer, following the schools of herring into Massachusetts Bay, for example.

Although the numbers of finback whales is still large, statistics already indicate that local declines occur where intensive hunting is carried on. Overfishing will undoubtedly lead to a repetition of the depletion suffered by other species, if persisted in for a long period. It is therefore a first step in correction of this abuse that the recent International Agreement for the Regulation of Whaling forbids the taking or killing of any finback whale less than 55 feet long. Calves, sucklings, or females accompanied by them are likewise protected, and there are restrictions as to the use of whale-catchers and floating factories and designated periods over which whales may be hunted. Thus in the 1937 regulations, any given area of waters may not be fished for more than six months of a year, and this period shall be continuous. No more whales than a given factory is equipped to handle shall be killed at a time, and the carcass must be as fully utilized as possible.

Apparently the chief use now made of the oil is in the manufacture of oleomargarine and soap.

LESSER RORQUAL; SEI WHALE; POLLOCK WHALE

BALAENOPTERA BOREALIS Lesson

Balaenoptera borealis Lesson, Hist. Nat. Gén. et Partic. Mamm. et Oiseaux, Cétacés, p. 342, 1828 (Gromitz, Lübeck Bay, Schleswig-Holstein).

SYNONYM: *Balaenoptera laticeps* Gray, Zool. Voy. *Erebus* and *Terror*, Mamm., p. 20, 1846 (coast of Schleswig-Holstein).

FIGS.: Andrews, R. C., 1916, pls. 29–42, text-figs.; Matthews, 1938b, pls. 18. 19.

The Sei whale, as it has come to be called by the whalers, is much like a small finback externally, attaining a length of up to 57 feet. The number of throat folds is less than in the finback, 40 to 62, more or less, including the shorter ones, between the pectoral limbs. These folds end evenly on a transverse line well anterior to the unbilicus. The general color of the body above varies a good deal but is some shade of gray, usually lighter than in the finback, but sometimes darker. The midventral region is white about as far back as the middle of the body and considerably in advance of the ends of the throat folds. The whalebone is distinctive in being black, and fraying into fine *white* fibers at the free end of the plates.

Harmer (1928) states that this species is "found rather farther from the poles than the Fin Whale, as a general rule, and is thus specially numerous off such localities as Cape Colony, Natal, and Angola in the south, and Japan and Norway in the north. It appears in tropical records from the French Congo and Ecuador . . . The numbers of this species in successive seasons are often very unequal." It feeds chiefly on small pelagic crustaceans. It is apparently nowhere so common as the finback but may be expected in the temperate seas of the world.

Although described by Rudolphi early in the nineteenth century, little was known of this whale until about 1881. In August of that year, Svend Foyn, who had previously paid little attention to these whales because of their small size, captured one in Varanger Fjord. In 1882 a whaling station was established at Sörvaer, near Hammerfest, western Finmark, and here the Sei whale proved to be a common species and became the object of a regular fishery. In the spring of 1885, according to Collett, it appeared "by thousands" along the entire Finmark coast and continued until early in September; another great invasion took place in the same waters in 1898. In 1903 Dr. F. W. True reported that four Sei whales had lately been taken at the whaling station in Placentia Bay, Newfoundland. In 1912, when Dr. Roy C. Andrews visited the whaling stations in Japan, he found the whalers taking it there and adduced reports of its capture at the Vancouver Island station in May, 1913. Meanwhile the first one to be reported from South African waters was taken off Saldanha Bay, Portuguese West Africa. Since these earlier reports, the Sei whale has been found to occur commonly in the southern oceans, as about South Georgia, where it is taken in numbers by the whalers in some seasons, while in others it appears to be nearly absent. Thus in the 16 seasons from 1913 to 1929, a total of 1,318 Sei whales was taken at South Georgia, of which 93 percent were killed in the months of February, March, and April (the southern summer), considerably after the peak season for the blue and finback whales, and at a time when the sea temperature is highest. Small numbers have been taken in the last decade off the coast of California.

Matthews (1938b, p. 277) has summarized the study made of these whales in southern waters, from which it appears that during several seasons from 1923 to 1927 the catch at Natal and in the Cape Province of South Africa has varied from some 50 or 75 to in some years as high as 350. The external characters of the southern whales do not seem to differ from those of the North Atlantic or Pacific animals. "The migrations of the Sei whale consist of a feeding migration to the south in the southern summer and a breeding migration towards the north in the winter. Parturition and pairing occur mainly in tropical and sub-tropical waters. Lactation is mainly finished by the time the whales arrive on their southern feeding grounds . . . The neighbourhood of South Georgia represents the approximate southern range of the migration." The main part of the pairing season in the southern oceans is from May to August, with the peak in July. The period of gestation is about 12 months. According to Matthews the evidence of the internal genitalia shows that the species "breeds once every two years, with a period of anoestrus of about 6 to 7 months between the end of lactation and the beginning of the next pregnancy." "Sexual maturity is reached at an age of about 18 months, and breeding first occurs at the end of the second year after the birth of the whale." It is clear from these facts that with only a single young at a birth, the rate of increase is bound to be relatively slow.

Though this whale is not as yet in any obvious danger of serious depletion, and on most of the world's whaling grounds is of minor importance, nevertheless, Matthews (1938b) points out that "when the serious diminution in numbers of the larger and more profitable species, which appears to be imminent, arrives, this species will suffer considerably and will be in danger of being reduced to a very small remnant in a short time." Among other factors that might conduce to this result is the sex ratio, in which it appears from a study of embryos and adults that males occur in a ratio of about 60 percent, so that the number of young would be less than in species in which the ratio were more nearly equal. Moreover, says Matthews, this ratio is often obscured in a study of whales killed, since the whalers select the larger females. The yield of oil is small, about 10–15 barrels per whale; those from South African waters are found to have thinner blubber than those from the Antarctic Ocean. While the International Agreement for the Regulation of Whaling, of 1937, does not specifically protect this whale, it seems likely that other general regulations may have that effect, such as the prohibition of the killing of finbacks under 55 feet long and the prohibition against killing females accompanied by suckling young; also the restriction of hunting in any given area to six consecutive months in a year may act as a further favoring condition in some regions.

BRYDE'S WHALE

BALAENOPTERA BRYDEI Olsen

Balaenoptera brydei Olsen, Tidens Tegn (Norwegian newspaper), Nov. 12, 1912; Proc. Zool. Soc. London, 1913, p. 1074 (Saldanha Bay, west coast of South Africa).

FIGS.: Olsen, 1913, pls. 109, 110 (exterior); Lönnberg, 1931, pls. 1–6 (skeleton).

Very little is known of this whale, which was first described in 1912. Dr. R. C. Andrews (1916) pointed out that it resembles the Sei whale in general, but the dorsal fin is less high. The distinguishing features are said by its describer to be, in addition to the shorter dorsal fin, the fewer ventral folds (42–54), extending back to the umbilicus instead of ending in advance of it; baleen plates fewer (250–280 in each rank) and shorter (longest 50 cm. long); bristles of the baleen very thick, long, and stiff, not curling, and gray in color; the anterior baleen more or less white, the rest grayish black; color of the throat dark bluish gray, the under side behind the anus white. Total length, 13–15 meters; females larger than males.

The species seems now to be recognized as probably valid. Nevertheless the whalers regard these whales as perhaps hybrids between the Sei whale and one of the other fin whales, as the common finback. More recently Lönnberg (1931) has figured and described the skeleton and believes the species a distinct one. Externally the extension of the throat folds to the umbilicus and the stiff bristles of the whalebone may be diagnostic, but on the other hand there are many resemblances to a small finback.

In addition to the coastal waters of South Africa, from Natal to Angola (13°–14° S.), where the species has been taken in small numbers, it has also been reported in the catches made in recent years on the coast of California, Grenada, in the West Indies, where two were said to have been killed in 1925, and on the coast of Norway in 1927, but these last records may hardly be accepted without confirmation and rest on identification by the whalers.

In South African waters this whale is said to come closer inshore than the other large species and to feed on small crustaceans (*Euphausia*) and small fishes. In 1911 six were taken at Durban, Natal, and sixteen the following year. In 1924, on the coast of southern Angola, 32 were reported taken, and in 1925 seventeen. Whaling there seems to have ended shortly after these years. It is evident that at present this species is taken in small numbers only and may not play much part in commercial whaling. However, with the increasing use of smaller whales, as the larger species diminish, it may eventually be more assiduously pursued.

BLUE WHALE; "SULPHUR-BOTTOM WHALE"

SIBBALDUS MUSCULUS (Linnaeus)

Balaena musculus Linnaeus, Systema Naturae, ed. 10, vol. 1, p. 76, 1758 ("In Mare Scotico," i. e., Firth of Forth, Scotland).
SYNONYMY: See Allen, G. M., 1939, p. 268.
FIGS.: True, 1904, pls. 13–21 (exterior); Miller, G. S., Jr., 1924b, pls. 1–3 (skull); pls. 4–9 (other parts of skeleton).

The blue whale is often referred to as the largest living mammal. As the prime object of the southern whalefishery during the past quarter century, it is now becoming reduced in numbers, at least in parts of its range, to a point indicating danger, if further depletion of the stocks continues.

Attaining a maximum length from tip of snout to notch of flukes up to 93.5 feet, it is characterized, among other features by the small, low, triangular fin far aft on the midline of the back; by the general dark blue-gray color of the body, mottled with paler oval marks and marbled irregularly on the throat with whitish flecks; by the convex margins of the rostrum; and by the coal-black whalebone plates, which fray out on their inner margin into coarse, black bristles. The number of these plates in a rank averages around 325, with a considerable variation according to sex and size. Females grow slightly larger than males. The ventral grooves extend as far back as a point slightly behind the umbilicus and average around ninety between the pectoral limbs, with again a wide variation.

On account of its great size, strength, and swiftness, the blue whale was not molested by whalers of earlier generations, whose hand tackle was quite inadequate for its capture, so that the species was known only from occasional individuals that were cast ashore from time to time. Various technical names were based on such individuals, but at the present time the evidence for recognition of more than the single species is insufficient. With the development of more powerful tackle and the application of the whaling gun, shooting a hundred-pound harpoon from the bow of a small steamer, this with the finback whale has become the main object of pursuit by modern whalers. The yield of oil, in spite of the relative thinness of the blubber as compared with that of the right whales, is proportionally more than in the finback, up to at least 70 or 80 barrels on an average as against 35 to 50 or more for a finback of adult size. Moreover, as with the latter, the oil is adaptable to the hardening process for making margarine, while the glycerine content is high, about 17 percent, so that it is in high demand as an ingredient of the finer grades of glycerine soap as well as of such explosives as nitroglycerine.

"The introduction of Svend Foyn's harpoon-gun, in 1865, revolutionized whaling, and the invention was made at a time when Right Whales and Sperm Whales were becoming difficult to obtain . . . When Svend Foyn had perfected the harpoon-gun in the latter part of the 'sixties, and had commenced operations in the Varanger Fjord on the Finmark coast of Norway, Blue Whales were the only object of his pursuit. With the entry of new companies, Fin Whales, Humpbacks, and Sei Whales were also caught" (Harmer, 1928). Ere long, however, the blue whales became scarcer and the pursuit shifted to more distant waters. Two whaling stations were started by Russians on the Murman coast, and in the later years of the century others were in operation at Spitsbergen, Iceland, the Faroe and Shetland Islands, and on the coasts of Newfoundland and Labrador, British Columbia, Japan, and Korea. The blue whale is a species that seems more particularly to be found in colder waters, although avoiding for the most part the Arctic seas; yet it occurs also in the Tropics and like other fin whales apparently makes seasonal migrations to and from the colder waters in summer and the warmer seas in winter. The discovery, early in the present century, of the abundance of fin whales in the Antarctic seas, especially in the region of South Georgia and in Ross Sea, resulted in centering the pursuit to southern waters beginning about 1905. The seas about South Africa, from Walvis Bay on the southwest coast around to Natal on the southeast, as well as the coast of Chile, likewise proved to be prolific "grounds." The catch of blue whales in these areas often exceeded that of the finbacks. Many have been taken also on the Lower California coast in recent years. In the statistics given by Harmer (1928) for various stations in the North Atlantic, the catch of blue whales appears in late years as a very small percentage of that for finbacks and humpbacks or other species. One may infer, therefore, that in this part of the ocean the numbers are much depleted, and probably at best did not compare with the abundance in the southern oceans.

The statistics published by Dr. Remington Kellogg (1931) for Alaska, British Columbia, Washington, and California, for the years 1919 to 1929, show that the blue whales taken were on the whole about half as many as finbacks and somewhat less than a fourth as many as the total of humpbacks. From 1925 to 1929, however, the figures were greatly increased by the taking of large numbers off Lower California, from 150 to 239 yearly, while the numbers for Alaskan stations ranged in the 11 years from only 16 to as high as 81, and in British Columbia usually considerably less. The numbers of blue whales frequenting the relatively shallow seas about Lower California were commented upon by Captain Scammon (1874) many years ago, and he recounts attempts to capture them by shooting bomb lances into them, but evidently the degree of success was slight, and the whale was usually lost even if hit. Dr. Kellogg's figures show a total of 1,994 blue whales taken on the west coast of North America between 1919 and 1929.

About 1906 the pursuit of the blue and other whales in the Antarctic commenced in earnest with the arrival of an expedition under Captain Christensen at the Falklands in December, 1905, and his subsequent departure for the South Shetlands in the following January. His total catch included 24 blue whales. In subsequent years the seas about South Georgia, the South Shetlands, and South Orkneys were the principal localities where whaling was carried on in the Antarctic. In 1923 Captain C. A. Larsen commenced operations on a larger scale with a floating "factory," accompanied by five "whale-catchers," and he extended his field into the Ross Sea. Meanwhile, from 1910 on, the cool waters about South Africa were being intensively searched for blue whales and other species. Laurie (1937, p. 270) has presented in tabular form the annual catches made in the Antarctic and South African seas, respectively, from 1904–5 to 1935–36. At the latter localities the catch is taken in the southern winter, and soon after 1913 it rose to large figures up to over 300 annually; in 1922–23 it was 1,074; and in the years 1925–26 and 1926–27 attained a maximum of over 1,700 (1,744, 1,743, respectively). Thereafter began a rapid decline to as few as 71 in 1933–34, the last year for which statistics were available.

In the past 15 years the numbers killed in the Antarctic seas have risen to an appalling total. Between the years 1927–28 and 1935–36 the number annually taken fell but once below 12,000 and in one year (1930–31) reached the peak figure of 29,410! It is pointed out by Laurie and others that the high percentage of immature whales taken on the African coasts makes "this fishery proportionately more destructive than the more southerly fisheries," in which a larger proportion consists of adults.

Studies of the whales caught, as carried on by the *Discovery* Investigations, demonstrate that the female blue whale becomes sexually mature when a length of about 78 feet is attained. At birth the young one is approximately 23 feet long, and attains breeding size at the age of about two years. The period of gestation is approximately a little over ten months. The whales continue to grow slowly for about ten years. Breeding takes place probably once in three years or "once every two years at best," as shown by the study of ovaries and the count of *corpora lutea* in those killed. It is obvious that this rate of increase is rather slow but is offset by the probability that under usual conditions a blue whale should live to be at least 30 years old.

As to the prospect for the future, it seems clear that the northern stocks of the blue whale are much depleted and that although the southern stock was perhaps originally the more abundant, it too has in recent years declined rapidly. This is in part proved by the fact that the average length of the total catch in the years from 1930 to 1936 is slowly falling off, with a particularly sharp drop of nearly two feet, in 1934–35, to 78.99 feet, or nearly the critical point when the whales become sexually mature. These newly mature individuals are thus killed before they have had opportunity to breed. Furthermore, the statistics compiled by Laurie (1937) for the southern stations show in the same years a rapidly rising increase in the proportion of immature females killed, amounting to over 41 percent of the total female catch in 1935–36, against nearly half as many in 1932–33. This means not only that an increasing proportion of the whales arriving at breeding stage leave no increase, but also that an increasing part of the young animals is destroyed before it attains reproductivity. "The consequences of continued intensive fishing under these conditions cannot fail to have a disastrous effect on the future of the stock. When killing has reached the point at which recruitment, already dangerously reduced, shall have virtually ceased, one may say that the future of Blue whaling will be limited to the lifetime of those whales now surviving" (Laurie, 1937, p. 266). The present rate of recruitment is believed insufficient to maintain the stock of blue whales in southern seas under the present intensity of whaling operations. "The stock is already seriously depleted and further hunting on the same scale bids fair to make Blue whales so scarce that they will cease to be a source of profit to the industry and so diminished in numbers that the stock even if completely protected may take many years to recover" (idem).

Hitherto little progress has been made in remedying these conditions. The only specific protection accorded blue whales by the International Agreement for the Regulation of Whaling, of 1937, is that none shall be killed less than 70 feet in length, thus removing most of the immature animals from the commercial class, but since the breeding condition is not reached for females until they attain a length of about 77 or 78 feet, the complete protection of near-breeding stock is not accomplished. Other general restrictions as to the killing of females accompanied by calves, the limited use of floating "factories," and the limitation of a hunting season to six months in any sector of waters will, it is hoped, prove beneficial, but it is clear that the present wholesale destruction must be reduced in intensity.

Humpback Whale

Megaptera novaeangliae (Borowski)

Balaena novae angliae Borowski, Gemeinnüzz. Naturgesch. Thierreichs, vol. 2, pt. 1,
p. 21, 1781 (New England coast).
Synonyms: *Balaena nodosa* Bonnaterre, Tabl. Encyclop. Méth., Cétologie, p. 5, 1789
(New England coast); *Balaenoptera australis* Lesson, Hist. Nat. Gén. et Partic. des
Mamm. et Oiseaux, Cétacés, p. 372, 1828 (Cape of Good Hope); *Balaenoptera
capensis* A. Smith, South African Quart. Journ., vol. 2, p. 130, 1834 (Cape of Good
Hope); *Megaptera versabilis* Cope, Proc. Acad. Nat. Sci. Philadelphia, 1869, p. 17.
For other synonyms see Allen, G. M., 1939, p. 266.
Figs.: True, 1904, pls. 29–41 (exterior and skeleton).

The humpback whale is at once distinguished from the other
large whales by the great length of the pectoral limb, which is
27 to 31 percent of the total length, with an irregularly knobbed
fore edge, and by the few throat folds, which number about 28
(21–36) between the pectorals. There is a low and irregularly
shaped dorsal fin at about the last third of the length. The
baleen and its bristles are coarse in texture, the plates varying
from gray to almost black, and the bristles from white to
grayish white. The color shows a wide range of variation from
nearly all blackish, with slight mottling on throat and lower
side, to a condition in which almost the entire throat and the
sides of the body fairly high up, as well as much of the pectoral
limb are white. Total length, about 45 to 47 feet.

This whale, though more agile than the right whales, was
nevertheless easily approached and often was killed without
great difficulty, so that occasional individuals were regularly
taken on the New England coast by the whalers as early at
least as 1757. The fishery seems to have been carried on in a
small way during Revolutionary times and into the first
quarter of the nineteenth century, when vessels from Nantucket
or Provincetown frequently went on short cruises to Mount
Desert, Nantucket Shoals, or other nearby waters in their
pursuit. With the coming into use of the bomb lance probably some of these whales were taken in Massachusetts waters
by whalers from Provincetown in the seventies and eighties,
using small steamers. The whales, if mortally hit, came to
the surface in a few days and, if retrieved, were towed ashore
and there tried out. This ceased, however, during the last
decade of the nineteenth century. Still earlier, at the close of
the seventeenth century and during the century following,

whales (probably in part of this species) were taken regularly about the Bermuda Islands.

In the last quarter of the nineteenth century the humpback became a regular object of pursuit at the whaling stations established on the coasts of Finmark, where the modern methods of capture with harpoon guns were instituted. At the close of the century, whaling stations were set up on the south coast of Newfoundland, and many humpbacks were taken during the summer season in those waters. Shortly after, stations were started on the Pacific coast, Alaska, British Columbia, and Washington, and in southern California, where, after about 1925, floating factories operated for a few years. Dr. Remington Kellogg (1931) has compiled statistics of the annual catches made by the stations at these four places for the period 1919–1929, from which it appears that the humpback "for a number of years outnumbered any other species . . . although the oil yield is not especially high in these waters. A yield of 33 barrels is generally expected of Humpbacks taken off the California coast, while at the Alaska stations the average yield is about 30 barrels for an adult whale." The total number of this whale taken in these eleven seasons was 7,295 or nearly half of the grand total of over 15,000 for six or more species.

Early in the present century intensive operations were begun against the humpbacks and other large species in the southern oceans, more particularly in the seas about South Africa and South Georgia, and to a less extent in the Australian waters.

At the South Georgia stations, Matthews (1937) has shown that while during the first season or so of intensive hunting large numbers of humpbacks were taken (in 1910 over 6,000), the catch after that dropped rapidly and, except for the 1915 season, never again exceeded a few hundred. This seems to be but a repetition of the story of other regions where humpbacks have been hunted; for "whenever new whaling grounds have been opened up the Humpback whale has always been the predominant species in the catch for the first few years, and has then rapidly declined in numbers. This is partly due to the fact that when whaling was started, in, for instance, South Georgia and South Africa, the plant then available was not suitable for dealing with any numbers of the larger species of whale. After a few years, when better facilities were installed, fewer Humpbacks were taken. Nevertheless the taking of the larger species coincided with a definite decrease in the numbers of Humpbacks available . . . The whalers state that the decrease in its numbers is due to its being frightened away from its former haunts, but there seems to be no valid reason why this species should be more easily frightened than any other, unless it is very attached to certain definite lines of migration. There appears to be some evidence in support of this possibility . . . The decrease in numbers, however, is probably due partly to excessive slaughter, because the Humpbacks have never returned in their former huge numbers to South Georgia. Their capture is now prohibited there, except under special license, given only when other species are very scarce" (Matthews, 1937, p. 82). At first, from 1908 onward, humpbacks were taken in very large numbers at the South African whaling stations as at Durban, but the more recent figures (Matthews, 1937) show a decline from the 1924 peak of nearly 200 to less than 100 in 1927. During the same years the catch of blue and finback whales was maintained at between 500 and 600 annually.

In the waters of Western Australia a similar phenomenon was observed. In 1913 a total of 654 was taken; in the next year, 1,900; in 1915, less than 900; and in 1916, less than 200. The whales taken were evidently "on their way to and from their breeding grounds a little to the north" so that as a result of the inroads on their numbers, the pursuit was abandoned as less profitable than other trades. It was renewed, however, in 1925, when of some 670 whales taken the greater part were humpbacks.

Matthews (1937) concludes that "the reason for the great decrease in numbers of Humpback whales, off the South African coast at any rate, is not far to seek . . . Most of the catch at the South African whaling stations consists of immature whales, and in addition . . . whaling in these localities is conducted during the breeding migration, so that it is small wonder that a species so harassed is becoming scarcer. In southern seas the catch consists predominantly of mature animals on their feeding migration, and the decrease in numbers there is probably due not only to excessive slaughter on the southern grounds but also to the killing of large numbers of breeding and pregnant whales in temperate and tropical latitudes."

In the southern oceans, the investigations of recent years show that the migrations of the humpback are seasonal. In the southern summer they have a "feeding migration" to the southward, and then in the southern winter they migrate toward the Tropics for breeding. "Parturition and pairing occur mainly in tropical and subtropical waters. On its northward migration the species regularly crosses the equator, at least on the west coast of Africa, for a distance of about 10° of latitude. Occasional migration of individuals from the schools of the southern hemisphere to those of the northern hemisphere is extremely probable" (Matthews, 1937). There is evidence that in the Northern Hemisphere there is migration northward in the northern summer, and southward toward the Tropics in autumn and winter, at a time when the southern schools would be in the reverse state of movement, so that much mingling of the two groups would be less likely.

The investigations of the *Discovery* Committee show that sexual maturity is reached at an age of 20–22 months, and breeding first occurs at the end of the second year after birth. Humpbacks probably breed once in two years, although occasionally pregnancies may occur twice in three years. The period of gestation is about 11 months; the single young at birth is about 4.5–5 meters long; it nurses for about five months and is weaned when about 7.5–8 meters long. The pairing season in the case of the southern schools is mainly from August to November, chiefly in September so that the peak of births falls in August, with a season from July to September.

Matthews (1937) further points out that "the great destruction of the stock of Humpback whales during the last thirty years is attributable solely to excessive slaughter both during the feeding and breeding migrations. The stock can only return to its former abundance, on which modern whaling in the south was founded, if the Humpback whale is afforded complete and world-wide protection for a long period of years. If, thereafter, the stock is to be maintained, catching would have to be carefully controlled, and restricted to the whaling grounds of the far south." By the International Agreement of June, 1937, it is forbidden to take humpback whales of less than 35 feet in length, while calves and suckling whales, or adult females accompanied by them, are not to be killed.

Order SIRENIA: Sea-cows

The sea-cows are completely aquatic in habit and somewhat fishlike in external form. They are thought to be distant relatives of the elephants. Three Recent families are recognized, each with a single genus:

(1) Dugongidae, the dugong. This sirenian occurs in the Red Sea, along the coasts of East Africa, Ceylon, the islands of the Indian Ocean, the Malayan Archipelago, the Philippines, and northern Australia. It is in need of protection.

(2) Hydrodamalidae, Steller's sea-cow. The single species had no teeth and was restricted to two small islands in the northern Pacific. It was exterminated by the Russian hunters.

(3) Trichechidae, the manatees. Three species (the Florida manatee is considered a race of the West Indian species) are still extant. Manatees occur in tropical and subtropical America and the west coast of Africa.—J. E. H.

Family DUGONGIDAE: Dugongs

Dugong

Dugong dugon (P. L. S. Müller)

Trichecus dugon P. L. S. Müller, Linnaeus's Vollständigen Natursystems, Suppl., p. 21, 1776 (Cape of Good Hope to Philippines).
Synonyms: *Halicore hemprichii* Ehrenberg, *in* Hemprich and Ehrenberg, Symbolae Physicae, Mamm., dec. 2, folio k, footnote, 1832 (Barkan Island, Red Sea); *Halicore lottum* Hemprich and Ehrenberg, Symbolae Physicae, Mamm., dec. 2, folio k, footnote, 1832 (Hauakel Island, Red Sea); *Halicore tabernaculi* Rüppell, Mus. Senckenbergianum, vol. 1, p. 113, pl. 6, 1834 (Red Sea); *Halicore indicus* Desmarest, Encycl. Méth., Mammalogie, pt. 2, p. 509, 1822.

Australian Dugong

Dugong australis (Owen)

Halicore australis Owen, *in* Jukes' Narr. Voyage *Fly*, vol. 2, p. 323, 1847 (Endeavour Strait, North Australia).
Figs.: Prater, 1928, pls. 1–4; Dollman, 1933, figs. 1–6 (exterior and skull).

The dugong is found in warm tropical and subtropical coastal waters from eastern Africa to the Philippines and Formosa, as well as southward to the east coast of Australia, and eastward again to the Solomon Islands. Although separate names have been given to those from the Red Sea and from Australian waters, it is not at all certain whether these represent distinguishable forms or what the characters are if they deserve recognition. Dollman (1933) found on comparing skulls from the East African coast with others of about the same age from Australia that the former were "much less massive and smaller" than the latter. In view of the present uncertainty the supposed forms may be considered together. On account of the palatability of the flesh this animal is much hunted wherever found and hence is in danger of reduction.

The dugong is in external form much like a cetacean, spindle-shaped in body, with the tail ending in lateral flukes, which are notched in the median line and pointed at the outer end. The skin is of a blue-gray color, lighter below. The fore limbs are flipperlike, but the hind limbs have disappeared in modern forms; eyes are small, the ear-opening a minute pore. The muzzle forms a flat disk, with a vertical cleft in the center, and with short spines on its lower part, while a few short bristles are present on the upper part. The nostrils open separately at the summit of the snout. The skull is remarkable for the downward bend of the rostrum, which in the male has a pair of short tusks, the second pair of upper incisors. The cheek teeth are six in number, but with age the smaller ones drop out in front, and the posterior ones wear down, until there may be but a single one left, the last in the series. Length, up to 10 feet.

Although the type locality of the dugong as given in Müller's original description is Cape of Good Hope to the Philippines, the former region is probably to be taken only in a general sense; at all events at the present day it is not apparently found farther south on the East African coast than Delagoa Bay, Mozambique (latitude 26° S.), where Barrett (1935) mentions seeing several adults and a "calf" caught in fish traps by the natives, in 1908–10. It is occasionally taken also in fish nets on the coasts of Madagascar and the neighboring small islands, and on the Tanganyika coast. According to Kaudern (1915) it was more often hunted formerly in Madagascar than now, though occasionally seen offered in the markets at Analalava; Petit shows that 20 years ago it was fairly common, but now is much more restricted among these islands. On the coast near Lamu, Kenya Colony, Arthur Loveridge (*in* G. M. Allen and B. Lawrence, 1936, p. 125) says that according to native report it is still fairly common, and one was brought to him there in 1934; but although the meat has a high commercial value, its captors refused to let him have the skull for $2.50!

Anderson and De Winton (1902), quoting a paper by Krauss, of 1870, on specimens collected by Klunzinger at Kosseir near the head of the Red Sea, speak of the dugong as then "apparently plentiful," going in small groups of two to ten. They appeared annually on the Nubian coast, especially near Aesa, and in December and January moved northward at least to the island of Safadje. They are little seen by day but appear to be more active, probably feeding inshore, by night. The single young one is born in winter, and the period of gestation seems to be about a year. Maj. S. S. Flower, writing in 1932, says that it is "now rare on the [Red Sea] coast of Egypt," seldom coming farther north than latitude 25° N., but to the southward it was not uncommon. The Arab fishermen prize the teeth highly. De Beaux (1931) writes that it is captured off Raheita, southeast of Assab, more frequently than elsewhere in the nets of the fishermen; the meat is said to be tender and well flavored and is much esteemed locally. He strongly urges its protection in the Red Sea and Somali coastal waters. It is an interesting fact that since the opening of the Suez Canal a female of this species was reported by Aharoni (1930, p. 330) as having been killed by fishermen from Tantura, about halfway up on the coast of Palestine, in a shore cave; but the possibility of this having been a monk seal should not be overlooked.

Passing eastward, Blanford (1876) writes that although reported by Murray as occurring on the Persian coast, he knew of no certain record of its presence on the west coast of India farther north than Canara, nor did he know of it from any part of the Arabian coast east of Aden. It is, however, still found on the coasts of Ceylon. In Tennent's time (before 1863) it was apparently common "from the bay of Calpentyn to Adam's Bridge," and about the Gulf of Manaar, but W. W. A. Phillips (1929) implies that it is no longer found in any numbers there and "appears to be in danger of extermination, if not protected." Millett (1914), however, speaks of it as "plentiful in and about the Gulf of Manaar . . . It is frequently caught in the large shallow lagoons near Trincomalie, where it enters the narrow mouths at high water in search of a certain kind of food of which it is very fond, and where it gets stranded by the receding tide, when it is easily captured." A more recent note from A. C. Tutein Nolthenius (October, 1936) states that small numbers may still be found in the shallow seas off the northwest coasts of Ceylon, to the north and northeast coasts. Fifty years ago it appears to have been much more common and somewhat more widely distributed than today. Its flesh is eagerly eaten by certain castes of the indigenous population and is in special demand because of its reputed aphrodisiacal properties. The animal is therefore taken whenever opportunity offers. Usually it is caught in nets spread among the coral reefs, to the vicinity of which it resorts during the northeast monsoon. At one time a considerable number were sent by train, alive, to Colombo, for sale in the fish market, but the practice has been stopped in recent years on the score of cruelty. The dugong is in no way protected at present, and its numbers are becoming much depleted. Unless given some measure of protection very soon its extermination in Ceylon waters may be accomplished at no very distant date. Prater (1928), a decade ago, wrote that the dugong was becoming increasingly scarce in Indian coastal waters and that recommendations were about to be put forward for its protection during part of the year.

Eastward, the dugong occurs in small numbers in the Straits of Malacca, on the Siamese coasts, on the coasts of Sumatra and Borneo, eastward to the Philippines, and thence follows the Japanese current northward even to Formosa and the

Australian dugong (*Dugong australis*)

Riu Kiu Islands, or farther. According to Ridley (1895, p. 165) it was "tolerably common in the Strait between Johore and Singapore; but one does not often see it. However, the Chinese sometimes catch it in nets when fishing, and sell it in the markets as food." In the Philippines it "occurs along all coasts from the Batan Islands at the northern extremity" of the group "to the Sibutu group east of the northern part of Borneo. It is not abundant anywhere, but is well known to all fishermen. It is harpooned or captured in fish corrals, but is taken more accidentally than otherwise" (Herre, 1928, p. 1072). While there are no recent records for Chinese waters, it very likely was once found on the southern coasts, for as lately as 1931 one was captured near Tai-jyu-bo, on the west coast of Formosa and its skull secured by Hirasaka (1932). This author also adduces some interesting information on the former abundance of the dugong in these seas. He adds the report of two others taken the same year at Haikau, a port near Koshun, and states further that many decades ago dugongs were "fairly abundant in the water[s] surrounding the Ryukiu Islands and Amami-oshima . . . and were hunted eagerly for flesh and oil. This hunting was carried on regularly once a year by feudal lords for tribute in Aragusuku Island, near Ishigakishima . . . I have heard from an old fisherman that once one was caught in a large trap seine for yellowtails, off Abratsu, a port on the eastern shore of Kyushu about thirty years ago." The present condition of these animals, he states, "is rather deplorable" as they are "on the point of extinction and are extremely rare" in these waters. However, the Government of Formosa, on advice of the Committee for the Preservation of Natural Monuments, "intends to forbid the capture of this animal or the disturbance of its resorts."

While the dugong seems to be mainly prized for its flesh, which is said to resemble pork or bacon (or "between beef and pork") and for its oil, hide, and even tusks, we learn from an old work published in 1665, concerning the famous mission of de Goyer and de Keyser from Batavia to Canton and Peking, that the Chinese held in high esteem certain stones found in the heads of these sea-cows, which they say have the property of clearing the kidneys of every kind of sand and gravel and of removing obstructions from the lower parts afflicted by them. These "stones" were very likely the dense tympanic bones of the dugong. Sowerby, in discussing this matter, states that so far as known to him there is no record in Chinese literature of the dugong's occurrence in the coastal waters of that country.

Whether the Australian dugong is identical with that of the East Indian and Formosan waters is still uncertain. It formerly ranged southward on the east coast to at least Moreton Bay, and probably still farther, for skeletal remains have been found at Botany Bay, New South Wales. It is common along the northern coast in tropical waters and occurs on the west coast at the present day, as far at least as Sharks Bay. Somewhat north of this point, in the Kimberly district, Dampier, in his account of 1688, found it in plenty, and relates that "our strikers brought home Turtle and Manatee [i. e., dugong] every day, which was our constant food" (Troughton, 1932, p. 176). Various recent writers agree that on the northern, western, and eastern coasts of Australia it is now getting scarcer owing to continued persecution.

In his excellent account of the dugong, Troughton (1928, 1932) says that in 1893 large herds were a common sight in Moreton Bay, Brisbane, and fishing or netting was carried out there and at Hervey Bay, but the slow breeding of the animals has usually put a stop to ungoverned slaughter. They are not so plentiful now between Brisbane and Cairns, eastern Queensland, and range round the north coast of Australia to Broome on the west coast. In July, 1893, a herd in Moreton Bay was reported as extending over a length of about 3 miles with a width of 300 yards. The main method of capture by whites was with strong coir nets of a yard mesh, which are not usually more than 300 feet long and 25 meshes deep, anchored at the ends and buoyed with floats. About 50 years ago (ca. 1890), fishing was conducted with the use of a schooner as a floating station and smaller boats for netting, but the venture proved unsuccessful, probably because of the rapid diminution of the quarry. In 1922 Banfield deplored the increasing rarity of dugong and attributed this largely to their slaughter by the crews of Japanese vessels fishing in the waters of northern Australia for trochus and trepang. They depended for meat on the dugong, which they harpoon from small boats. Pearling crews also kill many for food. In this destruction the aborigines also play a certain part, but though this, Troughton believes, "may hardly constitute a vital menace," their employment by Europeans in hunting dugongs may do so. He especially points out that "their increasing scarceness, defencelessness, and slow rate of breeding render it essential that the protection at present afforded them should be extended for all time and rigorously enforced."

The dugong is presumably altogether a vegetarian, browsing on certain marine plants that grow in shallow depths. In eastern Australian waters, stomach examinations by Drexler disclosed two species identified as a *Halophila* and a species of eel-grass (*Posidonia*). Hirasaka (1932) states that the stomach of the one reported killed in Formosa in 1931 was said to contain "quantities of marine algae and crabs," but the account was obtained at secondhand and one may doubt if the crabs were part of the diet. Perhaps other foods will be found to be eaten. Such knowledge is essential to any intelligent reservation of certain waters as sanctuaries for them.

Troughton (1928) summarizes the use made of the dugong in past years in Australia. "They are hunted for their flesh, which is both nutritious and tasty, and, when rolled and smoked can be converted into a substitute for bacon for which there was a ready sale some years ago. A more important product is the oil obtained from the blubber; this is cut into cubes and boiled in water from which the oil is skimmed and refined for medicinal use in the treatment of lung complaints and rheumatic troubles. It is estimated that a fully grown female in good condition will yield sufficient fat to supply from five to six gallons of oil. The hide, which is nearly an inch thick, makes very good leather when well tanned, and when cut up green and boiled can be converted into glue. Tusks attain a length of nine inches, and when polished make handsome carver handles, while the bones are said to provide the best charcoal for sugar-refining."

As long ago at least as 1863, the oil was believed to be of excellent medicinal value and was in considerable demand in lung troubles. Gould (1863, vol. 1, p. xxxix) wrote that it was "preferred to cod-liver oil, as being less disagreeable to the palate and more easily retained in the stomach." It is doubtful, however, if its properties are in any way superior to many other animal fats and oils.

There can be little doubt, writes Dollman (1933), that dugongs are in need of protection at the present day since they are being killed off wholesale for food purposes. This is especially true of those around the coast of Tanganyika Territory and Mafia Island, in the Red Sea, and probably Northern Australia.

Family HYDRODAMALIDAE

STELLER'S SEA-COW

HYDRODAMALIS STELLERI Retzius

Hydrodamalis stelleri Retzius, Kongl. Svenska Vet.-Akad. Nya Handl., Stockholm, vol. 15, p. 292, 1794 (Bering Island).
SYNONYMS: *Stellerus borealis* Desmarest, Mammalogie, pt. 2, p. 510, 1822 (Bering Sea); *Manati gigas* Zimmermann, Geographische Geschichte, vol. 2, p. 426, 1780 (Bering Sea).
FIGS.: Brandt, J. F., 1846, pls. 1–5 (outline of body; skeleton); Simpson, G. G., 1930, fig.; Stejneger, 1936, pl. 21.

The history of the extermination of this large sea-cow has been written. It was the largest of the known sirenians, attaining a length of about 24 feet, with a relatively small head in proportion to the body and with a tail of the dugong type, with lateral flukes. Its skin was of a dark brown color, sometimes spotted or streaked with white. The fore limbs were paddlelike and covered with short brushlike hairs, but the hind limbs as usual were absent. The skull showed a rostrum only slightly deflected downward and was entirely toothless. There were 19 pairs of stout ribs, with some 37 lumbar and caudal vertebrae.

In 1741 Bering and "his accomplished companion, the German naturalist Steller," were shipwrecked on what is now called Bering Island, one of the Commander Islands off the east coast of Kamchatka. While here Steller discovered this huge sea-cow, and his account of it is the basis of most of our knowledge. It seems to have been fairly numerous about the coasts of this and the adjacent Copper Island, living in the shallow bays and feeding upon the abundant growth of laminarians. Following the explorers came Russian traders and fur hunters, who found the animals easy to kill with harpoons and for a time slaughtered them in numbers and lived high on the meat. "Its restricted distribution, large size, inactive habits, fearlessness of man, and even its affectionate disposition towards its own kind when wounded or in distress, all contributed to accelerate its final extinction," which was practically accomplished hardly more than a quarter of a century later, by 1768.

On various occasions expeditions have since visited the islands without finding any further evidence as to the precise date of extermination. Nordenskiöld, however, believed from what he could learn that it might have persisted into the nineteenth century, but there seems no definite ground for this supposition. Bones have been collected by various naturalists. J. F. Brandt in his Symbolae Sirenologicae (1846 and 1861–68) described and figured the skeleton and added a résumé of the animal's history from the account of Steller. According to Kuntze (1932), the Russian naturalist Dybowski in 1879–85 collected reports and skeletal remains at Bering Island; he was told by the natives there that the great sea-cow still survived at the time of the arrival of the permanent settlers, which would extend the period of its existence to about 1830. He mentions also as a contributing factor to its extinction the formation of ice along the coast from time to time, thus restricting still further its available territory. Stejneger (1887), who visited the islands and collected many skeletal remains, has written an excellent account of the history of its passing. He believes that its supposed abundance may have been exaggerated, for Steller only says that he found it numerous. Stejneger would regard "fifteen hundred as rather above than below the probable number . . . There are hardly more than fifteen places on the [Bering] island which could afford them suitable grazing grounds, and if each of these were regularly visited by an average of one hundred animals, one would easily be impressed by their number." At the neighboring Copper Island there were probably even fewer, for in 1754, when Jakovleff visited it, the sea-cows had already been exterminated, only nine years after the island's discovery. From 1743 until 1763, "hardly a winter passed without one or more parties spending eight or nine months in hunting fur-animals there [Bering Island], during which time the crews lived almost exclusively on the meat of the sea-cow. But that is not all, for more than half of the expeditions which wintered there did so for the express purpose of laying in stores of sea-cow meat for their farther journey, which usually lasted two to three years more . . . From 1763 the visits to Bering Island seem to grow scarcer . . . probably due to the

very fact that sea-cows had now become so nearly exterminated
that the few left were insufficient to maintain any wintering
and foraging expedition." The animals were harpooned from
eight-oared boats or attacked by individual hunters who would
stealthily approach one lying close inshore or in shallow water,
and "wound it mortally by thrusting the iron-shod pole into it.
The animal, which was hardly ever killed outright, sought the
high sea and died there. If it drifted ashore the same day,
well and good; but in most cases it came in unfit to be eaten,
if it was not carried away altogether. So impressed was
Jakovleff with the extreme wastefulness of this method that
he predicted the speedy extermination of the sea-cow unless
some precautions be taken against this senseless slaughter."
Within thirteen years the result turned out as he expected!

As Stejneger (1887) points out, "there can hardly be any
doubt that these animals were the last survivors of a once more
numerous and more widely distributed species, which had been
spared to that late date because man had not yet reached their
last resort. It is, then, pretty safe to assume that this colony
was not on the increase and that, under the most favorable
circumstances, the number of surviving young ones barely
balanced the number of deaths caused by the dangers of the
long winters. Under this supposition, every animal killed by
a new agency—in this case by man—represents one less in the
total number." Slow and of stationary habits, unsuspicious,
and without means of defense or escape, its disappearance,
Stejneger asserts, "was simply due to man's greed." Brandt
(1846) in his monograph writes: "Stupiditas animalis summa
fuit!"

Steller's sea-cow (*Hydrodamalis stelleri*)

Family TRICHECHIDAE: Manatees

WEST INDIAN MANATEE

TRICHECHUS MANATUS MANATUS Linnaeus

Trichechus manatus Linnaeus, Systema Naturae, ed. 10, vol. 1, p. 34, 1758 ("In Mari Americano"; fixed by Thomas as West Indies).

SYNONYMS: *Manatus koellikeri* Kükenthal, Zool. Anz., vol. 20, p. 40, 1897 (Surinam). For other and older synonyms, see Hatt, 1934, pp. 534-537.

FIGS.: True, 1884b, pls. 33, 34 (exterior); Elliot, 1904, pt. 1, pls. 4, 5 (skull), fig. 14 (exterior).

While there is no evidence that any of the manatees is in immediate danger of extermination, the fact that wherever found they are sought by local populations for food makes their tenure at all times precarious on account of their limited range and inoffensiveness. At the present time three species are recognized, of which one, *T. inunguis*, is confined to the Amazon and Orinoco.

The West Indian manatee attains a total length of about 15 feet, usually less, and in form of body is somewhat cetacean-like, lacking hind limbs. The tail ends in a broad, rounded lobe unlike the flukes of the dugongs. The fore limbs are paddlelike, with four flat nails each and are rather freely movable, so that they are used in manipulating the food. The skin is hairless and of a dark gray-black color. The upper lip forms a broad, flat disk, somewhat bristly, with the nostrils opening separately at the summit. The rostrum of the skull is but slightly bent down, there are no upper tusks, and the end of the lower jaw is deflected and provided with a horny plate in lieu of teeth. The cheek teeth form a continuous row, with two tuberculate transverse ridges each. Their method of succession is peculiar in that the roots of the anterior ones gradually resorb; these teeth fall one by one and the posterior ones work forward, giving place to others coming in at the back of the row. There are two pectoral mammae.

The range of the West Indian manatee presumably includes the waters about the Bahamas and the Greater Antilles, thence across to the coasts of Yucatan and southern Mexico, and coastwise along the shores of Central America and northern South America to the Guianas. It often enters lagoons or the lower reaches of rivers emptying into the sea. Among the Bahamas there is almost no information of its status at the present time, but in 1904 I had a report of one killed in the Bimini Islands on the western edge of the group. Of course, it may have come over from the Florida coast. Among the Greater Antilles they were formerly present in some numbers on the coasts, at river mouths, and about the small outlying islands. Gundlach in 1877 wrote that around Cuba, though formerly abundant, they were then much reduced but not rare, though difficult to secure; at the present day, however, they are said to have become very scarce. Gosse and Hill (1851) speak of them as present in small numbers about Hispaniola, where in the eastern part of Haiti Hill had seen them about the mouth of the Yasica River. It is supposed, too, that the three "mermaids" that Columbus reported near Punta Roxa were manatees, the first record of the species in literature. In Oviedo's history there is a further account of the manatee, with which Columbus on his fourth voyage, in 1502, had then become more familiar. The translation of Herrera speaks of it as "a new sort of Fish, which was a considerable advantage to them" and relates the story of a tame one kept by the Cacique Carametex in a pond for 26 years; "it grew tame and sensible and would come when call'd by the name of *Mato*, which signifies Noble." In those times its flesh was eaten by the natives as attested by bones in their kitchen middens. On the north coast of Puerto Rico the town of Manati is said to have derived its name from the former abundance of the animal in nearby waters. According to Barrett (1935) their local disappearance here is due to the silting-up of the waters as well as to killing for meat and other products, so that "they now graze on bottom-growing marine plants in the shallow water one to two miles off shore, instead of on the malojillo grass" (*Panicum*) in the brackish or fresh waters along the coast. To the eastward of Puerto Rico I have found little evidence of its presence; but Miller (1918a) has recorded its bones dug up from a kitchen midden on St. Croix. Among the Lesser Antilles it seems not to occur at present and perhaps does not find suitable conditions there. In the middle of the last century, Gosse and Hill (1851) speak of it as frequenting the shores of Jamaica, but at that time it was evidently not very common, for they especially give an account of one with measurements, which became tangled in a fish net at Savanna-le-Mar; another at Spanish Town in 1848, that measured 10 feet long; and again one from Black River. Its meat was esteemed when brought to market, and an entire manatee if taken to Kingston would sell for £18 sterling, while at Port Royal the meat found a ready sale at 9 pence a pound.

One may suppose that originally manatees extended their range to the West Indian islands by way of the Yucatan Peninsula and the shallows intervening, for they formerly were common along its shores on both the east and the west side. How far to the westward along the coast of the Gulf of Mexico the range may have extended is uncertain, but in recent years apparently not farther than the province of Tabasco, at the western base of the peninsula, and southern Veracruz. Here, according to Gaumer (1917), the animals follow up the Grijalva River to its tributaries Chilapilla, Chilapa, Usumacinta, and Muscupana; he had seen them at a considerable distance from the mouth of the Hondo River and all along the east coast of Yucatan at the places where subterranean streams empty, and in 1886 and 1887 had hunted them by night on the unpopulated coasts of Quintana Roo. Their keen sense of hearing makes it imperative for the hunter to approach them with great care at this time when they come in to feed. He states that owing to constant hunting for their meat, bones, and hide, the number of manatees had notably diminished of late years, so that in many of the localities where they previously abounded, they were at that date (1917) either very scarce or no longer to be found. In Yucatan not only is the flesh much in demand, but the hide, which may be up to 4 centimeters thick, is sold for a good price to be made into canes, which, varnished yellow, are much prized locally. Likewise the fishermen play upon the credulity of their fellows, who believe that the bones of the manatee possess marvellous curative properties for certain complaints so that these are therefore largely used to make charms. Gaumer lists as further uses of the oil of the manatee at various times: Its employment as fuel for lamps in the churches; as a dressing for meat; as a lubricant; for softening leather; and frequently for adulterating "cod-liver oil."

Reports of manatees along the Gulf coast, north of Veracruz, are rare. In a recent paper, Gunter (1941) has summarized a number of records of manatees from extreme southern Texas. True (1884b) long ago reported a specimen in the U. S. National Museum from Brazos, which Gunter says must have been from the region of Brazos Island at the southern tip of Texas; another from the same source was said to be from Matamoros, Mexico, a short distance to the southward. In July, 1911, a large specimen over 15 feet long was captured near Port Isabel and kept in captivity. In the same and the succeeding year other reports were received of manatees seen or captured in the Laguna Madre, along the coast of extreme southern Texas. In July, 1928, a dead one was found at Copano Bay, slightly farther to the north, while in 1937 another dead one was reported from eastern Texas, at Cow Bayou, near the Louisiana line. Gunter supposes that all these cases represent "strays from Mexico" and points out that occasional cold waves might easily kill manatees in the northern part of the Gulf of Mexico.

Barrett (1935) has published some interesting notes on the occurrence and capture of the manatee on the east coast of Nicaragua, where, he writes, one of the best known herds on the Caribbean coast inhabits the Indio River and its bayous just north of Greytown. This group, variously estimated from a few score to several hundred, appears to be stationary and seems not to vary appreciably from year to year in spite of the heavy toll taken by the meat-hungry natives. Hunting is done at night, when the animals come in to feed from their places of concealment during the day. "Families consisting of a bull, a cow, and one or two immature calves, are usually met with; these groups merge into a loose herd of from 10 to 50 or more individuals living in a lagoon or certain stretch of river, concentrating during the day and scattering at night." Their food here seems to be mainly the Para grass (*Panicum molle*), which grows on the banks of fresh-water lagoons and rivers, with its roots "in the soil above the mean level of the water and the stems floating out some 6 to 10 feet from the bank. Only the tender vertical tips of the stems are eaten, the portions remaining in the water or forming a mat just above it being never touched." Mating is said to take place in shallow water, and the single young remains with the cow until half grown. Barrett states that the average adult is 8 to 10 feet in length, rarely 12 feet. Three kinds of meat are distinguished: The thick breast, back, and tail muscles, which are light-colored like veal; the red steak of the pelvic region; and the fat spare-rib slabs. "Bacon, salted and smoked from the belly regions,

is excellent; the thick chunks of flesh . . . corn well, and
may be jerked or smoke-dried. When roasted, fried, or stewed,
the flesh remains tender and holds its gamey taste, with none
of the tough dryness of turtle nor the oily fishiness of porpoise
meat." The cylindrical stapes of the inner ear are saved by
the Nicaraguans as charms against ill-luck. Near one end of
the stapes there is a natural perforation, which facilitates
stringing it; unless these bones are kept in the mouth an hour
or so it is believed that the hole will close up and thus "spoil
the charm's power" (Barrett, 1935).

More than two centuries ago Dampier, the famous bucca-
neer, found manatees common along the coasts of the Caribbean Sea from the Gulf of Campeche to Nicaragua and western
Panama. Goldman (1920) has quoted from his account,
which describes the method of harpooning them from canoes,
and tells that two natives from the coast brought him two
manatees every day for a week as provisions, for "the flesh is
white, both the fat and the lean, and extraordinary sweet
wholesome meat." At Bocas del Toro, where Dampier once
found them so common, Goldman writes in 1920 that manatees
are still "occasionally reported by native boatmen. The
species has probably become scarce here as in many other
localities where it was formerly common." He adds that he
has no record of it from any other part of the Panama coast,
but Dr. Maack in 1874 reported it as frequently caught by the
natives in the Atrato and the Cacarica Rivers, in eastern
Panama. In 1868 von Frantzius wrote that they were still
very common along the shores of Costa Rica, passing into
some of the larger rivers. They were found abundantly in the
San Juan and neighboring streams as the Río Colorado,
Sarapiqui, and San Carlos; but the rapids near the mouth of
the last-named prevent them from ascending far up the river
or passing into Lake Nicaragua.

Along the northern coast of South America manatees occur
still in some numbers as far east as the Guianas, especially
about the mouths of rivers. Carriker writes that in Colombia
they are not now much persecuted, though occasionally one is
killed by the natives for food. He mentions a group reported
from the Cienaga Grande, a lagoon on the coast between Santa
Marta and Barranquilla. Manatees occur in the Orinoco and,
in former times at least, on the Venezuelan coast, for True

(1884b) in his account of the aquatic mammals, quotes a translation of Acuña, which tells of the Spaniards about Margarita Island catching them for food. They "particularly value the stomach and belly part of it, roasted on spits. Others cut long slices of the flesh of its back, which they salt a little, only for two days, and then dry it in the air; after which it will keep three or four months. This they roast and baste with butter, and reckon delicious meat."

True (1884b) long ago called attention to the value of this animal as a source of food and of excellent oil to the people on whose coasts it occurs, and thus one whose abundance should be a matter of concern, for it is of large size, living in places readily accessible to man, and is easily taken, and with proper protection might furnish no small amount of food and revenue. Yet, he adds, "putting all the facts together, it seems evident that not many centuries will pass before Manatees will be extremely rare, especially in our own country."

Apparently the manatee does not occur on the northeastern coast of South America, from the Guianas to the mouth of the Amazon; at least I have come upon no record of it, and even in former days the people of French Guiana obtained manatee meat from the Amazon River, instead of from nearer waters. Possibly the coastal conditions on this shore are unfavorable; for, as Dr. R. C. Murphy writes (1936, vol. 1, p. 130), the water here becomes extremely muddy and very shoal, factors which, he believes, have made this coast practically uninhabitable for pelicans and prevented their spread east and south around Cape St. Roque to the apparently wholly suitable coasts of eastern Brazil.

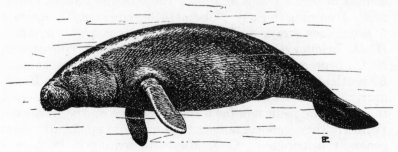

Manatee (*Trichechus manatus*)

544   EXTINCT AND VANISHING MAMMALS

FLORIDA MANATEE

TRICHECHUS MANATUS LATIROSTRIS (Harlan)

Manatus latirostris Harlan, Journ. Acad. Nat. Sci. Philadelphia, ser. 1, vol. 3, pt. 2,
  p. 394, 1824 (Near the capes of eastern Florida).
FIG.: Nelson, 1916, p. 467 (col. fig.).

In his original description of the Florida manatee, Harlan
was concerned chiefly in distinguishing it from the African
manatee and hence neglected to show clearly how it differed
from the West Indian and Caribbean animal. True (1884b),
also, long ago "satisfied" himself of the distinctness of the
Florida manatee from the Caribbean form, but again failed to
state the diagnostic characters; while the latest reviewer of the
subject (Hatt, 1934) regards the Florida manatee as a race of
the West Indian manatee, from which it differs in minor
skeletal characters. Even these, however, are subject to an
unascertained degree of individual variation, but are chiefly:
The first phalanx in the digits of the hand is proportionally
longer; the snout is apparently shorter in the Florida animal;
pterygoid process usually longer with palatine and pterygoid
points equal and longer than the alisphenoid, instead of one or
the other longer; and especially the shape of the foramen
magnum, which though oval in both (rather than roundish as
in the African and Amazon species), has its dorsal rim flat
instead of strongly curved. How far these differences may hold
with larger and more representative series remains to be shown.

Assuming that the Florida manatee is slightly different from
that of the Caribbean Sea and West Indies implies also the
distinctness of habitat and the failure of the two populations
to mingle except on rare occasions. The range of the Florida
manatee is in general the coastal waters, lagoons, and lower
courses of such streams as Indian River of the Florida Peninsula. According to E. W. Nelson (1916), however, "in summer
it sometimes strays as far north as the coast of Virginia."
H. H. Brimley (1931) reports one caught near Wilmington,
N. C., September 11, 1919. Ordinarily they are rare even as
far north as St. Augustine but are common in the Indian River,
nearly as far as its head, and south along the coast and around
the tip of the peninsula for a short distance on the west side.
Formerly they were commoner than now and apparently more
generally distributed. C. J. Maynard, writing in 1872, says
that he was informed by credible authorities that it was re-

markably abundant on the west coast in the various rivers and creeks between Tampa Bay and Cape Sable, but he had never seen it in Mosquito or Halifax Lagoons and believed it did not occur there. True (1884b) quotes Silas Stearns, a correspondent living formerly at Pensacola, in the western part of Florida, who states: "I have heard of their being taken in the Myakka River, Peace Creek, Caloosahatchie River and other small streams south of Charlotte Harbor and Okeechobee Lake, on the Gulf side . . . On the Gulf coast . . . the oldest settlers say that ten, fifteen, or twenty years ago Manatees were occasionally seen in nearly all the inland rivers from Key West westward to . . . Pensacola, Mobile, and New Orleans . . . During the summer of 1880 I saw one in Santa Rosa Sound, some twenty miles east of Pensacola, where there has been none seen for many years. While landing a sail-boat on the island we surprised the animal in shoal water and had a fine opportunity to examine it." Gunter (1941) reports as the only known record for Louisiana, a skull found at Calcasieu Lake, in January, 1929, but to which subspecies it may be referred he does not tell. Whether the range of the Florida manatee is continuous from the mouth of the Mississippi southward to the coast of southern Mexico does not seem clear, though one might suppose that it does not at the present time, occur so far to the westward, since the northern waters of the Gulf are probably too cool or subject to occasional cold spells.

Manatees have at various times been caught alive and kept in aquaria at zoological gardens, as at Philadelphia, New York, and London. Their natural food seems to be various species of such grasses as *Panicum*, which grows floating in shoal water; but in captivity they show somewhat more catholic taste, and at Philadelphia were found to take freely "various garden vegetables—cabbage, celery tops, spinach, kale, baked apples, and others, while they devoured as well quantities of the aquatic plant *Vallisneria spiralis*, and the sea-weed *Ulva latissima*. The Central Park [New York] specimen seems to have been more dainty, rejecting a variety of aquatic plants but at length accepting *Canna* and rockweed (*Fucus vesiculosus*)!" In the London Gardens a captive was offered a choice of various foods and finally selected watercress, cabbage, and lettuce, consuming an average of about 100 pounds of green food daily! It later refused to eat any cabbage, but continued its liking for lettuce. In Florida manatees are said to eat the leaves of mangrove trees hanging close to the water, but only when they are unable to obtain their favorite "manatee grass," as in the Sebastian River in the spring and summer of 1894, when on account of the dry season the salt water went nearly to the head of fresh-water streams and so killed it out (Bangs, 1895).

That the manatee is very sensitive to temperature is well known to those who have kept them in captivity, in aquaria. In a wild state, too, they sometimes suffer from a sudden "freeze." Bangs (1895, p. 785) records that in 1886 the late C. J. Maynard noted three large manatees killed by such a sudden cold and washed ashore at Palm Beach. In 1895 Bangs witnessed a similar thing himself, when there occurred two freezes of unprecedented intensity, with the thermometer at 20° F. at Oak Lodge (opposite Micco) on February 12, and only three degrees higher next morning. The intense cold of these two days and nights was later followed by another freeze. The result was that of a herd of eight manatees known for some time to have lived in the Sebastian River, all but three were wiped out, and nearly all the mangroves along the Indian River were killed. The mortality among the fish in shallow water, Bangs wrote, was "such as I never thought to witness." In both freezes the cold came without any warning and before the manatees could move into deeper water. Since the small herd of eight comprised all the individuals known to be in the vicinity, it is clear that such an occasional catastrophe might easily place the manatee population of all northern Florida in a critical state. A similar catastrophe resulted from the freeze of late January, 1940, when the air temperature in Charlotte and Lee Counties in southwestern Florida "hovered around 19° F.; the water temperature of Charlotte Harbor (Charlotte County) dropped from 68° F. to 46° F.," with the result that on January 28 five dead manatees were found in and about Charlotte Harbor. A. R. Cahn (1940), who reports these facts, remarks that "since manatees are very rare in the area, this mortality, which may well include others not found or reported, is a serious threat to the survival of the species."

About 1890 the manatee had become rather scarce in many parts of Florida. Bangs states that the small group of eight above mentioned was well known to have frequented the section of Indian River from the Sebastian to the St. Lucie, and represented most of if not all the animals in the region. He adds that he made many inquiries among the people along the river as to the diminution of the manatee in the recent years. One Mr. Ulrich said that he had come to the river first about 1880 when manatees were still common and he had often seen them from the door of his house at the Narrows, passing up and down the river; but he had seen none for eight years. Since 1893 the manatee has been in part protected by a State law, and netting them was prohibited with a penalty of $500 for killing one. As a result of protection the numbers have slowly increased, and at the present time it is once more fairly common in the Indian River. It is believed to be now quite safe, although the law is not always easy to enforce, nor is evidence that will pass in a court of law simple to obtain. On the other hand, it is quite possible that a certain amount of use of the animal as food is justified, although the rate of increase is not known.

West African Manatee

Trichechus senegalensis Link

Trichechus senegalensis Link, Beyträge Naturgesch., vol. 1, sect. 2, p. 109, 1795 (Senegal).

SYNONYMS: *Trichechus M. africanus* Oken, Lehrb. Naturgesch., vol. 3, sect. 2, p. 688, 1816 (Senegal); *Manatus nasutus* Wyman, Proc. Boston Soc. Nat. Hist., vol. 2, p. 190, footnote, 1847 (Caracalla River, Ivory Coast); *Manatus vögelii* Owen, Edinburgh New Philos. Journ., ser. 2, vol. 4, p. 346, Oct., 1846 (Benué River, northern Nigeria); *Manatus oweni* Du Chaillu, Proc. Boston Soc. Nat. Hist., vol. 7, p. 367, 1860 (Camma country, about the mouth of Gabun River).

FIGS.: Harlan, 1824, pl. 13, figs. 1-3; Hatt, 1934, pl. 27 (exterior).

The manatee of West Africa is very similar in general to the Florida manatee but differs in lacking a deep median anterior notch in the sternum; in its long, narrow scapula; slenderer arm bones; shorter snout; roundish foramen magnum; and strikingly in its short vomer, which extends approximately to the level of the middle of the orbit (Hatt, 1934).

This manatee lives in the lower reaches of the West African rivers from Senegal to Angola and in the coastal lagoons. Hatt (1934), from a search of the literature, has compiled a list of localities from which specimens have been recorded.

From this list it appears that in Senegal it occurs mainly in the coastal lagoons, but Rochebrune in 1883 notes that it no longer was found in the Sorres lagoon where Adanson recorded it in 1757. The presence of manatees in the Gambia River was reported in recent years, and there are old records for Sierra Leone. Büttikofer found it in the St. Pauls River, Liberia, below the rapids, and in the 1840's a specimen was secured by the missionary Perkins in Caracalla River, Ivory Coast. In more recent times it has been taken at Lagos and Benin, while from the Niger River manatees are known from "the lower reaches near the coast, the upper section above Timbuctu, and from the river Benué" (Hatt, 1934). In 1908 Maclaud found that the manatee was not uncommon in the lakes along the Niger near Timbuctu, but had almost disappeared from the large coastal rivers of Nigeria; Migeod found it common in 1924 in the Benué River, especially at Numan, below Yola. On the Gulf of Guinea there are many older records of its presence in the mouths of rivers as the Cameroon River, Rio Muni, Gabun and Ogowé Rivers, and it is said to occur in the mangrove regions of the Cameroons. In the lower Congo it is found in some numbers below the first rapids, particularly in the region about Boma, but is unknown above the rapids. Hatt's specimen was from Banana. In the mouths of rivers of northern Angola it is occasionally found, and here its southernmost limit seems to be the Quanza or Cuanza River, where it was first mentioned by David Livingstone, who on his famous journey states that at Loando the Portuguese were acquainted with it and called it the "Peixe-mulher" "woman-fish," doubtless on account of its pectoral mammae). Hatt further reviews the supposed occurrence of the manatee in the Lake Chad Basin, the upper Congo, and the Great Lakes, but concludes that the evidence for its presence in these waters is not conclusive. The reports of manatees about the island of St. Helena refer doubtless to elephant seals or some other pinniped.

Although in certain regions the manatee is much sought for its flesh and hide by the natives, there is little direct evidence of its extermination but rather of its gradual diminution in numbers. Woods (1937, pp. 23–28), writing of the Anambra system of creeks in Nigeria, says that "from present indications" the manatee has been "either practically exterminated or driven out," notwithstanding that it is now "totally protected." He mentions that a party of Ijaw fishermen had constructed a trap in which during the first year nearly 40 manatees were killed, in the second year 6, and in the third none. How large an area of the Izichi River this trap affected is unknown, but "the fact ren ains that from a yearly average of 15 to 20 brought into Agulérie up to 1932, a few only were obtained in 1933, and none "the year following, so that they must either have been killed out or driven away." Ordinarily, in this district, the manatees are killed with spears at night after being attracted to baits of freshly cut grass. "Calves" are occasionally netted. On the other hand, according to Woods, some native tribes hold the manatee in superstitious awe, believing it is certain death to even see one; while others hold special ceremonies over the dead body. He believes that they are probably still numerous in most of the larger rivers of southern Nigeria, but since the meat of a single animal may bring from five to eight pounds sterling, the incentive for killing them for food is great. In Senegal, according to Cligny (1900), "they have become very rare, but one still finds them from time to time, especially in the Falémé and the Casamance." They are rare now also in the French Cameroons, according to recent advices. In the Gaboon, at the present time, they are said to be strictly localized at the mouth of the Ogowé and in the coastal lagoons of Fernan-Vaz. Here, however, they have been protected since 1916, "but this protection appears to be merely platonic," for as lately as 1929 their meat was sold in the market of Port-Gentil, and the fishers, in view of the lucrative trade, eagerly pursued the animals; since 1930, however, the numbers brought in at Port-Gentil have much diminished (A. R. Maclatchy, *in litt.*). A. J. Jobaert writes, in reply to Dr. Harper's inquiry, that in the Belgian Congo the manatee "occurs in more or less considerable numbers in all the creeks of the Lower Congo from the river's mouth to Matade" but in the lower Congo "is on the verge of total extermination. The few remaining will not survive long under the merciless hunting of the river natives on both sides (Congo and Angola)." They are captured in special nets, kept alive in creeks or fish ponds, and sold as butcher's meat in the markets. The protection accorded them by law will remain illusory and will not prevent their disappearance as long as the use of these nets is tolerated, and the sale of the meat and hide is not strictly prohibited. In order to make any protection effective a complete accord between the Belgian and Portuguese Governments is necessary."

Thus it appears that the numbers in all the West African localities where manatees are found are slowly but certainly diminishing and that protection by law is ineffective unless the officials of the countries concerned take a more active interest in its enforcement. The manatee might be still a useful source of meat to local populations if the hunting could be better regulated, through the enforcement of close times and the prohibition of mass methods of killing. As yet there seems to be insufficient knowledge of the breeding season to make intelligent regulations for closed seasons.

AMAZONIAN, OR SOUTH AMERICAN, MANATEE

TRICHECHUS INUNGUIS (Natterer)

Manatus inunguis Natterer, *in* Pelzeln, Verhandl. Zool.-Bot. Ges. Wien, vol. 33, Beiheft, p. 89, 1883 (Rio Madeira, Brazil).
SYNONYMS: "Though several other older names have been used for this manatee, none of these names is clearly restricted to this one species" (Hatt, 1934, p. 537).
FIGS.: Hartlaub, 1886, pls. 1–4; Thomas and Lydekker, 1897, pl. 36, fig. 5.

"The species *inunguis* is, in all likelihood, constantly characterized by the absence of nails, a white breast patch, slender proportions, and elongated flippers" (Hatt, 1934, p. 540). Its sternum is smaller in proportion to the size of the animal and may further be distinguished from that of other species by its slenderness and backwardly directed processes. The cranial bones are characteristically soft, chalky, and rather elaborately roughened instead of smooth. The skull is long-snouted, the nasal bones may be lacking, the lacrimals are small and scale-like, the temporal ridges do not rise above the general level of the brain case, the pterygoid process is long, narrow, and high, and the molar teeth are small in diameter and more strongly furrowed as compared with those of other species. The vomer is short in young skulls but in those of adults may extend to within an inch of the incisive foramina. Total length of an adult skull, up to 360 mm.

The range of this manatee is said to be the "rivers of northeastern South America, particularly the Amazon and Orinoco systems" (Hatt, 1934). It is apparently still to be found in good numbers in the Amazon River and its larger affluents, although specific information is scarce. As an animal constantly in demand for its flesh, oil, and hide, however, it may be given brief mention here. In the Amazon it is found as far up at least as Iquitos on the eastern borders of Perú, and to the south is said by Wied to be known as far as St. Matthews River (lat. 19° S.), Brazil. True (1884b) quotes an account by Smyth and Lowe of the capture of a manatee in the Ucayali River at Sarayacu, in eastern Perú, in 1835. The basis for including the Orinoco drainage in the range of this species is not clear. Brandt mentions its occurrence in the lower reaches as far up as the first rapids, but this probably refers to *T. manatus;* and is quoted from old Oviedo. In general, the animal has become scarcer in inhabited regions, but in the upper waters, where natives are few or "civilization" has not reached, the numbers are probably little affected. An interesting account of French Guinea, by Barbot, published in 1732, tells us that at that time manatee meat was in much demand at Cayenne and was brought "ready salted from the river of the *Amazons;* several of the principal inhabitants sending the barks and brigantines thither with men and salt to buy it of the *Indians* for beads, knives, white hats of a low price, some linen, toys, and iron tools. When those vessels are enter'd the river of the *Amazons,* the *Indians,* who always follow the *Manati* fishery, go aboard, take the salt, and with it run up the river in canoes or *Piraguas* to catch the *Manáti's;* which they cut in pieces, and salt as taken, returning with that salt fish to the brigantines; which go not up, because the *Portuguese* who dwell to the eastward, at *Para,* and other places of *Brazil,* claim the sovreignty of the north side of that river . . . The brigantines having got their lading of salted *Manati,* return to *Cayenne,* and sell it there, commonly at three pence a pound" (quoted from True, 1884b). Here it was "preferred to beef. Its fat, also, is as sweet as butter, and can be used to advantage in all kinds of pastry, fricasees, and soups." In more recent times it must have been largely reduced in the lower Amazon, for Goeldi (1904), in mentioning it from the Rio Arary, says that at the mouth of the Amazon and the Isle of Marajó it was then altogether a rarity. Those, he adds, that from time to time come in to the markets at Belém generally show wounds or scars of harpoons and knives. Most of the specimens in the Museu Goeldi at Pará were from the middle and lower Amazon. More precise information as to the status of this species is desirable.

BIBLIOGRAPHY

ABBOTT, CLINTON G.
   1935.   Bears in San Diego County, California.   Journ. Mamm., vol. 16, pp. 148–151.
AHARONI, J.
   1930.   Die Säugetiere Palästinas.   Zeitschr. für Säugetierkunde, vol. 5, pp. 327–343.
ALLEN, ALEXANDER.
   1910.   Hunting the sea otter, 188 pp.   London.
ALLEN, GLOVER MORRILL.
   1901.   The Louisiana deer.   Amer. Nat., vol. 35, pp. 449–454, 3 figs.
   1910.   *Solenodon paradoxus.*   Mem. Mus. Comp. Zool., vol. 40, no. 1, pp. 1–54, 9 pl.
   1911.   Mammals of the West Indies.   Bull. Mus. Comp. Zool., vol. 54, no. 6, pp. 173–263.
   1917.   New fossil mammals from Cuba.   Bull. Mus. Comp. Zool., vol. 61, no. 1, pp. 1–12, 1 pl.
   1918.   Fossil mammals from Cuba.   Bull. Mus. Comp. Zool., vol. 62, no. 4, pp. 131–148, 1 pl.
   1920.   Bison remains from New England.   Journ. Mamm., vol. 1, pp. 161–164.
   1930.   The walrus in New England.   Journ. Mamm., vol. 11, pp. 139–145.
   1937.   *Geocapromys* remains from Exuma Island.   Journ. Mamm., vol. 18, pp. 369–370.
   1939.   A checklist of African mammals.   Bull. Mus. Comp. Zool., vol. 83, pp. 1–763.
ALLEN, G. M., AND BARBOUR, THOMAS
   1937.   The Newfoundland wolf.   Journ. Mamm., vol. 18, pp. 229–234, 1 fig.
ALLEN G. M., AND LAWRENCE, BARBARA.
   1936.   Scientific results of an expedition to rain forest regions in eastern Africa.   III: Mammals.   Bull. Mus. Comp. Zool., vol. 79, pp. 31–125, 4 pls.
ALLEN, G. M., AND SANBORN, C. C.
   1937.   Notes on bats from the Bahamas.   Journ. Mamm., vol. 18, pp. 226–228, fig.
ALLEN, JOEL ASAPH.
   1869.   Catalogue of the mammals of Massachusetts: with a critical revision of the species.   Bull. Mus. Comp. Zool., vol. 1, pp. 143–252.
   1870a. On the mammals of Iowa.   Proc. Boston Soc. Nat. Hist., vol. 13, pp. 178–194.

ALLEN, JOEL ASAPH.—*Cont.*

1870b. On the eared seals (Otariadae), with detailed descriptions of North Pacific species, together with an account of the habits of the northern fur seal (*Callorhinus ursinus*), by Charles Bryant. Bull. Mus. Comp. Zool., vol. 2, no. 1, pp. 1–108.

1876a. The American bisons, living and extinct. Mem. Geol. Surv. Kentucky, vol. 1, pt. 2, ix + 246 pp., 12 pls., map.

1876b. The American bisons, living and extinct. Mem. Mus. Comp. Zool., vol. 4, ix + 246 pp., 12 pls., map. (Same as 1876a but with different title page.)

1877. History of the American bison, *Bison americanus*. 9th Rept. U. S. Geol. and Geogr. Surv. Terr., F. V. Hayden in charge, pp. 444–587.

1880. History of North American pinnipeds, a monograph of the walruses, sea-lions, sea-bears and seals of North America. U. S. Geol. and Geogr. Surv. Terr., F. V. Hayden geologist in charge, Misc. Publ. no. 12, xvi + 785 pp., illustr.

1887. The West Indian seal (*Monachus tropicalis*). Bull. Amer. Mus. Nat. Hist., vol. 2, pp. 1–34, pls. 1–4.

1891. Description of a new species of *Capromys*, from the Plana Keys, Bahamas. Bull. Amer. Mus. Nat. Hist., vol. 3, pp. 329–336, figs 1, 3, 5–9.

1892. On a small collection of mammals from the Galapagos Islands, collected by Dr. G. Baur. Bull. Amer. Mus. Nat. Hist., vol. 4, pp. 47–50.

1894. On the mammals of Aransas County, Texas, with descriptions of new forms of *Lepus* and *Oryzomys*. Bull. Amer. Mus. Nat. Hist., vol. 6, pp. 165–198.

1895. List of mammals collected in the Black Hills region of South Dakota and in western Kansas by Mr. Walter W. Granger, with field notes by the collector. Bull. Amer. Mus. Nat. Hist., vol 7, pp. 259–274.

1896. On mammals collected in Bexar County and vicinity, Texas, by Mr. H. P. Attwater, with field notes by the collector. Bull. Amer. Mus. Nat. Hist., vol. 5, pp. 47–80.

1901. Description of a new caribou from Kenai Peninsula, Alaska. Bull. Amer. Mus. Nat. Hist., vol. 14, pp. 143–148, 4 figs.

1902a. A new caribou from the Alaska Peninsula. Bull. Amer. Mus. Nat. Hist., vol. 16, pp. 119–127, 6 figs.

1902b. Description of a new caribou from northern British Columbia, and remarks on *Rangifer montanus*. Bull. Amer. Mus. Nat. Hist., vol. 16, pp. 149–158, 6 figs.

1902c. A new caribou from Ellesmere Land. Bull. Amer. Mus. Nat. Hist., vol. 16, pp. 409–412, 2 figs.

1905. Mammalia of southern Patagonia. Rep. Princeton Univ. Exped. to Patagonia, 1896–1899, vol. 3 (Zoology), pt. 1, pp. 1–210, 29 pls.

1908. The Peary caribou (*Rangifer pearyi*). Bull. Amer. Mus. Nat. Hist., vol. 24, pp. 487–504, 12 figs.

ALLEN, JOEL ASAPH.—*Cont.*
1909. The white bear of southwestern British Columbia. Bull. Amer. Mus. Nat. Hist., vol. 26, pp. 233–238, figs. 1–4.
1912. Historical and nomenclatorial notes on North American sheep. Bull. Amer. Mus. Nat. Hist., vol. 31, pp. 1–29, 4 figs.
1913. Ontogenetic and other variations in muskoxen, with a systematic review of the muskox group, recent and extinct. Mem. Amer. Mus. Nat. Hist., ser. 2, vol. 1, pp. 101–226, pls. 11–18, 45 figs.
1916a. An extinct octodont from the island of Porto Rico, West Indies. Ann. New York Acad. Sci., vol. 27, pp 17–22, 5 pls.
1916b. List of mammals collected in Colombia by the American Museum of Natural History expeditions, 1910–1915. Bull. Amer. Mus. Nat. Hist., vol. 35, pp. 191–238.
ALLEN, J. A., AND CHAPMAN, FRANK M.
1897. On a second collection of mammals from the island of Trinidad, with descriptions of new species, and a note on some mammals from the island of Dominica, W. I. Bull. Amer. Mus. Nat. Hist., vol. 9, pp. 13–30.
ANDERSON, JOHN, AND DE WINTON, W. E.
1902. Zoology of Egypt: Mammalia, xvii + 374 pp., 63 pls., map. London.
ANDERSON, RUDOLPH MARTIN.
1934a. Effect of the introduction of exotic animal forms. Proc. 5th Pacific Sci. Congress, Canada, 1933, vol. 1, pp. 769–778.
1934b. The distribution, abundance, and economic importance of the game and fur-bearing mammals of western North America. Proc. 5th Pacific Sci. Congress, Canada, 1933, vol. 5, pp. 4055–4075, 17 maps.
1935. Mammals of the eastern Arctic and Hudson Bay. *In:* Canada's Eastern Arctic, Dept. of Interior, Ottawa, pp. 67–108.
1937. Mammals and birds of the western Arctic district, Northwest Territories, Canada. *In:* Canada's Western Northland, pp. 97–122, 4 figs., 1 map. Land, Parks, and Forests Branch, Ottawa.
1939a. Mammals of the Province of Quebec. Ann. Rept. Provancher Soc. Nat. Hist., Quebec, for 1938, pp. 50–114.
1939b. The present status and distribution of the big game mammals of Canada. Trans. 3d North Amer. Wildlife Conference, Baltimore, 1938, pp. 390–406, maps.
ANDREWS, C. L.
1937. The decline of the sea otter. Nature Mag., vol. 29 no. 2, pp. 107–108, fig.
ANDREWS, ROY CHAPMAN.
1914. Monographs of the Pacific Cetacea. I: The California gray whale (*Rhachianectes glaucus* Cope). Mem. Amer. Mus. Nat. Hist., new ser., vol. 1, pt. 5, pp. 227–287, 20 pls., 22 figs.
1916. Monographs of the Pacific Cetacea. II: The Sei whale (*Balaenoptera borealis*). 1: History, habits, external anatomy, osteology, and relationships. Mem. Amer. Mus. Nat. Hist., new ser., vol. 1, pt. 6, pp. 289–388, 38 figs., 14 pls.

ANTHONY, ALFRED WEBSTER.
1921a. The elephant seal off Santa Cruz Island, California. Journ. Mamm., vol. 2, pp. 112–113.
1921b. The California gray whale on the coast of southern California. Journ. Mamm., vol. 2, p. 174.

ANTHONY, HAROLD E.
1916. Preliminary report on fossil mammals from Porto Rico, with descriptions of a new genus of ground sloth and two new genera of hystricomorph rodents. Ann. New York Acad. Sci., vol. 27, pp. 193–203, 8 pls.
1917a. New fossil rodents from Porto Rico, with additional notes on *Elasmodontomys obliquus* Anthony and *Heteropsomys insulans* Anthony. Bull. Amer. Mus. Nat. Hist., vol. 37, pp. 183–189, pl. 5.
1917b. A new rabbit and a new bat from neotropical regions. Bull. Amer. Mus. Nat. Hist., vol. 37, pp. 335–337, 1 pl.
1917c. Two new fossil bats from Porto Rico. Bull. Amer. Mus. Nat. Hist., vol. 37, pp. 565–568, 1 pl.
1918. The indigenous land mammals of Porto Rico, living and extinct. Mem. Amer. Mus. Nat. Hist., new ser., vol. 2, pt. 2, pp. 329–435, 54 figs., 21 pls., 1 map.
1919. Mammals collected in eastern Cuba in 1917, with descriptions of two new species. Bull. Amer. Mus. Nat. Hist., vol. 41, pp. 625–643, 3 pls.
1920a. A zoologist in Jamaica. Nat. Hist., vol. 20, pp. 156–168, 9 figs.
1920b. New mammals from Jamaica. Bull. Amer. Mus. Nat. Hist., vol. 42, pp. 469–475, 4 figs., 1 pl.
1925–26. Mammals of Porto Rico, living and extinct. New York Acad. Sci., Sci. Surv. Porto Rico and Virgin Islands, vol. 9, pts. 1 and 2, pp. 1–238, 83 figs., 3 maps, 54 pls.
1928. Field book of North American mammals, xxv + 625 pp., 150 figs., 1 map, 48 pls. New York and London.

APLIN, OLIVER VERNON.
1894. Field-notes on the mammals of Uruguay. Proc. Zool. Soc. London, for 1894, pp. 297–315.

ARTHUR, STANLEY C.
1931. The fur animals of Louisiana. Louisiana Dept. Conservation Bull. 18, 433 pp., illus.

ASHBROOK, FRANK G.
1928. Fur-farming for profit, xxiii + 300 pp., illustr. New York.

ATKINSON, A. L. C., AND BRYAN, W. A.
1914. A rare seal [*Monachus schauinslandi*]. Bull. New York Zool. Soc., vol. 16, pp. 1050–1051.

AUDUBON, JOHN JAMES, AND BACHMAN, JOHN.
1846–54. The viviparous quadrupeds of North America, 1st 8vo ed.: Vol. 1, 1846; Vol. 2, 1851; Vol. 3, 1854.
1849–54. The quadrupeds of North America: Vol. 1, 1849; Vol. 2, 1851; Vol. 3, 1854.

BACHMAN, JOHN.
1839. Monograph of the genus *Sciurus*. Charlesworth's Mag. Nat. Hist., vol. 3, p. 161.

BAGGLEY, GEORGE F.
1936. Status and distribution of the grizzly bear (*Ursus horribilis*) in the United States. Proc. North American Wildlife Conference, 1936, pp. 646–650.

BAILEY, ALFRED M.
1928. An unusual migration of the spotted and ribbon seals. Journ. Mamm., vol. 9, pp. 250–251.

BAILEY, ALFRED M., AND HENDEE, R. W.
1926. Notes on the mammals of northwestern Alaska. Journ. Mamm., vol. 7, pp. 9–28, 3 pls.

BAILEY, VERNON.
1900. Revision of American voles of the genus *Microtus*. North Amer. Fauna, no. 17, 88 pp., 5 pls.

1905. Biological survey of Texas. North Amer. Fauna, no. 25, 222 pp., 24 figs., 16 pls.

1907. Wolves in relation to stock, game and the national forest reserves. Bull. Forest Service, U. S. Dept. Agric., no. 72, 31 pp., 5 figs., 3 pls.

1918. The mammals, with notes on physiography and life zones. *In:* Wild animals of Glacier National Park, 102 pp., 18 figs., 1 map, 21 pls. National Park Service.

1922. Beaver habits, beaver control, and possibilities in beaver farming. U. S. Dept. Agric. Bull. 1078, 29 pp., 7 figs., 8 pls.

1926. A biological survey of North Dakota. I: Physiography and life zones. II: The mammals. North Amer. Fauna, no. 49, vi + 226 pp., 20 pls., 9 maps.

1931. Mammals of New Mexico. North Amer. Fauna, no. 53, 412 pp., 22 pls., 58 maps.

1932a. Buffalo of the Malheur Valley, Oregon. Proc. Biol. Soc. Washington, vol. 45, pp. 42–43.

1932b. The north-western white-tailed deer. Proc. Biol. Soc. Washington, vol. 45, pp. 43–44.

1932c. The Oregon antelope. Proc. Biol. Soc. Washington, vol. 45, pp. 45–46.

1935. A new name for the Rocky Mountain elk. Proc. Biol. Soc. Washington, vol. 48, pp. 187–189.

1936. The mammals and life zones of Oregon. North Amer. Fauna, no. 55, 416 pp., 52 pls., map.

1937. A typical specimen of the eastern elk from Pennsylvania. Journ. Mamm., vol. 18, p. 104.

BAIRD, SPENCER FULLERTON.
1857. Mammals of North America. *In:* Reports of Explorations and Surveys for a Railroad from Mississippi River to Pacific Ocean, vol. 8, pt. 1, xv–xlviii + 757 pp., 44 pls.

BANGS, OUTRAM.
1895. The present status of the Florida manatee, *Trichechus latirostris*

BANGS, OUTRAM.—*Cont.*
        (Harlan) in the Indian River waters. Amer. Nat., vol. 29, pp
        783–787.
  1896. A review of the squirrels of eastern North America. Proc. Biol.
        Soc. Washington, vol. 10, pp. 145–167, 3 pls.
  1898. The land mammals of peninsular Florida and the coast region of
        Georgia. Proc. Boston Soc. Nat. Hist., vol. 28, pp. 157–235,
        7 figs.
  1908. Notes on the mammals of Block Island, Rhode Island. Proc.
        New England Zool. Club, vol. 4, pp. 19–21, 1 pl.
  1913. The land mammals of Newfoundland. Bull. Mus. Comp. Zool.,
        vol. 54, pp. 507–516, 1 fig.
BARABASH-NIKIFOROV, I.
  1935. The sea otters of the Commander Islands. Journ. Mamm.,
        vol. 16, pp. 255–261.
  1938. Mammals of the Commander Islands and the surrounding sea.
        Journ. Mamm., vol. 19, pp. 423–429.
BARBOUR, THOMAS.
  1916. Some remarks upon Matthew's "Climate and Evolution."
        Annals New York Acad. Sci., vol. 27, pp. 1–10.
BARBOUR, THOMAS, AND ALLEN, GLOVER M.
  1922. The white-tailed deer of eastern United States. Journ. Mamm.,
        vol. 3, pp. 65–78, 2 pls.
BARKER, ELLIOTT S.
  1936. [Wildlife management by public agencies.] Proc. North Amer-
        ican Wildlife Conference, 1936, pp. 175–181.
BARRETT, O. W.
  1935. Notes concerning manatees and dugongs. Journ. Mamm., vol.
        16, pp. 216–220.
BARRETT-HAMILTON, GERALD E. H.
  1901. Seals. *In:* Resultats du voyage du S. Y. *Belgica* en 1897–1898–
        1899, Rapports scientifiques, 19 pp., 1 pl.
BEDDARD, FRANK EVERS.
  1901. Contribution towards a knowledge of the osteology of the pigmy
        whale (*Neobalaena marginata*). Trans. Zool. Soc. London,
        vol. 16, pp. 87–114, 3 pls.
BEEBE, WILLIAM.
  1942. Book of bays, xviii + 302 pp., illus. New York.
BELL, WILLIAM B.
  1931. Experiments in re-establishment of musk-oxen in Alaska.
        Journ. Mamm., vol. 12, pp. 292–297.
BENNETT, EDWARD TURNER.
  1833. [On the family Chinchillidae.] Proc. Zool. Soc. London, for 1833,
        pt. 1, pp. 57–60.
BENNITT, RUDOLF, AND NAGEL, WERNER D.
  1937. A survey of the resident game and furbearers of Missouri.
        Univ. Missouri Studies, vol. 12, no. 2, 215 pp.
BENSON, SETH B.
  1933. A new race of beaver from British Columbia. Journ. Mamm.,
        vol. 14, pp. 320–325, 1 fig.

BENSON, SETH B.—*Cont.*
1938. Notes on kit foxes (*Vulpes macrotis*) from Mexico. Proc. Biol. Soc. Washington, vol. 51, pp. 17–24.

BERNARD, JOSEPH F.
1923. Local walrus protection in northeast Siberia. Journ. Mamm., vol. 4, pp. 224–227, 1 pl.
1925. Walrus protection in Alaska. Journ.Mamm.,vol. 6,pp. 100–102.

BIDLINGMAIER, THEODOR C.
1937. Notes on the genus *Chinchilla*. Journ. Mamm., vol. 18, pp. 159–163.

BLAKE, JAMES.
1938. The threatened whale. Journ. Soc. Preservation Fauna Empire, new ser., pt. 33, pp. 65–81.

BLANFORD, WILLIAM THOMAS.
1876. Eastern Persia, an account of the journeys of the Persian Boundaries Commission, 1870–72. Mammals: vol. 2, pp. 18–97, 8 pls. London.

BONNYCASTLE, R. H. G.
1936. Hudson's Bay Co. and fur conservation. Proc. North Amer. Wildlife Conference, 1936, pp. 625–628.

BORELL, ADREY E., AND ELLIS, RALPH.
1934. Mammals of the Ruby Mountains region of northeastern Nevada. Journ. Mamm., vol. 15, pp. 12–44, 6 pls.

BOURDELLE, E.
1939. American mammals introduced into France in the contemporary period, especially *Myocastor* and *Ondatra*. Journ. Mamm., vol. 20, pp. 287–291.

BRADT, G. W.
1933. Report on nuisance-beaver control. Papers Michigan Acad. Sci., vol. 17, pp. 509–513.

BRANDT, JOHANN FRIEDRICH.
1833. De solenodonte, novo mammalium insectivorum genere. Mém. Acad. Sci. St. Petérsbourg, ser. 6, vol. 2, pp. 459–478.
1846. Symbolae Sirenologicae, quibus praecique Rhytinae Historia Naturalis Illustratur. Mem. Acad. Imp. Sci. St. Petérsbourg, ser. 6, vol. 5, pp. 1–160, 5 pls.
1861–68. Symbolae Sirenologicae. Fasc. II et III. Sireniorum Pachydermatum, Zeuglodontum et Cetaceorum ordinis Osteologia Comparata, nec non Sireniorum Generum Monographiae. Mém. Acad. Imp. Sci. St. Petérsbourg, ser. 7, vol. 12, pp. 1–384, 9 pls.

BRAYTON, A. W.
1882. Report on the mammals of Ohio. Rept. Geol. Surv. Ohio, vol. 4, pt. 1, zool., pp. 3–185.

BRECKENRIDGE, W. J.
1935. Status of the Minnesota caribou. Journ. Mamm., vol. 16, pp. 327–328.

BRIMLEY, CLEMENT SAMUEL.
1905. A descriptive catalogue of the mammals of North Carolina.

BRIMLEY, CLEMENT SAMUEL.—*Cont.*
      exclusive of the Cetacea. Journ. Elisha Mitchell Sci. Soc.,
      vol. 21, no. 1, pp. 1-32.
BRIMLEY, HERBERT HUTCHINSON.
   1931. The manatee in North Carolina. Journ. Mamm., vol. 12, pp.
      320-321.
BROOKS, A. B.
   1923. Reappearance of beavers in West Virginia. Journ. Mamm.,
      vol. 4, p. 191.
BROOKS, ALLAN.
   1923. The Rocky Mountain sheep (*Ovis canadensis*) in British Colum-
      bia. Can. Field-Nat., vol. 37, pp. 23-25, map.
BROOKS, FRED E.
   1911. The mammals of West Virginia. Rept. West Virginia State
      Board Agric. for Quarter ending Dec. 30, 1910, Forestry, no.
      20, pp. 9-30.
BROWN, ROBERT N. RUDMOSE.
   1913. The seals of the Weddell Sea: Notes on their habits and distribu-
      tion. Scottish Nat. Antarctic Exped., Sci. Results Voyage
      Scotia 1902-4, vol. 4, zoology, pt. 13, pp. 181-198, 9 pls.
BRUCE, WILLIAM SPEIRS.
   1915. Some observations on Antarctic Cetacea. Scottish Nat. Ant-
      arctic Exped., Sci. Results Voyage *Scotia* 1902-4, pt. 20, pp.
      487-504, 1 fig., 2 pls.
BRYAN, WILLIAM ALANSON.
   1915. Natural history of Hawaii, 596 pp., 117 pls. Honolulu.
BUCHANAN, ANGUS.
   1920. Wild life in Canada, xx + 264 pp., 16 pls., 1 map. Toronto.
BUCHER, G. C.
   1937. Notes on life-history and habits of *Capromys*. Mem. Soc.
      Cubana Hist. Nat., vol. 11, pp. 93-107, 6 pls.
BURT, WILLIAM HENRY.
   1934. The mammals of southern Nevada. Trans. San Diego Soc. Nat.
      Hist., vol. 7, pp. 375-427, 1 map.
BUTLER, AMOS W.
   1934. Wild and domesticated elk in the early days of Franklin County,
      Indiana. Journ. Mamm., vol. 15, pp. 246-247.
CABOT, WILLIAM B.
   1912. In northern Labrador, xii + 292 pp., illustr. London.
CABRERA, ANGEL.
   1914. Fauna Iberica: Mamíferos, xviii + 441 pp., 22 pls. Madrid.
   1932. Los mamíferos de Marruecos. Trab. Mus. Nac. de Cienc. Nat.,
      zool. ser., no. 57, pp. 1-361, 34 figs., 12 pls.
CAHALANE, VICTOR H.
   1939a. Mammals of the Chiricahua Mountains, Cochise County,
      Arizona. Journ. Mamm., vol. 20, pp. 418-440, figs.
   1939b. The evolution of predator control policy in the national parks.
      Journ. Wildlife Management, vol. 3, pp. 229-237.

CAHN, ALVIN R.
  1937. The mammals of the Quetico Provincial Park of Ontario.
         Journ. Mamm., vol. 18, pp. 19–30.
  1940. Manatees and the Florida freeze. Journ. Mamm., vol. 21, pp.
         222–223.
CAMERON, T.
  1936. The conservation of fur in the Northwest Territories of Canada.
         Proc. North American Wildlife Conference, 1936, pp. 621–625.
CAMPBELL, CARLOS C.
  1939. Animals increasing in the Great Smokies. Amer. Forests, vol.
         45, p. 318.
CARY, MERRITT.
  1911. A biological survey of Colorado. North Amer. Fauna, no. 33,
         256 pp., 39 figs., 12 pls.
CHAMBERLAIN, MONTAGUE.
  1884. Mammals of New Brunswick. Bull. Nat. Hist. Soc. New Bruns-
         wick, no. 3, pp. 37–41.
CHAPMAN, FRANK M.
  1892. Notes on birds and mammals observed near Trinidad, Cuba,
         with remarks on the origin of West Indian bird life. Bull.
         Amer. Mus. Nat. Hist., vol. 4, pp. 279–350.
CHAPMAN, WENDELL AND LUCIE.
  1937. Wilderness wanderers: Adventures among wild animals in Rocky
         Mountain solitudes, 318 pp. New York.
CLARK, J. W.
  1876. On the eared seals of the islands of St. Paul and Amsterdam,
         with a description of the fur-seal of New Zealand, and an
         attempt to distinguish and rearrange the New-Zealand
         Otariidae. Proc. Zool. Soc. London, for 1875, pp. 650–677,
         8 figs., 3 pls.
CLIGNY, ADOLPHE.
  1900. Faune du Sénégal et de la Casamance.
COLLETT, ROBERT.
  1909. A few notes on the whale Balaena glacialis and its capture in
         recent years in the North Atlantic by Norwegian whalers.
         Proc. Zool. Soc. London, for 1909, pp. 91–98, 1 fig., 3 pls.
COLLINS, GRENOLD.
  1940. Habits of the Pacific walrus (Odobenus divergens). Journ.
         Mamm., vol. 21, pp. 138–144.
CONNERY, ROBERT H.
  1935. Governmental problems in wild life conservation, 250 pp.
         New York.
COOK, ARTHUR H.
  1940. Screwworms infest beaver in Texas. Journ. Mamm., vol. 21,
         p. 93.
COOK, NEWELL B.
  1936. Remarks of . . .   Proc. North Amer. Wildlife Conference,
         1936, pp. 187–190.

Cope, Edwin Drinker.
    1868. [On *Amblyrhiza inundata*.] Proc. Acad. Nat. Sci. Philadelphia,
            1868, p. 313.
Cory, Charles B.
    1896. Hunting and fishing in Florida, including a key to the water birds
            known to occur in the State, 304 pp., illustr. Boston.
    1912. The mammals of Illinois and Wisconsin. Publ. Field Mus. Nat.
            Hist., Zool. Ser., vol. 11, pp. 1–505, illustr.
Couch, Leo K.
    1937. Trapping and transplanting live beavers. U. S. Dept. Agr.
            Farmer's Bull., no. 1768, 18 pp., 15 figs.
Coues, Elliott.
    1877. Fur-bearing animals: a monograph of North American Musteli-
            dae [etc.]. Misc. Publ. U. S. Geol. Surv. Terr., F. V. Hayden,
            U. S. Geologist, xiv + 348 pp., 20 pls.
Cowan, Ian McTaggart.
    1936. Distribution and variation in deer (genus *Odocoileus*) of the
            Pacific coastal region of North America. California Fish and
            Game, vol. 22, pp. 155–246, 11 figs., 2 maps.
    1939. The vertebrate fauna of the Peace River district of British
            Columbia. Occas. Papers Brit. Columbia Provincial Mus.,
            no. 1, 102 pp., 5 pls.
    1940. Distribution and variation in the native sheep of North America.
            Amer. Midl. Nat., vol. 24, pp. 505–580, 5 figs.
Cox, William T.
    1941. The fight for the woodland caribou. Amer. Forests, vol. 47, pp.
            54–57, 93, 94.
Cutright, Paul R.
    1940. The great naturalists explore South America, xii + 340 pp.,
            illustr. New York.
Cuvier, F.
    1836. Caractères du genre Plagiodonte et description du Plagiodonte
            des habitations, *Plagiodontia aedium*. Ann. Sci. Nat., ser. 2,
            vol. 6, zool., pp. 347–353, 1 pl.
Danford, C. G., and Alston, E. R.
    1877. On the mammals of Asia Minor. Proc. Zool. Soc. London, for
            1877, pp. 270–281.
Darwin, Charles.
    1839. Narrative of the surveying voyages of His Majesty's ships
            Adventure and *Beagle*, between the years 1826 and 1836,
            describing their examination of the southern shores of South
            America, and the *Beagle's* circumnavigation of the globe, vol.
            3, xiv + 615 pp. London.
Davis, William B.
    1939. The recent mammals of Idaho, 499 pp., illustr. Caldwell, Idaho.
    1940. Critical notes on the Texas beaver. Journ. Mamm., vol. 21, pp.
            84–86, 2 figs.
Davis, William B., and Taylor, Walter P.
    1939. The bighorn sheep of Texas. Journ. Mamm., vol. 20, pp. 440–
            455, 3 figs.

DEARBORN, NED.
 1927. An old record of the mountain lion in New Hampshire. Journ.
  Mamm., vol. 8, pp. 311–312.
DE BEAUX, OSCAR.
 1931. Mammiferi. *In:* Spedizione del barone Raimondo Franchette
  in Dancalia. Ann. Mus. Civ. Stor. Nat. Genova, vol. 55, pp.
  183–217.
DELLINGER, S. C., AND BLACK, J. D.
 1940. Notes on Arkansas mammals. Journ. Mamm., vol. 21, pp. 187–
  191.
DEVINCENZI, GARIBALDI J.
 1935. Mamíferos del Uruguay. Anales Mus. Hist. Nat. Montevideo,
  ser. 2, vol. 4, no. 10, pp. 1–96, 5 figs., 12 pls.
DE WINTON, W. E.
 1896. On some mammals from Ecuador. Proc. Zool. Soc. London, for
  1896, pp. 507–513, 2 pls.
DIXON, JOSEPH S.
 1916a. Does the grizzly bear still exist in California? California Fish
  and Game, vol. 2, no. 2, 5 pp., 4 figs.
 1916b. The timber wolf in California. California Fish and Game, vol.
  2, pp. 125–128, 3 figs.
 1936. The status of the Sierra bighorn sheep. Proc. North American
  Wildlife Conference, 1936, pp. 641–643.
DOBSON, GEORGE EDWARD.
 1878. Catalogue of the Chiroptera in the collection of the British
  Museum, 567 pp., 30 pls. London.
 1884. On the myology and visceral anatomy of *Capromys melanurus,*
  with a description of the species. Proc. Zool. Soc. London, for
  1884, pp. 233–250.
DOLLMAN, GUY.
 1933. Dugongs from Mafia Island and a manatee from Nigeria. Nat.
  Hist. Mag., vol. 4, pp. 117–125, 7 photos. London (Brit. Mus.).
DUFRESNE, FRANK.
 1942. Mammals and birds of Alaska. Fish and Wildlife Service, U. S.
  Dept. Int., Circ. 3, 37 pp., 35 figs.
DUGMORE, A. RADCLYFFE.
 1913. The romance of the Newfoundland caribou, an intimate account
  of the life of the reindeer of North America, viii + 192 pp.,
  map, illustr. Philadelphia and London.
DURRANT, STEPHEN D.
 1935. Occurrence of the spotted bat in Utah. Journ. Mamm., vol. 16,
  p. 226.
DYMOND, J. R.
 1934a. Problems in the conservation of game and fur-bearing mammals.
  Proc. 5th Pacific Sci. Congress, Canada, 1933, vol. 5, pp.
  4077–4078.
 1934b. What of the predator? Proc. 5th Pacific Sci. Congress, Canada,
  1933, vol. 5, pp. 4079–4080.

EIDMANN, H.
　1935.　Zur Kenntnis der Säugetierfauna von Südlabrador. 2. Beitrag
　　　　zur Kenntnis der Fauna von Südlabrador. Zeitschr. für
　　　　Säugetierk., vol. 10, pp. 39–61, 1 fig., 8 maps.
ELLIOT, DANIEL GIRAUD.
　1901.　A synopsis of the mammals of North America and the adjacent
　　　　seas. Field Columbian Mus., zool. ser., vol. 2, xv + 471 pp.,
　　　　figs. 1–94, pls. 1–49.
　1904.　The land and sea mammals of Middle America and the West
　　　　Indies. Field Columbian Mus. Publ. 95, zool. ser., vol. 4,
　　　　pt. 1, pp. i–xxi, 1–439, i–xlix, figs., pls. 1–41; pt. 2, pp. i–xiii,
　　　　441–850, figs., pls. 42–68.
　1905.　Descriptions of three apparently new species of mammals.
　　　　Proc. Biol. Soc. Washington, vol. 18, pp. 79–82.
ELLIOTT, CHARLES, EDITOR.
　1942.　Fading trails, 279 pp., illus. New York.
ELLIOTT, HENRY WOOD.
　1875.　The sea otter and its hunting. In: A report upon the condition
　　　　of affairs in the Territory of Alaska. House Exec. Doc. 83,
　　　　44th Congress, 1st Sess., pp. 54–62. Washington.
ELY, ALFRED, ET AL.
　1939.　North American big game, xxii + 530 pp., illus. New York and
　　　　London.
EMMONS, EBENEZER.
　1840.　Report on the quadrupeds of Massachusetts, pp. 1–86. Cam-
　　　　bridge.
ENGLIS, BLYE.
　1939.　Death on Murderers' Creek. Amer. Forests, vol. 45, no. 2, pp.
　　　　58–59, 87.
EYERDAM, WALTER J.
　1933.　Sea otters in the Aleutian Islands. Journ. Mamm., vol. 14, pp.
　　　　70–71.
FIGGINS, J. D.
　1933.　The bison of the western area of the Mississippi basin. Proc.
　　　　Colorado Mus. Nat. Hist., vol. 12, pp. 16–33, 9 pls.
FISHER, ALBERT KENRICK.
　1896.　The mammals of Sing Sing, New York. The Observer, vol. 7,
　　　　no. 5, pp. 193–200.
FISHER, EDNA M.
　1930.　The early fauna of Santa Cruz Island, California. Journ.
　　　　Mamm., vol. 11, pp. 75–76.
　1934.　Early fauna of the Monterey region, California. Journ. Mamm.,
　　　　vol. 15, p. 253.
　1939.　Habits of the southern sea otter. Journ. Mamm., vol. 20, pp.
　　　　21–36, 27 figs.
FITZSIMONS, FREDERICK WILLIAM.
　1920.　The natural history of South Africa: Mammals (in 4 vols.), vol.
　　　　3, xiii + 278 pp.; vol. 4, xix + 271 pp. London.

FLEMING, JAMES H.
  1913. Mammals of Toronto, Ontario. *In:* The natural history of the
          Toronto region, reprint, 6 pp.
FLOWER, STANLEY SMYTH.
  1932. Notes on the recent mammals of Egypt, with a list of species
          recorded from that kingdom. Proc. Zool. Soc. London, for
          1932, pp. 369-430.
FOWLER, ROY L.
  1937. Changes in the natural history of the High River district,
          Alberta. Can. Field-Nat., vol. 51, pp. 15-16.
FRASER, F. C.
  1935. Sea elephant on St. Helena. Proc. Linn. Soc. London, sess. 147,
          pp. 33-35, pl. 2.
FREUCHEN, PETER.
  1920. Lidt om Polarulven. Some remarks on the occurrence of the
          polar wolf in East Greenland. Gronlandske Selskabs Aarsskr.,
          for 1919, pp. 17-29.
  1922. Om hvalrossens forkomst og vandringer ved Groenlands vest-
          kyst. The occurrence and wanderings of the walrus on the
          west coast of Greenland. Vid. Medd. Nat. For. Kjøbenhavn,
          vol. 72, pp. 237-249.
FRY, W.
  1923. The wolverine. California Fish and Game, vol. 9, pp. 129-134.
FRYXELL, F. M.
  1926. A horn of the prong-horn antelope (*Antilocapra americana*)
          found at Moline, Illinois. Journ. Mamm., vol. 7, pp. 333-334.
  1928. The former range of the bison in the Rocky Mountains. Journ.
          Mamm., vol. 9, pp. 129-139.
FUNKHOUSER, W. D.
  1925. Wild life in Kentucky. Kentucky Geological Survey, ser. 6,
          vol. 16, pp. [x] + 385, 89 figs., 1 pl.
GABRIELSON, IRA NOEL.
  1937. Rare and vanishing species. Amer. Field, vol. 127, no. 16, p. 436.
GARRETSON, MARTIN S.
  1938. The American bison: The story of its extermination as a wild
          species and its restoration under federal protection, xii + 254
          pp., illustr. New York Zoological Society.
GAUMER, GEORGE F.
  1917. Monografía de los mamíferos de Yucatán, 8vo, xxxviii + 331
          pp., 57 pls., map. Mexico City.
GAY, CLAUDIO.
  1847. Historia física y política de Chile, etc. Zoologia, vol. 1, Mamí-
          feros, pp. 1-182; atlas, pls. 1-11.
GEOFFROY-SAINT-HILAIRE, ÉTIENNE, AND CUVIER, FRÉDÉRIC.
  1825. Histoire naturelle des mammifères, vol. 3. (Each species illus-
          trated with colored plates and paged separately.)
  1830. *Idem*, vol. 4.
GILPIN, J. BERNARD.
  1867. On the Mammalia of Nova Scotia: No. III. Proc. and Trans.
          Nova Scotia Inst. Sci., for 1867, pp. 8-16.

GILSON, H. CARY.
1938. The Percy Sladen Expedition to Lake Titicaca. Geogr. Journ., vol. 91, no. 6, pp. 533–542, 5 pls., 1 map.

GOELDI, EMIL AUGUST.
1904. On the rare rodent *Dinomys branickii* Peters. Proc. Zool. Soc. London, for 1904, vol. 2, pp. 158–162, pl. 10.

GOELDI, EMIL A., AND HAGMANN, G.
1904. Catalogo da colecção de mammíferos no Museu do Pará. Bol. Mus. Goeldi, vol. 4, pp. 38–122.

GOLDMAN, EDWARD A.
1918. The rice rats of North America (genus *Oryzomys*). North Amer. Fauna, no. 43, 100 pp., 6 pls.
1920. Mammals of Panama. Smithsonian Misc. Coll., vol. 69, no. 5, pp. 1–309, pls. 1–39 (incl. map).
1928. The Kaibab or white-tailed squirrel. Journ. Mamm., vol. 9, pp. 127–129, pl. 16.
1932. A new beaver from Arizona. Journ. Mamm., vol. 13, pp. 266–267.
1935. New American mustelids of the genera *Martes*, *Gulo*, and *Lutra*. Proc. Biol. Soc. Washington, vol. 48, pp. 175–186.
1937. The wolves of North America. Journ. Mamm., vol. 18, pp. 37–45.

GOODWIN, GEORGE G.
1924. Mammals of the Gaspé Peninsula, Quebec. Journ. Mamm., vol. 5, pp. 246–257, pls. 28–29.
1936. Big game animals in the northeastern United States. Journ. Mamm., vol. 17, pp. 48–50.

GOSSE, PHILLIP H., AND HILL, RICHARD.
1851. A naturalist's sojourn in Jamaica, xxv + 508 pp., 8 pls. London.

GOULD, JOHN.
1863. The mammals of Australia, 3 vols., atlas. London.

GRANT, MADISON.
1902. The caribou. 7th Ann. Rept. New York Zool. Soc., 24 pp., 21 pls.
1933. The vanished game of yesterday. *In:* "Hunting Trails on Three Continents," pp. 1–22, 2 pls. New York.

GRAVES, HENRY S., AND NELSON, E. W.
1919. Our national elk herds. A program for conserving the elk on National Forests about the Yellowstone National Park. U. S. Dept. Agr. Dept. Circ. 51, 34 pp., 19 figs.

GRAY, JOHN EDWARD.
1859. On the eared seal of the Cape of Good Hope (*Otaria delalandii*). Proc. Zool. Soc. London, for 1859, pp. 107–110, 2 pls.
1872a. Notes on a new species of tapir (*Tapirus leucogenys*) from the snowy regions of the Cordilleras of Ecuador and on the young spotted tapirs of tropical America. Proc. Zool. Soc. London, for 1872, pp. 483–492, 1 fig., 2 pls.
1872b. On the sea-bear of New Zealand (*Arctocephalus cinereus*) and the North-Australian sea-bear (*Gypsophoca tropicalis*). Proc. Zool. Soc. London, for 1872, pp. 653–662, 4 figs.
1874. Hand-list of seals, morses, sea-lions, and sea-bears in the British Museum, 43 pp., 15 figs., 30 pls. London.

GRAY, PRENTISS N., EDITOR.
1932. Records of North American big game, ix + 178 pp., 26 figs., 30 pls. New York.

GRAY, R. W.
1935. Greenland whales and the Eskimos of N. E. Greenland. Scottish Nat., no. 213, pp. 75–77.

GREEN, ASHDOWN H.
1869. On the natural history and hunting of the beaver (*Castor canadensis*, Kuhl) on the Pacific slope of the Rocky Mountains: With supplementary notes by Robert Brown. Journ. Linn. Soc. London, vol. 10, pp. 361–372.

GRINNELL, GEORGE BIRD.
1928. Mountain sheep. Journ. Mamm., vol. 9, pp. 1–9.

GRINNELL, HILDA WOOD.
1918. A synopsis of the bats of California. Univ. California Publ. Zool., vol. 17, pp. 223–404, 24 figs., pls. 14–24.

GRINNELL, JOSEPH.
1933. Review of the recent mammal fauna of California. Univ. California Publ. Zool., vol. 40, pp. 71–234.

GRINNELL, JOSEPH; DIXON, JOSEPH S.; AND LINSDALE, JEAN M.
1930. Vertebrate natural history of a section of northern California through the Lassen Peak region. Univ. California Publ. Zool., vol. 35, pp. i–v, 1–594, figs. 1–181.
1937. Fur-bearing mammals of California, their natural history, systematic status, and relations to man, 2 vols., illus. Berkeley.

GRINNELL, JOSEPH, AND STORER, TRACY I.
1924. Animal life in the Yosemite. An account of the mammals, birds, reptiles, and amphibians in a cross-section of the Sierra Nevada, xviii + 752 pp., 62 pls. Berkeley.

GUNDLACH, JUAN.
1877. Contribución á la mamalogía cubana, 53 pp. Habana.

GUNTER, GORDON.
1941. Occurrence of the manatee in the United States with records from Mexico. Journ. Mamm., vol. 22, pp. 60–64.

HAHN, WALTER LOUIS.
1909. The mammals of Indiana. A descriptive catalogue of the mammals occurring in Indiana in recent times. 33d Ann. Rept. Indiana Dept. Geol. and Nat. Resources, for 1908, pp. 417–663, 36 figs., 5 pls.

HALE, HERBERT M.
1931. The pygmy right whale (*Neobalaena marginata*) in South Australian waters. Rec. South Australian Mus., vol. 4, pp. 314–319, 4 figs.

HALL, E. RAYMOND.
1928. A new race of black bear from Vancouver Island, British Columbia, with remarks on other Northwest Coast forms of *Euarctos*. Univ. California Publ. Zool., vol. 30, pp. 231–242, pls. 12, 13.
1932. Remarks on the affinities of the mammalian fauna of Vancouver Islands, British Columbia, with descriptions of new subspecies. Univ. California Publ. Zool., vol. 38, pp. 415–423.

HALL, E. RAYMOND.—*Cont.*
  1934. Certain osteological features of *Euderma maculatum.* Journ.
         Mamm., vol. 15, pp. 68–70, figs. 1–4.
  1935. Occurrence of the spotted bat at Reno, Nevada. Journ.
         Mamm., vol. 16, p. 148.
  1939. The spotted bat in Kern County, California. Journ. Mamm.,
         vol. 20, p. 103.
HANNA, G. DALLAS.
  1922. Why not protect the fur seal herds of the Southern Hemisphere?
         (With supplementary note by A. F. Bassett Hull.) Australian
         Zool., vol. 3, pt. 1, pp. 11–14.
  1923. Rare mammals of the Pribilof Islands, Alaska. Journ. Mamm.,
         vol. 4, pp. 209–215, pl. 23.
HARLAN, RICHARD.
  1824. On a species of lamantin resembling the *Manatus senegalensis*
         (Cuvier) inhabiting the coast of east Florida. Journ. Acad.
         Nat. Sci. Philadelphia, vol. 3, pt. 2, pp. 390–394, pl. 13.
HARMER, SIR SIDNEY F.
  1928. The history of whaling. Proc. Linn. Soc. London, sess. 140,
         1927–28, pp. 51–95.
  1931. Southern whaling. Proc. Linn. Soc. London, sess. 142, 1929–30,
         pp. 85–163.
HARPER, FRANCIS.
  1925. The wood buffalo and the proposed introduction of Plains
         buffalo. Can. Field-Nat., vol. 39, p. 45.
  1927. The mammals of the Okefinokee Swamp region of Georgia.
         Proc. Boston Soc. Nat. Hist., vol. 38, pp. 191–396, 4 figs., 4
         pls., 1 map.
  1929. Notes on mammals of the Adirondacks. New York State Mus.
         Handbook 8, pp. 51–118, 17 figs.
  1932. Mammals of the Athabaska and Great Slave Lakes region.
         Journ. Mamm., vol. 13, pp. 19–36, pls. 3–5.
HARTLAUB, CLEMENS.
  1886. Beiträge zur Kenntniss der *Manatus*-Arten. Zool. Jahrb., vol.
         1, pp. 1–112, pls. 1–4.
HATCHER, JOHN BELL.
  1896. Recent and fossil tapirs. Amer. Journ. Sci., ser. 4, vol. 1, pp.
         161–180, 2 figs, 4 pls.
HATT, ROBERT T.
  1934. The American Museum Congo Expedition manatee and other
         Recent manatees. Bull. Amer. Mus. Nat. Hist., vol. 66, pp.
         533–566, pl. 27.
HATTON, JOSEPH, AND HARVEY, M.
  1883. Newfoundland, the oldest British colony, 489 pp. London.
HAUTHAL, R.; ROTH, S.; AND LEHMANN-NITSCHE, R.
  1899. El mamífero misterioso de la Patagonia, *Grypotherium domes-
         ticum.* Rev. Mus. La Plata, vol. 9, pp. 409–474, pls. 1–5.
HAYASI, KYO.
  1928. A call for the protection of the whale. Proc. 3d Pan-Pacific
         Sci. Congress, Tokyo, 1926, vol. 1, pp. 1079–1085.

HEARNE, J.
   1835. [Notice of a specimen of *Solenodonta*, obtained by him in Hayti.]
        Proc. Zool. Soc. London, for 1835, p. 105.
HELLER, EDMUND.
   1904. Mammals of the Galapagos Archipelago, exclusive of the
        Cetacea. Proc. California Acad. Sci., Zool., ser. 3, vol. 3, pp.
        233–250, 1 pl.
HERMANN, JOHANN.
   1779. Beschreibung der Münchs-robbe. Beschäft. Berlin Ges. Naturf.
        Freunde, vol. 4, pp. 456–509.
HERRE, ALBERT W.
   1928. Rational methods for the protection of useful aquatic animals of
        the Pacific. Proc. 3d Pan-Pacific Sci. Congress, Tokyo, 1926,
        vol. 1, pp. 1072–1074.
HERRICK, CLARENCE LUTHER.
   1892. The mammals of Minnesota. A scientific and popular account
        of their features and habits. Geol. and Nat. Hist. Surv.
        Minnesota Bull. 7, pp. 1–301, 23 figs, 8 pls.
HIBBARD, CLAUDE W.
   1933. A revised check list of Kansas mammals. Trans. Kansas Acad.
        Sci., vol. 36, pp. 230–249.
HIRASAKA, KYOSUKE.
   1932. The occurrence of dugong in Formosa. Mem. Fac. Sci. and
        Agr. Taihoku Imp. Univ., vol. 7, pp. 1–3, pl. 1.
HOLLISTER, NED.
   1908. The last records of deer in Walworth County, Wisconsin. Bull.
        Wisconsin Nat. Hist. Soc., vol. 6, pp. 143–144.
   1912a. Mammals of the Alpine Club expedition to the Mount Robson
        region. Can. Alpine Journ., special no., pp. 1–44, pls. 1–13.
   1912b. New mammals from Canada, Alaska, and Kamchatka. Smith-
        sonian Misc. Coll., vol. 56, no. 35, pp. 1–8, pls. 1–3.
HOLZWORTH, JOHN M.
   1930. The wild grizzlies of Alaska. New York.
HONE, ELISABETH.
   1934. The present status of the muskox. Amer. Comm. for Internat.
        Wild Life Protection Spec. Publ. 5, 87 pp., 4 pls.
HOPWOOD, ARTHUR T.
   1926. A fossil rice-rat from the Pleistocene of Barbuda. Ann. Mag.
        Nat. Hist., ser. 9, vol. 17, p. 328–330, pl. 12.
HORNADAY, WILLIAM T.
   1889. The extermination of the American bison, with a sketch of its
        discovery and life history. Ann. Rep. U. S. Nat. Mus. for
        1887, pp. 367–548, 21 pls., map.
   1901. Notes on the mountain sheep of North America, with a descrip-
        tion of a new species. 5th Ann. Rept. New York Zool. Soc.,
        pp. 77–122, 14 pls., map.
   1905. A new white bear from British Columbia. 9th Ann. Rept.
        New York Zool. Soc., pp. 80–86.
   1911. The spectacled bear. New York Zool. Soc. Bull. 45, pp. 747–
        748, 4 figs.

HOWELL, A. BRAZIER, AND HUEY, LAURENCE M.
    1930. Food of the gray and other whales. Journ. Mamm., vol. 11,
        pp. 321–322.
HOWELL, ARTHUR H.
    1921. A biological survey of Alabama. I. Physiography and life
        zones. II. The Mammals. North Amer. Fauna, no. 45, pp.
        1–88, 10 pls., 11 maps.
HUDSON, WILLIAM HENRY.
    1892. The naturalist in La Plata, x + 388 pp., illus. London and
        New York.
HUEY, LAURENCE M.
    1924. Recent observations on the northern elephant seal. Journ.
        Mamm., vol. 5, pp. 237–242, pls. 24–27.
    1925. Late information on the Guadalupe Island elephant seal herd.
        Journ. Mamm., vol. 6, pp. 126–127.
    1927. The latest northern elephant seal census. Journ. Mamm., vol.
        8, pp. 160–161.
    1928. Notes on the California gray whale. Journ. Mamm., vol. 9,
        pp. 71–73.
    1930a. Past and present status of the northern elephant seal with a
        note on the Guadalupe fur seal. Journ. Mamm., vol. 11, pp.
        188–194.
    1930b. Capture of an elephant seal off San Diego, California, with notes
        on stomach contents. Journ. Mamm., vol. 11, pp. 229–231.
HUTTON, FREDERICK WOLLASTON, AND DRUMMOND, JAMES.
    1923. The animals of New Zealand; an account of the Dominion's
        air-breathing vertebrates, ed. 4, 434 pp., illus.
INTERDEPARTMENTAL COMMITTEE ON RESEARCH AND DEVELOPMENT IN THE
    DEPENDENCIES OF THE FALKLAND ISLANDS.
    1921. Extracts from report of. Journ. Soc. Pres. Fauna Empire, new
        ser., pt. 1, pp. 62–74.
ISACHSEN, GUNNAR.
    1929. Modern Norwegian whaling in the Antarctic. Geogr. Rev., vol.
        19, pp. 387–403, 21 figs.
JACKSON, C. F.
    1922. Notes on New Hampshire mammals. Journ. Mamm., vol. 3, pp.
        13–15.
JACKSON, HARTLEY H. T.
    1908. A preliminary list of Wisconsin mammals. Bull. Wisconsin
        Nat. Hist. Soc., vol. 6, pp. 13–34, pl. 3.
    1922. Wolverene in Itasca County, Minnesota. Journ. Mamm., vol. 3,
        p. 53.
    1928. A taxonomic review of the American long-tailed shrews. North
        Amer. Fauna, no. 51, 238 pp., 24 figs. (incl. 19 maps), 13 pls.
JACOBI, ARNOLD.
    1931. Das Renntier. Eine zoologische Monographie der Gattung
        Rangifer. Zool. Anz., Ergänzungsband to vol. 96, pp. 1–264,
        32 figs., 6 pls.

JENSEN, A. S.
    1928.   The fauna of Greenland. *In* "Greenland," vol. 1, pp. 319–355.
            Committee for the Direction of the Geological and Geographi-
            cal investigations in Greenland. Copenhagen and London.
JOHNSON, CHARLES E.
    1922.   An investigation of the beaver in Herkimer and Hamilton
            Counties of the Adirondacks. Roosevelt Wild Life Bull., vol.
            1, no. 2, pp. 117–186, 2 maps, 36 figs.
    1923.   A recent report of the wolverene in Minnesota. Journ. Mamm.,
            vol. 4, pp. 54–55.
JONES, FREDERIC WOOD. (See Wood Jones, F.)
JORDAN, DAVID STARR, et al.
    1899.   The fur seals and fur-seal islands of the North Pacific Ocean,
            4 vols., illus., maps.
JUKES, JOSEPH B.
    1842.   Explorations in and about Newfoundland.
JUNGE, G. C. A.
    1936.   Bones of a whale [*Rhachianectes*] from the Wieringermeer,
            Zuider Zee. Nature (London), vol. 138, p. 78.
KAUDERN, WALTER.
    1915.   Säugetiere aus Madagaskar. Arkiv Zool., vol. 9, no. 18, pp.
            1–101, pls. 1–4.
KEEN, J. H.
    1909.   Caribou in the Queen Charlotte Islands. Ottawa Nat., vol. 22,
            p. 260.
KELLOGG, REMINGTON.
    1918.   A revision of the *Microtus californicus* group of meadow mice.
            Univ. California Publ. Zool., vol. 21, pp. 1–42, fig.
    1931.   Whaling statistics for the Pacific coast of North America.
            Journ. Mamm., vol. 12, pp. 73–77.
    1937.   Annotated list of West Virginia mammals. Proc. U. S. Nat.
            Mus., vol. 84, pp. 443–479.
    1939.   Annotated list of Tennessee mammals. Proc. U. S. Nat. Mus.,
            vol. 86, pp. 245–303.
    1942.   Tertiary, Quaternary, and Recent marine mammals of South
            America and the West Indies. Proc. 8th Amer. Sci. Congress,
            Washington, 1940, vol. 3, pp. 445–473.
KENNEDY, WILLIAM ROBERT.
    1892.   Sporting sketches in South America, 268 pp., illus., map. London.
KIDDER, J. H.
    1876.   Contribution to the natural history of Kerguelen Island, made
            in connection with the United States Transit-of-Venus Expedi-
            tion, 1874–75, 122 pp. Washington.
KNOX, F. J.
    1871.   Observations on the Ziphidae, a family of the Cetacea: with
            notes by Dr. [James] Hector. Trans. New Zealand Inst., vol.
            3, pp. 125–129, 3 pls.
KOWARZIK, RUDOLF.
    1910.   Der Moschusochs und seine Rassen. Fauna Arctica, vol. 5,
            pp. 87–126, 16 figs.

KRIEG, HANS.
> 1931. Geographische Übersicht und illustrierter Routtenbericht, xii + 95 pp. Wissenschaftliche Ergebnisse der deutschen Gran Chaco Expedition [Bd. 2]. Stuttgart.

KUNTZE, R.
> 1932. Benedictus Dybowski als Säugetierforscher. Zeitschr. für Säugetierkunde, vol. 7, pp. 39–54, portr.

LANTZ, DAVID E.
> 1905. A list of Kansas mammals. Trans. Kansas Acad. Sci., vol. 19, pp. 171–178.
> 1907. Additions and corrections to the list of Kansas mammals. Trans. Kansas Acad. Sci., vol. 20, pp. 214–217.

LAMONT, JAMES.
> 1861. Seasons with sea-horses; or, sporting adventures in the northern seas, i–xvi, 17–282 pp., illus., map. New York.

LAURIE, ALEC H.
> 1937. The age of female blue whales and the effect of whaling on the stock. *Discovery* Reports, vol. 15, pp. 223–284.

LAWRENCE, BARBARA.
> 1934. New *Geocapromys* from the Bahamas. Occ. Pap. Boston Soc. Nat. Hist., vol. 8, pp. 189–196, 3 figs.

LE SOUËF, A. S.
> 1925. Notes on the seals found in Australian seas. Australian Zool., vol. 4, pp. 112–116, 7 figs.

LE SOUËF, A. S.; BURRELL, HARRY; AND TROUGHTON, ELLIS LE G.
> 1926. The wild animals of Australia embracing the mammals of New Guinea and the nearer Pacific islands with a chapter on the bats of Australia and New Guinea, 388 pp., illus. London.

LICHTENSTEIN, MARTIN HEINRICH CARL.
> 1830. Darstellung neuer oder wenig bekannter Säugethiere . . . . , [118] pp., 50 col. pls. Berlin.

LINSLEY, JAMES H.
> 1842. A catalogue of the Mammalia of Connecticut, arranged according to their natural families. Amer. Journ. Sci., ser. 1, vol. 43, pp. 345–354.

LLOYD, HOYES.
> 1936. Canada's fur resources. Proc. North American Wildlife Conference, 1936, pp. 628–630.

LÖNNBERG, EINAR.
> 1906. Contributions to the fauna of South Georgia. Kungl. Svenska Vet.-Akad. Handl., vol. 40, no. 5, 104 pp., 12 pls.
> 1910. Ein Exemplar von *Tremarctos ornatus* aus Venezuela. Zool. Anz., vol. 36, pp. 45–50.
> 1913. Notes on guanacos. Arkiv Zool., vol. 8, no. 19, 8 pp., 3 figs.
> 1923. Cetological notes. Arkiv Zool., vol. 15, no. 24, 18 pp., 6 figs.
> 1931. The skeleton of *Balaenoptera brydei* Ö. Olsen. Arkiv Zool., vol. 23A, no. 1, 23 pp., 6 pls.

LOOMIS, F. B.
> 1911. A new mink from the shell heaps of Maine. Amer. Journ. Sci., ser. 4, vol. 31, pp. 227–229.

LORD, CLIVE ERROL, AND SCOTT, H. H.
  1924. A synopsis of the vertebrate animals of Tasmania. viii + 340
      pp., illus. Hobart.
LOW, ALBERT PETER.
  1906. Report on the Dominion Government Expedition to Hudson
      Bay and the Arctic Islands on board the D. G. S. *Neptune*,
      1903-1904, xvii + 355 pp., illus. Ottawa.
LOWE, PERCY ROYCROFT.
  1911. A naturalist on desert islands. 8vo, xii + 300 pp., illus. London.
LYDEKKER, RICHARD.
  1898. The deer of all lands. A history of the family Cervidae living
      and extinct, xviii + 329 pp., 80 figs., 24 pls. London.
  1901. The great and small game of Europe, western and northern
      Asia, and America, xx + 445 pp., illus. London.
  1909. On the skull-characters in the southern sea-elephant. Proc.
      Zool. Soc. London, for 1909, pp. 600-606, 3 figs.
  1915. Catalogue of the ungulate mammals in the British Museum
      (Natural History), vol. 4: Artiodactyla, families Cervidae
      (deer), Tragulidae (chevrotains), Camelidae (camels and
      llamas), Suidae (pigs and peccaries), and Hippopotamidae
      (hippopotamuses), xxi + 438 pp., 56 figs. British Museum.
LYON, GRETCHEN M.
  1935. Some marine mammals from a southern California shellmound.
      Journ. Mamm., vol. 16, pp. 151-152.
LYON, MARCUS WARD, JR.
  1936. Mammals of Indiana. Amer. Midl. Nat., vol. 17, pp. 1-384,
      125 figs., 85 maps.
LYON, P. I., ET AL.
  1920. Report of Interdepartmental Committee on Research and Devel-
      opment in the Falkland Island Dependencies, 1920, pp. 1-164.
MACCAGNO, LUIS.
  1932. Los auquénidos peruanos, iv + 64 pp., 24 pls. Lima.
MACKINTOSH, N. A., AND WHEELER, J. F. G.
  1929. Southern blue and fin whales. *Discovery* Reports, vol. 1, pp.
      257-540, pls. 25-44.
MACMILLAN, DONALD B.
  1918. Four years in the White North, (18) + 426 pp., illus. New York.
MAJOR, C. I. FORSYTH.
  1901. The musk-rat of Santa Lucia (Antilles). Ann. Mag. Nat.
      Hist., ser. 7, vol. 7, pp. 204-206.
MANNICHE, A. L. V.
  1910. The terrestrial mammals and birds of north-east Greenland.
      Meddel. om Grønland, vol. 45, pp. 1-199, pls. 1-7.
MARR, JAMES W. S.
  1935. The South Orkney Islands. *Discovery* Reports, vol. 10, pp. 283-
      382, 14 pls., 11 maps.
MARSH, HADLEIGH.
  1938. Pneumonia in Rocky Mountain bighorn sheep. Journ. Mamm.,
      vol. 19, pp. 214-219.

MATSCHIE, PAUL.
  1918. Sechs neue Arten der Gattung *Gulo.* Sitzb. Ges. naturf. Freunde
          Berlin, 1918, pp. 141–155.
MATTHEW, W. D.
  1918. Affinities and origin of the Antillean mammals. Bull. Geol.
          Soc. Amer., vol. 29, pp. 657–666.
  1931. Genera and new species of ground sloths from the Pleistocene of
          Cuba, with prefatory note by W. Granger. Amer. Mus.
          Nov., no. 511, pp. 1–5.
MATTHEWS, L. HARRISON
  1937. The humpback whale, *Megaptera nodosa. Discovery* Reports,
          vol. 17, pp. 7–92, pl. 2.
  1938a. The sperm whale, *Physeter catodon. Discovery* Reports, vol. 17,
          pp. 93–168, pls. 3–11.
  1938b. The Sei whale, *Balaenoptera borealis. Discovery* Reports, vol.
          17, pp. 183–290, pls. 18, 19.
  1938c. Notes on the southern right whale, *Eubalaena australis. Dis-
          covery* Reports, vol. 17, pp. 169–182, pls. 12–17.
MAXWELL, MARCUSWELL.
  1930. Elephants and other big game studies, 28 pls. London.
MAYNARD, CHARLES J.
  1872. Catalogue of the mammals of Florida with notes on their habits,
          distribution, etc. Bull. Essex Inst., vol. 4, pp. 135–150.
MEARNS, EDGAR A.
  1907. Mammals of the Mexican boundary of the United States. U. S.
          Nat. Mus. Bull. 56, xv + 530 pp., 126 figs., 13 pls.
MERRIAM, C. HART.
  1882. The vertebrates of the Adirondack region, northeastern New
          York. Mammalia. Trans. Linn. Soc. New York, vol. 1,
          pp. 26–106.
  1884. The vertebrates of the Adirondack region, northeastern New
          York. (Second installment, concluding the Mammalia.)
          Trans. Linn. Soc. New York, vol. 2, pp. 9–214.
  1891. Results of a biological reconnoissance of south-central Idaho.
          2, Annotated list of mammals, with descriptions of new
          species. North Amer. Fauna, no. 5, pp. 32–87.
  1896. Preliminary synopsis of the American bears. Proc. Biol. Soc.
          Washington, vol. 10, pp. 65–83, pls. 4–6.
  1901. Preliminary revision of the pumas (*Felis concolor* group). Proc.
          Washington Acad. Sci., vol. 3, pp. 577–600.
  1905. A new elk from California, *Cervus nannodes.* Proc. Biol. Soc.
          Washington, vol. 18, pp. 23–25, 1 fig.
  1918. Review of the grizzly and big brown bears of North America
          (genus *Ursus*) with description of a new genus, *Vetularctos.*
          North Amer. Fauna, no. 41, pp. 1–136, pls. 1–16.
  1919. Is the jaguar entitled to a place in the California fauna? Journ.
          Mamm., vol. 1, pp. 38–40.
  1921. Former range of mountain sheep in California. Journ. Mamm.,
          vol. 2, p. 239.

MERRIAM, C. HART.—*Cont.*
1926. The buffalo in northeastern California. Journ. Mamm., vol. 7, pp. 211–214.
MESERVE, F. G., AND BARBOUR, E. H.
1932. Association of an arrow head with *Bison occidentalis* in Nebraska. Bull. Nebraska State Mus., vol. 1, pp. 239–242, fig.
MILLER, GERRIT S., JR.
1896. The beach mouse of Muskeget Island. Proc. Boston Soc. Nat. Hist., vol. 27, pp. 75–87, 1 pl.
1897a. Revision of the North American bats of the family Vespertilionidae. North Amer. Fauna, no. 13, 138 pp., 40 figs., 3 pls.
1897b. Notes on the mammals of Ontario. Proc. Boston Soc. Nat. Hist., vol. 28, pp. 1–44.
1898. Descriptions of five new phyllostome bats. Proc. Acad. Nat. Sci. Philadelphia, vol. 50, pp. 326–337, 5 figs.
1899. Preliminary list of the mammals of New York. Bull. New York State Mus., vol. 6, no. 29, pp. 271–390.
1904. Notes on the bats collected by William Palmer in Cuba. Proc. U. S. Nat. Mus., vol. 27, pp. 337–348, pl. 9.
1905. Mammals of the Bahama Islands. *In:* Shattuck's "The Bahama Islands," pp. 373–384, pls. 72–74. New York.
1907. The families and genera of bats. U. S. Nat. Mus. Bull. 57, xvii + 282 pp., 49 figs., 14 pls.
1912. The names of the large wolves of northern and western North America. Smithsonian Misc. Coll., vol. 59, no. 15, 5 pp.
1916a. Remains of two species of *Capromys* from ancient burial sites in Jamaica. Proc. Biol. Soc. Washington, vol. 29, p. 48.
1916b. Bones of mammals from Indian sites in Cuba and Santo Domingo. Smithsonian Misc. Coll., vol. 66, no. 12, 10 pp., 1 pl.
1918a. Mammals and reptiles collected by Theodoor de Booy in the Virgin Islands. Proc. U. S. Nat. Mus., vol. 54, pp. 507–511, pl. 81.
1918b. A new river-dolphin from China. Smithsonian Misc. Coll., vol. 68, no. 9, 12 pp., 13 pls.
1922. Remains of mammals from caves in the Republic of Haiti. Smithsonian Misc. Coll., vol. 74, no. 3, 8 pp.
1924a. List of North American recent mammals, 1923. U. S. Nat. Mus. Bull. 128, xvi + 673 pp.
1924b. Some hitherto unpublished photographs and measurements of the blue whale. Proc. U. S. Nat. Mus., vol. 66, art. 7, 4 pp., 9 pls.
1924c. A second instance of the development of rodent-like incisors in an artiodactyl. Proc. U. S. Nat. Mus., vol. 66, art. 8, 4 pp., 1 pl.
1927. The rodents of the genus *Plagiodontia*. Proc. U. S. Nat. Mus., vol. 72, art. 16, 8 pp., 1 pl.
1929a. A second collection of mammals from caves near St. Michel, Haiti. Smithsonian Misc. Coll., vol. 81, no. 9, 30 pp., 10 pls.
1929b. The characters of the genus *Geocapromys* Chapman. Smithsonian Misc. Coll., vol. 82, no. 4, 3 pp., 1 pl.

MILLER, GERRIT S., JR.—*Cont.*

1929c. Mammals eaten by Indians, owls, and Spaniards in the coast region of the Dominican Republic. Smithsonian Misc. Coll., vol. 82, no. 5, 16 pp., 2 pls.

1930. Three small collections of mammals from Hispaniola. Smithsonian Misc. Coll., vol. 82, no. 15, 10 pp., 2 pls.

1939. Note on the lectotype of *Lasiurus semotus* (H. Allen). Journ. Mamm., vol. 20, p. 369.

MILLER, GERRIT S., JR., AND GIDLEY, JAMES W.

1918. Synopsis of the supergeneric groups of rodents. Journ. Washington Acad. Sci., vol. 8, pp. 431–448.

MILLETT, MARCUS W.

1914. Jungle sport in Ceylon. London.

MILLS, HARLOW B.

1937. A preliminary study of the bighorn of Yellowstone National Park. Journ. Mamm., vol. 18, pp. 205–212.

MIVART, ST. GEORGE.

1890. Dogs, jackals, wolves, and foxes: A monograph of the Canidae, xxxvi + 216 pp., 45 col. pls. London.

MOHR, ERNA.

1936–37. Biologische Beobachtungen an *Solenodon paradoxus* Brandt in Gefangschaft. I–III. Zool. Anz., vol. 113, pp. 176–188, figs. 1–17, Feb. 1936; vol. 116, pp. 65–76, figs. 18–35, Oct. 1936; vol. 117, pp. 233–241, figs. 36–41, Mar. 1937.

1937a. Schlitzrüssler [solenodons]. Mitteil. Zool. Garten Stadt Halle, vol. 32, no. 4, 5 pp., 8 figs.

1937b. Vom Pacarana (*Dinomys branickii* Peters). Der Zool. Garten, new ser., vol. 9, pp. 204–209, 10 figs.

MOLINA, GIOVANNI I.

1782. Saggio sulla storia naturale del Chile, 367 pp., map. Bologna.

MOLTONI, EDGARDO.

1938. Escursione ornitologica all'Isloa delli Uccelli (Golfo della Gran Sirte, Cirenaica). Riv. Ital. Ornit., vol. 8, pp. 1–16, 9 figs., 1 pl.

MONOD, T.

1923. Note sur la presence du *Monachus albiventer* sur la côte saharienne. Bull. Mus. Hist. Nat. Paris, vol. 29, pp. 555–557.

MORRISON-SCOTT, T. C. S.

1939. Description of *Capromys nana* Allen, a supposedly extinct Cuban hutia. Ann. Mag. Nat. Hist., ser. 11, vol. 3, pp. 214–216, pls. 5–7.

MURDOCH, W. G. BURN.

1917. Modern whaling and bear hunting, pp. 1–320, illus. London.

MURIE, OLAUS J.

1930. An epizootic disease of elk. Journ. Mamm., vol. 11, pp. 214–222, pls. 13–14.

1935. Alaska-Yukon caribou. North Amer. Fauna, no. 54, 93 pp., 10 pls.

1940. Notes on the sea otter. Journ. Mamm., vol. 21, pp. 119–131, 3 figs.

MURPHY, ROBERT CUSHMAN.
1914. Notes on the sea elephant, *Mirounga leonina* (Linné). Bull. Amer. Mus. Nat. Hist., vol. 33, pp. 63–79, pls. 1–7.
1918. The status of sealing in the subantarctic Atlantic. Sci. Monthly, vol. 7, pp. 112–119, 9 figs.
1936. Oceanic birds of South America. A study of species of the related coasts and seas, including the American quadrant of Antarctica based upon the Brewster-Sanford collection in the American Museum of Natural History, 2 vols., illustr. New York.

NELSON, EDWARD WILLIAM.
1887. Report upon natural history collections made in Alaska between the years 1877 and 1881. U. S. Army Arctic Ser., no. 3, 337 pp., 21 pls.
1902. A new species of elk from Arizona. Bull. Amer. Mus. Nat. Hist., vol. 16, pp. 1–12, figs. 1–7.
1916. The larger North American mammals. Nat. Geogr. Mag., vol. 30, pp. 385–472, many col. illus.
1918. Smaller mammals of North America. Nat. Geogr. Mag., vol. 33, pp. 371–493, many col. illus.
1921. Lower California and its natural resources. Mem. Nat. Acad. Sci., vol. 16, 171 pp., 35 pls.
1923. The conservation of marine mammals. Science, new ser., vol. 58, pp. 135–136.
1925. Status of the pronghorned antelope 1922–1924. U. S. Dept. Agr. Dept. Bull. 1346, 64 pp., 6 pls., 21 maps.

NELSON, E. W., AND GOLDMAN, E. A.
1929. List of the pumas, with three described as new. Journ. Mamm., vol. 10, pp. 345–350.
1933. Revision of the jaguars. Journ. Mamm., vol. 14, pp. 221–240.

NEVEU-LEMAIRE, MAURICE, AND GRANDIDIER, G.
1907. Les cervidés de la Cordillera des Andes. Compt. Rend. Assoc. Fr. Av. Sci., vol. 35 (pt. 2), pp. 482–494.

NEWCOMBE, W. A.
1929. The sea-otter (*Enhydra lutris lutris* Linnaeus). Rep. Provincial Mus. Nat. Hist. for 1928, pp. F12–F14, pl. 5.

NORTON, ARTHUR H.
1930. The mammals of Portland, Maine, and vicinity. Proc. Portland Soc. Nat. Hist., vol. 4, pp. 1–151, map.

OBER, E. H.
1931. The mountain sheep of California. California Fish and Game, vol. 17, pp. 27–39.

OLIVER, W. R. B.
1922. A review of the Cetacea of the New Zealand seas. Proc. Zool. Soc. London, for 1922, pp. 557–585, 4 pls.

OLSEN, ØRJAN.
1913. On the external characters and biology of Bryde's whale (*Balaenoptera brydei*), a new rorqual from the coast of South Africa. Proc. Zool. Soc. London, for 1913, pp. 1073–1090, 5 pls.

OLSON, SIGURD F.
1938. A study in predatory relationship with particular reference to the wolf. Sci. Monthly, vol. 36, pp. 323–336, fig.

ORR, ROBERT T.
1938. A new rodent of the genus *Nesoryzomys* from the Galapagos Islands. Proc. California Acad. Sci., ser. 4, vol. 23, pp. 303–306, 1 pl.

OSGOOD, WILFRED H.
1900. Results of a biological reconnaissance of the Yukon River region. Annotated list of mammals. North Amer. Fauna, no. 19, pp. 21–45, pls. 4–7.
1901. Natural history of the Cook Inlet region, Alaska. North Amer. Fauna, no. 21, pp. 51–81, pl. 7.
1904. A biological reconnaissance of the base of the Alaska Peninsula. North Amer. Fauna, no. 24, 86 pp., 7 pls.
1908. The game resources of Alaska. U. S. Dept. Agr. Yearbook for 1907, pp. 469–472.
1912. Mammals from western Venezuela and eastern Colombia. Field Mus. Nat. Hist. Publ. 155, zool. ser., vol. 10, no. 5, pp. 33–66, 2 pls.
1914. Mammals of an expedition across northern Peru. Field Mus. Nat. Hist. Publ. 176, zool. ser., vol. 10, no. 12, pp. 143–185.
1916. Mammals of the Collins-Day South American expedition. Publ. Field Mus. Nat. Hist., zool. ser., vol. 10, pp. 199–216, 2 pls.
1929. A new rodent from the Galapagos Islands. Publ. Field Mus. Nat. Hist., zool. ser., vol. 17, pp. 21–24.

OSGOOD, W. H.; PREBLE, E. A.; and PARKER, G. H.
1915. The fur seals and other life of the Pribilof Islands, Alaska, in 1914. Bull. Bur. Fish., vol. 34 (1914), 172 pp., 18 pls., 24 maps.

PALMER, RALPH S.
1938. Late records of caribou in Maine. Journ. Mamm., vol. 19, pp. 37–43.

PARKER, GEORGE H.
1917. The fur-seals of the Pribilof Islands. Sci. Monthly, 1917, pp. 385–409, 25 figs.

PEDERSEN, ALWIN.
1934. Der Moschusochse in Ostgrönland. Zeitschr. für Säugetierk., vol. 9, p. 433.
1936. Der grönlandische Moschusochse, *Ovibos moschatus wardi* Lydekker. Medd. om Grønland, vol. 93, no. 7, pp. 1–82, 19 figs.

PERINGUEY, L.
1921. A note on the whales frequenting South African waters. Trans. Roy. Soc. South Africa, vol. 9, pp. 73–76, pl. 1.

PERKINS, R. C. L.
1903. Vertebrata. *In* "Fauna Hawaiiensis," vol. 1, pt. 4, pp. 365–466.

PETERS, WILHELM CARL HARTING.
1863. Über die Säugethiergattung *Solenodon*. Abh. Akad. Wiss. Berlin, 1863, no. 1, pp. 1–22, 3 pls.

PETERS, WILHELM CARL HARTING.—*Cont.*
1873. Über *Dinomys*, eine merkwürdige neue Gattung von Nagethieren aus Peru. Festschr. Ges. Naturf. Freunde Berlin, 1873, pp. 1–10, pls. 1–4.
1876. Über *Stenoderma* Geoffroy und eine damit verwandte neue Flederthier-Gattung, *Peltorhinus*. Monatsb. Preuss. Akad. Wiss. Berlin, 1876, pp. 429–434, 2 pls.

PETERSON, O. A.
1917. Report upon the fossil material collected in 1913 by the Messrs. Link in a cave in the Isle of Pines. Ann. Carnegie Mus., vol. 11, pp. 359–361, pl. 36.

PETIT, G.
1928. Sur un dugong femelle capturé à Mobombé (Madagascar). Bull. Mus. Hist. Nat. Paris, 1927, pp. 336–342.

PHILIPPI, RUDOLF AMANDUS.
1892. Las focas chilenas del Museo Nacional figuradas i descritas. Anal. Mus. Nac. Chile, sect. 1, zool., 50 pp., 23 pls.

PHILLIPS, JOHN C.
1912. A new puma from Lower California. Proc. Biol. Soc. Washington, vol. 25, pp. 85–86, 1 pl.
1913. The Lower California pronghorn antelope. Science, new ser., vol. 37, pp. 717–718.
1933. The pronghorn antelope. Journ. Soc. Preservation Fauna Empire, new ser., pt. 20, p. 14.
1935. Some remarks on the American game protective system and its limitations. Journ. Soc. Preservation Fauna Empire, new ser., pt. 25, pp. 44–54.
1936. [Address.] Proc. North Amer. Wildlife Conference, 1936, pp. 51–56.

PHILLIPS, W. W. A.
1929. A check list of the mammals of Ceylon. Spolia Zeylanica, vol. 15, pt. 2, pp. 119–152, map.

POCOCK, REGINALD INNES.
1913. The affinities of the Antarctic wolf (*Canis antarcticus*). Proc. Zool. Soc. London, for 1913, pp. 382–393, figs. 70–74.
1935. The races of *Canis lupus*. Proc. Zool. Soc. London, for 1935, pp. 647–686, pls. 1–2.

PRATER, S. H.
1928. The dugong or sea cow (*Halicore dugong*). Journ. Bombay Nat. Hist. Soc., vol. 33, pp. 84–99, 4 pls.

PREBLE, EDWARD ALEXANDER.
1902. A biological investigation of the Hudson Bay region. North Amer. Fauna, no. 22, 140 pp., 14 pls.
1908. A biological investigation of the Athabaska-Mackenzie region. North Amer. Fauna, no. 27, 574 pp., 25 pls.

PRELL, H.
1934. Die gegenwartig bekannten Arten der Gattung *Chinchilla* Bennett. Zool. Anz., vol. 108, pp. 97–104.

PRENTISS, DANIEL WEBSTER.
  1903. Description of an extinct mink from the shell-heaps of the Maine
         coast. Proc. U. S. Nat. Mus., vol. 26, pp. 887–888, 1 fig.
PRICHARD, H. HESKETH.
  1902a. Through the heart of Patagonia, xvi + 346 pp., illus. New York.
  1902b. Field-notes upon some of the larger mammals of Patagonia,
         made between September 1900 and June 1901. Proc. Zool.
         Soc. London, for 1902, vol. 1, pp. 272–277.
  1910. Hunting camps in wood and wilderness, xx + 274 pp., 54 pls.
         New York and London.
RADFORD, HARRY V.
  1908. History of the Adirondack beaver (*Castor canadensis*, Kuhl), its
         former abundance, practical extermination, and reintroduc-
         tion. 10th, 11th, and 12th Rep. Forest, Fish, and Game
         Comm. New York, pp. 389–418, 10 pls., 2 maps, figs.
RAINEY, FROELICH.
  1940. Eskimo method of capturing bowhead whales. Journ. Mamm.,
         vol. 21, p. 362.
RAND, A. L.
  1933. Notes on the mammals of the interior of western Nova Scotia.
         Can. Field-Nat., vol. 47, pp. 41–50.
RAUP, HUGH M.
  1933. Range conditions in the Wood Buffalo Park of western Canada
         with notes on the history of the wood bison. Amer. Comm.
         International Wild Life Protection Special Publ. no. 2, 52 pp.,
         1 map.
RENSHAW, GRAHAM.
  1931. The Antarctic wolf. Journ. Soc. Preservation Fauna Empire,
         new ser., pt. 13, pp. 16–20, 1 pl.
  1937. The northern sea-cow. Journ. Soc. Preservation Fauna Empire,
         new ser., pt. 31, pp. 51–54, 1 pl.
RHOADS, SAMUEL N.
  1896. Contributions to the biology of Tennessee, No. 3: Mammals.
         Proc. Acad. Nat. Sci. Philadelphia, vol. 48, pp. 175–205.
  1898. A contribution to a revision of the North American beavers,
         otters and fishers. Trans. Amer. Phil. Soc., ser. 2, vol. 19,
         pp. 417–439, pls. 21–25.
  1903. The mammals of Pennsylvania and New Jersey: A biographic,
         historic and descriptive account of the furred animals of land
         and sea, both living and extinct, known to have existed in
         these states, 266 pp., 9 pls., map. Philadelphia.
RICHARDSON, JOHN.
  1839. List of mammals hitherto detected in the country between the
         ridge of the Rocky Mountains and the Pacific, from North
         California to the northern extremity of the continent; with
         references to detailed descriptions in the Fauna Boreali-
         Americana. *In:* Zool. Beechey's Voyage, pp. 3–11, 2 pls.,
         London.
RIDGWAY, ROBERT.
  1912. Color standards and color nomenclature. Washington.

RIDLEY, H. W.
   1895.   The mammals of the Malay Peninsula. Nat. Sci., vol. 6, pp.
          23–29, 89–96, 161–165.
RING, T. P. A.
   1923.   The elephant-seals of Kerguelen Land. Proc. Zool. Soc. London,
          for 1923, pp. 431–443, 2 pls.
RISTING, SIGURD.
   1927.   Whales and whale foetuses. Conseil Permanent International
          pour l'Exploration de la Mer, vol. 50.
RITCHIE, JAMES.
   1921.   The walrus in British waters. Scottish Nat., 1921, pp. 5–9,
          77–86.
ROWLEY, JOHN.
   1921.   Elephant seals off the coast of California. Journ. Mamm., vol.
          2, pp. 235–236.
RUHL, HARRY D., AND LOVEJOY, PARISH S.
   1930.   Beaver plantings in Michigan. Papers Michigan Acad. Sci.,
          Arts and Lett., vol. 11, pp. 465–469.
RUUD, J. T.
   1937.   Grønlandshvalen, Balaena mysticetus (Linné). Nordkaperen,
          Balaena glacialis (Bonnaterre). Norsk Hvalfangs Tidende,
          Sandefjord, vol. 26, pp. 254–278, 3 figs.
SALVESEN, T. E.
   1914.   The whale fisheries of the Falkland Islands and their depend-
          encies. Trans. Roy. Soc. Edinburgh, for 1914, pp. 475–486;
          also Scottish Nat. Antarctic Exp., vol. 4, pp. 475–486, 10 pls.
SANBORN, COLIN CAMPBELL.
   1929.   The land mammals of Uruguay. Publ. Field Mus. Nat. Hist.,
          zool. ser., vol. 17, pp. 147–165.
   1931.   Notes on Dinomys. Publ. Field Mus. Nat. Hist., zool. ser.,
          vol. 18, pp. 149–155, pl. 5.
SARASIN, PAUL.
   1913.   Ueber die Ausrottung ser Walund Robbenfauna sowie der
          arktischen und antarktischen Tierwelt ueberhaupt. Verh.
          Ges. Deutsch. Naturf., vol. 84, pp. 117–137.
SCAMMON, C. M.
   1874.   The marine mammals of the northwestern coast of North
          America, described and illustrated; together with an account
          of the American whale-fishery, 319 + v pp., illus. San
          Francisco and New York.
SCHEFFER, VICTOR B.
   1938.   Notes on wolverine and fisher in the State of Washington.
          Murrelet, vol. 19, pp. 8–10, 2 figs.
   1940.   A newly located herd of Pacific white-tailed deer. Journ.
          Mamm., vol. 21, pp. 271–282, figs.
SCHORGER, A. W.
   1938.   A Wisconsin specimen of the cougar. Journ. Mamm., vol. 19,
          p. 252.
   1939.   Wolverine in Michigan. Journ. Mamm., vol. 20, p. 503.

Schorger, A. W.—*Cont.*
    1940. A record of the caribou in Michigan. Journ. Mamm., vol. 21,
          p. 222.
Schreuder, Ä.
    1933. Skull remains of *Amblyrhiza* from St. Martin. Tijdschr.
          Nederl. Dierkund. Vereen., ser. 3, vol. 3, pp. 242–266, 3 figs.
Sclater, Philip Lutley.
    1870. [Remarks on the hairy tapir.] Proc. Zool. Soc. London, for
          1870, pp. 51–52.
    1874. [Report on the additions to the Society's menagerie in November
          1874.] Proc. Zool. Soc. London, for 1874, pp. 664–666, 1 pl.
    1878. [On a hairy or Andean tapir.] Proc. Zool. Soc. London, for 1878,
          pp. 631–632, pl. 39.
Sclater, William Lutley.
    1900. The mammals of South Africa, vol. 1, 324 pp., illus. London.
Scoresby, William, Jr.
    1820. An account of the Arctic regions, with a history and description
          of the northern whale-fishery, 2 vols., illus. Edinburgh.
Serre, Paul.
    1910. [Lettre donnant des renseignements sur une race de mammifère
          insectivore, le *Solenodon paradoxus*, de Cuba et annonçant
          l'envoi de cristaux et de stalactites de la grotte de Bellamar.]
          Bull. Mus. Hist. Nat. Paris, vol. 16, p. 4.
Seton, Ernest Thompson.
    1900. *Rangifer dawsoni:* Preliminary description of a new caribou from
          Queen Charlotte's Islands. Ottawa Nat., vol. 13, pp. 260–261.
    1909. Life-histories of northern animals: An account of the mammals
          of Manitoba, 2 vols., illus. New York.
    1920. The jaguar in Colorado. Journ. Mamm., vol. 1, p. 241.
    1929. Lives of game animals: An account of land animals . . .
          north of the Mexican border, 4 vols., illus. Garden City.
    1931. Two records for New Mexico. Journ. Mamm., vol. 12, p. 166.
Sheldon, Charles.
    1912. The wilderness of the North Pacific coast islands, xvi + 246
          pp., 45 pls., 5 maps. New York.
    1930. The wilderness of Denali: Explorations of a hunter-naturalist in
          northern Alaska, xxv + 412 pp., illus., map. New York and
          London.
Sherman, H. B.
    1937. List of the recent wild land mammals of Florida. Proc. Florida
          Acad. Sci., 1936, vol. 1, pp. 102–128.
Shoemaker, Henry W.
    1914. The Pennsylvania lion or panther, 47 pp., illus. Altoona, Pa.
    1915a. Pennsylvania deer and their horns, 120 pp., illus. Reading, Pa.
    1915b. A Pennsylvania bison hunt, 60 pp., illus. Middleburg, Pa.
Shortridge, Guy C.
    1934. The mammals of South West Africa, a biological account of the
          forms occurring in that region, 2 vols., illustr. London.
    1936. Field notes (hitherto unpublished) on Western Australian mam-
          mals south of the Tropic of Capricorn (exclusive of Marsupi-

SHORTRIDGE, GUY C.—*Cont.*
> alia and Monotremata, and records of specimens collected during the Balston expeditions (November 1904–June 1907)). Proc. Zool. Soc. London, for 1936, pp. 743–749, 1 fig.

SIMPSON, GEORGE GAYLORD.
> 1930. Sea sirens. Nat. Hist., vol. 30, pp. 41–47, figs.

SKINNER, MILTON PHILO.
> 1923. The prong-horn. Journ. Mamm., vol. 3, pp. 82–105, pls. 6–9.
> 1928. The elk situation. Journ. Mamm., vol. 9, pp. 309–317.
> 1936. Browsing of the Olympic Peninsula elk in early winter. Journ. Mamm., vol. 17, pp. 253–256.

SKOTTSBERG, CARL.
> 1911. The wilds of Patagonia, xix + 336 pp., 34 pls., 3 maps. London.
> 1934. Report of the Standing Committee for the Protection of Nature in and around the Pacific for the years 1929–32, part 1. Proc. 5th Pacific Sci. Congress, Canada, 1933, vol. 1, pp. 385–437.

SNYDER, HARRY M.
> 1936. Report on Harry Snyder 1935 Barren Lands Expedition, Northwest Territories, Canada (manuscript, dated Jan. 31, 1936), 12 pp.

SOWERBY, ARTHUR DE CARLE.
> 1923. The naturalist in Manchuria, with photographs and sketches by the author, vols. 2 and 3: The mammals and birds of Manchuria, xxvii + 358 pp., illus., map. Tientsin.

STEFANSSON, VILHJALMUR.
> 1923. The musk ox in Arctic islands. Nature (London), vol. 112, p. 590.

STEJNEGER, LEONHARD.
> 1887. How the great northern sea-cow (*Rytina*) became exterminated. Amer. Nat., vol. 21, pp. 1047–1054.
> 1897. The Russian fur-seal islands. Bull. U. S. Comm. Fish and Fisheries, vol. 16 (for 1896), pp. 1–148, pls. 1–66.
> 1898. Report on the rookeries of the Commander Islands, season of 1897. U. S. Treasury Dept. Doc. 1997, 17 pp.
> 1936. Georg Wilhelm Steller: The pioneer of Alaskan natural history, 623 pp., 29 pls. Cambridge, Mass.

STIRLING, E.
> 1884. The grizzly bear in Labrador. Forest and Stream, vol. 22, p. 324.

STONE, ANDREW JACKSON.
> 1900. Some results of a natural history journey to northern British Columbia, Alaska, and the North-west Territory. Bull. Amer. Mus. Nat. Hist., vol. 13, pp. 31–62.

STONE, WITMER.
> 1908. The mammals of New Jersey. Ann. Rep. New Jersey State Mus., for 1907, pp. 33–110.

STONE, WITMER, AND CRAM, WILLIAM E.
> 1902. American animals, a popular guide to the mammals of North America north of Mexico, with intimate biographies of the more familiar species, xxiii + 318 pp., illus. New York.

STORER, TRACY I.
1932. Factors influencing wild life in California, past and present. Ecology, vol. 13, pp. 315–327.

STRASSEN, O. ZUR.
1914. Der Seeotter. Ber. Senckenb. Naturf. Gesell., vol. 45, Sonderheft, pp. 10*–15*, 3 figs.

STRONG, WILLIAM DUNCAN.
1926. Indian records of California carnivores. Journ. Mamm., vol. 7, pp. 59–60.

SURBER, THADDEUS.
1909. Some remarks on the game animals of West Virginia: with an annotated list of all species found in the State. Proc. 3d Ann. Meeting West Virginia Fish and Game Prot. Assoc., pp. 49–56.

SUTTON, GEORGE MIKSCH, AND HAMILTON, WILLIAM J., JR.
1932. The mammals of Southampton Island. Mem. Carnegie Mus., vol. 12, pt. 2, sect. 1, 111 pp., 10 pls.

SWANSON, GUSTAV.
1936. The Minnesota caribou herd. Proc. North Amer. Wildlife Conference, 1936, pp. 416–419.

SWARTH, HARRY S.
1912. Report on a collection of birds and mammals from Vancouver Island. Univ. California Publ. Zool., vol. 10, no. 1, pp. 1–124, 4 pls.
1936. Mammals of the Atlin region, northwestern British Columbia. Journ. Mamm., vol. 17, pp. 398–405.

TATE, G. H. H.
1931. Random observations on habits of South American mammals. Journ. Mamm., vol. 12, pp. 248–256.

TAYLOR, WALTER PENN.
1916. The status of the beavers of western North America, with a consideration of the factors in their speciation. Univ. California Publ. Zool., vol. 12, pp. 413–495, figs. A–P.
1936. The prong-horned antelope in the Southwest. Proc. North Amer. Wildlife Conference, 1936, pp. 652–655.

TAYLOR, WALTER P., AND SHAW, W. T.
1929. Provisional list of land mammals of the State of Washington. Occas. Pap. Conner Mus., no. 2, pp. 1–31.

THOMAS, OLDFIELD.
1880. On mammals from Ecuador. Proc. Zool. Soc. London, for 1880, pp. 393–403, 3 figs., 1 pl.
1902. On the bear of Ecuador. Ann. Mag. Nat. Hist., ser. 7, vol. 9, pp. 215–220.

THOMAS, OLDFIELD, AND LYDEKKER, RICHARD.
1897. On the number of grinding-teeth possessed by the manatee. Proc. Zool. Soc. London, for 1897, pp. 595–600, 1 pl.

TOMKINS, IVAN R.
1931. Some late records of the timber wolf in Pennsylvania. Journ. Mamm., vol. 12, pp. 165.

TORRE, CARLOS DE LA, AND MATTHEW, W. D.
1915. *Megalocnus* and other Cuban ground-sloths. Bull. Geol. Soc. Amer., vol. 26, p. 152.

TOWNSEND, CHARLES HASKINS.
1886. Present condition of the California gray whale fishery. Bull. U. S. Fish Comm., vol. 6, pp. 346–350, pls. 6, 7.
1909. The West Indian seal at the aquarium. Science, new ser., vol. 30, p. 212.
1923. The West Indian seal. Journ. Mamm., vol. 4, p. 55.
1912. The northern elephant seal, *Macrorhinus angustirostris* Gill. Zoologica, vol. 1, pp. 159–173.
1930a. Twentieth century whaling. Bull. New York Zool. Soc., vol. 33, no. 1, pp. 2–31, 1 pl., 34 figs.
1930b. The northern elephant seal herd in 1929. Bull. New York Zool. Soc., vol. 33, no. 1, pp. 31–32, 1 fig.
1931. The fur seal of the California islands with new descriptive and historical matter. Zoologica, vol. 9, pp. 443–457, figs. 345–356, pl. (col.).
1934. The fur seal of the Galapagos Islands. Zoologica, vol. 18, pp. 43–56, figs. 15–25.
1935. The distribution of certain whales as shown by logbook records of American whaleships. Zoologica, vol. 19, pp. 1–50, pl., 4 maps.

TROUESSART, ÉDOUARD LOUIS.
1881. Note sur le *Mus pilorides* ou rat musqué des Antilles, considéré comme type d'un sous-genre nouveau dans le genre *Hesperomys*. Le Naturaliste (Paris), vol. 3, pp. 355–357.
1885. Note sur le rat musqué (*Mus pilorides*) des Antilles type du sous-genre *Megalomys* (Trt.) et sur la place du ce sous-genre dans le group des rats Américains ou Hesperomyeae. Ann. Sci. Nat., zool., vol. 19, art. 5, 18 pp., pl.
1904–05. Catalogus mammalium tam viventium quam fossilium. Quinquennale supplementum, iv + 929 pp. Berlin.
1907. Mammifères pinnipèdes. *In:* "Expedition Antarctique Française (1903–1905) commandée par le Dr. Jean Charcot," Sci. Nat., Documents Sci., pp. 1–27, 4 pls., 5 figs.
1910. Faune des mammifères d'Europe (Conspectus mammalium Europae), xvii + 266 pp. Berlin.

TROUGHTON, ELLIS LE G.
1928. Sea-cows: The story of the dugong. Australian Mus. Mag., vol. 3, no. 7, pp. 220–228, 7 figs.
1932. Australian furred animals: Their past, present and future. Australian Zool., vol. 7, pp. 173–193.

TRUE, FREDERICK W.
1884a. On the skeleton of *Phoca* (*Histriophoca*) *fasciata*, Zimmermann. Proc. U. S. Nat. Mus., vol. 6, pp. 417–426, pls. 11–14.
1884b. The sirenians or sea-cows. The Fisheries and Fishery Industries of the United States, Section 1, Natural History of Useful Aquatic Animals, U. S. Comm. Fish. and ·Fisheries, part 1, art. C, pp. 114–136, pls. 33, 34.

TRUE, FREDERICK W.—*Cont.*

1885a. On the occurrence of *Loncheres armatus*, (Geoff.) Wagner, in the island of Martinique, West Indies. Proc. U. S. Nat. Mus., vol. 7, pp. 550–551.

1885b. A provisional list of the mammals of North and Central America, and the West India Islands. Proc. U. S. Nat. Mus., vol. 7, pp. 587–611.

1886. The almiqui. Science, ser. 1, vol. 8, p. 282, 1 fig.

1889a. The puma, or American lion: *Felis concolor* of Linnaeus. Rep. U. S. Nat. Mus., 1889, pp. 591–608, pl. 94.

1889b. A review of the family Delphinidae. U. S. Nat. Mus. Bull. 36, 191 pp., 47 pls.

1904. The whalebone whales of the western North Atlantic, with some observations on the species of the North Pacific. Smithsonian Contrib. Knowledge, vol. 33, 332 pp., 97 figs., 50 pls.

1910. An account of the beaked whales of the family Ziphiidae in the collection of the United States National Museum, with remarks on some specimens in other American museums. U. S. Nat. Mus. Bull. 73, v + 89 pp., 42 pls.

TRUE, FREDERICK W., AND LUCAS, F. A.

1884. On the West Indian seal (*Monachus tropicalis*, Gray). Rep. U. S. Nat. Mus. for 1884, pp. 331–335, pls. 1–3.

TSCHUDI, JOHANN JACOB VON.

1884. Therologie. *In:* "Untersuchungen ueber die Fauna Peruana," 262 pp., 18 pls. St. Gallen.

TUFTS, ROBIE WILFRID.

1939. Newfoundland caribou liberated in Nova Scotia. Can. Field-Nat., vol. 53, p. 123.

TURNER, WILLIAM.

1888. Report on the seals collected during the voyage of H. M. S. *Challenger* in the years 1873–76. *Challenger* Reports, zool., vol. 26, pt. 2, pp. 1–138, 10 pls., 2 figs.

VAN DEN BRINK, F. H.

1931. Catalogue des mammifères des Pays-Bas trouvés à l'état sauvage. Bull. Soc. Zool. France, vol. 56, pp. 163–190.

VERRILL, A. HYATT.

1907. Notes on the habits and external characters of the solenodon of San Domingo (*Solenodon paradoxus*). Amer. Journ. Sci., ser. 4, vol. 24, pp. 55–57, 1 fig.

VIGNEAU, P.

1908a. Capture d'un morse. Nat. Canad., vol. 35, pp. 49–51.

1908b. Les morses dans le Golfe Saint Laurent. Nat. Canad., vol. 35, pp. 140–142.

VORHIES, CHARLES T.

1935. The Arizona specimen of *Euderma maculatum*. Journ. Mamm., vol. 16, pp. 224–226.

WARD, HENRY L.

1908. The American elk in southern Wisconsin. Bull. Wisconsin Nat. Hist. Soc., vol. 6, pp. 145–146.

WARFEL, H. E.
1937. Moose records for Vermont. Journ. Mamm., vol. 18, p. 519.
WARREN, EDWARD ROYAL.
1910. The mammals of Colorado, an account of the several species found within the boundaries of the State, together with a record of their habits and of their distribution, xxxiv + 300 pp., illus. New York and London.
1922. The life of the Yellowstone beaver. Roosevelt Wild Life Bull., vol. 1, no. 2, pp. 187–228, figs. 37–70.
1926. Notes on the beaver colonies in the Longs Peak region of Estes Park, Colorado. Roosevelt Wild Life Annals, vol. 1, pp. 193–234, figs. 134–174.
1932. The grizzly bears of Colorado. Proc. Colorado Mus. Nat. Hist., vol. 11, pp. 19–24, map.
WATERHOUSE, GEORGE ROBERT.
1839. Zoology of the voyage of H. M. S. Beagle. Mammalia, 5 + 39 pp., 35 col. pls.
1848. A natural history of the Mammalia, vol. 2. Containing the order Rodentia, or gnawing mammals, 500 pp., 20 pls. London.
WETMORE, ALEXANDER, AND SWALES, BRADSHAW H.
1931. The birds of Haiti and the Dominican Republic. U. S. Nat. Mus. Bull. 155, iv + 483 pp., 25 pls., 1 map.
WILLIAMS, S. H.
1930. Mammalian fauna of Pennsylvania. Ann. Carnegie Mus., vol. 19, pp. 225–234, map.
WILSON, EDWARD ADRIAN.
1907. Mammalia (whales and seals). In: "National Antarctic Exped. 1901–1904," nat. hist., vol. 2, zool., pp. 1–69, 23 pls.
WILSON, GEORGE GRAFTON, AND WILLIAMS, JOHN FISCHER.
1931 (or later). Les fondements juridiques de la conservation des richesses de la mer. Avantprojet da rapport, 27 pp. mimeographed. Institut de Droit International Vingt-troisième Commission. [Appendice: Convention pour le Règlementation de la Chasse à la Baleine (approuvée par l'Assemblée de la s. D. N. Septembre, 1931), pp. i–viii.]
WOOD, F. J.
1937. Manatee. Nigerian Field, vol. 6, no. 1, pp. 23–28, 3 figs.
WOOD JONES, FREDERIC.
1925. The mammals of South Australia: Part III (Conclusion), containing the Monodelphia, pp. (4), 271–458, illus. Adelaide.
WOODWARD, ARTHUR SMITH.
1900. On some remains of Grypotherium (Neomylodon) listai and associated mammals from a cave near Consuelo Cove, Last Hope Inlet, Patagonia. Proc. Zool. Soc. London, for 1900, pp. 64–70, pls. 5–9.
WOOSTER, L. D.
1933. The present status of certain mammals in western Kansas. Trans. Kansas Acad. Sci., vol. 34, pp. 112–113.

Wyman, Leland C.
     1922. The validity of the Penobscot field mouse. Journ. Mamm.,
          vol. 3, pp. 162–166.
Yonge, C. M.
     1930. A year on the Great Barrier Reef. London and New York.
Young, Stanley Paul.
     1940. [Review of "North American Big Game."] Journ. Mamm.,
          vol. 21, pp. 96–98.
Zinser, Juan.
     1936. Remarks of . . . Proc. North Amer. Wildlife Conference,
          1936, pp. 6–11.

INDEX

abaconis, Geocapromys, 114
Abbott, W. L., on Hispaniolan hutia, 117, 118.
abieticola, Martes, 166, 170
    Mustela, 166
abietinoides, Martes, 166
Abrocoma, 390
absaroka, Ursus, 159
Academy of Natural Sciences of Philadelphia, viii
achradophilus, Ariteus, 23
    Artibeus, 23
Achras sapota, 24
Acratocnus, 39, 40, 124
    comes, 36
    major, 36
    odontrigonus, 36, 40
actuosa, Martes, 166, 170
    Mustela, 166, 167
Adams, James Capen, 255
Adanson, Michel, 548
aedium, Plagiodontia, 116, 119
africanus, Trichechus, 547
Agaphelus glaucus, 495
Agouti, Guadeloupe, 133
    St. Lucia, 132
    St. Vincent, 128, 131
Agoutis, 128
agrestis, Microtus, 97
aguti, Dasyprocta, 133
Aharoni, J., on dugong, 530
    on Mediterranean monk seal, 450
alascanus, Callorhinus, 442, 445
alascensis, Ursus, 160
albida, Dasyprocta, 128, 131, 132, 133
albiventer, Phoca, 449
albomaculatum, Stenoderma, 21
albus, Canis, 226
aleoutiensis, Balaena, 501
Alexander, Annie M., 97
alexandrinus, Rattus, 382
Allen, Glover M., vii, viii, 4
    on Atlantic walrus, 474
    on bison, 339
Allen, Harrison, 33
Allen, J. A., on Alaskan fur seal, 447
    on Atlantic walrus, 474, 476
    on cougar in Texas, 243, 244
    on Bahaman hutia, 112, 113, 114
    on barren-ground muskox, 329, 330, 331
    on beaver in Iowa, 67
    on cape fur seal, 436
    on bison, 337–340

Allen, J. A., on fisher in Colorado, 179
    on Greenland caribou, 305
    on Guadalupe fur seal, 440
    on Hudson Bay muskox, 332, 333
    on jaguar in Texas, 254
    on Kerguelen fur seal, 432, 433, 434
    on Kermode's bear, 139
    on kit fox in Iowa, 195
    on Lower California bighorn, 372
    on Merriam's elk, 272
    on mountain caribou, 320
    on mule deer in South Dakota, 280
    on New Zealand fur seal, 430
    on North Pacific fur seals, 443
    on Pacific walrus, 469
    on Philippi's fur seal, 437, 438
    on Plains wolf in Iowa, 220
    on southern fur seal, 426
    on Virginia deer in Massachusetts, 285
    on wapiti in Iowa, 266
    on West Indian seal, 452, 453, 454
    on white-faced muskox, 334
    on wood bison, 346
Allen, J. A., and Chapman, F. M., on St. Lucia agouti, 132
alexandrae, Ursus, 162
"Almiqui," 12
Alston, E. R., 450
Ambergris, 494
Amblyrhiza, 129, 389
    inundata, 127
Ameghino, F., on Patagonian giant ground sloth, 375
American Bison Society, 343
American Philosophical Society, viii
americana, Antilocapra, 323
    Antilope, 323
    Canis, 229
    Martes, 166, 167, 173
americanus, Bos, 337
    Canis, 229
    Euarctos, 136, 137
    Mustelus, 166
    Odocoileus, 280
    Ursus, 136
"Andaraz," 103
Anderson, John, and De Winton, W. E., on dugong, 530
    on Mediterranean monk seal, 451
Anderson, R. M., on Atlantic walrus, 474, 475
    on barren-ground caribou, 298
    on barren-ground muskox. 331, 332